Bombing to Win

A volume in the series

Cornell Studies in Political Economy

EDITED BY PETER J. KATZENSTEIN

A list of titles in this series is available at www.cornellpress.cornell.edu.

Bombing to Win

AIR POWER AND COERCION IN WAR

ROBERT A. PAPE

Cornell University Press

ITHACA AND LONDON

First published 1996 by Cornell University Press
First printing, Cornell Paperbacks, 1996

Printed in the United States of America

Library of Congress Cataloging-in-Publication Data

Pape Robert Anthony, 1960–
    Bombing to win: air power and coercion in war / Robert A. Pape.
      p.   cm. — (Cornell studies in security affairs)
    Includes bibliographical references and index.
    ISBN-13: 978-0-8014-8311-0 (pbk. : alk. paper)
    1. Bombing, Aerial—Case studies. 2. Air power—Case studies. I. Series.
UG700.P365   1996
358.4'24—dc20   95-45071

Cornell University Press strives to use environmentally responsible suppliers and materials to the fullest extent possible in the publishing of its books. Such materials include vegetable-based, low-VOC inks and acid-free papers that are recycled, totally chlorine-free, or partly composed of nonwood fibers. For further information, visit our website at www.cornellpress.cornell.edu.

Paperback printing   10   9   8

Contents

[v]

Acknowledgments

This book has benefited from the advice and support of a host of people and institutions. John Mearsheimer encouraged me to ask an important question and, more important, inspired me to produce the best answer I could both by the example he set and the counsel he gave at every stage of this project. Chaim Kaufmann was relentless in his demand for analytic clarity and endless in his generosity in helping my manuscript approach his rigorous standards. I am fortunate to have such fine scholars as friends. I also appreciate the remarkably keen and consistently constructive comments by Robert Art and Barry Posen who read, and immensely improved, the entire work.

The following people were kind enough to comment on large parts of the manuscript: Mark Clodfelter, Michael Desch, Matthew Evangelista, James K. Feldman, Charles Glaser, Paul Huth, Sean Lynn-Jones, Morton Kaplan, Craig Koerner, David Mets, Pat Pentland, Duncan Snidal, Stephen Walt, and William Zimmerman. In addition, many contributed their special expertise to improve specific chapters: Chris Achen, Andrew Blanar, Daniel Bolger, Michael Brown, Brian Downing, Joseph Grieco, Ted Hopf, Charles Horner, Akira Iriye, Fabrice Lehoucq, James Morrow, Karl Mueller, Kenneth Pollack, Wayne Thompson, Marc Trachtenberg, Stephen Van Evera, and Andrew Wallace. I am grateful to all of them, without whom the final product would be a shadow of itself. I also thank John Chapman, who inspired me to become a scholar and who has offered tough criticism and steadfast friendship ever since.

Several institutions have provided indispensable financial support as well as stimulating intellectual environments. The John D. and Catherine T. MacArthur Foundation furnished pre- and post-doctoral fellowship support, while the Earhart Foundation and the United States Air Force Historical Research Agency, Maxwell Air Force Base, Alabama, generously funded my archival research. The students and faculty of the Department of Political Science at the University of Chicago, the Program for International Peace and Security Research, University of Michigan, and the United States Air Force School of Advanced Airpower Studies vigorously debated the political and military issues I address and often saved me from misjudgments and errors of fact.

I also wish to thank Roger Haydon and Kristina Kelsey of Cornell University Press, whose superb editorial expertise and careful attention to detail made publishing this book a pleasure, and Judith Bailey, my copyeditor, whose prose clarified and brightened the text. No author could ask for a better publishing team.

Those who deserve the most credit are those I hold most dear. I owe a special thanks to my mother, Marlene, who not only made me, but alone made me capable of undertaking such an effort.

Most important, I thank my wife, Lisa. Her patience, sacrifice, and confidence not only made this work possible but made it worth doing. I dedicate this book to her.

R. A. P.

Bombing to Win

[1]

Why Study Military Coercion?

This book analyzes the dynamics of military coercion. It asks why some states decide to change their behavior when threatened with military consequences and other states do not. Why, for example, did the Japanese in 1945 and the Chinese in 1953 concede, whereas the British in 1940 and the North Vietnamese from 1965 to 1968 did not? This book seeks to determine the conditions under which coercion has succeeded and failed in the past in order to predict when it is likely to succeed and fail in the future.

The accepted wisdom is that successful coercion, whether nuclear or conventional, rests on the threat to inflict harm on civilians. In contrast, I maintain that coercion, at least in conventional wars, succeeds when force is used to exploit the opponent's *military* vulnerabilities, thereby making it infeasible for the opponent to achieve its political goals by continued military efforts.

The topic of military coercion is important for theoretical, policy, and moral reasons. Throughout history, states have repeatedly employed military force in attempting to persuade other states to do their bidding.[1] Both the successes and the failures merit careful attention. Successful coercion can bring about important changes in the distribution of power; for example, Nazi Germany's success in compelling Austria and Czechoslovakia to submit to its rule made Germany stronger in relation to—and much more dangerous to—England, France, and the Soviet Union. On the other hand, unsuccessful coercion can be costly for the victim but disastrous for the in-

[1] Peter Karsten, Peter D. Howell, and Artis Francis Allen, *Military Threats: A Systematic Historical Analysis of the Determinants of Success* (Westport, Conn.: Greenwood Press, 1984), counted 77 major cases of military coercion in international crises since ancient times. This figure underestimates the full universe of military coercion because it leaves out the coercive effect of military threats in wars.

stigator; for example, not only did Wilhelmine Germany's submarine campaign fail to compel England to withdraw from World War I, but it also led directly to the U.S. decision to enter the war and thus helped ensure Germany's ultimate defeat.

States involved in serious international disputes commonly engage in passionate debate over the utility of military (and nonmilitary) instruments of coercion.[2] Leaders are often drawn to military coercion because it is perceived as a quick and cheap solution to otherwise difficult and expensive international problems. Nonetheless, statesmen very often overestimate the prospects for successful coercion and underestimate the costs. Coercive attempts often fail, even when assailants have superior capability and inflict great punishment on the target state. Famous failures include German attempts to coerce Britain in 1917 and again in 1940, the French occupation of the Rhineland in 1923–1924, Italian efforts to coerce Ethiopia in 1936, the American embargo against Japan in 1941, Allied bombing of Germany in World War II, American efforts against North Vietnam from 1965 to 1968, and Soviet operations against the Afghan rebels from 1979 to 1988. The other side of the ledger is virtually blank. There are almost no instances in which coercion was not tried when a credible claim can be made that it would likely have succeeded.

Studying military coercion may be even more relevant to policy now than it was in the past. The end of the Cold War and the rise of potential regional hegemons are shifting national security policy away from deterring predictable threats toward responding to unpredictable threats after they emerge, making questions about how to compel states to alter their behavior more central in international politics. This trend is also apparent in the growing role of air power in U.S. military strategy. As the American public's willingness to bear military costs declines, the role of air power in overseas conflicts is increasing because it can project force more rapidly and with less risk than land power and more formidably than naval power. In Iraq and in Bosnia the first question in debates over American intervention has been,

---

[2] There have been three main cycles of policy advocacy. The first, between World Wars I and II, was dominated by advocates and critics of independent air operations. Advocates included J. F. C. Fuller, *The Reformation of War* (New York: Dutton, 1923); B. H. Liddell Hart, *Paris or the Future of War* (London: Kegan Paul, 1925); and Giulio Douhet, *Command of the Air*, trans. Dino Ferrari (New York: Coward-McCann, 1942). More critical of independent air operations is John C. Slessor, *Air Power and Armies* (London: Oxford University Press, 1936). The second, after World War II, centered on how to respond to potential Soviet nuclear blackmail: Hans Speier, "Soviet Atomic Blackmail and the North Atlantic Alliance," *World Politics* 9, no. 3 (1957): 307–28; Paul Nitze, "Atoms, Strategy, and Policy," *Foreign Affairs* 34 (January 1956): 187–98; and Arnold L. Horelick and Myron Rush, *Strategic Power and Soviet Foreign Policy* (Chicago: University of Chicago Press, 1966). The last occurred during the Vietnam War: e.g., the exchange between Colin S. Gray, "What Rand Hath Wrought," *Foreign Policy*, no. 4 (Fall 1971): 111–29, and Bernard Brodie, "Why Were We So (Strategically) Wrong?" *Foreign Policy*, no. 5 (Winter 1971–72): 151–87.

[2]

Can air power alone persuade states to alter their behavior? Some propose as a general defense policy to make strategic bombing the U.S. weapon of choice.[3]

Ironically, despite the growing importance of coercion as an instrument of statecraft, the study of coercion has stagnated in recent years,[4] partly because coercion is often identified with offensive rather than defensive national goals. In addition, coercion is seen as morally repugnant because it usually involves hurting civilians. Many considered the U.S. bombing of North Vietnam immoral as well as ineffective.[5] Coercion has thus come to be viewed as the "dark side" of international relations theory.

Dark or not, scholars of international politics cannot avoid the obligation to study how states use force to compel others to do their bidding. Although moral issues cannot be resolved on the basis of knowledge alone, social scientists have a responsibility to advance knowledge on subjects relevant to policy, especially when the decisions we make have great moral consequences. Moreover, the concern that studying coercion will provide strategic tools for international aggressors is misplaced. In fact, states tend to overestimate the prospects of coercion, and if humanitarian values deter scholars from studying the effectiveness of immoral practices in peacetime, we run the risk that ignorance could facilitate their use in wartime. As coercion becomes more prominent in policy debates, it is crucial to separate erroneous from valid beliefs, for an intellectual vacuum gives free rein to bad ideas and bad policies. Consider, for example, that in August 1990 strategic bombing advocates were able to lobby successfully for air strikes on Iraqi

---

[3] The clearest call for the United States Air Force to conduct power projection by relying on strategic bombing is found in Donald B. Rice, *The Air Force and U.S. National Security: Global Reach—Global Power* (Washington, D.C.: Department of the Air Force, June 1991). See also John A. Warden III, "Employing Air Power in the Twenty-first Century," in *The Future of Air Power in the Aftermath of the Gulf War*, ed. Richard H. Shultz Jr. and Robert L. Pfaltzgraff Jr. (Maxwell Air Force Base, Ala.: Air University Press, 1992), pp. 57–82. Other nations are considering the same option. See Ross Babbage, *A Coast Too Long: Defending Australia beyond the 1990s* (Sidney: Allen and Unwin, 1990), p. 113, who advocates taking any conflict to an enemy's decision-making elite.

[4] The landmark literature on the dynamics of military coercion was produced mainly in the 1960s, including Daniel Ellsberg, "Theory and Practice of Blackmail," P-3883 (Santa Monica, Calif.: Rand Corporation, 1968); Morton A. Kaplan, *The Strategy of Limited Retaliation*, Center of International Studies Memorandum no. 19 (Princeton: Center of International Studies, Woodrow Wilson School of Public and International Affairs, Princeton University, 1959); Thomas C. Schelling, *Strategy of Conflict* (Cambridge: Harvard University Press, 1960); idem, *Arms and Influence* (New Haven: Yale University Press, 1966); Alexander L. George, *Some Thoughts on Graduated Escalation*, RM-4844-PR (Santa Monica, Calif.: Rand Corporation, December 1965); and George, William E. Simons, and David K. Hall, *Limits of Coercive Diplomacy: Laos, Cuba, and Vietnam* (Boston: Little, Brown, 1971).

[5] In sharp contrast to the voluminous literature on coercion produced in the 1960s, the only major attempt by a social scientist to explain this failure in the decade after Saigon fell was Wallace J. Thies, *When Governments Collide: Coercion and Diplomacy in the Vietnam Conflict, 1964–1968* (Berkeley: University of California Press, 1980).

electric power plants in part because the American defense community did not remember the failure of such campaigns in Korea and Vietnam.

COMPETING EXPLANATIONS

"Coercion" means efforts to change the behavior of a state by manipulating costs and benefits. Both coercion and deterrence focus on influencing the adversary's calculus for decision making, but deterrence seeks to maintain the status quo by discouraging an opponent from changing its behavior. By contrast, coercion seeks to force the opponent to *alter* its behavior.[6] While coercion is thus the flip side of deterrence, the two can be intimately linked in practice. At the same time that the coercer hopes to force the target state to change its behavior, the target can hope to deter the coercer from executing the threat. Although states often use economic, diplomatic, or other forms of nonmilitary coercion, military coercion, the use of military instruments to change an opponent's behavior, deserves special attention because it is the form most often used when very important interests are at stake and because its use has the greatest physical and normative consequences.[7]

At the risk of oversimplifying, existing theories of coercion may be grouped into four broad families. The first family emphasizes the balance of resolve, contending that the state with the greater determination or reputation for determination is likely to prevail in coercive disputes.[8] The second family highlights the balance of interests, arguing that the state with the greater stake in a dispute's outcome will prevail.[9] The third focuses on the

---

[6] "Coercion" is the word I use to refer to the same concept as Schelling's "compellence." On the difference between coercion and deterrence, see Robert J. Art, "To What Ends Military Power?" *International Security* 4 (Spring 1980): 3–35; and Schelling, *Arms and Influence*, pp. 69–91.

[7] On nonmilitary sanctions, see David Baldwin, *Economic Statecraft* (Princeton: Princeton University Press, 1985); John Conybeare, *Trade Wars: The Theory and Practice of International Commercial Rivalry* (New York: Columbia University Press, 1987); and Michael Mastanduno, "Strategies of Economic Containment," *World Politics* 37 (July 1985): 503–31.

[8] Of the enormous literature on the role of resolve in international bargaining, three of the most important works are Fred C. Iklé, *How Nations Negotiate* (New York: Harper and Row, 1964); Schelling, *Arms and Influence*; and Robert Jervis, *The Logic of Images in International Relations* (Princeton: Princeton University Press, 1970).

[9] Robert E. Osgood and Robert W. Tucker, *Force, Order, and Justice* (Baltimore: Johns Hopkins University Press, 1967); George, et. al., *Limits of Coercive Diplomacy*; Andrew Mack, "Why Big Nations Lose Small Wars," *World Politics* 27 (January 1975), pp. 175–200. Some "balance of resolve" theorists should also be considered in this category because they think that often the balance of sheer political will is simply a reflection of the balance of interests. For instance, critical risk assessments generally turn on the interaction of actors' interests in the issue in dispute, because military costs are generally assumed to be equally high for both sides. See Ellsberg, "Theory and Practice of Blackmail." Similarly, Jervis, "Why Nuclear Superiority Doesn't Matter," *Political Science Quarterly* 94 (1979): 617–33; and Glenn H. Snyder and Paul Diesing, *Conflict among Nations* (Princeton: Princeton University Press, 1977), argue that resolve is primarily a function of interests.

vulnerability of the adversary's civilian population to air attack. Advocates of this view claim that coercive leverage derives from punishing large masses of civilians.[10] The fourth theory points to the balance of forces: striking military targets in the adversary's homeland shifts the military balance, thereby compelling the victim to modify its behavior.[11]

The key problem with these theories is that they are single-factor explanations that by themselves have limited explanatory power. Consider how each falls short as an explanation for the failure and success of coercive air power in the Vietnam War. If the balance of resolve had been crucial in Vietnam, why did Lyndon Johnson's coercive bombing from 1965 to 1968 fail but Richard Nixon's in 1972 succeed? The North Vietnamese were similarly determined to prevail in the two periods, and if anything, American resolve declined with the passage of time. Thus, the success of coercion does not correlate with a shift in determination toward the assailant. The balance-of-interests theory also fails. Regardless of how one appraises the geopolitical interests of the United States and North Vietnam in South Vietnam, those interests did not change over time and so cannot account for variation in the outcome of the cases.[12] The third theory, civilian vulnerability to air attack, is also inadequate, because the vulnerability of North Vietnam's population actually decreased as time went by. A comparable weakness confounds the final theory, changing the military balance through air attack. This theory leads to similar predictions in both cases, since the military targets subjected to attack were nearly identical in the two periods.

The existing theories are inadequate because they are incomplete. Although some authors have considered more than one of these factors, none has carefully defined the relations among variables, the strength of effects, and the conditions under which they occur, and the empirical testing of ex-

[10] Schelling, *Arms and Influence*; George H. Quester, *Deterrence before Hiroshima* (New York: Wiley, 1966); Liddell Hart, *Paris*; Fuller, *Reformation of War*; Douhet, *Command of the Air*; and Zeev Maoz, "Resolve, Capabilities, and the Outcomes of International Disputes, 1816–1976," *Journal of Conflict Resolution* 27 (June 1983): 195–229.

[11] Edward Luttwak, *The Strategic Balance, 1972*, Washington Papers no. 3 (New York: Library of Congress, 1972); Paul H. Nitze, "Assuring Strategic Stability in an Era of Detente," *Foreign Affairs* 54 (January 1976): 207–32; idem, "Deterring Our Deterrent," *Foreign Policy*, no. 25 (Winter 1976–77): 195–210; William R. Kintner and David C. Schwartz, *A Study on Crisis Management* (Philadelphia: University of Pennsylvania, Foreign Policy Research Institute, 1965); Richard K. Betts, *Nuclear Blackmail and Nuclear Balance* (Washington, D.C.: Brookings, 1987).

[12] South Vietnam was important to the United States largely for symbolic (reputational) reasons, and to the North for reasons of national cohesion. If one views American interests in Vietnam as declining during the war because of rapprochement with China, the balance of interest explanation does still worse, since the later bombing campaigns were more successful than the earlier ones. On American and North Vietnamese interests in South Vietnam, see Richard K. Betts, "Interests, Burdens, and Persistence: Asymmetries between Washington and Hanoi," *International Studies Quarterly* 24 (December 1980): 520–24.

isting hypotheses has been surprisingly thin.[13] Further, four analytic flaws common to nearly all work on the subject have impeded the advance of our understanding of how military coercion operates.

First, coercion is generally assumed to operate according to the same principles as deterrence. Although deterrence and coercion are complementary activities, however, they pose distinct theoretical problems because coercion is harder. Threats that deter may not coerce.

Deterrence is made easier by the "aggressor's handicap." In the era of nationalism, the homeland territory is normally much more valuable to the defender than it is to any assailant. Even if both value the stakes equally, the attacker, who stands to make gains, is likely to be more risk-averse than the defender, who stands to suffer losses. Attackers also bear the burden of disturbing the status quo.[14] As a result, deterrers will typically pay higher costs to retain possessions than attackers will to take them.

In situations of coercion, the victim assumes a role similar to the deterrer's. Hence, coercers operate under the same handicap as the attacker in deterrence. The victim is likely to value the stakes at issue more highly than the assailant, particularly when the coercer demands the surrender of homeland territory. Since the targets of coercion are normally willing to accept higher costs and risks than the coercers, potential assailants are likely to be deterred from even attempting coercion unless they possess superior military capabilities that can protect them from the victim's retaliation; by implication, thus, attempts by one nuclear superpower to coerce another will be rare because protection against retaliation is impossible. Furthermore, inasmuch as the coercer bears the ultimate responsibility for initiating hos-

---

[13] We have only one serious empirical study of military coercion, which is limited to nuclear cases and does not always distinguish coercion from deterrence: Betts, *Nuclear Blackmail*. Neither Walter J. Petersen, "Deterrence and Compellence: A Critical Assessment of Conventional Wisdom," *International Studies Quarterly* 30 (1986): 269–94, nor George, *Limits of Coercive Diplomacy*, systematically compares alternative explanations for success and failure. Barry M. Blechman and Stephen S. Kaplan with David K. Hall et al., *Force without War: U.S. Armed Forces as a Political Instrument* (Washington, D.C.: Brookings, 1978), studied 33 instances of peacetime uses of force but concluded little about military coercion except that it rarely achieves its objectives (pp. 89, 523–26).

[14] On these points, see Paul Kecskemeti, *Strategic Surrender: The Politics of Victory and Defeat* (Stanford: Stanford University Press, 1958); Robert Jervis, *The Illogic of American Nuclear Strategy* (Ithaca: Cornell University Press, 1984); Amos Tversky and Daniel Kahneman, "Judgment under Uncertainty," *Science* 185 (1974): 1124–30; and Morton A. Kaplan, "The Calculus of Deterrence," *World Politics* 11 (October 1958): 20–43. David Baldwin, "Power Analysis and World Politics," *World Politics* 31 (January 1979): 161–94, argues that compellence (coercion) and deterrence are indistinguishable and that the alleged difficulty of the former results from a practice of calling hard cases compellent and easy ones deterrent. But the distinction is not merely semantic. Changing the status quo is different from maintaining it, as well as harder. Petersen, "Deterrence and Compellence," finds that only 24 percent of compellent threats were successful in the cases he examined, compared to 63 percent of deterrent threats, although the difference disappears when both side's expected costs of war are controlled for. The meaning of this finding is unclear, however, because his samples are not comparable. The average severity of the coercive cases is lower than that of the deterrent ones (p. 282).

tilities if threats fail, coercive threats are inherently less credible than deterrent threats, which can shift the burden of the first hostile move to the target of the threat.[15] As a result, coercers tend to bolster their credibility by favoring threats that can be fulfilled in progressive stages and to rely on coercion in wartime when doubts about hostile action are moot.

Military coercion, in short, is about hard cases. Although the threat of a costly war of attrition may deter aggression,[16] successful coercion requires even stronger sanctions. The prospect of protracted war influenced the political calculations of all the major powers before World War II but had little effect on their decisions once they were involved in the war. Despite heavy costs, none of the powers on either side even considered surrender until faced with total defeat.

The second common flaw is to ignore one of the main strategies of coercion. Social scientists have long studied the effectiveness of both threats to civilians ("punishment") and threats of military failure ("denial") for deterrence. Punishment threatens to inflict costs heavier than the value of anything the challenger could gain, and denial threatens to defeat the adventure, so that the challenger gains nothing but must still suffer the costs of the conflict.[17] Most studies of military coercion have investigated only the punishment of civilians. They have omitted the use of coercive power to deny the target state the military capacity to control the contested territory.[18] The balance-of-interests school maintains, in effect, that the side more willing to risk punishment will prevail.[19] Even those who see the military balance as the key to coercion employ punishment-based logic; they assume the goal is to create a monopoly of force that enables the coercer to threaten the victim with unlimited punishment.[20]

Confining military coercion to countercivilian attacks raises both empirical and theoretical problems. On the empirical side, ignoring denial strategies distorts our understanding of important historical cases when military,

---

[15] Schelling, *Arms and Influence*, pp. 69–91.

[16] On requirements for successful deterrence, see John J. Mearsheimer, *Conventional Deterrence* (Ithaca: Cornell University Press, 1983).

[17] Glenn Snyder, *Deterrence by Punishment and Denial*, Research Monograph no. 1 (Princeton: Princeton University, Center of International Studies, 1959).

[18] George writes: "Coercive diplomacy can succeed only if the opponent accepts as credible the threat of punishment for non-compliance with the demands made upon him." *Limits of Coercive Diplomacy*, p. 238. Betts says: "The notion of blackmail in this study . . . means coercion by the threat of punishment." *Nuclear Blackmail*, p. 4. Ellsberg notes: "My problem as a blackmailer is to convince you that I am 'too likely' to respond with my second strategy, Punish, for you to accept the risk that your own second strategy, Resist, would entail." "Theory and Practice of Blackmail," p. 347. Schelling writes: "The ideal compellent action would be one that, once initiated, causes minimal harm if compliance is forthcoming and great harm if compliance is not forthcoming." *Arms and Influence*, p. 89.

[19] Robert Jervis, *The Meaning of the Nuclear Revolution: Statecraft and the Prospect of Armageddon* (Ithaca: Cornell University Press, 1989), p. 30.

[20] Betts, *Nuclear Blackmail*, pp. 15, 219–20, describes but does not endorse this logic.

as well as civilian, targets have been attacked for coercive purposes. During the bombing of Germany in World War II, the British focused on civilians while the Americans concentrated on military-related targets. Both strategies aimed to avoid a protracted land campaign, so as to achieve a political goal without paying the full cost of direct assault. Both are therefore properly considered coercive efforts. To study only the British bombing as coercion would be historically inaccurate and would miss an important part of the dynamics of the case.

In the realm of theory, studying only countercivilian attacks risks ignoring some of the most powerful mechanisms of successful coercion. Coercion sometimes succeeds even though civilians suffer only minor punishment, as in the American bombing of North Vietnam in 1972. Conversely, it sometimes fails despite very heavy punishment, as in Ethiopia in 1936, the Sino-Japanese war from 1937 to 1945, and the Allied bombing of Germany in World War II. Accordingly, a definition of coercion limited to punishment of civilians makes it impossible to explain many coercive outcomes.[21]

Third, the productive study of coercion must recognize that the vulnerability of target states to an assailant's coercive attacks varies. Societies differ in their vulnerability to countercivilian attacks according to such factors as their degree of urbanization, their use of burnable building materials, and the susceptibility of their food supplies to destruction. Similarly, target states with different military strategies vary in their vulnerability to denial attacks. Strategies that rely on large-scale mechanized operations are particularly vulnerable because they depend on massive logistic flows that make excellent targets for air attack. At the opposite end of the spectrum, guerrilla fighters are much less vulnerable to coercion because they need little logistic support. Matching the coercer's strategy to the target state's specific vulnerabilities can be decisive: it will determine how severe the effects of the coercer's attacks are and thus how strong the pressure on the target's political calculations. Theories that do not account for differences in vulnerability cannot accurately predict coercive outcomes.

Finally, the existing literature glosses over differences between conventional and nuclear coercion.[22] Most formal analyses have concentrated on nuclear coercion, and generally operate at levels of abstraction above the key causal factors in military coercion, namely, the military strategies of the assailant and victim. "Strategy" in formal models normally refers to decisions about whether to stand firm or make concessions, not to different

---

[21] Further, if policy makers believe that punishment threats are the best coercive strategy against all possible victims and if this premise is wrong, failing to examine the fundamental causes of coercion can have disastrous consequences in practice. Policy makers could easily assume that failure results from errors in execution, rather than the erroneous basic premise, and so repeat past mistakes again and again.

[22] Prominent examples are Schelling, *Arms and Influence*; George et al., *Limits of Coercive Diplomacy*; and, Quester, *Deterrence before Hiroshima*.

methods for translating force into coercive pressure by attacking different kinds of targets. Different military strategies available to an assailant are usually abstracted into a single variable in which different varieties of military costs are treated as wholly interchangeable.[23]

Although it makes no logical difference what type of weapon is used for coercion, in practice the vast gap in destructive power between nuclear and conventional weapons means that coercion in these two circumstances operates quite differently. Nuclear weapons can almost always inflict more pain than any victim can withstand; if the coercer's threat is credible, even the most determined opponents can be overwhelmed.[24] By contrast, the damage that conventional munitions can inflict is quite low when compared to the pain thresholds of modern nation-states. As a result, punishment strategies are rarely effective. If the coercer is not deterred from making a threat, therefore, nuclear coercion works better than conventional coercion.

To overcome the problems with these single-independent-variable approaches, we must, first, come up with a more comprehensive theory that incorporates the existing explanations into a set of conditional propositions about success and failure in military coercion. Second, we must test the new theory against an appropriate body of empirical evidence.

METHOD AND ARGUMENT

The overarching goal of this book is to present a theory that explains the success and failure of military coercion and to test it against the outcomes of all the strategic air offensives employed in international disputes during the twentieth century. The general propositions I propose in this book hold across space and time and account for a large amount of the variance, but they have limits. Nonmilitary variables, such as domestic political, organizational, and psychological factors—which can also affect outcomes—are treated as exogenous in order to study the specifically military elements of coercion. Although I do not construct a complete blueprint for coercion, my conclusions may help policy makers distinguish between strategies likely to succeed and those likely to fail. Also, in order to develop my theory of military coercion more fully, I have had to put aside many important related questions: whether availability of coercive tools makes states militant and helps to cause or to escalate wars; under what conditions states choose coercive over ordinary military strategies; and whether coercive force should

---

[23] For example, see Ellsberg, "Theory and Practice of Blackmail."
[24] Robert Jervis, "The Political Effects of Nuclear Weapons," *International Security* 13 (Fall 1988): 80–90.

have different legal and moral status from that accorded to other forms of influence in international politics.

Two kinds of tests are employed: quantitative analysis of all thirty-three strategic air campaigns to determine whether the theory's predictions correlate with outcomes, together with detailed case studies of five of the most important instances (Japan 1945, Germany 1945, Korea 1953, Vietnam 1965–1968 and 1972, and Iraq 1991) to determine whether the causal dynamics in specific cases match those expected by the theory.[25]

The evidence shows that it is the threat of military failure, which I call denial, and not threats to civilians, which we may call punishment, which provides the critical leverage in conventional coercion. Although nuclear weapons can make punishment the critical factor, in conventional conflicts even highly capable assailants often cannot threaten or inflict enough pain to coerce successfully. Conventional munitions have limited destructive power, and the modern nation-state is not a delicate mechanism that can easily be brought to the point of collapse. Moreover, governments are often willing to countenance considerable civilian punishment to achieve important territorial aims. Consequently, coercion based on punishing civilians rarely succeeds.

The key to success in conventional coercion is not punishment but denial, that is, the ability to thwart the target state's military strategy for controlling the objectives in dispute. To succeed the coercer must undermine the target state's confidence in its own military strategy. Precisely what capabilities must be denied to the target depends on the coercer's objectives. Thus, denial may require stopping the opponent from either gaining *or holding* territory, depending on whether the threatening assailant's goal is to prevent an attack, stop an ongoing attack, or force territorial concessions.[26] Once a state is persuaded that objectives cannot be achieved, levels of costs that were bearable as long as there was a chance of success become intolerable. The target then concedes in order to avoid suffering further losses to no purpose.

Nuclear coercion is different, because nuclear weapons have nearly unlimited capacity to do harm. No state can stand up under nuclear punishment. At the same time, denial does not matter, not because nuclear weapons are ineffective against military forces but because the threat to

---

[25] The theory originally developed from a probe of the explanatory power of commonly identified ingredients of coercion taken as single-factor propositions in two case studies— Japan and Vietnam. Although these initial hypotheses proved unsatisfactory, this effort enabled me to formulate a new theory, which has, as I hope to demonstrate, explanatory power not only for Japan and Vietnam but also for coercive air power in general. Further, though I have not tested the theory against cases that do not involve air power, comparison of the effects of land, sea, and air power in the cases I have studied suggests that the theory probably has explanatory power for all forms of military coercion.

[26] This is a broader definition of denial than that used by deterrence theorists, who usually refer only to defeat of an anticipated attack. See Snyder, *Deterrence by Punishment and Denial*.

civilians implied by any use of nuclear weapons is likely to overwhelm their military impact. Accordingly, successful nuclear coercion rests on threats to civilians rather than against military vulnerabilities. In short, the conventional wisdom is right for nuclear disputes but wrong for conventional cases.

The next chapter defines military coercion more precisely and builds and tests a new theory based on the interaction between coercers' strategies and target states' vulnerabilities. Chapter 3 explains the major coercive air strategies that have been used in international disputes; Chapters 4 through 8 investigate in detail how these strategies have fared in five important cases. Finally, Chapter 9 draws theoretical and policy implications from my findings.

[2]

Explaining Military Coercion

Coercion, like deterrence, seeks to affect the behavior of an opponent by manipulating costs and benefits. Deterrence, however, tries to persuade a state not to initiate a specific action because the perceived benefits do not justify the estimated costs and risks; coercion involves persuading an opponent to stop an ongoing action or to start a new course of action by changing its calculations of costs and benefits. Accordingly, coercion occurs whenever a state must choose between making concessions or suffering the consequences of continuing its present course of action. As a result, the universe of coercion includes nearly all attempts by states to force others to accept a change in the status quo, including virtually all wars. The two main exceptions are faits accomplis, which change the status quo so quickly that the opponent has no opportunity to resist, and wars of extermination, in which no concessions would be accepted.

Although it is often pursued deliberately, coercion is not defined by the intentions, or even the behavior, of the coercer but by the nature of the decisions faced by potential target states. Targets decide whether to make concessions and, as independent actors, can surrender without formal negotiations or explicit demands by the coercer. Even if the coercer makes no threats, no demands, and does not even imagine that the target might make concessions before being militarily defeated, if the coercer's actions cause the target to make concessions, coercion has succeeded. For instance, whereas the Allies in World War II had no expectations of achieving unconditional surrender of the Axis powers short of decisive victory, during the summer of 1943 it became clear that factions within the Italian government wished to leave the war, and in September Italy surrendered even though at that time the Allies controlled only a tiny part of the Italian mainland. Just as the success or failure of deterrence depends on calculations in the mind of the aggressor, so too does the success or failure of coercion rest in the decision of the target state.

There are two fundamental types of coercion: coercion by punishment and coercion by denial. Coercion by punishment operates by raising costs or risks to civilian populations. Punishment is not limited to hitting civilians in population centers. It may take the form of killing military personnel in large numbers to exploit the casualty sensitivities of opponents. Coercion by denial operates by using military means to prevent the target from attaining its political objectives or territorial goals. The coercing state could threaten, for example, to capture territory held by the opponent or to destroy enough of the opponent's military power to thwart its territorial ambitions. The coercer may try to stop the opponent from either gaining or holding territory, depending on whether the goal is to prevent an attack, stop an ongoing attack, or force territorial concessions.[1]

Both coercion by punishment and coercion by denial are logically distinct from the imposition of demands after complete military victory. Although coercers and war fighters may seek identical goals, such as the reduction of political aims, agreement to a cease-fire, withdrawal of forces, or even surrender, how they attain them is quite different. Brute force first routs opposing forces on the battlefield and then imposes political demands on a defenseless victim, bringing the defeated government to the point where it no longer controls organized forces capable of significantly impeding the victor's operations. For example, by early May 1945 the German government could no longer organize any concerted resistance to Allied occupation of the country, even though some combat units remained in the field. By contrast coercion seeks to change the behavior of states that still retain the capacity for organized military resistance.[2] As a result, coercion seeks to achieve the same goals as war fighting, but at less cost to both sides. While the coercer hopes to attain concessions without having to pay the full cost of military victory, the target may perceive that accepting the assailant's demands will be less costly than fighting to a finish. For example, Japan's surrender in August 1945 saved the lives of many thousands on both sides. In short, military coercion attempts to achieve political goals "on the cheap."

---

[1] This is a broader definition of denial than that used by deterrence theorists, who usually refer only to defeat of an anticipated attack. For an example of the narrower definition, see Glenn Snyder, *Deterrence by Punishment and Denial*, Research Monograph no. 1 (Princeton: Princeton University, Center of International Studies, 1959).

[2] Thomas C. Schelling includes bargaining between victor and defeated within the rubric of coercion, but this definition is too broad to be helpful. Since the victor must pay the full costs of winning the war to reach this situation, it gains no benefit from coercion, and since the victor has the ability to inflict unlimited harm on the defeated at little or no cost, coercion in this situation nearly always succeeds. These trivial successes tell us little about cases in which the victim can resist. See Schelling, *Arms and Influence* (New Haven: Yale University Press, 1966), pp. 12–15.

[13]

While logically distinct, efforts to coerce and efforts to achieve military victory are not completely separate activities, depending on the coercer's strategy. Coercion by punishment is relatively distinct from war fighting, for modern military forces often inflict civilian punishment without engaging opposing forces, and civilian pain, whether death, injury, illness, or hunger, is often observable and measurable separately from events on the battlefield. The distinction between coercion by denial and pursuit of military victory is more ambiguous, for both present the target state with military failure.[3] Moreover, coercers themselves often do not distinguish; instead, they pursue both options, hoping to attain their goals by coercion if possible and by decisive victory if necessary. However, distinguishing between coercion by denial and war fighting in actual military operations is easier in some circumstances than others. For example, when assailants have limited aims, coercion need only threaten the target's ability to control the disputed territory; it need not pose the risk of complete defeat. Alternatively, military strategies that depend on surprise for their effectiveness have no coercive value because they cannot be used to *threaten* the target with defeat.[4]

The gray area between coercion by denial and war fighting would be a problem only if war fighting ruled out coercion or if it were impossible to observe the difference between coercive success and complete military defeat. In fact, the pursuit of decisive victory does not necessarily rule out coercion. The coercer, whatever the set of demands for which it is prepared to use force, would almost always prefer to obtain them by the less costly method of coercion than by the more expensive alternative of winning total military victory first and imposing its demands afterward. In addition, the difference between successful coercion by denial and complete military victory depends on the particularities of the target state's military strategy. If the strategy is fairly ambitious, such as North Vietnam's effort to conquer the South through a massive conventional offensive in 1972, then relatively modest degradation of military capabilities may be sufficient to undermine

---

[3] Some analysts have attempted to draw a clear distinction between coercion and war fighting. The desirability of such a distinction is understandable in the work of Alexander George, for example, which explores usable alternatives to the unwinnability of nuclear war and the undesirability of an all-out military effort in Vietnam. Since war fighting itself can also be an effective coercive strategy, however, insisting on this distinction would exclude many important cases and ignore the most important coercive dynamics in others, such as Germany, Japan, Korea, North Vietnam, and Iraq. See Alexander L. George, William Simons, and David Hall, *The Limits of Coercive Diplomacy: Laos, Cuba, and Vietnam* (Boston: Little, Brown, 1971), pp. 16–19.

[4] The difference between coercion and war fighting is separate from the difference in decision making roles between national leaders and military officers in the field. Whether pursuing coercion or war fighting, the task of national leaders is to resolve trade-offs among societal values such as military power, territory, and civilian welfare, preserving all of them if possible or choosing among them if necessary. In contrast, military commanders try to widen the options of national leaders by resolving trade-offs among force-to-force considerations, terrain, and time; they do not weigh the relative importance of different social values.

it. Conversely, if the strategy is relatively unambitious, such as Iraq's effort to hold Kuwait by inflicting thousands of casualties on attacking ground forces, undermining it may require drastic reductions of the target's military capabilities. In this situation, the requirements for coercion by denial are almost identical to the requirements for complete military defeat.

The close conjunction between coercion and military victory tells us something important: if we find that coercive strategies based on denial are more effective than those based on punishment, then, by implication, the most effective way to compel concessions without achieving decisive victory is to demonstrate that one actually has the capacity to achieve decisive victory. Further, the overlap between coercion and military victory makes it possible to rate the magnitude of coercive successes. Surrender long before complete military defeat should be regarded an outstanding coercive success. By contrast, surrender only shortly before defeat should be considered only a minor success. This standard is important. If we find that coercion by denial does work but produces only minor successes, we must conclude that it is not worth pursuing in cases where coercers are not willing to fight almost all the way to victory.

Accordingly, the criteria for failure are simple. Coercion fails when the coercer stops its coercive military actions prior to concessions by the target, when the coercer's attacks continue but do not produce compliance by the target, or when the coercer imposes its demands only after complete defeat of the target. The last is crucial: if a coercive attempt is made but the war ends only when one side is decisively defeated, then *coercion* has failed, even if the coercer wins the war.

As this book shows, coercion by punishment rarely works. When coercion does work, it is by denial. Denial does not always work, either, of course, and sometimes states have no choice but to inflict a decisive defeat.

A Denial Theory of Military Coercion

A theory that predicts when military coercion will succeed and when it will fail must focus on the target state's decision-making process, which, in turn, is affected by the relationship between the coercer's military strategies and the target state's vulnerabilities.

The Logic of Coercion

The problem in coercion is to persuade the target state that acceding to the coercer's demands will be better than resisting them. Whether the state seeks to make gains or avoid losses is irrelevant for the purpose of explaining the logic of coercion. Success or failure is decided by the target state's decision calculus with regard to costs and benefits (that is, the state's value for its existing position compared to its [lower] value for its position if it makes the demanded concessions). When the benefits that would be lost by concessions and the probability of attaining these benefits by continued resistance are exceeded by the costs of resistance and the probability of suffering these costs, the target concedes. The logic of coercion can be described by a simple equation:

$$R = B\,p(B) - C\,p(C),$$

where: R = value of resistance
B = potential benefits of resistance
$p(B)$ = probability of attaining benefits by continued resistance
C = potential costs of resistance
$p(C)$ = probability of suffering costs.

Concessions occur when $R < 0$.

Coercive success must be a function of altering one or more of these factors by increasing the costs of continued resistance, raising the certainty that these costs will be suffered, lowering the benefits, or reducing the probability of success. Not all these components, however, are susceptible to manipulation.

First, benefits are not usually manipulatable by the coercer. While other issues may be involved, the principal issue in serious international disputes is usually control over territory. Territorial interests tend to be fixed within the time span of a dispute, because they emanate from pressures that change slowly, such as power-balancing considerations, or hardly at all, such as nationalism. Nationalist attachments to particular territories result from elements of the target state's linguistic, cultural, and political history, which the coercer is powerless to change. Interests based on security concerns derive from the balance of power and threat in the international system.[5] Since the coercer, by definition, poses a severe threat to the target state, it is in no position to persuade the target that territorial interests are unimportant. War itself, moreover, can occasionally increase the value of certain territory, especially territory with military significance, such as Norway in World War II. By implication, since the coercer cannot lower the value of the disputed territory to the target state, coercion must require either raising costs or reducing the probability that the territorial benefits can be attained even if the target continues to resist.

[5] Stephen M. Walt, *Origins of Alliances* (Ithaca: Cornell University Press, 1987). On the rise of nationalism and its effect on conceptions of national interest, see Ernest Gellner, *Nations and Nationalism* (Ithaca: Cornell University Press, 1983); and John Breuilly, *Nationalism and the State* (Chicago: University of Chicago Press, 1982).

The coercer can raise the costs of continued resistance, principally by exploiting civilian vulnerabilities. States are always concerned about protecting the welfare of their civilian populations. When a state participates in an international dispute, however, it does so because its territorial ambitions outweigh the expected costs and risks to its citizens. By threatening to harm civilians, the coercer seeks to raise the costs of continued resistance above the target state's value for the territory at stake. If the threat is sufficiently great, the target state will abandon the territory to preserve its greater interest in protecting its populace. The more important the territorial interests at stake, the higher the benefits, and therefore the higher must the coercer raise costs to compel concessions. If the concessions demanded include highly valued territory or even the target state's homeland (that is, surrender), the level of costs that must be inflicted to induce concessions is usually extremely high. By implication, moreover, economic inducements (bribery) are poor complements to military coercion over significant interests. Whether employed simultaneously or promised to sweeten deals, they are not likely to influence the victim's decision significantly, since they are likely to be trivial compared to the territorial interests at stake.

In principle the coercer can raise the probability that the threatened costs will actually be inflicted, but in practice the more important question is usually whether the coercer can inflict sufficient damage to compel concessions. Extremely high credibility that the coercer will impose damage is normally a minimum requirement. In fact, coercive threats are usually highly credible. They generally occur in war, when there is no reason to doubt the coercer's willingness to inflict damage. In addition, coercers usually possess military capabilities superior to their opponents' and so, except when both sides are nuclear armed, are unlikely to be deterred by fear of retaliation.

The final option for the coercer is to reduce the probability that continued resistance will bring the target state the hoped-for benefits. States are willing to pay costs in return for benefits only if they actually expect to gain the benefits. The task for the coercer, therefore, is to thwart the target state's military strategy, destroying confidence that it can take or hold the disputed territory. If the target no longer believes that it can achieve its goals at any price, it is likely to concede them.

Once there is no hope of military success, any further costs paid by the target state become futile, and its most important incentive becomes avoiding the costs of continued pointless resistance. Even if the coercer makes no special effort to punish the target, continued resistance inherently entails substantial additional costs, including the costs of military operations, economic costs, and loss of civilian lives through collateral damage and privation. Therefore, levels of costs that were insufficient to affect the target state's decision calculus as long as military success appeared possible become sufficient to cause surrender.

Denying the target the possibility of achieving benefits can compel abandonment only of those specific interests. If the coercer's attacks leave the target state still capable of defending its homeland but not peripheral territory, only the latter will be surrendered. For example, in 1972 the United States was able to prevent North Vietnam from continuing offensive operations but not from retaining control over territories it occupied in the South. Accordingly, Washington was able to pressure Hanoi into a cease-fire agreement but not into a withdrawal.

Coercion can succeed only when the costs of surrender are lower than the costs of resistance. If surrender were costless—beyond the value of the territorial interests conceded—states would always surrender when the probability of victory disappeared. Surrender, however, sometimes involves serious costs in addition to the territorial benefits abandoned, such as enforced change of government, destruction of social institutions, or the threat of genocide. When these costs equal or exceed the costs of continued resistance, coercion will fail. Surrender will not occur even if the military situation is hopeless.

Strategies of Military Coercion

Because the benefits of resistance are not manipulable by the coercer, strategy is limited to three options, each of which aims at one of the manipulable components of the target's decision calculus. Punishment strategies attempt to raise the costs of continued resistance; risk strategies, to raise the probability of suffering costs; denial strategies, to reduce the probability that resistance will yield benefits.

Punishment campaigns seek to raise the societal costs of continued resistance to levels that overwhelm the target state's territorial interests, causing it to concede to the coercer's demands. The common feature of all punishment campaigns is that they inflict suffering on civilians, either directly or indirectly by damaging the target state's economy. Cities may be bombed in order to kill or injure the inhabitants or render them homeless. Bombing or naval blockades can cause shortages of key supplies, such as food and clothing, or deprive residents of electrical power, water, and other essential services.

By contrast, risk strategies slowly raise the probability of civilian damage.[6] The crucial element here is timing. The coercer puts at risk essentially

---

[6] The idea of manipulating the risk of punishment for political purposes has largely come to be identified with the work of Thomas Schelling. Others also shared in the development of this idea, chief among them Morton A. Kaplan, *Strategy of Limited Retaliation* (Princeton: Center of International Studies, Woodrow Wilson School of Public and International Affairs, Princeton University, 1959); and Alexander L. George, *Some Thoughts on Graduated Escalation*, RM-4844-PR (Santa Monica, Calif.: Rand Corporation, December 1965).

the same targets as in punishment strategies, but the key is to inflict civilian costs at a gradually increasing rate rather than destroy the entire target set in one fell swoop. In order to convince the opponent that much more severe damage will follow if concessions are not made, operations are slowly escalated in intensity, geographical extent, or both. The coercer must signal clearly that the attacks are contingent on the target's behavior and will be stopped upon compliance with the coercer's demands. At the same time, the coercer must be careful not to "kill the hostage" by destroying everything of value to the target, for it would then be impossible to threaten more to come.[7] The coercer may interrupt the operations temporarily in order to provide time for reflection or negotiation or to reward the target state for concessions, thus encouraging minor demonstrations of willingness to accommodate the assailant's demands as well as major concessions.

Denial strategies target the opponent's military ability to achieve its territorial or other political objectives, thereby compelling concessions in order to avoid futile expenditure of further resources. Unlike countercivilian strategies, denial strategies make no special effort to cause suffering to the opponent's society, only to deny the opponent hope of achieving the disputed territorial objectives. Thus, denial campaigns focus on the target state's military strategy.[8]

Since coercive strategies correspond to specific elements in a target state's decision calculus, explaining when punishment, risk, and denial strategies are effective provides a general answer to the larger question of when military coercion succeeds and fails. To answer this question, I want to set out the main propositions of a denial theory of military coercion and then explain the logic behind each of them.

PROPOSITIONS ABOUT SUCCESSFUL MILITARY COERCION

No one coercive strategy is likely to succeed under all circumstances. Still, there are conditions under which one strategy is more likely to succeed than another. Specifically, in conventional disputes, coercion is most likely to succeed when directed at military, not civilian, vulnerabilities. Conversely, in nuclear disputes, coercion is likely to be predicated on civilian, not military, vulnerabilities.

---

[7] Schelling, *Arms and Influence*, p. 89. This logic would suggest that punishment strategies, which seek to maximize current rather than future costs, should never succeed unless targets are irrational. Punishment strategies would have to rely for their effectiveness on emotional reactions to sunk costs, such as frustration, grief, and anger. Architects of punishment-oriented air strategies, as I will show, do rely in part on such reactions.

[8] Decapitation, a recent proposal for pursuing both punishment and denial by attacking a single target set, is discussed in Chapter 3.

Conventional Coercion

Coercive success is a function of the interactions among the coercer's strategy, the target state's military strategy, and the target state's domestic politics. The denial theory of coercion incorporates six propositions about conventional coercion:

1. *Punishment strategies will rarely succeed.* Inflicting enough pain to subdue the resistance of a determined adversary is normally beyond the capacity of conventional forces. Punishment strategies will work only when core values are not at stake.

2. *Risk strategies will fail.* They are diluted, and therefore weaker, versions of punishment.

3. *Denial strategies work best.* They succeed if and when the coercer undermines the target state's military strategy to control the specific territory in dispute.

4. *Surrender of homeland territory is especially unlikely.* Nationalist sentiments demand resistance to foreign rule even when physical security cannot be guaranteed.

5. *Surrender terms that incorporate heavy additional punishment will not be accepted.* There is no incentive to concede when the costs of surrender outweigh those of continued resistance. Societies that expect to become victims of genocide will not surrender.

6. *Coercive success almost always takes longer than the logic of either punishment or denial alone would suggest.* Targets of coercion are usually slow to recognize the magnitudes of both increased civilian suffering and declining military prospects. Also, the domestic political costs of concessions encourage delay until the hopelessness of the situation becomes inescapably obvious. Even small hopes of success can cause coercion to fail.

Nuclear Coercion

In contrast to conventional coercion, the accepted wisdom on nuclear coercion is mostly right. It succeeds by manipulating civilian vulnerability, according to four propositions:

1. *Nuclear coercion requires superiority.* If the target state has an assured destruction capability, any coercer is likely to be deterred.

2. *Denial strategies are not useful in nuclear disputes.* The horrific levels of societal destruction in nuclear war are likely to so dominate decision making as to make the prospects for success or failure of military campaigns largely irrelevant.

3. *Risk strategies can be successful in nuclear disputes.* Unlike conventional threats, nuclear threats raise the prospect of so much harm that they can coerce without being fully implemented.

4. *Nuclear punishment should be effective but rare.* No target could resist. However, nuclear bombardment would not only reduce the value of the disputed territory, but would also earn the coercer a reputation for unparalleled barbarism.

These propositions are based on observations of the decision-making processes of modern nation-states and of how the industrial revolution has affected their powers of resistance. The rise of nationalism, industrialization, and bureaucratization have profoundly altered the abilities of modern states to limit the damage the coercer can inflict, to minimize the costs of damage suffered, and to endure costs that cannot be avoided. Because of the limited destructiveness of conventional weapons, outcomes of conventional coercion are determined mainly by the target state's powers of resistance, which explains why punishment and risk strategies generally fail, why denial strategies often succeed, and why success tends to come later than expected. Nuclear coercion works the other way: nuclear destructiveness overwhelms any possible resistance.

Why Conventional Punishment Rarely Succeeds

Punishment strategies seek to inflict enough pain on enemy civilians to overwhelm their territorial interests in the dispute. The hope is either that the government will concede or the population will revolt. Punishment strategies do not, however, usually offer significant coercive leverage, for six reasons. First, the territorial stakes in coercive disputes are often very important for either national security or nationalist reasons. As a result, states involved in coercive disputes are often willing to accept high costs, including civilian suffering, to achieve their objectives. Punishment can succeed when the target state has only minor interests at stake in the dispute, but these successes are likely to be rare because the coercer is likely also to have only low interests at stake and so is easily deterred from issuing a coercive threat. Thus, successful coercion based on punishment normally requires the conjunction of three conditions: low interest by the target; balance of interests favoring the coercer; and balance of capabilities favoring the coercer. Such easy cases tell us little about more serious disputes.

Second, individuals and states can value specific territories not only out of security concerns but also because of powerful drives for national identity and cohesion. Increasing ethnic conflict since the end of the Cold War indicates the cogency of this motivation. The prospect of the homeland, or part of it, or even co-nationals elsewhere being ruled by alien groups constitutes an intolerable injury to nationalist sentiments. Nationalism also imbues individual citizens with personal attachment to national goals, for which they are often willing to accept great sacrifice.[9]

This effect is intensified by democratization. The greater the sense of participation in the affairs of government, the more citizens see the state as the

[9] Carlton J. Hayes, *Essays on Nationalism* (New York: Macmillan, 1926); Boyd Shafer, *Faces of Nationalism* (New York: Harcourt Brace Jovanovich, 1972); and Quincy Wright, *A Study of War* (Chicago: University of Chicago Press, 1942), vol. 2.

embodiment of higher values and the deeper their commitment to protect and support the state and its goals.[10] Additionally, advances in communication technology have improved the ability of governments to use propaganda and education to enhance the legitimacy of the state and its policies.[11] Thus, modern states are often willing and able to countenance a great deal of civilian punishment to achieve goals articulated by the government. The resolve of democratic states can be further increased, moreover, when governmental efforts to sell (or oversell) foreign policy commitments lead to "blowback." Inflated images of the importance of foreign policy interests can trap governments into maintaining commitments long after they would have preferred to abandon them. Authoritarian states, to the extent they rely on public enthusiasm for their policies, are also susceptible to these pressures.[12]

Third, coercion often occurs in wartime, when the willingness of states to tolerate costs usually increases. As the economic and social suffering caused by war increases, states become less willing to abandon these sunk costs by making concessions. The experience of war and government propaganda can demonize the enemy and lead to an uncompromising "us or them" attitude in which anything less than victory comes to be seen as disaster. Doves may be constrained from participating in political debate; willingness even to consider negotiation can come to be seen as treasonous. The need to mobilize vast resources and to depend on large military organizations creates enormous institutional momentum that cannot easily be turned off.[13] As a result, the longer a society is at war, the greater are the costs it will bear and the less inclined it is to accept settlements, even ones that would have been acceptable in peacetime.

The fourth reason punishment rarely coerces is that conventional munitions can inflict only limited damage on civilians even when used deliber-

---

[10] Michael Howard, *War in European History* (New York: Oxford University Press, 1976), 110–11.

[11] Stephen Van Evera, "Causes of War" (Diss., University of California, Berkeley, 1984), pp. 407–21.

[12] For discussion of the resolve of democracies, see George Kennan, *American Diplomacy, 1900–1950* (Chicago: University of Chicago Press, 1951); and Van Evera, "Causes of War," who invented the term "Blowback." For discussion of the same dynamic in an authoritarian state (Wilhelmine Germany), see Ludwig Dehio, *Germany and World Politics in the Twentieth Century,* trans. Dieter Pevsner (New York: Norton, 1967); Fritz Fischer, *War of Illusions: German Policies from 1911 to 1914,* trans. Marian Jackson (New York: Norton, 1975); Paul M. Kennedy, *The Rise of the Anglo-German Antagonism, 1860–1914* (London: Allen and Unwin, 1980), chap. 18; Hans Kohn, *The Mind of Germany: The Education of a Nation* (New York: Harper Torchbook, 1965), chaps. 7–12; and Louis L. Snyder, *German Nationalism: The Tragedy of a People* (Harrisburg, Pa.: Telegraph Press, 1952).

[13] On these points, see John W. Dower, *War without Mercy: Race and Power in the Pacific War* (New York: Pantheon, 1986); Fred C. Iklé, *Every War Must End* (New York: Harper and Row, 1964); and John J. Mearsheimer, "The Theory and Practice of Conventional Deterrence" (Diss., Cornell University, 1981), chap. 4.

ately to cause massive casualties. Coercers can kill or starve significant numbers of civilians but rarely more than a small proportion of the population. There are no comprehensive data on civilian deaths in modern wars, but data on battle deaths, which nearly always exceed civilian losses, show that states rarely lose more than 2 percent of their prewar population. Even in World Wars I and II losses exceeded 5 percent of prewar population in only a few states.[14] Some populations are more vulnerable than others, depending on their degree of urbanization, type of housing construction, and susceptibility to flooding from dam destruction. Still, the most devastating of all countercivilian campaigns, the bombing of Japan in World War II, killed 900,000 people out of a prewar population of 70 million. Countercivilian attacks can lower morale, increase absenteeism, and cause some deurbanization as refugees flee vulnerable cities, but these problems rarely have serious effects on production or cause civilians to put effective pressure on the government to surrender. The worker absentee rate in Japanese industry during 1945 was approximately 8 percent.[15]

Fifth, modern states can minimize their vulnerability to countercivilian attacks by defense, evacuation of threatened areas, and rapid adjustment to economic dislocations.[16] States can protect themselves against naval blockades through defensive measures such as convoy systems, counteroffensive operations such as antisubmarine patrols and attacks on submarine bases, and by acceleration of shipping production to replace lost tonnage. In World War I, Germany's unrestricted submarine campaign against Britain initially inflicted very heavy losses, but the British were able to contain the problem with the introduction of convoys, later supplemented by laying a mine barrage across the North Sea which blocked German submarine access to the Atlantic. In World War II, Germany's submarine offensive against Britain was initially successful, even despite convoying, but was eventually defeated by a combination of improved antisubmarine escorts, air surveillance, and the enormous replacement tonnage provided by British and American shipbuilding industries.[17] Similarly, air attacks against population centers can be opposed by fighters, radar, antiaircraft artillery and missiles, and civil defense. During World War II bombing offensives in Europe by both Allied and German forces were greatly hampered by antiaircraft defenses, and in the Pacific the vul-

[14] J. David Singer and Melvin Small, *The Wages of War, 1816–1965: A Statistical Handbook* (New York: John Wiley, 1972), pp. 351–57.

[15] United States Strategic Bombing Survey (USSBS), *The Effects of Strategic Bombing on Japanese Morale* (Washington, D.C.: GPO, 1947), pp. 65, 249.

[16] Modern precision guided weapons and stealth do not fundamentally alter this. See Chapter 9.

[17] Karl Lautenschlager, "The Submarine in Naval Warfare, 1901–2001," *International Security* 11 (Winter 1986–87): 94–140.

nerability of the Japanese homeland was greatly increased by the relative lack of such defenses.[18]

Evacuation of population centers threatened by bombing or by the advance of enemy troops can further reduce civilian vulnerability. Once city populations have been greatly reduced, additional raids inflict lighter losses, and the outlying districts in which refugees are resettled make very poor targets for bombing.

Substitution for shortages further reduces the effects of countercivilian attacks. The relatively slow place at which damage caused by bombing or blockade accumulates allows states to substitute for shortages and thus to ameliorate indirect costs to civilians. The economies of modern nation-states do not have "break points," thresholds of shortages below which sudden collapse occurs; they deteriorate incrementally by a process of successive substitution. Modern techniques in science and administration can compensate for the shortage of a primary good by conservation, more efficient allocation, or discovery of alternatives. The history of wartime food shortages in Britain during the Napoleonic wars, World War I, and World War II, illustrates this point. Attempts to blockade Britain into submission by exploiting its excessive dependence on food imports failed in part because the ability of the British to compensate for food shortages actually grew faster than their dependence on food imports during each period.[19]

Finally, the citizenry of the target state is not likely to turn against its government because of civilian punishment. The supposed causal chain—civilian hardship produces public anger which forms political opposition against the government—does not stand up. One reason it does not is that a key assumption behind this argument—that economic deprivation causes popular unrest—is false. As social scientists have shown, economic deprivation does often produce personal frustration, but collective violence against governments requires populations to doubt the moral worth of the political system as a whole, as opposed to specific policies, leaders, or results. Political alienation is more important than economic deprivation as a cause of revolutions.[20]

---

[18] Robin Higham, *Air Power: A Concise History* (New York: St. Martin's, 1972), pp. 114–19.

[19] Mancur Olson Jr., *The Economics of the Wartime Shortage: A History of British Food Supplies in the Napoleonic War and in World Wars I and II* (Durham, N.C.: Duke University Press, 1963), p. 142.

[20] On the causes of popular unrest, see David Snyder and Charles Tilly, "Hardship and Collective Violence in France, 1830 to 1960," *American Sociological Review* 37 (October 1972): 520–32; Charles Tilly, Louise Tilly, and Richard Tilly, *The Rebellious Century, 1830–1930* (Cambridge: Harvard University Press, 1975); Edward N. Muller, *Aggressive Political Participation* (Princeton: Princeton University Press, 1979); and Steven Finkel and James Rule, "Relative Deprivation and Related Psychological Theories of Civil Violence: A Critical Review," in *Research in Social Movements, Conflicts, and Change*, ed. Louis Kriesberg (Greenwich, Conn.: JAI Press, 1986), 9: 47–69.

Nationalism, moreover, almost always translates into a corresponding disdain for other nations, which is easily exacerbated by governments. Indeed, serious international disputes tend to produce a "rally around the flag" effect, which increases support for the government even among groups who tend to oppose government policies in peacetime. In many instances, people continue to follow instructions even though they no longer believe in government reports or policies. German and Japanese civilians continued to work in support of their countries' war efforts even after they ceased to believe their governments' claims that victory would be achieved.[21]

In fact, punishment generates more public anger against the attacker than against the target government. Punishment does produce emotional stress, but this *reduces rather than increases* collective action against the government, because heavy punishment induces a "survival" response and light punishment, a "Pearl Harbor" effect. Populations that survive heavy air attack commonly suffer temporary emotional disorders, more prolonged and severe when they experience a near miss, and heavily bombed populations may develop feelings of hostility toward their own government, but these feelings are overwhelmed by the need for personal safety. As a result, heavy punishment does not produce disruptive behavior; it induces political apathy. English workers lost an average of only six days from work after even the largest bombing raids, and then only when their house was destroyed. Even when heavily bombed populations show increasing resentment toward national leaders, this effect is not dramatic. In Germany, 62 percent of the people in unbombed towns expressed trust in their national leaders, as against 48 percent in heavily bombed towns, hardly a decisive effect. The level of trust in national leaders in unbombed cities suggests that Germany's defeat on the ground had more impact than attack from the air. Moreover, even if resentment of national leaders increased in heavily bombed communities, this does not mean that populations shift their loyalties toward the attacker. Many of the Germans and Japanese who were interviewed and who said that the enemy was not responsible for the

---

[21] The United States Strategic Bombing Survey, *The Effects of Strategic Bombing on German Morale* (Washington, D.C.: GPO, 1947); and USSBS, *Effects on Japanese Morale*. For discussion of how nationalism influences the way nations view each other, see Kenneth R. Minogue, *Nationalism* (New York: Basic Books, 1967), pp. 7–32; Boyd Shafer, *Nationalism: Myth and Reality* (New York: Harcourt, Brace, 1955); Hans Kohn, *The Idea of Nationalism* (New York: Macmillan, 1944); and Mearsheimer, "Theory and Practice of Conventional Deterrence," pp. 121–22. On foreign conflict and domestic divisions, the seminal study is Rudolph J. Rummel, "Dimensions of Conflict Behavior within and between Nations," *General Systems* 8 (1963): 1–50. For a review of follow-on studies, see Dina A. Zines, *Contemporary Research in International Relations* (New York: Free Press, 1976): 160–75. Some research suggests that international conflict actually increases domestic support for governments; see Jack Levy, "The Diversionary Theory of War: A Critique," in *Handbook of War Studies*, ed. Manus Midlarsky (Boston: Unwin Hyman, 1989), pp. 259–88.

bombings, nevertheless had extremely hostile attitudes toward the Allies elsewhere in their interviews. In response to the question, "How did you feel about the Americans during the war?" one-fourth of Japanese gave no answer, 40 percent spoke in terms of hatred, and only 11 percent answered that they had no ill feelings. This breakdown probably underestimates the actual incidence of antienemy sentiment, since the interviews were conducted by Americans who had their countries under military occupation.[22] In Germany and Japan bombing did contribute to wartime increases in petty crime (looting, black marketeering, and juvenile delinquency), but obvious forms of subversive activity were extremely rare.[23] That subversive activity did not increase in Great Britain as well suggests that loyalty to the state may have been as important a factor as the conditions of repressive and coercive control exercised by totalitarian governments.

In contrast, light punishment produces popular anger toward the attacker and, often, demands for reprisals. In World War II, Americans justified the bombing of Japan as retribution for Pearl Harbor. Similarly, in both World Wars, British civilians who had *not* experienced heavy air attacks were more likely to favor an aggressive "Bomb Berlin" policy than those who had.[24]

It is also true that forcible removal of the regime by popular opposition groups is unlikely as long as military forces are loyal to the government. To overturn a government, opposition groups must do more than passively resist government orders; they must wrest possession of important instruments of national control, such as communication, transportation, and administrative centers. Opposition groups are at a great disadvantage in any contest of force, however, since they usually lack organization, training, and heavy weapons. Quite small contingents of well-armed forces loyal to the regime can disperse, decapitate, and deter most mass movements against the government or collective civil disobedience. In major disputes capabilities for repression grow, both because governments are likely to mobilize significant additional forces and because repression of dissent is likely to be supported by nationalist groups. Unless the society is so badly divided by domestic cleavages before the dispute that the government lacks authority, opponents criticizing government policy labor under a legitimacy disadvantage, and if necessary, dissent can be forcibly repressed. As a result, it is unlikely that either government policy or the regime itself can be changed by popular pressure. In short, punishment does not empower opposition groups.[25]

[22] USSBS, *Effects on German Morale* 1: 13; USSBS, *Effects on Japanese Morale* 1: 38, 41.

[23] Irving L. Janis, *Air War and Emotional Stress: Psychological Studies of Bombing and Civilian Defense* (Santa Monica, Calif.: Rand Corporation, 1951), pp. 126–52.

[24] Dower, *War without Mercy*, pp. 36–37; R. H. Thouless, "Psychological Effects of Air Raids," *Nature* 148 (1941): 183–85; P. E. Vernon, "Psychological Effects of Air Raids," *Journal of Abnormal Social Psychology* 36 (1941): 457–76.

[25] Charles Tilly, "Revolutions and Collective Violence," in *Handbook of Political Science*, ed. Fred Greenstein and Nelson Polsby (Reading, Mass.: Addison-Wesley, 1975), 3: 483–556.

Attackers can sometimes precipitate revolution in target states, but only by smashing the state's army. Successful revolution depends on the disintegration of rank-and-file military support for the government. The supreme solvent of military forces is large-scale battlefield defeat. As large numbers of disgruntled soldiers (and deserters) return home, they may feel highly motivated to take revenge for their sufferings on the government and so may form the nucleus of revolutionary forces, making collective action possible for political opposition groups.

Both the Russian Revolution in 1917 and the German Revolution in 1918 occurred when significant parts of their militaries mutinied shortly after battlefield disasters that demonstrated that the war was lost. As early as 1916 there were 1.5 million deserters from the Russian army. The Brusilov offensive, Russia's largest offensive of the war, ended in disaster on 20 September with over a million casualties. By February 1917, Russian cities were swarming with deserters who were only too willing to join, rather than oppose, a revolution. Moreover, the other pillar of the tsarist system—the bureaucracy—was disintegrating. Thus, when the popular revolts started, there were no organized social forces strong enough to support the regime. In Germany by the summer of 1918 the Allies had defeated the last major German offensive and achieved a succession of breakthroughs, clearly indicating that Germany had lost the capacity to hold its front. When in October 1918 the Kiel sailors were ordered to put to sea for a grand-scale raid on England which could not conceivably alter the course of the war, they refused to sail. This mutiny spread like a windblown fire throughout Germany, led to the formation of local councils, and in early November caused the Kaiser to abdicate and the October Government to resign in favor of a government that ended the war.[26]

Similarly, the uprisings in Iraq in 1991 occurred after its army had suffered a catastrophic battlefield defeat. Many of the defeated soldiers returning home were Shi'as and Kurds who already hated the regime for previous repression and for placing them in the way of Coalition firepower. They linked up with civilians also already so disaffected with from ruling regime that they did not require the additional motive of civilian cost to revolt. Thus, those who believe that states can be coerced by encouraging popular unrest that avoids messy battles have it backward; smashing the army, not punishing civilians, is the key to revolution in serious international disputes.

[26] Feliks Gross, *The Seizure of Political Power in a Century of Revolution* (New York: Philosophical Library, 1958), pp. 192–95; Katherine Chorely, *Armies and the Art of Revolution* (Boston: Beacon Press, 1973), pp. 110–23; Vincent J. Esposito, *A Concise History of World War I* (New York: Praeger, 1964).

Why Conventional Risk Strategies Fail

The alternative countercivilian strategy relies on the manipulation of risk of future damage rather than on inflicting maximum actual damage. Risk strategies are usually less effective than punishment campaigns, for three reasons.

First, the argument on which the strategy is based, that coercive leverage can come only from fear of future damage rather than actual damage, does not address a real distinction in the causal mechanism of the strategies. Given the limits of conventional weapons, punishment strategies never actually "kill the hostage"; damage accumulates slowly, so the coercer can always inflict still more by continuing the assault.

Second, for any given level of coercer capabilities, damage threatened under a risk-based strategy cannot exceed the actual damage imposed by a punishment strategy. In fact, by further slowing the already slow pace at which damage accumulates, risk strategies may improve the ability of opponents to adjust and so may be unable to threaten even as much damage as punishment strategies. In principle, risk-based strategies could be used to threaten denial, but in practice they hardly ever are. The slow and pre-dictable pace provides the target state with too many opportunities to adjust tactics or regenerate losses, making this strategy inherently ineffective. The one exception is the unusual case where the target cannot regenerate damaged capabilities. Iraq in the fall of 1990 may have been in this position, having no indigenous capability to produce high-technology equipment and being subject to an effective arms blockade.

Third, the pattern of gradually increasing damage which is supposed to increase the credibility of threatened future damage is actually more likely to reduce credibility because the coercer's restraint tends to be attributed to political constraints rather than free strategic choice. Instead of being convinced of the coercer's resolve to inflict maximum damage if demands are not met, the opponent is more likely to be convinced that the coercer will never escalate far above current restrained levels. The result is that the costs and risks perceived by the target state are likely to be much lower than intended by the coercer and lower than those produced by a punishment strategy with correspondingly less coercive effect. In fact, risk strategies are rarely used except when coercers are subject to political constraints that prevent them from waging full-blown punishment campaigns. Domestic political constituencies may be unwilling to countenance the large-scale suffering that would result from prosecuting a punishment campaign, for instance, or the coercer's government may fear that more intensive attacks would provoke third-party intervention on behalf of the target state. The U.S. bombing of Libya in 1986 was limited to a single raid because neither the American public nor U.S. allies in Europe would have supported exten-

[28]

sive operations.[27] This case also demonstrates that credibility may be lost if the assailant becomes less determined to continue inflicting costs as the campaign progresses.

When Conventional Denial Works

The key to the success of denial strategies rests in the interaction of the two sides' military strategies. Simply destroying targets of military value is not sufficient, for such attacks may not necessarily undermine the opponent's prospects of controlling the territory at issue. Thus, the German submarine blockade of Britain in World War I did reduce British imports of raw materials with some effect on aggregate industrial production but not sufficiently to prevent Britain from continuing to execute its strategy for liberating northern France and Belgium. Of course, complete destruction of all the victim's military capabilities will undermine any strategy, but it is achieved only by decisive military victory—with all its costs—and thus counts as a coercive failure, not a success.

Although the target usually cannot change its basic strategy, because this is fixed by its capabilities or form of political organization, it often has great ability to minimize the effects of the coercer's attacks. The target state may have a considerable cushion above military requirements, allowing it to absorb significant losses without endangering its objectives. Also, some military strategies are much more sensitive to losses of certain types of forces than others; in certain categories even heavy losses may have little effect on the outcome. For example, the United States inflicted heavy losses on North Vietnamese POL stockpiles in 1965–1968, but these had hardly any effect on the progress of the war. Similarly, because Germany's strategy in World War II did not depend on the ability to move resources overseas, the loss of the German surface navy had little affect on the outcome of the war. If losses can be regenerated quickly enough, moreover, they may not affect ultimate outcomes. For example, during the course of 1941 the Red Army lost over 3 million men, compared to its prewar strength of 3.5 million, but it was substantially rebuilt by the next summer.[28] Finally, the opponent can often compensate for losses by abandoning low-priority missions and reallocating remaining resources to the most important objectives. To compensate for heavy naval losses in the early years of World War II, Britain substantially withdrew its fleet from the Pacific and the Mediterranean to concentrate on the vital Atlantic, and in late 1941, the Soviets withdrew large numbers of

[27] Aside from increasing the risk of further attacks if Libya did not stop supporting terrorism, a second objective appears to have been to kill Khaddafi himself. Tim Zimmermann, "The American Bombing of Libya: A Success for Coercive Diplomacy?" *Survival* 29 (May–June 1987): 195–214.

[28] John Keegan, *The Second World War* (New York: Viking, 1990), pp. 173–208.

their forces in the Far East to commit to the battle for Moscow.[29] To succeed, therefore, coercers must not only thwart the opponent's strategy but also any possible countermeasures.

For coercion through denial to succeed, the coercer must exploit the particular vulnerabilities of the opponent's specific strategy. All military strategies do not share the same weaknesses. Modern nation-states employ two main types of strategies in conflicts with other states: mechanized (or "conventional") war and guerrilla (or "unconventional") war. In this context, "mechanized" refers to the dominance of the types of mechanical weapons and transport provided by the industrial revolution, *not* to battle tactics that rely on armored vehicles and rapid mobility, such as the German blitzkrieg. The objective in mechanized war is destruction of enemy forces, by means of massive, heavily armed forces that fight intense, large-scale battles along relatively well-defined fronts. Success means routing opposing forces on the battlefield by inflicting sufficient losses to destroy the cohesion of units so they cannot execute combat functions. Guerrilla warfare, in contrast, aims to gain control over population, usually beginning with villages located in remote areas, and to use these as anchors to control still larger segments of the population and thus undermine support for the government. Guerrillas fight in small units dispersed over large areas with no well-defined front line. Combat is intermittent and at low intensity, avoiding major battles. The objective is gradually to wear down the opponent government's political authority and thus its ability to field military forces, rather than to destroy those forces in battle.[30]

From a coercer's point of view, the most important difference between these two strategies is that mechanized war is highly dependent on logistics and communications networks, and guerrilla war is not. Mechanized war strategies depend on tremendous amounts of ammunition, fuel, and other supplies, which flow from rear areas to forward combat units. Supply consumption is especially high in intense battles, and the strategy breaks down quickly when the flow of needed supplies is interrupted; logistical demands are inelastic. Both battlefield operations and logistics are coordinated by centralized headquarters in the rear; if communication is disrupted, frontline forces become sluggish and vulnerable to defeat in

---

[29] B. H. Liddell Hart, *History of the Second World War* (New York: Putnam's, 1970), pp. 159–70, 370–96.

[30] Andrew T. Krepinevich, *The Army and Vietnam* (Baltimore: Johns Hopkins University Press, 1986), pp. 3–10. Representative of the extensive literature on guerrilla warfare are David Galula, *Counterinsurgency Warfare* (New York: Praeger, 1964); Robert G. K. Thompson, *No Exit from Vietnam* (London: Chatto and Windus, 1969); and Douglas S. Blaufarb, *The Counterinsurgency Era* (New York: Free Press, 1977).

[31] James F. Dunnigan, *How to Make War: A Comprehensive Guide to Modern Warfare* (New York: Morrow, 1982), pp. 308–22; Martin Van Creveld, *Supplying War: Logistics from Wallenstein to Patton* (New York: Cambridge University Press, 1977).

[30]

detail.[31] Lightly armed guerrillas, however, have minimal logistics and communication requirements. Small amounts of weapons, ammunition, and fuel are needed, but the bulk of the necessary material support, such as food, is derived from the population under their control. Additionally, guerrillas require much less coordination and central control than conventional forces. Since individual units operate autonomously, only rudimentary communications networks are necessary and temporary disruptions rarely jeopardize operations.

The implication is that the most effective denial strategy in any dispute depends on the strategy of the opponent. If it is mechanized warfare, disrupting logistical flows and communication networks is likely to be effective. If it is guerrilla warfare, cutting logistics and communications will have little effect; instead, the coercer must separate the guerrillas from the population that forms the basis of their support, such as by re-locating villages to more secure areas. For instance, American attempts to coerce North Vietnam from 1965 to 1968 by interdicting supply lines failed because the North was pursuing a guerrilla war strategy; in 1972 a similar air campaign did coerce Hanoi because the North had shifted to a conventional war strategy.

Denial strategies offer more coercive leverage than punishment or risk, but they are subject to three limitations. First, coercers can obtain concessions only over the specific territory that has been denied to the opponent. If the target state is persuaded it will lose one territory but not another, it will concede only the one that is lost. If the coercer demands more than it can persuade the target state it would lose in continued fighting, coercion will fail even though denial was partly achieved. By June 1945 the Japanese were willing to give up Korea, Formosa, and their positions in China, which they considered to be certainly lost, but were not willing to surrender the home islands, which they thought might still be held by inflicting such high costs on American forces that they would abandon a final invasion.

Second, military pressure must be maintained continuously until a satisfactory settlement is reached. Any premature relaxation of military efforts gives the target state breathing space to restore its military capabilities, improving its chances of controlling the disputed territory. Thus, truces for the purpose of facilitating negotiation or as rewards for partial concessions are likely to be counterproductive, for they have the effect of placing the target state in a stronger position to resist the coercer's demands or even to "backslide" from concessions already made. At the start of negotiations with China in 1951, the United States substantially ended offensive ground operations, with the result that the peace talks dragged on for two more years. In 1972 the United States terminated bombing of North Vietnam after Hanoi had agreed to a cease-fire but before Saigon's agreement had been secured; Hanoi subsequently repudiated parts of the deal and bombing had to be resumed. Thus traditional theories of coercion which emphasize carefully timed pauses for signaling and negotiation have it exactly backward, providing a recipe for frustration and failure. This mistake follows from the excessive focus on punishment and neglect of denial.

Finally, denial is an inherently expensive coercive strategy, for it requires the coercer to demonstrate the capacity to control the disputed territory by force. Accordingly, whereas assailants can sometimes avoid the full costs of achieving victory, they cannot succeed without paying the costs of preparing for military victory.

Why Success Comes Late

Outstanding successes in which the coercer achieves objectives while paying only a small fraction of the battlefield costs are virtually unknown. Although the United States successfully compelled the Japanese in 1945, the Chinese in 1953, the North Vietnamese in 1972, and Iraq in 1991 to change their behavior, it achieved only minor gains from coercion in all these cases. At most, coercion saved the United States the costs of a final round of military action. In fact, coercion usually takes longer than the logic of either punishment or denial alone would suggest, partly because governments tend to hold out longer than societies and partly because states evaluate costs and military performance poorly.

Even when the costs of further resistance clearly outweigh any attainable benefits, governments tend to hold out longer than the society wants because there are domestic costs to admitting defeat. Once a nation is deeply involved in an international dispute, any concessions are likely to result in the fall of the government that demanded sacrifices in pursuit of national goals. Appeasing the enemy allows domestic political rivals to charge the ruling regime with incompetence, betrayal, or both. Even worse, the enemy might demand removal of the existing regime or even institute war crimes trials.

The possibilities of domestic political change determine how strongly the government will resist. Incentives to resist are weaker when regime change involves replacing individuals rather than the destruction of the ruling class and allied social institutions; so the likelihood of concessions is higher when replacement of the target state's ruling elite can be accomplished by evolutionary rather than revolutionary change. Regime members have less reason to resist if their main social values are not under threat. More important, when sacrificing the current individual leaders is the only real domestic cost to concessions, even their strongest social and political allies may withdraw their support. Similarly, the rulers themselves may offer up the top leader as a sacrificial lamb if doing so will save the remainder of the government. For example, in 1943 the Italian government jettisoned Mussolini in an unsuccessful effort to persuade the Allies not to replace the nonfascist ruling circles in power.[32] If regimes expect concessions to result in the destruction of the ruling group and social institutions, either by an occupying opponent or by a new, hostile domestic regime, the government is likely to resist to the end regardless of the consequences.

The ruling elite can survive loss of power if the political system has a tradition of peaceful change and if the ruling elite has deep sources of power in society aside from its control of the current government. For example, the German Nazis were a purely political elite; once discredited and out of power, they could expect to retain no source of social, economic, or political influence.[33] In contrast, the former daimyo and samurai families that ruled Japan in 1945 had staffed every modern Japanese government and faced no real social or political opposition. Thus, the Japanese government could contemplate surrender, whereas the Nazis could not.

Further, the power of governments to control societies increases in coercive disputes. Governments possess advantages in domestic political competition, and their resistance to concessions is likely to control policy even when it is not in the interest of the society as a whole. The cushion of legitimacy provided by nationalism permits the government to maintain the allegiance of the population, especially for mobilization against an external threat.

Even when governments do not have incentives to oppose surrender, military elites often do. Aside from the reasons affecting government regimes, the military has reason to fear that its very institution will be dismantled because of externally imposed disarmament or domestic demilitarization initiatives. Although militaries lack the legitimacy advantages of civilian governments, they possess powerful capabilities to prevent concessions they oppose. The vast resources that must be mobilized to meet serious threats force governments to depend heavily on the military as an organization and give it great political influence.[34] An additional threat to the government is that the military usually also has a monopoly of force, enabling it to disobey or even remove the government if necessary.

Aside from the disincentives to make concessions, states also often poorly evaluate both civilian costs and military failures.[35] Governments in serious disputes tend to become less tolerant of criticism of their policies, for example. Since decisions have more momentous consequences, criticism is per-

[32] Ernest May, *"Lessons" of the Past: The Use and Misuse of History in American Foreign Policy* (New York: Oxford University Press, 1973), pp. 125–43.

[33] Karl Dietrich Bracher, *The German Dictatorship* (New York: Praeger, 1970).

[34] Mearsheimer, "Theory and Practice"; Bernard Brodie, *War and Politics* (New York: Macmillan, 1973), chap. 1; and Gordon Craig, *The Politics of the Prussian Army, 1640–1945* (New York: Oxford University Press, 1955).

[35] The following discussion applies Stephen Van Evera's pathbreaking analysis of "nonevaluation of strategy" by modern nation-states to the problem of understanding coercive pressures. See Van Evera, "Causes of War," pp. 453–99.

ceived as more serious, threatening the public support needed to mobilize resources against the opponent and possibly threatening the political survival of the regime. The reaction to criticism increases as the costs of state policy rise and as the likelihood of success falls. Accordingly, governments tolerate less dissent within their ranks, suppress leaks, and censor information that might tend to undermine support for state policy, such as civilian costs being suffered or risks of military defeat. Within the government, information is restricted to a smaller circle of officials who believe in the regime's policy.[36]

The result is that the public, as well as most of the government, is presented with a rosier picture of the performance of state policy than is actually the case. Dissenters operate at a disadvantage because of the cushion of legitimacy usually enjoyed by nationalist states. Most people will defer to government statements unless the gap between the official line and reality becomes inescapably obvious.[37]

Militaries of states involved in disputes also control information and suppress criticism, for the same reasons as government leaders and because evaluation threatens organizational stability. Evaluation promotes change and innovation, which threatens jobs and the status of incumbent leaders of the organization. Hence incumbents tend to oppose, disrupt, or punish serious evaluation.[38] Although they do not usually enjoy the same legitimacy as governments, their special expertise gives militaries important advantages in avoiding evaluation. Military expertise is largely confined to military institutions; outside evaluators are usually less knowledgeable about military operations than the military itself, putting them in a poor position to compete with in-house evaluations, which may be corrupted, ignored, or kept to a minimum. Further, the need for secrecy means that information about the likely success or failure of military strategies is usually tightly controlled, making evaluation difficult.[39] In wartime, when any security breach can cost lives, secrecy becomes tighter and evaluation correspondingly harder.

Suppression of criticism is made easier because neither the elites nor the public wants to recognize the possibility of failure. When confronted with high-stakes decisions and ambiguous information, people normally prefer to discount the risks rather than confront the possibility of disaster. Evi-

---

[36] Philip Knightly, *The First Casualty* (New York: Harcourt Brace Jovanovich, 1975); David Wise, *The Politics of Lying: Government Deception, Secrecy, and Power* (New York: Random House, 1973); David M. Kennedy, *Over Here: The First World War and American Society* (New York: Oxford University Press, 1980), chap. 1.

[37] Van Evera, "Causes of War," pp. 683–85.

[38] Aaron Wildavsky, "The Self-Evaluating Organization," *Public Administration Review* 32 (September–October 1972): 509–20. Van Evera, "Causes of War," pp. 453–99. On obstacles to military innovation, see Barry R. Posen, *The Sources of Military Doctrine* (Ithaca: Cornell University Press, 1984).

[39] Edward Shils, *The Torment of Secrecy* (Chicago: University of Chicago Press, 1956).

dence that current policies may lead to unacceptable costs and risks tends to be ignored or discredited until its import is indisputably clear.[40]

Additional reasons why coercion tends to come late include unwillingness to abandon sunk costs and states' interests in protecting their reputations for future conflicts. States could resist, or at least mask, concessions not on the basis of the dispute in isolation but because they believe that a defeat or retreat on one issue is likely to encourage further demands on the state by its adversaries and defections from its allies.[41]

The combined effect of discouraging criticism and hampering evaluation is that risks of disastrous defeat are often not recognized by either governments or publics until events make them inescapably obvious. This tendency makes the coercer's task of demonstrating the consequences of failure to concede all the more difficult. Even when costs escalate beyond the apparent value of the issues at stake or when the prospects for achieving goals through further resistance are bleak, states may not recognize the need to surrender until all ambiguity has been eliminated.

Nuclear Coercion

Unlike conventional coercion, the accepted wisdom on nuclear coercion is mostly right, though incomplete. The focus on civilian punishment which has retarded our understanding of conventional coercion is more accurate for nuclear cases. Current theories, however, focus excessively on coercion under conditions of mutual assured destruction and so exaggerate the role of the balance of interests in successful nuclear coercion. A general understanding should incorporate other nuclear situations.

The principal source of nuclear coercion is manipulation of civilian vulnerability. Nuclear weapons have made it possible to launch sudden, devastating attacks on the vast majority of a state's population simultaneously.[42]

---

[40] Irving L. Janis and Leon Mann say that such "defensive avoidance" is likely whenever people face choices between highly unpalatable options, such as between making concessions and military defeat. Janis and Mann, *Decision Making: A Psychological Analysis of Conflict, Choice, and Commitment* (New York: Free Press, 1977). For examples of failure to recognize impending defeats, see Geoffrey Blainey, *Causes of War* (New York: Free Press, 1973); and Iklé, *Every War Must End.*

[41] On sunk costs, see Iklé, *Every War Must End.* For discussion of the importance leaders attach to protecting state reputation, see Robert Jervis, "Domino Beliefs and Strategic Behavior," in *Dominos and Bandwagons: Strategic Beliefs and Great Power Competition in the Eurasian Rimland,* eds. Robert Jervis and Jack Snyder (New York: Oxford University Press, 1991), pp. 20–50; Betty Glad and Charles Taber, "The Domino Theory," in *War: The Psychological Dimension,* ed. Betty Glad (Syracuse: Syracuse University Press, 1988); and Ross Gregory, "The Domino Theory," in *Encyclopedia of American Foreign Policy,* ed. Alexander DeConde (New York: Scribner's, 1978), 1: 275–80.

[42] It is possible that modern chemical and biological weapons have, or soon will have, nearly equivalent capability. For comparison of the destructive effects of nuclear, chemical, and biological warheads against civilian targets, see Steve Fetter, "Ballistic Missiles and Weapons of Mass Destruction," *International Security* 16 (Summer 1991): 5–42.

Meaningful defense is not possible, because nuclear weapons are so destructive that penetration of even a small proportion of weapons can devastate a great power's society.[43] The adjustment to gradually accumulating damage which is possible under conventional attack cannot be made either, for the destruction can be inflicted all at once. Further, the nuclear revolution largely overturns the effects of nationalism on the conduct of war. The willingness of individuals to bear costs and risks for national goals loses all meaning when large-scale nuclear war endangers not only national interests or fractions of the population but, for all practical purposes, the existence of the nation itself.[44] Accordingly, it is hardly surprising that during the nuclear age publics have not been enthusiastic about pursuit of national goals at the risk of nuclear war.

Risk strategies, which are not effective in conventional disputes, can be successful in nuclear disputes. Since the destructive power of nuclear weapons magnifies the risks the coercer can threaten beyond levels that any state can accept, perfect credibility is not required. In nuclear disputes, risk strategies are likely to be preferred over punishment strategies. If a nuclear threat is credible at all, the threat alone, or a few attacks, is likely to be sufficient; actually executing large-scale nuclear attacks would be coercive overkill. Moreover, intensive nuclear punishment runs the risk of destroying all governmental authority in the target state, making it impossible to terminate the conflict.[45] Nuclear punishment would be tantamount to genocide, which except in cases of the most extreme ethnic or religious hatreds is likely to be repulsive to the coercer's citizenry, as well as to third parties. Finally, nuclear punishment is likely to cause collateral damage, including radioactive contamination, beyond the boundaries of the target state, possibly reaching even the attacking state and its allies.[46]

By contrast, denial makes little difference in nuclear cases. Nuclear weapons do increase the coercer's ability to inflict military as well as civilian damage, but not so dramatically.[47] More important, the horrific levels of societal destruction in nuclear war are likely to dominate decision making so as to make the prospects for success or failure of military campaigns largely irrelevant.

The existing literature on nuclear coercion, as on conventional coercion, has been heavily influenced by ideas imported from work on deterrence. On

---

[43] For a comprehensive discussion, see Charles Glaser, *Analyzing Strategic Nuclear Policy* (Princeton: Princeton University Press, 1990).

[44] Arthur Katz, *Life after Nuclear War* (Cambridge, Mass.: Ballinger, 1982).

[45] Stephen Cimbala, *Strategic War Termination* (New York: Praeger, 1986).

[46] American nuclear planners do not appear to have considered this last possibility in the massive-retaliation era. If early plans had been executed against the Soviet Union, millions of people in Japan, China, and Europe would have been killed. David A. Rosenberg, "The Origins of Overkill," *International Security* 7 (Spring 1983): 3–71.

[47] Bernard Brodie, *Escalation and the Nuclear Option* (Princeton: Princeton University Press, 1968).

the nuclear side, however, this dependence has been much less damaging because of the huge destructiveness of nuclear weapons. When both sides can inflict virtually unlimited pain on each other and when states are normally willing to endure more risk of pain to defend the status quo than to change it, nuclear coercion is hard for the same reasons and in the same proportion that nuclear deterrence is easy.

Under mutually assured destruction (MAD), any potential coercer must consider the possibility of nuclear retaliation and will be unlikely even to attempt coercion unless enormously important interests are at stake. As a result, nuclear coercion attempts are very rare, and when they do occur, the outcome will likely be determined by the balance of interests between the two sides.[48] Unless there is a large asymmetry in its favor, however, the coercer is not likely to fear nuclear escalation any less than the target. Any concessions are therefore likely to be on peripheral issues, inasmuch as a coercer that challenges major territorial interests is unlikely to enjoy the necessary advantage.

While the standard wisdom is right for MAD, it misses important features of cases in which the coercer has a large advantage in nuclear forces, although the target has some retaliatory capability and cases in which the target cannot retaliate. Most authors have treated the first group of cases as equivalent to MAD and have ignored the second altogether. When nuclear capabilities are quite unequal, the outcome is determined primarily by relative civilian vulnerability, not the balance of interests; the less vulnerable state is likely to prevail. The prospect of one party suffering assured destruction while the other does not implies that one must fear elimination and the other, only very high costs. Assuming this situation is common knowledge, the asymmetry between damage and elimination creates tremendous coercive pressure on the opponent, because any increase in the risk of nuclear war will create a large divergence in the expected outcome for each side. Thus, once the coercer indicates a credible willingness to risk starting a nuclear war, the prospect of unequal damage exerts coercive leverage on the opponent to accept the coercer's demands. Although Britain in the Suez crisis and the Soviet Union in the Cuban missile crisis had some nuclear retaliatory capabilities, both were tremendously overmatched and both conceded.[49] Although the assailant may prevail despite an equal or unfavorable balance of interests, we should not expect nuclear coercion attempts over trivial issues. Potential assailants will be quite concerned by the significant costs that even modest nuclear retaliation would bring, and will attempt coercion only when they have important interests at stake.

---

[48] Richard K. Betts, *Nuclear Blackmail and Nuclear Balance* (Washington, D.C.: Brookings, 1987); Robert Jervis, *The Illogic of American Nuclear Strategy* (Ithaca: Cornell University Press, 1984).
[49] Betts, *Nuclear Blackmail*, pp. 62–65 and 109–22.

When nuclear capabilities are completely one-sided, the outcome is also determined by the vulnerability of the target's civilian population. If the coercer's capability is relatively unlimited, coercive success is virtually assured. Even if the coercer's nuclear resources are limited, the prospect of damage far worse than the most intense conventional assault will likely coerce all but the most resolute defenders. Potential coercers may, however, still be constrained by humanitarian, domestic political, or alliance considerations.

Using a nuclear-based risk strategy, the United States was able to compel China to make the necessary concessions to end the Korean War. By 1953 the broad outlines of an armistice in place had been agreed, but the Chinese were inflexible on several minor issues, the most important of which was the repatriation of Chinese POWs. To break the deadlock, the United States threatened nuclear bombing and lent the threat credibility by gradually escalating conventional air attacks during the spring of 1953 and warning that nuclear attacks would follow. Meanwhile, two political events may also have enhanced credibility. The election of Eisenhower reduced domestic constraints on U.S. action, and the death of Stalin in March reduced American fears of possible Soviet retaliation. The Chinese agreed to the U.S. terms in June.

Coercion succeeds if the coercer can alter key components in the target state's decision calculus sufficiently to compel concessions. In major international disputes, the main stakes generally involve control over territory, the value of which the coercer cannot significantly alter. Accordingly, there are three main coercive strategies. Punishment strategies seek to inflict maximum damage on civilian targets in order to raise costs above the value of the stakes at issue. An alternative countercivilian strategy relies on manipulating risk of future damage rather than inflicting maximum actual damage. Denial strategies attack military-related targets in order to undermine the opponent's strategy for controlling the territory in dispute.

Of these three strategies, denial is most effective. Given the limited destructiveness of conventional munitions and the relative insensitivity of modern nation-states to civilian costs, punishment is likely to succeed only when the opponent's resolve or the stakes are low. Risk strategies are likely to be even less effective since at best they can threaten no more damage than is actually inflicted under a punishment strategy. Only when the threat is virtually unlimited damage from nuclear weapons will this approach work. Denial is effective more often, but success depends on the coercer's ability to undermine the opponent's strategy for protecting or capturing the territory at issue. If the coercer lacks the capability to attack the specific vulnerabilities of the opponent's military strategy, denial will fail. Consequently, no one coercive strategy is likely to succeed under all circumstances, and in some cases no effective strategy may be available.

Of the major components of modern military power—land, sea, and air power—each of which can be used for coercive purposes, air power, particularly strategic bombing, most cogently reveals the relative effectiveness of different coercive strategies. The utility of each of the major instruments of military coercion has been modified over time by changes in the organization of the modern nation-states.[50] Democratization and industrialization, in particular, have led to changes in military technologies, the costs of war, and the ability of modern societies to absorb these costs.

Land power has always been a formidable coercive tool, but whereas it was used primarily for punishment in the Middle Ages, now its role is almost pure denial because massive growth in the size of armies allows them to form continuous fronts that shield society from punishment as long as they are undefeated. Sea power is the weakest instrument of coercion, potent only against states whose economies are exceptionally dependent on trade. Further, because naval blockades affect enemy economies as a whole, they have both punishment and denial effects, whose relative weight coercers cannot fully control. Air power, by contrast, the newest coercive instrument, has grown more and more powerful as both aircraft and weapons have improved. Also, air power can be employed much more selectively than the other two instruments for either punishment or denial.

In feudal times, land power was more effective at inflicting punishment than for denial. Control of territory revolved around fortified castles, which were extremely difficult to capture, and armies were small enough that they could and often did raid deep into enemy territory, sowing destruction and disease over wide areas. Indeed, armies invaded hostile territory less to seize strategic points than simply to pillage the land, and they rarely engaged each other in battle.[51]

During the early modern period, a host of factors, including changes in military technology, rivalry between monarchs and nobility, and the rise of state bureaucracy, brought about a shift from small feudal and mercenary forces to large standing armies.[52] The rise of nation-states able to maintain standing armies equipped with cannon and siege trains increased land

---

[50] The modern nation-state has been defined by consolidation of the entire population within territorial limits under a common organ of government; differentiation among economic, judicial, administrative, and military functions; recognition of the state by other states as a sovereign authority within its borders; a conscious sense of community of feeling; and a common sense of political allegiance. See Samuel E. Finer, "State- and Nation-Building in Europe: The Role of the Military," in *The Formation of National States in Western Europe*, ed. Charles Tilly (Princeton: Princeton University Press, 1976), pp. 84–163.

[51] C. W. C. Oman, *The Art of War in the Middle Ages* (Ithaca: Cornell University Press, 1953), pp. 61–63.

[52] Michael Roberts, *The Military Revolution, 1560–1660* (Belfast: Queen's University of Belfast, 1956).

power's ability to seize territory. Still, punishment remained important. Armies of a hundred thousand could devastate agricultural and commercial resources en route to battle, whether they were foraging for supplies or simply engaged in plunder. So great was the devastation wrought by marauding armies during the Thirty Years' War that all the parties eventually agreed to a settlement even though none of them attained its original territorial objectives. In addition, wartime diseases cost more lives prior to the French revolutionary wars than did battle casualties.[53]

The Thirty Years' War was a watershed. Advances in fortification technology countered cannon, and more centralized and wealthier states proliferated border defenses, leading to a period of limited, positional warfare. Denial capabilities were limited by the logistic and time requirements of sieges, which made conquest of territory an excruciatingly slow process. At the same time, punishment capabilities declined. Although foraging and pillaging still took place, fortification belts shielded the major portions of a state's population from marauding armies.[54]

The industrial revolution, together with increasing democratization and nationalism, led to changes that ended the punishment role of land power and made it into a tool for denial. Industrialization made possible the mass production of weapons, greatly increased their firepower, and expanded the capacity of military transport and logistics. Intense nationalism motivated citizens to accept great personal sacrifice, including military service, for the purposes and goals of the state. These advances, together with improved administrative controls, enabled states to mobilize, arm, and maintain in the field armies of unprecedented size.

Since no fixed fortification can resist the firepower of industrial armies for long, land armies are now the only means of defense against each other. Battle has become decisive and the defeat of the enemy army opens the way to unlimited territorial gains. In short, denial has become the main function of land power. As long as the enemy army remains undefeated, however, the reach of modern armies is very limited. The size of modern armies and lethal-

---

[53] John Childs, *Armies and Warfare in Europe, 1648–1789* (Manchester: Manchester University Press, 1982); and William H. McNeill, *Plagues and Peoples* (New York: Anchor Press, 1976).

[54] For excellent discussions of the nature of land warfare in the seventeenth and eighteenth centuries, see Richard Preston and Sydney Wise, *Men in Arms* (New York: Praeger, 1956), chap. 9; and Robert S. Quimby, *The Background of Napoleonic Warfare: The Theory of Military Tactics in Eighteenth-Century France* (New York: AMS Press, 1968). The strategic consequences of industrialization are discussed in Bernard Brodie and Fawn M. Brodie, *From Crossbow to H-Bomb: The Evolution of the Weapons and Tactics of Warfare* (Bloomington: Indiana University Press, 1973), pp. 124–71; John U. Nef, *War and Human Progress* (Cambridge: Harvard University Press, 1950), pp. 302–28; and Van Creveld, *Supplying War*. The best brief discussions of the relationship between nationalism and the conduct of war are R. R. Palmer, "Frederick the Great, Guibert, Bulow: From Dynastic to National War," in *Makers of Modern Strategy*, ed. Edward Meade Earle (Princeton: Princeton University Press, 1943), pp. 49–74; and Howard, *War in European History*, pp. 75–93.

ity of their weapons makes possible the formation of effectively continuous fronts, which prevent access to the enemy's population centers until its forces in the field are destroyed. As a result, land power has virtually ceased to be an important instrument of punishment, for punishment by land power is usually possible only after decisive victory. For example, William Tecumseh Sherman's march through Georgia and the Carolinas was made possible by the decimation of John Hood's Confederate army at Atlanta and Hood's subsequent decision to invade Tennessee rather than oppose Sherman. Similarly, the French occupation of the Ruhr in 1923 was enabled by Germany's defeat in World War I and subsequent disarmament.[55] With continuous fronts, land power can inflict punishment only through attrition of the enemy army, in the hope that heavy casualties will levy such pain on the opposing society that it will concede rather than face further losses. Although attrition often plays a large role in denial campaigns, however, it is rarely pursued as a punishment strategy because the coercer is likely to suffer as much as the target. In 1916 German leaders planned a protracted attrition operation against the French lines at Verdun. Their purpose was partly denial, for they hoped that "bleeding its forces to death" would so weaken the French army that the specter of ultimate defeat would compel France to peace negotiations. At the same time, they also hoped that the heavy loss of life would inflict such pain on French society that the government would be compelled to change its policies. The operation was a failure; German casualties were nearly as high as French and after five months the attack was abandoned.[56]

By contrast to land power, sea power has usually been a weaker instrument of coercion. It can contribute to the application of land power. Command of the sea allows amphibious operations against enemy coasts or overseas possessions, while denying these types of operations to the opponent. The value of amphibious operations has declined since the industrial revolution, however, both because railroads improved the efficiency of land transportation and because increased army size and firepower have made landings much more likely to be stiffly opposed. Speaking against a proposal to land on Germany's Baltic coast in 1914, a British general said, "The truth was that this class of operation possibly had some value a century ago, but now when they were excellent they were doomed to failure. Wherever

---

[55] On Sherman's march, see John Bennett Walters, "General William T. Sherman and Total War," *Journal of Southern History* 14 (November 1948): 447–80; and Joseph T. Glatthaar, *The March to the Sea and Beyond: Sherman's Troops in the Savannah and Carolinas Campaigns* (New York: New York University Press, 1986). On the French occupation of the Ruhr, see Marc Trachtenberg, *Reparation in World Politics: France and European Economic Diplomacy* (New York: Columbia University Press, 1980).

[56] Erich von Falkenhayn, *The German General Staff and Its Decisions, 1914–1916* (New York: Dodd, Mead, 1920), p. 249; Michael Geyer, "German Strategy in the Age of Machine Warfare, 1914–1945," in *Makers of Modern Strategy*, ed. Peter Paret, 2d ed. (Princeton: Princeton University Press, 1986), pp. 530–37.

we threatened to land, the Germans could concentrate superior force."[57] Although many amphibious operations were mounted in World War II, they required huge ratios of superiority to succeed.

Another way to coerce with sea power is gunboat diplomacy, which involves local naval demonstrations in peacetime. Sea power's relative weakness compared to land power, however, means that this can work effectively only against very weak states or those especially dependent on access to the sea. For example, the British, the greatest practitioners of gunboat diplomacy applied this tactic primarily against weak states in peripheral regions such as Latin America, Greece and Portugal, and the Far East, but not against the great powers of Europe.[58]

The principal coercive naval strategy is blockade to cut the target state's access to overseas trade. A blockade's effectiveness is determined by the target state's dependence on overseas trade, which in turn is primarily a function of geography and economic structure. In principle, a peaceful economic embargo can serve the same function, but in practice, embargo is ineffective if any major supplier fails to cooperate. A main purpose of naval blockade is to cut off supplies from neutral or uncooperative sources. In general, blockade has been potent only against states whose economies are exceptionally dependent on trade.

Prior to the industrial revolution, mercantilist economies depended on external trade for large fractions of state income, loss of which could significantly reduce the capacity of the state to make war, though not as much as proponents of blockade imagined. During the War of the Spanish Succession, the British twice intercepted Spain's annual treasure *flota*, but French and Spanish conduct of the war was little affected because domestic sources of revenue were more important.[59] Blockades also imposed punishment on sectors of civilian society heavily involved in trade, such as the New England ports in the Revolutionary War and the War of 1812.[60] Nevertheless, both the denial and the punishment effects of blockade were limited. Some shortages could result, but the economies of the day were not heavily dependent on imports of food or important war materiel. As Adam Smith remarked about the effects of a French blockade: "Sir, there is a great deal of ruin in a nation."[61] The seventeenth- and eighteenth-century efforts of France, Britain, and Spain to blockade each other never did great harm to

---

[57] Quoted in Alfred J. Marder, *From the Dreadnought to Scapa Flow* (London: Oxford University Press, 1961), p. 391.

[58] Antony Preston and John Major, *Send a Gunboat: A Study of the Gunboat and Its Role in British Policy, 1854–1904* (London: Longmans, Green, 1967); and Paul M. Kennedy, *The Rise and Fall of British Naval Mastery* (London: Macmillan, 1976), pp. 167–71.

[59] Kennedy, *Rise and Fall of British Naval Mastery*, pp. 83–84.

[60] Alfred Thayer Mahan, *The Influence of Sea Power on History* (New York: Hill and Wang, 1957).

[61] Quoted in Bernard Brodie, *Strategy in the Missile Age* (Princeton: Princeton University Press, 1959), p. 6.

the target economies. In fact, despite the loss of nearly eleven thousand merchant vessels from 1793 to 1815 and the loss of trade with the Continent, British overseas trade nearly doubled during the Napoleonic wars.[62] The Dutch economy, which was much smaller and more trade dependent, suffered heavily from wartime trade interruptions in this period.

At first glance, the industrial revolution might appear to increase the vulnerability of states to sea power coercion both because of the vast growth of the volume of sea trade and because of the development of new anticommerce weapons such as the submarine and the sea mine. Further, modern industrial war production is often dependent on key raw materials such as oil, rubber, iron ore, aluminum, and other metals. In actuality, however, technical advances in the defense of sea transport and, even more important, the improved organizational ability of modern state bureaucracies, have kept pace with these increased vulnerabilities.

Submarines can be countered by the defender's own submarines, mines, land-based aircraft, and most important, carrier-based aircraft. Further, merchant shipping can be concentrated into well-guarded convoys, reducing the raider's attack opportunities as well as providing direct defense for the cargo vessels.[63]

Blockades, moreover, can often be evaded by overland trade. The coming of railroads so improved land transportation that, unless the target country is an island, needed materials can usually be obtained from continental allies or neutrals.[64] In 1939 Germany imported over 10 percent of its food, 66 percent of its iron ore, 50 percent of lead, 70 percent of copper, 90 percent of tin, 95 percent of nickel, 99 percent of bauxite, 66 percent of oil, 80 percent of rubber, as well as large fractions of its zinc, manganese, molybdenum, mercury, sulfur, cotton, and wool. It managed to obtain all but the rubber and part of the oil requirement by intra-European trade or conquest.[65]

Modern industrial states with efficient administrative and technical services organized and coordinated through bureaucratic institutions have dramatically improved their ability to adjust to most types of blockade-induced shortages by conservation, substitution, or technical innovation. For instance,

---

[62] Kennedy, *Rise and Fall of British Naval Mastery*, pp. 131–32, 143–45. For a broader survey of the effect of blockades in this period, see Alfred Thayer Mahan, *The Influence of Sea Power upon the French Revolution and Empire* (Boston: Little, Brown, 1894), 2: 199–351.

[63] The relationship between the submarine and the conduct of war is discussed in Brodie and Brodie, *Crossbow to H-Bomb*, pp. 180–89; Lautenschlager, "Submarine in Naval Warfare"; and Robert E. Kuenne, *The Attack Submarine: A Study in Strategy* (New Haven: Yale University Press, 1965).

[64] Paul Kennedy, "Mahan versus Mackinder: Two Interpretations of British Sea Power," in *Strategy and Diplomacy, 1870–1945* (London: Allen and Unwin, 1983), pp. 41–86.

[65] Kennedy, *Rise and Fall of British Naval Mastery*, pp. 307–8; W. N. Medlicott, *The Economic Blockade* (London: H.M. Stationery Office, 1952), 1: 43; and Mancur Olson Jr., "The Economics of Target Selection for the Combined Offensive," *Royal United Services Institution Journal* 108 (November 1962): 313.

although Britain became increasingly dependent on food imports after the industrial revolution, it was better able to compensate for blockade-induced shortages in World Wars I and II than in the Napoleonic wars, and Japan managed to feed itself throughout World War II although it was essentially totally blockaded by the end of the war. In World War I, Germany was totally cut off from nitrates, a crucial ingredient in the manufacture of explosives, but was able to develop synthetic substitutes in time to avoid serious disruption of its war effort. Although totally cut off from rubber imports in World War II, the United States was able to satisfy its needs by conservation and recycling.[66]

This is not to say that blockades have no effect on modern industrial economies. In World War I, Russia was chronically short of explosives, and in World War II, Germany was never able, despite synthetic production, to satisfy its oil and rubber requirements fully. Together with battlefield pressures, these shortages ultimately contributed to the defeat of both countries. Nevertheless, only in cases of extreme import dependence is blockade decisive. Import losses can cripple the war economy of a modern industrial state only when the imported materials are indispensable for war production, no substitutes are available, and shortfalls cannot be made up by conservation. In World War II, Japan had to import nearly all of its oil, rubber, aluminum, and tin, and most of its iron ore. When its merchant fleet was destroyed and stockpiles exhausted, Japan's war economy collapsed.

Blockade is also an indiscriminate instrument, because it affects the target economy as a whole. Coercers cannot choose between punishment and denial, for even if they selectively block war-related materials, the target state can often shift resources within its economy. Germany in World War I suffered food shortages because government deliberately shifted manpower, animals, and chemical production from agriculture to the war effort. In effect, Germany punished itself rather than submit to the Allies' denial efforts. Moreover, governments can choose who gets punished by shifting the burden to politically weak groups. Thus, in World War II, Germany starved Poland and occupied Soviet territory, and conscripted slave labor.[67]

Air power, initially a minor instrument, has become a more and more powerful coercive tool as the range and payload of aircraft have increased and weapons have become more accurate and more destructive.[68] Also, to a

[66] On the ability of modern state bureaucracies to offset blockade-induced shortages, see Olson, *Economics of Wartime Shortage*; Gerd Hardach, *The First World War, 1914–1918* (Berkeley: University of California Press, 1977), pp. 53–138; and Alan S. Milward, *War, Economy, and Society, 1939–1945* (Berkeley: University of California Press, 1977).

[67] Hardach, *First World War*, pp. 112–20; Edward L. Homze, *Foreign Labor in Nazi Germany* (Princeton: Princeton University Press, 1967).

[68] The relationship of air power to the conduct of war is discussed in Walter Millis, *Arms and Men: A Study in American Military History* (New Brunswick, N.J.: Rutgers University Press, 1956); Brodie, *Strategy in the Missile Age*, pp. 71–106; Edward Warner, "Douhet, Mitchell, Seversky: Theories of Air Warfare," in *Makers of Modern Strategy*, ed. Earle, pp. 457–84; and Schelling, *Arms and Influence*, chap. 1.

much greater extent than with either land or sea power, coercers can employ air power selectively for either punishment or denial. Aerial bombing capacities in World War I were extremely limited, but by World War II long-range bombers could deliver a few tons of bombs against a target hundreds of miles away. Now, modern aircraft can carry many tons thousands of miles. High-explosive bombs have been augmented, first by incendiary munitions, which can burn large urban areas or even start fire storms, and then by atomic weapons. Navigation difficulties, which made targets hard to find, were overcome by the end of World War II. Finally, from the 1960s onward, precision munitions, from laser-guided bombs to cruise missiles, have drastically reduced the number of weapons needed to destroy specific targets.[69]

This is not to say that air attack is always easy; defense is possible and often quite effective. Although air defenses rarely enjoy a great tactical advantage over the attacker, they are much cheaper. Interceptors require little range or payload and so can be much smaller, simpler, and cheaper than bombers or even long-range escort fighters. Surface-to-air missiles are cheaper still. Although the defender can rarely prevent penetration of its air space or inflict decisive losses on individual missions, even moderate losses can accumulate over time to make a protracted air campaign prohibitively expensive for the attacker. The usual standard of prohibitive losses on any single mission is 5 percent. The high loss rates suffered by American daylight raids over Germany in 1943 (over 10 percent) forced the United States to curtail these operations until long-range fighters became available to escort the bombers in 1944.[70] To wage a successful coercive air campaign, therefore, the coercer must normally be substantially the stronger military power, because it must achieve air superiority over the disputed territory and still retain sufficient resources for bombing operations. Nuclear bombing is an exception since individual missions are so destructive that much higher losses can be accepted. In fact, American strategic plans do not call for achieving air superiority before sending in the bombers, and it is not clear that there are plans for multiple missions by each aircraft.

Air power offers assailants advantages over either land or sea power. Unlike land power, it can reach deep into the enemy's homeland from the outset of a conflict, and it promises to achieve its effects at sharply lower cost in lives than land power. Unlike sea power, bombing can focus on specific categories of targets, attacking either political, economic, population, or military targets in isolation or combination. Given adequate intelligence, air power can also attack selective target sets within these categories, which may be helpful if, for example, there are bottlenecks in key industries— whether in raw materials production (or importation), transportation to

[69] Higham, *Air Power*.
[70] Wesley Frank Craven and James Lea Cate, *The Army Air Forces in World War II* (Washington, D.C.: GPO, 1948), 2: 699–704.

manufacturing sites, manufacturing, or delivery of finished goods. Naval blockade can affect only the first link (and only to the extent that the material must be imported), but air power can attack any of them.

There are two major types of coercive air operations: strategic bombing, which attacks fixed military, industrial, or civilian targets in and near political or economic centers, and interdiction, which strikes at lines of supply between military production and the combat theater as well as theater logistics, command centers, and fielded forces, usually in support of friendly ground operations. Strictly speaking, interdiction, which strikes at targets behind the front, is separable from ground support, which attacks frontline units, but both are forms of theater air attack as opposed to strategic bombing. Strategic bombing campaigns can pursue either a punishment strategy, by harming enemy civilians in order to lower their morale and motivate them to force their governments to end the war, or a denial strategy, by damaging the opponent's war economy to the point that sufficient production cannot be maintained to continue the war successfully. Theater air campaigns are virtually pure denial. They seek to weaken enemy battlefield forces by starving them of needed logistic support or by direct attrition so that their collapse becomes inevitable.

Accordingly, air power is a more flexible coercive tool than land power, which is useful only for denial, or sea power, whose effects depend at least as much on the choices of the target as on those of the coercer. Air campaigns can be, and often are, tailored to a specific coercive strategy through selective attack of targets identified with that strategy but not others. Still, the ability of coercive air power to discriminate between punishment and denial is not perfect, particularly when strategic bombing rather than theater air attack is used. Punishment targets, such as residential areas, may be located close to denial targets, such as bridges, although proximity matters less as weapons accuracy improves. Nor is this problem as common as is sometimes believed. For example, in World War II, German, Japanese, and British cities all tended to have residential neighborhoods near the center with industrial plants around the outskirts. This is a common pattern because industry requires large stretches of low-priced land.[71] Although the target government may compensate for damage by shifting resources from civilian consumption to military use, the potential for such adjustment is less than under naval blockade because strategic bombing can destroy specific war plants or military transportation links that are hard to replace at any price. Indeed, almost all losses in aircraft, vehicle, or explosives production must reduce military resources because in wartime little of such production is allocated to civilian use.

[71] Kenneth Hewitt, "Place Annihilation: Area Bombing and the Fate of Urban Places," *Annals of the Association of American Geographers* 73, no. 2 (1983): 257–84.

In nuclear coercion, strategic nuclear forces fulfill much the same role as conventional strategic air power, although they are vastly more destructive, to the point that there are no real limits on their ability to inflict punishment or to damage an opponent's war economy. Further, when both sides are nuclear armed, both sides will have this capability, in contrast to conventional strategic bombing, which can normally be carried out only by the stronger side. Similarly, tactical nuclear forces can fulfill the same role as theater air power, although again with much greater destructive power. Distinguishing denial and punishment uses is harder, however, since any use of nuclear weapons may generate considerable radioactive fallout. Tactical nuclear weapons may also play a large role in coercive strategies based on risk, since any use of nuclear weapons threatens escalation to strategic nuclear war.

In brief, given the limited vulnerability of modern industrial states to naval blockades and the costliness of coercive ground strategies, air power has emerged as the main tool of military coercion. Strategic air power cases are ideally suited for testing theories of military coercion because such cases can isolate the effects of various coercive threats and differences in the target states' vulnerabilities on decisions whether to make concessions. They differentiate better than sea, land, or theater air power cases because they include variation on both independent and dependent variables, whereas the others do not. Given the limited vulnerability of modern industrial states to naval blockades and commerce raiding, coercion with sea power is so ineffective that these cases inevitably consist mainly of failures. Thus, any sample would have insufficient variation on the dependent variable to distinguish among a variety of causes. Likewise, land power and theater air power cases have little variation on the independent variable. Since modern ground forces are rarely able to attack economic or military targets without first penetrating enemy lines and achieving decisive victory, coercion with land power must be based mainly on denial rather than punishment or risk. Similarly, theater air power is primarily a denial instrument, usually used together with land power. Inasmuch as these instruments are not used punitively, studying them cannot help discern the relative effectiveness of different coercive strategies.

Identifying different coercive strategies is also easier in air power cases. This task can sometimes be problematic because assailants often do not explicitly identify the coercive strategy they are pursuing and because most sea and some land operations have both denial and punitive effects. By contrast, in air power cases coercive strategies can nearly always be distinguished according to target sets and bombing techniques. Punishment strategies most often employ area bombing of urban centers, whereas denial strategies use precision attacks on industrial, transportation, and military targets.

[47]

TESTING THE DENIAL THEORY

To test my theory, I employ a methodology that combines the features of focused-comparison and statistical-correlative analysis using the universe of coercive air campaigns.[72] Correlative analysis of this universe enhances confidence that my theory can predict future events by showing that the patterns predicted by the theory actually occur over a broad class of cases. It also increases the robustness of my findings; even if ambiguity of evidence leaves my interpretation of certain cases open to debate, my conclusions are likely to be valid as long as most of the analysis is sound. Detailed examination of five cases enhances confidence that the correlations found in the larger universe are not spurious, that is, that my theory accurately identifies the causal dynamics that determine outcomes.

Testing the denial theory requires three steps. First, relevant historical evidence must be identified. Second, the theory must be put into operation to provide falsifiable predictions that can be easily observed in historical cases. Third, the predictions of the theory must be compared to the evidence.

This study investigates the universe of coercive attempts using strategic air power, thirty-three in all, most of which occurred in war (see Table 1). Cases were identified according to three criteria. First, cases are restricted to those in which the target was asked to give up important interests. Typical examples are efforts to compel reduction of political aims, agreement to a cease-fire, withdrawal of forces, or even surrender, by states that retain the capacity for continued military operations. Cases in which the demands on the target involved minor or insignificant loss, such as extortion of tribute, are excluded. If the target of coercion incurs little or no cost in complying with the coercer's demands, it might comply even if subjected to little or no pressure. Such cases, therefore, have little value for explaining cases where compliance is expensive for the target. Thus, I excluded a number of cases of British air policing in the Middle East in the 1920s and 1930s because they involved minor issues such as payment of taxes or fines and surrender of criminals for trial. A typical example was the bombing of Quteibi tribesmen in Aden in 1934 in order to compel their leaders to pay a fine of five hundred dollars and surrender criminals who had raided a caravan. Total casualties were three tribesmen killed while trying to take apart a dud bomb.[73]

Second, I exclude situations involving a monopoly of military force by one side, such as domestic police actions or postwar concessions. (This is another reason for excluding the British policing cases.) Some (such as

---

[72] For a test of the balance of interests, balance of forces, and relative expected punishment, see Robert A. Pape, "Coercion and Military Strategy: Why Denial Works and Punishment Doesn't," *Journal of Strategic Studies* 15 (December 1992): 423–75.

[73] Charles F. A. Portal, "Air Force Co-operation in Policing the Empire," *Journal of the Royal United Service Institution* 82 (May 1937): 351–54.

Table 1. Coercive air campaigns

Year	Coercer	Target	Issue
1917	Germany	Britain	British withdrawal from World War I
1920	Britain	Somalis	Rebellion
1920s	Britain	Turkey	Northern Iraq
1936	Italy	Ethiopia	Ethiopian sovereignty
1936–39	Spanish nationalists	Spanish loyalists	Spanish sovereignty
1937–45	Japan	China	North/Central China
1938	Germany	Britain/France	Czechoslovakia
1939	Germany	Britain/France	Poland
1939	Germany	Poland	Polish sovereignty
1939–40	USSR	Finland	Finnish sovereignty
1940	Germany	Netherlands	Dutch sovereignty
1940	Germany	Britain	British withdrawal from World War II
1943	U.S./Britain	Italy	Italian sovereignty
1942–45	U.S./Britain	Germany	German sovereignty
1944–45	Germany	Britain	Reduction of surrender demands
1944–45	United States	Japan	Japanese sovereignty
1950–53	United States	China	North Korea
1954–62	France	Algerian rebels	Algerian sovereignty
1956	Britain/France	Egypt	Control of Suez Canal
1956	USSR	Britain/France	Withdrawal from Middle East War
1962	United States	USSR	Missiles in Cuba
1965–68	United States	North Vietnam	South Vietnam
1972	United States	North Vietnam	South Vietnam
1969–70	Israel	Egypt	Cessation of artillery attacks
1970s	Israel	PLO	Terrorism
1979–88	USSR	Afghan rebels	Government of Afghanistan
1979–86	USSR	Pakistan	Support for Afghan rebels
1983–85	Israel	PLO	Terrorism
1980–88	Iraq	Iran	Border territories
1986	United States	Libya	Terrorism
1991	United States	Iraq	Kuwait
1991	Iraq	Saudi Arabia	Kuwait
1991	Iraq	Israel	Provoke military response[a]

[a]This is the only instance of a state attempting to coerce another into initiating military action against itself.

Schelling) might refer to "bargaining" or coercion when the coercer has a monopoly or near monopoly of power, but such cases are not useful for distinguishing between competing theories in important cases. If the coercer can inflict unlimited harm on the target at little or no cost to itself, then the cause of coercive success is trivial and tells us little about the more important case in which the coercer does not have a monopoly of force. Moreover, whereas postwar concessions from defeated to victor might be called coercive success, if war must be pursued to its ultimate conclusion, coercion has failed in its more important task of enabling the victor to win concessions without paying the costs of achieving decisive victory.

Third, cases are limited to those in which coercive threats can be clearly identified. These cases include explicit statements of the form "Do X or I'll do Y" or implicit threats where there is evidence they were understood by the target state. Cases that involve highly ambiguous threats are excluded, as are those in which it is not certain that the target perceived a coercive threat. This coding rule, for example, does not count Truman's movement of B-29s to Britain during the Berlin crisis as nuclear coercion because there is no evidence that the Soviets understood this as a threat to launch an attack if the blockade continued, but it does include Soviet coercion of the British and French during the 1956 Suez crisis because the record indicates that the British and French understood themselves to be victims of coercion. This rule has the effect of defining coercive attempts from the target's perspective, which is appropriate given that the theory is about changes in the target state's decisions. If we cannot establish that the substance of the threat and the conditions of its execution were communicated to the target, we cannot determine whether a coercive failure was due to insufficient threats or to communication gaps. This rule might exaggerate the effectiveness of countercivilian threats based on risk, since excluding instances of highly ambiguous threats may disproportionately eliminate cases of low-credibility threats.

To make operationalization easier for purposes of a statistical-correlative test, I test only a parsimonious version of the denial theory which includes only its main propositions. This procedure has the effect of reducing the power of the theory somewhat because any variance accounted for by its subsidiary propositions will count against the theory in this test. The full power of the theory cannot be tested without understanding concrete air strategies and their application in specific cases, because appropriate operationalization of all the variables depends on the context of a particular coercive dispute.

The two independent variables are civilian vulnerability and military vulnerability. Since risk strategies, which affect the probability of costs, are only a weaker version of punishment strategies, which affect the magnitude of costs, I combine them to test for the expectation of suffering due to the coercer's attacks. In terms of the equation $R = B\,p(B) - C\,p(C)$, previously discussed, civilian vulnerability represents the combined effects of C and $p(C)$.

Civilian vulnerability, or punishment, is coded as "low," meaning that although there is some risk to individuals, no major part of the population must make adjustments or compromises in daily life to avoid the threat; "medium," meaning that the risks to individuals has risen to the point that major parts of the population must make compromises or adjustments in their daily life, such as evacuation or substitution, to lower the threat; "high," meaning that 1 percent or more of the population may die despite the best countermeasures; and "very high," meaning that 5 percent or more

[50]

of the population is at risk.[74] The denial theory expects that coercion should fail in conventional disputes even if civilian vulnerability is high or very high.

Military vulnerability, or denial, refers to leaders' expectations of being able to take or hold the disputed territory with military force. In terms of the equation $R = B\,p(B) - C\,p(C)$, military vulnerability represents the combined effects of B and $p(B)$. Military vulnerability is coded as "low," meaning that while there is some risk that the current position could not be maintained, it has not reached the point of requiring additional military measures to maintain confidence in success; "medium," meaning that control over the disputed territory is definitely in jeopardy but the threat can be reduced by added military measures, such as further mobilization of society; "high," meaning that the successful defense or conquest of the territory cannot be assured even with added military measures, but it may be possible to inflict enough attrition to reduce the opponent's commitment to control the territory; and "very high," meaning that the likelihood of loss of control over the territory approaches certainty because both defense and heavy attrition of enemy forces are impossible. The denial theory expects coercion to succeed if military vulnerability is high or very high.

The key question in assessing the significance of correlations between independent and dependent measures is how they compare to chance. There are two possible outcomes, success and failure, which are defined as meeting or failing to meet the coercer's demands prior to final defeat. Accordingly, we can easily determine whether the success rate for each theory is the same or higher than would be obtained by simply flipping a coin (see Table 2).[75] The denial theory predicts thirty-seven of forty cases successfully, a result that could be achieved by chance less than once in a thousand times. This is an extremely robust result; for the denial theory to fail the 0.05 standard benchmark significant level it would have to be wrong in more than ten additional cases. Such a robust result has the advantage that quibbles over one or a few cases cannot invalidate the theory.

Moreover, the results of this analysis demonstrate that military vulnerability, not civilian vulnerability, accounts for most of the variance in the cases. Table 3 shows that achieving high or very high military vulnerability

---

[74] In Singer and Small's study of casualties in modern warfare, 1 percent is half of the average total losses and 5 percent is near the upper limit of total losses. See *The Wages of War*, pp. 351–57. In some cases, either civilian or military vulnerability is described as "nil," meaning that there was no current or foreseeable threat, without excluding the possibility that a threat might arise in the future.

[75] I justify assuming that the underlying distribution of outcomes is random by the observation that the distribution of success and failure in the original 33-case universe appears to be random with 14 successes and 19 failures. For a useful methodological guide, see William Gamson and André Modigliani, *Untangling the Cold War: A Strategy for Testing Rival Theories* (Boston: Little, Brown, 1971).

Table 2. Predictions of the denial theory

Case	Punishment	Denial	Prediction	Outcome
1917/Britain	medium	medium	failure	failure
1920/Somalis	low	high	success	success
1920s/Turkey	nil	high	success	success
1936/Ethiopia	high	medium	failure	failure
1936–38/Spanish Republic	low	medium	failure	failure
1939/Spanish Republic	low	high	success	failure*
1937–45/China	high	medium	failure	failure
1938/Britain/France	high	high	success	success
1939/Britain/France	high	high	success	failure*
1939/Poland	high	very high	success	success
1939–40/Finland	medium	high	success	success
1940/Netherlands	high	very high	success	success
Aug. 1940/Britain	medium	medium	failure	failure
Sept. 1940/Britain	high	medium	failure	failure
1942–44/Germany	high	medium	failure	failure
1945/Germany	very high	very high	success	failure*
1943/Italy	medium	high	success	success
1944–45/Britain	medium	low	failure	failure
1944–45/Japan	high	medium	failure	failure
Aug. 1945/Japan	very high	very high	success	success†
1950–51/North Korea & China	medium	high	success	success
1953/North Korea & China	very high	medium	success	success†
1954–62/Algeria	medium	low	failure	failure
1956/Egypt	low	medium	failure	failure
1956/Britain/France	very high	medium	success	success†
1962/USSR	very high	very high	success	success†
1965–68/North Vietnam	medium	low	failure	failure
1972/North Vietnam	medium	very high	success	success
1969–70/Egypt	low	medium	failure	failure
1970s/PLO	medium	low	failure	failure
1979–88/Afghanistan	high	low	failure	failure
1979–86/Pakistan	low	low	failure	failure
1980–88/Iran	low	medium	failure	failure
July 1988/Iran	medium	high	success	success
1982/PLO	high	high	success	success
1982–85/PLO	low	low	failure	failure
1986/Libya	low	low	failure	failure
1991/Iraq	low	high	success	success
1991/Saudi Arabia	medium	low	failure	failure
1991/Israel	medium	nil	failure	failure

NOTE: The success rate is 93 percent and the significance <0.001. When a coercer pursues a single set of coercive demands through two or more parallel military campaigns, this is still coded as a single case because it still involves a single set of decisions by the target state on whether to concede, regardless of whether only one of the campaigns or both contribute to the decision. Conversely, when independent variables shift during the course of a single campaign these are counted as separate cases because they present the target with different decisions. Accordingly, although the universe of strategic bombing campaigns totals thirty-three disputes, the test of the denial theory recognizes forty distinct cases. For data underlying codings, see Appendix. Air power alone may not account for the outcome of all the cases, for in many instances, other instruments were also used.

* Cases in which the denial theory failed to predict the outcome.

† Cases involving nuclear coercion.

Table 3. Civilian vs. military vulnerability (successes/cases)

	Military vulnerability		
	Very high/high	Medium/low	Success rate
Civilian vulnerability			
Very high/high	6/8	2/8	50%
Medium/low	8/9	0/15	33%
Success rate	82%	9%	

is far more important than achieving high or very high civilian vulnerability. Success rates vary only slightly across civilian vulnerability (50 percent to 33 percent), whereas they vary dramatically across military vulnerability (82 percent to 9 percent).

Further, the four nuclear cases account for half of the successes with very high civilian vulnerability, including both of the ones without high military vulnerability. If these cases are excluded, success rates are completely unrelated to civilian vulnerability—33 percent in each row—confirming the proposition that conventional coercion is a function of military vulnerability and nuclear disputes are determined by civilian vulnerability.

The strong results of this test indicate that even the parsimonious version of the denial theory accounts for nearly all the variance in the pattern of success and failure in the universe of coercive air campaigns. We may derive confidence that future cases are likely to follow a similar pattern, but only if I can show that the results are not spurious (accounted for by as yet unidentified factors) and that the causal dynamics expected by the theory actually appear in individual cases. For these purposes, detailed case studies are required.

In the next six chapters I intensively investigate five disputes involving strategic bombing campaigns. Chapter 3 explains the major coercive air strategies that have been developed and used by coercers in this century. Chapters 4 through 8 show how these strategies were actually implemented in five of the largest coercive air campaigns: U.S. coercion of Japan in World War II, of North Korea and China in the Korean War, of North Vietnam in the Vietnam War, and of Iraq in the Gulf War, and Allied coercion of Germany in World War II.

Why did I select these cases? The purpose of this test is to discover whether states make decisions to accept or reject coercer's demands according to the patterns expected by the denial theory. To compare the effects of different military threats, I first control for the credibility of the coercer's threat by comparing the largest air campaigns in the universe, which are those in which the coercer's willingness to attack is least in doubt. Next, I seek cases that test relative effects of civilian and military vulnerability especially well. Accordingly, I investigate one dispute from each of the three key boxes in Table 3: Japan is a case of very high civilian and military vulnerability, Korea is a case of medium military but very high civilian vulnerability, and Vietnam is a case of very high military but medium civilian vulnerability. The Gulf War is included because it is the first real test of a new coercive air strategy, decapitation, which seeks to achieve both punishment and denial effects by destroying a small collection of crucial leadership targets. Finally, Germany is a case in which denial success did not produce coercive success, and I investigate it in order to discover whether the reasons for this failure require revision of the theory.

All the case studies are structured in a similar way in order to show the pattern of decision making both within and across cases. To illuminate the causal dynamics within cases, I analyze cause and effect by dividing each case into time-slice sequences. Since the richness of the evidence on coercer's actions and target state's reactions varies case by case and within cases, I discriminate time periods more finely in some cases than others. For example, the evidence on Japanese decision making is so rich that I can divide Japanese decisions in the last two years of the war into seven distinct periods, but the less rich evidence on North Vietnamese decision making limits the divisions to but three periods over eight years.

To illuminate the causal patterns across cases, I organize each around four main questions: First, what were the goals of the air offensive? Was it pursued for coercive purposes alone, or were other goals also important? Second, what coercive strategies were considered and adopted? Were the strategies pursued in their most ambitious form, or were they truncated to conform to political and organizational constraints? Third, how was the campaign conducted? How fully were the requirements of each proposed strategy achieved in practice? Finally, how did the target's decision making change over time and how did it correlate with the stages of the coercer's bombing campaign?

[3]

Coercive Air Power

The most important instrument of modern military coercion, and the most useful for investigating the causes of coercive success and failure, is air power. This instrument has been used to execute concrete coercive strategies that correspond to the conceptual categories of punishment, risk, and denial. A fourth strategy which pursues both punishment and denial effects simultaneously is decapitation. This chapter explains how to identify coercive air strategies from the coercer's concrete military actions, how to measure their success, and how the major strategies were developed, and it evaluates the historical effectiveness of each strategy.

IDENTIFICATION OF COERCIVE AIR STRATEGIES

Coercive air strategies can be identified by either of two criteria. The first criterion is a set of specific indicators, such as timing, target sets, and munitions used. A maximal punishment strategy would simply blot out whole residential and commerical areas of cities. Missions could be flown at night since high standards of accuracy are not needed. Munitions would include a high proportion of incendiaries to start fires or fire storms. The campaign would be prosecuted as intensively as possible to maximize shock effects. A somewhat more genteel punishment strategy might attack civilian sectors of the economy, such as power, water, or agricultural targets such as irrigation systems, causing hardship but fewer immediate deaths.

The ideal risk campaign would resemble punishment, except that rather than inflict as much harm as possible as fast as possible, it would smoothly and gradually increase the tempo of air operations, interrupting them only by pauses for diplomatic signaling. Civilian targets would be attacked, with a gradual progression from less painful to more critical targets.

The ideal denial campaign would attack military targets and military production centers. Targets could include fielded forces; theater-level command, communications, and logistics; weapons plants; and critical raw materials used in war production. Denial missions generally require pinpoint accuracy, and are likely to be flown in daylight if air superiority allows. Munitions would include fewer incendiaries and more high explosives, and precision-guided munitions (PGMs) might be used if available. The campaign would be prosecuted at the maximum intensity the coercer could sustain and might restrike certain critical targets many times to prevent their repair.

The ideal decapitation campaign would attack key leadership facilities and communications networks in the opponent's political centers, in addition to vital nodes in a nation's economic infrastructure such as electric power and petroleum refining. Since many leadership and communications targets are room size, PGMs are required. Because the total number of targets is very small, the campaign would take only a few days.

Although air strategies can be defined in terms of the targets to be struck and the timing of their destruction, this approach is not fully satisfactory. Co-location and multipurpose economic installations make these distinctions difficult to apply. Residential, transportation, and industrial targets may be located close together, so that—absent PGMs—any attack on one may damage the others. More important, certain economic targets, such as electric power and transportation systems, might be attacked either because of the harm this would do the civilian economy or because destroying them might reduce war production.

A second and more satisfactory criterion focuses on the mechanisms by which the destruction of a target set is supposed to translate into changed enemy behavior. Mechanisms provide the intellectual guidance for operational air planners who then translate strategy into actual campaigns with the forces at their disposal. This alternative schematic for identifying differences between coercive air strategies is based on the means-to-ends chain assumed by each, as follows: force → targets → mechanism → political change. Table 4 shows the chains developed by some major theorists. Each of the strategies described in this book depends on assumptions about how destruction of a specific set of targets (unique in each particular case) will trigger a specific mechanism (which is believed to be generally applicable) to produce a concrete policy outcome.

MEASURING EFFECTIVENESS

The effectiveness of military operations can be measured as either *combat* effectiveness or *strategic* effectiveness. Combat effectiveness describes how efficiently a given force destroys a given target set, that is, how well bombs

Table 4. Coercive air strategies

Strategy	Theorist	Target set	Mechanism
Punishment	Douhet	cities	popular revolt
	Trenchard	cities	popular revolt
	Air Corps Tactical School	key economic nodes	social disintegration
Risk	Schelling	gradual civilian damage	avoid future costs
Denial	Luftwaffe	frontline forces	battlefield breakthrough
	Committee of Operations Analysts	weapons plants	equipment shortages
	Enemy Objectives Unit	POL/transportation	operational paralysis
Decapitation	Warden	leadership	leadership change or strategic paralysis

destroy targets, and strategic effectiveness focuses on whether the destruction of target sets attains political goals.[1]

The usual index of combat effectiveness is the number of sorties needed to deliver enough bombs to cripple a specific target, most often judged by visible destruction. As technology improves bombing accuracy, air power necessarily becomes more combat effective, because fewer sorties are necessary to destroy targets. At best, measures of combat efficiency are measures of how quickly or cheaply forces perform military missions. They do not gauge whether mission success will achieve political purposes.

Measuring the overall success of an air campaign only in terms of combat effectiveness can cause one futile mission to be succeeded by another, while more worthwhile missions are neglected. Against Japan, precision bombing in 1944 was condemned as a failure because it produced no visible damage to industrial plants, and incendiary attacks against Japanese cities beginning in March 1945 were hailed as a great success because burned acreage was easy to observe and quick to accumulate. However, incendiary bombing ultimately made little difference to the war's outcome. Because Japan's main industries had already been shut down by the naval blockade, their destruction merely made unused rubble bounce, and the Japanese government was willing to countenance the civilian costs that the fire bombing caused. Bombers could have contributed more to the collapse of the Japanese economy had they been dedicated to a third mission: mine laying

[1] Barry Watts has proposed a somewhat similar categorization between combat effectiveness and "second order effects." This broader concept than strategic effectiveness includes all noncombat consequences whether or not they affect political goals. Thus, they are less useful for our present purpose. James G. Roche and Barry D. Watts, "Choosing Analytic Measures," *Journal of Strategic Studies* 14 (June 1991): 165–209.

along shipping lanes. Thus, since the goal of coercion is political change, my discussion of coercive air strategies focuses on strategic effectivness, not combat effectiveness.

COERCIVE AIR STRATEGIES

The four main categories of coercive air strategies are punishment, risk, denial, and decapitation. Air superiority is sometimes named as a separate air strategy, but it is not. Indeed, all coercive air strategies require command of the air, for aircraft cannot systematically place bombs on any target set if air operations encounter strong opposition from enemy forces. Air superiority need not extend over the enemy's entire territory, but only over the target set the attacker intends to strike and the air corridors to it.

The importance of air superiority to coercive air power is illustrated by Germany's attempt to coerce Britain in 1940, which failed because Germany could not achieve command of the air. After the fall of France, the Germans tried to coerce Britain to accept a position of neutrality by threatening an invasion across the English Channel. The Luftwaffe was supposed to play a decisive role in this invasion both by direct support of German ground forces and, even more important, by keeping the Royal Navy, which was far superior to the German surface fleet, from wreaking havoc on German amphibious operations. Before the Luftwaffe could carry out these missions, however, it first had to eliminate the capacity of the Royal Air Force to operate over southern England and the English Channel. Accordingly, the Luftwaffe attempted to knock out the main airfields of the RAF in southern England. Initially the campaign achieved considerable success in wearing down British airfields, fighter direction systems, and pilot reserves. Later, however, the Germans shifted their attacks from these weak points in the British air defense system to bombing the city of London, allowing the air defenses to recover. As a result, the Germans never gained air superiority and so could not even begin to implement their threat to invade the United Kingdom.[2]

Air superiority is not a separate coercive air strategy but a necessary step in the pursuit of all four coercive air strategies. The central question in air strategy is what to attack once air superiority has been achieved.

---

[2] Len Deighton, *Fighter: The True Story of the Battle of Britain* (London: Johnathan Cape, 1977); Derek Wood and Derek Dempster, *The Narrow Margin: The Battle of Britain and the Rise of Air Power, 1930–1940* (London: Hutchinson, 1961); and John Terraine, *A Time for Courage: The Royal Air Force in the European War, 1939–1945* (New York: Macmillan, 1985). For German intentions in the Battle of Britain, see F. M. Sallagar, *The Road to Total War: Escalation in World War II*, R-465-PR (Santa Monica, Calif.: Rand Corporation, 1969), p. 7.

Punishment and the Theories of Giulio Douhet

Aerial *punishment* attempts to inflict enough pain on enemy civilians to overwhelm their territorial interests in the dispute and to cause either the government to concede or the population to revolt against the government. Air power can impose terrible costs on civilians by saturation bombing of population centers, as occurred in World War II. Or it can cause pain indirectly by wrecking the civilian economy. Destroying electric power grids, oil refineries, water and sewer systems, and domestic transportation can substantially lower a nation's ability to distribute and refrigerate food, purify water, and heat homes, thus, over time, increasing poverty, disease, and hunger in the general population.

Punishment was the first coercive strategy to be put into practice when airpower was developed. The earliest significant use of what can be called "strategic" airpower was the German air offensive of 1917, in which both Gotha bombers and Zeppelins struck British population centers. The seeds of this coercive strategy were planted in late 1914 and early 1915 once it became evident that a quick end to the war was unlikely to be won on the battlefield. In late 1914 German naval memoranda recommended air attacks against British civilians: "In general air attacks with aeroplanes and airships from the Belgian and French coasts, particularly with airships, promise considerable material and moral results. . . . We dare not leave untried any means of forcing England to her knees, and successful air attacks on London, considering the well-known nervousness of the public, will be a valuable measure." Admiral Alfred von Tirpitz himself supported these raids on the basis of their punitive effects on British civilian morale. "All available ships should be concentrated on London," he wrote, adding, "The measure of the success will lie not only in the injury which will be caused to the enemy, but also in the significant effect it will have in diminishing the enemy's determination to prosecute the war, which will be greater than if the bombs are scattered singly."[3] All together, some nine thousand German bombs totalling 280 tons were delivered in fifty-one Zeppelin and fifty-two Gotha raids against Britain. These raids killed 1,413 and wounded 3,408.[4] Although German air raids failed to compel Britain to withdraw support for the war, the British responded with their own countercity offensive in 1918 and planned for a much larger strategic air campaign in 1919.

During the interwar period, intense debates occurred in industrialized countries about the role of the bomber in a future war. Although all these debates were putatively focused on lessons learned from World War I combat experience, British, German, and American air doctrines were actually

[3] Douglas H. Robinson, *The Zeppelin in Combat* (London: Foulis, 1962), pp. 50, 52, 54.
[4] Robin Highham, *Air Power: A Concise History* (New York: St. Martin's, 1972), p. 49; George H. Quester, *Deterrence before Hiroshima* (New York: Wiley, 1966), p. 28.

shaped by a combination of experience in that war, domestic politics, inter-service rivalry, and grand strategy. The nature of these factors varied from country to country as did the doctrines that emerged.[5]

One strategy, pivotal in all these debates, can be called the Douhet model, because it was first laid out in the writings of the Italian air theorist Giulio Douhet.[6] The Douhet model rests on the belief that infliction of high costs can shatter civilian morale, unraveling the social basis of resistance, so that citizens pressure the government to abandon its territorial ambitions.[7] The logic of this model proposes that civilian morale is damaged by exposing large portions of the population to the terror of destruction or by causing severe shortages of consumer goods and services (such as food, textiles, and industrial goods). "Take the center of a large city," Douhet wrote, "and imagine what would happen among the civilian population during a single attack by a single bombing unit. . . . I have no doubt that its impact on the people would be terrible." Lowered civilian morale, it is said, then produces internal turmoil: "What civil or military authority could keep order, public services functioning, and production going under such a threat?" Finally, domestic unrest causes grass-roots opposition against the home government: "A complete breakdown of the social structure cannot but take place in a country subjected to this kind of merciless pounding from the air. The time would soon come when, to put an end to horror and suffering, the people themselves, driven by the instinct of self-preservation, would rise up and demand an end to the war."[8]

The first air force to put the Douhet model into practice in its doctrine and force posture was that of Great Britain. Following Germany's punishment attacks, the Royal Air Force was born and the goal of its first chief, Hugh Trenchard, was to build a force capable of striking at the heart of German civilian morale. According to the British representatives to the Inter-Allied Aviation Committee, the effect of Trenchard's strategy "would be that the German government would be forced to face very considerable and constantly increasing civil pressure which might result in political disintegra-

---

[5] This discussion generally supports Walter Millis's assessment of the general pattern of the evolution of air doctrine: "Independent power came first; to attain the goal it was next necessary to develop a 'doctrine' which would make it military valid; finally, with the doctrine established, it was necessary to invent a weapon which would justify the strategy." *Arms and Men: A Study in American Military History* (New Brunswick, N.J.: Rutgers University Press, 1956), p. 231.

[6] Although historians continue to debate the influence that Douhet's writings had on American, British, and German air theorists, there is no doubt that the set of ideas contained in his writings were common knowledge. See R. R. Flugel, "United States Air Power Doctrine: A Study of the Influence of William Mitchell and Giulio Douhet at the Air Corps Tactical School" (Diss., University of Oklahoma, 1965).

[7] Giulio Douhet, *Command of the Air*, trans. Dino Ferrari (New York: Coward-McCann, 1942), esp. pp. 28, 47–48, 57–58, 309.

[8] Ibid., pp. 57–58.

tion." After the war, Trenchard lost no time in applying this thinking to conflict with Britain's most likely continental adversary, France: "I feel that although there would be an outcry, the French in a bombing duel would probably squeal before we did. . . . The nation that would stand being bombed longest would win in the end." Whether bombing the enemy population would have a long-term material effect on the enemy's industrial capacity hardly mattered, because air wars were expected to be short and intense. Rather, Trenchard believed that strategic air attack would trigger popular revolts: "The end of war is usually attained when one nation has been able to bring such pressure to bear on another that public opinion obliges the government to sue for peace."[9] He became famous for arguing that in air wars, the ratio of the "moral effect" on populations to material effect stood at twenty to one. Additionally, the possibility that the enemy might retaliate made getting in the first blows just that much more critical. National character, not battlefield forces, would determine the outcome of counterpopulation air wars, and in this respect the British were favored over their potential continental adversaries. As one senior British officer noted, "Casualties affected the French more than they did the British. That would have to be taken into consideration too, but the policy of hitting the French nation and making them squeal before we did was a vital one—more vital than anything else."[10] Such notions of the vulnerability of civilian morale to air attack sometimes also stemmed from the overt contempt that many military men felt for civilians in general and from racism. J. F. C. Fuller believed that it was the Jewish element in the East End that had panicked in the bombing of 1917.[11]

Moreover, based on their fears of how German air attack would compel British surrender, the British seemed to place their own stamp on Douhet's theory by marrying the air scare to the red scare of the 1920s. Air power, according to this logic, would bomb industrial centers, creating mass unemployment and panic, especially among the working classes, who in turn would overthrow the government. In short, air attack against populations would cause workers to rise up against the ruling classes.[12]

Douhet-style thinking had its strongest supporters in Great Britain for several reasons. First, as a result of German bombing of London in 1917, the British public generally supported the idea of an air force designed to punish an enemy's population centers. Public enthusiasm for this policy culminated in April 1918 when widespread passion to bomb German cities led the British Cabinet to push an Air Law through Parliament which estab-

---

[9] Williamson Murray, *Luftwaffe* (Baltimore: Nautical and Aviation, 1985), pp. 299, 301.
[10] Barry D. Powers, *Strategy without a Slide Rule: British Air Strategy, 1914–1939* (London: Croom Helm, 1976), p. 201.
[11] Malcolm Smith, *British Air Strategy between the Wars* (Oxford: Clarendon Press, 1984), p. 61.
[12] Powers, *Strategy without a Slide Rule*, pp. 124–26.

lished the Royal Air Force as an independent service equivalent to the Army and Navy.[13] In other words, the creation of the RAF was closely linked to the doctrine of bombing the enemy's population.

Second, British practical success in bombing rebellious Iraqi and Afghan tribesmen into submission during the 1920s encouraged belief in the efficacy of punishment, even though such small campaigns over relatively minor issues against primitive peoples with no means of defense had limited relevance to a future European war. The less successful RAF bombing campaign against Germany in 1918 would have been a far superior foundation on which to build an air doctrine, but no scientific investigation of it was ever undertaken.[14]

Finally, the RAF's organizational interests influenced its preferred doctrine. During the interwar years, the RAF was competing for autonomy, wealth, and size with the Royal Navy, whose first priority was to protect British interests in the Pacific, and the Army, which placed primary importance on various imperial policy duties. To succeed in this competition, the RAF needed its own mission (bombing Germany) and a doctrine that promised cheap victory, relative to World War I, if it were endowed with superiority over its continental opponents. Winning through bombing civilians was made to order for these purposes, since it promised a swift victory without the commitment of ground forces to the Continent.[15]

In contrast to the British, American air strategy aimed not at killing large numbers of civilians directly but at causing general social collapse through the precision bombing of key industrial nodes. The theory of the industrial web was developed in the mid-1930s by a group of young air officers at the U.S. Air Corps Tactical School (ACTS), then the highest educational establishment for American airmen, who later wrote *AWPD-1*, the first U.S. air strategy plan in World War II.

The key assumption embedded in the industrial web theory was that fighting modern wars would stretch an industrial state's economy so taut that small amounts of destruction, carefully concentrated on certain critical nodes, would cause the entire economic system to fold in on itself. The industrial web tied in several key producers, including basic industry and its sources of raw materials, plant machinery, power supplies, and the work force. The thread that tied workers to the web was called the industrial fab-

---

[13] Malcolm Cooper, *The Birth of Independent Air Power: British Air Policy in the First World War* (London: Allen & Unwin, 1986), p. 26. For an interesting argument that before World War I many British elites manipulated civilian fears of air attack to speed the growth of British air power, see Alfred Gollin, *The Impact of Air Power on the British People and Their Government, 1909–1914* (Stanford: Stanford University Press, 1989).

[14] David Divine, *The Broken Wing: A Study in the British Exercise of Air Power* (London: Hutchinson, 1966), p. 162.

[15] Barry R. Posen, *The Sources of Military Doctrine* (Ithaca: Cornell University Press, 1984), pp. 159–63.

ric: sources of food, clothing and utilities.[16] Since industrial economies were thought to be fragile, it was believed that a small number of bombers could destroy the entire economic base of an enemy, wreaking havoc on both civilian welfare and an opponent's military power. When the people witnessed the paralysis of the economy, the general will to fight would be shattered and the state would surrender. Like the British and German strategies of economic blockade in World War I, but far more efficiently, the enemy population would be attacked indirectly, as Michael Sherry puts it, "by disrupting and starving it rather than by blasting and burning."[17]

Although this strategy contained elements of both punishment and denial, the punitive elements were dominant. Advocates occasionally alluded to how strategic air attack would support a future land invasion, but air officers built this strategy precisely to avoid depending on land and sea power to achieve political goals in future wars. Because there is some dispute among historians about the essential logic of this strategy, it is useful to quote directly from three ACTS lectures, given to most of the Air Corps "best and brightest" officers, which elucidate the core of the theory.[18]

The first of these, "The Aim in War", states: "The ultimate object of all military operations, then, is to destroy the will of the people at home, for that is the real source of the enemy's national policy. . . . None of the props which bolster the soldier's morale are present to the same degree to support the will of the civilian. And yet the loss of that morale in the civilian population is far more conclusive than the defeat of the soldier on the battlefield. . . . Air forces [in contrast to land and sea forces] are capable of immediate employment toward accomplishing the ultimate aim. They can be used directly to break down the will of the mass of the enemy people."[19]

The second lecture explains how to achieve this aim by attacking an enemy's national economic structure. "Modern warfare places an enormous load upon the economic system of a nation, which increases its sensitivity to attack manifold. Certainly a breakdown in any part of this complex interlocked organization must seriously influence the conduct of war by that nation, and greatly interfere with the social welfare and morale of its nationals. . . . The application of the additional pressure necessary to cause a breakdown—a collapse—of this industrial machine . . . is the maximum contribution of which an air

[16] Thomas A. Fabyanic, *Strategic Air Attack in the United States Air Force: A Case Study*, Air University Report no. 5899 (Maxwell AFB, Ala.: U.S. Air Force, April 1976).

[17] Michael S. Sherry, *The Rise of American Air Power: The Creation of Armageddon* (New Haven: Yale University Press, 1987), p. 58.

[18] On the historical debate, see Ronald Schaffer, *Wings of Judgment: American Bombing in World War II* (New York: Oxford University Press, 1985), chap. 2, and Conrad C. Crane, "Evolution of U.S. Strategic Bombing of Urban Areas," *The Historian* 50 (November 1987): 14–39.

[19] M. S. Fairchild (instructor), "Air Force: The Aim in War," March 28, 1939, pp. 10, 12, 15, copy in United States Air Force Historical Research Agency (USAFHRA), Maxwell Air Force Base, Ala., file K248.2019A-2.

force is capable towards the attainment of *the ultimate aim in war.*" If, for example, the American national economic structure is destroyed, "what happens to our capacity to wage war? Under such circumstances, what is the amount of pressure that would be applied to our civil population? Would it be sufficient to cause our capitulation before the threat of continued action? . . . if we picture section after section of our great industrial system ceasing to produce all those numberless articles which are essential to life as we know it, we can form an idea of the pressure that would be exerted."[20]

The third lecture, "New York Industrial Area," translates these ideas into actual targeting plans against New York City as "a typical great city." Three target systems are identified. Attacking aqueducts would make the distribution of water impossible, undermining sanitation, causing thirst, and raising the threat of fire, with the result that "this method of attack on the city could force its almost complete evacuation." Striking railroad bridges would make the distribution of foodstuffs equally difficult: "Feeding this great metropolitan area depends upon the continuance of uninterrupted rail communications into the area. With any interruption, shortages in various items would become apparent almost immediately. . . . the area would become untenable and the population could have to be evacuated." Bombing electric power stations would cut water distribution in half by disabling pumping stations, would cause refrigerated food to spoil, and would leave households without power.[21]

Although the official Air Force history of the period claims that the ACTS strategy aimed to destroy an enemy's "military power," these lectures hardly mentioned the effects of bombing on the capacity to produce military goods or to operate forces on the battlefield. Instead, the argument was that bombing can destroy a nation's economy and cause so much discomfort among civilians that they will demand political acquiescence regardless of any military effects.[22]

ACTS thinking is remarkably similar to ideas developed in the interwar period by the Russian turned American air theorist Alexander P. de Seversky. Rather than depend on air power's ability to sow panic throughout the population, Seversky believed in breaking civilian will "by destroying effectively the essentials of their lives—the supply of food, shelter, light, water, sanitation, and the rest. . . . Bombardment from on high must fit strictly to the pattern of aerial blockade, systematically wrecking the implements and channels of normal life until a complete breakdown of the will to

[20] M. S. Fairchild (instructor), "Air Force: National Economic Structure," April 5, 1939, pp. 8–9, USAFHRA, file K248.2019A-10.

[21] M. S. Fairchild (instructor), "Air Force: New York Industrial Area," April 6, 1939, pp. 3, 12, 14, 15–21, USAFHRA, file K248.2019A-12.

[22] Wesley Frank Craven and James Lea Cate, *The Army Air Forces in World War II* (Washington D.C.: GPO, 1948), 1: 50–52.

fight and the ability to fight is accomplished." In contrast to a naval blockade that aims to reduce the flow of goods into an area, an aerial blockade aims at the inverse, to increase the flow of people out of cities.[23]

Three factors drove the American interwar air strategy.[24] First, unlike the RAF, which was created during World War I, and the Luftwaffe, which was not created until the late interwar years, the air force in the United States fought a protracted battle for autonomy throughout the entire period and did not actually win it until after World War II. Thus, the pioneers of air doctrine had to demonstrate that air power could achieve cheaply a military purpose that the other services could achieve only at unacceptable cost. They also had to show that air power was more efficient (and therefore more worthy of resources) than sea or land power. These pressures led the pioneers of U.S. air doctrine, such as General William Mitchell and officers at the Air Corps Tactical School, to argue during the 1920s that bombing attacks on the enemy's civilian population at the beginning of a war would effectively destroy the enemy's will to resist, producing a far cheaper victory than the Army could achieve.

The choice of the industrial web approach rather than Douhet-style area bombing also helped the Air Corps in a separate resource competition with the Navy. The United States was so geographically isolated from European centers of power that American leaders believed their cities were immune from enemy bombing and that the principal threat would come across the seas. Accordingly, to win resources, proponents of air power had to argue not for the preemptive strike on enemy cities favored in Britain but that aircraft could destroy approaching ships more effectively than the Navy. Since coastal defense required precision bombing, it made sense for the Air Corps to adopt a precision-based rather than area attack approach to strategic bombing. In short, the complementarity of precision attack on the industrial web and and precision bombing of ships at sea satisfied the Air Corp's twin needs for a "strategic" function to gain independence from the Army and for tactical superiority against enemy ships to win resources from the Navy.[25]

U.S. air doctrine was also shaped by the liberal tradition in American politics and by economic conditions during the Great Depression. In essence,

---

[23] Alexander P. de Seversky, *Victory through Air Power* (New York: Simon and Schuster, 1942), pp. 146–47.

[24] This discussion is generally informed by Flugel, "United States Air Power Doctrine"; Schaffer, *Wings of Judgment*, chap. 2; Sherry, *Rise of American Air Power*, chap. 3; I. B. Holly, *Ideas and Weapons* (New Haven: Yale University Press, 1953); Robert Futrell, *Ideas, Concepts, Weapons: Basic Thinking in the United States Air Force* (Maxwell Air Force Base, Ala.: Air University Press, 1989).

[25] Both arguments are reflected in Mitchell's writings. If anything, he is more enthusiastic about the capabilities of aviation against ships than against any other kind of target. See, for example, William Mitchell, "Air Power vs. Sea Power," *American Review of Reviews* 58 (March 1921): 273–77. For an example of Mitchell's argument in favor of bombing cities, see *Winged Defense* (New York: Putnam's, 1925), pp. 126–27.

domestic political and economic considerations influenced how the duality in U.S. air doctrine matured into a focus on precision bombing of key points in a state's economy. By the mid-1930s, air planners ceased to favor direct attacks on civilian populations, although such attacks were never excluded as an option for the later stages of an air offensive. Attacking the enemy's will through the more humane and economical method of selective attack made sense in the 1930s because the total budgets of the Army, of which the Air Corps was a part, were in decline. Accordingly, the Air Corps required a doctrine that promised victory not only at less cost relative to the Army and Navy but cheaply in absolute terms. Greater financial scarcity also made it impolitic to affront American liberal values by advocating the mass slaughter of civilians. Thus, unlike Mitchell, who assumed that strategic air power would wipe away cities, Generals Ira C. Eaker and H. H. Arnold wrote in 1941: "Human beings are not priority targets except in special situations. Bombers in far larger numbers than are available today will be required for wiping out people in sufficient numbers by aerial bombardment to break the will of a whole nation."[26]

Thomas Schelling and the Manipulation of Risk

In the two decades after World War II, social scientists devoted considerable attention to the problem of military coercion. The most important product of this effort was the concept of manipulation of *risk*. The nuclear revolution and in particular the advent of mutual assured destruction created both new restrictions and new opportunities for coercion. Since full-scale thermonuclear war would devastate both sides, any threat to carry out a full-scale punishment campaign lost all credibility. At the same time, since damage from even limited nuclear strikes would outweigh the national interest at stake in almost any dispute, the way was opened to coercion through manipulation of that risk. Later, these ideas were applied to purely conventional conflicts as well.

The idea of manipulating the risk of punishment for political purposes has largely come to be identified with Thomas Schelling's book *Arms and Influence*.[27] The heart of this strategy is to raise the risk of civilian damage slowly, compelling the opponent to concede to avoid suffering future costs.

[26] H. H. Arnold and Ira C. Eaker, *Winged Warfare* (New York: 1941), p. 134. For the impact of pacifism and antimilitarism on the U.S. Army between the world wars, see Ronald Schaffer, "The War Department's Defense of ROTC, 1920–1940," *Wisconsin Magazine of History* 53 (Winter 1969–70): 108–20.

[27] Thomas C. Schelling, *Arms and Influence* (New Haven: Yale University Press, 1966). Others also shared in the development of this idea, chief among them Daniel Ellsberg, "Theory and Practice of Blackmail," P-3883 (Santa Monica, Calif.: Rand Corporation, 1968); Morton A. Kaplan, *The Strategy of Limited Retaliation*, Center of International Studies Policy Memorandum no. 19 (Princeton: Center of International Studies, Woodrow Wilson School of

Like the Douhet model, the Schelling model focuses on population and economic targets. Civilian punishment can be inflicted both directly by killing large numbers and indirectly by destroying economic infrastructure, depriving the population of essential goods and services. There is, however, a fundamental difference. The Schelling model holds ultimate ruin in abeyance. Douhet called for immediate devastation: "Inflict the greatest damage in the shortest possible time."[28] The campaign need not be launched at the opening of a dispute to succeed, but the damage must be inflicted in a concentrated period of time. By contrast, Schelling argued that the key is not to destroy the entire target set in one fell swoop. Since coercive leverage comes from the anticipation of future damage, military action must be careful to spare a large part of the opponent's civilian assets in order to threaten further destruction: "To be coercive, violence has to be anticipated. . . . It is the expectation of *more* violence that gets the wanted behavior, if the power to hurt can get it at all."[29]

This logic calls into question the coercive usefulness of punishment strategies. Since, according to Schelling, sunk costs do not influence decisions, inflicting massive damage actually reduces the coercer's leverage. Punishment theories avoid this dilemma by assuming, explicitly or implicitly, that sunk costs do matter. In Douhet's model, for instance, victims of bombing are moved to revolt more by their emotional reaction to current suffering than by their rational consideration of future risks.

According to Schelling's view, the coercer must convince the opponent that targets will in fact be destroyed. Under this strategy, bombing is gradually escalated in intensity, geographical extent, or both. For example, a Schelling campaign might destroy targets in a sequence from demonstration targets to military targets to economic targets to population centers. The coercer must signal clearly that the bombing is contingent on the opponent's behavior and will be stopped upon compliance with the coercer's demands. "The ideal compellent action," Schelling writes, "would be one that, once initiated, causes minimal harm if compliance is forthcoming, and great harm if compliance is not forthcoming, is consistent with the time schedule of feasible compliance, is beyond recall once initiated, and cannot be stopped by the party that started it but *automatically* stops upon compliance, with all this fully understood by the adversary."[30]

Public and International Affairs, Princeton University, 1959); J. David Singer, "Inter-Nation Influence: A Formal Model," *American Political Science Review* 56 (June 1963): 420–30; and Alexander L. George, David K. Hall, and William E. Simons, *The Limits of Coercive Diplomacy: Laos, Cuba, and Vietnam* (Boston: Little, Brown, 1971). For a more recent discussion, see Richard K. Betts, *Nuclear Blackmail and Nuclear Balance* (Washington, D.C.: Brookings, 1987).

[28] Douhet, *Command of the Air*, p. 47.
[29] Schelling, *Arms and Influence*, pp. 2–3.
[30] Ibid., p. 89.

The most important instance of a risk strategy in action was the American bombing campaign against North Vietnam from 1965 to 1968, by which the United States sought to compel North Vietnam to cease supporting the insurgency in the South. The Johnson adminstration felt constrained to limit bombing of North Vietnam, both because important sectors of the American public would not support indiscriminate bombing and, even more important, because officials feared that massive bombing throughout North Vietnam would bring China into the war.[31] The aim was to coerce Hanoi by increasing the risks that existing limits would be crossed, leading to the loss of industrial production.

This campaign failed both because the political constraints on the Johnson administration ruled out indiscriminate countercivilian attacks and because the threat of limited bombing of industrial targets did not pose the risk of sufficiently brutal civilian hardship to overwhelm Hanoi's territorial interests. North Vietnam viewed the South as part of its homeland and its commitment to unify the country was based on the powerful motive of national cohesion. Threatening to destroy North Vietnam's tiny industrial base did not create sufficient risks to affect the government's political calculus.

Air attack on civilian populations, whether it seeks to kill large numbers or destroy the civilian economy, is not likely to coerce states in serious international disputes. Over more than seventy-five years, the record of air power is replete with efforts to alter the behavior of states by attacking or threatening to attack large numbers of civilians. The incontrovertible conclusion from these campaigns is that air attack does not cause citizens to turn against their government. Air power slaughtered British, German, and Japanese civilians in World War II; threatened Egyptian civilians in the 1970 "war of attrition" with Israel; and depopulated large parts of Afghanistan in the 1980s. In each case, the citizenry remained loyal to its leaders. In fact, in the more than thirty major strategic air campaigns that have thus far been waged, air power has never driven the masses into the streets to demand anything.

Although bombing economic structures can weaken an opponent's military capabilities in long wars, the first effects are generally felt by civilians. Since nearly all military and governmental facilities have backup power generation, the loss of electric power mainly shuts down public utilities (water pumping and purification systems), residential users (food refrigeration), and general manufacturing in the economy. Since the military generally has first call on oil, the effects of oil shortages fall mainly on civilians, cutting the fuel available for heating and civilian transportation (food distribution). Destroying rail and road bridges throughout the country further degrades the food distribution system.

[31] Mark Clodfelter, *The Limits of Air Power: The American Bombing of North Vietnam* (New York: Free Press, 1989), pp. 39–72.

Since World War II, Western publics have shrunk from using indiscriminate means against noncombatants to pressure other states. Western air campaigns have, however, inflicted indirect punishment on civilian populations by attacking economic targets. Electric power grids, internal transportation networks, and dams were destroyed in Korea; electric power grids, oil refining, and internal transportation were also wrecked in Vietnam; and electric power, oil refining, and internal transportation were demolished in Iraq. In none of these cases, however, did civilian pressure induce governments to surrender.

The key reason is that air attack against civilian infrastructure is even less effective than direct punishment in stimulating disruptive behavior. Inadequate food, lack of transportation, poor sanitary facilities, and the breakdown of public utilities and services (gas, water, electricity, heat supply, etc.) produce less effect on civilians than direct attack. Although emotional stress increases with the amount of deprivation, the changes in morale are not as great as with personal exposure to bombing.[32]

Denial: Attacking the Enemy's Military Strategy

Using air power for *denial* entails smashing enemy military forces, weakening them to the point where friendly ground forces can seize disputed territories without suffering unacceptable losses. Denial strategies seek to thwart the enemy's military strategy for taking or holding its territorial objectives, compelling concessions to avoid futile expenditure of further resources. Accordingly, denial campaigns generally center on destruction of arms manufacturing, interdiction of supplies from homefront to battlefront, disruption of movement and communication in the theater, and attrition of fielded forces.

Coercive air strategies based on denying the enemy victory on the battlefield developed without the benefit of an air theorist to organize the ideas into a coherent set of principles, though John C. Slessor, a British airman who wrote in the 1930s, came the closest. Concerned that the Germans might capture the Low Countries, from which the Luftwaffe could attack British economic and political centers, he stressed the importance of attack-

[32] James M. Mackintosh, *The War and Mental Health in England* (New York: Commonwealth Fund, 1944); Richard M. Titmuss, *Problems of Social Policy* (London: HMSO, 1950); and Max Seydewitz, *Civil Life in Wartime Germany* (New York: Viking, 1945). Although bombing in Germany caused water shortages and widespread pollution of the water supply, it did not significantly reduce public health because personal health habits, medical services, and government emergency measures controlled the spread of disease. USSBS, *The Effect of Bombing on Health and Medical Care in Germany* (Washington, D.C.: GPO, 1947), pp. 230–37. For an analysis of the civilian and military effects of attacking electric power, see Thomas E. Griffith Jr., "Strategic Attack of National Electric Systems" (Thesis, Maxwell Air Force Base, Ala.: School of Advanced Airpower Studies, 1993).

ing theater military targets until the German army had been pushed back to its borders, after which the final "decision will only be gained by direct action against the hostile centers."[33] Several organizations developed ideas about how to use air power to enhance the prospects for victory on the battlefield and then as a way to achieve independent political effects. Though some of these strategies, such as interwar Luftwaffe air doctrine, did not consider political effects at all, they are important instances of coercive air strategies and were in some cases extremely effective. For instance, the Dutch government surrendered on 14 May 1940 although it still retained substantial military forces in the field because it was persuaded that the fronts could not be held under continued Luftwaffe bombing. There are three main kinds of denial strategies.

The first to be developed was direct support of ground forces. All the major combatants in World War I used air power for such purposes, including operational reconnaissance and attacks on enemy front lines and logistic centers immediately behind the front. These were ad hoc efforts that threw newly available capabilities at existing problems. The first attempt to articulate an integrated theory of the role of air power in land warfare occurred in interwar Germany. German thinking on air power held that bombers should support the army's ability to take and hold territory by attriting enemy frontline forces. Proponents declared that the chief purpose of air power was to contribute to a combined arms assault that would break through an enemy's front lines. Bombers would be used as "flying artillery" to strike both fixed and moving targets very close to the point of attack but out of range of army artillery. Most important, bombers would strike reinforcements in the rear areas and near the "shoulders" of breakthrough points, disrupting the ability of the enemy to counterconcentrate tactical reserves to defeat the initial penetrations of the front.[34]

The use of air power directly on the battlefield had its strongest support in Germany for three reasons. First, because the Versailles Treaty proscribed an independent German air force, the Reichswehr was forced to maintain and develop its reservoir of air power expertise clandestinely, under the tutelage of the army until 1935. Thus, airmen had no choice but to cooperate with the army and had no incentive to produce a doctrine underwriting an independent air force. Second, the Luftwaffe learned from its experience during the Spanish Civil War that counterpopulation bombing had much less effect on civilian morale than expected and that accurate bombing of in-

[33] Slessor, *Air Power and Armies* (London: Oxford University Press, 1936), p. 3.

[34] On the emergence of Luftwaffe doctrine, see James S. Corum, "The Reichswehr and the Concept of Mobile War in the Era of Hans von Seeckt" (Diss., Queen's University, Kingston, Ont., 1990); Williamson Murray, "The Luftwaffe Experience, 1939–1941," in *Cast Studies in the Development of Close Air Support*, ed. Benjamin Franklin Cooling (Washington, D.C.: Office of Air Force History, 1990), pp. 71–114; and Matthew Cooper, *The German Air Force, 1933–1945: An Anatomy of Failure* (New York: Janes, 1981).

dustrial targets was beyond the limits of their technology. As a result, early Luftwaffe operations tended to reinforce rather than challenge doctrinal preferences established under the auspices of the army.[35] Finally, strategic bombing of industrial centers did not contribute to, and indeed subtracted from, Germany's grand strategic requirements. Germany's central military vulnerability was that it possessed within its own territory insufficient raw materials to support a wartime economy. Consequently, a basic principle of Germany's grand strategy was to acquire the economic assets of the European continent. Successful achievement of this goal required the domination rather than destruction of economic structures.[36]

The second major denial strategy, strategic interdiction, involves large-scale operations either to destroy the enemy's sources of military production or to isolate them from combat theaters or fronts. Its purpose is to reduce the aggregate quantities of weapons and war materiel available to the opponent. Two forms of strategic interdiction emerged.

The first was the "critical component" theory, the first instance of which was the industrial web strategy. Although the main purpose of the strategy was to reduce civilian will to continue by inflicting punishment, complete destruction of the enemy economy would obviously impede war production as well, reducing the quantity and quality of military equipment and supplies that could be delivered to a theater of operations. The crucial assumption, however, was that there exists some small, and therefore inexpensive to destroy, target set that produces a key item or service indispensable to the economy as a whole, such as national transportation and power resources. Moreover, economic infrastructures themselves were systems with critical nodes. Thus, strategic bombing planners could bring an entire economy to a halt by researching its industrial structure to determine which supplies were used in a wide variety of industries and which of the sources of supplies could be destroyed with least effort.

The next instance of the critical component theory applied it more narrowly to military production, as opposed to the economy as a whole. The Committee of Operations Analysts, a group of leading civilians (mainly economists, political scientists, and industrial managers) and air planners (including some from the ACTS) recommended targets for strategic bombing in Germany in 1943. The COA believed it was beyond current capabilities to cause a general industrial collapse and that such a strategy would not in any case achieve decisive military effects quickly. The analysts rec-

---

[35] Williamson Murray, "British and German Air Doctrines between the Wars," *Air University Review* 31 (March–April 1980): 39–58; Posen, *Sources of Military Doctrine*, p. 214.

[36] On Germany's goals during the interwar years, see Williamson Murray, *The Change in the European Balance of Power, 1938–1939: The Path to Ruin* (Princeton: Princeton University Press, 1984); E. M. Robertson, *Hitler's Pre-war Policy and Military Plans, 1933–1939* (New York: Citadel, 1963); Burton H. Klein, *Germany's Economic Preparations for War* (Cambridge: Harvard University Press, 1959).

ognized that the civilian sectors of the economy could absorb so much damage that the combat power of German forces could not be reduced until the huge civilian cushion had been destroyed. Therefore, they looked instead for components early in the military production cycle, the destruction of which would make the large-scale manufacture of heavy military equipment such as tanks, aircraft, and artillery impossible: "It is better to cause a high degree of destruction in a few really essential industries or services than to cause a small degree of destruction in many industries."[37] Consequently, their targets for strategic interdiction were special primary and semifinished products such as ball bearings, machine tools, rubber, aluminum, magnesium, nickel, steel, and nitrates that are used in the assembly of finished military goods. Even after the experience of World War II, many civilian students of strategic bombing have advocated critical component theories.[38]

Another form of strategic interdiction is a "systemwide" strategy that seeks to stop flows of resources and manufacturing by attacking all parts of very large systems rather than selecting critical components within systems. This strategy also emerged from World War II, deriving mainly from operations against Japanese sea commerce and the German national railway. Transportation is an effective target set for this purpose because it is large and connects primary goods to industries and industries to each other. Since the purpose is to attack the movement of resources and goods at all stages of the production cycle (raw materials to heavy industry to intermediate industries to finished products), air attacks are directed not only against key nodes such as marshalling yards, bridges, and ports but also against moving traffic, rolling stock, and cargo vessels. In contrast to attacks on critical components this form of strategic interdiction applies pressure as widely as possible in order to affect many industries simultaneously.[39]

The third major denial strategy, operational interdiction, attacks rear-area combat support functions in a theater of operations, the most important of which are tactical supply networks, reinforcements, and command-and-control facilities. The purpose of these attacks is to induce operational paralysis, which reduces the enemy's ability to move and coordinate forces in the theater.

[37] Report of the Committee of Operations Analysts, 8 March 1943, quoted in Charles Webster and Noble Frankland, *The Strategic Air Offensive against Germany, 1939–1945* (London: HMSO, 1961), 2: 213.

[38] Bernard Brodie, *Strategy in the Missile Age* (Princeton: Princeton University Press, 1959), pp. 110, 115, 116; Stefan T. Possony, *Strategic Air Power: The Pattern of Dynamic Security* (Washington: Infantry Journal Press, 1949), pp. 48–73. The Summary Report of the U.S. Strategic Bombing Survey implicitly accepted the critical component theory by suggesting that small, key industries, such as the German tetra-ethyl lead industry, should have been attacked.

[39] The main advocate of systemwide economic attack in order to cause economic collapse is Mancur Olson Jr., "The Economics of Target Selection for the Combined Bomber Offensive," *Royal United Services Institution Journal* 108 (November 1962): 308–14.

This strategy also arose in World War II. As the date for the invasion of Europe grew nearer, the Allied air services were called upon to develop plans to support the ground offensive. It was necessary to shift away from both Douhet and strategic interdiction because these would require an uncertainly long period to translate damage inflicted on specific targets to measurable weakening of German resistance. The pressure to reduce Allied ground casualties compelled development of a strategy designed to diminish German ground force mobility and fighting capacity in the western theater with effects that Allied ground forces could immediately exploit to their advantage.

Emphasis on operational paralysis led to the development of two sets of plans. The British plan aimed to destroy the rail, road, and river communications on which the German army depended in the theater. The core target set was the French railway network, because it carried the vast majority of very heavy loads, including military vehicles and other heavy equipment.[40] Railroad marshaling yards and bridges were struck, virtually shutting down rail movement west of Paris. Since reinforcing divisions had to march by road from Paris to Normandy, it took those that came from Poland as long to move the last two hundred miles by road as it had taken to move the first thirteen hundred miles by train.[41]

In contrast, American air planners selected oil instead of transportation. Believing that German-controlled railroads had too great a cushion of capacity for civilian and long-term industrial use above the minimum required by fighting units, the U.S. Enemy Objectives Unit maintained that a determined effort against oil would quickly reduce German military capabilities by reducing tactical and strategic mobility and frontline delivery of supplies.[42] Both the British and the American plans were executed, and debate continues over which contributed more to the war's outcome.[43]

This focus on affecting the fighting effectiveness of the German army also caused tactical air doctrine to evolve along similar lines. Until 1944, tactical air forces were largely seen as most effective in direct attacks against enemy

[40] Arthur William Tedder, *With Prejudice: The War Memoirs of the Marshal of the Royal Air Force* (Boston: Little, Brown, 1966), pp. 502–4, 509, 529–40; Solly Zuckerman, *From Apes to Warlords* (New York: Harper and Row, 1978), pp. 222, 232–33, 289–90; and Alfred C. Mierzejewski, *The Collapse of the German War Economy, 1944–1945: Allied Air Power and the German National Railway* (Chapel Hill: University of North Carolina Press, 1988), pp. 81–82.

[41] Price T. Bingham, *Interdiction in Italy and France* (Maxwell AFB, Ala.: Air University M-43796-4, 1986), p. 11.

[42] Enemy Objectives Unit, "The Use of Strategic Air Power After 1 March 1944," 28 February 1944, pp. 3–4, app. 8, USAFHRA K519.3171-2. Memorandum, Carl Spaatz to General Dwight D. Eisenhower, Supreme Allied Commander, "Plan for the Completion of the Combined Bomber Offensive," 5 March 1944, USAFHRA K519.318-1.

[43] On the historical debate, see David R. Mets, *Master of Air Power: General Carl A. Spaatz* (Novato, Calif.: Presidio Press, 1988) and its review by Solly Zuckerman, "The Doctrine of Destruction," *New York Review of Books*, March 29, 1990, pp. 33–35.

ground units, albeit at deeper distances than artillery could reach. The imperative to weaken the German army in preparation for the Normandy landings and to permit the advance of Allied ground troops, however, led to the use of air power against German command posts and logistic networks throughout the theater. The purpose of this first "battlefield air interdiction" campaign was not so much to destroy reserve units deep behind the front as to prevent them from being moved to reinforce the front. Disrupting communications would keep theater commanders ignorant of the true situation of units; attacking headquarters would impair the ability of staffs to coordinate units; and bombing logistic networks would reduce the mobility and firepower of German forces.[44] The campaign succeeded, as Field Marshal Erwin Rommel, the German commander reponsible for defending the French coast, noted: "The movement of our troops on the battlefield is almost completely paralyzed, while the enemy can maneuver freely."[45] Thus, by the end of World War II, a complete set of denial strategies—from attrition of ground units to operational and strategic interdiction—had been developed.

In general, denial air strategies are more likely to succeed against conventional forces than against guerrillas. The inelastic dependence of mechanized forces on logistics and central control means that shortages can undermine the ability of organized units to take or hold the disputed territory, and the complexity of conventional war planning means that these can be anticipated in advance. In contrast, guerrilla wars depend on the willingness of overlapping small groups to continue to resist central authorities, and this type of collective action is both less sensitive to shortages and less predictable. Guerrillas should be largely immune to coercion; coercers should expect to pay the full costs of military success to extract political concessions.

American coercion of North Vietnam in 1965 to 1968 failed because U.S. bombing could not address any important vulnerability of Hanoi's guerilla strategy. During this period, the United States tried to undermine the North's strategy for unifying Vietnam by interdicting the flow of logistics from Hanoi to Communist forces in the South. Although considerable damage was inflicted on the enemy logistic system, this had little effect on the feasibility of Hanoi's military strategy because the guerrilla campaign being fought in this period required little in the way of supplies and next to nothing at all from North Vietnam. Even with well over 200,000 troops in the field, their requirements for food, ammunition, medical supplies, and POL never exceeded roughly 380 tons a day, of which only some 34 tons came from the North. Given these tiny supply requirements, aerial bombardment

---

[44] Alfred Price, *Instruments of Darkness: The History of Electronic Warfare* (London: Macdonald and Jane's, 1977), pp. 97–250.

[45] B. H. Liddell Hart, ed., *The Rommel Papers* (New York: Harcourt, Brace, 1953), p. 476.

could not significantly hinder the insurgency, and consequently coercion failed.

If denial is more likely to succeed against conventional than against guerrilla strategies, when are the three forms of denial—strategic interdiction, operational interdiction, and attrition of military forces—most effective?

The purpose of strategic interdiction, which destroys production of military equipment and national transportation networks, is to reduce available quantities of weapons, munitions, and other military supplies. Strategic interdiction is an effective denial strategy only in protracted wars of attrition, and even then may require the attacker to pay heavy costs before coercive success is achieved.

In short wars, attacking economic targets rarely affects battlefield capabilities. The long lead times of production and conversion of civilian to military manufacturing means that industry can hardly contribute to wars lasting less than six months or a year. Accordingly, demolishing weapons plants, and even the entire economy, is often futile. The destruction of civilian transportation also rarely matters. The transportation requirements of military units and their logistics is generally small compared to the capacity of national transportation systems. Because military transportation can receive priority passage, national transportation capacity generally cannot be reduced below the level required by the military. Moreover, destroying national power grids does not weaken military capabilities in the theater. The widespread use of backup power generation, the positioning of POL reserves, and the low power requirements of military units means that military forces do not depend on national power grids to execute their functions. Instead of weakening battlefield capabilites, the greatest effect of strategic interdiction in short wars is to punish civilians, whose welfare is always tightly linked to the health of the economy.

By contrast, in long wars of attrition strategic interdiction can be an effective denial strategy. Wars of attrition occur when states seek victory by pushing the opponent back along a broad front in a series of set-piece battles. Rather than attempt to score a single knockout punch, opponents seek to overwhelm each other with numbers, and battles are fought to wear down opposing military capabilities. Accordingly, the side with greater manpower and a larger material base will ultimately win.[46] In essence, wars of attrition are economic wars in which outcomes are determined by relative manufacturing capability.[47]

[46] John Mearsheimer, *Conventional Deterrence* (Ithaca: Cornell University Press, 1983), pp. 33–34.

[47] On the connection between the economic foundations of military power and the nature of war, see Paul M. Kennedy, "The First World War and the International Power System," *International Security* 9 (Summer 1984): 37–40.

Strategic interdiction can undermine attrition strategies, either by attacking weapons plants or by smashing the industrial base as a whole, which in turn reduces military production. Of the two, attacking weapons plants is the less effective. Given the substitution capacities of modern industrial economies, "war" production is highly fungible over a period of months. Production can be maintained in the short term by running down stockpiles and in the medium term by conservation and substitution of alternative materials or processes. In addition to economic adjustment, states can often make doctrinal adjustments. Even when production of an important weapon system is seriously undermined, tactical and operational adjustments may allow other weapon systems to substitute for it. In 1944–1945 the Germans compensated for their shortage of tanks by introducing more effective infantry antitank weapons, notably the Panzerfaust and Panzerschreck. As a result, efforts to remove the "critical" component in war production generally fail. The Allies won air superiority over Germany in World War II not because bombing aircraft engine plants caused the numbers of German aircraft to decline but because air battles killed the Luftwaffe's most highly trained pilots. Iraq's ability to disperse its nuclear weapons plants indicates that the industrial bases of even Third World countries are elastic. In addition to nuclear facilities, the Iraqis also appear to have dispersed much of the equipment for their national telecommunications network and other key industrial systems prior to the start of the air war to enable the rapid restoration of these systems after the war.[48]

Strategic interdiction is most effective when attacks are against the economy as a whole. The most effective plan is to destroy the transportation network that brings raw materials and primary goods to manufacturing centers and often redistributes subcomponents among various industries. Attacking national electric power grids is not effective because industrial facilities commonly have their own backup power generation. Attacking national oil refineries to reduce backup power generators typically ignores the ability of states to reduce consumption through conservation and rationing. Against an exceptionally import-dependent economy, such as Japan in World War II, disruption of transportation can best be accomplished by blockading sea routes, using air power less for bombing than for shipping attack and mining. If imports can be totally cut off, the target economy will collapse when domestic stockpiles are exhausted; the Japanese merchant marine was essentially destroyed by the end of 1944, leading to collapse of war production by the middle of 1945. Against a relatively resource-rich economy, such as Nazi-controlled Europe, strategic interdiction requires stopping the flow of commerce along domestic railroad, highway, and canal

[48] See the remarks by William Arkin in "Defeat of Iraq Sparks Debate on Which Air Role Was Crucial," *Aviation Week and Space Technology*, 27 January 1992, pp. 62–63.

systems by destroying key nodes (bridges, canal locks, and railroad marshaling yards), moving traffic, and rolling stock and cargo vessels. This mission is hard because commercial transportation systems are large and redundant and are rarely used to full capacity. Thus, the United States could not bring the German economy to quick collapse even though U.S. air forces were vastly superior.

The weakness of strategic interdiction as a coercive strategy is that the attacker must still pay a heavy price for victory. Strategic interdiction reduces the quantity of weapons, munitions, and supplies reaching the battlefield, but it does not thin frontline forces or rapidly reduce their effectiveness. Thus defenders can still extract a considerable toll on attacking forces. Weakened states may "deter" an opponent from pressing its advantage to final victory by threatening to exact a very high price in casualties during the final battles to overcome their still-powerful frontline forces.

The purpose of operational interdiction, which destroys logistic networks, reinforcements, and command headquarters behind the front lines, is to stop the movement and coordination of forces throughout the theater. Disrupting these combat support functions matters most when adversaries are racing to concentrate (or counterconcentrate) forces at particular decisive points. As a result, attacking rear-area military targets is likely to be most effective when fronts are fluid rather than static.

Fronts become fluid when one side either breaks though the opposing line or maneuvers around the opponent's open flank. In order to achieve a breakthrough or a flank attack, the attacker must suddenly concentrate a large amount of force against a narrow sector before the defender can react. Air power can disrupt the attacker's combat support functions, slowing the attacker's concentration and giving the defender time to counterconcentrate. Likewise, disrupting the defender's logistics, reinforcements, and command and control delays reorganization of the defense, so that the attacker can punch through before the weak point is strengthened. Once a breakthrough is achieved, the main tasks of the attacker are to penetrate deeply into the opponent's rear and annihilate the defender's rear-area logistic and communications networks; the main task of the defender is to block the breakthrough, counterattack the vulnerable flanks of the penetrating spearheads, and form a new front. For both sides, timely movement of reserve forces and lateral movement of frontline forces is crucial. Accordingly, the more air power can disrupt logistic networks, reinforcements, and command headquarters behind the front lines, the more it stops the movement and coordination of forces throughout the theater, and the more it can affect the outcome.

In contrast, efforts to achieve operational paralysis by attacking rear-area targets is much less effective when fronts are static, as they are when either natural obstacles or force concentrations are so dense that breakthroughs and flank attacks are virtually impossible. Timely movement of reinforcements is less critical because strong fronts act as a cushion to permit even delayed forces to enter the battle in time to be effective. As a result, partial operational paralysis, which could significantly affect outcomes when fronts are fluid, weakens the opponent's ability to maintain a static front much less. For operational paralysis to matter when fronts are static, the attacker must achieve virtually complete destruction of the opponent's transportation and communications throughout the theater, completely isolating front forces from rear support. Even then, achieving a breakthrough could be costly and time-consuming.

The purpose of close air support, which attacks frontline fielded forces, is to thin the front, creating weak spots that the attacker's ground forces can exploit. Ground support is most effective when fronts are static rather than fluid.

When fronts are static, ground support is the most effective denial strategy because achieving a breakthrough is the only way to thwart the opponent's strategy without waging a costly war of attrition. In essence, air power adds additional firepower that can be used to create holes or to stop initial penetrations in a front. Air power has the advantage that it can be concentrated more easily in space and time than ground power because it ranges farther from supply bases and sees over the horizon. Thus, air power makes it more difficult for the defender to anticipate where the main weight will initially fall and, likewise, easier for the attacker to shift weight between separate axes when an advance is in progress.

When fronts are so static that breakthroughs are impossible, however, air power's ability to concentrate is less valuable than simply the aggregate firepower it adds to ground weapons. In this situation air power is likely to be less cost-effective than ground firepower, especially artillery.

When fronts are fluid, air support, while important, is less crucial to the success of a ground offensive. Once spearheads penetrate a front and head for rear areas, they no longer face solid resistance as they did at the front. The attacker seeks to reach and destroy the defender's rear logistics and communications centers, overwhelming weak enemy concentrations that may be encountered on the way and bypassing stronger ones. To defeat the attacker, the defender attempts to reestablish a continuous front to block further penetration and to counterattack the vulnerable flanks of the attacking spearheads. Thus, while air support immediately in front of spearheads is important, interdicting the movement of defending reserves is the most crucial mission. Interdiction blunts the threat to the spearheads' flanks and delays the defender's efforts to re-form a solid front. At the same time, direct support of the attacking spearheads is less effective because their rapid movement makes distinquishing friend from foe difficult. In this case, ground support merges into operational paralysis, since both are oriented toward stopping the effective movement of opposing reserve forces. Simi-

[78]

larly, after a breakthrough, the defender's main concern is with stopping the forward advance of the attacking spearheads, by blocking their supply lines and operational reserves, after which the spearheads themselves become significantly less mobile and more vulnerable to counterattack.

In guerrilla warfare, when meaningful counterconcentration does not occur and when logistic requirements are minuscule, air power is most effectively used directly against guerrillas rather than against their combat support functions. The ability of air power to substitute for ground power is significantly constrained by tremendous difficulties in identification of friend and foe from the air, however, which can be offset only partially by increasing loiter time over the target and coordination between air and ground units.

Decapitation

The use of air power for *decapitation*—a strategy spawned by precision-guided munitions and used against Iraq—strikes against key leadership and telecommunication facilities. The main assumption is that these targets are a modern state's Achilles' heel. Regardless of the strength of a state's fielded forces or military-industrial capacity, if the leadership is knocked out, the whole house of cards comes down. These counterleadership raids also cause little collateral damage if intelligence about the targets is right. The air theorist most closely identified with decapitation is Colonel John A. Warden III, one of the principal architects of the Desert Storm air campaign. He sees leadership as the most critical element in determining a nation's will to fight:

> The command structure . . . is the only element of the enemy—whether a civilian at the seat of government or a general directing a fleet—that can make concessions. In fact, wars through history have been fought to change (or change the mind of) the command structure—to overthrow the prince literally or figuratively or to induce the command structure to make concessions. Capturing or killing the state's leader has frequently been decisive. In modern times, however, it has become more difficult—but not impossible—to capture or kill the command element. At the same time, command communications have been more important than ever, and these are vulnerable to attack. When command communications suffer extreme damage . . . the leadership has great difficulty in directing war efforts. In the case of an unpopular regime, the lack of communications not only inhibits the bolstering of national morale but also facilitates rebellion on the part of dissident elements.[49]

[49] John A. Warden III, "Employing Air Power in the Twenty-first Century," in *The Future of Air Power in the Aftermath of the Gulf War*, ed. Richard H. Shultz Jr. and Robert L. Pfaltzgraff Jr. (Maxwell Air Force Base, Ala.: Air University Press, 1992), p. 65; see also Bruce A. Ross, "The Case for Targeting Leadership in War," *Naval War College Review* 46 (Winter 1993): 73–93.

Three variants might be pursued, each with a slightly different mechanism for success. The first is leadership decapitation, seeking to kill specific leaders on the assumption that they are the driving force behind the war and that eliminating them will lead to peace, either because their successors are not as committed to the objectives of the war or because they fear that they too will become targets in turn. The second variant is political decapitation, the use of air power to create the circumstances in which domestic opposition groups overthrow the government and replace it with one more amenable to concessions. Whether the mechanism is popular revolt or a coup d'etat, air power can increase the chances of success by attacking the regime's instruments of internal control (such as counterintelligence, security forces, and loyal military units) and knocking out communications to isolate leaders from their sources of support. The last variant is military decapitation, which attacks national command and communications networks in order to isolate the central leadership from its units in the field, so that the leaders can no longer give strategic direction or adjust to enemy moves. Deprived of central direction, the enemy's field forces will collapse under even light military pressure.

According to this strategy, a nation's leadership is like a body's brain: destroy it and the body dies; isolate it and the body is paralyzed; confuse it and the body is uncontrollable. The logic of decapitation is part punishment and part denial. As a punishment strategy, it aims to overcome a key weakness in such strategies: the increased ability of governments to repress dissent in war. As a denial strategy, it aims to extend the logic of operational paralysis to "strategic" or national decision makers.

Although there have been sporadic efforts to attack leaders or their national communications, only recently has this strategy became the cornerstone of air campaigns. Government buildings were bombed in Berlin and Pyongang and Hanoi's radio station was attacked, but the inaccuracy of bombing limited the ability of air strikes to destroy targets. With the Libya raid, however, which just missed Moamar Qaddafi, and the inclusion of Saddam Hussein's palaces and command bunkers on Desert Storm's target lists, decapitation is gaining attention.[50] The main attraction of targeting political leadership with conventional weapons is that it offers the possibility of successful coercion with minimal commitment of resources and risk of life, and it can be justified on the grounds that national command and control should be a legitimate target in conventional war, just as political leadership became a legitimate nuclear target in the 1970s.

Political leadership targeting is not likely to produce coercive leverage, however, for three reasons. First, it is very hard to find individuals and kill them. National leaders often have domestic enemies and so are well protected even in peacetime. The outbreak of war is generally accompanied by the tightening of security measures throughout society, especially those de-

---

[50] Ross, "Case for Targeting Leadership."

signed to protect the lives of government and military leaders. To circumvent the security surrounding leaders requires extremely detailed intelligence about their movement patterns, which can change without warning.[51] It took American troops days to find General Manuel Noriega after the Panama invasion, and they were looking for him on the ground. In fact, there has been only one successful wartime assassination by military forces of an important enemy military or political leader (Japanese Admiral Isoroku Yamamoto in World War II), and it had no effect on the outcome of war.[52] Moreover, success resulted more from opportunity than from planning. On 13 April 1943 Yamamato planned a series of morale-building visits to frontline bases. On 18 April United States intelligence intercepted a radio message indicating his flight schedule and an air attack destroyed his aircraft.[53] Of all possible instruments, air power is among the least effective at such work because there is likely to be a significant time delay between locating a leader and sending an aircraft to attack him, a delay that is all the more critical in today's era of mobile command posts. Thus, using air power to strike at leaders probably requires reflex targeting, which assumes that the first attack will be unsuccessful but will drive the leader to his favorite hideout, which is subjected to a a follow-on attack. This strategy multiplies the uncertainty.[54]

Second, truly idiosyncratic wars are rare in modern times. It is common for states to mobilize public support for war by demonizing their opponents, and personalizing conflicts (Churchill vs. Hitler, Reagan vs. Qaddafi, Bush vs. Saddam) plays an important role in these efforts. Outsiders frequently exaggerate the degree to which enemy leaders' policies express their personal preferences rather than those of the larger society. This tendency is exacerbated by intelligence provided by internal dissidents who have an interest in minimizing the degree of popular support for the leader's policies. In fact, the death of a leader in war commonly brings less change in policies than outsiders expected. The German general staff and the Nazi leadership continued to fight for months after Hitler removed himself from public view and for weeks after his suicide.

Third, succession in most states is highly unpredictable in war, the more so in closed societies. The problem is not intelligence but that tools for forecasting succession are indeterminate. In democratic systems, predictions of suc-

[51] Roger G. Herbert, "Bullets with Names: The Deadly Dilemma" (Monterey, Calif.: Naval Postgraduate School, 1992), pp. 93–99.

[52] The many instances in European colonial wars and in America's Indian wars in which native military leaders were captured by military forces and then killed in captivity are not comparable to decapitation in the context of coercion, since the native leaders' forces had to be defeated before the leader could be captured. See Dee Brown, *Bury my Heart at Wounded Knee* (New York: Rinehart and Winston, 1970); and Thomas Pakenham, *Scramble for Africa* (New York: Random House, 1991).

[53] R. Cargill Hall, *Lightning over Bougainville* (Washington, D.C.: Smithsonian Institution, 1991), p. 7; and John Dean Potter, *Yamamoto* (New York: Viking, 1965), pp. 303–4.

[54] John T. Stark, "Unconventional Warfare—Selective Assassination as an Instrument of National Policy" (Maxwell AFB, Ala.: Air University, n.d.).

cession are difficult because of the vagaries of public opinion. In authoritarian states, successions are even more uncertain because lieutenants commonly mute their voices and opinions, making it particularly difficult to know the political power they would have in a succession crisis or the direction in which they would move the country once in power. Efforts to predict the Soviet leadership succession in the late 1970s are an important case in point. Brezhnev's actual successor, Yuri Andropov, and his successor, Konstantin Chernenko, and his successor, Mikhail Gorbachev, are hardly mentioned, let alone predicted as future rulers, by the most detailed treatment at the time.[55] Similarly, few would have known that Saddam Hussein was the strong man in Baghdad before he replaced Ahmad Hasan al-Bakr in 1979.

Another variant on decapitation is to use air power to create the circumstances in which local groups overthrow the government, either by popular revolt or a coup, replacing it with one more amenable to concessions. Decapitation, however, has never toppled a government. The only attempt to execute such a strategy occurred during the air campaign against Iraq, in which some air planners hoped that strikes against Baghdad would weaken Saddam's political control and permit the overthrow of his government.[56] Nonetheless, after the most ambitious decapitation air campaign in history, in which over 44 leadership and 156 command-and-control facilities were attacked, and despite the fact that Iraq, with a long history of coups and an unpopular leader, was an ideal case for this strategy, Saddam did not fall.

Decapitation, like punishment, is not likely to topple governments, by fomenting either popular rebellion or a coup. Air attack is a weak instrument for producing popular rebellions, mainly because conflict with a foreign power typically unleashes political forces (such as nationalism and fear of treasonous behavior) which make collective action against even unpopular regimes unlikely until the opportunity for military victory has been lost.

Although decapitation might reduce a regime's ability to monitor and communicate with the population, it is unlikely to disrupt these functions for long unless the country is also occupied. The redundancy and miniaturization of modern telecommunications (telephone, television, and radio) makes it practically impossible to cut all the communication links between elites for any appreciable time. The destruction of civilian telecommunications can be hampered by housing transmitters in facilities that that attackers may want to avoid (hospitals, schools, and churches). Even if air power destroys the telecommunication network, it is not clear that a leader's ability to talk to his population would be limited in any meaningful way. Newspapers alone could keep communication open. Nor would the destruction of telecommunications free the population from fear of surveillance or

[55] Seweryn Bialer, *Stalin's Successors: Leadership, Stability, and Change in the Soviet Union* (New York: Cambridge University Press, 1980).

[56] Gulf War Air Power Survey, *Summary Volume* (Washington, D.C.: U.S. Air Force, 1993), p. 20.

reprisal, because the visibility, brutality, and perhaps even size of domestic security services can be increased.

Decapitation is also not likely to provoke coups, which, like popular revolts, are rare in wars and never occur in the early stages. When they happen, as when Mussolini was successfully overthrown in July 1943 or the famous attempt was made on Hitler in July 1944, they occur in the later stages, after battlefield defeats. The reason is that coup plotters want to control the country, not just remove the old guard. Unless the war is already clearly lost, the successor regime could be blamed for losing the war and quickly deposed in turn.[57]

More specifically, coups generally require the cooperation of the army, for only the army has the power to overcome the ruler's security forces. At a minimum, a segment of the army must actively participate and the rest must tacitly cooperate. In a conflict with a foreign power, such cooperation is unlikely. Armies are typically among the most patriotic national institutions and especially unlikely to cooperate with the enemy. Moreover, armies are responsible for winning wars. Since a coup will interfere with that goal, it is not surprising that armies have been interested in coups only when war is clearly lost and their leaders can blame the government for losing it.

Even if a state is ripe for a coup, moreover, disabling communications is not sufficient to provoke one or to ensure its success. Knowing the leader's location and overcoming his security forces are far more important. Successful coups always involve the arrest or murder of the top leader because rulers can commonly summon loyal forces to oppose the coup by meeting with them face-to-face. Thus, coup attempts do not pose significantly easier intelligence problems for foreign powers than assassinations. Indeed, air attack against national telecommunications can complicate the mission of coup plotters because they too are denied access to communication networks as they plan and execute operations.[58]

Finally, coups backed by the opponent in a serious international conflict are among the least likely to succeed. International enmity makes foreign cooperation with the indigenous military difficult before the coup and provokes resistance to the insurgents by the people and army during it, which is why the Iranian-backed coup in Iraq (1970) and the Libyan-backed coup in the Sudan (1976) failed. Indeed, unless foreign ground troops are committed, the key predictor of the success of a foreign-backed coup is the degree of po-

---

[57] Some of the standard works on coups are Samuel E. Finer, *The Man on Horseback: The Role of the Military in Politics* (New York: Praeger, 1962); Eric A. Nordlinger, *Soldiers in Politics: Military Coups and Governments* (Englewood Cliffs, N.J.: Prentice-Hall, 1977); Samuel P. Huntington, *Political Order in Changing Societies* (New Haven: Yale University Press, 1968); and Amos Perlmutter, *The Military and Politics in Modern Times* (New Haven: Yale University Press, 1977).

[58] For the mechanics of coup operations, see Edward Luttwak, *Coup d'Etat: A Practical Handbook* (Cambridge: Harvard University Press, 1979); and Gregor Ferguson, *Coup d'Etat: A Practical Manual* (Dorset, England: Arms and Armour Press, 1987).

litical affiliation between the foreign state and local regime. If the survival of the targeted regime already depends on the outside power backing the coup, as in the case of the United States in South Vietnam (1963–1965) or the French in the Central African Republic (1981), the chances of success are high. If the foreign power's influence is weak compared to the indigenous political base of the existing regime, as with the Soviet Union in the Sudan (1971), the chances of success are low.[59]

In theory, the growing centralization of military operations could mean that attacks against the most senior military commanders and their communication links to the theater could paralyze military forces. If the leaders cannot communicate with theater commanders, they cannot coordinate any meaningful national strategy, nor can they adjust strategy to meet enemy moves. In short, if attacking military headquarters in the theater causes operational paralysis, then attacking national military headquarters should be even better because it causes "strategic" paralysis.[60]

Strategic paralysis is virtually impossible to achieve, however, for three reasons. First, strategic direction does not demand high-volume real-time communication. The sheer size, spatial dispersion, and complexity of modern forces makes it impossible for national leaders to direct units in battle. The complexity and speed of modern operations means that the flow of information to and from units cannot be sufficiently detailed or arrive sufficiently fast to allow close control by a commander sitting at the seat of government, modern communications notwithstanding; control over actual combat must be exerted in the theater.[61] Lyndon Johnson did involve himself in picking air targets for strategic bombing (a type of operation more easily centrally planned than most), but he could not and did not get involved in the enormous number of decisions required for day-to-day management of land, tactical air, and naval operations. National leaders generally give theater-wide direction (choosing when and where the main effort is to be applied), sometimes authorize operational plans prepared by lower echelons to implement these broad decisions, and only sporadically intervene in decisions about how to coordinate forces, and then on an ad hoc basis. Characterizations of military command and control systems as centralized and decentralized can be misleading. These terms generally relate to the discretion given tactical unit commanders (e.g., divisions and brigades) by theater commanders (e.g., corps and armies). Even in militaries famous for centralized command styles and major roles for political leaders in operational affairs, national leaders are

[59] For an excellent analysis of foreign-backed coups, see Steven R. David, *Third World Coups d'Etat and International Security* (Baltimore: Johns Hopkins University Press, 1987), pp. 138–52.

[60] Jason B. Barlow, "Strategic Paralysis: An Air Power Strategy for the Present," *Airpower Journal* 7 (Winter 1993): 4–15.

[61] Hans Rosenberg, *Bureaucracy, Aristocracy, and Autocracy* (Boston: Beacon Press, 1958); and Martin Van Creveld, *The Transformation of War* (New York: Free Press, 1991).

still mainly concerned with broad decisions regarding fronts to be defended and attacked and not the orchestration of tactical units or their battlefield support to execute those decisions. Except in smallest contingencies, national leaders normally cannot plan and coordinate in-theater military operations.[62]

Thus, communication between national and theater commanders need not be voluminous and instantaneous. Major changes in strategic direction involve so much planning and logistic effort that they take days or weeks to implement theaterwide. Accordingly, short delays in receiving such orders rarely matter.

Second, strategic communications cannot be cut for long. Since national orders can be extremely short messages, many means can be used to send them effectively (land lines, radio transmissions, couriers, and face-to-face meetings). Moreover, disruptions of any of these methods is easily repaired because breaking strategic communication does not cause the same traffic jams that breaking intratheater communication does. Because theater warfare is analogous to railroad management—that is, it must dispatch large loads along a limited number of high-capacity routes on a tight schedule—traffic jams make it necessary to plan new routing, and therefore they have major and long-lasting effects. Strategic direction is more like a car trip. If the car does not start, one can borrow or rent another; if the road is closed or there are traffic jams, one can take a different route; if the weather is bad, one can go another day.

Third, theater commanders frequently are predelegated to act without higher authorization in emergencies. Although the normal practice in the United States is for unified commanders to seek authorization from the Joint Chiefs of Staff to implement measures beyond basic peacetime routines, the unified commanders have discretionary power to take whatever measures they consider necessary to preserve the security of the forces under their command, including moving them to locations anywhere in their area of responsibility.

Delegation of authority occurs even in authoritarian regimes. In principle, the tendency of authoritarian leaders to limit decision making to a very few and to avoid predelegation of authority could make them more vulnerable to strategic paralysis. In practice, however, centralization is limited by the extreme complexity of modern military operations. Even if they would like to, central authorities cannot micromanage all the command and logistic coordination that occurs in the theater. Militaries of authoritarian regimes often do perform poorly, but for a different reason. Such regimes often select and train officers primarily for political loyalty, not military skill. Thus, their most important battlefield weakness is simply poor generalship, not excessive dependence on strategic communications.

[62] Martin Van Creveld, *Command in War* (Cambridge: Harvard University Press, 1985); Paul Stares, *Command Performance* (Washington, D.C.: Brookings, 1991), pp. 112–13.

Table 5. Success and failure of coercive air strategies

Cases	Punishment	Risk	Strategic interdiction	Denial Operational interdiction, close air support, ground threat	Decapitation
Japan, 1944–45	failure	uncertain*	failure	success	—
Korea, 1950–51	failure	—	—	success	—
Korea, 1952–53	failure	success*	—	failure	—
Vietnam, 1965–68	failure	failure	—	failure	—
Vietnam, 1972	—	failure	—	success	—
Iraq, 1991	—	—	—	success	failure
Germany, 1942–45	failure	—	failure	failure	—

* Instances of nuclear coercion.

Stalin's command of the Soviet military in World War II illustrates how the limits of centralization limit the potential for causing strategic paralysis by interrupting communications between the rear and the front. Stalin formed his own supreme command body, called the Stavka, which in principle had the authority to intervene in local decisions anywhere. In practice, however, its members recognized that, being in the rear, they could not obtain enough timely information for detailed operational direction to be useful in many circumstances. As a result, the Stavka developed a procedure to exert close control over a local battle by sending a member with plenipotentiary authority to the front to issue orders to local commanders in the name of the Stavka. For instance, when Stalin could not obtain information about the course of the battle for Moscow in September 1941, he sent Marshal Georgi K. Zhukov to the front, not only to collect information but also to issue orders on the spot.[63]

STRATEGIES AND CASES

All the coercive air strategies I have described were used in one or more of the cases studied in Chapters 4 through 8 (see Table 5). In most cases the coercer pursued several different strategies either in series or in parallel. The case studies detail the effects of each strategy on the target state's willingness to make demanded concessions in order to determine which strategies were responsible for coercive successes.

[63] Georgi K. Zhukov, *Marshal Zhukov's Greatest Battles* (New York: Harper and Row, 1969), p. 44.

[4]

Japan, 1944–1945

The end of World War II in the Pacific provides the most successful case of modern military coercion. On 15 August 1945 Japan unconditionally surrendered to the United States, although it still possessed a two-million-man army in the home islands, prepared and willing to meet any American invasion, as well as other forces overseas. Indeed, Japan's surrender represents a rare instance in which a great power surrendered its entire national territory to an opponent that had not captured any significant portion of it. This coercive success saved the lives of tens of thousands of Allied soldiers and many times more Japanese.[1]

From the standpoint of coercion, what matters is not the exact date of surrender but that Japan did surrender without offering last-ditch resistance. The key question is why Japan capitulated before invasion and decisive defeat of its home army? Three principal explanations have been offered during decades of debate, all of which assume that civilian vulnerability was the key to coercion. The first declares that the decisive factor was fear of future punishment from atomic bombing: "It was not one atomic bomb, or two, which brought surrender," writes Karl T. Compton. "It was the experience of what an atomic bomb will actually do to a community, *plus the dread of many more*, that was effective."[2] Japan surrendered, it is said, to avoid the risk of having its population centers annihilated.

---

[1] Contrary to exaggerated claims at the time that Japan's surrender saved half a million American lives, Rufus Miles persuasively estimates that the invasion of Kyushu, the southernmost of Japan's four main islands, would have cost perhaps twenty thousand American deaths. Japanese casualties would likely have occurred in the same proportion as those during Pacific operations from March 1944 through May 1945, in which Japanese losses were over twenty times higher than American casualties. Rufus E. Miles Jr., "Hiroshima: The Strange Myth of Half a Million American Lives Saved," *International Security* 10 (Fall 1985): 121–40.

[2] Karl T. Compton, "If the Atomic Bomb Had Not Been Used," *Atlantic Monthly* (December 1946): 54; Louis Morton, "The Decision to Use the Atomic Bomb," *Foreign Affairs* 36 (January

The second explanation focuses on the effects of conventional strategic bombing on Japan's population. This position is largely identified with the United States Strategic Bombing Survey: "It was not necessary for us to burn every city, to destroy every factory, to shoot down every airplane or sink every ship, and starve the people. It was enough to demonstrate that we were capable of doing all this."[3] The decline in morale had a profound effect on Japan's political leadership, according to the USSBS: "At the time surrender was announced, [low morale] was rapidly becoming of greater importance as a pressure on the political and military decisions of the rulers of the country."[4]

The third explanation stresses American demands, contending that Japan's decision resulted from a concession by the United States to permit retention of the emperor. This concession reduced the costs of surrender, and so made Japan willing to give in rather than face continued suffering.[5]

The principal implication of all three of these arguments is that had American air power not driven up the costs and risks to civilians, Japan would not have surrendered prior to invasion of the home islands. Yet, none of these explanations is consistent with the facts. The argument that Japan was coerced by the threat of atomic attack fails because conventional bombing had already achieved such a high level of destruction that atomic bombs could not inflict dramatically more damage; the "hostage" was already dead. The argument that bombing collapsed Japanese morale is also wrong. Despite being subjected to the most harrowing terror campaign in history, Japan's civilian population did not pressure the government to surrender, industrial workers did not abandon their jobs, and army discipline remained excellent. The argument that a reduction of American demands can explain the outcome misreads the facts. The United States never communicated any commitment to retain the emperor or willingness to reduce any other demands.[6]

1957): 334–53; Herbert Feis, *The Atomic Bomb and the End of World War II* (Princeton: Princeton University Press, 1966).

[3] USSBS, *Japan's Struggle to End the War* (Washington, D.C.: GPO, 1946), p. 10. Army Air Forces Commanding General Henry Arnold later contended, "the Japanese acknowledged defeat because air attacks, both actual and potential, had made possible the destruction of their capability and will for further resistance." Quoted in Martin Caidin, *A Torch to the Enemy: The Fire Raid on Tokyo* (New York: Ballantine, 1960), p. 23.

[4] USSBS, *The Effects of Strategic Bombing on Japanese Morale* (Washington, D.C.: USGPO, 1947), p. 6. The USSBS also claims that strategic bombing of industry, helped accelerate surrender by hastening the collapse of the economy. As I discuss, it was the blockade rather than bombing that gutted Japanese industrial production, as the USSBS itself recognizes in several subsidiary reports.

[5] Paul Kecskemeti, *Strategic Surrender: The Politics of Victory and Defeat* (Stanford: Stanford University Press, 1958), p. 198. See also Feis, *The Atomic Bomb.*

[6] Leon Sigal, whose work is perhaps the most important since the early 1960s, debunks this myth. He contends that Japanese decision makers were motivated by their own interests in preserving their institutions and domestic power, and thus, intervention by the emperor to

I argue that a fourth explanation is correct. Military vulnerability, not civilian vulnerability, accounts for Japan's decision to surrender. Japan's military position was so poor that its leaders would likely have surrendered before invasion and at roughly the same time in August even if the United States had not employed strategic bombing or the atomic bomb. Rather than concern for the costs and risks to the population, or even Japan's overall military weakness vis-à-vis the United States, the decisive factor was Japanese leaders' recognition that their strategy for holding the most important territory at issue—the home islands—could not succeed. As Japanese leaders came to doubt whether they could prevent the home islands from being invaded and overrun, they preferred surrender to the costs of continuing the war.

Three key events persuaded Japanese leaders that their military position was untenable. First and most important, by the summer of 1945 the Allied sea blockade had completely cut off all outside sources of supply, crippling the key economic and military pillars supporting Japan's strategy. Second, the fall of Okinawa in June placed American tactical air power in range of the southernmost home island of Kyushu. Finally, the rapid collapse of the Japanese armies in Manchuria under Soviet attack indicated by analogy that the home army was unlikely to perform as well against the Americans as had been expected.[7]

To establish which of these four explanations is correct, four questions must be answered. First, what were the American coercive goals, and what strategies were employed to achieve them? Second, how faithfully and capably were these strategies executed? Third, what were the relationships among the progress of the American coercive campaigns, changes in the prospects for Japan's diplomatic and military strategies, and changes in Japanese leaders' willingness to surrender? Finally, can alternative explanations account for Japan's surrender?

AMERICAN GOALS AND STRATEGIES

American planning for the end of the war against Japan took shape very slowly, for two reasons. First, the United States and Britain had agreed in

---

overcome the domestic logjam accounts for the surrender. Yet if actors behaved according to domestic considerations and if the United States made no concession to preserve the imperial institution, then the emperor would have acted against his own interest, jeopardizing the throne by surrendering. Leon V. Sigal, *Fighting to a Finish: The Politics of War Termination in the United States and Japan, 1945* (Ithaca: Cornell University Press, 1988).

[7] On this point my argument agrees with the official British history, which says, "The Russian declaration of war was the decisive factor in bringing Japan to accept the Potsdam declaration, for it brought home to all members of the Supreme Council the realization that the last hope of a negotiated peace had gone and that there was no alternative but to accept the Allied terms sooner or later." Major General S. Woodburn Kirby, *The Surrender of Japan*, vol. 5 of *The War against Japan* (London: HMSO, 1969), pp. 433–34.

1941 on a "Germany first" strategy, because Germany was considered the more dangerous opponent. Accordingly, the conduct of the war against Japan was held hostage to the defeat of Germany, with only limited resources initially allocated to the Pacific. The United States allocated more than originally intended, though still less than to the European theater, and the British allocated very little in the Pacific until late 1944.[8] Second, the rapid and unexpected success of Japan in seizing the Philippines and other Pacific islands during 1942 unhinged Plan Orange, the American prewar plan for offensive operations against Japan, and temporarily forced the United States onto the defensive. Senior military and political leaders were compelled to make important strategic choices on the basis of immediate operational concerns, instead of forming a coherent long-term plan for ultimate victory.[9] It was not until the strategic tide turned in 1943 that American leaders became confident enough of the final outcome to begin considering how to force Japan to surrender.

By early 1943, the United States and Great Britain had both determined that, as with Germany, the only acceptable goal in the Pacific was the "unconditional surrender" of Japan. Although the meaning of this phrase was not unpacked in great detail, the clear implication was that Japan would be asked to surrender to the Allies not only its armed forces, all territories seized in the war, and its prewar overseas possessions, but also to accept occupation of its national homeland.[10] According to the Allied division of military labor, under which Britain would be chiefly responsible for Asiatic mainland operations (China-Burma-India), the United States would take the lead in any direct offensive against the Japanese islands.

Once it was announced, powerful domestic forces prevented the United States from altering its demand of unconditional surrender. Eager to obtain retribution for Japanese atrocities and for the surprise attack against Pearl Harbor, the American polity readily accepted the goal and political leaders were quickly locked in. Consequently, as the war progressed, the United States could not make surrender more appealing to Japan by reducing the concessions demanded and so searched for and adopted a host of military strategies to bend Japan to its will.[11]

---

[8] Maurice Matloff, *Strategic Planning for Coalition Warfare, 1943–1944* (Washington, D.C.: U.S. Department of the Army, 1959), p. 135.

[9] Louis Morton, *Strategy and Command: The First Two Years* (Washington, D.C.: U.S. Department of the Army, 1962).

[10] Unconditional surrender of Japan, however, was less onerous than unconditional surrender of Germany.

[11] The problems the unconditional surrender doctrine caused for American and Japanese leaders are discussed in Anne Armstrong, *Unconditional Surrender: The Impact of the Casablanca Policy upon World War II* (New Brunswick, N.J.: Rutgers University Press, 1961); and Akira Iriye, *Power and Culture: The Japanese-American War, 1941–1945* (Cambridge: Harvard University Press, 1981).

During 1944 and 1945, American military and civilian leaders conceived four strategies to finish Japan, all of which were adopted and pursued as they became feasible. These were interdiction using sea and air power, a Douhet strategy using incendiary bombing of population centers, a mixed Douhet and Schelling strategy based on the atomic bomb, and invasion.

Support for these strategies fluctuated. Initially all the services favored interdiction because it appeared to promise the surest (if not necessarily the fastest) results, and at the lowest cost in American lives. As the war progressed and Japan became increasingly vulnerable to all forms of American military pressure, this cooperation splintered into interservice rivalry to secure postwar credit for victory. Each service and President Truman's civilian advisers came to advocate a strategy to end the war which would dovetail with their interest in obtaining public credit for Japan's surrender. The Army argued for an invasion; the Army Air Forces changed from air interdiction to Douhet-style bombing; and the Navy remained wedded to interdiction. Finally, Truman's advisers, concerned to justify the cost of the Manhattan Project, advocated using the atomic bomb.[12]

Strategic Interdiction: Bombing and Blockade

Some senior naval and air officers believed that Japan could be forced to surrender by naval blockade and precision air bombardment of industry, without invading the Japanese homeland or resorting to terror bombing of civilians.[13] Although the Army Air Forces had pursued interdiction until General Curtis LeMay took command of B-29 operations in January 1945 and the Army, including General Douglas MacArthur, was agreeable until after the Philippines were liberated in March 1945, by 1945 its principal proponents were Commanding Admiral of the U.S. Fleet Ernest J. King and Admiral William D. Leahy, the president's representative on the Joint Chiefs of Staff.[14] The chief motive behind the strategy was to achieve the surrender of Japan at minimum cost. Economy of resources and lives was especially important because of the tremendous demands of the European theater.

This strategy had two components. First, precision air bombardment would successively destroy the key industries making up Japan's war manufacturing capacity. Aircraft production would be targeted first, in order to

---

[12] This pattern in the evolution of military doctrine for the Pacific war supports Barry Posen's general claim that external concerns tend to determine military doctrine when threats are high, while organizational interests dominate when threats diminish. Barry R. Posen, *The Sources of Military Doctrine* (Ithaca: Cornell University Press, 1984), chap. 2.

[13] See Haywood S. Hansell, Jr., *Strategic Air War against Japan* (Washington, D.C.: GPO, 1980), pp. 31–35, 90–91.

[14] Admiral Ernest J. King and Walter Muir Whitehead, *Fleet Admiral King* (New York: Norton, 1952), pp. 598, 605; and William D. Leahy, *I Was There* (New York: McGraw-Hill, 1950), pp. 383–85.

leave Japan completely vulnerable to protracted air attack. Second, U.S. naval forces would blockade Japan, cutting off the flow of crucial raw materials (especially oil, iron ore, and rubber) to Japan, and causing even those war industries not destroyed by bombing to collapse. The naval blockade would also bar the return of Japanese forces overseas to the home islands, preventing Japan from reinforcing its dwindling military capacity to defend the islands. Although advocates of these measures emphasized their contribution to invasion, they hardly concealed their hopes that they would make a major landing in Japan itself unnecessary.[15]

In addition to blockading sea lanes and bombing aircraft and other factories, this group also favored a schedule of amphibious operations, but ones that would be at odds with the prescriptions of the invasion strategy. Rather than prepare to land in Kyushu, they advocated a preliminary campaign to seize areas along the China coast, in Korea, and in the Tsushima Strait region for use as interdiction bases.[16]

Douhet: Burning Cities

In March 1945 the American bombing campaign shifted from interdiction to attacking civilian morale. The principal supporters of the change were Assistant Secretary of War for Air Robert Lovett, Army Air Forces Commanding General Henry Arnold, and Chief of Staff of the Twentieth Air Force General Lauris Norstad. In the field, General LeMay also advocated this strategy.

This strategy used incendiary raids on urban areas to compel Japan to surrender by shattering the will of the Japanese people. LeMay's theory reduced bombing to the essentials of Douhet: first establish bases, then "bomb and burn them until they quit."[17] Japan's wooden cities had long been considered more vulnerable than German cities to fire attack, and Japanese society susceptible to the terror effects of bombing.[18] During the war, this view was reinforced by social scientists who worked for the Air Force's Committee of Operations Analysts. For instance, Charles Hitch thought that reducing morale would depress the ability to recuperate from industrial bombing, for a spirited populace could repair the economic damage by gathering materials and rebuilding. Others expected that fire bombing would trigger wholesale administrative, psychological, and economic breakdown, cracking the backbone of the enemy's will to resist.[19]

[15] Feis, *Atomic Bomb*, pp. 5–6.

[16] Ibid., p. 6.

[17] Le May quoted in Michael S. Sherry, *The Rise of American Air Power: The Creation of Armageddon* (New Haven: Yale University Press, 1987), p. 300.

[18] Sherry, *Rise of American Air Power*, chap. 4.

[19] Ronald Schaffer, *Wings of Judgment: American Bombing in World War II* (New York: Oxford University Press, 1985), pp. 107–27.

The standard explanation for the change to Douhet-style bombing is that the air staff became dissatisfied with the meager results of the precision bombing campaign. As the official history explains, during the winter of 1944–1945 Washington "became progressively more interested in an all-out incendiary campaign." Although other arguments were advanced, "they had less influence than the failure of the precision attacks."[20]

This is not what actually happened. The air staff was interested in area incendiary bombing from at least the middle of 1944, before the precision-bombing campaign had even begun. As soon as the Twenty-First Bomber Command started operations, pressure was put on its precision-bombing-oriented commander, General Haywood S. Hansell, Jr., to adopt area incendiary bombing. Washington ordered test incendiary raids as early as 11 November, before the first precision strikes had been flown.[21] The pressure intensified after a successful incendiary raid on Hankow, China, by India-based B-29s on 18 December. Finally, on 20 January 1945, when Hansell would not agree to abandon precision attacks for fire bombing, he was replaced with LeMay, who had commanded the B-29s in India, and was known as an advocate of night incendiary attacks.[22]

The principal motive driving the shift to night area attacks was the air staff's need to demonstrate to the Joint Chiefs of Staff and civilian authorities that strategic bombing was decisive. As the Pacific war approached conclusion, the desire to make a visible contribution to victory led air planners to endorse the idea of morale bombing. The disadvantage of precision bombing was that it could not provide impressive statistical measures of its accomplishments, especially in comparison with the naval blockade, which by late 1944 could already claim to have sunk about three-quarters of Japan's merchant shipping. Only the small number of direct hits on factories could be reported, and it was very difficult to measure the effects of destroying a factory on the enemy's ability to meet specific economic and military needs. When poor weather over Japan forced planes to bomb by radar, as was often the case, even immediate results could not be observed, hits could not be reported, and damage assessment was rendered more uncertain. By contrast, photographs of burned-out cities seem to speak for themselves. Similarly, statistics of tons of bombs dropped and square miles of urban area burned are easily compiled, seem factual and specific, and are

[20] Wesley Frank Craven and James Lea Cate, *The Army Air Forces in World War II* (Washington, D.C.: GPO, 1948), 5: 610–11.

[21] The first fire raids were flown against Tokyo on November 29 and Nagoya on January 3. Craven and Cate, *Army Air Forces* 5: 564–65.

[22] Gary J. Shandroff, "The Evolution of Area Bombing in American Doctrine and Practice" (Diss., New York University, 1972), pp. 134–38; John W. Mountcastle, "Trail by Fire: U.S. Incendiary Weapons, 1918–1945" (Diss., Duke University, 1979), pp. 204, 210–20; Craven and Cate, *Army Air Forces* 5: 143–44, 609, 612–14; and Hansell, *Strategic Air War against Japan*, pp. 46–49.

impressive.[23] Accordingly, battlefield commanders identified with precision bombing were replaced by a new generation eager to experiment with incendiary raids.

The mission of the incendiary raids, writes Ronald Schaffer, would be chiefly psychological: to "affect directly the largest number of Japanese people . . . in the shortest period of time." Their "secondary purpose" would be to eradicate Japan's industrial system. The goal was to win through air power alone. Although the airmen tried not to project untamed enthusiasm, at times their ebullience was hardly contained. General LeMay wrote General Norstad that incendiary bombing gave the AAF for the first time "the opportunity of proving the power of the strategic air arm." Norstad, who saw early fire raids on Japan as "nothing short of wonderful," told LeMay in April 1945 that the Twenty-first Bomber Command, more than any other branch or service, was in position to strike a decisive blow. As the Strategic Bombing Survey states, "The implicit strategy now was to mount such an air offensive that Japan would be forced to surrender because of the disruption of its organized economic, political, and social life, without an actual military invasion of the home islands."[24]

Mixing Douhet and Schelling: The Atomic Bomb

The atomic bombings of Japan were intended to compel surrender both through their shock effect on civilian morale, as in a Douhet strategy, and through the threat of horrendous further devastation, as in a Schelling strategy. Among those who supported use of the atomic bomb were Presidents Roosevelt and Truman, Secretary of War Henry L. Stimson, General George C. Marshall, and the commander of the Manhattan Project General Leslie R. Groves. Although initially opposed, military commanders later lent their support.

The decision to use the atomic bomb was overdetermined. Its basic purpose was coercion, but it had the potential to solve other problems as well. If successful, atomic coercion would end the war without Soviet intervention, and so its use could reduce the political influence of the Soviet Union in the aftermath of the war.[25] It was expected, too, that a factual demonstra-

---

[23] Hansell, *Strategic Air War against Japan*, p. 48; Arthur Hezlet, *The Submarine and Sea Power* (New York: Stein & Day, 1967), pp. 218–21.

[24] Schaffer, *Wings of Judgment*, p. 139, LeMay and Norstad quoted p. 138; USSBS, *Effects on Japanese Morale*, p. 34.

[25] For a reasoned argument that assigns weight to the political opportunity costs of relying on Soviet intervention rather than the atomic bomb, see Kenneth M. Glazier Jr., "The Decision to Use Atomic Bombs against Hiroshima and Nagasaki," *Public Policy* 18 (Summer 1970): 463–516. Glazier essentially takes a middle position between those who contend that the atomic bombs were employed primarily to coerce the Soviet Union in Europe and those who ascribe little weight to the Soviet factor in American decision making.

tion of the enormous power of the new weapon might deter nations from pursuing aggressive policies for years to come: The immense cost of developing the weapon would eventually have to be disclosed, and there was some concern that Congress might be critical if the expenditure had not contributed to the end of the war. Finally, the attempt at atomic coercion would not interfere with plans for the invasion of Japan, should this prove to be necessary. If it failed, the Soviet invasion of Manchuria and U.S. invasion of Kyushu could proceed as scheduled.[26]

The basic goal was to manipulate civilian vulnerability, although no single strategy appears to have guided the use of the atomic bomb. Elements of both Douhet and Schelling models are detectable in the discussions of the Target Committee. Some meetings emphasized the importance of civilian morale: "We should seek to make a profound psychological impression on as many of the inhabitants as possible." Kyoto was initially attractive because its people were "more highly intelligent and hence better able to appreciate the significance of the weapon." Other discussions stressed the importance of signaling the unprecedented destructive power of the atomic weapon: virgin targets would reveal the true force of the atomic bomb (hence, Tokyo was ruled out). Another goal was to make "the initial use sufficiently spectacular for the importance of the weapon to be internationally recognized when publicity on it is released." The committee explicitly rejected military importance as the chief criterion, deciding "to neglect location of industrial areas as pin point targets." Psychological and political effects were clearly paramount.[27]

Despite the extensive targeting discussions, analysis of exactly how the atomic bomb would produce these psychological and political effects was remarkably casual, especially given the years of debate among senior political and military leaders about exactly this issue with respect to conventional bombing. Afterwards, some recalled greater clarity about the expected role of the atomic bomb in producing surrender than existed at the time. For instance, Leslie Groves later wrote, "I had set as the governing factor that the targets chosen should be places the bombing of which would most adversely affect the will of the Japanese people to continue the war."[28] In fact, the committee's main efforts went into producing a list of several cities which could be struck given operational considerations, such as

[26] The landmark works regarding the atomic bomb decision are Henry L. Stimson, "The Decision to Use the Atomic Bomb," *Harper's* (February 1947): 97–107; Morton, "Decision to Use the Atomic Bomb"; Len Giovannitti and Fred Freed, *The Decision to Drop the Bomb* (New York: Coward-McCann, 1965); and Feis, *The Atomic Bomb*. The best brief descriptions are Kirby, *Surrender of Japan*, pp. 184–87; and Giovannitti and Freed, *Decision to Drop the Bomb*, pp. 199–236.

[27] For close analysis of the Target Committee's deliberations, see Sherry, *Rise of American Air Power*, pp. 316–21.

[28] Leslie R. Groves, *Now It Can Be Told* (New York: Harper, 1962), p. 276.

weather. One reason for such loose strategic planning may have been the small number of nuclear weapons available for use. The Target Committee was formulating not an overall plan for atomic warfare but how best to use the few weapons at its disposal.[29]

But the decision for atomic coercion did not mean that American decision makers were highly confident that the atomic bomb alone would necessarily produce surrender. Stimson, for instance, was concerned with operational problems: "Even the New Mexico test would not give final proof that any given bomb was certain to explode when dropped from an airplane. Quite apart from the generally unfamiliar nature of atomic explosives, there was the whole problem of exploding a bomb at a predetermined height in the air by a complicated mechanism which could not be tested in the static test of New Mexico." Truman himself was only cautiously optimistic. As Louis Morton summarized his reaction, "Here at last was the miracle to end the war and solve all the perplexing problems posed by the necessity for invasion. But because no one could tell what effect the bomb might have 'physically or psychologically,' it was decided to proceed with the military plans for invasion."[30]

Invasion

The first three strategies—interdiction, Douhet, and the atomic bomb—were intended primarily for coercive purposes. Invasion could also coerce if the threat or the actual capture of one home island led to the complete surrender of Japan. American decision makers, however, thought of invasion primarily as the alternative to coercion; it would guarantee decisive military victory if coercion failed.

Initially, it was thought that an invasion would likely be unnecessary, but the consensus changed during 1944. American leaders, under domestic pressure to finish the war quickly, sought means to complete the defeat of Japan within twelve months after victory in Europe. It seemed at that time that the war in Europe would reach a speedy conclusion, making it critical to decide on Pacific strategy promptly.

The primary advocate of invasion was the Army, which rested its case on three arguments. First, an invasion of the home islands would guarantee decisive defeat of Japan, whereas coercion could not be counted on given the limits of American intelligence about the state of Japan's economy and morale. In April 1944 the Army's Operation's Planning Division declared: "a. The collapse of Japan as a result of blockade and air bombardment

---

[29] For detailed accounts of military plans regarding the atomic bombs, see Craven and Cate, *Army Air Forces* 5: 704–26.

[30] Henry L. Stimson, *On Active Service in Peace and War* (New York: Harper, 1948), p. 617; Morton, "Decision to Use the Atomic Bomb," p. 348.

alone is very doubtful. b. The collapse of Japan can be assured only by invasion of Japan proper." Moreover, the failure of Germany to surrender in April 1944, as many had predicted, discouraged confident assessments of when Japan would surrender. Second, invasion would produce results more rapidly than alternative strategies, and this possibility was especially important because of the pressure to finish the war within twelve months after the defeat of Germany. Finally, the interdiction strategy would waste many American lives in seizing ultimately irrelevant peripheral bases, whereas invasion would get the bloodletting over as quickly and as cheaply as possible.[31]

The leaders of the Army Air Forces and the Navy opposed invasion. The air staff contended that the Army's arguments underrated blockade and bombardment and contradicted the JCS goal of defeating Japan "by other means than invasion, while preparing for invasion as an ultimate alternative requirement."[32] The navy took a similar position. Admirals King and Leahy wanted to augment air and sea assault with operations against Japanese forces on the China coast, south of Shanghai and north of Formosa, and perhaps a lodgment on Korea. Together, these operations would sever Japan's communications with the Asiatic mainland and complete the blockade.[33]

The army gained the upper hand in this debate in the summer of 1944, when the progress of the island-hopping campaign made clear that an invasion would be feasible. The Joint War Plans Committee took the position that "while the bombing and blockade of Japan will have a considerable effect upon Japanese morale and their ability to continue the war, there is little reason to believe that such action alone is certain to result in the early unconditional surrender of Japan." It recommended, therefore, that "our concept of operations against Japan, subsequent to a lodgment in Formosa, should envisage an invasion of the industrial heart of Japan." The recommendations were officially adopted by the JCS on 11 July 1944:

> Our successes to date, our present superiority in air and sea forces, and the prospective availability of forces following the defeat of Germany, lead us to believe that our concept of operations against Japan following Formosa should envisage an invasion into the industrial heart of Japan. While it may be possible to defeat Japan by sustained aerial bombardment and the destruction of her sea and air forces, this would probably involve an unacceptable delay.[34]

---

[31] Ray S. Cline, *Washington Command Post: The Operations Division* (Washington, D.C.: Office of the Chief of Military History, U.S. Department of the Army, 1951), pp. 333–51, quote p. 337.

[32] Quoted in ibid., p. 337.

[33] Feis, *The Atomic Bomb*, pp. 5–8; King and Whitehead, *Fleet Admiral King*, p. 605; Leahy, *I Was There*, pp. 384–85.

[34] Quotations from Leahy, *I Was There*, pp. 338–39.

Plans for the invasion of Japan built on previous plans for blockade and bombardment, which had led to the capture of the Marianas, Iwo Jima, and Okinawa for use as naval and air bases. In addition to their value in cutting Japanese communications, these bases could now be used to support amphibious operations against the home islands. Although it was considered highly doubtful that Japan would surrender before the vital industrial areas of the main island, Honshu, were captured, an immediate assault against Honshu was considered too formidable without preliminary occupation of one of the smaller home islands. Thus, in November 1944 it was decided that southern Kyushu would be occupied first. From this vantage point the main invasion would be launched against the Tokyo plain on Honshu.[35]

A key component of this strategy was the participation of the Soviet Union, which, it was hoped, would launch a full-bore offensive against Manchuria to contain Japanese forces that might otherwise be redeployed to the defense of the home islands. Soviet entry would be of greatest advantage if it attacked prior to the invasion of Kyushu. Soviet participation in the actual invasion was neither expected nor desired.[36]

Execution of Military Operations

Military pressure to end the war progressed through three stages, as more and more coercive implements and strategies were brought to bear. In the first stage, the United States employed an interdiction strategy, based on a submarine blockade and precision bombing of industrial targets. The second stage, which began in early 1945, incorporated both interdiction and Douhet-style bombing of cities. While the naval interdiction effort continued, strategic bombing shifted from interdiction targets to attacking civilian morale. In the final stage, in the summer of 1945, the interdiction and conventional Douhet strategies were supplemented with an invasion threat and a mixed Schelling-Douhet strategy based on the atomic bomb.

Strategic Interdiction

Once American forces gained the initiative in 1943, coercion rather than invasion became the preferred means of ending the war. The naval blockade actually began on a small scale shortly after Pearl Harbor and escalated continuously until, by the summer of 1945, Japan was cut off virtually com-

[35] Grace Person Hayes, *The History of the Joint Chiefs of Staff in World War II: The War against Japan* (Annapolis: Naval Institute Press, 1982), pp. 655–59.
[36] U.S. Department of Defense, *The Entry of the Soviet Union into the War against Japan: Military Plans, 1941–1945* (Washington, D.C.: GPO, September 1955), pp. 39–41.

pletely.[37] Success in early island operations, the growing superiority of the American fleets organized around aircraft carriers, the progress of the submarine campaign, and the new B-29 long-range bomber all persuaded American strategic planners that the main pressure applied to Japan should come from the sea and air. Although much of the planning for blockade and bombardment of Japan occurred in 1943, these components of U.S. strategy took some time to execute fully. American submarines did not achieve great success in sinking Japanese shipping until late 1943 and 1944, and large-scale bombing could not begin until the Marianas Islands were seized in mid-1944.

The naval component of the interdiction strategy was based on commerce warfare. The essence of commerce warfare is that, rather than attempt to stop especially important cargos, the attacker simply tries to sink as much merchant shipping tonnage as possible, reducing the defender's stock of shipping by destroying vessels faster than they can be replaced. If the strategy is successful, the effects are exponential, for fewer supplies are available to produce replacement ships and attacking forces can concentrate against a dwindling number of targets. The ultimate goal is to reduce the defender's shipping capacity below the minimum needed to maintain its war economy.

Japan was exceptionally vulnerable to commerce warfare, for 75 percent of the country's most important raw materials and high percentages of other basic goods and foodstuffs were imported from overseas. The Japanese merchant fleet was fairly small, moreover, and highly sensitive to small losses because it was already used to nearly full capacity at the start of the war. In fact, only 65 percent of Japan's domestic trade was carried by its own shipping in 1941.[38] Japan's shipbuilding industry was small, too; so its capacity to replace losses was very limited. Counting all vessels of five hundred tons or more, Japan had 6 million tons of shipping available when the war began and built or captured another 4 million tons during the war, making a total of only 10 million tons, compared to the 85 million tons of Allied shipping confronted by the German commerce warfare effort in the Atlantic.[39] According to Japanese prewar estimates, Japan required an absolute minimum of 5 million tons to continue a protracted war.[40]

The U.S. strategy to cut Japanese lines of communication depended primarily on submarines, operating singly or in small groups, which destroyed far more tonnage than all other instruments combined, although land- and carrier-based air power also played a role toward the end of the

---

[37] Karl Lautenschlager, "The Submarine in Naval Warfare, 1901–2001," *International Security* 11 (Winter 1986–87): 121.

[38] Jerome B. Cohen, *Japan's Economy in War and Reconstruction* (Minneapolis: University of Minnesota Press, 1949), p. 251.

[39] Lautenschlager, "The Submarine in Naval Warfare," pp. 114, 119, 122.

[40] Cohen, *Japan's Economy*, p. 104.

war. The submarine campaign was initially hampered by problems in weapons design, particularly torpedoes, and excessively cautious tactics based on submerged approach rather than surface attack at night. Also, few modern submarines could make the long voyages from central Pacific and western Australian bases to the main shipping lanes off the Asian mainland. By mid-1943, however, all these difficulties had largely been solved. The number of U.S. submarines on patrol at any given time rose from an average of 13 in 1942 to 18 in 1943, to 27 by January 1944, and to 43 by October.[41]

By contrast, geographical limitations prevented air power from contributing much to the blockade until late 1944. Although the Fourteenth Air Force, stationed in China, made limited attacks against the Japanese shipping routes between Singapore, China, and Japan, it was not until the capture of the central Philippines in late 1944 that land-based air power could cut into Japan's economic lifeline on a significant scale.[42] Carrier-based air power was allocated to major operations against Japanese naval forces and island bases and was hardly used for commerce raiding until 1945.

The naval interdiction succeeded completely in destroying the Japanese economy. Shipping losses were so severe that by August 1945 Japan's merchant fleet had been reduced to just half a million tons.[43] In fact, over 75 percent of the tonnage destroyed was sunk prior to 1 January 1945.[44] Thus, submarines had essentially won the tonnage war before air power could intervene to help.

The economic effects of the blockade were devastating, although they did not materialize immediately because Japan had stockpiled large quantities of raw materials prior to the war. Despite heavy shipping losses, during the first two years of the war it was able to increase output in most categories. These reserves could be spent only once, however. By late 1944—prior to the initiation of strategic air attacks—the raw material base of Japan's war economy had been undermined and its industry was in steep decline.

By 1945 commodity imports had practically ceased, with disastrous effects on industrial production. Oil was the most critical problem. Japan depended on overseas supplies of oil for 90 percent of its requirements. Aware of this weakness, U.S. forces gave priority to sinking tankers, drastically cutting Japan's import capacity; after March 1945 no oil entered Japan.[45] Although Japan had a stockpile of over 40 million barrels in 1941 compared to an estimated annual requirements of 35 million, this had dwindled to 3.7 million barrels by the end of March and just 800,000 by July. In addition to

---

[41] Hezlet, *The Submarine and Sea Power*, pp. 210–27.
[42] USSBS, *The Effects of Strategic Bombing on Japan's War Economy* (Washington, D.C.: GPO, 1946), p. 36.
[43] Cohen, *Japan's Economy*, p. 104.
[44] Kirby, *Surrender of Japan*, 475.
[45] Hezlet, *The Submarine and Sea Power*, p. 223.

Table 6. Production in key industries as proportion of peak, 1945

Industry	Peak production	1st quarter	2d quarter	July
Rubber	1944 (1st qtr)	18% (4th '44)	10%	—
Aluminum	1944 (2d qtr)	26%	15%	8%
Oil refining	1941	27%	9%	—
Steel	1943	32%	—	13%[a]
Motor vehicles	1941	18%	6%	0%
Ordnance[b]	1944 (3d qtr)	42%	31%	22%
Aircraft engines	1944 (2d qtr)	42%	39%	29%
Airframes	1944 (3d qtr)	67%	61%	36%
Explosives	1945 (1st qtr)	100%	75%	45%

SOURCE: Cohen, *Japan's Economy,* pp. 129, 133, 134, 155, 185–86, 231, 235–36, 243, 247, 248, 249.

NOTE: Where quarter is specified for peak production, this is the only quarter for which data are available.

[a]The quality of what steel was produced declined because of increasing shortages of high-grade coking coal, cobalt, nickel, chrome, and molybdenum. Aluminum quality also declined as an increasing proportion of production consisted of reprocessed scrap. Cohen, *Japan's Economy,* pp. 125–26, 156.

[b]Small arms, artillery, tanks, half-tracks, ammunition, and military electronics, by yen value at 1945 prices. Calculated from detailed figures for naval ordnance and reported fraction of the total spending accounted for by the navy.

the economic effects, lack of fuel drastically curtailed Japanese air and naval operations.[46] Finally, by July 1945, with stockpiles of all major materials exhausted and no more coming in, Japan's economy was completely shattered (see Table 6).

Interdiction also involved precision bombing against key Japanese war industries. The primary instrument was the B-29, the product of an ambitious project to develop a very long range bomber by 1944. Before it was developed U.S. heavy bombers did not have the range to strike Japan from Pacific or Chinese bases, and carrier aircraft lacked the weight of striking power for sustained bombardment of a major industrial state like Japan.[47]

Precision bombing began in June 1944 and ended in March 1945. It started with Project Matterhorn, which used B-29s of the Twentieth Bomber Command, stationed in India and staging through forward bases at Chengtu in China. From this distance the bombers could just reach the southernmost home island of Kyushu but not the main industrial areas on Honshu. Therefore, Matterhorn dropped a mere eight hundred tons of bombs on Japan in nine missions; forty other missions were flown against targets in China, Manchuria, Korea, and Southeast Asia. The target directive included aircraft production, steel, ball bearings, electronics, and merchant

---

[46] Kirby, *Surrender of Japan,* app. 11; Cohen, *Japan's Economy,* pp. 134–35, 144.
[47] Craven and Cate, *Army Air Forces* 5: 3–33.

shipping, but in practice, only steel offered significant targets within range of the forward base at Chengtu.[48] Matterhorn demanded excessive logistic support in relation the weight of bombs dropped and so was deemphasized once the Marianas became available.[49]

The main American bombing effort was based in the Marianas, which were captured in the summer of 1944. Heavy bomber bases were quickly prepared and the Twenty-first Bomber Command began precision bombing in November, continuing until early March 1945. Even this was a small effort, amounting to just twenty missions, which dropped 5,400 tons of bombs, compared to the overall total of 160,800 tons ultimately dropped on Japan and the 1.36 million tons dropped on Germany.[50]

The JCS target directive specified that bombers should attack, in order of priority, aircraft engine manufacturers, airframe manufacturers, port areas, and urban areas. In fact, nearly all the effort (fifteen of twenty raids) was dedicated to attacking aircraft production.[51]

The campaign was a failure, partly because operations were hindered by the long flying distances that restricted payloads to three tons out of the nominal ten, poor weather, Japanese fighter opposition, a suboptimal ordnance mix of too many high explosives and too few incendiaries, and an initial shortage of aircraft. Thus, little damage was done. Of Japan's nine principal aircraft engine and assembly plants, only three suffered any lasting damage.[52]

More important, any damage inflicted by bombing could contribute little to reducing Japan's fighting capacity, for aircraft production was already in steep decline because of the shortages of key materials caused by the naval blockade. Production of aircraft engines had already fallen off sharply and airframes slightly in the last two months of 1944, *before* the plants were struck by B-29s. For example, output at the Ota aircraft plant had fallen from a peak of three hundred per month to less than a hundred before the plant was first attacked in February. Allocation of aluminum to the industry had declined 70 percent by the first quarter of 1945.[53] In addition, the quality of Japan's remaining industrial output had fallen so far that the equipment still being produced was highly unreliable. For instance, aircraft availability rates fell from 80 percent at the beginning of the war to 20 percent, and noncombat ferrying losses reached 40 percent.[54] Thus, even if left

[48] Craven and Cate, *Army Air Forces*, 5: 551–54.
[49] Shandroff, "Evolution of Area Bombing," p. 130; Craven and Cate, *Army Air Forces* 5: 175.
[50] Craven and Cate, *Army Air Forces* 5: 574; USSBS, *Summary Report (Pacific War)*, (Washington, D.C.: GPO, 1946), p. 16. Two additional major B-29 missions were sent against Iwo Jima as well as some minor raids against both Iwo Jima and Truk.
[51] Craven and Cate, *Army Air Forces* 5: 554–74.
[52] Ibid., pp. 554, 573.
[53] Ibid., p. 570; Cohen, *Japan's Economy*, p. 227.
[54] Cohen, *Japan's Economy*, pp. 144, 230.

undestroyed, the remaining industries could contribute little to the combat capability of Japanese forces.

Douhet: March–August 1945

Starting with the fire raid against Tokyo on 9 March 1945, the American strategic bombing effort shifted from an interdiction strategy to a Douhet strategy meant to inflict maximum damage on population centers. Chemical and biological weapons were not used, primarily because of strong opposition by Churchill, who feared that use of gas against Japan would encourage German gas attacks against Britain. In 1944 the United States agreed not to initiate the use of gas or to retaliate unilaterally without prior consent by the British.[55]

The transition in strategies can be dated by tracing changes in targeting, mission profiles, and munitions. An ideal interdiction strategy would pinpoint key war industries and raw materials, whereas an ideal Douhet strategy would simply blot out whole residential and commercial areas of cities. Interdiction missions would be flown in daylight for maximum accuracy and at high altitude to avoid air defenses, whereas Douhet missions, requiring less accuracy, could be flown at night when air defenses would be weaker. Finally, although bombloads for both types of missions might include a mix of high explosives and incendiary bombs, Douhet strikes would employ a higher proportion of incendiaries. The high-explosive bombs would break up structures so that the incendiaries could set the pieces on fire. Since homes are normally more flammable than factories and the industrial equipment in them, fewer high explosives are needed for residential area bombing.[56]

Following a pair of small, experimental raids against Kobe (4 February) and Tokyo (25 February), the incendiary campaign began in earnest with a spectacular fire raid against Tokyo on 9 March, which remains the most devastating air attack in history, exceeding even the atomic attacks on Hiroshima and Nagasaki. Eighty-four thousand people died and sixteen square miles (25 percent of the city) were rubbed out.[57] Next a series of fire raids from 11 to 19 March against Nagoya, Osaka, and Kobe destroyed another sixteen square miles of Japan's most important cities.

Tactics for the fire raids were designed for effective incineration. Since precision accuracy would be unnecessary, missions were flown at night. In addition, LeMay developed a set of special tactics to reduce fuel requirements and enable the planes to carry heavier payloads. Since the Japanese had very little short- and medium-range flak, the bombers flew at very low altitudes (five thousand instead of the usual twenty thousand feet). Because Japan had

[55] Sigal, *Fighting to a Finish*, p. 163.
[56] For a detailed account of the development of American incendiary tactics, see Mountcastle, "Trial by Fire."
[57] Craven and Cate, *Army Air Forces*, 5: 617.

no real night fighter capability, moreover, bombers could attack individually instead of flying in formation and needed to carry no armament.[58]

The fire blitz was temporarily halted only because LeMay ran out of incendiary bombs.[59] For the next two months, the B-29s were diverted to support the Okinawa invasion by bombing airfields on Kyushu and aircraft factories in Japan and by mining Japanese coastal waters. Even so, LeMay managed to send two major fire raids against Tokyo, which burned away another twenty-two square miles.[60]

The next major round of incendiary raids, between 14 May and 15 June, attempted to finish off Japan's six largest cities (Tokyo, Nagoya, Kobe, Osaka, Yokohama, and Kawasaki). Attention then turned to secondary cities (with populations over 100,000), and fifty-eight of sixty-two were burned. The war ended before the tertiary cities (those with populations of over 30,000) could be bombed.[61]

The extent to which the Douhet strategy was implemented is often unappreciated. One reason may be that political leaders have understated its magnitude in memoirs, and media coverage at the time largely neglected the countercity campaign. Both Churchill and Truman hardly mention it. They give the impression that countercity attacks were just under way when the war ended. Likewise, press reports during the war paid scant attention to the incendiary campaign against Japanese civilians.[62] Actually, the degree of destruction to Japan's population centers was extreme. In all, 178 square miles were razed, amounting to 40 percent of the urban area of the sixty-six cities attacked. 22 million people, 30 percent of Japan's entire population, were rendered homeless. 2.2 million civilian casualties were inflicted, including 900,000 fatalities, more than exceeding Japan's combat casualties of approximately 780,000.[63]

Mixed Douhet-Schelling: The Atomic Bomb

The final decision to drop the atomic bombs was taken by President Truman following Japan's rejection of the Potsdam Declaration on 28 July 1945.

---

[58] Ibid., pp. 612–14; Brooks E. Kleber and Dale Birdsell, *Chemicals in Combat*, vol. 3 of U.S. Department of the Army, Office of Chief of Military History, *The U.S. Army in World War II*, ser. 11: The Technical Services, 7: Chemical Warfare Services (Washington, D.C.: GPO, 1966), pp. 626–27; and Mountcastle, "Trial by Fire," pp. 135–65.

[59] Shandroff, "Evolution of Area Bombing," p. 143.

[60] Craven and Cate, *Army Air Forces* 5: 627–35.

[61] The best short overview of the urban area attacks is ibid., chap. 20.

[62] Sherry, *Rise of American Air Power*, pp. 315–16.

[63] Craven and Cate, *Army Air Forces* 5: 643, 674–75; USSBS, *Effects on Japanese Morale*, p. 34; and USSBS, *Summary Report (Pacific War)*, pp. 17, 20. Official Japanese figures, based on unscientific data collection and reporting procedures, were considerably lower (930,000 total civilian casualties). The USSBS built its estimate from a sample survey and is probably more representative of actual casualties. For a detailed discussion of Japanese casualty estimates, see Sherry, *Rise of American Air Power*, p. 413.

Hiroshima was bombed on 6 August and Nagasaki on 9 August. Some eighty thousand died at Hiroshima and the city was leveled; at Nagasaki thirty-five thousand died and less of the city was destroyed because hills shadowed large parts of the city from the blast. Many more died later from radiation.[64]

Evaluating the effectiveness of the atomic bombings as a Douhet strategy requires assessing their additional contribution beyond what was already being done by conventional fire bombing. This can be measured in two respects: morale or shock effect, and additional damage and suffering inflicted on the population.

Surprisingly, the shock effect of the atomic bomb was minor. Because the Japanese government tightly controlled information, news of the bombings spread slowly and the war ended before much of the population learned what had really happened at Hiroshima and Nagasaki.[65] While the emotional effects on the survivors were devastating, it is not certain that citizens of unattacked cities would have been equally affected even if there had been time for the news to spread. The Strategic Bombing Survey argues that morale effects of conventional and atomic bombing were similar in that those closest to the blast were affected substantially more than those not in the immediate vicinity.[66]

As far as damage is concerned, atomic bombs could contribute much less than is commonly thought. The two bombs that were dropped killed about one-seventh as many people as the conventional incendiary attacks. The Strategic Bombing Survey later estimated that damage equivalent to that caused by both atomic bombs could have been matched by 330 B-29 sorties using incendiaries—210 for Hiroshima and 120 for Nagasaki—only a fourth of the sorties that the Twenty-first Bomber Command was flying every week by August 1945.[67]

To be effective as a Schelling strategy, the atomic bombings should have been employed to threaten vast future damage, rather than to maximize current damage, and the time between detonations should have been measured to allow the import to sink in and to permit the Japanese to reconsider whether to accede to American demands. Neither of these criteria was met. The first could not be met, because the fire bombings had already inflicted such tremendous damage. By the time the atomic bombs fell, a vast portion of the urban population had either become casualties or fled to

[64] Craven and Cate, *Army Air Forces* 5: 724–25.

[65] For discussion of Japanese control of the media and confusion of the population regarding the atomic bombs, see Ben-Ami Shillony, *Politics and Culture in Wartime Japan* (New York: Oxford University Press, 1981), pp. 91–109; and Michihiko Hachiya, *Hiroshima Diary: The Journal of a Japanese Physician, August 6–September 30, 1945* (Chapel Hill: University of North Carolina Press, 1955).

[66] USSBS, *Effects on Japanese Morale*, p. 34.

[67] USSBS, *The Effects of Atomic Bombs on Hiroshima and Nagasaki* (Washington, D.C.: GPO, 1946), p. 33.

the countryside. By the end of the war, Japan's sixty-eight largest cities were shadows of their prewar incarnations; those with over 100,000 had lost 58 percent of their 1940 populations, and those with over a million had lost two-thirds. If one defines the hostage as major and secondary cities with over 100,000 people, then the hostage was nearly dead before the atomic bombs fell.[68]

Without many more bombs—perhaps dozens—which the United States did not have, atomic bombing certainly could not have overshadowed the effects of incendiary attacks. In fact, no more bombs were on hand at the end of the war, and only two were produced by the end of 1945.[69] Probably the most damaging use for atomic bombs would have been in restriking the largest cities, which had already been badly burned but still had people living among the rubble. These targets would have been quickly used up, forcing the atomic campaign to turn to smaller cities where its advantage over conventional bombing would have been smaller.

The timing requirement was also not satisfied. Since the Schelling strategy aims to coerce by increasing future risks, it is necessary to permit the opponent to assess those risks and act accordingly. The second atomic bomb was dropped only three days after the first, however, barely sufficient time for the Japanese government to carry out a cursory investigation of the effects of a wholly revolutionary weapon, and not enough to develop a reasoned assessment of the danger it presented.

Despite these weaknesses, one possible Japanese miscalculation could have made the atomic bombings an effective Schelling strategy. This strategy usually depends on signaling fairly clearly the scale of punishment that the attacker intends to inflict, but the coercive potential of the atomic bomb depended precisely on the fact that the Japanese had no way of knowing how much destruction would be visited upon them. Having no way to estimate how many bombs were in the U.S. arsenal, they might have believed that we had an unlimited number, and therefore feared that they would suffer devastation on an even greater scale than they had already.

Invasion

In fall 1944 the timetable for ending the war against Japan was disrupted by events in Europe, when it became clear that the collapse of Germany was not imminent. Since the invasions of Kyushu and especially Honshu depended on redeployment of large numbers of troops from Europe, which

---

[68] More than 10 million Japanese, one-seventh of the national population and one-fourth of urban dwellers, fled to the farms for refuge. Thomas R. H. Havens, *Valley of Darkness: the Japanese People in World War II* (New York: Norton, 1978), pp. 154–73.

[69] "U.S.-Soviet Nuclear Weapons Stockpile, 1945–1989: Numbers of Weapons," *Bulletin of the Atomic Scientists* (November 1989): 53.

would require from four to six months, plans for these operations had to put on hold. Hence, during the winter and spring of 1945, air and sea operations against the Japanese homeland continued, but without a fixed timetable for invasion.[70]

The final debate over the timing of the invasion took place following Germany's collapse in May 1945. The Navy and the Army Air Forces still objected to invasion. General Arnold tried to persuade MacArthur that air attack would make invasion unnecessary, while Admiral Leahy lobbied President Truman for an extension of the blockade.[71] Despite these objections, the final schedule of amphibious operations against the Japanese homeland was established in late May and confirmed by Truman, the JCS, and senior civilian advisors on 18 June.

The reasoning behind the decision was contained in a JCS staff study which argued that while the Japanese home army lacked aircraft and fuel, it consisted of 2 million men plentifully supplied with ammunition and under powerful discipline. Although Japan was virtually cut off from the Asian mainland, its food supplies were thought to be adequate at least through 1945. So, despite the close blockade and intense bombardment of Japan, the JCS "doubted whether the general economic deterioration had yet reached, or would reach for some time, the point at which it would affect the ability of the nation to fight or repel an invasion."[72] Moreover, if the Allies were to forgo occupation, the Japanese government might withdraw from occupied territory on the Asiatic mainland but not agree to unconditional surrender. With some misgivings, Truman accepted the JCS recommendation, although, according to Stimson, "he had hoped there was a possibility of preventing an Okinawa from one end of Japan to the other."[73]

The invasion of Kyushu (Operation Olympic) would begin on 1 November 1945, followed by invasion of the Tokyo plain on Honshu (Operation Coronet) on 1 March 1946.[74] The last preliminary step, completed in mid-June, was the capture of Okinawa, without which American tactical aircraft could not reach Kyushu. According to the plan for Kyushu itself, strategic air bombardment would continue the destruction of Japanese industrial power and communications. Next, the southern part of Kyushu would be isolated from the rest of the island, the mainland, and Honshu

---

[70] Cline, *Washington Command Post*, pp. 340–42.

[71] Feis, *The Atomic Bomb*, pp. 5–8; King and Whitehead, *Fleet Admiral King*, p. 605; Leahy, *I Was There*, pp. 384–85.

[72] Kirby, *Surrender of Japan*, p. 182.

[73] Stimson quoted in Feis, *The Atomic Bomb*, p. 11.

[74] Kirby, *Surrender of Japan*, p. 152. No formal directive for Coronet was ever issued by the JCS, since Japan surrendered well in advance of the start of Olympic. Planning for this operation during the summer and fall of 1945 involved more logistics than strategy, more about how to redeploy large numbers of army formations from Europe than about how to employ them in the Japanese theater. Hayes, *History of the Joint Chiefs*, pp. 701–10.

by a close naval blockade and tactical air interdiction. Finally, fourteen U.S. Army and Marine divisions would commence an assault against the estimated fifteen to eighteen Japanese divisions defending southern Kyushu.[75] The American forces would enjoy greater superiority in air, ground, and naval firepower than ever before in the Pacific war and were expected to overrun the objective area within thirty days. If the campaign took longer, reinforcements could be brought in from Europe at the rate of three divisions a month.[76]

In summary, the interdiction, Douhet, and invasion strategies all satisfied their basic requirements, but at different times. Although air interdiction contributed little, the naval blockade had achieved most of its military objectives by the end of 1944, leading inevitably to Japan's economic collapse in 1945. The Douhet strategy was implemented quite effectively from its inception in March 1945, largely depopulating Japan's cities by August. Although it could not be carried out before November, the invasion strategy was highly credible, especially after the fall of Okinawa in June provided the necessary forward bases. By contrast, the atomic bomb contributed little to the Douhet strategy, but could have been effective as a Schelling strategy, provided the Japanese miscalculated U.S. capabilities.

EXPLAINING JAPAN'S DECISION TO SURRENDER

In order to determine whether it was military or civilian vulnerability that played the decisive role in Japan's decision to surrender, three tasks are required. First, we must understand how the Japanese government made consequential decisions. Second, we need to know Japan's political objectives in the Pacific war and its military and diplomatic strategies for achieving them. Finally, we must measure the relationship between, on the one hand, the increasing vulnerabilities of the population and Japan's military strategy and, on the other, changes in Japanese leaders' willingness to surrender.

Japanese Decision Making

In some cases the military and political calculations of the target state's leadership cannot be measured directly and so must be inferred from the behavior of the state as a whole. In the Japanese case, however, there is sufficient evidence to reconstruct the analyses and positions of various groups within the governing elite, although we do not have sufficient evidence for all individuals to treat each as a separate case.

[75] Kirby, *Surrender of Japan*, p. 154.
[76] Ibid., p. 155.

Japan was an authoritarian state governed by an oligarchy composed of three principal elements. Popular opinion played no direct role and in practice was merely one factor to be considered among others by elites.[77]

The first and most powerful group was the military, which controlled strategic planning without civilian oversight. Also, because the Japanese constitution provided that a cabinet could not be formed without a War and Navy minister, the military had effective veto power over all government actions. Of the two branches, the Army was by far the more dominant. Civilian, Navy, and even senior Army officials who opposed Army interests were often simply assassinated by radical junior officers. In addition, the formation of the Kwantung Army after the seizure of Manchuria in 1931 gave the Army an instrument wholly beyond central control. The Navy was much weaker but did have the advantage over the civilians that it had the military information and skills occasionally to raise a credible dissent to the Army.

The second group was the civilian leadership, which included the senior statesmen serving in the Cabinet, some of whom were retired military officers, and the Emperor's chief adviser, Lord Privy Seal Koichi Kido. This group had the formal responsibility for running the country but in practice did not act against the wishes of the military. Their most important function was to serve as counselors to the emperor, who would occasionally summon one or more of them to offer analysis and recommendations. Although the emperor did not express his own opinion directly, the simple fact of an audience would lend weight to the summoned official's recommendations.

Last was Emperor Hirohito, who served primarily as a religious symbol to unify the national consciousness of the country. Although in principle he had the power to make law, in practice he took no formal part in government, with the exception of the requirement that Cabinet decisions be reported to him.

In theory, national policy decisions were made by unanimous consent. The Cabinet, which combined the Army and civilian groups, worked out a decision and then presented it to the Emperor, who never departed from it. In practice, the Army had overwhelming dominance, for it controlled the military police, a prime instrument for repression of dissent. For instance, in April 1945 War Minister General Korechika Anami ordered the arrest of some four hundred persons suspected of harboring end-the-war sentiments, including a former ambassador to England and a judge of high rank.

[77] For discussion of prewar and wartime Japanese politics, see Iriye, *Power and Culture*; David J. Lu, *From the Marco Polo Bridge to Pearl Harbor* (Washington, D.C.: Public Affairs, 1961); Saburo Ienaga, *The Pacific War, 1931–1945* (New York: Pantheon, 1978); and Michael A. Barnhart, *Japan Prepares for Total War* (Ithaca: Cornell University Press, 1987). For descriptions of the oligarchical and consensual nature of Japanese government during this period, see Robert J. C. Butow, *Japan's Decision to Surrender* (Stanford: Stanford University Press, 1954), pp. 10–17; and USSBS, *Japan's Struggle to End the War*.

Civilians recognized the dominant role of the Army. After the war, Prime Minister Kantaro Suzuki said, "The Cabinet would have collapsed immediately had the War Minister submitted his resignation. Because Anami refrained from submitting his resignation, the Suzuki Cabinet was able to attain its major goal, namely, the war's termination."[78]

Japanese Goals and Strategies

Japan's main territorial goals in World War II were driven by a need for economic and military autarky. Japan sought to control the major agricultural and raw-materials-producing areas of East and Southeast Asia, including Manchuria, much of China, and the Dutch East Indies. The Philippines, Malaya, and Burma all had some economic value, but were attacked for strategic reasons.[79] War with the United States was precipitated partly by the American, British, and Dutch economic embargo of July 1941, which cut off most of Japan's oil supplies.[80]

During the war against the United States, Japanese strategy passed through four phases. In the first, Japan aimed to capture the East Indies quickly, together with strategic points along a defensive ring from the northern Pacific all the way to Burma, including the Philippines, Central Pacific islands, New Guinea, the Bismarck Archipelago, Siam, and Malaya. This perimeter, the Japanese believed, would defy any U.S. counteroffensive, forcing acceptance of Japan's gains. The strategy enjoyed some success until the Japanese tried to extend the perimeter to include Midway Island and Attu and Kiska in the Aleutians, enabling the United States to destroy the Japanese carrier fleet at Midway in June 1942.[81]

Once the Japanese lost command of the sea, the initiative passed to the United States. During the second phase, Japan fought a defensive war, seeking to "hold the ring" in the central and southern Pacific in order to present the United States with the prospect of a long-drawn-out war and thus induce it to abandon its counteroffensive.[82]

The third phase began in July 1944. Following the loss of Guadalcanal, New Guinea, the Marshalls, and the Marianas, it became clear to most Japanese elites that Japan could not achieve the original objectives for which it had waged war against the United States in the first place. The cabinet of General Hideki Tojo, which had begun the war, fell and was replaced by a

[78] Butow, *Japan's Decision to Surrender*, pp. 75, 204.

[79] Barnhart, *Japan Prepares for Total War*, pp. 237–262.

[80] For a discussion of how Western economic coercion backfired, see Jonathan G. Utley, *Going to War with Japan, 1937–1941* (Knoxville: University of Tennessee Press, 1985).

[81] On Japan's initial strategy in the South Pacific, see Butow, *Japan's Decision to Surrender*, pp. 7–12; Paul M. Kennedy, "Japanese Strategic Decisions, 1939–1945," in *Strategy and Diplomacy* (London: Allen and Unwin, 1983), pp. 179–96.

[82] Kirby, *Surrender of Japan*, pp. 393–406.

new government headed by Premier Kuniaki Koiso. Some had begun to doubt Japan's ability to maintain control over its newly acquired territories as early as 1943, but the fall of Tojo was the first real opportunity to change fundamental policy.[83] Japan did not immediately sue for peace, however, because Japanese leaders believed that continued resistance would inflict enough costs on the Americans to induce them to lighten their terms. In particular, Japan hoped to end the war with its most important mainland possessions intact.[84]

Toward this end, Japan began to seek intermediaries to facilitate negotiations, hoping to find an ally who would help moderate the unconditional surrender demands of the United States.[85] Japan was not willing to accept peace at any price. An indication of the commitments Japan still believed itself capable of defending can be gained from the September 1944 Cabinet discussions about the concessions Japan would have to offer the USSR to "mediate" between Japan and the United States. Estimating that the Soviets would demand much of Manchuria, Inner Mongolia, part of the Kuriles, and other territories, the Cabinet decided not to proceed at that time.[86] China, Sweden, and Britain were also approached as possible intermediaries, with no result.

The fourth and final stage began with the U.S. invasion of Okinawa in April 1945. Koiso fell and was replaced by Admiral Suzuki, but Suzuki's Cabinet was not formed to produce a negotiated settlement. The Japanese expectation that after Okinawa the Americans would invade the home islands did not trigger a decision to open surrender negotiations. To the contrary, the army, the emperor, and Suzuki himself believed that Japan should fight an intense battle on the home islands rather than accept surrender.

Specifically, this plan had two tracks. The first was an approach to the Soviet Union, beginning in June, in search of diplomatic or military aid.[87] The second track was to prepare for a major battle against the invasion forces.

Japanese leaders were divided over the goals of Soviet mediation. For the civilians, the purpose was to get help in encouraging the United States to reduce its surrender terms. For the military, which was not interested in surrender, the purpose was to ensure Japan's ability to continue the war. In particular, the military intended to purchase Soviet oil and aircraft in return for Southeast Asian rubber, tin, lead, and tungsten or, if necessary, for territorial concessions. At best, some in the Navy hoped eventually to draw the Soviet Union into the war on Japan's side. At a minimum, they wanted to

---

[83] Butow, *Japan's Decision to Surrender*, p. 15.
[84] Ibid., p. 43 n. 41.
[85] Kirby, *Surrender of Japan*, p. 174.
[86] Butow, *Japan's Decision to Surrender*, p. 89.
[87] Statements by some Japanese officials to the effect that Japan first approached the Soviets in February 1944 are erroneous, according to Butow, *Japan's Decision to Surrender*, p. 127.

prevent a Soviet attack. Because of the lack of consensus, contact with the Soviet Union was not pursued with any sense of urgency or with a consistent set of priorities. In any case, the Soviets were unresponsive.[88]

In April 1945 the Japanese military began planning for homeland defense.[89] Remarkably prescient, Japanese Army intelligence predicted that American forces would follow up the capture of Okinawa with an invasion, first of Kyushu and then of the Tokyo plain area of Honshu. They estimated that the United States would invade Kyushu with fifteen to twenty divisions and Honshu with approximately thirty divisions. They thought the invasion might come as early as July, but considered it more likely that the United States would not be prepared to attack Kyushu until 1 October.[90]

Japan's strategy was to inflict such heavy losses on American forces, both at sea as they approached the landing zones and on the beach once they landed, that the United States would be compelled to retreat.[91] The key was not to defeat the American forces militarily but to raise the price of conquering Japanese territory higher than American society would be willing to stand. According to General Shuichi Miyazaki, Chief of the Operations Bureau, the Army "hoped to concentrate its strength entirely in the area where the American forces would make their first landing, and it hoped to strike a decisive blow, thereby forcing the enemy to abandon [its] intention of attempting a second landing or else seriously delay this move."[92]

The high command's defense plan, Ketsu-Go, called for augmenting the homeland's existing defenses with divisions brought back from China and Manchuria, newly raised divisions and air fleets, supplemented with large numbers of lightly armed guerrillas. Operationally, the American assault would be countered by large conventional forces positioned in and near the likely landing areas, while guerrilla forces covered lower-priority regions. Accordingly, southern Kyushu and the Tokyo area were allotted more than half of the sixty-seven divisions and thirty-five independent brigades available, and provision was made for rapid reinforcement of the initial invasion area. For instance, should Kyushu be attacked first, its fifteen divisions would be augmented with three others from Honshu. Given Japan's mountainous terrain, the possible landing beaches were well demarcated. These beaches were to be heavily fortified with obstacles, mines, entrenched troops, and artillery emplacements. If possible, the invaders were to be defeated on the beaches; otherwise, mobile assault divisions would counterattack and destroy the beachheads.

[88] Ibid., pp. 77, 112–41.

[89] Kirby, *Surrender of Japan*, p. 147.

[90] Ibid., p. 149; Donald S. Detwiler and Charles B. Burdick, eds., *Defense of the Homeland and End of the War*, vol. 12 of *War in Asia and the Pacific, 1937–1949* (New York: Garland, 1980), p. 75.

[91] Kirby, *Surrender of Japan*, pp. 96, 149.

[92] Quoted in Sigal, *Fighting to a Finish*, p. 49.

Rather than provide close air support for the army, Japan's air power was to be used in Kamikaze units against troop transports approaching the landing zones. Because of a dearth of trained pilots and aviation fuel, Kamikaze tactics were expected to be more effective in inflicting losses than standard types of air operations.[93] It was estimated that cannibalizing reconnaissance and training units could make some eight hundred Army fighter and bomber aircraft and three thousand Kamikaze aircraft available.[94] All these preparations were to be completed by the end of August.[95]

Causes of Change in Japanese Behavior

To evaluate the relative effects of civilian and military vulnerability on Japan's decision to surrender, we must trace the effects of changes in vulnerabilities on the positions of the major groups in the Japanese government regarding surrender. To do so, I divide the case into discrete time slices and measure the degree of Japan's vulnerability to each type of threat—nuclear, conventional fire attack, and invasion—in each period. If the preferences of one group changed at the same time as one type of vulnerability increased and the other remained constant, then the first and not the second must be the cause of that group's decision.

Carrying out this analysis reveals that the only factor to influence all principal groups was Japan's military vulnerability to invasion. Japan's vulnerability to nuclear attack had some influence on some groups but not on the Army, the critical group. The vulnerability of Japanese civilians to conventional attack had hardly any effect on any decision makers.

The two independent variables are civilian vulnerability and military vulnerability. Civilian vulnerability is coded as "low" where civilian costs were not sufficient to merit the costs of civilian defense procedures, "medium" where large civilian costs could be avoided with defensive steps, "high" where major parts of the population were uncertain about whether they would survive even with defenses, or "very high" where major parts of the population were certain not to survive because avoiding the enemy's attacks was impossible.

Measurement of military vulnerability focuses on the home islands, because control of the national homeland was the most important value Japan was being asked to surrender. Vulnerability is coded as "low" where there was no risk of the home islands being overrun in the short term, "medium" where the risk was considerable but could be reduced by added defensive measures, "high" where the risks of losing were great despite the best avail-

---

[93] Butow, *Japan's Decision to Surrender*, p. 99.
[94] Actually, Kamikaze air strength totaled more than 4,800. Detwiler and Burdick, *Defense of the Homeland*, document no. 119, p. 2.
[95] Kirby, *Surrender of Japan*, pp. 147–48.

able countermeasures but it might be possible to inflict enough casualties to reduce the enemy's commitment to control the territory, and "very high" where the likelihood of loss of control over the territory approached certainty because it was impossible either to defeat the enemy or to impose heavy attrition.

Before June 1944 Japanese society was not vulnerable to attack, and Japan was not bombed except by the fifteen-plane Doolittle raid of April 1942. In October 1943 the government ordered nonessential civilians to evacuate urban areas, but few did and no resources were devoted to enforcing the order.[96]

From June to November 1944, civilian vulnerability was low. During this period, China-based B-29s bombed Japan on several occasions, but only a few cities in Kyushu were affected and damage was extremely light.

In November civilian vulnerability increased to medium, when Marianas-based B-29s began bombing industries throughout the country. Although thousands of civilians were killed or injured, protective measures such as air defenses, evacuations, and fire lanes cut through city neighborhoods worked to keep costs and risks low. For example, the relative ineffectiveness of early experimental incendiary raids convinced the Japanese that their fire-prevention systems were highly efficient.[97]

After March 1945, however, civilian vulnerability was quite high. The massive American incendiary raids inflicted high levels of casualties which Japanese protective measures could not significantly reduce.[98] As the summer wore on, the problem grew as Japanese air defenses weakened, American bomber strength grew, and the campaign spread out to strike smaller cities, so that fewer and fewer safe places remained.[99]

Following the atomic bombing of Hiroshima, the vulnerability of Japan's population to nuclear attack is rated as very high. Current costs and risks were not significantly higher than those from incendiary attack. The atomic bombs were not much more lethal than the largest incendiary raids, certainly not by the orders-of-magnitude increase in lethality that has come to be associated with hydrogen weapons. More people died in the first major incendiary raid on Tokyo than at Hiroshima. Nevertheless, the ultimate risks faced by Japan had escalated markedly. Given sufficient time for the United States to produce weapons, Japan's vulnerability to nuclear attack was unlimited.

In fact, the degree of vulnerability perceived by Japanese leaders varied, depending on whether they understood immediately what these revolutionary weapons implied and how many more they thought the United

[96] Havens, *Valley of Darkness*, pp. 161–62.
[97] Craven and Cate, *Army Air Forces* 5: 565.
[98] Alvin Coox, *Japan: The Final Agony* (New York: Ballantine, 1970), pp. 28, 33, 41.
[99] Craven and Cate, *Army Air Forces* 5: 658.

States might possess. Some civilian leaders were at once convinced that Japan could not sustain this new form of warfare; at the same time, some Army and Navy representatives denied that an atomic bomb had been used at Hiroshima. Not until 10 August, after the Nagasaki bombing, did the investigators finally agree that Japan faced the prospect of an enemy equipped with atomic power.[100] By then, however, the government had already decided to surrender.

Prior to July 1944, military vulnerability was nil. Japan's strategy for holding the defensive perimeter in the Pacific had not yet been decisively defeated. Japanese leaders still hoped that at some point escalating losses would deter the United States from continuing the war, allowing Japan to keep its territorial gains.

Beginning in July 1944 with the fall of the Marianas, military vulnerability rose, although it remained low. The Marianas were the first positions to fall in Japan's inner defensive perimeter, and the battle for the islands destroyed much of its remaining naval power. The defeat brought down Tojo's cabinet. Japan was clearly losing the war, and invasion of the home islands had to be considered as a remote possibility. Also by this date, submarines had stripped Japan of much of the shipping needed to continue a protracted war.

In April 1945 military vulnerability increased to medium with the landings on Okinawa, the strategic gateway to the invasion of Japan. With all raw materials imports blocked and stockpiles largely consumed, production in key war industries had fallen from 25 percent to 50 percent or more. While the military recognized the risk of an invasion by powerful American forces, it believed that Japan still retained sufficient resources to make Ketsu-Go effective. With the morale advantage of fighting on home soil, Japanese forces would be capable of defeating the attackers. In addition, there was still hope that the Soviet Union would provide diplomatic and military assistance, although it had announced on 5 April that it would not renew the Russo-Japanese Neutrality Pact when it expired in April 1946. Nevertheless, Imperial General Headquarters insisted that a decisive battle on Japanese shores would end in victory.[101]

In June 1945 military vulnerability rose to high. With Okinawa in American hands, invasion had to be expected as soon as support bases could be made ready. The connection with the Asian mainland was now completely cut, making it impossible to bring back any forces to reinforce Ketsu-Go.[102] With stockpiles exhausted, production of war equipment was running down rapidly, falling from 55 percent to 100 percent in different categories

---

[100] Butow, *Japan's Decision to Surrender*, pp. 151–52.

[101] Ibid., pp. 73–77.

[102] For a summary of a Japanese army report, "The Present State of National Power," see ibid., p. 94. For a similar American appraisal, see Sigal, *Fighting to a Finish*, p. 109.

by July. A report by the premier's cabinet secretary concluded that Japan could not continue the war, because of the decline in munitions, shipping, and food.[103] In addition, the Soviet Union had failed to respond to Japan's requests for assistance.

Under these conditions, it was clear that Japan could not prepare for Ketsu-Go as fully as was expected in April.[104] On 12 June, Admiral Kiyoshi Hasegawa reported to the Emperor that the Navy had not been able to carry out preparations as planned. In particular, the Kamikaze units would be unable to cope with the demands of an invasion. At about the same time, General Yoshijiro Umezu, Chief of Staff of the Army, was forced to admit that the Army was encountering serious difficulties in preparing even basic defenses for the Tokyo plain area.[105]

Still, the Army remained confident that even if ultimate victory was beyond any realistic possibility, the Japanese strategy of inflicting punishing losses on the invading forces would succeed despite these problems. Lieutenant General Seizo Arisue, chief of the Army's Intelligence Bureau, said, "If we could defeat the enemy in Kyushu or inflict tremendous losses, forcing him to realize the strong fighting spirit of the Japanese Army and people, it would be possible, we hoped, to bring about the termination of hostilities on comparatively favorable terms."[106]

The Soviet invasion of Manchuria on 9 August raised Japan's military vulnerability to a very high level. The Soviet offensive ruptured Japanese lines immediately and rapidly penetrated deep into the rear.[107] Since the Kwangtung Army was thought to be Japan's premier fighting force, this quick mastery had a devastating effect on Japanese calculations of the prospects for home island defense. The Kwantung Army retained a reputation earned by its performance in the late 1930s and early 1940s, but by 1945 nonreplacement of aged equipment and repeated drafts for Pacific island service had greatly reduced its prowess. Even so, it still maintained better

[103] USSBS, *Japan's Struggle to End the War*, p. 7.

[104] "While a full-scale suicide effort could have been supported by the supplies on hand, they not only would have been exhausted in a few months of full-scale combat but were qualitatively inadequate, with such essential items as tanks, heavy artillery and field communications equipment largely lacking. . . . Under these circumstances it was obvious that the invasion would find Japan without means for prolonged resistance, and that even if it were initially repelled, disintegration of the entire economy would occur in a short time." USSBS, *Effects on Japan's War Economy*, p. 41.

[105] Butow, *Japan's Decision to Surrender*, pp. 115–16 n. 13.

[106] General Miyazaki was somewhat less confident, saying that victory "was beyond all expectation. The best we could hope for [was to inflict] a major blow on the enemy." Miyazaki and Arisue quoted in Sigal, *Fighting to a Finish*, p. 228.

[107] For an excellent history, see David M. Glantz, *August Storm: The Soviet 1945 Strategic Offensive in Manchuria*, Leavenworth Papers no. 7 (Fort Leavenworth, Kans.: U.S. Army Command and General Staff College, 1983); and idem, *August Storm: Soviet Tactical and Operational Combat in Manchuria, 1945*, Leavenworth Papers no. 8 (Fort Leavenworth, Kans.: U.S. Army Command and General Staff College, 1983).

equipment and training than could be provided for most of the make-shift Ketsu-Go forces.[108] If their best forces were so easily sliced to pieces, the unavoidable implication was that the poorly equipped, poorly trained forces assembled for Ketsu-Go had no chance of success against American forces even more capable than the Soviets.

Japan's depleted ability to execute Ketsu-Go made it unlikely that U.S. forces invading Kyushu would meet strong opposition. Contemporary American analyses estimated that conquering Kyushu would cost about twenty-five thousand Allied lives. American planners were still more optimistic about taking Honshu, which they estimated would cost fifteen thousand lives, presumably because they expected that the battle for Kyushu would consume the last of Japan's war production.[109] These figures are not high compared with the thirteen thousand lost at Okinawa against a much smaller but better-supplied Japanese force.

The dependent variables are the policy preferences of each of the three major groups in the Japanese government. To determine the effect of increasing civilian and military vulnerability on Japanese decision making, the views of each major group on surrender must be measured for each period when there was an increase in either type of vulnerability. Policy views are measured as "no surrender," which means not willing to surrender prior to invasion; "limited surrender," which means willing to surrender most overseas possessions but not the home islands; "flexible surrender," which means willing to surrender before invasion but not without attempting to obtain more favorable terms; and "immediate surrender," which means willing to accept unmodified American terms at once.

Much of the evidence for Japanese officials' views is problematic, because it comes from statements made by the principals to American interrogators after the war. Evidence may be biased toward presenting officials as favoring surrender earlier or more strongly than they in fact did. Given the anticipation of war crimes trials, senior officials had powerful incentives to maximize the extent to which they personally, and the emperor in particular, favored surrender. They tended to paint the military as responsible for continuation of the war. Also, because many of the interviews were conducted by the U.S. Strategic Bombing Survey, which was concerned to demonstrate the effectiveness of strategic bombing, the interviewees had an incentive to agree that air power had played the decisive role in bringing about the surrender.[110]

---

[108] See Kirby, *Surrender of Japan*, pp. 193–96.

[109] Barton J. Bernstein, "A Postwar Myth: 500,000 U.S. Lives Saved," *Bulletin of the Atomic Scientists* (June–July 1986): 39.

[110] For a collection of statements that conventional air power won the war assembled by the air force from postwar interviews, see *Mission Accomplished: Interrogations of Japanese Industrial, Military, and Civil Leaders of World War II* (Washington, D.C.: GPO, 1946).

Despite these difficulties, knowing the likely direction of any bias helps us separate more reliable from less reliable evidence. First, we should be more confident of views if we have corroboration from two or more sources. In particular, we should rely more strongly on statements made in official meetings whose date and attendance can be verified and of which multiple accounts often exist, than on the accounts by single individuals of informal conversations or of their private preferences. Second, we should give more credence to statements that could not reduce the witness's war crimes liability or enhance his reputation. Accordingly, an individual's statement that he did not favor surrender until well after he assumed official responsibility (e.g., Premier Koiso, who consistently advocated a decisive battle rather than surrender) should be trusted, whereas a claim that he worked for surrender from the start of his tenure in office (e.g., Premier Suzuki) should not be accepted uncritically. Similarly, claims that the emperor was kept uninformed until late in the war may reflect attempts to preserve his reputation, although evidence from major government meetings of his statements favoring negotiations can probably be considered reliable. Third, our assessments of individuals' statements should be affected by evidence of their previous preferences prior to their involvement in surrender decisions. For example, Shigenori Togo was well known as a member of the "peace party" from an early stage in the war. By contrast, Suzuki was chosen as Premier partly because the Army saw him as more reliably committed to continuing the war than the major alternative candidate, Prince Fuminaro Konoye. Indeed, Togo initially decline to enter Suzuki's Cabinet for this reason.[111] Taken together, these methods permit us to characterize Japanese leaders' views with fairly high confidence. Instances where codings remain uncertain despite the best available evidence are noted.

Given Japan's political system, only a small number of civilians could influence policy on the war. The key figures on whom we have detailed evidence are Kuniaki Koiso and Mamoru Shigemitsu, Premier and Foreign Minister from July 1944 to April 1945, Kantaro Suzuki and Shigenori Togo, who took over these positions in April, Prince Fumimaro Konoye, a former premier and influential noncabinet adviser,[112] and Lord Keeper of the Privy Seal Koichi Kido, the Emperor's personal adviser. Of these, Suzuki was the most important in the surrender decisions.

Changes in these leaders' positions on surrender correspond only weakly to increases in the vulnerability of civilians. None of them changed his views in response to the escalations of conventional bombing in November 1944 or March 1945, although several were influenced by the dropping of the atomic bomb on 6 August. By contrast, all of them were strongly influ-

[111] Sigal, *Fighting to a Finish*, p. 48.
[112] Konoye had been premier three times in the 1930s and was also considered for premier in April 1945. Sigal, *Fighting to a Finish*, p. 46.

enced by the worsening of Japan's military vulnerability, particularly the invasion of Okinawa in April 1945 and the collapse of Japan's war economy during the summer.

The attitudes of civilian leaders were determined largely by their loss of confidence in Japan's ability to execute the Army's Ketsu-Go plan. Some individuals required more evidence than others, however. Togo and Kido seem to have lost confidence in Ketsu-Go in June 1945, but Suzuki appears to have harbored hopes of inflicting a major defeat on American forces up until the Soviet invasion of Manchuria. Toshikazu Kase, Foreign Minister after the war, emphasized that Suzuki's primary concern was military vulnerability: "The more the prime minister learned of the extensive depletion of our war potential and our military helplessness the more convinced he became of the hopelessness of our position."[113] Suzuki himself told Air Force interrogators that the fire bombing of the cities by B-29s had been his main concern, but if this were so, he would have advocated surrender in March, not August.[114]

Further evidence that the primary focus was the military situation is the failure of the government to sacrifice military requirements to offset the miseries being inflicted on the populace. While Japanese leaders in public and private expressed frequently their sympathy for the hardships suffered by the general population, they did not hesitate to shift burdens to civilians when military requirements were unfulfilled. For example, Japanese leaders were well aware that food shortages had caused per capita consumption to decline well below two thousand calories per day during 1945, but they nonetheless ordered massive quantities to be stockpiled for the military to use in defending the homeland.[115]

Prior to July 1944, when both civilian and military vulnerability was nil, the civilian leadership did not favor surrender. Some senior statesmen such as Konoye, Kido, and Shigemitsu had growing doubts about Japan's military position in 1942 and 1943, and by the spring of 1944 had come to believe that Japan could not ultimately win a war of attrition against the United States. A principal factor in this change was a secret study completed in February 1944 by Rear Admiral Sokichi Takagi, which showed that air, fleet, and merchant marine losses had created insurmountable difficulties in acquiring essential imported materials, and concluded that Japan could not possibly win the war and therefore should seek a compromise peace.[116] Nev-

---

[113] Toshikazu Kase, *Journey to the Missouri* (New Haven: Yale University Press, 1950), p. 148.

[114] Suzuki said, "It seemed to me unavoidable that in the long run Japan would be almost destroyed by air attack so that merely on the basis of the B-29's alone I was convinced that Japan should sue for peace." Craven and Cate, *Army Air Forces* 5: 756.

[115] Kase, *Journey to the Missouri*, p. 196; USSBS, *Japan's Decision to Surrender*; Saburo Hayashi and Alvin Coox, *Kogun: The Japanese Army in the Pacific War* (Quantico, Va.: Marine Corps Association, 1959), p. 155.

[116] Butow, *Japan's Decision to Surrender*, pp. 7–26.

ertheless, these leaders had no concrete plans for surrender; instead, they spoke and behaved as ardent supporters of continuing the war.

Following the loss of the Marianas in July 1944, several senior statesmen called for Tojo's resignation, leading to the Cabinet's fall on 18 July. By this point, some individual civilians had come to favor limited surrender, but the civilians as a group still did not take action toward ending the war. Lord Kido, for example, suggested that the new government should consider concessions, albeit ones that would provide some measure of victory for Japan; in particular, Japan would retain Manchuria.[117] Shigemitsu, the new Foreign Minister, suggested asking the Soviet Union to mediate a limited surrender, but the cabinet rejected this proposal on the grounds that excessive concessions would be required. Koiso, the new Premier, still favored seeking a decisive victory in battle prior to opening negotiations.[118]

The successive increases in civilian vulnerability as bombing escalated in November 1944 and March 1945 had no apparent effect on the views of civilian leaders. For instance, during March the major topic among them was the prospect of a separate peace with China, not the devastation caused by the fire bombings. The negotiations fell through because the Chinese demanded that Japan withdraw from China, open separate negotiations over Manchuria, and make peace with the United States and Britain.[119] There was still no consensus among the civilian leadership in favor of any form of surrender.[120]

The civilian leaders accepted the idea of limited surrender when Okinawa was invaded in April 1945, raising Japan's military vulnerability from low to medium. The Koiso cabinet fell and was replaced by a new government that represented a compromise between civilians who wanted to end the war and the Army, which wanted to fight to the last. With Suzuki as Premier to satisfy the Army and the dovish Togo as Foreign Minister, the new government's policy was to prepare for a tenacious defense of the home islands while exploring opportunities to obtain peace on acceptable terms. Togo, supported by Kido and Navy Minister Admiral Mitsumasa Yonai, advocated approaching the Soviet Union for mediation and offering substantial concessions, including all of Manchuria. Suzuki went along but supported Army demands that the primary objective should be obtaining Soviet aid rather than exploring surrender terms. Suzuki was more hawkish perhaps

---

[117] Kido recorded these thoughts in his diary in January 1944 but did not act on them until the fall of the government in July 1944. Sigal, *Fighting to a Finish*, pp. 30–31.

[118] Ibid., pp. 33–38.

[119] Butow, *Japan's Decision to Surrender*, pp. 53–54.

[120] One reason Konoye opposed surrender was that he feared a leftist revolution in the aftermath of defeat. Though there was apparently no evidence, he thought that the lower and middle ranks of the Army had been infiltrated by communist sympathizers who would use surrender as an excuse to revolt. Kido thought Konoye's fears exaggerated but not wholly unfounded. See ibid., p. 50.

because he still believed that Japan could continue to fight two or three more years. Togo personally thought any hope of Soviet assistance was a chimera.[121]

In June, when Okinawa fell and communications with the mainland became impossible, the civilians began to accept the idea of flexible surrender. They preferred to drop efforts to gain Soviet assistance and to concentrate on getting Soviet mediation for terms other than unconditional surrender.[122] Kido was willing to pursue peace through mediation regardless of the price Japan would have to pay.[123] Togo persuaded Suzuki and Yonai to send Konoye as a special emissary to Moscow. Konoye agreed to go despite the risk of assassination by military diehards, and Togo instructed him to "try for anything at all short of unconditional surrender."[124] Clearly, civilians had not yet reached the point of accepting immediate unconditional surrender, for they unanimously rejected the Potsdam Declaration.

The final straws that led to acceptance of immediate surrender were the dropping of the atomic bomb on 6 August and the Soviet attack on 9 August, which raised both civilian and military vulnerability to very high levels. Immediately after learning about Hiroshima, Togo asked Suzuki to convene an emergency meeting of the Supreme War Council and also went to the emperor to advocate accepting unconditional surrender.[125] Suzuki, however, did not come around to this viewpoint until the Soviet attack on 9 August. Informed that Manchuria would be quickly overrun, Suzuki replied, "Is the Kwantung Army that weak? Then the game is up."[126] Kido and Konoye supported the decision to surrender, but there is no evidence of exactly when they came to this view. Thus, for this final change in civilian views, it is impossible to determine whether military or civilian vulnerability had the greatest impact.

The Emperor's views on surrender were dominated by military vulnerability, although his final shift to immediate surrender was triggered by the atomic bomb. Prior to February 1945 the Emperor took no role in trying to end the war. Major Japanese officials later claimed he had been largely uninformed, but since they had powerful incentives to protect the Emperor's reputation, it is not clear whether these reports represent the truth or whether they were intended to mask the Emperor's actual support for the war.

During February 1945 the Emperor held a series of meetings with senior Japanese statesmen about the war situation and plans for the future. Although several advised him that the situation was serious, no one recom-

[121] Sigal, *Fighting to a Finish*, pp. 48, 50–54; Butow, *Japan's Decision to Surrender*, pp. 86–89.
[122] Iriye, *Power and Culture*, pp. 257–60.
[123] Butow, *Japan's Decision to Surrender*, p. 88 n. 33.
[124] Sigal, *Fighting to a Finish*, pp. 76–78.
[125] The meeting was not held, because the military representatives refused to attend. Ibid., p. 237.
[126] Quoted ibid., p. 226.

mended surrender. In response, the Emperor took no action other than com-
missioning a study of Japan's military capabilities by Admiral Hasegawa.[127]

The first change in the Emperor's position occurred in June, when he came
to favor flexible surrender. As late as a Cabinet conference on 8 June, the emperor was still committed to waging a decisive battle on the home islands,
but the contents of Hasegawa's report on 12 June shocked him. Not only was
production low as a result of inadequate facilities and a shortage of raw materials, but also what did roll off the assembly line was frequently defective.
Morale was sufficiently high to continue, but basic capabilities were not, and
therefore, the final battles would fail. Army Chief of Staff Umezu also presented an appraisal, which although concluding that the final battles would
be victorious, detailed Japan's abundant military weaknesses at length.

On 20 June the Emperor told Togo that the reports from Hasegawa and
Umezu had convinced him that the military's preparations in both China
and Japan were so inadequate as to make it necessary to end the war without
delay. On 22 June the Emperor suddenly summoned the key Cabinet officials
and personally opened the proceedings by declaring that it was necessary to
consider means other than the Army's strategy to end the war.[128] Since the
Emperor did not explicitly discuss possible surrender terms, whether he favored limited or flexible surrender at this stage is difficult to say. One piece of
evidence does point to the more conciliatory position. On 7 July he suggested
to Suzuki that the government send a special envoy to Moscow, undoubtedly in the knowledge that Togo and Konoye intended to have the envoy
pursue any terms short of unconditional surrender.[129]

The second and final change in the Emperor's views was caused by the
bombing of Hiroshima, which increased Japan's civilian vulnerability. According to Kido, when the Emperor received the first reports, he said,
"Under these circumstances, we must bow to the inevitable. No matter what
happens to my safety, we must put an end to this war as speedily as possible so that this tragedy will not be repeated." The Emperor also sent Togo to
ask Suzuki to secure a prompt end to the war.[130]

Although the atomic bomb was the catalyst of the Emperor's decision, his
statement to the Cabinet meeting at which surrender was decided on the
night of 9–10 August stressed Japan's military vulnerability.

> I cannot bear to see my innocent people suffer any longer. Ending the war is
> the only way to restore world peace and to relieve the nation from the terrible
> distress with which it is burdened.

[127] Butow, *Japan's Decision to Surrender*, pp. 43–50.
[128] Ibid., pp. 117–19.
[129] As of mid-June, Kido had arranged for Togo to report directly to the emperor. Sigal,
Fighting to a Finish, pp. 234–36.
[130] Butow, *Japan's Decision to Surrender*, p. 152; Sigal, *Fighting to a Finish*, p. 237.

I was told by those advocating a continuation of hostilities that by June, new divisions would be placed in fortified positions at Kujukurihama so that they would be ready for the invader when he sought to land. It is now August and the fortifications still have not been completed. Even the equipment for the divisions which are to fight is insufficient and reportedly will not be adequate until after the middle of September. Furthermore, the promised increase in the production of aircraft has not progressed in accordance with expectations.

There are those who say that the key to national survival lies in a decisive battle in the homeland. The experience of the past, however, shows that there has always been a discrepancy between plans and performance. I do not believe that the discrepancy in the case of Kujukurihama can be rectified. Since this is the shape of things, how can we repel the invaders?[131]

Thus, the Emperor's argument was that, because defense of the homeland was hopeless, Japan was compelled to surrender to avoid pointless losses.

The views of senior military leaders, the most important group in the surrender decision, were completely determined by military vulnerability. Army leaders were extremely resistant to any form of surrender. They refused to consider even limited surrender prior to the fall of Okinawa in June 1945 and accepted immediate surrender only after the Soviet attack on 9 August.

Of the two services, the Army was dominant and almost unanimous in its views from War Minister Anami and Chief of Staff Umezu on down. If anything, some junior officers were even more opposed to surrender, and in fact, senior officers feared insubordination in case of surrender. The Navy, by contrast, was divided. Some Navy leaders such as Chief of Staff Admiral Soemu Toyoda consistently supported the Army line. Others, such as Admiral Yonai, supported the more dovish civilian line, although they based their arguments for surrender entirely on Japan's military situation.[132] Given its basic political weakness and its internal divisions, the Navy could offer no organized opposition to the Army's no-surrender policy.

Until June 1945, the Army opposed any form of surrender. When the new government was being formed in April, the Army vetoed the more peace-oriented Konoye as premier in favor of Suzuki and even then demanded guarantees that the Cabinet would continue to prosecute the war fully if any overtures were made to the Soviets. The Army also insisted that the objective of the overtures would be obtaining military aid, not diplomatic mediation.

---

[131] Kujukuri is on the Boso Peninsula near Tokyo. The most detailed reconstructions of the Emperor's speech are nearly identical. See Butow, *Japan's Decision to Surrender*, p. 175; Thomas M. Coffee, *Imperial Tragedy: Japan in World War II, the First Days and the Last* (New York: World, 1970), p. 354.
[132] Butow, *Japan's Decision to Surrender*, pp. 159–65.

After Okinawa fell in June 1945, the Army relaxed its adamant opposition and accepted the idea of limited surrender. The Army agreed to permit overtures to the Soviets to seek peace, but Anami insisted that since Japan was still holding most of the territory it had conquered, it had not lost the war and peace terms had to reflect that fact.[133] Similarly, both Togo, a strong supporter of surrender, and Toyoda, a strong obstacle to surrender, testified that by the end of July no one (including Umezu and Anami) was opposed to the Potsdam terms, providing certain additional terms were attached.[134]

When Japan's military vulnerability became very high following the Soviet attack on Manchuria, the Army's commitment to Ketsu-Go finally evaporated. Army and prowar Navy officials had recognized Japan's weak resource base for some time. As early as April 1945 both the Army and Navy chiefs of staff expressed deep concern over Japan's lack of oil, believing that stocks would last only until June 1945.[135] This, however, did not influence their views on surrender until the Soviet entry, after which the military chose not to veto the surrender. Prior to 9 August, the Army led the Cabinet in rejecting the Potsdam Declaration. When Suzuki called a cabinet meeting on 8 August to discuss reports of the atomic bombing of Hiroshima, it had to be canceled because the Army representatives claimed to have had "more pressing business." The next day, after the Soviet invasion had begun, the Army agreed to a special meeting of the Supreme War Council. News of the Nagasaki bombing arrived during the meeting.[136]

Even at this point, Anami, Umezu, and Toyoda all argued that Japan should not surrender without certain conditions. Following a direct plea from the Emperor, however, they no longer blocked the civilians' efforts to make peace, although they had the power to do so. Anami could simply have refused to endorse the Emperor's decision since, under the Meiji constitution, Cabinet decisions required unanimous consent. Alternatively, Anami could have resigned, thus dissolving the government and effectively vetoing the decision for surrender, for a new government could not be formed without the Army's approval of a new War Minister.[137]

In comparison to the Soviet entry, the atomic bomb had little or no effect on the Army's position. The Army initially denied that the Hiroshima blast had been an atomic bomb, and then it went to great lengths to downplay its importance. When Togo raised it as an argument for surrender on 7 August, Anami explicitly rejected it. The Army vigorously argued that minor civil-

[133] Sigal, *Fighting to a Finish*, p. 78.
[134] Butow, *Japan's Decision to Surrender*, p. 161.
[135] Butow, *Japan's Decision to Surrender*, pp. 121–22.
[136] Sigal, *Fighting to a Finish*, p. 257.
[137] Makoto Iokibe, "Japan Meets the United States for the Second Time," *Daedalus* 119 (Summer 1990): 97–98.

ian defense measures could offset the bomb's effects. Interviewed after the war, Toyoda said, "I believe the Russian participation in the war against Japan rather than the atom bombs did more to hasten the surrender."[138] Similarly, Army Vice-Chief of Staff Torashiro Kawabe said, "Since Tokyo was not directly affected by the bombing, the full force of the shock was not felt. ... In comparison, the Soviet entry into the war was a great shock when it actually came. ... It gave us all the more severe shock and alarm because we had been in constant fear [that] the vast Red Army forces in Europe were now being turned against us."[139]

Japan's leaders made the decision to surrender on the night of 9–10 August. Following Suzuki's abortive attempt to meet the previous day, the Supreme War Council met on 9 August but could not reach a consensus. A Cabinet meeting that same afternoon also reached no result. To break the deadlock, an imperial conference was held at midnight, at which the Emperor expressed his desire that the Allied terms, as contained in the Potsdam Declaration, be accepted immediately. Finally, the Cabinet met again and agreed at four o'clock in the morning to accept the Allied terms, subject to the one condition that the imperial institution would be retained.

The American response, received by the Japanese on 12 August, contained no promise to retain the Emperor, but the government accepted it anyway on 14 August. Concerned about the possibility of a coup by diehard officers, Anami, Umezu, and the third-highest-ranking officer, General Kenji Doihara, ordered their principal subordinates to pledge that "the Army will act in obedience to the Imperial decision to the last."[140] Nonetheless, on 14 August a group of Army officers did attempt a coup, aiming to subvert negotiations entirely and fight to the bitter end. The plotters assassinated the commander of the palace guard division and attempted to seize the palace and the Tokyo radio station but were stopped by loyal troops. Approached by the plotters for his support during the coup, Anami committed suicide instead. The Emperor's speech announcing surrender was broadcast to the country at noon on 15 August.[141]

Table 7 summarizes the changes in Japan's civilian and military vulnerability and the corresponding changes in the policy preferences of the major groups of the Japanese leadership. Clearly, changes in views about surrender were associated with increases in military vulnerability much more often than with enhanced civilian vulnerability. Of three changes in civilian leaders' attitudes, only one corresponded to a change in civilian vulnerability (the atomic bomb), and even that instance affected the views of only

---

[138] John Toland, *The Rising Sun: the Decline and Fall of the Japanese Empire, 1936–1945* (New York: Random House, 1970), p. 807.
[139] Quoted in Sigal, *Fighting to a Finish*, p. 226.
[140] Ibid., pp. 273–74.
[141] Sigal, *Fighting to a Finish*, pp. 259–78; Butow, *Japan's Decision to Surrender*, pp. 189–227.

Table 7. Changes in Japan's vulnerabilities and surrender policies

Date	Event	Vulnerability		Leaders		
		Civilian	Military	Civilian	Emperor	Military
before 7/44		nil	nil	ns	ns	ns
7/44	Marianas fall, first bombing (6/44)	low	low	ns[a]	ns	ns
11/44	Bombing from Marianas	medium	low	ns	ns	ns
3/45	massive fire raids	high	low	ns	ns	ns
4/45	Okinawa invaded	high	medium	ls	ns	ns
6/45	Okinawa falls	high	high	fs	fs	ls
8/6/45	Hiroshima	very high	high	is[b]	is	ls
8/9/45	Soviet attack	very high	very high	is	is	is[c]

NOTE: I thank Chaim Kaufmann for helping me to design this table and for educating me on a host of methodological issues involved in testing theories in single cases, many of which appear in his "Deterrence and Rationality in International Crises" (Diss., Columbia University, 1990) and "Out of the Lab and into the Archives: A Method for Testing Psychological Models of Foreign Policy Decision Making in Historical Cases," *International Studies Quarterly* 38 (December 1994): 557–86.

[a] Tojo's government fell and Shigemitsu sought Soviet mediation.

[b] Some civilians (e.g., Togo) advocated immediate surrender, whereas others (e.g., Suzuki) did not do so until 9 August.

[c] Army leaders still wanted some conditions for surrender but abandoned them in obedience to the emperor's request.

ns = no surrender
ls = limited surrender
fs = flexible surrender
is = immediate surrender

some civilian officials. Of the two changes in the Emperor's position, one was caused by military vulnerability and the other by civilian vulnerability (the atomic bomb). Of the two changes in the Army's position, both were associated with increases in military, not civilian, vulnerability. Thus, of seven major instances when leaders altered their views on surrender, at most two can be associated with civilian vulnerability to nuclear weapons and none to civilian vulnerability to conventional attack.

Because of the dominance of the Army in Japanese decision making, military vulnerability actually played an even more decisive role in the decision to surrender than the table depicts. The Army paid absolutely no attention to civilian vulnerability, even after the atomic bomb. Further, an extremely high level of military vulnerability was required to persuade it to accept surrender. Even after the Soviet attack and despite clear indications that Japan could not defend itself, some officers attempted to overthrow the government rather than obey the surrender decision. Most important, no surrender was possible without the Army's consent both because of the constitutional requirement for the War Minister's agreement and because of the Army's monopoly of force in domestic politics.

Compared to increasing military vulnerability, the escalating costs and risks to the population hardly mattered in Japanese decision making. If they had, Japanese leaders would have moved rapidly to end the war when the massive and devastating incendiary raids began in March 1945. In fact, the final crisis that brought surrender did not come until five months later, by which time nearly all major Japanese cities lay in ruins. In addition, military plans for the defense of the home islands would actually have inflicted yet greater hardships on the civilian population. In the event of invasion, the Army was to take control of the railways and so give precedence to the transportation of troops over the shipment of supplies to the civilian population. These plans were made in the knowledge that local inhabitants in the coastal areas would suffer great hardship.[142]

Altogether, it seems clear that the decisive U.S. coercive strategies were interdiction and invasion, not the Schelling or Douhet strategies. Japanese leaders agreed to surrender not because civilians were at risk but because the home islands were vulnerable to an impending American invasion. Once Japanese leaders became convinced that their strategy for defending to homeland would not succeed, they preferred surrender to the costs of continuing the war.

ALTERNATIVE EXPLANATIONS

Four major alternative explanations are worth considering: the atomic bomb, the conventional fire bombing of Japanese cities, the Emperor's intervention to demand that the government make peace, and reduction in American demands to permit Japan to retain the imperial institution.

Atomic Bomb

The most widely accepted explanation of Japan's surrender is atomic coercion. To avoid the prospects of many more Hiroshimas and Nagasakis, so the argument runs, the Japanese agreed to accept American terms for ending the war. The key problem with this argument is that it focuses excessively on identifying the immediate catalyst that led Japanese decision makers to accept the Potsdam Declaration on 9 August, as if preceding events mattered hardly at all. In effect, the atomic argument is limited to explaining the *timing* of surrender as if explaining this outcome were equivalent to explaining the larger issue of why coercion succeeded.

---

[142] Kirby, *Surrender of Japan*, p. 148.

In fact, Japan's decision to surrender developed gradually, not overnight. All three major leadership groups gradually shifted their views in several stages from April 1945 onward, although at somewhat different rates. No one suddenly altered his position from no surrender to immediate surrender after the atomic bombing. All groups had demonstrated their willingness to accept at least some forms of surrender before the bombs were dropped.

Regardless of the pace of Japanese decision making, moreover, the atomic bomb did little to increase the vulnerability of Japan's civilian population. By 6 August over 800,000 Japanese civilians had already been killed and more than 20 million rendered homeless. Sixty-four of Japan's sixty-six largest cities had already been so thoroughly burned out that LeMay's B-29s had begun to rub out smaller cities and towns. Secretary of War Stimson said shortly after the war, "Had the war continued until the projected invasion date of 1 November 1945, additional fire raids would have been more destructive of life and property than the limited number of atomic raids which we could have executed in the same time period."[143]

In any case, the atomic bombings were not decisive even in the timing of the surrender. Hiroshima did convince the Emperor and some civilian leaders to favor immediate surrender, but it did not influence the Army, which refused to attend a meeting called to discuss surrender. Had the civilians tried to surrender at this point, senior military leaders would likely have supported a coup.[144] Only the following day, after the Soviet invasion of Manchuria, did senior military leaders agree to attend surrender discussions.[145] Although army leaders opposed to surrender contended either that no atomic bomb had been dropped or that it was of little significance, none ever tried to maintain that defeat in Manchuria was irrelevant to Japan's prospects for defense. Thus, the timing of surrender was determined by the Soviet attack and not by the atomic bomb. Inasmuch as the invasion occurred just two days after Hiroshima, however, we cannot know whether additional time to reflect on the awesome effects of nuclear attack would have moved Japanese army leaders or whether additional bombs (had they been available) could have produced a decisive collapse of Japanese society.

[143] Stimson quoted in Mountcastle, "Trial by Fire," p. 222.

[144] Indeed, at an imperial conference on 5 April 1945, Tojo threatened an army coup d'etat if Japan accepted unconditional surrender and thereby, according to Kido, succeeded in preventing explicit discussion of peace moves. Butow, *Japan's Decision to Surrender*, pp. 60–61; Sigal, *Fighting to a Finish*, p. 260.

[145] Feis's contention that the Nagasaki bomb hastened the surrender is refuted by the fact that the army had already agreed to discuss surrender before the bombing occurred. Feis, *The Atomic Bomb*, p. 200.

Conventional Bombing

The second most common argument, originally made by the Strategic Bombing Survey, is that the conventional fire bombing of Japanese cities was the main cause of Japan's surrender: "It is the Survey's opinion that certainly prior to 31 December 1945, and in all probability prior to 1 November 1945, Japan would have surrendered even if the atomic bombs had not been dropped, even if Russia had not entered the war, and even if no invasion had been planned or contemplated."[146] This explanation is composed of two parts. The first is that strategic bombing depressed morale, putting irresistible pressure on Japanese leaders to surrender. Bernard Brodie maintains that the rain of death induced a mood of urgency which "hastened the end of the war and sufficed to make invasion unnecessary."[147] The second is that strategic bombing so devastated the economy that it was impossible for the Japanese to continue fighting and surrender was hastened.[148]

Neither of the causal connections claimed in these two arguments holds. The tremendous suffering strategic bombing inflicted on civilians did not affect the calculations of Japanese leaders. It is true that the collapse of Japan's war economy did hasten the surrender, by contrast, but strategic bombing was not responsible.

The morale argument rests on Douhet's theory that inflicting extreme civilian costs causes publics to rise up against their own governments to demand peace at nearly any price. If this model could succeed anywhere, it should have been in Japan. Sixty-four cities were subjected to urban area saturation tactics, with an average of 43 percent of each burned to the ground. Over two-thirds of the civilian population experienced air raids; more than a third had bombs fall in their residential neighborhood.[149] Despite the smaller tonnage of bombs dropped, the heavy use of incendiaries against crowded wooden cities resulted in vastly heavier casualties than those suffered by Germany; 900,000 Japanese civilians (1.2 percent of the population) were killed by bombing compared to 330,000 Germans (0.5 percent of the population).[150]

While bombing did depress individuals' spirits, it failed to stimulate, and indeed impeded, collective political action against the government. Nearly everyone considered air-raid protection and postraid services inadequate.

[146] USSBS, *Japan's Struggle to End the War*, p. 13.
[147] Bernard Brodie, *Strategy in the Missile Age* (Princeton: Princeton University Press, 1959), p. 141.
[148] USSBS, *Effects on Japan's War Economy*, p. 2.
[149] USSBS, *Effects on Japanese Morale*, p. 34.
[150] Japanese casualty figures are from USSBS, *Effects on Japanese Morale*, p. 1; Japanese population estimated at 73 million in 1940 from USSBS, *Effects on Japan's War Economy*, p. 98. German casualties are reported in USSBS, *The Effects on German Morale* (Washington, D.C.: GPO, 1947), 1: 7; German population estimated at 67 million in 1939: USSBS, *The Effects on the German War Economy* (Washington, D.C.: GPO, 1945), p. 202.

According to the Strategic Bombing Survey, 67 percent of those who experienced bombing felt intense fright and fear of death. Most believed they were better off after the surrender than during the war.[151] Yet despite the brutal suffering, the social and political fabric of Japan did not unravel. There were no mass demonstrations against the government, or any other form of popular political activity. Civil disobedience was insignificant. The labor absenteeism rate between January and August 1945 was approximately 8 percent, the same rate as estimated for the United States during a similar period. The only organized opposition was from underground communists, who remained numerically insignificant throughout the war. Far from generating collective action against the government, bombing made people "more and more obsessed with finding individual solutions to their own severe and urgent personal problems." Just 325 individuals were prosecuted for antiwar proclamations during 1945, twice the 1944 level but still a trivial number.[152]

There are three reasons why public feeling did not directly influence Japanese political calculations to any important degree. First, Japan was an oligarchical society in which the leaders did not feel compelled to respond to popular concerns. Although Japanese leaders frequently expressed their sympathy for the hardships suffered by the general population, they never sacrificed military requirements to relieve popular misery. For example, Japanese leaders were well aware of the suffering caused by severe food and fuel shortages, but nevertheless appropriated much of Japan's dwindling food stocks and all available fuel for the military to use in defending the homeland.[153]

Second, the government controlled education, the news media, and religion, and therefore the state could indoctrinate the population, instilling belief in the evil nature of its enemies and the value of sacrifice for national goals. In 1945 more than two-thirds of the population expected enslavement, starvation, or annihilation if Japan were to lose the war. A majority was stunned and dismayed to hear the Emperor's surrender announcement, and only a relatively small minority later admitted to being relieved that the war was over.[154]

Third, the state anticipated dissent and subversion and took active measures against them. As the war went on, greater resources were allocated to repression. While the personnel of Japan's civil police declined, the military police increased from fourteen hundred in 1937 to twenty-four thousand in 1945 and, by acquiring a reputation for brutality, created an atmosphere of passivity.[155]

---

[151] USSBS, *Effects on Japanese Morale*, pp. 35, 38, 41.
[152] Ibid., pp. 65, 236–37, 249.
[153] Hayashi and Coox, *Kogun*, p. 155; and Kase, *Journey to the Missouri*, p. 196.
[154] USSBS, *Effects on Japanese Morale*, p. 150; Brodie, *Strategy in the Missile Age*, pp. 138–40.
[155] USSBS, *Effects on Japanese Morale*, p. 117.

In fact, the movement of Japan's leaders to surrender can hardly be called urgent. During the period of greatest suffering, March to July 1945, the maneuvers of the peace party were delicate and phlegmatic in the extreme. Even the first atomic attack did not bring a meeting of the Supreme War Council, whereas the Soviet invasion triggered a meeting within hours.[156]

The second of the two arguments is that the incendiary campaign against cities contributed significantly to Japan's economic problems. Although proponents of this argument admit that the blockade was responsible for the greater part of Japan's economic collapse, they contend that strategic air attack did contribute in an important way. The key argument is that, by destroying many thousands of the feeder system of small cottage industries, air bombardment counteracted the dispersal of Japanese war production. Furthermore, incendiary attacks drove approximately 8.5 million people to the countryside, diminishing Japan's industrial labor pool.[157] Finally, just as the war was ending, bombers were turning to attacks against the transportation infrastructure, principally railroads. These attacks would have destroyed Japan's ability not only to move military resources but also to distribute food to the scattered population.[158]

The fundamental problem with this argument is that once the main industries began to go quiet for lack of imported raw materials, the feeder system hardly mattered. The decline of Japan's war-making powers started before the main weight of the bombing attack began in March 1945. With stockpiles of key raw materials such as oil, rubber, and bauxite virtually exhausted, production was rapidly running down to zero, regardless of remaining industrial capacity. Unbombed factories simply sat unused.[159] To be sure, incendiary raids burned the physical structures of urban plants, big and small. Bombing, as Michael Sherry puts it, "simply made the rubble of Japan's war economy bounce."[160]

Imperial Intervention

The third alternative explanation focuses on the Emperor's intervention. Traditionally, the Emperor was not expected to participate in policy decisions, and Hirohito's actions in August were the only direct political interventions of his reign. Nonetheless, Japanese society invested the Emperor with such enormous prestige that it would be virtually impossible for any-

[156] Stephen Harper, *Miracle of Deliverance: The Case for the Bombing of Hiroshima and Nagasaki* (New York: Stein and Day, 1986), p. 128.
[157] B. H. Liddell Hart, *History of the Second World War* (New York: Putnam's, 1970), p. 691.
[158] USSBS, *Effects on Japan's War Economy*, pp. 63–64.
[159] Cohen, *Japan's Economy*, p. 107.
[160] Sherry, *Rise of American Air Power*, p. 286.

one to refuse his directly expressed wish. This power was not unlimited; as long as the government remained united on continuation of the war, there was little scope for the Emperor to act. But, once the government became deeply divided in April 1945, the Emperor could have demanded surrender at virtually any point, and those who favored continuing the war could not have been able to resist him. Thus, according to this view, surrender occurred when it did because the emperor chose to intervene then.[161] An implication of this argument is that had he intervened at any earlier point, Japan would have surrendered at that point. Thus, the Emperor's decisions *not* to intervene in July 1944 or early 1945 were responsible for the prolongation of the war.

This argument overstates the Emperor's actual power. Many in the military had no compunction about defying the Emperor. One school at the Army General Staff College taught that if a man believes that the Emperor's decision is incorrect, he can still be loyal to the throne even though he does not obey, because the chief goal is preservation of the imperial system for posterity, not reflexive obedience to the reigning Emperor. In fact, Toyoda said that "apart from the intervention of Soviet Russia, it is difficult for me to say [if] at any time prior to the actual termination of the war, the Emperor had issued a rescript terminating the war, the Navy would have been willing to say that is not a mistake, because so long as one feels there is any chance left, it is very difficult to say that the time to quit [has come]."[162] The August plotters planned to establish an old-style shogunate system, under which the Army would exercise all real power in the name of a figurehead. Had the Emperor attempted to force through a surrender decision before the Army chiefs were prepared to accept it, the Army quite likely would have attempted to seize power.[163] In direct opposition to the expressed will of the Emperor, however, it is uncertain whether they could have succeeded.

A greater problem with this argument is that the difference between the concerns that influenced the Emperor and those that influenced Army leaders was not great, because both were significantly affected by Japan's increasing military vulnerability. Only in June 1945 did the Emperor become convinced that the Army's strategy would not succeed, and accordingly, it

---

[161] Kecskemeti, *Strategic Surrender*, pp. 199–200; Sigal, *Fighting to a Finish*, p. 279.

[162] Butow, *Japan's Decision to Surrender*, p. 210 n. 2; Sigal, *Fighting to a Finish*, p. 279.

[163] The Army had seized power before. On 26 February 1936 a group of junior officers succeeded in overturning civilian authority and murdering the Lord Keeper of the Privy Seal and other ministers and high-ranking officials. The plot succeeded largely because senior Army leaders supported the rebels and welcomed the removal of civilians who opposed a more vigorous foreign policy and bigger military budgets. That plot stands in contrast to the August 1945 coup, which failed mainly because senior Army leaders chose not to support it. When Anami, who was to become the new head of state, committed suicide on 14 August, he decapitated the conspiracy. For details on the Army's coup activities, see Butow, *Japan's Decision to Surrender*, p. 211 n. 4; Kazuo Kawai, "Militarist Activity between Japan's Two Surrender Decisions," *Pacific Historical Review* 22 (November 1953): 383–89.

was at that point that he first asked the government to seek means of ending the war. Not until August, when he was persuaded both that the war was lost and that the continuation would involve horrendous costs, did he intervene in a governmental decision. Thus, while it may be possible that imperial intervention could have ended the war slightly earlier, there is no evidence that such an intervention was ever likely.

Imperial intervention apparently did have a slight effect, at least on the timing of the decision. In two meetings on 9 August the Army chiefs refused to relax their conditions for negotiation, but after the Emperor's plea for peace, Anami assented to the Cabinet decision to surrender. Had the Emperor not intervened, it might have taken an even greater demonstration of Japan's military vulnerability to persuade the Army to give in. Surrender might have come days later as the import of the disasters in Manchuria and at Nagasaki had time to sink in, or not until weeks later when invasion appeared imminent, or not at all; we cannot know.

Reduction in American Demands

The last alternative explanation for the change in Japan's position on surrender focuses on a supposed change in American demands, namely, an assurance that the imperial institution would be preserved. According to this view, the Japanese would not have consented to surrender without this concession.[164]

This argument misstates the facts. Prior to the surrender the United States never communicated to the Japanese any such assurance, either publicly or through covert channels. A group of Truman's civilian advisers, led by Assistant Secretary of State Joseph Grew, recommended that Truman publicly interpret the unconditional surrender doctrine to permit retention of the Emperor, because, Grew maintained, "the hands of the Emperor and his peace-minded advisors would be greatly strengthened in the face of the intransigent militarists."[165] Henry Stimson, James Forrestal, and William Phillips, as well as some sectors of military intelligence, supported Grew.[166] Others, including Harry Hopkins, Dean Acheson, Archibald MacLeish, and the State Department as a whole, opposed such a concession and advocated extensive social engineering for Japan, Acheson and MacLeish believed the imperial institution must be abolished because it was closely associated

[164] See Kecskemeti, *Strategic Surrender*, pp. 204–5.

[165] Joseph Grew, *Turbulent Era: A Diplomatic Record of Forty Years, 1904–1945* (Boston: Houghton Mifflin, 1952), 2: 1421–22.

[166] For details, see Ellis Zacharias, *Secret Missions* (New York: Putnam's, 1946), pp. 342–50; Alexander Leighton, *Human Relations in a Changing World* (New York: E. P. Dutton, 1949), pp. 60, 93, 227–91; Cline, *Washington Command Post*, pp. 341–45; and Brian L. Villa, "The U.S. Army, Unconditional Surrender, and the Potsdam Proclamation," *Journal of American History* 63 (June 1976): 71.

with "the current coalition of militarists, industrialists, large land owners and office holders."[167]

The critical decision on the position of the Emperor was made at the Potsdam Conference. The new Secretary of State, James F. Byrnes, cast the deciding vote against a public reassurance on the retention of the Emperor. He took the view that any public statement by the Allies could be detrimental to one of the various competing factions in Japan.[168] Thus, article 12 of the Potsdam Declaration read, "The occupying forces of the Allies shall be withdrawn from Japan as soon as these objectives have been accomplished and there has been established in accordance with the freely expressed will of the Japanese people a peacefully inclined and responsible government."[169] Even after the Japanese message of 10 August accepting the Potsdam Declaration on condition that the imperial institution be spared, the American position did not change. The U.S. responded: "With regard to the Japanese Government's message accepting the terms of the Potsdam proclamation but containing the statement, 'with the understanding that the said declaration does not compromise any demand which prejudices the prerogatives of His Majesty as a sovereign ruler,' our position is as follows: . . . The ultimate form of government of Japan shall, in accordance with the Potsdam Declaration, be established by the freely expressed will of the Japanese people."[170] Despite this discouraging response, on 15 August Japan surrendered anyway.[171]

The principal cause of Japan's surrender was the ability of the United States to increase the military vulnerability of the home islands sufficiently to persuade Japanese leaders that their defense was highly unlikely to succeed. The key military factor causing this effect was the sea blockade, which crippled Japan's ability to produce and equip the forces necessary to execute

[167] Villa, "U.S. Army," p. 89.

[168] On this matter, Byrnes apparently followed the advice of former secretary of state Cordell Hull, who said: "We did not want to come out against the institution [of the Emperor] lest this give the Japanese militarists live coals to blow upon. . . . Nor did we wish to come out for the institution lest this discourage whatever popular movement there might be in Japan to erase it." Giovannitti and Freed, *Decision to Drop the Bomb*, p. 220.

[169] Kirby, *Surrender of Japan*, p. 487.

[170] Kirby, *Surrender of Japan*, pp. 184, 211–12, 488.

[171] Even if the United States had offered assurances concerning the Emperor, there is no reason to believe that they would have affected the Japanese decision. The divisions within the Supreme War Council over whether to surrender did not turn on the position of the Emperor. Prior to 14 August both hawks and doves assumed that any acceptance of the Potsdam Declaration would be conditional on retention of the Emperor. Suzuki, Togo, and Yonai favored acceptance subject to this one condition; Anami, Umezu, and Toyoda would accept it only with three additional provisos: that Allied forces not occupy the home islands, that Japan would disarm and demobilize its forces itself, and that Japan would prosecute its own war criminals. Only on 14 August did the Supreme War Council agree, unanimously, to drop all conditions. Thus, a declaration by the United States on the position of the emperor would not have altered the position or the influence of either faction.

its strategy. The most important factor accounting for the timing of surren-der was the Soviet attack against Manchuria, largely because it convinced recalcitrant Army leaders that the homeland could not be defended.

Contrary to the assertion of the Strategic Bombing Survey that bombing was so effective that even if there had been no atomic bomb, Soviet attack, or planned American invasion, surrender would have occurred at nearly the same time, in actuality the naval blockade, invasion threat, and Soviet attack ensured that surrender would have occurred at *precisely* the same time even if there had been no strategic bombing campaign.

The end of World War II in the Pacific offers students of coercion three major lessons. First, terror bombings, however effective in inflicting wide-spread terror and death on civilian societies, is not effective in coercing gov-ernments to abandon highly valued territorial goals. Second, although strategic air power may be effective when used for interdiction, the success of this strategy depends greatly on careful and detailed understanding of the enemy's specific economic and military weaknesses. Finally, successful coercion depends on a credible threat to capture the specific territories the opponent is asked to surrender. In the Japanese case, only the prospect of successful invasion of the home islands could bring about surrender.

If terror bombing was ever going to work, it should have worked against Japan. Despite tremendous damage, the population learned to live under bombing and the government was not influenced at all. Conventional mu-nitions, even under the optimal conditions that prevailed in 1945, cannot damage a modern society so rapidly as to shock it into collapse. "Morale" or terror bombing, under whatever name, is not only immoral but futile.

Strategic air power could have contributed to ending the war if it had been used appropriately. Air planners would have had to understand where Japan's true vulnerabilities lay. Precision bombing of industry and fire bombing were both ineffective because Japan's main weakness was neither its manufacturing base nor its morale but its extreme dependence on imported raw materials. Once the sources of supply were cut off, Japan's industrial capacity and the population's morale became irrele-vant. The naval blockade was so effective precisely because it concen-trated on this weak link. Strategic air power directed at this same link could have made a significant contribution, principally through aerial mining of key shipping lanes. Aerial mines were actually more effective than submarines during the last four months of the war, accounting for 50 percent of all tonnage sunk during that period.[172] Rather than wait until the end of March 1945, B-29s should have begun mining operations as early as possible, that is, in June 1944 from China and in November 1944 from the Marianas). If B-29s could have cut off Japan's oil imports earlier,

[172] Hezlet, *The Submarine and Sea Power*, pp. 221–22.

the collapse of Japan's war effort would have been hastened by the same amount of time.

Not only strategic air power but also general purpose forces could have been better used to bring about the surrender of Japan. What counted in the minds of Japanese leaders was the threat of invasion of the home islands. Accordingly, once the United States had completed the destruction of the Japanese navy at the Battle of Leyte Gulf in October 1944 and had decimated Japan's merchant fleet, the most effective coercive strategy would have been preparation for the earliest possible invasion of the home islands. Other objectives, such as consolidation of the Philippines, no longer mattered. Thus, the invasions of Luzon (January 1945), and Iwo Jima (February) were unnecessary, and the thousands of lives lost in these operations were wasted.[173] The best choice would have been to go straight to Okinawa, the gateway to Kyushu and the other home islands.

Most of all, the Japanese case shows that strategic air power is limited not by the capabilities of the attacker, but by the vulnerabilities of the victim. In the coercion of Japan, the instruments that mattered were naval power, tactical air power, and land power. Properly used, strategic air power could have made a noticeable contribution but could not have been decisive.

---

[173] Iwo Jima–based aircraft flew some missions in support of the invasion of Okinawa, but the main air support was supplied by aircraft carriers. Although Iwo Jima was useful as a base for fighters that escorted B-29s on raids against heavily defended Japanese cities, mining missions would have been flown against offshore areas and shipping lanes to the west and south of the home islands where air defenses were minimal or nonexistent.

[5]

Korea, 1950–1953

The end of the Korean War represents a mixture of conventional and nuclear coercion. After the seesaw battles of 1950 and 1951 demonstrated that neither the United Nations nor the Communist forces could drive the other from Korea, the UN set out to compel the Communists to accept a territorial division of Korea as well as a permanent UN military presence to guarantee the security of the South. This effort succeeded, leading to the signing of an armistice on 27 July 1953.

The debate over the causes of this success has never been resolved. Some attribute it to the risk of nuclear escalation threatened by the United States in 1953, some to conventional punishment inflicted by American air power, and some to a political change unrelated to U.S. military efforts, namely the death of Stalin. The entire debate, however, overlooks the most important instance of coercive success in Korea because it focuses on the endgame in 1952 and 1953 over the prisoners of war issue. The most important Communist concessions, those that occurred in 1951 and related to the territorial settlement, are neglected, perhaps because the war did not end at that point. These were the concessions that achieved the goals for which the United States went to war and would have ended the war, thereby saving nearly half of America's ultimate casualties, if the United States had not escalated its demands. This gap in the debate has not only limited our historical understanding of the Korean War, but has also confused its lessons for coercion. Although nuclear risks played a role at the end, the earlier critical concessions were due to conventional denial, not punishment or nuclear pressure.

The Korean armistice negotiations began on 10 July 1951. The critical issues concerned control over territory: the line along which Korea would be divided and the continued presence of foreign forces in Korea after peace.

The Communists initially demanded restoration of the pre-war boundary at the Thirty-eighth Parallel as well as the withdrawal of all American troops, while the UN demanded the "Kansas Line" (the existing front line, which by mid 1951 was north of the Parallel in most places) and acceptance of a permanent U.S. garrison to guarantee the security of the South.[1]

Although there were other issues, such as supervision of the cease-fire and repatriation of prisoners, the territorial issues must be considered the most important because they concerned the security of South Korea and therefore the security of all the other participants. In its rapid collapse in June 1950, South Korea had already demonstrated its inability to defend itself alone, while the line of contact would provide U.S. and South Korean forces with a shorter and more defensible line than would the Thirty-eighth Parallel. By comparison, the UN decision whether to forcibly repatriate those Chinese and North Korean POWs who did not wish to return home would have no direct security implication, while the U.S. military believed that the membership of the Neutral Nations Supervisory Commission, on-site inspection, and whether the North Koreans would be permitted to improve airfields would not be crucial to the stability of the peace. Although formal recognition that many Chinese and North Korean prisoners did not want to be repatriated involuntarily would be useful in the global ideological struggle, the political value of moving the boundary northward from the Thirty-eighth Parallel to the line of contact would be even greater since this could be presented by the West as punishment for North Korean aggression.[2]

Communist negotiators conceded the presence of foreign troops in Korea on 25 July 1951 and agreed to divide Korea at the line of contact on 26 November.[3] In return the UN agreed to fix the line of contact for thirty days while minor issues were negotiated. The war did not end at this point because the United States further insisted that prisoners could only be repatriated voluntarily. Originally U.S. officials seem to have assumed that all prisoners would be repatriated, but as it became clear that many North Korean and Chinese prisoners did not want to return U.S. policy shifted. While some U.S. officials and other UN members favored dropping this demand in order to get a quick settlement, Secretary of State Dean Acheson and President Harry Truman refused on the grounds that many returnees would be

---

[1] Barton J. Bernstein, "The Struggle over the Korean Armistice: Prisoners or Repatriation," in *Child of Conflict: The Korean-American Relationship, 1943–1953*, ed. Bruce Cumings (Seattle: University of Washington Press, 1983), pp. 266–67; Dean Acheson, *The Korean War* (New York: Norton, 1969), p. 115.

[2] Rosemary Foot, *A Substitute for Victory* (Ithaca: Cornell University Press, 1990), pp. 45–46, 76–87.

[3] To save face for the Communists, the armistice included a recommendation for a postwar conference on withdrawal of foreign troops, although both sides understood that this recommendation was empty because the United States would never agree.

executed for cooperating with the UN.[4] The Communists initially rejected the U.S. position as contrary to the 1949 Geneva Convention, which provided for the return of all prisoners of war.[5] They did not accept this last demand until 4 June 1953.

Had the United States been less insistent on the POW issue, it is likely that a settlement could have been reached quickly in late 1951. While one could suppose that the Communist concessions of 26 November were a disingenuous ploy, made only to gain a thirty-day respite from combat, the evidence is against this. First, the thirty-day limit was a condition set by the UN carrying the implied threat of renewed ground offensives if negotiations stalled. Although the expiration of the thirty-day limit in December theoretically put the demarcation line up for grabs, in practice the Communists never raised the issue again in negotiations and never attempted to seize more than tiny amounts of territory by ground attack. The final line fixed on 17 June 1953 was almost exactly where it had been in November 1951.

Second, a judgment that the territorial concessions were not sincere requires one to assume that if the United States had back off from its demand for voluntary repatriation only, the Communists would have raised new difficulties on other issues in order to prolong the war. Chairman of the Chinese Communist Party Mao Zedong argued in August 1952 that protracted war would pressure the United States to seek peace but did not suggest that previous concessions could be repudiated.[6] In fact, the Communists proved forthcoming on the remaining issues other than POWs, including the width of the demilitarized zone, rotation rates and port access for foreign troops, repair and improvement of airfields, the Neutral Nations Supervisory Commission, and the Military Armistice Commission. By 7 May 1952 the repatriation was the only issue not formally resolved.[7]

Although primary evidence on the Communists' intentions during the negotiations is thin, all of their tangible behavior is consistent with a belief on their part that they had settled all the issues except repatriation. It may be that privately the Communists were not completely sincere in their 1951 concessions in the sense that, although they fully expected to honor their commitments given the existing military situation, they might have reneged

---

[4] Foot, *Substitute for Victory*, p. 89; Bernstein, "Struggle over the Korean Armistice," pp. 276–79.

[5] The logic of the Convention was that prisoners could otherwise be pressured to remain, as in fact happened in both Communist and UN prisoner of war camps during the Korean War. For this reason initial UN estimates of non-returnees proved to be too high. Allen E. Goodman, ed., *Negotiating While Fighting: The Diary of Admiral C. Turner Joy at the Korean Armistice Conference* (Stanford: Hoover Institution Press, 1978), p. 355.

[6] Mao Zedong, "United and Clearly Draw the Line Between the Enemy and Ourselves," 4 August 1952, *Mao's Selected Works* (Peking: Foreign Language Press, 1977), 5: 80.

[7] Foot, *Substitute for Victory*, pp. 104–6; Richard Whelan, *Drawing the Line: The Korean War, 1950–1953* (Boston: Little, Brown, 1990), p. 321; Walter C. Hermes, *Truce Tent and Fighting Front* (Washington, D.C.: GPO, 1966), p. 174.

if the situation had shifted dramatically in their favor. But they had little hope or expectation of this.

Ultimately, 21,839 Communist and 347 UN POWs refused repatriation. To purchase this right for these men the war was extended for nearly two years, costing the United States alone 63,200 casualties, of whom 12,300 were killed (45 percent of the total casualties for the war), while other UN forces, mainly the South Korean Army, lost over 50,000 and the Communists well over a quarter of a million men.[8]

Accordingly, the Korean War includes two instances of coercion that are worthy of investigation: the 1951 territorial concessions, because they achieved the UN's principal war objectives, and the 1953 POW concessions, which ended the war and which also provide one of the few opportunities to compare the effectiveness of conventional and nuclear coercion.

The 1951 concessions were caused by conventional denial, not punishment. Further, the critical pressure was applied by ground and tactical air power, not strategic air power. In spring 1951 UN forces were advancing against overextended Communist troops and defeated major Communist counter-offensives in early Summer. By mid-June it was clear that the UN could defend the Kansas Line and that any attempt by the Communists to retake ground would be prohibitively costly. Strategic air interdiction was also employed from May 1951 on, but was largely ineffective. Punishment bombing had been suspended at the end of 1950 and was not resumed until April 1952.

The final armistice of 1953 has attracted considerably more attention than the 1951 concessions. There are three schools of thought. The dominant view is that the decisive factor was fear of future punishment from atomic bombing. President Dwight Eisenhower bluntly stated that the armistice resulted from "danger of an atomic war. . . . We told them we could not hold it to a limited war any longer if the communists welshed on a treaty of truce. They didn't want a full-scale war or an atomic attack. That kept them under some control."[9] China and North Korea capitulated to avoid the risk of having their population centers annihilated.

The second theory, put forward by the official U.S. Air Force history, focuses on the effects of conventional strategic bombing on North Korea's

[8] Hermes, *Truce Tent and Fighting Front*, pp. 500, 515.

[9] Sherman Adams, *First Hand Report: The Inside Story of the Eisenhower Administration* (London: Hutchinson, 1962), p. 102; see also Dwight D. Eisenhower, *The White House Years: Mandate for Change, 1953–1956* (Garden City, N.Y.: Doubleday, 1963), pp. 179–80. For agreement by other high-ranking members of the Eisenhower administration with this claim, see James Shepley, "How Dulles Averted War," *Life*, 16 January 1956, pp. 70–72; and C. Turner Joy, *How Communists Negotiate* (New York: Macmillan, 1955), pp. 161–62. Prominent scholars who agree with this position are David Rees, *Korea: The Limited War* (New York: St. Martin's, 1964), pp. 418–20; Bernard Brodie, *War and Politics* (London: Macmillan, 1973), p. 105; Alexander L. George and Richard Smoke, *Deterrence in American Foreign Policy: Theory and Practice* (New York: Columbia University Press, 1974), p. 239.

population: "During the last year of Korean hostilities, American air power executed the dominant role in the achievement of the military objectives of the United States and of the United Nations. . . . no single air operation so gravely affected the Communists as the simple destruction of two agricultural irrigation dams, for this operation, too terrible to execute in its entirety, portended the devastation of the most important segment of the North Korean agricultural economy."[10] Wrecking North Korea's rice crop threatened its survival as a nation and promised to deprive the Communist troops on the Thirty-eighth Parallel of food.[11]

The third explanation contends that Soviet rather than American pressure compelled the Chinese and North Koreans to capitulate. Seeking to diminish East-West tensions so as to turn more attention to domestic troubles, the Soviets are said to have been searching for an end to the war. Stalin's death in March 1953 accelerated this movement because of the attendant uncertainty in the succession crisis in Soviet domestic politics. In the spring of 1953 the Soviets stressed their desire for an end to Korean hostilities in diplomatic contacts with Americans, which some scholars interpret as indirect evidence of Moscow's possible role in encouraging concessions.[12]

I argue that nuclear coercion, and not the other explanations, accounts for the Communist concessions on the POW issue in 1953. The claim based on the threat of starvation from conventional attack against the dams fails because after the first few attacks the North Koreans discovered ways to prevent breaches in the dams. The argument that Soviet pressure drove the Chinese and North Koreans to the armistice is not supported by any direct evidence. Only the nuclear explanation accounts for the timing of the final concessions. The U.S. nuclear threats were communicated to China, via several channels simultaneously, near the end of May, and the Communist ne-

[10] Robert F. Futrell, *United States Air Force Operations in the Korean Conflict, 1 July 1952–27 July 1953*, USAF Historical Study no. 127 (Maxwell Air Force Base, Ala.: USAF Historical Division, Research Studies Institute, Air University, 1956), pp. 93, 126, Air University Library M-U 27218 no. 127. Although Futrell later published an unclassified history, *The United States Air Force in Korea, 1950–1953* (New York: Duell, Sloan, and Pearce, 1961), important detail was omitted, including the quoted passage. It is important to note that some lower-ranking members of the Truman administration, such as Dean Rusk, who was Truman's assistant secretary of state for far eastern affairs, later agreed with the Air Force's position. See Mark Clodfelter, *The Limits of Air Power: The American Bombing of North Vietnam* (New York: Free Press, 1989), p. 24.

[11] A punishment argument that does not depend on strategic bombing is that the economic hardships caused by the war had strained Chinese and North Korean civilian morale near to the breaking point, putting pressure on both governments to make concessions. Rosemary Foot, "Nuclear Coercion and the Ending of the Korean Conflict," *International Security* 13 (Winter 1988–89): 92–112, esp. 108–9.

[12] Marshall D. Shulman, *Stalin's Foreign Policy Reappraised* (Cambridge: Harvard University Press, 1963), pp. 197–98. Robert Simmons argues similarly, but in fact his evidence suggests tepid Soviet support for the Korean War from 1951 onward. Simmons, *The Strained Alliance: Peking, Pyongyang, Moscow, and the Politics of the Korean Civil War* (New York: Free Press, 1975), pp. 175–246.

gotiators accepted UN terms on 4 June. The bombing of the dams likely mattered, not because it threatened starvation, but because it raised the credibility of the threat to resort to nuclear warfare. Similarly, Stalin's death probably affected the outcome, not because it caused Soviet pressure on China, but because it called into question the Soviet commitment that the Chinese had relied on as their guarantee against American nuclear blackmail.

To establish the causes of each set of concessions, three questions must be answered. First, what were the American coercive goals, and what strategies were employed to achieve them? Second, how faithfully and capably were these strategies executed? Third, what were the relationships among the progress of the American coercive campaigns, changes in the prospects of the Chinese and North Korean diplomatic and military strategies, and changes in the Communist negotiators' willingness to concede? Since primary evidence for Chinese and North Korean decisions is scanty, I rely principally on the sequence of UN coercive actions and Communist diplomatic responses.

THE TERRITORIAL ISSUES

In February 1951, the United Nations determined that it would seek negotiations to terminate the war on terms that would secure an independent, non-Communist South Korea. By 26 November, the Communists had agreed to the critical conditions that would make this possible: the division of Korea on the basis of the military status quo and a permanent U.S. garrison in the South.

American Goals, 1950–1951

Although the anti-Communist military effort in the Korean War was nominally a police action of the United Nations, in practice the United States and South Korea provided the overwhelming majority of the UN forces and the United States held the main decision-making power. While American ambitions fluctuated throughout the war, as did strategies to achieve them, the bedrock goal was always to maintain the independence of South Korea.

This goal was driven by reputational rather than strategic concerns. Korea's value was related to America's ideological and diplomatic competition with the USSR rather than to military considerations of Korea's importance in a war against the Soviet Union. Since 1945, when the American military was reluctant to occupy Korea, American policy about its interests in Korea followed a consistent pattern: the State Department saw Korea as important to U.S. security, but military planners did not.

Specifically, the State Department placed a high value on Korea's importance as a symbol of American success at stopping the spread of communism: "The U.S. cannot at this time withdraw from Korea under circumstances which would inevitably lead to Communist domination of the entire country. The resulting political repercussions would seriously damage U.S. prestige in the Far East and throughout the world." One interdepartmental report was more explicit: "It is important that there be no gaps or weakening in our policy of firmness in containing the USSR because weakness in one area is invariably interpreted by the Soviets as indicative of an overall softening. A backing down or running away from the USSR in Korea could very easily result in a stiffening of the Soviet attitude on Germany or some other area of much greater intrinsic importance to us."[13] Although reluctant to extend a defense commitment to Korea, the military often agreed that the political value of Korea justified economic aid. On 29 April 1947 the JCS declared: "From the security viewpoint the primary reason for current assistance to Korea would be that . . . this is the one country within which we alone have for almost two years carried out ideological warfare in direct contact with our opponents, so that to lose this battle would be gravely detrimental to U.S. prestige, and therefore security, throughout the world."[14]

In general, however, the War Department depreciated America's interest in Korea, believing that in a general war troops and bases in Korea would be a liability. American planning for general war in the late 1940s assumed the Soviets would begin by seizing all of continental Europe and that the United States, Britain, and Canada would have to refight World War II by standing on the defensive in the Pacific while seeking to reinvade Europe from England. In one plan, Offtackle, Great Britain, Okinawa, and Egypt would be important bases for launching an atomic air offensive against the Soviet Union. To ensure the success of this plan, the Americans would have to concentrate their limited conventional forces and withdraw from Korea.[15] Accordingly, Secretary of War Robert Patterson urged on 4 April 1947 that the United States should quickly withdraw its military forces from Korea.[16] Two years later, Truman authorized American withdrawal from Korea after he had concluded that Stalin would not resort to open aggression to extend Soviet influence over the peninsula but would rely instead on subversion and political penetration.[17]

[13] Quoted in Bruce Cumings, "Introduction: The Course of Korean-American Relations, 1943–1953," in *Child of Conflict*, ed. Cumings, pp. 21, 19.
[14] Thomas Etzold and John Lewis Gaddis, eds., *Containment: Documents on American Foreign Policy and Strategy, 1946–1950* (New York: Columbia University Press, 1978), pp. 71–83.
[15] Stephen Pelz, "U.S. Decisions on Korean Policy, 1943–1950: Some Hypotheses," in *Child of Conflict*, ed. Cumings, p. 116.
[16] Cumings, Introduction to *Child of Conflict*, p. 20.
[17] James I. Matray, "Korea: Test Case of Containment in Asia," in *Child of Conflict*, ed. Cumings, pp. 170–71.

American political objectives vacillated during the Korean conflict. When North Korea invaded the South in June 1950, Truman's goal was to preserve the independent, non-Communist South Korean government and to restore its territory to preinvasion boundaries. Initial aspirations were limited by the fear that the North Korean attack was a feint to test the willingness of the United States to confront Communist aggression, a prelude to the main assault, which would come in Europe.[18] Following the success of the Inchon landing in September, Truman enlarged American goals to include destruction of the North Korean army and the unification of Korea under a single democratic government. After Chinese intervention in November forced the UN once again to the defensive, the more ambitious goals were abandoned in favor of a return to the initial objective—a decision that ultimately led the containment-minded Truman to fire the rollback-oriented General Douglas MacArthur as commander of the United Nations forces in Korea.[19]

Coercive Strategies

To intensify the military pressure on the Communists to accept an armistice on UN terms, three military strategies were conceived and pursued, all of which relied heavily on air power. The first, employed in 1950 against North Korea alone, sought to compel complete surrender with a Douhet strategy using conventional bombing of North Korean cities and major economic nodes, but this was abandoned after China's entry into the war. The second, employed against both China and North Korea, used a strategy of nuclear threats to compel an armistice, but was given up after the movement of nuclear-armed B-29s failed to persuade the Chinese to call off their largest offensive of the war. Finally, in May 1951 the United States shifted to air interdiction because it saw undermining the Communist forces' ability to maintain their positions as the best way to ensure that an armistice would be signed quickly.

On 31 July 1950, the U.S. Far East Air Forces and Strategic Air Command began a strategic bombing campaign by B-29s using incendiary area bombing to weaken North Korean morale. Although industrial targets were attacked, the primary goal was to compel the government to surrender or cause its collapse, not merely to weaken its military capabilities. Major General Emmett O'Donnell, who carried the plan from its designers in the Strategic Air Command to Japan, said:

---

[18] For a rich account, see Marc Trachtenberg, "A 'Wasting Asset': American Strategy and the Shifting Nuclear Balance, 1949–1954," *International Security* 13 (Winter 1988–89), pp. 18–32.

[19] For a concise history of the vacillation in American political goals, see Whelan, *Drawing the Line*, pp. 144–50, 193–202, 288–94. On the decision to seek negotiations, see Rosemary Foot, *The Wrong War: American Policy and the Dimensions of the Korean Conflict, 1950–1953* (Ithaca: Cornell University Press, 1985), pp. 132–39.

It was my intention and hope that we would be able to get out there and to cash in on our psychological advantage in having gotten into the theater and into the war so fast by putting a very severe blow on the North Koreans, with an advance warning, perhaps, telling them that they had gone too far . . . and [then] *go to work burning five major cities in North Korea to the ground*, and to destroy completely every one of about 18 major strategic targets."[20]

Similarly, the FEAF plan for strategic bombing argued that "the psychological impact of bringing the war to the people is a catalyst that destroys the morale and will to resist" and that "destruction of urban areas adjoining industrial plants would erode the morale of the North Korean people and undermine their obedience to the communist government."[21] Washington ultimately disapproved the use of incendiaries so as not to give the Communists propaganda advantages from raids that produced heavy civilian casualties, but did permit high-explosive raids. As North Korea had only five major industrial centers (Wonsan, Pyongyang, Hungnam, Chongjin, and Rashin), the B-29s quickly ran out of targets and were stood down on 27 October, having achieved no perceptible effect on the course of the war.[22]

At the same time that China's entry into the war forced the United States to scale down its territorial ambitions, it also led American leaders to consider escalating the use of force to the nuclear level. As early as 24 December 1950, MacArthur requested nuclear weapons for use against China.[23] These were never granted, but atomic threats were issued in March and April 1951.

In February 1951 as UN troops were poised to advance across the Thirty-eighth Parallel, the Chinese appeared to be preparing a massive ground offensive of their own. While official Washington struggled to resolve differences over whether direct military and economic pressures on China could lead to a negotiated end to the war, General MacArthur took matters into his own hands. On 24 March 1951 he published an ultimatum to Peking, threatening that if the Chinese Communists did not withdraw their troops at once and permit the unification of Korea, the U.S./UN forces would bring China to its knees. In addition to denigrating the capacity of the Chinese to conduct high-intensity conventional warfare, MacArthur warned them of the dire consequences of any extension of the war onto their territory: "The enemy . . . must by now be painfully aware that a deci-

---

[20] Futrell, *Air Force in Korea*, p. 186. My emphasis.
[21] FEAF, Plan for Employment of FEAF Bomber Command Against North Korea, ca. 2 August 1950, quoted in Futrell, *Air Force in Korea*, p. 42.
[22] Futrell, *Air Force in Korea*, pp. 183–207. See also Robert F. Futrell, *United States Air Force Operations in the Korean Conflict, 25 June–1 November 1950*, USAF Historical Study no. 71 (Maxwell Air Force Base, Ala.: Air University, 1 July 1952), p. 84, Air University Library M-U 27218 no. 71.
[23] Foot, *Wrong War*, p. 114.

sion by the United Nations to depart from its tolerant effort to contain the war to the area of Korea through expansion of our military operations to his coastal areas and interior bases would doom Red China to the risk of imminent military collapse."[24]

Two weeks later, Truman undertook his own brand of atomic diplomacy. In early April Washington had indications that Moscow had moved three divisions into Manchuria and had positioned other forces for an attack on Japan. Soviet planes were packed onto Manchurian airfields, submarines appeared ready to surge from Vladivostok, and Soviet ground forces had moved south on Sakhalin. Fearing Soviet offensive action, Truman decided on 6 April to send B-29s with complete atomic weapons aboard across the Pacific. Truman then authorized General Matthew Ridgeway (who had replaced MacArthur) to use nuclear weapons if the situation arose and let his domestic rivals know of his willingness to use the bomb.[25]

To the extent MacArthur's and Truman's actions were designed to move the Chinese toward accepting a negotiated settlement and away from launching a massive attack across the Thirty-eighth Parallel, they failed. On 22 April the Chinese began their largest offensive of the war.[26]

Truman's response was to step up rather than abandon atomic coercion. On 28 April Truman sent a nuclear command-and-control team to Tokyo, approved a second westward movement of nuclear-configured aircraft, and authorized reconnaissance aircraft to fly over the airfields in Manchuria and Shantung to obtain target data, all of which indicated something more serious than a training exercise. Soon after, a secret envoy was sent to Hong Kong to contact persons capable of getting a message to leaders in the People's Republic of China, warning them against misreading MacArthur's relief as a rejection of his call for expanding the war and reminding them of Washington's ability to set their nation's development back for decades.[27]

These actions also failed to produce tangible results. Discouraged, Truman ordered the nuclear-armed B-29s home late in June 1951. Shortly thereafter, to his surprise, the Communists opened the door to peace talks.

The third coercive strategy employed by the United States was conventional denial. There were two components, a ground offensive in spring and early summer 1951, which demonstrated that the Communists could not obtain a better territorial settlement than that offered by the UN, and an air interdiction campaign from May 1951 onward, which sought to demon-

---

[24] Roger Dingman, "Atomic Diplomacy during the Korean War," *International Security* 13 (Winter 1988–89), pp. 69–71; MacArthur is quoted in Foot, *Wrong War*, p. 134. MacArthur was relieved for this act of insubordination on 11 April 1951. John W. Spanier, *The Truman-MacArthur Controversy and the Korean War* (New York: W. W. Norton, 1965), pp. 200–207.

[25] Dingman, "Atomic Diplomacy," pp. 71–74; and Roger M. Anders, ed., *Forging the Atomic Shield* (Chapel Hill: University of North Carolina Press, 1987), pp. 134, 137, 217.

[26] For details of the attack, see Whelan, *Drawing the Line*, pp. 307–21.

[27] Dingman, "Atomic Diplomacy," pp. 75–76.

strate that the Communists could not hold their current positions. While it is clear that the UN intended the air component as coercive, there is no comparable evidence for a coercive intent behind the ground operation, which was designed principally to secure the position of UN forces in Korea initially by attrition of over-extended Communist forces and later by seizing especially defensible terrain that lay just north of the Thirty-eighth Parallel. Any coercive impact may have been an unanticipated bonus.

The limit of UN forces' retreat after Chinese intervention was reached on 25 January 1951, along a line well below the Thirty-eighth Parallel and somewhat south of Seoul. At this point, the tide turned and UN forces were able to return to the offensive against the seriously over-extended Communist forces. By the middle of April the UN had recaptured Seoul and reached a short, defensible line slightly north of the Thirty-eighth Parallel. UN forces then defeated two major Communist counter-offensives, which began on 22 April and 15 May. Although the line seesawed during these battles, each was followed by a renewed UN advance so that by the beginning of June the UN was back on about the same line that it had held in April.

At this point, the commander of the Eighth U.S. Army in Korea, General James Van Fleet, wanted to order a general advance against Communist forces which he argued had been badly battered in the spring battles and so could be defeated easily. General Ridgeway and the Joint Chiefs disagreed, doubting that a general offensive would succeed in part because any further advance would over-extend UN supply lines while shortening those of the Chinese and North Koreans. Conversely, halting the advance would actually increase the pressure on the Communists because the further south they tried to maintain themselves the more vulnerable their logistics would be to air interdiction. As a result, only very limited offensive operations were authorized to capture especially valuable defensive terrain just in front of the UN lines. These were carried out with partial success from 1 to 13 June. By mid-June, the line of contact ran about 40 miles north of the Thirty-eighth Parallel for most of its length, although it dipped a few miles south of the parallel at its western end. With only trivial differences, this would be the final armistice line. Once formal armistice negotiations opened on 10 July, further ground offensives were generally stood down except for occasional operations to seize very small areas in order to strengthen the UN position.[28]

As the ground war along the Thirty-eighth Parallel approached a stalemate and armistice negotiations were about to start, American leaders turned to air interdiction in the hope it could quickly bring the war to an end. All the services and many civilian leaders in Washington supported the new strategy, the heart of which was to demonstrate to the enemy, as Air

[28] Whelan, *Drawing the Line*, pp. 307–20; Matthew B. Ridgeway, *The Korean War* (New York: Da Capo Press, 1967), pp. 170–83.

Table 8. Total U.S. combat sorties by type of mission, 1950–1953

Mission	Number
FEAF	
interdiction (+ armed reconnaissance)	220,168
close support	92,603
counterair—offensive	73,887
counterair—defensive	12,931
Navy / marines	
offensive	204,995
defensive	44,160
reconnaissance	26,757
Total	737,466

SOURCE: Edmund Dews and Felix Kozaczka, "Air Interdiction: Lessons from Past Campaigns," N-1743 (Santa Monica, Calif.: Rand Corporation, September 1981), p. 51.

Force Commander General Otto P. Weyland expressed it, "the innumerable advantages of air power as a predominant weapon for destroying the enemy fighting machine."[29] It was thought that the destruction of the rail system, supplemented by air attacks against roadways and trucks, would force the enemy to retire northward to shorten lines of communication, even without the pressure of a ground offensive.

The main source of optimism about the success of air interdiction came from the large dividends that limited air interdiction had paid earlier in the war in retarding Communist ground movement. The Chinese and North Korean armies lacked large quantities of modern transportation, and UN air attacks had forced them to disperse their supply dumps, adding to their distribution troubles. As a result, previous Communist offensives tended to collapse after two weeks because of casualties in forward units and a failure of their supplies to keep pace.[30]

Enormous effort was devoted to air interdiction throughout the war. If one assumes (conservatively) that half of the Navy's offensive air missions involved interdiction, then about half of the nearly 740,000 combat sorties flown by the Air Force, Navy, and Marines were allocated to interdiction or armed reconnaissance (see Table 8).

Air interdiction achieved significant military results. Although the only available figures count claimed rather than confirmed damage, the aggregate damage to the enemy supply transportation system would have been

[29] Weyland, "Requirements of Increased Combat Effectiveness," 19 June 1951, quoted in Robert F. Futrell, *United States Air Force Operations in the Korean Conflict, 1 November 1950–30 June 1952*, USAF Historical Study no. 72 (Maxwell Air Force Base, Ala.: Air University, 1 July 1955), p. 138, Air University Library M-U 27218 no. 72.
[30] Futrell, *Air Force Operations, 1 November 1950–30 June 1952*, pp. 145–49.

Table 9. Interdiction targets claimed as damaged or destroyed

Target type	FEAF	Navy	Total
Bridges	3,082	2,005	5,087
Rail cuts	22,828	unknown	22,828+
Locomotives	1,954	391	2,345
Rail cars	35,986	5,896	41,882
Vehicles	104,186	7,437	111,623

SOURCE: Dews and Kozaczka, "Air Interdiction," p. 55.

enormous even if the claims exaggerate real achievements by a factor of two or three (see Table 9).

The air interdiction effort was conducted in two stages, an operational interdiction campaign from May to August 1951, followed by a strategic interdiction campaign from August 1951 to June 1952. The operational interdiction campaign aimed to interrupt enemy logistics in a sixty-mile belt north of the line of contact.[31] Attacks focused on the roadways between major rail centers in central North Korea and the Communist forces manning the frontline.[32] Initially successful while the Eighth Army was pressing northward, the attacks against the enemy's roads lost effectiveness as the Eighth Army attained its objectives and slackened its ground pressure, reducing the Communists' need for large flows of replacements and supplies. The attacks reduced the enemy's use of trucks, but they were never able to knock out a road completely because repair materials and abundant labor were readily available.[33]

Beginning on 18 August 1951, Far East Air Forces implemented a strategic interdiction campaign against North Korean railroads especially in the northern half of the country between the Yalu River and Pyongyang, code named Operation Strangle.[34] Except for the tiny output of North Korea's few small arms factories, all war materiel for the Communist forces in Korea came from Manchuria along a rudimentary rail and road network. The FEAF estimated that the Communists, with sixty divisions forward, each re-

[31] This operation later came to be called Strangle I.

[32] Frank J. Merrill, *A Study of the Aerial Interdiction of Railways during the Korean War* (Fort Leavenworth, Kans.: U.S. Army Command and General Staff College, 1965), pp. 74–91.

[33] Futrell, *Air Force in Korea*, p. 437.

[34] Normally, strategic interdiction is defined as undermining war production, while operational interdiction concerns interrupting the flow of finished military goods from economic centers in the homeland to engaged forces. However, because North Korea produced only a tiny amount of war materiel, most of which had to be imported from China and the Soviet Union (whose production centers were not targeted), the more useful place to draw the distinction in this case is between transportation of bulk goods into the country and their subsequent distribution from major transportation nodes in the center of the country to specific units. A similar situation occurred in North Vietnam during the Vietnam war.

quiring 40 tons of supply a day when not engaged in combat, needed to receive 2,400 tons a day—about 1,200 truck loads or 120 boxcars. The plan was to destroy the North Korean rail system and force the enemy to wear out its trucks. The FEAF estimated that if denied the use of rail lines and forced to depend entirely on trucks, the Communists would have to replace 5,000 to 7,500 vehicles a month. Inasmuch as Communist China and the Soviet Union together were manufacturing only about 33,000 trucks per month, it was believed that the Communists could not long depend exclusively on road movement.[35]

Strangle was designed "to interfere with and disrupt lines of communication to such an extent that [the enemy] will be unable to contain a determined offensive by friendly forces or be unable to mount a sustained major offensive himself." An even more enthusiastic air planner assured Air Force Chief of Staff General Hoyt Vandenberg, "We are optimistic enough . . . to believe that with this program we can force [the enemy] to retire without any major battle to a line generally from Pyongyang through Kowon, which is a line generally 100 miles from and parallel to the Yalu River."[36]

Although the Communists had conceded on the territorial issues by November 1951, Strangle continued until June 1952 to try to coerce the enemy to concede on the POW issue as well.

Operation Strangle fizzled. The enemy supply cushion was so great that months of air strikes were needed to achieve any effect and during this time the enemy was able to develop effective countermeasures. During October 1951, rail track was being destroyed faster than the enemy could rebuild it. By December, however, repair crews were stationed at every rail junction and along every four miles of track. As a result, rail cuts were repaired in two to six hours and bridges in two to four days.[37] In the fall of 1951 the Communists also built an extensive tunnel system in mountain caves at the front to conceal stockpiles of material that were virtually immune to air attack.[38] These responses came as a surprise to UN air planners, who had failed to anticipate enemy countermeasures and in fact hardly studied potential enemy "reactions" until after the interdiction campaign had misfired.[39]

A second major weakness of the campaign was that supply interdiction was not combined with ground attack. The enemy was allowed to dictate

[35] Futrell, *Air Force in Korea*, pp. 432–42.
[36] Ibid., pp. 440, 442.
[37] Merrill, *Aerial Interdiction of Railways*, pp. 91–93; Futrell, *Air Force in Korea*, p. 473. The North Koreans relied on government agencies to organize these repair efforts, following a pattern similar to how advanced industrial states have dealt with wartime shortages. For details on Communist logistics, see James A. Huston, *Guns and Butter, Power and Rice: U.S. Army Logistics in the Korean War* (Toronto: Associated University Press, 1989), pp. 350–64.
[38] Robert Jackson, *Air War over Korea* (London: Ian Allan, 1973), p. 102.
[39] Futrell, *Air Force Operations, 1 November 1950–30 June 1952*, p. 155.

the pace of battle and so husband resources optimally, according to an undisrupted schedule. During the period of Strangle, Communist forces were able to accumulate as much as 500 tons of supplies a day above requirements.[40] Although air interdiction reduced rail traffic to some 5 percent of capacity, the operational success could produce no effect on the ability of the enemy to hold positions on the battlefield without a major UN offensive to force the Communists to use up supplies faster than they could be replaced, but no such offensive was launched.[41]

Why the Communists Conceded the Territorial Issues

UN coercive efforts succeeded in compelling the Communists to concede the UN's demands that foreign (i.e., American) forces could remain in Korea after an armistice and that the current line of contact, not the pre-war line at the Thirty-eighth Parallel, serve as the basis for the division of Korea. Conventional denial, not conventional punishment or atomic risk threats, explains the outcome. To show why, I examine each strategy in turn, with particular attention to the sequence of UN coercive efforts and Communist concessions. Finally, I explain why the Communists conceded on the territorial issues in the summer and fall of 1951 but did not concede on the POW issue at that time.

The punishment strategy which sought to bring North Korea to terms by weakening civilian morale failed for three reasons. First, the damage inflicted appears to have been light. While figures for North Korean casualties are unavailable, according to the FEAF Bomber Command the bombing of Pyongyang was so accurate that while the industrial areas of the city were gutted, civilian neighborhoods suffered almost no damage. While incendiaries were used, the bombing of North Korea caused no fire-storms similar to those in World War II.[42] North Korean military casualties from 24 June to 1 November 1950 were approximately 72,000, or about one half of one percent of the prewar population.[43] By the standards of wartime coercion, this is not high. Germany in World War II suffered 7.2 million military casualties, equal to nearly 10 percent of the prewar population.

Second, both China and North Korea were willing to countenance great civilian costs and risks to achieve their goals, which for both countries were driven by nationalism. For North Korea, the Korean War was the culmination of a civil war between various factions of indigenous political groups for control of the Korean peninsula after the Japanese were ousted after

[40] Ibid., p. 159.
[41] Merrill, *Aerial Interdiction of Railways*, p. 147.
[42] Futrell, *Air Force in Korea*, p. 198.
[43] Roy Appleman, *South to the Naktong, North to the Yalu* (Washington, D.C.: Department of the Army, 1961), pp. 263, 540.

World War II.[44] For their part, Chinese leaders feared that the United States would use Korea as a beachhead on the mainland from which it would try to reverse the Communist revolution and return the Chinese Nationalists on Taiwan to power in Peking.[45]

Third and most important, once Chinese forces entered the war in October 1950, North Korea was not in imminent danger of losing the war, even though MacArthur's headquarters did not realize this until late November when the main Chinese offensive flow fell. Indeed, in the winter of 1950–51, it seemed to most observers more likely that the Communists would conquer all of Korea than that they would not.

Having failed to produce North Korean concessions, the city bombing campaign was abandoned in 1950 and thus cannot possibly account for concessions in mid-1951.

Similarly, Truman's and MacArthur's attempts to manipulate atomic risks also cannot account for the change in Communist behavior on the territorial issues. The success of a risk strategy depends on making a threat of extreme punishment credible by constructing a pattern of escalations, which the opponent can easily recognize and can avoid only by conceding to the assailant's demands. In other words, for a risk strategy to succeed, the assailant must be willing to lock itself into executing the threatened penalty, shifting control over its ultimate execution to the opponent. America's 1951 attempt at atomic diplomacy lacked both qualities. The nuclear threats were not part of a pattern of escalation, and no steps were taken to shift the burden of initiation to the Communists.

The main reason why the Truman administration appeared hardly willing to wage nuclear war was that it in fact was not willing to do so. MacArthur certainly was willing, but his removal for insubordination in April 1951 eliminated his influence. During the early Cold War, U.S. leaders were deeply concerned about the weaknesses of American military power in a global war and worried that the Soviet Union could prevent the United States from winning a protracted war in Europe.[46]

American military weakness affected Truman's willingness to escalate the Korean War in three ways. First, early atomic weapons were not seen as certainly decisive in a global war. American leaders believed that no

[44] Bruce Cumings, *The Origins of the Korean War: Liberation and the Emergence of Separate Regimes, 1945–47* (Princeton: Princeton University Press, 1981); and John Merrill, *Korea: The Peninsular Origins of the War* (Newark: University of Delaware Press, 1989).

[45] See also Allen S. Whiting, *China Crosses the Yalu* (New York: Macmillan, 1960); Hao Yufan and Zhai Zhihai, "China's Decision to Enter the Korean War: History Revisited," *China Quarterly*, no. 121 (March 1990): 94–115; and Melvin Gurtov and Byong-Moo Hwang, *China under Threat* (Baltimore: Johns Hopkins University Press, 1980), pp. 25–62.

[46] As the primary documents have become available, a virtual consensus among historians of the early cold war has emerged on this point. See Trachtenberg, "Wasting Asset"; Harry Borowski, *A Hollow Threat: Strategic Air Power and Containment before Korea* (Westport, Conn.: Greenwood, 1982).

atomic blitz could be counted on to destroy the war-making power of the Soviet Union and so guarantee ultimate victory. The stockpile of atomic weapons was small in the early 1950s, and the power of early fission bombs was relatively limited compared to the high-yield thermonuclear weapons then under development. The U.S. Strategic Bombing Survey had found that despite the absence of precautions against atomic attack in Hiroshima, three-fourths of the city's industrial plants could have resumed normal operation within thirty days, and this analysis deeply impressed American "insiders."[47] In short, American leaders considered the atomic monopoly more impressive for what it could not do than for what it could.

Second, the perceived need to avoid global war convinced most American leaders, including the JCS and the State Department, that the United States could not run the risk of escalating the Korean War to a general war involving the Soviet Union. On 12 January 1951 Army Chief of Staff General J. Lawton Collins was specific: "Since the United States is not now prepared to engage in global war, and will not be ready before 1 July 1952, we should take all honorable means to avoid any action that is likely to bring Russia into open conflict with the United States prior to that date."[48]

Finally, U.S. leaders believed that air strikes on targets in Manchuria would bring American forces directly into a heated air battle with Soviet air forces. On 18 April 1951, Air Force Chief of Staff Vandenberg noted rumors of the formation of a Soviet "volunteer" air force, and Dean Rusk reported that conversations in Russian had been intercepted between enemy planes and the ground. By 10 May national intelligence estimates indicated that the Soviet Union had the ability to "ensure successful defenses of the Chinese mainland against any force." Later, Vandenberg assessed the air balance over China in May 1951 as clearly favoring the Soviets: "These groups that we have over there now doing this tactical job are really about a fourth of our total effort that we could muster today [but] four times that amount of groups in that area over the vast expanse of China would be a drop in the bucket." The Soviets, in contrast, could launch two thousand planes—"much more than I have."[49]

In essence, American atomic threats lacked credibility because, given the reluctance to risk global war, the Soviet Union could extend deterrence to the Chinese. In any case, they could not account for the Communist concessions in July and November 1951, since the principal tangible instruments of the threat, the nuclear-equipped B-29s, were brought home in June, ending the threat before armistice negotiations began.

---

[47] Trachtenberg, "Wasting Asset," pp. 22–23.
[48] Collins quoted ibid., p. 26.
[49] Vandenberg quoted in Foot, *Wrong War*, pp. 136–37.

In contrast to conventional punishment and nuclear risk, conventional denial can account for the Communists' concessions on the territorial issues in 1951. Further, the logic of denial can explain why the Communists did not also concede on the POW issue at the same time. Finally, although one would like to discriminate the independent effects of ground and air pressure, the evidence on Communist decision making in this case is insufficient to enable this to be done with certainty.

The Communists' most important goals in the Korean War concerned territory: at maximum, they hoped to unify Korea under communist rule and at minimum to restore the status quo anti at the Thirty-eighth Parallel. After the failure of North Korea's first attempt in 1950, China's entry into the war made unification again seem feasible. From late November 1950 to late January 1951, a series of ground offensives carried out primarily by Chinese forces inflicted heavy losses on UN forces and pushed them back from a line that had almost reached North Korea's northern border to a line well south of Seoul, reducing the fraction of Korean territory controlled by the UN from almost 90 percent to about 30 percent. As Commander-in-General Peng Dehuai cabled to Mao on January 16, 1951, "the most fundamental principle should be to have all the foreign troops withdraw from Korea within a limited period of time; a second goal is to restore the status quo prior to June 25, 1950, with a demarcation at the 38th parallel. . . . other issues than these two [for instance, the repatriation of POWs] are only of minor significance and merely concern technical questions."[50] If the Communists had been able to continue their advance, they would shortly have overrun all of Korea, and if they would have been able, on a continuing basis, to inflict heavy losses on UN forces, the United States and other UN powers might have given up their resolve to defend South Korea.

In fact, the Communists were unable to meet either requirement of their strategy. By late January 1951, Communist supply lines were seriously overextended, enabling UN ground and tactical air forces to mount a series of offensives, which by mid-April had regained nearly all of South Korea as well as some territory north of the Thirty-eighth Parallel. Communist counter-offensives in April and May were bloody failures and actually led to small additional UN territorial gains. Further, throughout the spring of 1951 Communist casualties were much greater than those of the U.N.[51]

Thus, by June 1951 UN ground action had undermined the Communists' military strategy. First, the failure of Communist offensives in January, April, and May showed that they could not overrun all of Korea. Second,

[50] Peng quoted in Shu Guang Zhang, *Deterrence and Strategic Culture: Chinese-American Confrontations, 1949–1958* (Ithaca: Cornell University Press, 1992), p. 170.

[51] An extreme example was the UN's defeat of the Communists' May 15, 1951 offensive after three days, which cost the UN 900 casualties and the Communists 35,000. Ridgeway, *Korean War*, p. 175.

the casualty ratios during the spring showed that with their existing capabilities and operational methods the Communist forces could not break UN resolve through attrition, because they would have run out of men first. Further, the UN's ability to strengthen its positions in May and June by both fortification and seizures of additional defensive terrain threatened to make Communist advances even more prohibitively expensive in the future. It is important to point out, however, that in mid-1951 UN operations did not threaten to overrun North Korea in the short term. Offensive ground operations were all but suspended after mid-June and had not been mounted on a large scale since mid-April. During the spring air power contributed significantly to the success of ground operations, primarily through close air support, not through an independent air interdiction effort.

With their mobile offensive strategy in tatters, the Communists shifted from the summer of 1951 onward, and especially after October, to a static attrition strategy, intended to hold down their own casualties to an acceptable level while still retaining the ability to inflict losses on UN forces. This strategy relied on deeply dug fortified positions combined with artillery bombardment and occassional limited ground attacks in place of the massive human wave assaults used previously.[52] These fortifications, which became known as the "underground Great Wall," were built, according to the commander of Chinese forces in Korea, "in anticipation of enemy counterattacks and a prolonged war."[53] Chinese leaders decided on 27 June that "if the enemy will not increase forces in the front or attempt any amphibious operations against our rear, we should always stay in the line between the 38th and 38.5th parallels. . . . If tactically we need to take offensives, we should not go too far [into the South] and should always stop at the Wanhan and Shaokiang Rivers."[54]

For its part, the air interdiction effort, which began in May 1951, added little to what had already been accomplished by ground power. Although the purpose of the air effort was to undermine the Communists' attrition strategy by starving their frontline forces of supplies, the Communists' logistic capacity was not reduced enough to prevent them from maintaining and actually increasing the ability of their ground forces to wage attrition warfare. Despite 87,552 interdiction sorties that claimed 19,000 rail cuts plus the de-

---

[52] Max Hastings, *The Korean War* (New York: Simon and Schuster, 1987), p. 277; Mark A. Ryan, *Chinese Attitudes toward Nuclear Weapons: China and the United States during the Korean War* (Armonk, N.Y.: M.E. Sharpe, 1989), pp. 129–30; Jonathan D. Pollack, "The Korean War and Sino-American Relations," in *Sino-American Relations, 1945–1955: A Joint Reassessment of a Critical Decade*, ed. Harry Harding and Yuan Ming (Wilmington, Del.: Scholarly Resources, 1989), p. 229.

[53] Peng Dehuai, *Memoirs of a Chinese Marshal: The Autobiographical Notes of Peng Dehuai (1898–1974)*, trans. Zheng Longpu (Beijing, China: Foreign Language Press, 1984), p. 479.

[54] Minutes from meeting of Chinese high commanders quoted in Zhang, *Deterrence and Strategic Culture*, p. 173

struction of 34,211 rail cars, the Chinese and North Korean armies were able to supply their frontline troops and even to build up logistical dumps. Perhaps the key indicator of interdiction's failure is the increase in Chinese artillery fire, the biggest killer in conventional war, from 8,000 rounds in July 1951 to 102,000 in May 1952. On 21 May 1952 General Ridgeway reported that "the hostile forces opposing the Eighth Army . . . have a substantially greater offensive potential than at any time in the past."[55]

Under these conditions, the denial theory would predict that the Communists would concede those UN demands which they could not militarily prevent, but none which they could still foresee some chance of resisting. This is what happened. The fact that the Chinese were compelled to abandon offensive ground operations meant that the Chinese no longer had any chance to drive the UN command off the Korean peninsula by force. Although they could still have hoped that continuing attrition would break UN and especially U.S. resolve, this would have been a faint hope at best. While the shift to an attrition strategy reduced Communist casualties to tolerable levels, it also sharply reduced their ability to inflict casualties on the UN. While the United States lost an average of about 1,700 dead a month during the first year of the war, this fell to about 500 a month in the last two years. Further, although more and more Americans were becoming frustrated with the stalemate in Korea, most critics of the Truman administration's policy preferred to resolve the stalemate by escalation, not by reducing U.S. objectives.[56] Accordingly, the Communists conceded the UN demand that an American garrison be allowed to remain in Korea on 25 July 1951.

In addition, the commanding defensive prowess demonstrated by UN forces in defeating the April and May Communist offensives made it extremely unlikely that the Communists could improve upon the line of contact of late June 1951 in even a small way, let alone push the UN back to the Thirty-eighth Parallel. However, the Communists did not concede this immediately, possibly because they still entertained hopes of regaining some territory. Communist negotiators first hinted that they might be willing to accept the line of contact on 20 August 1951, but negotiations were then suspended for two months because of accusations that UN forces had violated the negotiation site at Kasong. In September, a small UN offensive advanced a part of the line of contact slightly and inflicted 80,000 casualties against 20,000 suffered by the UN, thus destroying any remaining hopes that the Communists might still have had of improving their territorial position. The

---

[55] Ridgeway quoted in Futrell, *Air Force in Korea*, p. 471.

[56] In June 1950 Senator Robert Taft said, "my quarrel is with those who wish to go all-out in Europe . . . and who at the same time refuse to apply our general program and strategy to the Far East," a theme the Republican Party would increasingly sound over the next two years. Quoted in Spanier, *Truman-MacArthur Controversy*, p. 161.

Communists returned to the bargaining table on 25 October and agreed to divide Korea along the then current line of contact on 26 November.[57]

Since the Communists were not in imminent danger of losing the vast majority of the territory they controlled in Korea, the denial theory would expect that they would refuse demands for the surrender of additional territory. Similarly, the loss of their offensive military prospects did nothing to undermine the Communists' bargaining power on the POW issue. Neither side could get its prisoners back without the consent of the other and the Communists faced no danger of total defeat. Accordingly, denial did not provide the UN with any coercive leverage on this issue and the Communists did not concede.

Perhaps the most controversial aspect of the division of Korea agreement on 26 November was that the demarcation line would remain fixed for thirty days provided the other outstanding issues were resolved within that time. This provision has been criticized for giving the Communists valuable time to strengthen their defenses, thus rendering their concessions on the presence and boundary lines meaningless. However, as shown above, the evidence does not support this; the Communists never attempted to withdraw those concessions. A more reasonable criticism might be that the thirty-day truce reduced U.S. leverage on the still-outstanding POW issue by reducing the threat of a major UN offensive. In fact, the UN had no such plans. After September 1951 Ridgeway suspended further offensive operations in order to reduce casualties.[58]

THE PRISONERS OF WAR ISSUE

Despite Communists concessions on the territorial issues in 1951, the Korean War did not end because the UN also demanded that prisoners be returned only on a voluntary basis. As a result, the armistice talks and the fighting dragged on for nearly two years until the Communists conceded on the POW issue on 4 June 1953.

America's New Goal

After five months of negotiations on the remaining non-territorial issues, on 7 May 1952 the UN and Communists announced to the world that their stalemate on POW repatriation was now the single issue separating the belligerents from an armistice agreement. This deadlock had been evident

[57] Hermes, *Truce Tent and Fighting Front*, pp. 113, 508.

[58] Rosemary Foot also doubts that the thirty-day respite made much difference to Communist defensive capabilities, as they had been fortifying continuously at least since August 1951. Foot, *Substitute for Victory*, p. 105.

since February when the United States first clearly opposed forcible repatriation. Although the Communists insisted on the Geneva Convention standard of repatriation of all prisoners,[59] they also agreed to a poll of UN-held prisoners, which indicated that just over half the Korean prisoners wished to return home and that 16,000 of 21,000 Chinese prisoners said they did not want to return to the People's Republic of China, although the number refusing repatriation was exaggerated by intimidation.[60] On notification that only 70,000 POWs would be returned, the Communist negotiators rejected "voluntary" repatriation. On 21 March, the Communists consented to nonforcible repatriation of North Korean prisoners, but adamantly insisted that all Chinese prisoners had to be returned.[61]

Why did the United States insist on voluntary repatriation? Until armistice negotiations were about to begin in the summer of 1951, American leaders fully expected that all prisoners would be automatically returned after a settlement. However, on 5 July, General Robert A. McClure, Army chief of psychological warfare, argued that, because many Communist prisoners would be put to death or imprisoned for their surrender to the UN, returning prisoners only voluntarily would be humane and aid in future psychological warfare operations. Although Ridgeway, the JCS, and Secretary of Defense Robert Lovett argued that voluntary repatriation would violate the Geneva convention and probably jeopardize the return of Allied POWs, President Truman and Secretary of State Acheson disagreed. After World War II, both the United States and Britain returned many reluctant soldiers to the Soviet Union who had met a terrible fate. Truman and Acheson had no wish to repeat this. During the fall of 1951, their inclination for voluntary repatriation hardened into an irrevocable moral principle, one indicating democracy's moral superiority over Communism.[62]

By the time President Dwight Eisenhower entered office in January 1953, the American coercive effort in Korea appeared stalemated. Although some American leaders, especially military commanders, maintained in the fall of

[59] The common practice was to exchange all prisoners of war at the end of a conflict. In fact, the 1949 Geneva Conference strengthened the relevant articles to a flat statement prescribing quick and compulsory repatriation so as avoid a recurrence of the situation following World War II when the Soviet Union retained large numbers of POWs for long periods as forced labor. Hermes, *Truce Tent and Fighting Front*, p. 135.

[60] Because the Chinese POWs were guarded by Nationalist Chinese troops from Taiwan, they were not able to speak freely, as Ridgeway and Turner Joy knew. Joy recorded in his diary that those who said they wished to return to the People's Republic of China "were either beaten black and blue or killed." He believed that an honest screening would find 85 percent, not the recorded 15 percent, seeking repatriation. Joy, *How Communists Negotiate*, pp. 140–44.

[61] Foot, *Substitute for Victory*, p. 98.

[62] For a rich account, see Bernstein, "The Struggle over the Korean Armistice," in *Child of Conflict*, ed. Cumings, 261–308.

1952 that UN military pressure was having a "material effect on the civilian morale in North Korea," peace talks had been adjourned since 8 October.[63] During this period, the supposedly demoralized Communist forces had continued their military buildup and by January had fielded nearly one million men in Korea, more than half of them at or just behind the front.[64]

Eisenhower had a reputation for commitment to ending the Korean War on America's terms and for willingness to use nuclear weapons to do it. Although Truman and Acheson occasionally contemplated the use of nuclear weapons, Eisenhower and Secretary of State John Foster Dulles frequently discussed these weapons, both publicly and privately, as though they were just bigger bombs.[65]

The new administration's principal goal, however, was not fundamentally different from Truman's: the establishment of an independent, non-Communist South Korea secure from future attack. It was also firmly committed, for reputational reasons, to prevailing on the POW issue. Dulles wrote in December 1952 that the Soviets "expect the Republican administration to be tougher and if it is not tougher, they will enlarge their estimate of what they can get away with."[66]

Coercive Strategies

To achieve this goal, U.S. leaders fashioned two major coercive strategies in 1952 and 1953, a punishment strategy using conventional bombing and a nuclear risk strategy based on more explicit threats than those issued by Truman in 1951. Conventional denial was not seriously considered, as it would have been costly to break the military stalemate with conventional weapons alone.

If the first two strategies had failed, Eisenhower planned to shift in 1954 to what can best be termed a nuclear denial strategy. This would have combined a major land offensive in Korea, a naval blockade of China, and nuclear air strikes directly against airfields and other targets in Manchuria and China proper. These operations would have aimed to destroy Communist military power in Korea, reduce China's capabilities more generally, and advance South Korea's boundary from the Kansas line to the "narrow waist" of the peninsula, giving the South 80 percent of the Korean population.[67] Because the armistice was settled in 1953, the nuclear denial strategy was never implemented.

---

[63] General Clark quoted in Foot, *Substitute for Victory*, p. 143.
[64] Whelan, *Drawing the Line*, p. 351.
[65] Foot, *Wrong War*, pp. 204–5.
[66] Dulles quoted in Foot, *Substitute for Victory*, p. 159.
[67] U.S. leaders estimated that the United States would not be ready to mount such a strike until the spring of 1954. Foot, *Wrong War*, pp. 206–10, 214.

[159]

By the spring of 1952, air interdiction had clearly failed to compel the Chinese and North Koreans to accept UN terms, so in May the American bombing campaign shifted to a new strategy focused on attacking civilian morale. This shift was supported by Generals Weyland and Vandenberg and the JCS as well as by important civilian leaders such as George Kennan, ambassador to the Soviet Union, Secretary of Defense Lovett, and officials in the CIA. General Ridgeway opposed it, however, and it was not initiated until General Mark Clark replaced him as UN Commander in May 1952.[68]

The key concepts of this strategy, called "air pressure," were outlined in a staff study by Colonel Richard L. Randolph and Lieutenant Colonel Ben I. Mayo completed on 12 April 1952.[69] The central goal was to employ air power "to inflict maximum pressure on the enemy by causing him permanent loss," focusing on critical targets of such significance to the Soviet bloc that their destruction would influence political decisions in Moscow and Peking.[70] Inasmuch as North Korea had few "strategic" targets to begin with, and most of those had been destroyed in 1950, the emphasis on "destruction" triggered an intense search for lucrative new targets. The FEAF intelligence chief, General Don Zimmerman, was convinced that "a dynamic and constant expansion of the target horizon . . . will always reveal that efficient employment of air power can be made regardless of the circumstances of the operation, the geographic location, the composition, deployment, and tactics of the enemy forces."[71]

Despite public claims that only military targets would be attacked, in fact target selection focused on undermining civilian morale. To hide the true nature of the attacks from public scrutiny, FEAF's Deputy for Operations, General Jacob E. Smart, planned that "whenever possible attacks will be scheduled against targets of military significance so situated that their destruction will have a deleterious effect upon the morale of the civilian population."[72]

---

[68] Kennan suggested that any air attack that could "frighten the Chinese and increase their demands on Russia would be good." The CIA concluded in July 1952: "Despite the capability to continue the war in Korea, we believe that internal economic and political considerations are probably exerting pressure on the Chinese Communists to conclude hostilities." Lovett commented: "If we stay firm [on the POW issue] we can tear them up by air. We are . . . hurting them badly. . . . If we keep on, tearing the place apart, we can make it a most unpopular affair for the North Koreans." Futrell, *Air Force in Korea*, pp. 487–88; Bernstein, "Struggle over the Korean Armistice," pp. 291–92, 294, 296.

[69] Colonel R. L. Randolph and Lieutenant Colonel B. I. Mayo, "The Application of FEAF Effort in Korea," Staff Study for Deputy for Operations FEAF, 12 April 1952, USAF HRA K720.01.

[70] Ibid., p. 11. This idea went back at least to June 1951; see Weyland, "The Air Campaign in Korea," pp. 24–27.

[71] Futrell, *Air Force Operations, 1 July 1952–27 July 1953*, pp. 94–95.

[72] Futrell, *Air Force in Korea*, p. 481. The reasons for obfuscation were as much to avoid injuring Communist prestige as to avoid domestic criticism. The JCS stated that it was "considered important to avoid public statements ascribing the high level of air activity as bringing pressure on the Communists to agree to an armistice, so that Communist prestige is not so seriously engaged as to make more difficult ultimate Communist agreement to an acceptable armistice." Futrell, *Air Force Operations, 1 July 1952–27 July 1953*, p. 37.

The air pressure strategy consisted of three separate operations. The first was a concerted attack on North Korea's five hydroelectric power facilities at Fusen, Chosen, Kyosen, Funei, and Kongosan. Since air power had already destroyed all large industry, power from these stations went primarily to the civilian economy in Korea and secondarily to Chinese industrial complexes in Manchuria.[73] Starting on 23 June, the hydroelectric plants were hit repeatedly over several weeks, destroying or severely damaging all of them. As a result, North Korean electric power production was reduced to less than 10 percent of installed capacity, causing a power blackout in North Korea for fifteen days and resulting in a loss of 23 percent of Manchuria's power requirements for 1952.[74]

The second operation, Pressure Pump, involved incendiary raids on North Korea's capital, Pyongyang. Following General Weyland's belief that there were psychological benefits to be derived from punishing the enemy at the seat of government, on 11 July and 29 August, FEAF dropped thousands of tons of napalm against thirty "military" targets within the city.[75]

The last operation, called Strike, identified seventy-eight towns and villages sheltering Communist supplies as targets. To disrupt civil order, aircraft first dropped leaflets titled "You Are Next," and then followed up with massive night assaults by B-26s with incendiary and delay-fused bombs. After two towns had been fire bombed, Strike was ended by pressure from the U.S. State Department, which was concerned about the propaganda advantages accruing to the Communists.[76]

To minimize possible civil disturbances, the Communists responded by reorganizing their counterintelligence system and dispatching special subversion control agents to those cities that had received the heaviest air attacks. In addition, they permitted large numbers of civilians to evacuate population centers for the safety of farms and villages. Government authorities compelled only civilians performing essential services to remain.[77] Although FEAF pointed to enemy objections that the bombing was immoral as evidence that it was actually undermining Communist morale, none of the voluminous unit histories mentions any more substantial indicator of Communist civilian morale, such as subversive activities against Pyongyang or

[73] James F. Schnabel and Robert J. Watson, *The Korean War*, vol. 3 of *The History of the Joint Chiefs of Staff* (Washington, D.C.: Historical Division of the Joint Secretariat, Joint Chiefs of Staff, March 1979), pt. 2, pp. 843–44.

[74] Foot, *Wrong War*, p. 178.

[75] Futrell, *Air Force Operations, 1 July 1952–27 July 1953*, pp. 98–99.

[76] By August the Douhet-style campaign had begun to produce negative reactions toward the United States in friendly and neutral countries, especially in Great Britain and India. Futrell, *Air Force Operations, 1 July 1952–27 July 1953*, pp. 36–37; and Schnabel and Watson, *Korean War*, pt. 2, p. 847.

[77] Futrell, *Air Force Operations, 1 July 1952–July 27 1953*, p. 103.

Peking, problems in recruiting military manpower, or public demonstrations against the war.[78]

Given the price the Communist states had already paid to achieve their goals by June 1952, the additional costs of the "air pressure" campaign seem minor indeed. Overall, about 900,000 Chinese Communist and 520,000 North Korean soldiers were killed or wounded during the war, and during the last year of the war, Communist casualties ranged from 10,000 to 70,000 per month.[79] In any case, these punishment operations had no discernable effect on the armistice negotiations, so, from September 1952 to May 1953, air power was redirected toward enemy troop concentrations.

American air strategies returned to morale bombing in May 1953, this time a much more aggressive punishment strategy that aimed to destroy North Korea's food supply. The principal supporters of this shift were operational commanders in the field, especially the FEAF's target staff and General Clark. Unlike "air pressure," General Weyland was not a supporter of this strategy.[80]

The strategy used high-explosive raids against the North Korean irrigation dams to inundate and destroy most of the country's rice crop, which, the FEAF's target intelligence chief believed, "would cause a serious food shortage in North Korea which could seriously hamper the overall war effort in North Korea and possibly result in an economic slump of serious proportions accompanied by a lowering of morale and possibly the will to fight."[81]

The FEAF's air planners were confident that North Korea's rice crop was highly vulnerable to air attack. It grew in some 422,000 acres along the northwest coast and produced about 283,000 tons of rice annually. Approximately 70 percent of the rice lands required some form of controlled irrigation, and the Koreans customarily stored water in reservoirs for use in the April and May rice-planting season. Most of the required irrigation water was impounded in reservoirs behind earth and stone dams. The key was to cause floods. If the dams were breached, not only would the irrigation waters be lost but the released flood waters would destroy the current year's rice planting in the lowlands and jeopardize future crops by silting over and washing away topsoil. The best times to attack the dams were in early May, at the end of the transplanting season when flood waters would uproot young plants, and in early August, during the blooming season, when flood

[78] FEAF unit histories are located at the USAF Historical Research Agency, Maxwell Air Force Base, Ala.

[79] Whelan, *Drawing the Line*, p. 373; Hermes, *Truce Tent and Fighting Front*, pp. 198–99, 477.

[80] Jackson, *Air War over Korea*, pp. 156–57; John Gittings, "Talks, Bombs and Germs: Another Look at the Korean War," *Journal of Contemporary Asia* 5 (Winter 1975): 215; and Futrell, *Air Force in Korea*, pp. 666–71.

[81] Quoted in Futrell, *Air Force Operations, 1 July 1952–27 July 1953*, p. 126.

waters would destroy a large portion of the plants and thus the year's crop. Of these, strikes in August would be more disastrous, because farmers could replant after damage done in May.[82]

The target set for this strategy consisted of twenty dams irrigating the rice fields in northwest Korea. Destroying these dams would, General Clark estimated, cause "damage or destruction of an estimated one quarter million tons of rice, thereby curtailing the enemy's ability to live off the land and aggravating a reported Chinese rice shortage and logistic problem." To mitigate Communist propaganda advantages following these strikes and to obfuscate the true nature of the raids, FEAF planners also targeted interdiction nodes such as rail bridges and track.[83]

In all, five dams were attacked. On 13 May fifty-nine F-84 Thunderjets attacked the Toksan irrigation dam twenty miles north of Pyongyang, a twenty-three-hundred-foot dike that impounded a large reservoir. The strike was an operational success, causing swirling floodwaters to wash out five square miles of crop lands. "The damage done by the deluge," said the Fifth Air Force directorate of operations, "far exceeded the hopes of everyone." Similar results occurred from air strikes on 15 and 16 May against the dikes of the mile-wide lake at Chason, which caused onrushing waters to surge over a number of fields of young rice.[84]

Repeating these results, however, proved increasingly difficult, for the North Koreans speedily engineered countermeasures to offset the damage caused by the air strikes. The 21 May direct hit of the Kuwonga dam produced no flooding, because the enemy had reduced the water level in the reservoir, thus increasing the thickness of the earth that had to be breached by some ninety feet. A second strike on 29 May also failed to produce the desired flood, although it did compel the North Koreans to slowly drain the lake. From 13 to 18 June, F-84s, F-86s, and B-29s attacked Kusong and Toksang dams many times but again failed to produce a flood. The North Koreans not only lowered the water level with each attack just enough to avert a breach, but also stationed labor battalions to refill craters immediately after they were made. The water was lost, but flood damage to the current rice crop was averted. By this time it was clear that further attacks would be fruitless, so strikes against dams were discontinued in favor of attacks against airfields.[85]

There is good reason to doubt whether forcing the North Koreans to drain their reservoirs posed much threat of starvation; certainly the threat was not

[82] Ibid., pp. 126–27.
[83] See Clodfelter, *Limits of Air Power*, p. 18.
[84] Futrell, *Air Force Operations, 1 July 1952–27 July 1953*, pp. 127–29.
[85] Ibid., pp. 129–30; Hermes, *Truce Tent and Fighting Front*, p. 461; Schnabel and Watson, *Korean War*, pt. 2, p. 980; Director of Targets and Director of Reconnaissance, HQ FEAF, "The Attack on the Irrigation Dams in North Korea," *Air University Review* 6 (Winter 1953–54): 40–61.

nearly so severe as that which would have been posed by large-scale flooding. Large amounts of rice could have been grown without any irrigation, although the average annual yield in areas with controlled irrigation was about double that of areas without it. Indeed, about a third of the rice crop was not irrigated and so would not have been damaged by the air raids. In addition, rice paddies might have been double cropped in an emergency. Thus, it seems likely that significant amounts of rice could have been grown even without controlled irrigation.[86] In any case, the water in the reservoirs was returned to normal levels shortly after the attacks. By 22 July 1953, photographic intelligence revealed that the reserviors controlled by two of the attacked dams were more than half full and repair work was well advanced on the other three.[87]

In essence, the air campaign against North Korea's food supply could not, alone, have produced much coercive leverage because no significant threat to the rice crop emerged.

Simulaneously with the campaign against the irrigation dams, in May 1953 the United States issued atomic threats against China that were intended to compel acceptance of an armistice mainly through the prospect of horrendous devastation. This strategy was supported by President Eisenhower, the Joint Chiefs, and Secretary of State Dulles, as well as military commanders in the field.

The core of this strategy was to communicate a credible intention to use large numbers of atomic weapons in a future expansion of military operations to China. Although no specific targets were identified in any communications to the Communists, American leaders clearly thought atomic attacks were more important for their ability to exploit civilian, not military, vulnerabilities. Eisenhower later recalled: "The Joint Chiefs of Staff were pessimistic about the feasibility of using tactical atomic weapons on frontline positions, in view of the extensive underground fortifications which the Chinese Communists had been able to construct; but such weapons would obviously be effective for strategic targets in North Korea, Manchuria, and on the China coast."[88] Paul Nitze, head of the State Department's Policy Planning Staff, explained the effects of such strikes: "If the bomb should be used for strategic purposes through attacks on Manchurian cities such as Mukden, Fushen, Anshan, Harbin, and Dairen, this action would result in the destruction of many civilians and would almost certainly bring the Soviet Union into the war."[89]

---

[86] "Reservoirs and Irrigation Complexes," enclosure no. 3, "Minutes of the FEAF Formal Target Committee Meeting, 24 March 1953," pp. 1–2, USAF HRA K720.151A.

[87] "Highlights of North Korean Target Spectrum," enclosure no. 3, "Minutes of the FEAF Formal Target Committee Meeting, 22 July 1953," p. 1, USAF HRA K720.151A.

[88] Eisenhower, *White House Years*, pp. 179–80.

[89] Nitze quoted in Ryan, *Chinese Attitudes*, p. 33.

It has been alleged that far from pursuing coercive policies, the Eisenhower administration acted even more cautiously than had its predecessor in threatening to use nuclear weapons to end the Korean War.[90] To be sure, Eisenhower sought to contain Communist expansion rather than roll it back. Nonetheless, there is persuasive evidence that he was more willing to employ the atomic instrument than was Truman.

First, the Eisenhower administration formally approved contingency plans for the use of nuclear weapons, something that Truman never did. In March 1953 Eisenhower ordered a study of how to reach the waist of Korea while doing maximum damage to Chinese forces, which identified six options, three intensifying hostilities on the Korean peninsula and three expanding the war into China. Only one option—a limited conventional effort in Korea—did not involve the use of nuclear weapons. On 20 May the JCS recommended "air and naval operations directly against China and Manchuria" and "a coordinated offensive to seize a position generally at the waist of Korea," using atomic weapons "on a sufficiently large scale to insure success." Eisenhower supported the JCS plan on the ground that it would reduce UN casualties: "To keep the attack from becoming overly costly, it was clear that we would have to use atomic weapons." He also noted that the more rapid the military operation, the less risk of Soviet retaliation against Japan's cities.[91]

Second, the Eisenhower administration sent a package of signals to the Chinese which indicated the growing willingness of the United States to escalate the level of violence in the war. This package was deliberately designed to avoid swaggering public threats that might alarm domestic and foreign opinion and create too much pressure on the enemy.[92] Rather, it

[90] Dingman, "Atomic Diplomacy," pp. 79–91.

[91] This evidence is in Foot, "Nuclear Coercion," pp. 97–98; Daniel Calingaert, "Nuclear Weapons and the Korean War," *Journal of Strategic Studies* 11 (June 1988): 193. Dingman depreciates the importance of the 20 May National Security Council meeting on the grounds that Dulles was not present and that Eisenhower frequently made idle, tentative, or educational remarks at such meetings. "Atomic Diplomacy," pp. 80–85. The JCS had already produced its recommendations before the meeting, however, and Dulles was already on his way to deliver signals of the administration's intent to China through third parties. Under these circumstances, his absence more likely indicates that de facto agreement on the policy had already been reached. Moreover, Eisenhower explicitly asked that his decision on the recommendation be officially recorded, indicating that he took the matter seriously and was not merely engaged in a "rambling conversation."

[92] Eisenhower's policy to avoid the appearance of ultimatum also has its roots in the Truman administration. As early as November 1950, Bedell Smith, CIA director, favored a policy of "quiet exploration with implied threats." Instead of parading colorful threats in front of the enemy and the world at large, he advised a "simple statement of facts" about what would and would not happen if an arrangement could not be completed. See Trachtenberg, "Wasting Asset," p. 32 n. 113. This tactic, which seeks to reduce the embarrassment involved in accepting an opponent's terms, runs counter to the advice of some coercive theorists to produce a sense of urgency which requires publicity. See Alexander L. George, William E. Simons, and David K. Hall, *Limits of Coercive Diplomacy: Laos, Cuba, and Vietnam* (Boston: Little, Brown, 1971).

aimed to deliver the message shrewdly and quietly, so that "a foreign G-2," piecing together bits of information, would conclude that "he had pierced the screen" of Washington's intentions. "With a little handling," Eisenhower concluded, "the desired effect could certainly be secured."[93]

To convey the message to the Chinese that further delays in settling the war would not be tolerated, the United States employed four parallel diplomatic channels. First, assuming the message would reach Peking, Dulles told Prime Minister Jawaharlal Nehru of India on 21 May that "if armistice negotiations collapse, the United States would probably make a stronger rather than a lesser military exertion and that this might well extend the area of conflict." Although Nehru may not have made specific reference to nuclear weapons in transmitting it, there is evidence that he passed Dulles's message to other states. The Indian foreign minister told a British diplomat that if the negotiating terms were rejected, the United States would "break off the negotiations and have recourse to dramatic action."[94] Second, at U.S. behest, the UN negotiator, General William K. Harrison, explained to the Communist negotiators that the United States was offering its "final" position; if, after a one-week recess, it were rejected, talks would be terminated. Third, General Mark Clark, the UN commander, was authorized on 27 May to write to his counterparts commanding Communist forces in Korea: "It is not our purpose to engage in prolonged and fruitless repetition of arguments. It is our earnest hope that you will give urgent and most serious consideration to our delegation's alternative proposals. . . . you are urged to take advantage of the present opportunity." Finally, on 3 June, the U.S. ambassador to Moscow, Charles Bohlen, met with Soviet Foreign Minister V. M. Molotov to explain the "extreme importance and seriousness of the latest UNC proposals, pointing out the lengths to which UNC has gone to bridge the existing gap and making it clear these represent the limit to which we can go."[95]

At roughly the same time, the United States also established a pattern of escalation in force, although we do not have evidence that this was deliber-

---

[93] Dingman, "Atomic Diplomacy," p. 84, interprets this as evidence of Eisenhower's intention to bluff. This interpretation is mistaken because it confuses two preference orderings: preferring nonescalation to failed negotiations and actual escalation and preferring negotiated settlement to actual escalation. Dingman's evidence supports the second but not the first, which requires evidence that Eisenhower did not intend to escalate the war even if negotiations failed.

[94] Subsequently, Nehru distanced himself from Dulles's suggestion that he transmitted nuclear signals to Beijing. He claimed not to have recorded in the May meeting any note of a threat to use nuclear weapons and not to have passed any such threat on to the Chinese. It is probable that Dulles did not use the words "nuclear weapons," for he and other administration representatives relied on diplomatic euphemisms. Thus, Nehru's denial is not as absolute as it at first appears.

[95] Edward C. Keefer, "President Dwight D. Eisenhower and the End of the Korean War," *Diplomatic History* 10 (Summer 1986): 267–89.

ately coordinated with the atomic risk strategy. In February American B-29s bombed Communist frontline forces and then attacked the Suiho power installation. In May another target system came under attack when the United States bombed irrigation dams in North Korea.[96]

A principal reason why the United States was more willing to employ atomic threats and, if necessary, actually use atomic weapons, was that the global military balance had shifted in its favor. The Truman administration was reluctant to escalate from 1950 to 1952 because key policy makers saw a window of Western vulnerability to Soviet aggression. By 1953, after an extraordinary buildup of American military power in Europe and the Far East, the window of vulnerability seemed closed, and the United States was correspondingly more willing to escalate in Korea if the war could not otherwise be ended favorably.

When the Korean War began, contrary to myths of American atomic omnipotence, atomic strikes could not be counted on to destroy the industrial power of the Soviet Union because early fission bombs were so much less powerful than the thermonuclear weapons on the horizon and they were in quite short supply. Strategic Air Command planners estimated that, given the inadequacy of forward bases and overseas fuel supplies, any world war would involve months of atomic bombing and even longer conventional warfare. A long war meant an uncertain war. General Omar N. Bradley, Chairman of the Joint Chiefs of Staff, warned senior officials in November 1950 that if a global war broke out, "we might be in danger of losing." Acheson argued in February 1951 against a general advance north of the Thirty-eighth Parallel because of the "risk of extending the Korean conflict to other areas and even into general war at a time when we are not ready to risk general war."[97]

By 1953, the global military balance had fundamentally changed. After several years of ramping-up, Truman's mobilization policies had sharply increased available conventional forces, logistics, and munitions. Monthly production of military items expanded over fivefold between June 1950 and August 1952, and the annual cost of military deliveries rose from $6.4 billion in 1951 to $17.8 billion in 1952.[98] U.S. nuclear capability expanded even more dramatically. On 30 June 1950, the U.S. arsenal had about 292 atomic bombs. Owing to Truman's orders to increase production in October 1950 and again in January 1952, the stockpile increased to over 1,000 by the summer of 1953. U.S. aircraft capable of delivering strategic nuclear weapons increased from 250 in June 1950 to 1,000 by the end of 1953. Further, the development of small "tactical" nuclear weapons meant that atomic bombs

---

[96] Foot, *Substitute for Victory*, p. 166.
[97] Dingman, "Atomic Diplomacy," p. 53; Trachtenberg, "Wasting Asset," pp. 21–28.
[98] Ibid., p. 29.

could also be dropped by fighter aircraft such as the F-84.[99] U.S. ability to deliver rapid atomic strikes was also enhanced by the advent of jet bombers, growth of overseas bases, and modifications that made aircraft carriers capable of delivering nuclear weapons.[100]

The United States now had enough weapons for a major war in Europe and some to spare. In December 1952 General Bradley told Eisenhower that "we have so many atomic bombs now that we could spare a considerable number of them for the Korean War, should it be deemed advisable to use them." Similarly, in January 1953 Nitze expressed the belief that the United States possessed "a stockpile of sufficient size to enable us to use these weapons locally," that is, in Korea.[101] As a result of these changes, the same JCS that had been cautious in 1950 and 1951 had begun to advocate nuclear escalation by late 1952 and early 1953.

Why the Communists Conceded the POW Issue

Without access to their records, no explanation for why the Chinese and North Koreans changed their behavior can be definitive. Nonetheless, the weight of available evidence supports the conclusion that Eisenhower's nuclear threats, made more credible by a reduction in Soviet willingness to deter the use of atomic weapons in the Korean War, were the decisive factor that induced the Communists to abandon their previous reluctance to accept the UN's demands.

The evidence comes in three parts. First, the record of negotiations establishes that the timing of the change in Communist behavior corresponds perfectly with Eisenhower's use of nuclear threats. Second, the evidence indicates that the Chinese were far more sensitive to atomic strikes than the bombastic public rhetoric of their leaders would suggest, and that they recognized the American ultimatum when it was issued in May 1953. Finally, the failure of alternative explanations to account for the Communist shift independently of the atomic signals casts considerable doubt on the counterfactual case that Chinese and North Korean behavior would have changed even without atomic coercion.

---

[99] Prior to 1953, atomic weapons were large (the MK 6 weighed eighty-five hundred pounds, and the MK 4, eleven thousand pounds) and had to be delivered by B-29s and other bombers that would have been extremely vulnerable to enemy fighters. During 1952 the United States developed the MK 7, a seventeen-hundred pound weapon that could be fitted to the external carriage of the F-84G, the first fighter with in-flight refueling capability. In December 1952 a wing of F-84Gs moved to Japan "to train its aircrews in the delivery of tactical atomic weapons." Ryan, *Chinese Attitudes*, pp. 138–39.

[100] David A. Rosenberg, "Origins of Overkill: Nuclear Weapons and American Strategy, 1945–1960," *International Security* 7 (Spring 1983): 23–24; Trachtenberg, "Wasting Asset," p. 30.

[101] Bradley and Nitze quoted in Calingaert, "Nuclear Weapons and the Korean War," pp. 184, 191.

By the summer of 1953, peace talks had been at an impasse for over a year over the fate of prisoners of war, although the principal Korea would be divided at the line of contact between the two armies was not still in dispute. The only movement toward peace occurred in early 1953. On 22 February General Clark proposed an exchange of sick and wounded prisoners, which Premier Zhou Enlai accepted on 28 March. Two days later, Zhou proposed that POWs who were unwilling to be repatriated should be transferred to a neutral state; the United States rejected the proposal.

On 25 May, in conjunction with the other signals that comprised Eisenhower's atomic coercion strategy, the UN negotiators put forward "final" terms. It was the first time such definite language was formally employed. On 4 June the Chinese and North Korean negotiators indicated they would accept the latest UN proposal, which would basically release any POWs not wishing repatriation as civilians after their original government had an opportunity, under supervision, to persuade them to return home. On 8 June a formal agreement on the POW question was completed, and the demarcation line was fixed on 17 June, the same day the president of South Korea tried to disrupt the armistice by releasing North Korean prisoners who rejected repatriation. On 27 July the armistice agreement was formally signed.[102]

The timing of these final concessions indicates that the Chinese and North Koreans did fear and expect an expanded war if the negotiations were further delayed. Although the final concessions were small, those issues had held up the negotiations for over a year, mainly because no significant pressure could be brought to bear on either side to abandon any hopes of its goal.

Chinese officials could not help knowing in early 1953 that a thoroughgoing shift of American military strategy in Korea toward greater reliance on nuclear weapons was under way. To be sure, they could not know the full details, which have only recently been declassified. Nonetheless, the general outlines and some vital details were documented in the Western press and signaled by administration officials through diplomatic channels.

Dwight Eisenhower's election campaign gave great prominence to the war and to his pledge to bring truce negotiations to a rapid and successful conclusion, which was a core means by which he established his presidential credentials. Soon after Eisenhower's famous visit to Korea in December 1952, his administration leaked word of a new strategic plan that would "induce communist aggressors to want peace."[103]

The Chinese recognized the implications of these faint hints. Following Eisenhower's inaugural address, the official Chinese news agency de-

---

[102] Excellent descriptions of the negotiations are in Foot, *Substitute for Victory*, pp. 130–58; and Hermes, *Truce Tent and Fighting Front*, pp. 112–74, 263–82.

[103] John Wilson Lewis and Xue Litai, *China Builds the Bomb* (Stanford: Stanford University Press, 1988), p. 13.

nounced U.S. plans to "resort to the use of atomic weapons." Moreover, recent sources indicated that Chinese representatives at the armistice talks and in the Ministry of Foreign Affairs had intelligence on the UN command's proposals for expanding the war.[104] The Chinese could easily monitor U.S. nuclear doctrine and the basic progress of the American nuclear weapons program during the Korean war. Nuclear tests were nationally televised, and data on systems, kilotonnages, and weapons were published by major American newspapers. It was hardly necessary for the Chinese to be informed of U.S. progress via Soviet espionage agents in the West.[105]

U.S. nuclear capability stimulated the interest of the Chinese in acquiring their own nuclear weapons. Although Mao's 1946 quip that a rural country like China was immune to nuclear threats was official Chinese policy during the war, in fact Chinese thinking had begun to change. In October 1951 a representative of a Chinese scientific association said, "Only when we ourselves have the atomic weapon, and are fully prepared, is it possible for the frenzied warmongers to listen to our just and reasonable proposals." At roughly the same time, a *People's Daily* editorial stressed the deterrent effects of nuclear weapons: "Only the fact that other countries [than the United States], in the first place the Soviet Union, possess the atomic weapon can bring America to believe that there is not the slightest advantage in atomic militarism."[106]

Recent revelations by historians with access to some Chinese sources indicate that the Korean War precipitated China's independent nuclear program, though it was not formally announced until 1956. By 1951 the People's Republic of China had begun joint operations with the Soviet Union to mine uranium in Xinjiang, and construction of an "atom town" was begun to accommodate scientists and technicians developing nuclear weapons in Xian. In 1953 China launched a two-pronged nuclear research project in both peaceful applications and weapons development, which included a research visit by Chinese nuclear scientists to the Soviet Union in February and the construction of a number of atomic facilities.[107]

Although historians have not unearthed conclusive evidence of how Chinese officials perceived individual U.S. messages sent through the four channels Eisenhower used, there is significant evidence that the Chinese recognized a major change in U.S. policy. On 19 May, for instance, the New China News Agency reported rumors from Tokyo that the United States was preparing a "new ultimatum." Moreover, Chinese, Soviet, and North

[104] Ibid., p. 14.
[105] Hastings, *Korean War*, p. 394.
[106] Both quoted in William R. Harris, "Chinese Nuclear Doctrine: The Decade Prior to Weapons Development (1945–1955)," *China Quarterly*, no. 21 (January–March 1965): 94.
[107] Chong-Pin Lin, *China's Nuclear Weapons Strategy* (Lexington, Mass.: Lexington Books, 1988), pp. 45, 143.

Korean leaders conferred with each other after 28 May, the date on which Bohlen met with Molotov in Moscow and on which the talks recessed, but before their resumption on 4 June.[108] The fact that the Communists accepted UN terms almost immediately upon resumption of the talks strongly suggests that the Chinese were swayed by U.S. nuclear threats.

Further, the Chinese may have recognized that the atomic bomb was better suited to destroying population centers than to attacking battlefield targets. A bomb with a blast and radiation radius of several miles can wreak havoc on densely populated areas, and China's and North Korea's cities would have been highly vulnerable. The same would not have been true for attacks against troop or supply concentrations. Communist troops were well-entrenched and widely dispersed in the rugged terrain of Korea, where the effects of an atomic explosion would have been mainly confined to individual valleys, while hills would have protected troops on the other side. In May 1952 the United States tested this proposition. Troops were dug into 4½-foot-deep foxholes located 3½ miles from ground zero and, after an atomic explosion, climbed out without injury. The underground "great wall" was estimated at four times this depth. The most effective means of destroying troops is not by a massive single blast but by many smaller separate explosions spread over a wide area. Among conventional munitions, clusters of fragmentation-type bombs are more effective against personnel than are large high-explosive weapons. Again, even if an atomic bomb blasted an enemy off the side of a hill, it could not prevent replacements from moving into the old positions. One simulation of the use of nuclear attacks to support ground operations, Operation Hudson Harbor, found that "timely identification of large masses of enemy troops [had] been extremely rare" and that "troops in the forward areas" were generally "dug in in such a manner as to be afforded protection from airburst of atomic weapons." Finally, the main targets of aerial interdiction (supply lines) could most expediently be destroyed by conventional munitions. In short, the battlefield offered few suitable targets for atomic weapons, and when it did, they were hard to detect in time for attack.[109]

Two facts indicate that the Chinese were impressed with the effects of atomic blasts against population centers. First, beginning at the end of 1950, raw materials and industrial machinery were shifted from coastal areas into the interior. Second, during the Korean War, Chinese leaders began to consider civil defense problems related to nuclear weapons and to implement concrete defensive measures. U.S. intelligence reported air-raid drills and the building of air-raid shelters and anti-aircraft facilities in Shanghai, Beijing, Shenyang, Guangdong, Hubei, and other places. Also reported were

---

[108] Foot, *Substitute for Victory*, p. 177.
[109] Calingaert, "Nuclear Weapons and the Korean War," pp. 186–88.

evacuations of population, heavy industrial equipment, and other supplies from Shenyang, Guangzhou, Beijing, Shanghai, and cities along the Manchuria-Korea border.[110]

Finally, the Soviet extended nuclear deterrence on which the Chinese relied was withdrawn. Chinese wartime rhetoric indicated heavy reliance on Soviet Union to discourage the United States from employing atomic weapons: "The atomic bomb is now no longer monopolized by the U.S. The Soviet Union has it too. If the U.S. dares to use the atomic bombs, she naturally will get retaliation, and deservedly." Similarly, "The possession by the Soviet Union of the atomic weapons . . . means, first of all, that the American atom monopolists have been deprived of the possibility of carrying out threats and blackmail against other countries." U.S. intelligence and others reported that during much of the war, "the Chinese were certain that if Manchuria were attacked the Soviets would intervene."[111]

However, just as American nuclear capability and offensive intentions were increasing in Korea during the spring of 1953, Soviet willingness to extend deterrence was on the wane, and the Chinese recognized as much. Stalin's death may have contributed to this shift, although Soviet foreign policy appears to have been seeking reduced tensions with the West even before he died in March 1953. From the end of 1952 onward, Soviet official rhetoric called for peace and improved economic relations with the West. In March, Soviet leaders took the occasion of Stalin's funeral to indicate to foreign diplomats their desire to see Korean hostilities ended.[112]

The Soviet Union responded to the nuclear buildup and threats by reducing, rather than increasing, its commitment to defend China. Most important, the Soviets withdrew their pilots in May 1953, and the Chinese and North Koreans had to go it alone. Throughout the war, Chinese and North Korean pilots had fared substantially worse than Soviet pilots against better-trained American pilots. The Chinese problems in air-to-air combat were confirmed in May, when, in the absence of Soviet-piloted fighters, fifty-six MiGs were downed for the loss of a solitary F-86.[113] The upshot of the withdrawal of Soviet pilots was that China's capacity for defense against nuclear air strikes was substantially reduced.

In the Korean War, American military pressure achieved two coercive successes. First, during the summer and fall of 1951 conventional denial compelled the Communists to concede the future presence of U.S. troops in

---

[110] Ryan, *Chinese Attitudes*, p. 108.

[111] Quotations from Whiting, *China Crosses*, p. 142; Ryan, *Chinese Attitudes*, p. 75; Claingaert, "Nuclear Weapons and the Korean War," p. 196.

[112] Simmons, *Strained Alliance*, pp. 223–28; Shulman, *Stalin's Foreign Policy Reappraised*, chap. 10; and Foot, "Nuclear Coercion," pp. 107–9.

[113] Futrell, *Air Force in Korea*, pp. 653, 698; Jackson, *Air War over Korea*, p. 153.

South Korea as well as the movement of the inter-Korean boundary from the Thirty-eighth Parallel to the military frontline somewhat north of the parallel. Second, in June 1953 Eisenhower's nuclear threats persuaded the Chinese and North Koreans to accept the principle of voluntary repatriation of prisoners of war, thus ending the war.

Four implications from this case can be drawn for the denial theory of coercion I offer in this book. First, the conventional air campaigns of the Korean War support the proposition that conventional coercion is not a function of civilian vulnerability. Despite several attempts to use air power to attack civilian morale, there is no evidence that any coercive leverage was generated.

Second, strategic air interdiction also contributed relatively little to coercive success. The concessions in 1951 were due to the successes of UN ground forces assisted by close air support and operational interdiction. Once the territorial issues were settled and ground war became static, air planners' confidence that strategic interdiction could by itself force an armistice was unwarranted. Ignorance of how conventional armies work, how engineers can work around various problems, and how supply shortages can be overcome in the absence of intense ground action to strain logistic networks foiled the plans of airmen searching for a pure air solution to the conflict. The effects of this ignorance should worry future air power advocates who might value expertise in air operations to the exclusion of comparable expertise in other areas.

Third, the Korean case supports the proposition that nuclear coercion can work when it is credible, but it is likely to be credible only when the coercer enjoys superiority so great that it need not fear retaliation in kind. Nuclear coercion succeeded in 1953 where it had failed in 1951 because the Chinese could no longer depend on Soviet extended deterrence.

Finally, even when it succeeds the rewards of military coercion are often meager. All that was accomplished by conventional denial was to ratify a territorial status quo that neither side had much prospect of changing, while nuclear coercion achieved even less, purchasing for the UN the right to return some 16,000 Chinese prisoners of war.

[6]

Vietnam, 1965–1972

The American bombing of Vietnam is a classic example of conventional coercion. Unable or unwilling to commit the ground forces necessary to win decisively in the South, the United States attempted to compel Hanoi to alter its behavior by using powerful air forces to bypass the battlefield and strike directly at North Vietnam. The aim was to force Hanoi to cease supporting the insurgency in the South and to enter serious negotiations for peace between North and South Vietnam. The United States conducted two major series of bombing campaigns against North Vietnam, Lyndon Johnson's Rolling Thunder from 1965 to 1968, which failed, and Richard Nixon's Freedom Train and Linebacker campaigns in 1972, which succeeded in forcing concessions. The failure of Rolling Thunder extended the war by four years, during which approximately twenty thousand Americans and hundreds of thousands of Vietnamese lost their lives, whereas the success of the Linebacker bombings finally enabled the United States to escape the unpopular war.[1]

Although the bombing of the North has generated heated debate on many different dimensions,[2] my task is to explain why American coercive efforts succeeded or failed. In fact, the air war against North Vietnam is the

[1] Rolling Thunder's failure also contributed to the collapse of Johnson's presidency, whereas the later success may have contributed to Nixon's reelection. Herbert Y. Schandler, *The Unmaking of a President: Lyndon Johnson and Vietnam* (Princeton: Princeton University Press, 1977).

[2] For the moral and legal controversy over the bombing of North Vietnam, see Ernest W. Lefever, *Ethics and World Politics: Four Perspectives* (Baltimore: Johns Hopkins University Press, 1972); Hays W. Parks, "Rolling Thunder and the Law of War," *Air University Review* 33 (January–February 1982): 2–23; idem, "Linebacker and the Law of War," *Air University Review* 34 (January–February, 1983): 2–30; William V. O'Brian, *The Conduct of Just and Limited War* (New York: Praeger, 1981), pp. 91–126; and Richard A. Falk, ed., *The Vietnam War and International Law*, 4 vols. (Princeton: Princeton University Press, 1969–76).

most studied case of conventional coercion. The most extreme position holds that coercion is likely to fail under almost any set of circumstances.[3] Another group contend that coercion succeeds only when powerful ultimatums are issued under political, military, and diplomatic circumstances that all favor the assailant.[4] Still another sees the major obstacle to success as excessive civilian control over military operations.[5] Contrary to these views, the air war against North Vietnam suggests that success is possible, but that the critical leverage in conventional coercion comes from exploiting the vulnerabilities in the opponent's military strategy, not from threats or costs to civilians.

The principal goals of the first major bombing campaign, Rolling Thunder, which ran from 2 March 1965 through 31 October 1968, were to coerce the North Vietnamese into halting the infiltration of men and supplies into South Vietnam and entering into peace negotiations. In pursuit of these aims, Rolling Thunder inflicted costs and risks primarily on civilians. Military targets were also bombed, but these attacks had little effect on Hanoi's military strategy, because the guerrilla campaign being fought in this period was largely immune to conventional air attack. As a result, the North Vietnamese were not coerced.

In 1972 Richard Nixon began another series of air campaigns against the North. Freedom Train, in April, sought to compel North Vietnam to cease its ground offensive in the South and to accept a cease-fire. Freedom Train also focused on civilian vulnerabilities, and also failed completely. Nixon then launched another air offensive, known as Linebacker I, lasting from 10 May until 23 October 1972. Linebacker I did succeed in persuading Hanoi to halt its ground offensive and to accept U.S. terms for the peace accords. Yet the accords were not signed immediately, because South Vietnam stalled negotiations, and this hiatus encouraged Hanoi to back away from the agreement. To force the North back to the table, Nixon ordered another air

---

[3] Wallace J. Thies, *When Governments Collide: Coercion and Diplomacy in the Vietnam Conflict, 1964–1968* (Berkeley: University of California Press, 1980); Andrew Pierre, "America Down, Russia Up: The Changing Political Role of Military Power," *Foreign Policy*, no. 4 (Fall 1971): 163–87; and Colin S. Gray, "What Rand Hath Wrought," *Foreign Policy*, no. 4 (Fall 1971): 111–29.

[4] Alexander L. George, *Some Thoughts on Graduated Escalation*, RM-4844-PR (Santa Monica, Calif.: Rand Corporation, December 1965); and William E. Simons, "The Vietnam Intervention, 1964–65," in Alexander L. George, Simons, and David K. Hall, *Limits of Coercive Diplomacy: Laos, Cuba, and Vietnam* (Boston: Little, Brown, 1971), pp. 144–210.

[5] William W. Momyer, *Air Power in Three Wars* (Washington, D.C.: Department of Defense, Department of the Air Force, 1978); and Admiral U. S. Grant Sharp, *Strategy for Defeat: Vietnam in Retrospect* (San Rafael, Calif.: Presidio Press, 1978). In addition to these basic camps, more nuanced approaches are Guenter Lewy, *America in Vietnam* (New York: Oxford University Press, 1978); Tad Szulc, *The Illusion of Peace: Foreign Policy in the Nixon-Kissinger Years* (New York: Viking, 1978); Leslie H. Gelb with Richard K. Betts, *The Irony of Vietnam: The System Worked* (Washington, D.C.: Brookings, 1979); Mark Clodfelter, *The Limits of Air Power: The American Bombing of North Vietnam* (New York: Free Press, 1989).

campaign on 18 December 1972 known as Linebacker II. It lasted eleven days and led to the achievement of a cease-fire agreement. Both Linebacker campaigns ignored civilian vulnerabilities and concentrated instead on damaging Hanoi's military capabilities. They succeeded because Hanoi had switched from a guerrilla to a conventional war strategy, which was vulnerable to an air offensive.[6]

JOHNSON'S AIR WAR AGAINST NORTH VIETNAM

Why did the Rolling Thunder air campaign, which pounded the North Vietnamese homeland with hundreds of thousands of bombs over three years fail to coerce a settlement? I believe that North Vietnam during the Johnson years was essentially immune to coercion with air power. The Johnson administration hoped that bombing could successfully conclude the war more quickly and cheaply than large-scale ground warfare by inflicting costs and risks primarily on civilians. Military targets were also bombed in conjunction with events on the battlefield. Conventional air power, however, especially as used here, was not destructive enough to affect civilian morale decisively, nor could it seriously hamper the North's military strategy, because the guerrilla campaign being fought in this period was largely immune to conventional air attack. Rolling Thunder, therefore, could not compel Hanoi to abandon its territorial ambitions. The United States and North Vietnamese did reach an "understanding" on 10 May 1968, but this did not represent a coercive success. The North made no significant conces-

---

[6] The relation between North Vietnam's strategy and the effectiveness of U.S. air power is briefly discussed in many articles and books, but only two scholars deal with the subject at any length. Guenter Lewy demonstrates that Rolling Thunder and Linebacker both destroyed large numbers of military targets, but Rolling Thunder had no effect on the guerrilla war, whereas Linebacker played a significant role in thwarting North Vietnam's 1972 massive conventional offensive. Mark Clodfelter goes a step farther, contending that the principal differences in the political impact of air power had less to do with tactical and technological improvements by the U.S. Air Force than with North Vietnam's shift from a guerrilla to a conventional military strategy. Both books are valuable contributions that should be studied closely by anyone seriously interested in understanding the air war against North Vietnam; their comprehensive research explodes key myths. Lewy demonstrates that American leaders were far more careful to avoid collateral civilian damage than was recognized at the time. Clodfelter shows that as of 1989 the Air Force, though professing to have taken the lessons of Vietnam to heart, had in fact ignored those that are most significant for the future of American air strategy.

My analysis goes beyond these works by developing propositions about military coercion that are generally applicable across space and time. Because Lewy and Clodfelter are solely interested in explaining the Vietnam case, they do not disentangle factors unique to a particular case from those common to a range of cases. In addition, I want to test the explanatory power of competing propositions. Lewy and Clodfelter do not distinguish among Schelling, Douhet, and denial models of coercion, or even between civilian and military vulnerabilities as a basis for coercion. Thus, neither provides much insight into the general conditions when coercive air power succeeds.

sions, refused to confirm the existence of the agreement publicly, and in any case began violating it immediately.[7]

Any explanation of failure or success in a specific case must address four questions. First, what were the goals of the air offensive? Was it pursued for coercive purposes alone, or were other goals also important? Second, what coercive strategies were considered and adopted? Were they pursued in their most ambitious form or truncated to conform to political and organizational constraints? Third, how was the campaign conducted? How fully were the requirements of each proposed strategy achieved in practice? Finally, what ultimately explains the failure or success of each strategy?

Goals of Rolling Thunder

Rolling Thunder is often characterized as a policy undermined by rival objectives. President Johnson's advisers, so the argument goes, agreed on the necessity for bombing, but each sought different and divergent aims. This bureaucratic disunity was exacerbated by tensions in civil-military relations. The military, it is said, relentlessly advocated more bombing, and the civilians backed a restrained policy of gradualism. In this environment of "consensus without agreement," the air campaign was stillborn.[8]

This diagnosis is not accurate. In fact, there was broad consensus among administration officials about the goals of Rolling Thunder: it was meant to dissuade the North from infiltrating men and supplies into the South and to force Hanoi to negotiate a peace settlement. Although some officials, particularly McGeorge Bundy, believed that the air campaign would also bolster South Vietnamese morale and reaffirm the credibility of the American commitment to resist revolutionary activity in the Third World, these additional goals were not inconsistent with the objective of coercing North Vietnam. In fact, their achievement depended at least in part on the ability of the United States to conduct a successful coercive campaign.

The debate within the administration was not over aims; it was over strategy. Ordered to initiate contingency planning for coercion, Johnson's advisers made an exhaustive search for options and produced three competing strategies. Johnson's civilian advisers, the Air Force, and the Army each favored a different coercive strategy, variants of the Schelling, Douhet, and denial models.[9] In the event, these three strategies took turns dominating the conduct of Rolling Thunder.

---

[7] Lewy, *America in Vietnam*, pp. 388–89.

[8] These arguments are made most persuasively by James Clay Thompson, *Rolling Thunder: Understanding Policy and Program Failure* (Chapel Hill: University of North Carolina Press, 1980), pp. 25–26.

[9] The military chiefs were not completely at odds with each other. They agreed that the air war should escalate rapidly and that negotiations with Hanoi should not begin until after the main weight of the air effort had been delivered. Thus they were in accord on timing issues

Coercive Strategies in Rolling Thunder

Johnson's civilian advisers believed North Vietnam could be coerced by threats against its population and economy, and they proposed what is best described as a "lenient" Schelling strategy, which threatened relatively mild penalties compared to the scale of damage the United States could have inflicted. Limited bombing would subject the North's industrial economy to gradually increasing risk, and direct attacks on the population, such as hitting cities or dikes, would be avoided. The key proponents of this scheme were Defense Secretary Robert McNamara, his assistant John McNaughton, Joint Chiefs of Staff Chairman Maxwell Taylor, Director of Central Intelligence John McCone, Ambassador Henry Cabot Lodge, Deputy National Security Adviser Walt W. Rostow and Assistant Secretary of State William Bundy. The attraction of senior civilian advisers to Schelling's ideas was not an accident, since his views on coercive warfare were widely respected within the national security community, and John McNaughton, one of Robert McNamara's closest advisers on Vietnam strategy, was a dedicated devotee of Schelling.[10]

This strategy had four components. First, North Vietnam was to be coerced by the threat to destroy its nascent industrial base. Throughout 1964, the intelligence community stressed that "we have many indications that the Hanoi leadership is acutely aware and nervously aware of the extent to which North Vietnam's transportation system and industrial plant is vulnerable to attack."[11] Johnson's civilian advisers agreed, as signified by Rostow's famous quip: "Ho has an industrial complex to protect: he is no longer a guerrilla fighter with nothing to lose."[12] The connection between air raids on the North Vietnamese homeland and the insurgency in the South is perhaps best revealed in Rostow's memo to Dean Rusk: "If, despite communist efforts, the U.S. attacks continued, Hanoi's leaders would have to ask themselves whether it was not better to suspend their support of Viet Cong military action rather than suffer the destruction of their major military facilities and the industrial sector of their economy. . . . Our most basic problem is, therefore, how to persuade them that a continuation of their present policy

---

and concurred that civilian micromanagement had no place in the conduct of military operations, but they disagreed about the sources of coercive leverage, the relative importance of types of targets, and the ways in which the air campaign would influence Hanoi's behavior. On the views of the military, see Clodfelter, *Limits of Air Power*, pp. 101–58; and Gelb and Betts, *Irony of Vietnam*, pp. 96–180.

[10] See Fred Kaplan, *The Wizards of Armageddon* (New York: Simon and Schuster, 1983), pp. 332–35.

[11] "Probable Consequences of Certain U.S. Actions with Respect to Vietnam and Laos," DDRS (Declassified Documents Reference System), 1986, no. 39, 23 May 1964, p. 7. These volumes are published by Carrollton Press of Washington, D.C.

[12] Rostow quoted in *The Pentagon Papers: The Defense Department History of United States Decision-making in Vietnam*, Senator Gravel edition, vol. 3 (Boston: Beacon Press, 1971), p. 153.

will risk major destruction in North Vietnam."[13] The civilians were convinced that placing its industrial assets at risk would create a powerful incentive for Hanoi to abandon its support for the insurgency.

Second, the use of force was to be controlled to keep the hostage healthy. This group recognized that coercion based on the risk of punishment imposed strict boundaries on the scale of the campaign. If the hostage were killed, the threat of future damage would be nullified. As McNamara wrote to the president, the campaign "should be structured to capitalize on fear of future attacks. At any time, 'pressure' on the DRV [Democratic Republic of Vietnam—North Vietnam] depends not upon the *current* level of bombing but rather upon the credible threat of *future* destruction which can be avoided by agreeing to negotiate or agreeing to some settlement in negotiations."[14]

Third, the campaign would be orchestrated to tighten the noose gradually in recognizable and conspicuous ways, creating a discernible pattern of escalation which would convince Hanoi of American willingness to inflict ever-increasing costs to achieve its political goals. Thus, Maxwell Taylor favored "a gradual, orchestrated acceleration of tempo measured in terms of frequency, size, number and/or geographic location. . . . An upward trend in any or all of these forms of intensity will convey signals which, in combination, should present to the DRV leaders a vision of inevitable, ultimate destruction if they do not change their ways."[15] Indeed, politically driven timing considerations took priority over operational planning. Although a number of campaign scenarios were drafted, no firm targeting schedule was ever made. As long as the campaign moved from noneconomic toward main industrial targets, advance preparation of the details was not considered especially important. The key was to adhere to a pattern of mounting pressure on industry. As McNaughton explained, "The escalating actions might be naval pressures or mining of harbors or they might be made up of air strikes against North Vietnam moving from southern to northern targets, from targets associated with infiltration . . . to targets of military then industrial importance."[16]

The fourth component was coordination between military action and secret diplomacy. In order to tailor military pressure to the course of diplomacy, careful civilian control over the conduct of air operations would be required. William Bundy, in particular, repeatedly emphasized that progressive military pressure "would be designed for maximum control at all stages to permit interruption at some appropriate point or points for nego-

[13] "Memorandum for Secretary of State from W. W. Rostow," DDRS, vol. 1988, no. 326, 23 November 1964, p. 2.
[14] "Memorandum for the President from Robert S. McNamara (TOP SECRET)," DDRS, vol. 1987, no. 1344, 30 July 1965, p. 4.
[15] Taylor quoted in *Pentagon Papers*, 3: 316.
[16] McNaughton quoted ibid., p. 200.

tiations, while seeking to maintain throughout a credible threat of further military pressures."[17]

In short, the civilians' vision of coercive air power would work by threatening industrial assets, creating a powerful incentive for Hanoi to bargain away its support for the insurgency to ensure the survival of its nascent industrial economy.

The air force proposed a different strategy, a "genteel" Douhet plan, which also focused on civilian vulnerabilities but aimed at raising current costs rather than future risks. The architect of this strategy was General Curtis E. LeMay, then Air Force Chief of Staff, assisted by his successor, General John P. McConnell. Battlefield commanders also lent their support to this strategy.

The air chiefs did not intend to target civilians or the civilian economy directly, but unlike Johnson's nonmilitary advisers, they preferred to destroy, rather than simply threaten, the North's industrial base. They believed destruction of North Vietnam's industrial war potential would wreak havoc on the country's political and social fabric. In LeMay's words, "The military task confronting us is to make it so expensive for the North Vietnamese that they will stop their aggression against South Vietnam and Laos. If we make it too expensive for them, they *will* stop."[18] Destroying the North's industrial economy appears to have been valued more for its effect on civilian morale than for reducing the flow of military goods into the South. For instance, the rationale for closing the port of Haiphong was not to interdict battlefield hardware (all military goods arrived by land from China) but to weaken civilian morale: "The sustained effects would result in a gradual degradation of the will and morale of the populace. The risk of degrading the viability of the North Vietnamese governmental processes would be increased."[19] With this emphasis on weakening civilian morale, the air staff held true to the essentials of Douhet. Nevertheless, the strategy can be called "genteel," inasmuch as civilian lives would not be intentionally attacked. This forbearance also had the virtue of helping to shield the strategy from domestic criticism.

The air force planners meant to hit not just a small number of critical targets in critical industries, as had been done in precision bombing against Germany in World War II. Rather, they planned to obliterate *all* industrial and major transportation targets as well as air defense assets. Indeed, although genuine industrial targets numbered fewer than thirty, the Rolling Thunder campaign would actually destroy ninety-four economic and military sites. Further, speedy execution was seen as important for its shock

[17] Bundy quoted ibid., p. 611.
[18] Curtis E. LeMay with MacKinlay Kantor, *Mission with LeMay* (Garden City, N.Y.: Doubleday, 1965), p. 564.
[19] "JCS View of Military Campaign against North Vietnam," DDRS, 1986, no. 132, June 1967, p. 38.

value among civilians.[20] The sudden violence of the campaign would create panic and divert Hanoi's attention away from the South toward its own internal problems. Admiral U.S. Grant Sharp, commander in chief, Pacific, said destruction of the North's industrial war potential would induce "a feeling of helplessness among the military and general frustration, anxiety, and fear among the people."[21]

The third proposed strategy aimed to exploit military vulnerabilities, thwarting Hanoi's ability to succeed on the battlefields of the South. The main supporter of this strategy was JCS Chairman General Earle G. Wheeler, who had replaced Taylor in August 1964. Army Chief of Staff General Harold K. Johnson also backed it, as did theater commanders such as General William Momyer and Admiral U.S. Grant Sharp.

The nucleus of this plan was the use of air power to limit the infiltration of men and equipment into the South, thus undermining Hanoi's support for the southern insurgency. If the battlefield were isolated, Viet Cong (VC) combat capabilities would depreciate rapidly. Unable to achieve military victory in South Vietnam, Hanoi would be compelled to seek negotiations.

In accordance with this view, General Wheeler and his representatives stressed the importance of diminishing infiltration from North Vietnam over other aspects of the air campaign. Wheeler said, "Most important, in my view, is the application of as much force as we possibly can in a given period against the lines of communication in order to destroy, hopefully, and at least disrupt and attrite the flow of supplies to the south."[22] The strategy was stated even more clearly by a JCS representative: "The actual U.S. requirement with respect to the DRV is reduction of the *rate of delivery* of support to the VC, to levels below their minimum necessary sustaining level."[23]

Executing Rolling Thunder

Rolling Thunder was conducted in four phases, distinguished by different guiding strategies. Driven by swelling congressional and public pressure to find coercive leverage over North Vietnam, all three of the strategies advocated by Johnson's civilian and military advisers were tried in turn. At first the bombing followed the civilians' lenient Schelling strategy, next the

[20] Initially, destruction of all ninety-four targets was to occur in just sixteen days. Subsequent plans, however, extended the schedule to forty-six days to take account of delays from bad weather. Still, these recommendations consistently followed the same pattern: first to strike infiltration targets in Laos and the North Vietnamese panhandle, then to suppress the North's air defense network, and finally to attack the remaining military and industrial targets and restrike missed or regenerated sites. *Pentagon Papers* 3: 629.

[21] Sharp quoted in Clodfelter, *Limits of Air Power*, p. 106.

[22] U.S. Congress, Senate Committee on Armed Services, Preparedness Investigating Subcommittee, *Air War against North Vietnam*, 90th Cong., 1st sess., pt. 2 (16 August 1967), p. 150, hereinafter cited as Senate Hearings.

[23] *Pentagon Papers* 3: 213.

Army's strategy of denial by interdiction, and finally the Air Force's genteel Douhet. This evolution can be identified by tracing the changes in targeting and timing considerations guiding the campaign.

In each period, the tonnage allocated to and damage inflicted on each target set measures the weight of each strategy, for each would emphasize a different mix of strikes against fixed-site economic, transportation, and military targets, and armed reconnaissance missions against broad areas in which mobile or temporary military targets might be found. If appropriately implemented, perfect execution of the lenient Schelling strategy would not include any armed reconnaissance and would progress gradually from fixed military targets northward toward economic targets. Perfect execution of interdiction would concentrate on armed reconnaissance, transportation, and military missions. Perfect execution of the genteel Douhet strategy would avoid armed reconnaissance and emphasize economic and transportation targets.

With respect to timing, the perfect Schelling strategy would smoothly and gradually increase the tempo of air operations, interrupting it only for diplomatic signaling. The perfect interdiction strategy would apply steady pressure at the highest sustainable level to grind down the enemy's military capacity. The perfect Douhet strategy would destroy as many targets as possible in a sudden, vicious thunderclap for maximum psychological effect.

Unfortunately, there are important gaps in the month-by-month figures on combat sorties flown and tonnages dropped against North Vietnam. Therefore, the evolution of air strategies during the campaign cannot be reliably reconstructed based on timing. Accordingly, I rely on target selection patterns to identify the strategies. This approach requires data about the types of targets struck in each period but not detailed sequences of sortie rates (see Table 10).

The first phase, spring-summer 1965, was dominated by the lenient Schelling model, whose main objective was to elevate the risk to industry by establishing an obvious pattern of escalation. Bombing focused on a list of fixed targets prepared by the Joint Chiefs of Staff (58 percent of total tonnage), rather than armed reconnaissance (42 percent). Moreover, of bombs dropped on the JCS target set, most were on military (65 percent) and transportation (32 percent) targets, compared to only 3 percent on industry.[24] The bombing was also orchestrated to move progressively farther north. Rolling Thunder 8, in March 1965, attacked targets in the North Vietnamese "panhandle," south of the nineteenth parallel; Rolling Thunder 14 and 15, in May, included targets up to the twentieth parallel; and Rolling Thunder 21 in July struck several isolated targets above the twentieth parallel, such as the port of Hon Gay.[25]

[24] CIA memo, "Effectiveness of the Air Campaign," table A13; "Memorandum for the President from McNamara," p. 6.
[25] "Joint Message Rolling Thunder 8," DDRS, vol. 1988, no. 1546, 24 March 1965; "Rolling Thunder 14," DDRS, vol. 1987, no. 2006, 16 May 1965; "Thunder 15, Air Strikes against Objectives in North Vietnam," DDRS, vol. 1987, no. 1339, 17 May 1965; "Joint Message Rolling Thunder 21," DDRS, vol. 1987, no. 2011, 1 June 1965.

Table 10. Fixed targets in North Vietnam hit in 1965

Target type	JCS Target list		Hit in 1965	
Transportation	74	(31%)[a]	49	(32%)
Military	141	(58%)[b]	97	(65%)
Industrial	27	(11%)[c]	7	(3%)
Totals	242		153	

SOURCE: CIA intelligence memorandum, "The Effectiveness of the Air Campaign Against North Vietnam, 1 January–30 September 1966", DDRS, vol. 1986, no. 2539, December 1966, table A19. Figures for total targets are as of September 1966.
[a]61 bridges, 5 rail yards, 8 locks.
[b]91 barracks and depots, 13 petroleum, oil, and lubricant sites, 15 port and naval facilities, 5 communication sites, 11 airfields, 6 radar and surface-to-air missile sites.
[c]19 power plants, 8 manufacturing plants.

The second phase, summer 1965 through winter 1966–1967, concentrated on air interdiction, with the main objective of disrupting the North's ability to infiltrate men and supplies. The period from August 1965 to September 1966 is representative. During this time, the weight of the campaign shifted from the JCS list (7 percent) to armed reconnaissance (93 percent); only twenty-two JCS fixed targets, most of them petroleum facilities, were struck for the first time.[26] The Joint Chiefs had maintained that these POL targets were the core of North Vietnam's infiltration potential and that their destruction would have an immediate and significant impact on its ability to send war materiel south.[27] The attacks were an operational success; some 70 percent of the North Vietnamese POL storage capacity was destroyed.[28] The increasing emphasis on interdiction is also apparent in the geographic distribution of the air effort. In 1966 about 70 percent of the total sorties were concentrated in the North Vietnamese panhandle south from Thanh Hoa to the demilitarized zone, and only 7 percent were flown in the northeastern area of Hanoi and Haiphong.[29]

The third phase, spring-fall 1967, saw the dominance of the Douhet model. By this point, nearly all the JCS fixed targets located in the panhandle had been destroyed. With success nowhere in sight and under pressure from Congress and public opinion, Johnson removed the remaining political constraints on bombing. A rapid "sharp knock" was struck against the

[26] CIA Memo, "Effectiveness of the Air Campaign," table A13.
[27] *Pentagon Papers* 4: 66.
[28] Raphael Littauer and Norman Uphoff, eds., *The Air War in Indochina* (Boston: Beacon Press, 1972), p. 39.
[29] CIA memo, "Effectiveness of the Air Campaign," pp. 1–7.

vast majority of the industrial and transportation targets situated in and around Hanoi, Haiphong, and the Chinese buffer zone. Targets included electric power facilities, steel, cement, explosives, and chemical plants, and key rail bridges such as the Paul Doumer and Canal des Rapides bridges near Hanoi. Following this assault, few options for increasing the bombing pressure against the North remained because nearly all the targets had been destroyed. As one study noted, "the only remaining possibilities for increased military action against the North were mining and bombing of ports, bombing dikes and locks, and a land invasion of North Vietnam."[30]

In the fourth and final phase of Rolling Thunder, from April to November 1968, the bombing was gradually deescalated. Public opinion had turned against the war, and Johnson was under intense political pressure to reduce American involvement.[31] During this phase, the bombing was rolled back from the Hanoi-Haiphong area, first to the twentieth parallel, then to the nineteenth. Although the bombing retracted geographically, the number of sorties flown for interdiction purposes actually increased as resources were released from missions farther north. After November 1968 aerial bombardment of North Vietnam effectively came to an end, with air interdiction continuing only in the immediate area above the demilitarized zone.[32]

In order to assess how well each strategy performed, we must know how faithfully actual operations adhered to the intended strategies. The conventional view is that the Rolling Thunder campaign failed to execute coherently any of the three proposed strategies. Not surprisingly, military officers charge that civilian intervention doomed operations that would have worked, and civilian analysts blame the bluntness of the military instrument for making signals ambiguous and for disrupting the delicate orchestration of force and diplomacy. In effect, both sides contend that errors in execution eroded the coercive effectiveness of Rolling Thunder.[33]

This conventional view is wrong. Although implementation problems existed, they did not cause coercion to fail. As a whole, the campaign largely satisfied the fundamental requirements of each strategy.

Rolling Thunder implemented the essential components of the lenient Schelling strategy. As the civilians intended, the structure of the bombing presented an obvious pattern of escalation toward industrial targets; it escalated progressively in conspicuous measures of intensity. The weekly average of sorties grew from 883 in 1965, to 1,050 in January–June 1966, to

[30] Ibid., p. 41.

[31] John E. Mueller, *War, Presidents, and Public Opinion* (New York: Wiley, 1973).

[32] Littauer and Uphoff, *Air War in Indochina*, p. 41.

[33] For standard civilian critiques, see Theodore Draper, in *No More Vietnams?* ed. Richard Pfeffer (New York: Harper and Row, 1968); Stephen Peter Rosen, "Vietnam and the American Theory of Limited War," *International Security* 7 (Fall 1982): 83–113; Thies, *When Governments Collide*; and Simons, "The Vietnam Intervention." The military's view is ably represented by Momyer, *Airpower in Three Wars*; and Sharp, *Strategy for Defeat*.

2,637 in July–December 1966; it declined slightly to 1,985 in January–March 1967 but soared to 3,150 in April–June 1967. Bomb tonnage also rose from 63,000 in 1965, to 136,000 in 1966, and to 226,000 in 1967.[34] Target selection matched the geographical prescriptions of the Schelling model, starting with military targets near the DMZ and gradually advancing northward toward the industrial areas of Hanoi and Haiphong and the China buffer zone. Especially important, North Vietnam's industrial base was left intact until quite late in the air campaign, thus preserving the health of the hostage so that the victim would still fear its loss. Only mission types did not match an ideal Schelling strategy, in that the campaign included a large number of armed reconnaissance missions of more relevance to an interdiction strategy. This was not a serious failing, however, because the campaign did adhere to the key requirement of continually escalating risk.

Bombing and diplomacy, moreover, were closely coordinated. The charge that ambiguous signals were conveyed to Hanoi is overdrawn. It is based mainly on the public rhetoric of the Johnson administration and does not consider the secret channels through which Washington and Hanoi communicated.[35] Blair Seaborn, a Canadian official acting as an agent of the U.S. government in talks with Prime Minister Pham Van Dong, made a clear presentation of the U.S. position to Hanoi on 18 June 1964. Seaborn presented a carefully prepared statement that the United States wished Hanoi to cease its support for the Viet Cong, and containing the "explicit threat that if the conflict should escalate, the 'greatest devastation' would result for the North." Afterward, Seaborn reported that he had left the North Vietnamese in little doubt about U.S. intentions.[36] Thus what we know about communication with the North Vietnamese suggests that confusion over threats and demands did not seriously hinder U.S. coercion.[37]

---

[34] "Research Memorandum by Thomas Hughes, Director of Intelligence and Research, Department of State," DDRS, vol. 1986, no. 268, 16 November 1967; Littauer and Uphoff, *Air War in Indochina*, p. 281.

[35] Spokesmen for the Johnson administration, including the president himself, waffled in public about their intentions and demands toward North Vietnam. See *Pentagon Papers* 3: 291–92.

[36] Thies, *When Governments Collide*, p. 37.

[37] The bombing pauses are also wrongly accused of obstructing the success of the Schelling strategy. Some complain that they signaled weak resolve and so were counterproductive. Pausing as an incentive to initiate negotiations is perfectly appropriate to the Schelling strategy, however, and this was in fact the reason (other than holidays) for the three major pauses that occurred. Others criticize the military for disrupting the coordination of pauses and diplomatic initiatives, but the military did not bomb without the president's authorization during any of the halts, and Johnson was able to continue the longest pause (of thirty-seven days), despite vehement objections from senior military officers, until he became convinced that peace was not at hand.

The connection between force and diplomacy may have broken down, however, in taking advantage of possible diplomatic initiatives by Hanoi. In November 1966 there were indications from Warsaw that North Vietnamese representatives wished to meet with American representatives to initiate peace talks (the "Marigold" case). These discussions were not con-

The available evidence strongly indicates that Rolling Thunder did create an expectation of industrial damage in the minds of North Vietnamese leaders. Soon after the campaign began, Hanoi went to great lengths to improve its air defense network by coaxing its allies, the Soviet Union and China, to provide large numbers of surface-to-air missiles and some fighter aircraft. In addition, to reduce dependence on highly vulnerable industrial facilities, imports of industrial goods were increased and some light industries were dispersed. Finally, the rhetoric that North Vietnamese leaders directed toward Western audiences suggests that the geographic progression of the air campaign increased their anxiety about the risk that Hanoi and Haiphong would be bombed.[38]

Nor did implementation problems prevent the air interdiction strategy from being effective. The notion that interdiction was undermined by civilian control of air operations is a myth. To be sure, President Johnson and his advisers directly supervised the release of new targets for bombing.[39] Civilian planners agreed, however, that attacks should emphasize infiltration targets. During the second phase of Rolling Thunder in 1966, the Johnson administration permitted complete freedom for armed reconnaissance and restrikes of previously released targets throughout all of North Vietnam except for small areas around Hanoi, Haiphong, and the Chinese border.[40] By the late summer and fall of 1967, nearly all infiltration targets were subject to air attack. The rail lines between the Chinese border and Hanoi and between Hanoi and the port of Haiphong were severed many times and were essentially closed to traffic from September 1967 to January 1968.[41] With nearly the entire country open to air attack, military leaders had vast autonomy to interdict supplies before they reached South Vietnam.

It is also a myth that civilian-enforced bombing pauses seriously hindered the effectiveness of interdiction. The military complained that each pause in

summated because the North Vietnamese representatives failed to appear after American aircraft struck two targets near Hanoi. Nevertheless, blaming the military for the failure of Marigold is problematic. It is possible that the channel may not have been serious, for the North made no good-faith efforts, such as temporarily halting infiltration. Further, the circumstances surrounding the two air strikes, one on a railroad yard and the other on a vehicle depot, make it implausible that they were responsible for the failure of Marigold. At this point, the United States was launching thousands of sorties a month against North Vietnam, had only brief notice of the onset of these negotiations, and had in the past demonstrated its willingness to cease bombing. Under these circumstances, if the Marigold channel was so frail that it could wilt after just two air strikes, negotiations would likely have failed anyway.

[38] For example, see Harrison Salisbury, *Behind the Lines—Hanoi* (New York: Harper and Row, 1967), pp. 107–8.

[39] On Johnson's target selection, see David C. Humphrey, "Tuesday Lunch at the Johnson White House: A Preliminary Assessment," *Diplomatic History* 8 (Winter 1984): 81–101.

[40] The loosening of political restraints on targeting during 1966 is discussed in Sharp, *Strategy for Defeat*, pp. 119–20.

[41] CIA/DIA Bombing Appraisals, DDRS, vol. 1988, nos. 2032–34, October–December 1967.

the bombing would permit the North to rush through massive amounts of men and materiel. Because the insurgency was employing a guerrilla strategy which required very little logistic support from the North compared to the North's resupply capacity, pauses did in fact present a potentially serious problem. Thus, the insurgents could take advantage of a pause to stockpile supplies for future use, especially if the timing were known in advance. In fact, pauses were severely limited precisely because the military succeeded in persuading the civilians of this possibility. The bombing was halted eight times for a total of fewer than 60 days out of the 1,337 days of the campaign, and a single pause of 37 days, beginning at Christmas 1965, accounts for over half of the total.[42]

Field commanders were not starved for air assets to perform this mission. When General Momyer, the commander of the Seventh Air Force, was questioned on the subject before the Senate in summer 1967, he remarked: "We are operating at about maximum effort. And I do not believe under the circumstances putting in additional forces would significantly increase your disruption in the movement of men and supplies to the South."[43]

Finally, timing and mission types during most of Rolling Thunder were consistent with the requirements for air interdiction. Between summer 1965 and spring 1967, the campaign placed far greater emphasis on armed reconnaissance than on fixed targets, as interdiction advocates preferred.[44] With respect to timing, urgent destruction of military targets was not necessary because the North had a long-war strategy.[45] Consequently, the coercive potential of denial by interdiction did not depend on a swift campaign.[46]

[42] Clodfelter, *Limits of Air Power*, p. 119, lists the pauses.

[43] Senate Hearings, p. 132.

[44] When General Wheeler was asked in Senate hearings whether he would exchange a reduction of armed reconnaissance for authorization to strike the full package of fixed targets, he shunned the deal: "I would prefer to keep the present level . . . and slowly but surely obtain approval on the other points." Ibid., p. 151.

[45] Hanoi frequently indicated that it was prepared to wage a long war. In 1966 Pham Van Dong said, "We are preparing for a long war. How many years would you say? Ten, twenty— what do you think about twenty?" In Salisbury, *Behind the Lines*, p. 196. For similar statements, see Melvin Gurtov, *Hanoi on War and Peace*, P-3696 (Santa Monica, Calif.: Rand Corporation, 1967).

[46] To be sure, senior military commanders, particularly air force officers, vigorously advocated rapid destruction of as many targets as possible. Organizational motives can account for this preference. The military has a strong institutional bias toward quick over long wars, largely because of its desire to avoid casualties. Thus, it is not surprising to find military officers reluctant to wage protracted campaigns when quick blows are feasible. On the bias against casualties in military institutions, see Samuel P. Huntington, *The Soldier and the State: The Theory and Politics of Civil-Military Relations* (Cambridge: Harvard University Press, 1957), pp. 68–69. In the Vietnam case this bias explains why officers generally blame gradualism for the growth of North Vietnam's air defenses, an effect that increased the costs of air attack but not the eventual vulnerability of targets. For example, Admiral Sharp said: "Gradualism enabled North Vietnam to mount the most formidable air-defense system that has ever been used in combat history. . . . The result is that we have lost nearly 1000 planes over North Vietnam." Sharp, "We Could Have Won in Vietnam Long Ago," *Reader's Digest*, May 1969, p. 121.

During the first two phases of Rolling Thunder, the destruction of military and industrial infrastructure was postponed. These restraints were lifted in summer 1967 when the administration, responding to military complaints and congressional pressure, finally permitted the Air Force to execute its preferred strategy. The best benchmark against which to measure the destruction of North Vietnam's industrial war potential is the JCS list of fixed targets. Indeed, the air chiefs consistently favored the destruction of the entire set of these targets, which initially numbered 94, grew to 242 soon after Rolling Thunder began, and remained stable at about that level.[47]

How many of these targets were destroyed? In 1965, 158 of the targets were destroyed, but nearly all of these were military targets located below the twentieth parallel. In 1966, an additional 22 were hit. By summer 1967, only 57 targets remained unscathed, but these included the key industrial and transportation sites in the Hanoi-Haiphong quadrant.[48] In late summer and early fall 1967, Johnson released nearly all these targets, and by November all but five had reportedly been hit.[49] By December, nearly all North Vietnam's industrial war potential had been destroyed.[50]

What about the issue of timing? It has become almost commonplace for military leaders to complain about the gradual way in which the JCS target set was destroyed. They believe that the slow progression of Rolling Thunder violated the basic Douhet precept that the assailant must slam the adversary all at once for coercion to succeed. This possibility can be heavily discounted by the ineffectiveness of the 1967 "sharp knock," the pace of which closely approximated the Douhet model's prescription. The Air Force, accounting for delays in its program due to bad weather, planned for a campaign of eight to ten weeks: in fact, the assault lasted twelve weeks, from August to October, and restrikes continued during November and De-

[47] The best measure of implementation of the Douhet strategy would be the proportion of North Vietnamese industrial and transportation targets destroyed, but these data are not available for the crucial year 1967. We do know, however, that all the relevant targets were included in the JCS fixed target set, although that set also included a large number of purely military targets. Accordingly, the status of the JCS target set is the best substitute measure.

[48] For a detailed description of these 57 targets, see U.S. Congress, House Committee on Appropriations, Subcommittee on Department of Defense, *Department of Defense Appropriations: Bombings of North Vietnam*, Hearings, 93d Cong., 1st sess., 9–18 January 1973, pp. 278, 302, hereinafter cited as House Hearings.

[49] *Pentagon Papers* 4: 216. Because data on the sharp knock remain classified, there is still some ambiguity about the exact number of targets left untouched. A list of "major targets" struck by air in North Vietnam released at the end of 1968 by the Defense Department lists 228: 57 military barracks, 18 ammunition depots, 13 petroleum storage areas, 75 dispersed petroleum storage sites, 25 supply depots, 15 power plants, 8 port facilities, the country's only iron plant and cement plant, 11 airfields, and 4 naval facilities. If these figures are correct, 14 of the 242 JCS targets were not hit. The discrepancy may be accounted for by the possibility that the JCS did not recommend striking all the targets on its list. For the 1968 Department of Defense list, see Jon M. Van Dyke, *North Vietnam's Strategy for Survival* (Palo Alto, Calif.: Pacific Books, 1972), p. 27.

[50] Van Dyke, *North Vietnam's Strategy for Survival*, p. 27.

cember. Thus its duration closely approximated the air chiefs' plans. There is no evidence that executing the sharp knock in 1965 instead of 1967 would have produced better results.

Explaining the Failure of Rolling Thunder

All things considered, implementation problems cannot explain why Rolling Thunder failed. In fact, it failed because none of the strategies could exert much leverage against North Vietnam.

To understand why the Schelling strategy was ineffective, we must consider how Hanoi perceived the territorial interests it had at stake and the extent to which the Schelling strategy raised the risks of civilian damage. At stake in Rolling Thunder was the status of South Vietnam. North and South Vietnam had been separate only since 1954, and indeed, until the Tet offensive in 1968, the insurgents were mostly South Vietnamese. North Vietnam viewed the South as part of its homeland. Consequently, Hanoi's commitment to its territorial interest was based on the powerful motive of national cohesion.[51] In light of the importance Hanoi attached to South Vietnam, the lenient Schelling strategy did not create risks of sufficient magnitude to affect the North's political calculus.

The principal problem was that the threat of limited conventional bombing of industrial targets did not pose the risk of especially brutal civilian hardship. The industrial sector of North Vietnam's economy was not a highly valued asset. It was tiny by any standards, producing only about 12 percent of a gross national product of $1.6 billion in 1965. Indeed, few heavy industrial targets could be found to attack. When North Vietnam was first targeted, the JCS listed only eight industrial installations, and even after standards were lowered in 1965, the list included only twenty-four. Nor was this sector on the verge of rapid growth. North Vietnam's tiny industrial base was a legacy from the French, and its Communist allies showed little inclination or ability to assist with further development. Industrial progress was also stunted by domestic inadequacies—shortages of capital, skilled labor, and management—as well as by the government's preference to allocate resources according to ideological rather than economic criteria.[52]

Rolling Thunder did not pose high risks to the civilian economy as a whole either. Throughout the war, Hanoi waged an ardent propaganda campaign against the United States, claiming that U.S. bombing had damaged civilian sectors of the economy. For example, North Vietnam charged the United States with devastation of the dike system, the bulwark of North

[51] Richard K. Betts, "Interests, Burdens, and Persistence: Asymmetries between Washington and Hanoi," *International Studies Quarterly* 24 (December 1980): 520–24.

[52] *Pentagon Papers* 4: 57; CIA, "Outlook for North Vietnam," DDRS, vol. 1988, no. 72, 1964, p. 4.

Vietnam's agricultural economy. The destruction of dikes could flood rice paddies and so threaten a basic staple of the civilian diet, and floods could threaten civilians directly. In fact, however, North Vietnam's ninety-one dikes were never methodically targeted. Eight were struck because they supported waterways used for the transportation of military and economic goods.[53] In fall 1967 Hanoi claimed that twenty-four dikes had been breached, but U.S. intelligence determined that only four had been partially damaged by accident, with no evidence of flooding.[54]

Most important, the risks to population centers were low, Hanoi's propaganda again notwithstanding.[55] Civilians actually became less vulnerable to attack as the war progressed. In 1965 evacuation programs were initiated in all major cities and villages. U.S. intelligence estimated that the population of Hanoi fell from 475,000 in 1965 to 235,000 in 1967, and Haiphong declined from 220,000 to 55,000 during the same period.[56] More significant, the physical pattern of Rolling Thunder indicated no intention to kill large numbers of civilians. The great majority of destroyed targets were isolated from population centers. Also, Johnson's political advisers went to great lengths to avoid civilian casualties. Theater commanders were ordered to follow discriminating tactics that minimized collateral damage and estimates of civilian casualties were made before JCS targets were released. Thus, it is hardly surprising that actual civilian casualties were exceedingly low. From March 1965 to September 1966, for instance, U.S. intelligence estimated that 17,900 civilians had been killed or injured.[57] The entire Rolling Thunder campaign appears to have slain 52,000 civilians, or about 0.3 percent of North Vietnam's 1965 population.[58] This total is small in comparison to strategic bombing in World War II, when Japan suffered 2.2 million civilian casualties (3 percent of its population) and Germany 1.1 million (1.6 percent of its population).[59]

[53] Clodfelter, *Limits of Air Power*, pp. 126–27.

[54] CIA/DIA, "An Appraisal of the Bombing of North Vietnam through 16 October 1967," DDRS, vol. 1988, no. 2032, October 1967, p. 16.

[55] In September 1965 Hanoi asserted that Rolling Thunder had caused seventy-five thousand casualties; American intelligence estimated a much lower figure of about seven thousand. CIA memo, "Effectiveness of the Air Campaign," p. 13.

[56] CIA/DIA, "An Appraisal of the Bombing of North Vietnam through 16 November 1967," DDRS, vol. 1988, no. 2034, November 1967, p. 16.

[57] CIA Director Richard Helms, "Bombing Casualties in North Vietnam," DDRS, vol. 1985, no. 2319, 16 January 1967.

[58] NSSM (National Security Study Memorandum) 1 (1969), *Congressional Record*, vol. 118, part 13 (May 10, 1972), p. 16833.

[59]German casualties are reported in USSBS, *The Effects of Strategic Bombing on German Morale* (Washington, D.C.: GPO, 1947), 1: 7; German population in 1939 estimated at 67 million in USSBS, *The Effects of Strategic Bombing on the German War Economy* (Washington, D.C.: GPO, 1945), p. 202. Japanese casualty figures are from USSBS, *The Effects of Strategic Bombing on Japanese Morale* (Washington, D.C.: GPO, 1947), p. 1; Japanese population estimated at 73 million in 1940 from USSBS, *The Effects of Strategic Bombing on Japan's War Economy* (Washington, D.C.: GPO, 1946), p. 98.

Evaluation of the air interdiction aimed at choking off the logistical flow must address three questions: What was Hanoi's strategy from 1965 to 1968? What resources were required to carry on? Could aerial attack diminish these resources below the level necessary to continue? The character of North Vietnam's military strategy from 1965 to 1968 is still the subject of heated debate. The core issue is whether it was a conventional or a guerrilla strategy.[60] This debate continues despite the stark differences between these two forms of war. The principal objective in conventional war is destruction of enemy forces, generally by means of large-scale battles along relatively well defined fronts, with logistics flowing from rear areas to forward combat units. Guerrilla warfare, in contrast, aims to gain control over population, usually beginning with villages located in remote areas, and to use these as anchors to control still larger segments of the population and thus undermine support for the government. Guerrillas fight in small units and derive material support from the population under their control. This last point is critical: logistic support in guerrilla war flows from forward areas to the insurgent's rear bases, the reverse of the flow in conventional warfare. Further, these flows are generally very small.

During the Johnson years, the U.S. Army tried to fight the war largely as a conventional war. From its inception, the priorities of the Military Assistance Command–Vietnam were to seek out and destroy the enemy through large-scale operations relying on massive firepower in the form of helicopters, airpower, and defoliants.[61] Hanoi, however, followed an almost pure guerrilla strategy until after the Tet offensive in spring 1968. Viet Cong guerrillas were the principal force in the field. Even by August 1967, North Vietnamese troops (conventional forces) in the South totaled only 55,000, whereas the VC (guerrillas) numbered approximately 245,000.[62] Furthermore, the overwhelming number of engagements involved small units. By 1967 over 96 percent of all engagements took place at company strength or less, and battalion-size attacks by the enemy had dropped off from an average of 9.7 per month in late 1965 to 1.3 per month. Finally, much of the ground combat was at low levels of intensity, with enemy battalions averaging only one day of combat out of thirty.[63]

The next issue concerns the logistic support required by the guerrilla forces. Despite the Army's claims that the Communists could be forced to do battle and so rapidly exhaust their resources, it was the enemy that determined the frequency and length of combat. Far from being cornered, the

---

[60] The position that the war was conventional is prominently advocated by Harry G. Summers Jr., *On Strategy: A Critical Analysis of the Vietnam War* (Novato, Calif.: Presidio Press, 1982), pp. 76–77, 90. The best critique of this position is Andrew T. Krepinevich, *The Army and Vietnam* (Baltimore: Johns Hopkins University Press, 1986).

[61] Krepinevich, *Army and Vietnam*, pp. 58–65.

[62] Clodfelter, *Limits of Air Power*, p. 184.

[63] Krepinevich, *Army and Vietnam*, p. 188.

Communists initiated 88 percent of all engagements.[64] This ability to dictate the pace of battle allowed the Communist forces to wage war with minimal logistical support because they had the luxury of being able to expend stocks slowly and intermittently. Although they maintained well over 200,000 troops in the field from 1965 to 1968, their requirements for food, ammunition, medical supplies, and POL never exceeded roughly 380 tons a day. By contrast, *one* American infantry division consumes approximately 750 to 2,000 tons per day, depending on the intensity of battle.[65]

Their control over major segments of the rural population permitted the Communist forces to extract large resources from South Vietnam, greatly reducing their dependency on North Vietnam for supplies. Estimates of the tonnage of supplies that the southern insurgents had to receive from the North varied from 15 to 34 tons a day throughout this phase of the war.[66] Thus, as Senator Henry Jackson vividly put it, to run the war, the North needed to supply each soldier only ten ounces of provisions a day.[67] In short, guerrilla warfare required little in the way of supplies and next to nothing at all from North Vietnam.

The final issue is whether aerial bombardment could hinder North Vietnam's ability to support the insurgency. About this, there is no question: it could not. North Vietnamese industry was not an important source of war materiel—a fact that has received curiously little mention by the U.S. military. Its only factory of direct military importance, a small explosives plant, was destroyed. North Vietnam was primarily a funnel for military-related equipment produced in the USSR and the People's Republic of China.

Nor was North Vietnam's transportation system a good target for air attack. At first glance, it seemed highly vulnerable, largely because of the small number of narrow arteries.[68] In fact, however, this rudimentary system was amply durable and redundant. Rail and road lines were not used to full capacity and were supplemented by extensive waterways and a honeycomb of trails. For instance, truck traffic on Route 15 was estimated by the CIA to have used only 10 percent of the road's capacity in summer 1967. Given that the maximum reduction by U.S. bombing of the road capacity was 25 percent, even a doubled rate of effectiveness would still have left five

[64] Ibid.
[65] Clodfelter, *Limits of Air Power*, p. 134; James F. Dunnigan, *How to Make War: A Comprehensive Guide to Modern Warfare* (New York: Morrow, 1982), p. 318.
[66] For 15 tons, see McNamara in Senate Hearings, p. 299. For 34 tons, see Clodfelter, *Limits of Air Power*, p. 134.
[67] Jackson in Senate Hearings, p. 302.
[68] The keys to the North Vietnamese transportation network were four highways and two rail lines connecting China with Hanoi, and two highways and one rail line connecting Haiphong with Hanoi. Below Hanoi the network reduced to a single road before diverging between Route 15 (over the Mu Gai pass to the Ho Chi Minh trail) and Route 115 (to the DMZ). For a detailed description, see Keith R. Tidman, *The Operations Evaluation Group* (Annapolis: Naval Institute Press, 1984), p. 239.

times more than required.[69] Effective measures to circumvent cuts in the transportation network were also developed, which, together with the low requirements of the insurgency, gave the shipment of supplies a generous cushion. One ingenious technique, the use of cable bridges with removable decks, greatly reduced the vulnerability of bridges to aerial interdiction, for the cables were exceedingly hard to destroy, and the wooden decks could be prefabricated and rapidly replaced.[70] As a result, according to the *Pentagon Papers*, bombing could "put a low 'cap' on the force levels which North Vietnam can support in the South—but the 'cap' is well above present logistic supply levels."[71]

Evaluation of the Douhet strategy, which aimed to destroy the North's industrial base in one fell swoop, inflicting extreme civilian costs that would overwhelm Hanoi's territorial interests in the South, depends on whether destruction of the industrial economy would have significantly increased the costs North Vietnam had to pay. By this criterion, the strategy had little hope of success. The basic problem was that North Vietnam was already paying a tremendous price in blood to achieve its goals. Estimates of Communist losses from 1965 to 1974 range from 600,000 to 950,000.[72] Even the more conservative figure amounts to about 3 percent of the prewar population; it demonstrates a willingness to tolerate tremendous civilian punishment.

The genteel Douhet strategy added little to these costs, for it caused few additional casualties. In addition, not only was North Vietnam's industry puny but alternative methods of providing needed industrial services were cheap. For example, the loss of North Vietnam's major power plants in 1967 resulted only in temporary power shortages, and two thousand portable generators were sufficient to compensate for the absence of these facilities.[73] There were textile shortages and the 1967 rice harvest was below average, but no worse than in 1966.[74] In general, lost production was effectively offset by economic assistance from Hanoi's Communist allies. Prior to Rolling Thunder, North Vietnam received about $95 million a year in economic aid and almost no military aid. From 1965 to 1968, however, North Vietnam received approximately $600 million in economic aid and $1 billion in military

[69] CIA, "Evaluation of Alternative Programs for Bombing North Vietnam," DDRS, vol. 1986, no. 54, 1 June 1967, pp. 2–6.

[70] CIA intelligence memorandum, "Cable Bridges in North Vietnam," DDRS, vol. 1985, no. 2316, 20 September 1966.

[71] *Pentagon Papers* 4: 137.

[72] John E. Mueller, "The Search for the 'Breaking Point' in Vietnam," *International Studies Quarterly* 24 (December 1980): 507–9.

[73] Clodfelter, *Limits of Air Power*, p. 187.

[74] Drought contributed as much as bombing to the below-average harvest. CIA/DIA, "Appraisal of the Bombing through 16 October 1967," p. 14; CIA/DIA, "Appraisal of the Bombing through 16 November 1967," p. 16.

assistance, while sustaining a loss of $370 million in measurable physical damage from bombing.[75]

Despite the intensity of the third phase of bombing, there was little discernible effect on North Vietnamese civilian morale.[76] U.S. intelligence reported: "There have been no indications that difficulties associated with the bombing have been sufficient to force the regime to alter its policy on the war."[77]

Would a stern Douhet strategy have succeeded? Although the possibility of success cannot be completely dismissed, there are good reasons to doubt that more ambitious conventional air strategies would have worked. Haiphong could have been blockaded, and many military officers and political leaders contend in retrospect that such a blockade would have added enormously to the North's economic difficulties. This claim, however, is dubious. Although Haiphong was not actually blockaded during the Johnson years, the routes between Haiphong and Hanoi, the major redistribution center, were attacked, and this interdiction was particularly successful during the fall of 1967. Moreover, even a highly successful attack against Haiphong would not have reduced import capacity below normal requirements. Total daily import capacity was 17,200 tons compared to actual daily imports of only 4,200, and the Department of Defense estimated that capacity would not drop below 7,200 tons even after unrestricted air attack and mining.[78]

Many believe if the Red River dikes had been hit, there would have been enormous loss of life and destruction of the rice crop, but no documentary evidence exists to support this assertion and there is important evidence against it. General John McConnell, a key proponent of the Douhet strategy, believed that attacking the dikes would have been "a pretty fruitless operation," and a declassified Department of Defense option paper claims that only 20 percent of the rice crop would have been lost even in high-water season.[79] A key factor that may account for these bleak expectations is that the dikes, built by the French to resist erosion, were constructed of enormous amounts of earth over many years—a program accelerated by Hanoi during the war. Some were forty feet across.[80]

---

[75] *Pentagon Papers* 4: 226. For analysis of Soviet assistance to North Vietnam, consult William Zimmerman, "The Korean and Vietnam Wars," in *Diplomacy of Power: Soviet Armed Forces as a Political Instrument*, ed. Stephen S. Kaplan (Washington, D.C.: Brookings, 1981), pp. 314–56.

[76] CIA/DIA, "Appraisal of the Bombing through 16 October 1967," p. 11; CIA/DIA, "Appraisal of the Bombing through 16 November 1967," pp. 13–14.

[77] CIA/DIA, "Appraisal of the Bombing through 16 November 1967," p. 14.

[78] *Pentagon Papers* 4: 146.

[79] Clodfelter, *Limits of Air Power*, p. 126; Department of Defense, "Military Actions against North Vietnam and Laos," DDRS, vol. 1986, no. 131, n.d., p. 6.

[80] Van Dyke, *North Vietnam's Strategy for Survival*, pp. 46, 183–86.

The final option was to attack population centers directly. Yet only 10 percent of North Vietnam's population lived in major population centers.[81] Nonurban demographics, combined with the extensive evacuation of cities and villages, meant that there simply were not large numbers of civilians vulnerable to conventional air attack. To be sure, bombing of cities would have been exceedingly painful for North Vietnam. Still, it is not clear that the additional loss of life, compared to the tremendous costs the North was already paying for its prosecution of the war, would have been enough to have any political effect.

It seems clear that Rolling Thunder failed not because coercive strategies were poorly executed but for the fundamental reason that during the Johnson years North Vietnam was largely immune to conventional coercion. The denial model was impotent because air power could not thwart Hanoi's guerrilla strategy, and the Schelling and Douhet models could not raise either civilian risks or costs high enough to overwhelm Hanoi's territorial interests in South Vietnam.

Nixon's Air War against North Vietnam

After a three-and-a-half-year hiatus, Nixon resumed large-scale bombing of North Vietnam in 1972. Although the initial campaign failed, the Linebacker I and II campaigns succeed in compelling Hanoi to sign the 27 January 1973 Paris agreements, ending America's role in the war. Nixon's coercive efforts succeeded where Johnson's had failed mainly because Hanoi's military strategy had changed between 1968 and 1972. In March 1972 Hanoi launched a conventional offensive aimed at achieving a series of limited battlefield victories that would precipitate the downfall of the Saigon regime. This strategy, in sharp contrast to the earlier guerrilla tactics, was highly vulnerable to interdiction by conventional air attack. As a result, the United States was able to undermine the North's battlefield strategy and force political concessions.

To explain why Nixon's use of coercive air power ultimately succeeded, we must address five questions. First, how did the North's strategy change? Second, what were the goals of American bombing? Third, what were the coercive strategies employed and were they executed faithfully? Fourth, what was the relationship between U.S. bombing strategies and changes in North Vietnamese behavior? Finally, can alternative explanations account for the change in Hanoi's behavior?

[81] Judith Banister, *The Population of Vietnam*, International Population Reports Series P-95, no. 77, U.S. Department of Commerce, October 1985.

The Change in North Vietnamese Strategy

Hanoi's strategy for the ground war changed during the Nixon years. Their goal for 1972 was to defeat significant portions of the Army of the Republic of Vietnam (ARVN) and to capture a series of provincial capitals through an enormous conventional invasion. Execution of this plan would ultimately involve all fourteen divisions and twenty-fix separate regiments of the North Vietnamese Army (NVA). Its overall purpose was to reverse the deteriorating battlefield prospects of Communist forces. Despite the withdrawal of nearly all American combat forces, the North's influence over territory had waned, principally because by 1972 the combination of Vietnamization and pacification had become effective.[82] The VC/NVA controlled or actively contested areas containing about 23 percent of South Vietnam's populace in 1968, but this figure had declined to 3 percent by the end of 1971.[83]

To counter this trend, North Vietnamese leaders decided to confront Vietnamization head on. An article in *Tien Phong*, the organ of the South Vietnamese Communists, stated: "Our general offensive is designed to defeat the enemy's Vietnamization plan, force the enemy to acknowledge his defeat, and accept a political settlement on our terms."[84] Apparently the Hanoi leadership believed that seizing and holding a number of key cities in the face of ARVN opposition would discredit Vietnamization. At least a successful conventional offensive would enhance Hanoi's bargaining leverage for a coalition government in the South. At best, the remaining ARVN forces would be demoralized and South Vietnam's President Nguyen Van Thieu crippled, precipitating the downfall of the entire Saigon government. The key to either outcome was a series of conventional victories over ARVN combat units defending provincial capitals.[85] During 1971, North Vietnam received large numbers of T-54, T-55, and light amphibious PT-76 tanks, 130mm and 152mm artillery pieces, 160mm mortars, 23mm and 57mm anti-aircraft guns as well as MiG aircraft, surface-to-air missiles, and ammunition from the Soviet Union and China.[86]

---

[82] By March 1972 the United States had withdrawn all but six thousand combat troops from South Vietnam and about ninety thousand other military personnel. George C. Herring, *America's Longest War: The United States and Vietnam, 1950–1975* (New York: Wiley, 1979), p. 240. Pacification was able to succeed despite the reduction of American combat forces, largely because of improved counterinsurgency methods adopted by ARVN and U.S. intelligence agencies. See Krepinevich, *The Army and Vietnam*, pp. 237–57.

[83] Lewy, *America in Vietnam*, p. 192.

[84] Quoted in David W. P. Elliott, *NLF-DRV Strategy and the 1972 Spring Offensive*, International Relations of East Asia Project, Report no. 4 (Ithaca: Cornell University, January 1974), p. 35; Elliott provides other evidence to support this conclusion.

[85] There is no definitive account of North Vietnam's strategy in the Easter Offensive, and hence the available evidence must be used with care. The best sources on the matter are Elliott, *NLF-DRV Strategy*; and General Ngo Quang Troung, *The Easter Offensive of 1972* (Washington D.C.: U.S. Army Center of Military History, 1980), pp. 157–60.

[86] G. H. Turley, *The Easter Offensive: Vietnam, 1972* (Novato, Calif.: Presidio Press, 1985), p. 27.

The first wave of the so-called Easter Offensive was launched on 30 March, and the initial stages were an unqualified success. Spearheaded by over six hundred tanks and artillery pieces, 120,000 NVA troops struck across the DMZ, across the Cambodian border northwest of Saigon, and in the central highlands. Although American intelligence recognized the impending invasion by late 1971, it had miscalculated its timing, scope, and location. Achieving both local superiority and surprise, Communist forces easily broke through the ARVN forward lines of defense. Three NVA divisions rapidly overran all fourteen fire bases in the DMZ area, decimated the ARVN Third Division, captured the provincial capital of Quang Tri, and moved toward Hue. In the highlands, another two divisions mauled the ARVN Twenty-second Division and laid siege to Kontum. Three other NVA divisions destroyed the ARVN Fifth Division and threatened to capture An Loc, a provincial capital just sixty miles north of Saigon.[87] By early May, Communist forces had the initiative and ARVN morale was on the verge of a collapse that would have meant the end of Thieu's regime and the achievement of Communist control over the entire country.

Goals of Nixon's Air War

In response to the North Vietnamese invasion, the United States launched a series of air offensives against the North: "Freedom Train," in April 1972; "Linebacker I," from May to October; and "Linebacker II," dubbed the "Christmas bombing," in December. The purpose of the bombing was to compel Hanoi to halt its conventional offensive and accept a standstill cease-fire agreement. The U.S. definition of a standstill cease-fire changed from the time it was first offered, however. In October 1971 it had meant the removal of all American forces from the South if Hanoi released American POWs and stopped fighting throughout all of South Vietnam, a meaning to which Thieu consented. On 8 May 1972, when Nixon reiterated the demand after the Freedom Train campaign, it had a different import, since the North occupied significant, albeit thinly populated, chunks of the South. Thus, the goals of the 1972 air campaigns were to compel the North to terminate a specific ground offensive and to rescue an ally from imminent defeat but not to recapture lost territory.

Coercive Strategies

President Richard Nixon and Henry Kissinger, his national security adviser, pursued two coercive strategies in succession. First they tried a type of

---

[87] This summary is derived from Turley, *Easter Offensive*; and Troung, *Easter Offensive*.

Schelling strategy, even less threatening than Johnson's. When this failed, they adopted an interdiction strategy that was ultimately successful.

Freedom Train in April 1972 was a superficial effort to manipulate civilian fears according to a ceremonious version of the Schelling model. It observed the rituals of the strategy without establishing a threat to any core value of the North. As in the early stages of Rolling Thunder, the main aim was to create a physical pattern of escalation easily recognizable to the victim. As Kissinger later explained, "If we wanted to force a diplomatic solution, we had to create an impression of implacable determination to prevail."[88] Its threat, however, was even more ethereal than that of Johnson's lenient Schelling strategy. Nixon's variant observed the model's timing considerations but gave no concrete signals of what civilian targets were at risk.

This strategy entailed massive redeployment of U.S. air forces to Southeast Asia and bombing that progressed incrementally northward. Available U.S. air power was visibly enhanced by sharp increases of B-52s in the region from 40 to 171, tactical aircraft from 76 to nearly 400, and aircraft carriers from 2 to 6.[89] In the first week of April, the bombing of North Vietnam resumed with a limited number of strikes against military targets up to sixty miles north of the DMZ. By the second week, raids were authorized up to the eighteenth parallel and, by the end of April, up to the twentieth parallel.[90] In addition, a single strike of twenty B-52s in mid-April attacked POL storage areas in Haiphong as "a warning" writes Kissinger, "that things might get out of control."[91] This application of the ceremonious Schelling strategy also had a diplomatic component, which took the form of a secret initiative to Hanoi's allies, the Soviet Union and China, to persuade them to cut off their economic and military assistance to North Vietnam.[92]

This strategy soon came to a critical test. On 2 May Kissinger met with Le Duc Tho, the North's negotiator, to work out a diplomatic settlement to the offensive. These talks proved that the ceremonious Schelling strategy used in Freedom Train had failed. Tho told Kissinger flatly that Hanoi had no intention of pulling back from the offensive. Far from moderating, Tho's demeanor was more resolute than in the past. Kissinger understandably

---

[88] Henry A. Kissinger, *White House Years* (Boston: Little, Brown, 1979), p. 1116.

[89] A summary of B-52, F-4, and F-105 tactical aircraft and aircraft carrier deployments is found in Donald D. Frizzell and Ray L. Bowers, eds., *Air Power and the Spring Invasion* (Washington D.C.: Office of Air Force History, United States Air Force, 1985), pp. 15–30.

[90] *USAF Air Operations against North Vietnam, 1 July 1971–30 June 1972*, June 1973, pp. 52–79, Maxwell Air Force Base, Ala., Air University Library, M-U 38245–263.

[91] Kissinger, *White House Years*, p. 1118.

[92] Kissinger met covertly with Premier Leonid Brezhnev in April. He indicated that American terms for a standstill cease-fire had been redefined. No longer would the United States insist that NVA troops withdraw to the North. If Hanoi would cease the Offensive, then its forces could remain in possession of the territory they had seized. He also tried to pressure the Soviet Union to terminate its material support for the offensive. Ibid., pp. 1134–64.

inferred "Hanoi's conviction that it was so close to victory that it no longer needed even the pretense of negotiations."[93]

Following the failure of Freedom Train, the United States shifted to an interdiction strategy in a new air campaign called Linebacker I. Since the beginning of the Easter Offensive, B-52s had been engaged in operational interdiction against troop and supply concentrations behind the enemy lines. On 8 May Nixon announced a strategic air interdiction campaign and proclaimed that, for the first time, North Vietnam's ports would be mined. JCS Chairman Admiral Thomas Moorer delineated the three military objectives of the air strikes: "(a) destroy war material already in North Vietnam, (b) to the extent possible, prevent the flow of war material already in Vietnam, and (c) interdict the flow of troops and material from the North into combat areas."[94] Planners expected that destruction of North Vietnam's war assets and supply delivery system would make it impossible for Hanoi to continue its conventional offensive.

Linebacker I involved air strikes against a broad set of military targets in both North and South Vietnam, including logistical centers and transportation arteries, such as the Paul Doumer bridge in Hanoi, bridges along the northwest and northeast rail lines from China, fuel dumps, warehouses, marshalling yards, rolling stock, vehicles, power plants, a POL pipeline running from China, and a large number of surface-to-air missile and antiaircraft artillery sites.[95] Civilian and economic targets appear not to have been pursued. There is no evidence that cement, steel, chemical, or light industries were part of the target set, and the rules of engagement strictly prohibited hitting dikes, fishing craft, houseboats, and third-country shipping.[96] In short, Linebacker I was a pure case of interdiction bombing.

Linebacker I largely achieved the goal of thwarting the Easter Offensive. Prior to the massive bombing campaign, the NVA had appeared to be on the way to complete defeat of the ARVN. By June, a month after air interdiction began, the Easter Offensive had stalled. The NVA abandoned the sieges of Kontum and An Loc and assumed the defensive in Quang Tri. By October the ARVN had recaptured significant portions of previously lost territory, including Quang Tri. The momentum of the Communist steamroller had been checked, and the NVA no longer controlled any of the forty-four provincial capitals.[97]

American air power played a principal role in thwarting the North's strategy, though the efforts of ARVN ground forces were also necessary. Air interdiction reduced the flow of resources to NVA units, diminishing the

---

[93] Ibid., p. 1175.
[94] Quoted in Clodfelter, *Limits of Air Power*, p. 216.
[95] Momyer, *Air Power in Three Wars*, p. 32.
[96] *USAF Air Operations*, p. 98.
[97] Troung, *Easter Offensive*, p. 158.

North's combat ability by creating firepower shortages and disrupting mobility. American air power succeeded largely because Hanoi had adopted a military strategy vulnerable to interdiction bombing.

The switch to conventional operations increased the North's vulnerability to air attack in two ways. First, the demand for logistics is an order of magnitude greater in conventional compared to guerrilla operations. The Easter invasion involved large quantities of tanks, heavy artillery, and other mechanized equipment, which provided a substantial increase in firepower but also consumed far greater quantities of POL, ammunition, and spare parts than had guerrilla operations.[98] In 1972 North Vietnam's conventional forces regularly consumed ammunition and POL at an estimated rate of several thousand tons per day compared to a few hundred tons per day in 1968.[99] Second, the demand for logistics in conventional operations is inherently inelastic. Because battles are intense, shortages appear quickly if supply lines are interdicted, and brief lapses can be exploited by the enemy.

During the Easter Offensive, air power greatly reduced the flow of resources to NVA units in battle. Strategic interdiction created aggregate shortages, while operational interdiction intensified local shortages and created coordination and mobility problems at battlefronts in the South. On the aggregate supply level, North Vietnam's import capacity was reduced by about 80 percent. Overland imports were reduced by interdiction of the railways to China from 160,000 tons to 30,000 tons a month, and the mining of the port of Haiphong cut seaborne imports from 250,000 tons a month to a trickle. The criticial item was oil, most of which before Linebacker had come from Haiphong. Hanoi's only other sources were a pipeline running south from China and stores in dispersed sites. By the end of June, air attack had shut down the pipeline as well as destroyed all large POL tank farms, totalling 25 percent of stocks. Intelligence estimated that the NVA was left with only two months of supplies.[100]

Operational interdiction intensified these shortages, reducing shipments to troops in the South by 75 percent, sharply limiting their mobility and firepower.[101] There were frequent reports of NVA tanks running out of gas, while by early June the number of shells fired at An Loc had fallen to less than 300 from about 8,000 daily in April.[102] Local air strikes also seriously weakened each of the prongs of the Easter offensive. At Quang Tri, strikes

[98] Office of Air Force History, Air War—Vietnam, intro. by Drew Middleton (New York: Arno Press, 1978), p. 203.

[99] Robert Thompson, Peace Is Not at Hand (London: Chatto and Windus, 1974), p. 114.

[100] Clodfelter, Limits of Air Power, p. 228.

[101] House Hearings, p. 43; Aviation Week and Space Technology, 30 October 1972, pp. 12–13.

[102] John Morrocco, Rain of Fire: Air War, 1969–1973 The Vietnam Experience (Boston: Boston Publishing, 1985), p. 136; Lewy, America in Vietnam, p. 200; Pacific Air Forces Headquarters, Linebacker: Overview of the First 120 Days (Maxwell Air Force Base, Ala.: Air Force Historical Research Agency, 27 September 1973), p. 42, file number K717.0414-42.

against supply points and lines of communications disrupted the coordination and resupply of enemy forces and destroyed large troop concentrations. At Kontum, the enemy ran into supply difficulties because B-52 raids forced him to store supplies at great distances from the city. Finally, a captured enemy report blamed the failure of the 9th NVA division to take An Loc on the devastating effects of U.S. tactical air power and B-52s.[103]

Linebacker I halted the Easter Offensive, but the NVA had not been decisively defeated and still retained the capacity to continue fighting indefinitely, though it was now on the defensive. The CIA and DIA reckoned that Communist forces could have continued to fight at their September levels for another two years.[104] Hanoi's prospects of further territorial gains in the short term were slim, and its hopes for a quick end to the war had been frustrated. Unable to execute its battlefield strategy, on 22 October North Vietnam agreed to a cease-fire.

The North began backing away from the agreement, however, when the South refused to sign. To bring Hanoi back to the table, the United States launched a new air offensive starting on 18 December, nicknamed the "Christmas bombing." Linebacker II's purpose and target set largely paralleled those of Linebacker I.[105] The campaign, said the Air Force, "was designed to coerce a negotiated settlement by threatening further weakening of the enemy's military effort to maintain and support his armed forces."[106] The target set consisted of military targets north of the twentieth parallel which had not been bombed since 23 October. The Linebacker I and II target sets were so similar both because Linebacker II was deliberately designed to repeat the earlier operation and because North Vietnam had used the bombing halt to regenerate key choke points and facilities in its logistics network. For example, after the cessation of bombing north of the twentieth parallel, Hanoi rebuilt supply depots, made railroad lines from China serviceable again, resumed coastal shipping north of the twentieth parallel, and reopened rail lines between Hanoi and Haiphong.[107] Linebacker II, however, followed a quicker pace than before; in twelve days the United States flew almost half as many sorties against Hanoi, Haiphong, and the Chinese buffer zone as in the six months of Linebacker I (see Table 11).[108]

---

[103] Troung, *Easter Offensive*, pp. 64, 103, 123.

[104] See Tad Szulc, "Hanoi Held Able to Fight Two Years at Present Rate," *New York Times*, 13 September 1973.

[105] Linebacker II did not include armed reconnaissance missions, partly because the Easter Offensive had already been defeated and partly because as many aircraft as possible were dedicated to finishing off targets in the Hanoi-Haiphong and Chinese border areas.

[106] Norman R. Thorpe and James R. Miles, "Comments on Air Warfare—Christmas 1972" in *Law and Responsibility in Warfare: The Vietnam Experience*, ed. Peter D. Trooboff (Chapel Hill: University of North Carolina Press, 1975), p. 145.

[107] PACAF Headquarters, *Linebacker II USAF Bombing Survey* (April 1973), AFHRA file K717.64-8; House Hearings, p. 4.

[108] PACAF, *Linebacker II Bombing Survey*, p. 1.

Table 11. Linebacker II targets and damage assessment

Category	Targets struck	Damage assessment
Rail yards	13	55%
Storage facilities	14	35
Radcom facilities	5	32
Power facilities	6	29
Airfields	5	9
SAM sites	13	10
Bridges	3	33
Totals	59	32%

SOURCE: PACAF, *Linebacker II USAF Bombing Survey*, p. 20.

Linebacker II ruined the North's efforts to rebuild its logistic network, reinforcing the lesson that American air power would make resumption of the conventional offensive against the South futile. Consequently, the North returned to the bargaining table and signed the Paris Accords.

Impact on North Vietnamese Behavior

The effect of American air power on the Paris Accords is often distorted, mainly because excessive attention is given to the December raids against Hanoi and Haiphong. Some contend that these raids alone were responsible for the agreement.[109] Others maintain that they were irrelevant, since they were launched to reassure South Vietnam about the American commitment of air power to its defense rather than to influence the North.[110] In my view, Linebacker I persuaded Hanoi to accept the terms of the Paris Accords. Linebacker II became necessary when President Thieu delayed the signing of the agreement and the North began to backslide from its commitments. The second Linebacker campaign restored Hanoi's commitment to the accords.[111]

The effect of air power on Hanoi's behavior is apparent from the course taken by the Paris peace talks. Prior to June, with its offensive still on the move, Hanoi had avoided serious negotiations. Once the offensive stalled in

[109] For instance, see Sharp, *Strategy for Defeat*, pp. 252–55; Momyer, *Air Power in Three Wars*, p. 339; Carl Berger, ed., *The United States Air Force in Southeast Asia, 1961–1973* (Washington, D.C.: Office of Air Force History, United States Air Force, 1984), p. 95.

[110] Gabriel Kolko, *Anatomy of a War: Vietnam, the United States, and the Modern Historical Experience* (New York: Pantheon, 1985), p. 450; and Seymour Hersh, *Price of Power: Kissinger in the Nixon White House* (New York: Summit, 1983).

[111] My explanation largely agrees with the views of Lewy and Clodfelter, but I go beyond their views in seeking to establish which aspect of air power (civilian vulnerability or military vulnerability) was responsible for the change in Hanoi's behavior and in testing the argument against competing explanations.

July under the pressure of American air power, earnest talks between Kissinger and Tho began. The diplomatic breakthrough came on 8 October, a few weeks after the NVA had lost Quang Tri City and assumed the defensive. Le Duc Tho dropped Hanoi's long-standing demand that the Thieu regime be replaced with a coalition government in favor of a national commission to oversee a future presidential election. In essence, Hanoi accepted the American diplomatic position of first settling the military issues and leaving the political issues for the Vietnamese to negotiate.

To exploit this opportunity, Kissinger reiterated Nixon's May proposal for a standstill cease-fire instead of pressing for withdrawal of North Vietnamese forces. Both negotiating teams spent the next few days working through the language of the agreement. Finally, it was arranged that Kissinger and Tho would initial the treaty on 24 October and the formal signing would follow in Hanoi on 31 October. After being briefed by Kissinger, Nixon accepted the terms of this accord provided that Hanoi agreed to four modest changes. By 21 October, Hanoi had conceded to all U.S. demands and even the exact text in most cases.[112] Nixon cabled Hanoi on the 22 October declaring the agreement "complete," and the Linebacker I bombing ended the next day.

The negotiations did not end there, however, because President Thieu balked. His main concern, not surprisingly, was that the treaty did not require the North to withdraw elements of its armed forces from South Vietnam. Quite the opposite, it would legitimate the presence of North Vietnamese regulars and guerrillas in the South. Thieu demanded sixty-nine changes in the terms of the accord.[113] Nixon, unwilling to pressure Thieu just two weeks before the U.S. presidential election, ordered Kissinger to cancel his trip to Hanoi, effectively killing any hope of an agreement by the end of October.

Thieu's refusal tarnished Washington's reputation as a reliable negotiating partner and encouraged Hanoi to back off. Nixon wanted to abide by the existing substance of the agreement, but he had no interest in appearing to compel an ally to sign against its will. So the administration decided, on the one hand, to reassure Thieu that U.S. power would be available to force Hanoi to comply with the cease-fire and, on the other, to push for cosmetic improvements in the text, alterations that Kissinger later called "window-dressing."[114] In the November and December negotiations between Tho and

---

[112] Kissinger, *White House Years,* 1361, 1371, 1380. The changes related to the precise formulations on the ban on infiltration, military aid to South Vietnam, weakening the powers of the national council, and terms of cease-fire in Laos and Cambodia.

[113] For details and analysis of Thieu's demands, see Gareth Porter, *A Peace Denied: The United States, Vietnam, and the Paris Agreement* (Bloomington: Indiana University Press, 1976), pp. 145–48; Allan E. Goodman, *The Lost Peace: America's Search for a Negotiated Settlement of the Vietnam War* (Stanford: Hoover Institution Press, 1975), pp. 148–49.

[114] Kissinger, *White House Years,* p. 1447.

Kissinger, however, Hanoi refused to go along with Kissinger's scheme to placate Thieu, perhaps sensing an opportunity to embarrass its long-standing enemies or renew military operations.[115] Its policy was, as Kissinger informed Nixon at the time, "to give us just enough each day to keep us going but nothing decisive which would conclude an agreement."[116] Finally, Kissinger walked away.

Peace negotiations were on the brink of failure. To save the accords, the United States had to compel Hanoi to return to its earlier position and to accept enough cosmetic changes to mollify Thieu. Just days after Kissinger walked out of the negotiations, bombing above the twentieth parallel was resumed with the Linebacker II offensive. From 18 to 25 December, B-52 bombers and tactical aircraft blasted fifty-nine military-related targets in and around Hanoi and Haiphong with twenty thousand tons of high explosives. On 29 December Hanoi indicated its willingness to resume serious talks.[117]

When negotiations resumed in January, Hanoi's diplomatic behavior changed. Although Saigon got little of the substance of its demands, Hanoi permitted Kissinger to placate Thieu by inserting enough cosmetic alterations to allow the United States to defend itself from the charge that it had forced the treaty upon its ally. There were some twelve changes from the October draft.[118] Significantly, there was no concession by Hanoi on troop withdrawal, and so the security of South Vietnam was not improved. Equally significant, the new language did not alter the behavior demanded of the North Vietnamese. Thus, whereas it compelled Hanoi to return to serious bargaining, Linebacker II made no substantial difference in the terms of the agreement.

The effect of American air power on Hanoi's calculations is reinforced by evidence that it deterred conventional aggression beyond 1972. Once the

[115] The consensus among North Vietnamese leaders in favor of the accords seems to have been exceedingly fragile. Thieu's refusal appears to have unwound this consensus and led the Politburo to back away from its earlier position. See Tad Szulc, "Behind the Vietnam Cease-Fire Agreement," *Foreign Policy*, no. 15 (Summer 1974): 60–61.

[116] Kissinger, *White House Years*, p. 1442.

[117] Karl J. Eschmann reports total tonnage as 15,287. *Linebacker: The Untold Story of the Air Raids over North Vietnam* (New York: Ivy Books, 1989), p. 202. Clodfelter adds an additional 5,000 tons for navy and air force fighters, *Limits of Air Power*, p. 194. For details on sorties and targets, see PACAF, *Linebacker II Bombing Survey*. NVA General Tran Van Tra, commander of Hanoi's forces in South Vietnam, explained the effects of Linebacker II in the following terms: "Our cadres and men were fatigued, we had not had time to make up for our losses, all units were in disarray, there was a lack of manpower, and there were shortages of food and ammunition . . . The troops were no longer capable of fighting." Tran Van Tra, *Concluding the 30 years War* (Ho Chi Minh City, 1982), pp. 6, 33, 34.

[118] The most significant changes were deletion of the words "administrative structure" as a description of the national council; a reference implying that the DMZ was a military boundary; a signing procedure that did not require South Vietnam to recognize the southern Communists formally; and some bolstering of the inspection mechanism for the cease-fire. These are described in detail by Kissinger, *White House Years*, pp. 1466–1467; and Goodman, *The Lost Peace*, pp. 144–149.

Paris Accords were signed, the North quickly resupplied and reinforced its troops. By November 1973 intelligence analysts estimated that the NVA had sufficient strength to launch a full-scale offensive if it wished.[119] Despite minor skirmishes between NVA and ARVN forces, however, Hanoi essentially stuck by its agreement until 1975, when it unleashed the final offensives that crushed ARVN and the Thieu regime. A key consideration for North Vietnam's leaders during this period, according to the CIA station chief in Saigon, was the risk that American air power might return to the region.[120] Not until fall 1974, after the resignation of President Nixon, was Hanoi sufficiently confident that the air threat had disappeared to authorize the final offensives. By implication, even in late 1974 or 1975 the threat of a resumption of American bombing would have been likely to discourage Hanoi from launching the final offensives.

In summary, air power coerced North Vietnam to accept a negotiated cease-fire. Linebacker I played a key role in defeating the North's ground offensive and so compelled Hanoi to accept U.S. terms for the peace accords. When South Vietnam derailed negotiations, Hanoi had to be discouraged from retreating from the negotiated position and compelled to accept cosmetic changes that placated South Vietnam. Linebacker II achieved these purposes.

Could the United States have gotten more? Some believe that the United States could have extracted much more substantial concessions from Hanoi in return for ending the Christmas bombing. For instance, Robert Thompson said: "They [the North] and their whole rear base at this point were at your mercy. They would have taken any terms. And that is why, of course, you actually got a peace agreement in January, which you had not been able to get in October."[121] I disagree. Linebacker II, like Linebacker I, damaged the North's ability to carry out its conventional military strategy for overrunning the ARVN, but it did not seriously impair its ability to defend already-held territories. Thus my theory predicts that more substantial concessions could not have been obtained.

Alternative Explanations

There are four major alternatives to my explanation for Hanoi's concessions: reduction in American demands; Soviet and Chinese pressure on Hanoi; South Vietnamese resistance; and civilian suffering inflicted by Linebacker II.

The first alternative explanation focuses on the reduction in American demands between Rolling Thunder in 1968 and the Linebacker campaigns in

[119] Elliott, *NLF-DRV Strategy*, p. 63.
[120] Frank Snepp, *Decent Interval* (New York: Random House, 1977), pp. 91–141.
[121] Thompson quoted in W. Scott Thompson and Donald D. Frizzell, *The Lessons of Vietnam* (New York: Crane, Russak, 1977), p. 105.

1972. In Rolling Thunder, according to this view, the United States was seeking to coerce the North into abandoning the entire effort to unify Vietnam. In Linebacker, the United States was seeking to coerce the North into accepting a "decent interval" before it eventually achieved its goal. The United States no longer required Hanoi to change its territorial interests in South Vietnam.[122]

There is some truth in the premise of this argument. Johnson was demanding a cease-fire agreement at a time when Hanoi had captured little territory below the DMZ compared to the sizable areas it controlled at the time of the 1972 negotiations. Nevertheless, the implication that Johnson could have obtained an agreement had he been willing to reduce his demands does not follow. In fact, he tried this tactic. On 10 May 1968, the United States and the North Vietnamese did reach an "understanding." In return for a cessation of the bombing, the North agreed not to infiltrate troops through the DMZ, shell cities, or attack unarmed American reconnaissance planes over North Vietnam. Since most infiltration came through Laos and Cambodia, these were not important concessions. Further, Hanoi refused to confirm the agreement publicly. The United States stopped bombing on 1 November, whereupon the North immediately began violating the terms.[123] Given the failure of Rolling Thunder to put any real pressure on Hanoi's military strategy, it is unlikely that the North would have committed itself to any territorial concessions.

Similarly, the concessions Nixon could and could not obtain were determined by the limits of the ability of American air power to undermine Hanoi's military strategy, not by changes in territorial demands. When the NVA was still advancing at the peak of the Easter Offensive in early May 1972, Hanoi refused to discuss a standstill agreement, even though it would have left the North in possession of more territory, including the provincial capital of Quang Tri, than they controlled at the time of the final accords. Conversely, once the Linebacker I campaign stalled the offensive, Hanoi accepted a less favorable standstill agreement than it could have obtained earlier.

The second alternative explanation accepts that Hanoi's failure in the ground war changed its behavior but credits the Soviet Union and China with exerting the leverage that caused the change. Indeed, there is evidence that the Russians and Chinese did try to pressure Hanoi to negotiate, but they did so at the end of 1971, not in 1972. In spite of reductions in Chinese aid, the North rejected these requests and launched the Easter Offensive instead.[124] There is no evidence of any direct Soviet or Chinese pressure on

---

[122] Snepp, *Decent Interval*, 1–91; Clodfelter also stresses the significance of the differences in goals, *Limits of Air Power*, pp. xi, 204.

[123] Lewy, *America in Vietnam*, pp. 388–89.

[124] Raymond L. Garthoff, *Detente and Confrontation: American-Soviet Releations from Nixon to Reagan* (Washington, D.C.: Brookings, 1994), pp. 255–56, 258; Hersh, *Price of Power*, pp. 442, 502.

Hanoi after the beginning of the Offensive or that either ever asked Hanoi to abandon any of its ultimate goals in South Vietnam.[125] Most important from Hanoi's perspective, the Soviets maintained their level of aid throughout 1972, and in mid-June the Chinese increased theirs, restoring the earlier cuts.[126] Later, during Linebacker II, the USSR and China publicly declared their support for Hanoi and fervently denounced the bombing.[127] In short, Soviet or Chinese pressure does not explain the change in North Vietnam's behavior.

The third competing view also accepts that Hanoi's failure in the ground war changed its behavior but emphasizes the role of the South Vietnamese. According to this view, the ARVN success in stabilizing its defensive lines deserves the credit for thwarting the North's military plans in 1972 and therefore for the Paris Accords.[128] It is not likely, however, that the ARVN would have held without the support of American air power, judging from the local balance of forces in the summer of 1972 in the main battle areas. NVA forces enjoyed overwhelming superiority in two of the three battle areas and a significant edge in the third. At An Loc, the NVA had a seven-to-one advantage over ARVN units. At Quang Tri City, the NVA enjoyed a two-to-one advantage, though on the defensive. At Kontum, on the offensive, the NVA had about a two-to-one advantage.[129] The South Vietnamese recognized that U.S. air power was decisive. General Ngo Quang Troung, the ARVN commander in Quang Tri, admitted that the city "certainly could not have been retaken, nor could ARVN forces have held at Kontum and An Loc, had it not been for the support provided by the U.S. Air Force."[130] General Tran Van Minh, commander of the South Vietnamese Air Force, later contrasted the successful campaign at An Loc in 1972 to defeats under sim-

---

[125] Douglas E. Pike reports that during the April 1972 summit the Soviets promised Kissinger that they would "deliver" Hanoi to the bargaining table but says they were unable to do so. *Vietnam and the Soviet Union: Anatomy of an Alliance* (Boulder, Colo.: Westview Press, 1987), p. 96. Daniel S. Papp reports no pressure by the Soviets and says that although the Chinese were initially opposed to the Easter Offensive as excessively risky, they changed their views when the early stages were successful. *Vietnam: The View from Moscow, Peking, Washington* (Jefferson, N.C.: McFarland, 1981), pp. 145–172, passim.

[126] Joseph Kraft reports that in a July 1972 interview Le Khac Vien, the editor of the Communist publication *Vietnamese Studies*, acknowledged "that Hanoi had lost some political support from Moscow and Peking. But in the same breath he said that 'what counts is material support.' " Kraft, "Hanoi's Communism," *Washington Post*, 25 July 1972. In addition, in June the Soviets offered additional surface-to-air missiles, to be manned by Russian crews; the North Vietnamese declined. Papp, *Vietnam*, pp. 169–70, 157.

[127] Kolko, *Anatomy of a War*, p. 442.

[128] Jeffrey J. Clark, *United States Army in Vietnam: Advice and Support, the Final Years, 1965–1973* (Washington, D.C.: Center of Military History, United States Army, 1988), pp. 481–90.

[129] The numbers were An Loc, seven NVA regiments to four thousand ARVN defenders; Quang Tri, six NVA divisions to three ARVN divisions; Kontum, five NVA regiments to one ARVN division. Troung, *Easter Offensive*, pp. 64, 103, 123.

[130] Ibid., p. 172.

ilar circumstances in 1975. At An Loc, he pointed out, the battle turned on the use of B-52s, which were not available at Phuoc Long and Ban Me Thout in 1975.[131] Since the Easter Offensive would probably not have failed against ARVN resistance alone, the ARVN cannot be credited with successful coercion of North Vietnam.

Finally, a myth has sprung up that Nixon's air offensives, especially Linebacker II, worked because they terrified civilians. Some American journalists turned the Christmas bombing of Hanoi into a terror bombing legend akin to the fire bombing of Dresden in World War II.[132] As a result, Linebacker II is viewed as a robust Douhet strategy that succeeded by shocking civilians into forcing their government to give way.[133]

The fundamental problem with this myth is that civilian fears played no role in the success of Linebacker I or II. Nixon was keenly aware of the domestic political criticism to which he would be subjected if large numbers of civilians were killed. Accordingly, both campaigns avoided civilians and pinpointed military targets with discriminate tactics and weapons. For instance, B-52 navigators were directed not to drop bombs unless they were 100 percent sure of the aim point and they were supplied with the locations of schools, hospitals, and POW camps.[134] Indeed, bombing caused relatively little loss of life. Laser-guided smart bombs allowed the military to wreak havoc on the North's logistical infrastructure while minimizing casualties. Air raids against the North in 1972 caused an estimated 13,000 deaths; even the intense Linebacker II raids killed 1,318 in Hanoi and 305 in Haiphong, by North Vietnam's count.[135] The significance of these small numbers becomes manifest when compared to the estimated 125,000 deaths that Communist forces sustained in South Vietnam during 1972 and the reported 851,000 total deaths from 1964 to 1972.[136] Nor was the North Vietnamese agricultural economy harmed. Linebacker I did not hit the irrigation system, despite widespread reports that the United States had begun a concerted effort to raze the dikes.[137] A few bombs fell close to dams located near military targets, but not a single

[131] A. J. C. Lavalle, *Airpower and Spring Invasion* (Washington, D.C.: Office of Air Force History, 1985), p. 104.
[132] For years after the fact, Anthony Lewis dedicated columns in the *New York Times* to commemoration of the terror inflicted by Linebacker II. A provocative study of how the news media purveyed this illusion is Martin Herz, *The Prestige Press and the Christmas Bombing, 1972* (Washington, D.C.: Ethics and Public Policy Center, 1980).
[133] Many military officers share this perception. See Sharp, *Strategy for Defeat*, p. 252, 255.
[134] Clodfelter, *Limits of Air Power*, p. 260.
[135] Lewy, *America in Vietnam*, p. 451; Stanley Karnow, *Vietnam: A History* (New York: Viking, 1983), p. 653.
[136] Thomas C. Thayer, *War without Fronts: The American Experience in Vietnam* (Boulder, Colo.: Westview, 1985), p. 104.
[137] See testimony by Ramsey Clark and media reports collected in U.S. Senate, Committee on the Judiciary, Subcommittee to Investigate Problems Connected with Refugees and Escapees, *Problems of War Victims in Indochina*, pt. 3: *North Vietnam*, Hearings, 92d Cong., 2d sess., 16–17 August 1972.

major dike was breached and no flooding occurred.[138] Finally, there is no evidence that bombing disrupted the social and political fabric of North Vietnam. Civilians may have been frightened, but there was no general panic, civil disobedience, or grass-roots opposition to the Hanoi government. The Air Force's survey reports that air strikes had marked psychological effects on North Vietnamese civilians, such as general disorientation. It goes on to say, however, that "despite this obvious decline in morale, there was no evidence indicating that the North Vietnamese leadership could not maintain control of the situation."[139] None of the available evidence suggests that civilian vulnerability contributed to the success of American coercion.

Coercion succeeded in 1972 where it had failed from 1965 to 1968 because in the interim Hanoi had changed from a guerrilla strategy, which was essentially immune to air power, to a conventional offensive strategy, which was highly vulnerable to air interdiction. Freedom Train, an attempt to manipulate civilian vulnerability through a ritualized version of the Schelling model, was a failure, but the Linebacker interdiction campaigns, which disabled Hanoi's conventional strategy, produced coercive success. Later, when American air power no longer posed a risk to Hanoi's strategy, it delivered the final blows to South Vietnam.

The American bombing of Vietnam offers three major lessons for students of coercion. Most important, not every adversary is susceptible to coercion by air power. Some target states are not sensitive to the exploitation of civilian vulnerability because they are willing to pay higher costs than the assailant can inflict. Exploitation of civilian vulnerability is ineffective against adversaries who are fighting for such important interests that they are willing to countenance considerable costs to attain them. North Vietnam and Communist forces in the South accepted over half a million losses rather than abandon their quest for unification. When the adversary is willing to bear costs on such a scale, the additional harm that an assailant can levy against the population using conventional munitions may not make any significant difference. In Vietnam, these problems were exacerbated by the American aversion to the deliberate infliction of civilian casualties.

Coercion based on military vulnerability will not work either, if the adversary has a military strategy whose ultimate prospects of success cannot be significantly reduced by air attack. Air power is very effective against conventional forces and the logistic flows on which they depend because these present concentrated and easily located targets for air strikes. Guerrilla forces, such as those fielded by the Vietnamese Communists during the Johnson years, are inherently poorer targets because they are normally mobile,

[138] Photographic reconnaissance showed only two slight nicks in two dikes. See PACAF, *Linebacker: Overview of the First 120 Days*, p. 61; see also Lewy, *America in Vietnam*, p. 411.
[139] PACAF, *Linebacker II Bombing Survey*, p. 37.

dispersed, and difficult to locate, and they depend very little on logistic support. Terrain can make a difference, however. In Vietnam the cover provided by jungle terrain made the already stealthy guerrillas prohibitively difficult to locate. In desert terrain, on the other hand, even very mobile guerrilla forces may be relatively easy to locate and attack effectively.[140] Thus, in some cases effective coercion of guerrilla opponents may be possible.

Even if these principles are well understood, accurately assessing the adversary's vulnerabilities and choosing an effective coercive strategy can be problematic. In Vietnam both the Air Force and civilian leaders failed to recognize that North Vietnamese morale and commitment were too high to be affected by threats or costs to civilians, and the Army wrongly expected that air interdiction would be effective against Hanoi's guerrilla strategy during 1965–1968. In fact, the Nixon administration's coercive success in 1972 was due more to fortune than to perceptive analysis. Air interdiction was selected primarily by trial and error, following the failure of the Schelling-oriented Freedom Train offensive and under the pressure of the Easter Offensive. Even then, Linebacker succeeded only because Hanoi had shifted to a conventional strategy vulnerable to air attack.

Many analysts of the Vietnam War say that the United States lost primarily because—contrary to Clausewitz's dictum—American leaders did not pay careful attention to the connection between American military action and achievement of U.S. political goals.[141] In fact, however, the decisive error was a different one, at least as far as coercion is concerned. American leaders, both civilian and military, paid insufficient attention to the relationship between American military action and the *enemy's* goals. Proponents of Schelling and Douhet strategies considered means of attacking civilian morale but failed to consider how firm North Vietnamese morale might actually be. Similarly, proponents of interdiction strategies during 1965–1968 planned operations for attacking military targets but failed to consider how much difference destruction of those targets would make to Hanoi's military strategy. Consequently, American leaders failed to realize that no coercive air power strategy could have succeeded during 1965–1968. The cheap, quick solution they so badly wanted did not exist.

[140] In the desert and mountain terrain of Algeria, French air power was highly effective for both reconnaissance and direct attack against guerrilla forces, despite limited numbers of aircraft and some technical difficulties. According to a report by the Concepts Division of the Aerospace Studies Institute, the French failure to defeat the Algerian insurgency was partly due to insufficiently rapid adaptation to the terrain and special conditions of the country. *Guerrilla Warfare and Airpower in Algeria, 1954–1960* (Maxwell AFB, Ala.: Air University Press, March 1965).

[141] Summers, *On Strategy*; Clodfelter, *The Limits of Air Power*.

[7]

Iraq, 1991

People's views on the future of coercive air power are likely to be determined by their interpretation of the Persian Gulf War. The many televised films of modern precision-guided weapons making deadly accurate strikes on all types of targets have fed a perception that a technological revolution has made it possible to win wars with air power alone.

This chapter examines air power in the Gulf War to determine whether this perception is true. The key question is not whether air power has become extremely powerful but whether it has become so powerful that it can decide international disputes, not simply without costly ground campaigns but even without deployment of any credible ground threat. The answer is no. Air power did succeed in coercing Iraq to withdraw from Kuwait, but it did so by undermining its ability to defend against the Coalition's ground threat.

The Gulf War is also important as the first major use of strategic bombing to decapitate an opponent's leadership in order to achieve victory by changing or paralyzing the enemy government. Unlike prior strategic bombing campaigns, which tried to inflict enough pain on enemy civilians to overwhelm their interests in the dispute or to attack national armaments industries in order to reduce the enemy's overall military resources, decapitation focuses on political and military leaders and national communications networks. It is important to evaluate its effectiveness because in future crises the main choice may well be between strategic bombing for decapitation and theater bombing for denial. The pinpoint accuracy of modern precision-guided weapons which encouraged strategic bombing advocates to propose the first systematic decapitation campaign in air history could encourage such efforts in the future, especially since the strategy ultimately requires only a small number of aircraft to destroy just a handful of targets. At the same time, denial rather than war fighting has become the main alternative for theater air power. There are few potential conflicts that are likely to appear worth the costs of fighting a lengthy combined-arms campaign. Thus, there has been a major shift from the traditional debate about air power, which usually pitted strategic bombing that emphasized punishing civilians or attacking arms industries against theater bombing for war fighting, in conjunction with the advance of friendly ground forces.

The debate between decapitation and denial is being fought out mostly in arguments over which approach was most effective in the Gulf War. Strategic bombing advocates assert that Iraq was done in primarily by strikes against leadership and communication targets in Baghdad. Theater air power proponents allege that strikes against the army were decisive.[1]

Desert Storm is ideal for testing decapitation against denial strategies because the Coalition carried out both types of air campaigns during the war. The decapitation campaign, known as Instant Thunder, pursued victory solely through strategic bombing of a small number of political and economic targets in the hope of isolating Saddam Hussein's regime from its political and military control structures, thus leading to its overthrow or strategic paralysis, either of which would force Iraq to abandon Kuwait. The theater air campaign actually aimed more at annihilating the Iraqi army than at coercion through denial.[2] It is worth studying as a denial campaign both because it did in fact coerce Iraq into withdrawing from Kuwait and because the reluctance of Americans to risk heavy casualties means that future war planners may be asked to coerce an enemy with air power alone.

---

[1] Those who stress the decisive role of the strategic air campaign in Desert Storm include Richard P. Hallion, *Storm Over Iraq: Air Power and the Gulf War* (Washington, D.C.: Smithsonian Institution Press, 1992), esp. pp. 188–200; Mark Clodfelter, "Of Demons, Storms and Thunder: A Preliminary Look at Vietnam's Impact on the Persian Gulf Air Campaign," *Airpower Journal* 5 (Winter 1991): 17–32; John F. Jones, "Giulio Douhet Vindicated: Desert Storm 1991," *Naval War College Review* 45 (Autumn 1992): 97–101; James P. Coyne, *Airpower in the Gulf* (Arlington, Va.: Air Force Association, 1992); and John A. Warden III, "Employing Air Power in the Twenty-first Century," in *The Future of Air Power in the Aftermath of the Gulf War* ed. Richard H. Schultz and Robert L. Pfaltzgraff (Maxwell Air Force Base, Ala.: Air University Press, 1992), pp. 57–83. Proponents of theater air power, who tend to focus on its employment only after the ground war began, include Trevor N. Dupuy, "How the War was Won," *National Review*, 1 April 1991, pp. 29–31; R. A. Mason, "The Air War in the Gulf," *Survival* 33 (May/June 1991): 211–29; Harry G. Summers, Jr., *On Strategy II: A Critical Analysis of the Gulf War* (New York: Dell, 1992); and Michael R. Gordon and Bernard E. Trainor, *The General's War: the Inside Story of the Conflict in the Gulf* (Boston: Little, Brown, 1994). Future researchers should also consult the five volume study produced by the Air Force, "The Gulf War Air Power Survey" (Washington, D.C.: GPO, 1993), whose forthright presentation and rich data are likely to make it the standard reference work on the subject.

[2] It is very often difficult to separate warfighting and denial in theater air campaigns, both because planners themselves often do not distinguish and because there may be few or no observable differences. The difference is not so much in the design of the campaign but in how far it must be prosecuted.

If decapitation mattered, we should find evidence relating change in Saddam's willingness to abandon Kuwait to the destruction of strategic targets. Decapitation strikes might threaten leaders with death, a coup by other elites, a popular revolt against the Ba'ath party, or loss of ability to direct the war. Thus, decapitation's effectiveness can be assessed by measuring the impact of strategic air power on these factors and the correlation between these effects and Iraq's willingness to abandon Kuwait.

Alternatively, if denial mattered, we should find that Saddam's calculations varied according to the expected success of his military strategy for holding Kuwait. Iraq depended on a conventional military strategy, which requires tremendous amounts of ammunition, fuel, and other supplies to flow from rear areas to forward combat units; maneuver of large reserve forces to meet enemy spearheads that break through the front; and large numbers of heavy weapons (tanks, armored personnel carriers, and artillery) to kill enemy forces. Accordingly, denial's effectiveness can be assessed by measuring the impact of theater air power on these target sets and the correlation between damage to these targets and Iraq's willingness to surrender Kuwait.

Three main findings emerge from this test. First, coercion succeeded. The facts show that Saddam Hussein's willingness to abandon Kuwait changed during the air war. Although Saddam adamantly opposed negotiations from 2 August 1990 to 14 February 1991, from 15 to 23 February, Iraq negotiated and accepted a Soviet-brokered peace including "full and unconditional withdrawal" from Kuwait. This agreement did not avoid a ground campaign because the United States additionally demanded that Iraq leave its military equipment behind, and Saddam Hussein refused.

Second, denial and not decapitation accounts for Iraq's willingness to abandon Kuwait. The first week of the air war was dedicated to destroying the Instant Thunder target set, but Saddam's regime was not overthrown and his army continued to receive strategic direction. In contrast, the denial campaign wreaked havoc on Iraq's strategy of waging a protracted war of attrition against a Coalition ground offensive by sharply interdicting supply lines, preventing military units from moving on the battlefield, and destroying heavy forces. As a result, Saddam began negotiating with the Soviet Union to abandon Kuwait.

Third, Desert Storm shows that advances in military technology have improved the effectiveness of theater air campaigns against an opponent's military strategy more than strategic air campaigns against an enemy's political and economic centers. While it has long been possible to destroy a small number of key targets by mounting massive air raids, today's precision-guided weapons make it possible to destroy many more targets using one or a few weapons each. Thus, the revolution in precision weapons benefits strategies that would attack many targets more than those that would strike only a few. Since political and economic targets have always been few compared to military targets, these advances increase the power of denial strategies while improving the effectiveness of strategic air power hardly at all.

This chapter proceeds in five parts. The first describes the changes in Iraq's willingness to abandon Kuwait over the course of the war. The next three sections explain that change. They describe the Coalition's goals and the two strategies—decapitation and denial—conceived to achieve them, and they explain the execution and effects of the decapitation campaign and the denial campaign. Finally, the conclusion discusses how advances in military technology are likely to effect America's ability to influence regional conflicts using air power.

COERCION SUCCEEDED

Although many observers of the Gulf War have not realized it, Saddam Hussein was coerced into agreeing to abandon Kuwait. The problem is not Iraq's behavior prior to war; everyone agrees that Iraq remained firmly opposed to withdrawal from Kuwait from the time of the invasion on 2 August 1990 to the start of the air war on 16 January 1991. What is in dispute is Iraq's behavior after the war began, specifically whether its mid-February offers to withdraw were genuine.[3] The evidence shows that these concessions were serious.

Without extensive access to Iraqi records, the key to resolving this controversy is separating the issues at stake. Iraq's rapid and unexpected seizure of all of Kuwait gave Saddam Hussein control of 20 percent of the world's oil reserves. U.S. leaders were concerned that he could double that percentage by next seizing Saudi oil fields, thereby gaining single-handed control over the world price of oil. To avoid this prospect, the United States wanted not only to reverse Iraq's conquest of Kuwait but also to contain its expansion in the future.[4] Thus, from the beginning, the Coalition had two main

---

[3] Richard Herrmann believes that Saddam was not serious about leaving Kuwait; Lawrence Freedman and Efraim Karsh maintain that Saddam, in agreeing to the Soviet proposal, in effect accepted the loss of Kuwait. Richard K. Herrmann, "The Middle East and the New World Order: Rethinking U.S. Political Strategy after the Gulf War," *International Security* 16 (Fall 1991), p. 53; Lawrence Freedman and Efraim Karsh, *The Gulf Conflict, 1990–1991: Diplomacy and War in the New World Order* (Princeton: Princeton University Press, 1993), p. 382.

[4] Bush announced America's national objectives in "Address to the Nation Announcing the Deployment of United States Armed Forces to Saudi Arabia, 8 August 1990," in *Public Papers of the Presidents of the United States: George Bush, 1990 (Book II)* (Office of the Federal Register, National Archives and Record Administration), p. 1108. Secretary of Defense Richard Cheney stressed that "if Iraq's ambitions are not curbed they will just grow stronger. . . . Its military power will be greater. It will come armed not just with 5,600 tanks, a million-man army, chemical weapons, and ballistic missiles [but could also] possess nuclear weapons and long-range missiles to deliver them." Hearings before the Committee on Armed Services, Senate, *Crisis in the Persian Gulf Region: U.S. Policy Options and Implications*, 101st Cong., 2d sess., p. 657.

demands: that Iraq withdraw from Kuwait and that conditions for "future regional stability" be established, which over time came to mean the destruction of Iraq's offensive military capability and the replacement of Saddam's regime. The available evidence shows that in mid-February 1991 Iraq agreed to the first demand, but it never agreed to the second.

The appropriate benchmark to measure change in Iraq's willingness to leave Kuwait is Saddam's initial set of conditions for withdrawal, which he announced on 12 August 1990. Without mentioning withdrawal, he tied even the consideration of a change in Kuwait's status to a prior agreement by Israel and Syria to withdraw from contested territories and the United States to disengage completely from Saudi Arabia and the Gulf region. The specific conditions were: unconditional Israeli withdrawal from Palestine, Syria, and Lebanon; Syrian withdrawal from Lebanon; immediate American and Egyptian withdrawal from Saudi Arabia; formulation of arrangements in Kuwait "taking into consideration the historical rights of Iraq in its territory and the Kuwaiti people's choice"; and an immediate end to the boycott against Iraq.[5] Despite many diplomatic initiatives by UN, French, Soviet, and U.S. representatives, these conditions not only remained unchanged, but Iraq took no initiatives of its own to start negotiations until the war began.

In mid-February 1991 Iraq's diplomatic behavior changed significantly. On 15 February Iraq's highest governing body, the Revolutionary Command Council, in publicly announcing Iraq's conditions for peace, mentioned the idea of withdrawal from Kuwait for the first time. It was a sharp turn from Iraq's previous position that the annexation of Kuwait was "permanent."

By itself the announcement is not a reliable indicator of intent to withdraw, primarily because it also could be interpreted as a way to weaken Arab support for the war. If Iraq's purpose was to use diplomacy to split away Arab members from the UN Coalition, the key was to continue to assert linkage between resolution of Kuwait's status and the Israeli-Palestinian conflict and American presence in the Middle East. The announcement included a list of demands that linked Kuwait to just these issues. The specific conditions were a cease-fire; abolition of UN resolutions related to the crisis; international withdrawal from the Gulf region within one month; Israeli withdrawal from occupied territories; recognition of Iraq's historical rights on land and sea; free elections in Kuwait; international payments to Iraq to cover war damages; cancellation of outstanding Iraqi debt; and declaration of the Gulf region as a zone free from foreign military bases or presence.[6]

---

[5] "Text of Saddam Husayn Initiative on Situation," 12 August 1990, reported in *Foreign Broadcast Information Service: Near East and South Asia [FBIS-NESA]*, 13 August 1990, pp. 48–49.
[6] "RCC Issues Statement of Terms for Peace," *FBIS-NESA*, 15 February 1991, pp. 17–19.

The 15 February announcement is best viewed as the opening gambit in a flurry of diplomatic activity during the second half of February in which Iraq dropped the linkage of Kuwait to other issues and accepted unconditional withdrawal. On 11 February, Iraq had quietly received the personal envoy of Soviet President Mikhail Gorbachev, Yevgeny Primakov, in Baghdad, and on 12 February he met with Saddam and Foreign Minister Tariq Aziz to discuss a Soviet initiative to stop the war. In his memoirs, Primakov describes his conversation with Saddam:

> I said that I would like us to left tete-a-tete, and when this was the case I unambiguously emphasized that the Americans were decidedly in the mood for starting a broad-based ground operation, as a result of which the grouping of Iraqi forces in Kuwait would be crushed. You understand, would be crushed. . . . I proposed to him the following: that he declare a withdrawal of forces from Kuwait . . . and that this withdrawal had to be complete and unconditional. It was here that there really was for the first time a change. Saddam Husayn began to put questions in point of substance: Could he be sure that "the soldiers leaving Kuwait will not be shot in the back"?[7]

Primakov cabled Moscow on 13 February that "the Baghdad talks were encouraging" and that Aziz would travel to Moscow to "continue Soviet-Iraqi contacts on instructions from Saddam Husayn" on 16 February.[8] After Aziz assured Gorbachev that Iraq would agree to the unconditional withdrawal of its troops from Kuwait in six weeks, Gorbachev presented Aziz with a peace proposal, which caught the international community as a whole by surprise.[9]

On 21 February Moscow announced that Saddam had accepted the Soviet plan for Iraq's "full and unconditional withdrawal" from Kuwait. Most important, the Soviet plan contained no linkage to other Middle East disputes and outlined the order in which hostilities would end. Iraqi withdrawal would begin on the second day after a cease-fire; it would be completed in a fixed time period; economic sanctions against Iraq would lapse when Iraq had withdrawn two-thirds of its forces from Kuwait; all other UN resolutions against Iraq would lapse when all Iraqi forces had left Kuwait; all POWs would be released immediately after the cease-fire; and the UN Security Council would designate countries not involved in the conflict to oversee the Iraqi withdrawal.[10] This second concession marks the first coer-

---

[7]"Primakov on Gulf Diplomacy," *FBIS-SOV*, 12 March 1991, p. 24. Quotations in the original.
[8] "Soviet Envoy Arrives in Baghdad," *FBIS-NESA*, 12 February 1991, p. 27; "Soviet Spokesman: Primakov Talks 'Encouraging,' " *FBIS-NESA*, 14 February 1991, p. 20.
[9] "Aziz Allegedly Says Iraq Wants to Withdraw," *FBIS-NESA*, 19 February 1991, p. 45; "Gorbachev Offers Peace Plan to Iraq," *Washington Post*, 19 February 1991, p. 1; "Primakov on Gulf Diplomacy," *FBIS-SOV*, p. 26.
[10] "Soviets Say Iraq Accepts Kuwait Pullout," *New York Times*, 22 February 1991, p. 1.

cive success during the Gulf War, since Iraq, although not militarily defeated, had conceded one of the Coalition's two main demands.

The Bush administration was not satisfied, however. On 22 February the United States denounced the Soviet plan as too soft because it lacked a timetable for withdrawal and ended economic sanctions prematurely.

Iraq responded later that day with its third set of concessions. It agreed, through a Soviet spokesman, to complete withdrawal from Kuwait in twenty-one days and from Kuwait City in four days and to the end of economic sanctions only after the withdrawal was complete. Primakov's memoirs explain that to agree to the twenty-one-day timetable, Aziz cabled Saddam from Moscow via Soviet transmitters directly to the Soviet embassy in Baghdad in Iraqi code and that Saddam responded positively on the evening of February 22.[11]

Still dissatisfied, the Bush administration responded with an ultimatum: Iraq must withdraw from Kuwait in seven days and from Kuwait City in two days and must announce "publicly and authoritatively" acceptance of these terms by noon on 23 February. As administration spokespersons explained at the time, these terms were designed to force Saddam to abandon his heavy conventional forces, many of which were disabled or dug in and to admit defeat in a public manner that would weaken his political support in Iraq and throughout the Arab world.[12]

Indeed, far from wanting Saddam to withdraw, American leaders by mid-February appear to have sought to prevent the withdrawal of his army in Kuwait. In his memoirs, CENTCOM (Central Command) Commander in Chief General H. Norman Schwarzkopf recounts multiple phone calls between himself and Joint Chiefs of Staff Chairman General Colin Powell. These make clear that American leaders knew in detail about the Iraqi-Soviet negotiations and wanted Schwarzkopf to speed up the timetable for a ground war before the Soviet initiative could be consummated.

On 18 February Powell called Schwarzkopf to say: "The National Security Council is saying we may need to attack a little early. Can you let me know by tomorrow if you can manage it?" The next day, when Schwarzkopf told Powell that he could not speed up the timetable because his commanders objected that this would increase the number of casualties, Powell responded that "This [Soviet] peace initiative may be for real," and that the State Department was pushing for an even harder line: "They want to demand unconditional surrender." Further, when Schwarzkopf called Powell

[11] "Primakov on Gulf Diplomacy," p. 27.
[12] For discussions of specific Iraqi conditions, see Associated Press, "8 Points of the Soviet-Iraqi Peace Plan," *International Herald Tribune*, 23 February 1991; Peter Riddell, "Bush Regains the Initiative," *Financial Times*, 23–24 February 1991; Anatoly Repin, "The Chance Has Been Missed," *Novosti Gulf Bulletin* (Moscow), 27 February 1991; and stories in the *New York Times*, 23 February 1991.

on the twentieth to say that bad weather was forecast for 24 February and that his commanders wanted a two-day delay, Powell said:

> I've already told the President the twenty-fourth. How am I supposed to go back and tell him the twenty-sixth? You don't appreciate the pressure I'm under. I've got a whole bunch of people here looking at this Russia proposal and they're all upset. My President want to get on with this thing. My secretary wants to get on with it. *We need to get on with this.*[13]

Schwarzkopf also makes clear that the main objection with the Soviet plan was not that Kuwait would not be returned but that Saddam would be permitted to keep his army intact. When discussing whether the Iraqis should be given six weeks to withdraw, Schwarzkopf told Powell on 21 February: "Give him six weeks to pull out, and he packs up his weapons, goes home, and tells everybody he defied the United States. And he still has enough force to threaten his neighbors. It's the Arabs nightmare." Instead, Schwarzkopf suggested the U.S. offer a cease-fire of one week which he believed would be enough time for Saddam to withdraw his solders but not his supplies or the bulk of his equipment, most of which was dug in or disabled. "This would work," he told Powell, "but I doubt Iraq would buy it."[14]

As is well known, Saddam did not comply with the ultimatum, which he denounced as a double-cross since Iraq had already made concessions to meet American objections to the Soviet plan. Less well known, however, is that he did make a fourth, final concession. Early on the twenty-third, before the ultimatum expired, Foreign Minister Aziz held a news conference in Moscow in which he reaffirmed Iraq's acceptance of the second Soviet plan. Thus, Iraq accepted Bush's first demand for a public commitment, but rejected a shorter time table—since that would have meant abandoning Iraq's army, Saddam's only incentive for withdrawing prior to the ground war.[15]

There are three reasons to believe that Iraq was sincere about leaving Kuwait. First, Iraq made numerous concessions in response to American complaints that Iraq's offers were insufficient, and met the demand for public, direct Iraqi acceptance of concessions in place of announcements through Soviet spokesmen. Second, disingenuous concessions would have been pointless. The twenty-one days allowed for a withdrawal under the second Soviet plan was so short that the Coalition would still have been in

---

[13] H. Norman Schwarzkopf, *It Doesn't Take a Hero* (New York: Bantam Books, 1992), pp. 511–514. Emphasis in the original.

[14] Schwarzkopf, *It Doesn't Take a Hero*, p. 516.

[15] "US and Britain Insist on Deadline," *New York Times*, 21 February 1991, p. 1; "War is to Continue," *New York Times*, 22 February 1991, p. 1; "RCC Statement of Bush's 'Disgraceful' Ultimatum, 22 Feb 1991," *FBIS-NESA*, 25 February 1991, pp. 33–34; "Transcripts of Statements by Bush and Fitzwater on Unconditional Pullout," *New York Times*, 23 February 1991, p. 4; and "Transcript of Aziz's Comments in Moscow," *New York Times*, 24 February 1991, p. 4.

position to resume the war if Saddam did not comply fully. If Iraq had ceased its withdrawal at a certain point, at oil fields in northern Kuwait, for example, the war could have resumed before the Iraqis could do much to fortify their new position. Third, the final U.S. demands that Iraq rejected had little to do with withdrawal from Kuwait but centered instead on forcing Iraq to abandon its military equipment in Kuwait and on undermining public support for Saddam's regime. This pattern continued even after the ground war began. When Saddam publicly announced on 26 February, after two days of ground fighting, that his army was withdrawing from Kuwait, President Bush responded by declaring that the ground war would continue unless Iraqi soldiers abandoned their equipment:

> [Saddam] is not withdrawing. His defeated forces are retreating. . . . As we announced last night, we will not attack unarmed soldiers in retreat. We have no choice but to consider retreating combat units as a threat. . . . The best way to avoid further casualties on both sides is for the Iraqi solders to lay down their arms. . . . It is time for all Iraqi forces in the theater of operations, those occupying Kuwait, those supporting the occupation of Kuwait, to lay down their arms. And that will stop the bloodshed.[16]

In effect, Bush was demanding that Iraqi troops surrender, not withdraw.[17]

Thus, the record indicates that Iraq was coerced. By 23 February 1991 Saddam agreed to complete withdrawal from Kuwait, although not to surrendering his military equipment in addition. The key question is what happened in mid-February that caused Saddam to change his behavior and look for a way to avoid a ground war.

GOALS AND AIR STRATEGIES IN DESERT STORM

To liberate Kuwait and to assure "the security and stability of the Persian Gulf region," which came to mean stripping Iraq of its military capability to threaten its neighbors, the United States and the UN Coalition mounted a military campaign that incorporated two alternative, but not mutually exclusive, air strategies. "Instant Thunder" aimed to win with a six-day strategic air campaign alone, which would decapitate the Saddam Hussein

[16] George Bush, "The Iraqi Retreat," public address on 26 February 1991, reprinted in *Vital Speeches of the Day*, 16 March 1991, p. 325.

[17] I reported in a *Boston Globe* editorial on November 17, 1994 that a U.S. aircraft that can monitor the movement of ground forces with radar had detected that Iraq withdrew one or two of its 42 divisions from Kuwait on the nights immediately preceding the ground war. If true, this partial withdrawal would provide further evidence that Saddam's acceptance of the Soviet Peace plan was sincere. However, subsequent analysis by the U.S. Air Force revealed that the underlying data was spurious. It was not based on moving forces, but on radar anomalies associated with static ground structures.

[219]

regime, rendering it unable to govern Iraq or control military forces. It was so named to distinguish it from the graduated and failed Rolling Thunder campaign during the Vietnam War. The denial campaign assumed that a American ground campaign would be necessary to force the Iraqis out of Kuwait. For this strategy, the purpose of air power was to shift the military balance on the ground, crippling Iraq's military strategy to defeat the ground attack.

Rather than choose one over the other, General Schwarzkopf melded both strategies together in his 25 August 1990 briefing to Chairman Powell and Secretary of Defense Richard Cheney. Originally, the decapitation campaign was planned to come first. Phase I would be the "strategic air campaign," which would achieve air superiority over Iraq and cripple its political and military leadership. Phase II would be a "Kuwait air campaign" to gain air superiority over Kuwait and allow "unchallenged use of the skies for fixed wing and [helicopter] operations." Phase III would be "ground combat power attrition" to "reduce Iraqi ground force capability, soften ground forces to assure successful penetration and exploitation, reduce ability to lay down chemicals, and destroy Republican Guard capability to reinforce Kuwait." Finally, Phase IV would be the "ground attack" to "eject Iraqi forces from Kuwait."[18] As additional air assets were allocated to the theater, it became possible to carry out both air strategies at the same time. By 20 December, plans called for executing Phases I, II, and III simultaneously, with Phase I lasting six days, Phase II two days, and Phase III fourteen days, followed by an eighteen-day ground campaign.[19]

Three factors drove senior political and military leaders to pursue both decapitation and denial strategies. First, even though Army leaders might be expected to favor air attacks on Iraqi forces in the Kuwaiti theater of operations (KTO) as the surest way to reduce ground casualties, decapitation advocates were able to present the Instant Thunder plan to General Schwarzkopf first, on 8 August, and no competing denial plan was available until October. Second, the shadow of Vietnam discouraged political leaders from rejecting any military strategy that did not have insuperable political costs, with the result that organizational rivalry produced more logrolling than victory for one strategy over another.[20] Finally, the abundance of military resources ultimately available to the Coalition muted competition over which strategy to pursue. With sixteen hundred Coalition combat aircraft available and the Iraqi air force expected to offer only meager opposition,

---

[18] Diane T. Putney, *Air Power Advantage: Planning the Gulf Air Campaign* (Washington, D.C.: Office of Air Force History, 1993), p. 7; Department of Defense, *Conduct of the Persian Gulf War: Final Report to Congress* (Washington, D.C.: GPO, April 1992), 1: 92.

[19] Gulf War Air Power Survey (GWAPS), *Planning and Command and Control* (Washington, D.C.: GPO, 1993), vol. 1, pt. 1, p. 175.

[20] Clodfelter, "Of Demons, Storms and Thunder."

air power could destroy targets both in Baghdad and in the KTO without compromising either mission.[21]

The Decapitation Strategy

Senior air force leaders believed that the Instant Thunder strategic air campaign would force Iraq to withdraw from Kuwait without a ground offensive or even significant strikes against Iraqi ground forces. The principal architect of this plan was Colonel John A. Warden III, the Air Staff's Deputy Director of Plans for Warfighting Concepts, who was supported by Air Force Chief of Staff General Michael Dugan. This strategy also received some support from the chief of strategic air planning in Saudi Arabia, General Buster C. Glossen, and, most important, from General Schwarzkopf, who was looking for something that could be done in the fall before the Coalition had much in the way of ground or even air forces, especially to retaliate against Saddam if he were to execute hostages or launch a preemptive chemical or biological attack. The chief advantage of this strategy was that the air campaign could be assembled in a matter of weeks and executed in a matter of days. When Warden briefed Schwarzkopf on Instant Thunder, he reportedly told him that bombing Baghdad would form a "left hook of sorts, thus delivering a 'quick knockout blow' to the Iraqis. . . . General you have here the opportunity to attain the greatest military victory since Inchon!"[22]

Instant Thunder sought to kill, overthrow, or isolate Saddam Hussein and his regime or to use the threat of these events to compel Saddam to withdraw from Kuwait. The decapitation campaign failed to accomplish any of these objectives.

The most explicit statement on assassination comes from General Dugan, who said in comments that led to his dismissal: "Saddam is a one-man show. If for any reason he went away, it is my judgment that those troops would all of a sudden lose their legitimacy and they would be back in Iraq in a matter of hours, in disarray. That kind of thinking has been at the heart of the advice that I've brought to discussions in the past couple of weeks."[23]

[21] For the bureaucratic details of the merger, see DoD, *Conduct of the Persian Gulf War*, pp. 122–24.

[22] GWAPS, *Summary Volume* (Washington, D.C.: GPO, 1993), pp. 27–53; Warden quoted in Edward O'Connell, "A Look into Air Campaign Planning," (manuscript, Defense Intelligence College, March 1992), p. 5.

[23] "U.S. War Plan: Air Strikes to Topple Hussein Regime," *Aviation Week and Space Technology*, 24 September 1990, pp. 16–18. For similar comments by Dugan, see "U.S. to Rely on Air Strikes if War Erupts," *Washington Post*, 16 September 1990, p. 1. Dugan also referred to the idea of overthrowing Saddam: "You would attempt to convince his population that he and his regime cannot protect them. If there is a nation that cannot defend its people against intruding foreigners—protect their lines of communication, their means of production, their cities—that brings a great burden for their ruler." "U.S. War Plan in Iraq: 'Decapitate' Lead-

After the war, General Schwarzkopf explained: "After the shooting started we repeatedly asserted that the United States was not trying to kill Saddam Hussein . . . and that was true, to a point. But at the very top of our target list were the bunkers where we knew he and his senior commanders were likely to be working."[24]

An early August planning document on Instant Thunder focuses more on overthrowing and isolating the regime, listing as its goals, "to induce: A. Saddam Hussein to withdraw all Iraqi forces completely from Kuwait and restore the legitimate Kuwaiti government; B. create conditions conducive to the overthrow of the Saddam Hussein regime by patriotic Iraqi elements who may be more amenable to withdrawal from Kuwait; C. render Iraq incapable of providing strategic and operational support to its forces in Kuwait and significantly reduce Iraq's offensive and defensive potential for a prolonged period." The Gulf War Air Power Survey agrees that Instant Thunder "would not just neutralize the government, but change it, by inducing a coup or revolt that would result in a government more amenable to the Coalition's demands." John Warden summarized the plan in one short sentence: "The Saddam Hussein regime is our target—not the Iraqi people."[25]

To accomplish these objectives, Instant Thunder planned to attack eighty-four targets in six days (see Table 12), attacking the main target sets simultaneously. First, air power would gain command of the air, destroying the Iraqi air force, long-range missiles, and weapons of mass destruction. The object was not only to render Iraq defenseless to stop subsequent attacks but also to signal Saddam's weakness to the population. "The psychological impact on the Iraqi populace of being open to unremitting air attack will be a powerful reminder of the bankruptcy and impotence of the Saddam Hussein regime."[26] Second, precision aircraft would attack the regime by striking key leadership facilities (presidential residences and VIP bunkers),

---

ership," *Los Angeles Times*, 16 September 1990, p. 6. Although President Bush, General Powell, and General Schwarzkopf publicly declared that "individuals" were not specifically targeted, the Gulf War Air Power Survey reports that "the chief architects of the air campaign targeted Saddam Hussein. . . . Planners believed that Hussein, as a military commander, was a legitimate target during the war." GWAPS, *Planning*, p. 99. Moreover, on the eve of the war, General Merrill McPeak, Dugan's successor, is reported to have estimated the odds of killing the Iraqi leader with air strikes as three in ten. Rick Atkinson, *Crusade: The Untold Story of the Persian Gulf War* (New York: Houghton Mifflin, 1993), p. 273.

[24] Schwarzkopf, *It Doesn't Take a Hero*, p. 319.

[25] "Strategic Air Campaign against Iraq to Accomplish NCA Objectives," 16 August 1990, pp. 1–2, USAF Historical Research Agency, Maxwell AFB, Ala., GWAPS files, CHSH 1–5; GWAPS, *Summary*, pp. 44–45; Colonel John A. Warden III, "Instant Thunder: A Strategic Air Campaign Proposal for CINCENT," 17 August 1990, USAFHRA, GWAPS files, portions declassified by author on 9 May 1992 during briefing at School of Advanced Airpower Studies, Maxwell AFB.

[26] "Strategic Air Campaign," p. 3.

Table 12. Instant Thunder target set

Leadership (24)*	Production (24)	Infrastructure (3)	Population	Forces (33)
Hussein Regime Incapacitate	Electricity Oil	Railroads Bridges	Psyops —Iraqis	Air Defense Offense
Telecom and C3 Military Civil	NBC		—for workers	—bombers —missiles
Internal Control Organs				

SOURCE: "Instant Thunder," A Strategic Air Campaign Proposal for CINCCENT, 17 August 1990.
*Number of targets in each major category.

telecommunication nodes (telephone exchanges and television and radio stations), and internal security organs (Ba'ath party and secret police headquarters, and government ministries). Finally, air power would hit economic infrastructure (electric power, oil facilities, railroads, and bridges) in order to harass and frustrate the Iraqi public, "to convince the Iraqi populace that a bright economic and political future would result from the replacement of the Saddam Hussein regime."[27] Thus, Instant Thunder also incorporated civilian punishment logic, although the punishment effort was mild by World War II standards. Civilians would only be inconvenienced, not killed. Iraqi ground forces were not targeted.

The Denial Campaign

In contrast to Instant Thunder, which hoped for victory through air power alone, a second camp proposed a combination of air and land power.[28] Led by Chairman Powell, General Schwarzkopf, and General Charles Horner, this group did not believe that strategic air attack would coerce Saddam into pulling out of Kuwait. Further, some members of this group were less interested in coercing withdrawal than in destroying the

[27] GWAPS, *Summary*, p. 44. The goal of inconveniencing the population is also indicated in the comments of the air planners in Riyadh during the war. A 28 January report states: "Results to date—no electricity, water in Baghdad—100% electricity out in Baghdad—no water—50% out nationwide." GWAPS, *Operations and Effects and Effectiveness* (Washington, D.C.: GPO, 1993), vol. 2, pt. 1, p. 197.
[28] Some U.S. Army officers, such as Colonel Harry Summers, argue that Desert Storm vindicated AirLand Battle Doctrine, the vision of how to employ air power developed by the army during the 1980s. The denial campaign, however, did not adhere to this doctrine, which ties air power closely to the ground scheme of maneuver of the friendly field army. Since Coalition ground forces did not move until after the air campaign had made practically any ground scheme of maneuver viable, AirLand Battle was not tested in this case. Summers, *On Strategy II.*

Iraqi army. Thus, the denial campaign was not intended primarily for coercive purposes, although in the event it did succeed in coercing Saddam Hussein.[29]

When first briefed on Instant Thunder on 11 August, Chairman Powell dropped his bombshell question: "OK, It's day six . . . now What?" Colonel Warden expressed confidence that the strategic air campaign would "induce" the Iraqis to withdraw from Kuwait, but Powell wanted more. He insisted, "I don't want them to go home—I want to leave smoking tanks as kilometer fence posts all the way to Baghdad."[30] For his part, Horner doubted whether Instant Thunder could induce withdrawal at all: "There is no way the Iraqis are going to turn tail and head home after six days of bombing!"[31] Schwarzkopf, in a conference with his commanders on 14 November 1990, was even more emphatic that the goal was annihilation of Iraq's army, not withdrawal: "We need to destroy—not attack, not damage, not surround—I want you to *destroy* the Republican Guard. . . . We're not gonna say we want to be as nice as we possibly can, and if they draw back across the border that's fine with us. That's bullshit! We are going to destroy the Republican Guard."[32] "Our strategy to go after this army," Powell crisply explained on 23 January 1991, "is very, very simple. First, we're going to cut it off, and then we're going to kill it."[33]

The denial campaign was built around a "hammer and anvil" concept. First, air power would fix the Iraqi ground forces in position, preventing them from retreating or redeploying, and then, air power would attack the Iraqi army where it stood, to weaken its combat power as much as possible. Finally, a massive ground attack would destroy the forces that remained.

Air interdiction would block the Iraqi army's withdrawal from Kuwait as well as wreck its morale by reducing the flow of supplies (ammunition, POL, food, and water). On blocking withdrawal, the 17 January 1991 operations order for Desert Storm could not have been clearer: "Cut key bridges, roads, and rail lines immediately south of Basra to block withdrawal of RGFC [Republican Guard] forces."[34] On logistics, although no target goal

[29] GWAPS, *Planning*, p. 164.

[30] Putney, *Air Power Advantage*, p. 5.

[31] O'Connell, "Look into Air Campaign Planning," p. 10.

[32] Schwarzkopf, *It Doesn't Take a Hero*, pp. 381–82. Schwarzkopf appears to have adopted annihilation as *the* main goal only after his one-corps plan, which had as its main objective seizing Kuwaiti oil fields in a frontal assault into Kuwait, was rejected in October. For the details of the plan, see Richard M. Swain, *Lucky War: Third Army in Desert Storm* (Ft. Leavenworth, Kans.: U.S. Army Command and General Staff College Press, 1994), pp. 107–8; Robert Scales, *Certain Victory: United States Army in the Gulf War* (Washington, D.C.: Office of the Chief of Staff, 1993), pp. 145–53.

[33] Powell news briefing, *New York Times*, 23 January 1991.

[34] Quoted in GWAPS, *Operations and Effects and Effectiveness*, vol. 2, pt. 2, p. 161. Hereinafter GWAPS vol. 2, pt. 2 is referred to as *Effects and Effectiveness*. Schwarzkopf viewed the Republican Guard as the center of gravity of Iraq's military forces, and was especially keen to see it

for reducing throughput capacity was stated, the purpose was to lower capacity below subsistence levels, not merely to weaken the army's ability to conduct fast-paced combat operations. General Glossen declared in October 1990 that the interdiction campaign would make it "for all practical purposes impossible for [Saddam] to resupply the troops that he has in Kuwait. . . . Once you've done that, the only thing you have to have is the *patience to wait out the effect of what you've already accomplished*. . . . It's impossible for that military force of 500,000 people and 4,000 tanks, to eat and drink and have resupplies for more than about 10 days."[35]

Air power would then annihilate large parts of Iraq's field army by direct attack. As early as 14 August 1990, Schwarzkopf set a goal of destroying 50 percent of the enemy's combat power (later defined to mean armor, artillery, and personnel) before launching a ground offensive.[36] In November air attrition of ground forces became tightly linked to the Coalition's plan to launch a surprise "left hook" against the Iraqi army's exposed right flank, because both goals—50 percent attrition and the westward movement of 255,000 Coalition troops some two hundred miles to their jumping-off points—were estimated to require two to three weeks.[37] This attrition would dramatically shift ground-force ratios in the Coalition's favor, increasing the speed at which the ground campaign could be prosecuted and reducing casualties.[38] To orient attacking aircraft, the theater was divided into some thirty-six "kill boxes," thirty nautical miles on a side, and aircraft were assigned to specific corners of boxes to attack either predesignated targets or targets of opportunity. Plans called for the kill boxes associated with the Republican Guard to be attacked first, followed by those associated with Iraq's

---

annihilated. Given its position between Iraq's regular army and Iraq, blocking the Republican Guard's withdrawal effectively blocked withdrawal for the army as a whole. Lieutenant General John J. Yeosock, "Army Operations in the Gulf Theater," *Military Review* 71 (September 1991), p. 7; Scales, *Certain Victory*, pp. 112–18.

[35] Quoted in GWAPS, *Effects and Effectiveness*, p. 171.

[36] This goal was established for a one-corps attack. Although the United States later planned a two-corps attack, the 50 percent goal did not change because Saddam had also deployed more forces to Kuwait. GWAPS, *Planning*, p. 170.

[37] To keep the left hook a surprise, repositioning of ground forces could not begin until after the Air Force stopped Iraqi reconnaissance flights. Thus, Coalition ground forces could not shift westward until after the air war started, and the Air Force was guaranteed a window to attrite the enemy's military forces. In early November Warden's planners estimated that twenty-three days would be required to achieve 50 percent destruction of Iraqi armor, artillery, and troops in the Kuwaiti theater of operations, and Glossen, taking account of additional aircraft, projected twelve days. The plan to target Iraqi personnel appears to have been dropped before the air war began. GWAPS, *Planning*, pp. 172–86. On the timetable for the westward positioning of ground forces, see Schwarzkopf, *It Doesn't Take a Hero*, p. 392.

[38] While the overall ratio of Coalition to Iraqi brigades in the Seventh Corps sector was assumed to be no better than 1.3 to 1, with the assumption of 50 percent attrition by the air campaign, the Seventh Corps would have an advantage of 11.5 to 1 at the breach site, 3.8 to 1 en route to the Republican Guard, and 2 to 1 in the decisive encounter with the Republican Guard. Swain, *Lucky War*, p. 146.

regular army units. The Republican Guard, thus, appeared as targets in both Phase I and Phase III.

The ground plan was built around a two-corps left hook, which would "maneuver deep West of Kuwait to destroy the [Republican Guard] and cut off [lines of communications] to Iraqi forces in the KTO." A consolidation phase would follow, which was expected to last up to four weeks, during which remaining Iraqi forces in Kuwait would be mopped up. The left hook involved the Seventh Corps attacking west of Wadi al Batin (the western boundary of Kuwait), driving north and east to attack the Republican Guard south of Basra, while the Eighteenth Corps would attack even farther west in a secondary effort designed both to distract the Iraqi high command by appearing to threaten Baghdad and, more important, to cut the major axis of withdrawal along Highway 8 south of the Euphrates River. Three other attacks by U.S. Marine and other Western and Arab ground forces would seek to penetrate the Iraqi front line along the Saudi-Kuwait border, fix tactical reserves, and liberate Kuwait City.[39]

There appears to have been no predefined decision rule for when to launch the ground offensive once the forces were in position. Glossen's planners projected that air power could continue the attrition of Iraqi forces beyond the 50 percent level, if given the time. The same model that predicted 50 percent attrition of enemy forces in twelve days also predicted 80 to 100 percent attrition in eighteen days.[40] Central Command was not confident such time was available, however, and prepared for the possibility of staging an earlier-than-planned ground attack if it was discovered that the Republican Guard was about to retreat back into the interior of Iraq before the planned ground offensive got under way.[41] Thus, plans were based on the goal of destroying Iraqi forces, not coercing withdrawal.

EXECUTION AND EFFECTS OF DECAPITATION

The air campaign against Iraq progressed through four stages, shifting between decapitation and denial. In the first, the United States executed the Instant Thunder decapitation strategy, based on precision bombing of leadership and economic infrastructure targets. The second, which began in early February, incorporated both decapitation and denial strategies. While the decapitation effort continued, bombing shifted from strategic targets to interdiction and Iraqi army targets in southern Iraq and Kuwait. In the third stage, beginning after the Al-Firdos bunker incident on 14 February, decapitation ceased as Baghdad was placed off limits and bombing focused ex-

[39] Swain, *Lucky War*, pp. 126, 130–31.
[40] GWAPS, *Operations*, p. 256.
[41] GWAPS, *Effects and Effectiveness*, p. 161.

Figure 1. Air campaign—Sorties by phase

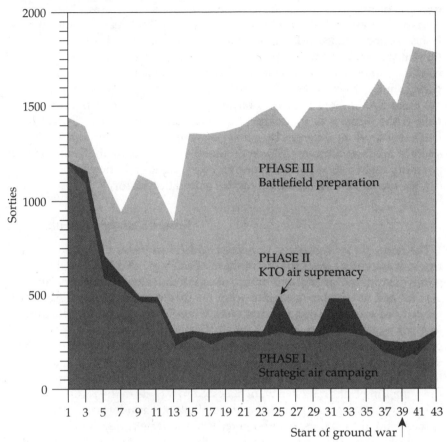

SOURCE: U.S. Department of Defense, *Conduct of the Persian Gulf War* (Washington, D.C.: GPO, April 1992), p. 101.

clusively on military targets in the KTO. Finally, on 23 February, the night before the ground offensive, a final spasm of decapitation attacks supplemented the denial strategy. Figure 1 indicates this general pattern.

The Coalition could shift strategies at will because it had air superiority from the outset. Qualitatively inferior in both pilot training and aircraft technology, the Iraqi air force mostly rode out the initial bombing raids inside hardened aircraft shelters. Its most ambitious opposition, on the first night, only involved 25 fighters, 8 of which were shot down.[42] The main threat came

[42] Less than 50 percent of Iraqi pilots met Soviet standards and less than 20 percent, French standards. GWAPS, *Operations*, p. 76. Less than half of Iraq's 700 combat aircraft on 2 August 1990 were third generation (MiG-23 / 25 and F-1, comparable to the U.S. A-6 or late-model F-4)

[227]

from Iraq's ground-based air defenses, hundreds of medium and high altitude radar-guided surface-to-air missiles and thousands of low-altitude antiaircraft artillery (AAA) guns and infrared SAMs. The Coalition suppressed Iraq's radar-guided SAMs by attacking the command-and-control network that integrated early warning radars, acquisition and intercept radars, and missile control radars. Iraq's radar network was neutralized to the point that during the last four weeks of Desert Storm only about 15 percent of the nearly 480 radar SAMs fired appear to have been guided. After 23 January Iraq's radar SAM threat was so meager that coalition aircraft chose to deal with Iraq's low-level air defenses by simply avoiding them, flying almost exclusively at medium altitudes (fifteen thousand feet). Overall, the Coalition lost just thirty-eight aircraft, or about one for every eighteen hundred combat sorties, the lowest rate for sustained combat in aviation history.[43]

Instant Thunder's Execution

The strategic air campaign remained faithful to Instant Thunder's chief tenets. It is evident from the distribution of strategic and KTO sorties, categories of strategic targets, and timing of attack that almost all important targets related to Saddam's regime were hit in the opening days. The vast majority of sorties during the first week were flown against targets in Iraq and not against targets in the Kuwait theater of operations. Of approximately fourteen hundred combat sorties launched on each of the first three days, some twelve hundred were dedicated to strategic attack and counterair, about a hundred were assigned to strike the Republican Guard, and the remaining hundred or so were allocated to targets in the KTO.[44] The distribution of strategic targets also matched Instant Thunder's conceptual design. As Table 13 shows, over 90 percent of the targets attacked in the first seventy-two hours (235 of 257) fell into the original Instant Thunder categories, despite the fact that the target list had expanded since August. The timing of attacks also remained faithful to Instant Thunder's goal of speed; almost 70 percent of the Instant Thunder-related targets were hit in the first three days (235 of 347).

The air campaign was combat effective against Instant Thunder's target categories. By 25 January Iraqi electric power capacity had dropped by more than 75 percent and the national power grid had collapsed in central and southern Iraq; oil-refining capacity had dropped by more than 35 per-

---

or fourth generation (MiG-29, comparable to U.S. F-14/F-15/F-16). The rest of its aircraft were 1950s and 1960s Soviet and Chinese technology. DoD, *Conduct of the Persian Gulf War*, p. 13.

[43] GWAPS, *Effects and Effectiveness*, pp. 130–44; GWAPS, *Summary*, pp. 57–62; and Benjamin S. Lambeth, *The Winning of Air Supremacy in Operation Desert Storm*, P-7837 (Santa Monica, Calif.: Rand Corporation, 1992).

[44] DoD, *Conduct of the Persian Gulf War*, pp. 135, 165.

Table 13. Strategic targets and plans for attack in the first three days

Categories	Instant Thunder 17 August 1990	Strategic targets 15 January 1991	Planned strikes first 72 hours
Decapitation			
Leadership	5	33	29
Telecommunications	19	59	27
Electricity	10	17	17
Oil	6	12	10
Other strategic			
Railroads, bridges	3	33	23
Nuclear, chemical,			
biological sites	8	23	20
Strategic air defense	10	58	49
Airfields	7	31	28
Naval	1	19	9
Military support	15	62	23
Subtotals	84	347	235
Republican Guard	na	37	6
Scud missile sites	na	43	16
Breach areas	na	6	0
SAMs	na	43	0
Totals	84	477	257

SOURCE: GWAPS, vol. 1, pt. 1, *Planning*, pp. 185 and 189.

cent.[45] On 30 January Coalition commanders could confidently claim that twenty-six leadership targets had been struck and 60 percent severely damaged or destroyed, 75 percent of Iraq's command-and-control and communications facilities had been struck and one-third destroyed, and all known nuclear facilities and most known biological and chemical facilities had been destroyed.[46] Thus, in terms of targets destroyed, Instant Thunder achieved what it had hoped to accomplish within the time frame it had established.

While strategic air attacks continued, after the first 6 days, they were concentrated mainly on nonleadership targets such as nuclear, chemical, and biological weapons sites, Scud missile sites, bridges, and military industries. Decapitation attacks also continued, although at a reduced level of effort, rarely climbing above a hundred sorties per day.[47] With the main strategic targets already hit, subsequent attacks were limited to restriking old targets to keep them out of operation and striking new targets identified after the air war began.

[45] GWAPS, *Effects and Effectiveness*, pp. 302–3, 309.
[46] Central Command Briefing, General Schwarzkopf and Brigadier General Glosson, *New York Times*, 30 January 1991.
[47] For the most complete daily record of strategic air attacks, see "Target Attacks by Day by Aircraft," n.d., USAFHRA, GWAPS files, BH-56.

There were two brief spikes in the decapitation attacks. From 9 to 13 February Coalition aircraft attacked secondary leadership bunkers in Baghdad's suburbs which had been activated after the beginning of the war and re-struck places where Saddam might be and other government ministries and security service facilities. This campaign was cut short by the Al-Firdos bunker incident. This secondary bunker was targeted after intelligence reported that senior Iraqi officials were using its communications equipment.[48] Destruction of the target also accidentally killed hundreds of civilians, and Iraq was quick to exploit the tragedy for propaganda purposes. Thereafter the Coalition instituted higher-level control over strikes in Baghdad in general and against leadership targets in particular.[49] As a result, only five targets in Baghdad were hit during the remainder of the war.[50] Finally, leadership targeting was renewed on 22 February, just before the beginning of the ground war, with strikes on Saddam's non-Baghdad residences and on a command "Winnebago," and continued until the end of the war.[51]

Instant Thunder's Results

Instant Thunder failed to kill, overthrow, or isolate Saddam or his regime. It posed no significant threat to Iraq's senior political and military leadership at all. None of Iraq's top political or military leaders were killed during Desert Storm. Although Iraq is a closed society, Baghdad regularly announces leadership changes in key positions, such as head of state, the Revolutionary Command Council, Council of Ministers, the Chief of General Staff and commanders of the Popular Army, Air Force, and Republican Guard, as well as some heads of the intelligence and security services. All of the top forty-three Iraqi political and military leaders on 15 January 1991 were still alive after 1 March.[52] Nor is there any evidence that relatives of

[48] DoD, *Conduct of the Persian Gulf War*, p. 189.
[49] Schwarzkopf thereafter personally reviewed all targets nominated for air attack in Baghdad. GWAPS, *Summary*, pp. 68–69.
[50] GWAPS, *Summary*, p. 219.
[51] Saddam purchased twenty-four motor homes during the 1980s, which he used as conference vehicles, and he appeared in one on American television early in the air campaign. GWAPS, *Operations*, p. 241.
[52] For the civilian government (President, Vice-President, and members of the Revolutionary Command Council and Council of Ministers), I compared pre-war data good as of January 1990 to post-war data good as of 23 March 1991 from *The Europa World Year Book*, vols. 1990 and 1991 (London: Europa Publications, 1990, 1991). I verified this information with the Iraq branch of Europa Publications on 1 March 1994. For leaders of defense and intelligence organizations (Chief of General Staff, Commander of the Popular Army, Commander of the Air Force, Commander of the Republican Guard, and heads of the Mukhaburat, Amn al-Khass, and Special Security Apparatus), I compared pre-war data from September and November 1990 to post-war data from June and September 1991 from *The Middle East and North Africa*, vols. 1991 and 1992 (London: Europa Publications Limited 1990, 1991); FBIS-NESA, 8 November 1990; *Agence France Presse*, 19 June 1991; *Los Angeles Times*, 14 July 1991; and *Middle East Report* 22 (May–June 1992): 15–21.

Revolutionary Command Council members were killed, although it is possible that some family members of second-ranking officials may have died in the Al-Firdos bunker.[53]

Instant Thunder did not pose a significant threat to Iraqi leaders partly because individuals can move about and change schedules so easily, especially in war when they are constantly reacting to fast-changing events, that the intelligence task of locating leaders in time and place is inherently difficult. Even if located, an individual is not likely to remain in place long enough to mount a strike and get bombs on target. The one known effort to kill a senior Iraqi military leader by matching real-time intelligence to air attack (the Iraqi Third Corps commander on 26 January) failed not because bombs were late but because the commander did not show up.[54] Iraqi leaders, moreover, always take extreme measures to disguise their whereabouts to avoid assassination attempts by domestic and regional foes. Saddam, a former assassin, adheres to no fixed schedule, often spontaneously changes his itinerary, and never announces his rare public appearances in advance.[55] In addition, General Dugan's public remarks in September 1990 in effect gave Saddam four months' warning that he would be targeted.

Strategic bombing advocates claim that destroying leadership targets explains Iraq's change of heart in mid-February.[56] The 15 February announcement followed only a day after the Al-Firdos bunker incident, in which, according to Iraqi reports, hundreds of members of "leading families" were killed. Thus, so the argument goes, to avoid the death of top leaders or their families, Saddam agreed to abandon Kuwait.

The main problem with this argument is that the political fallout over the loss of Iraqi civilian lives in fact *reduced* the vulnerability of leadership bunkers almost immediately. Just hours after the bunker was destroyed, the Bush administration announced a halt to bunker attacks and required future attacks to receive authorization from the highest levels.[57] Air operations against Baghdad ceased completely for the next four days and only 5 targets

---

[53] After the war, Foreign Minister Aziz denied that the Al-Firdos bunker raid killed anyone close to Saddam. "Nobody in my family was injured, nor were any of those from other members of the leadership." Since we do not know exactly whom Aziz meant to include as 'members of the leadership,' it remains unclear whether his statement excludes all Iraqi officials. See *Washington Post*, 8 May 1991.

[54] On 26 January 1991, American intelligence intercepted an Iraqi transmission that proposed a commander's conference be held in the Iraqi Third Corps sector two hours after the intercept. Two F-111s attacked the target within minutes of the planned meeting with one-ton bombs, and the next day reconnaissance confirmed that the building and some surrounding military transportation vehicles had been obliterated. Intelligence later learned that the Third Corps commander was not at the meeting. Scales, *Certain Victory*, pp. 189–90.

[55] Efraim Karsh and Inari Rautsi, *Saddam Hussein: A Political Biography* (New York: Free Press, 1991).

[56] Warden, "Employing Air Power in the Twenty-first Century," p. 82.

[57] "Allies to Review Air Target Plans to Avoid Civilians," *New York Times*, 15 February 1991, p. 1.

in Baghdad were attacked during the remainder of the war.[58] Thus, if Iraq's political calculations were driven by the vulnerability of leadership bunkers, the Coalition's reaction should have stiffened Iraq's position on withdrawal, not softened it.

Instant Thunder also failed to overthrow Saddam's regime, by either coup or popular revolt. The campaign might have succeeded by precipitating a coup that not only removed Saddam from power but also replaced him with a new elite more sympathetic to American policies. Specifically, targeting leadership facilities and communications networks between the leadership and the instruments of state power could weaken Saddam's control, while attacks on economic infrastructure brought the war home to the general population and encouraged the formation of counterelites. Consequently, evaluation of this strategy must address three questions: What are the minimum requirements for a coup to succeed? How vulnerable to a coup was Saddam's regime prior to air attack? How much could Instant Thunder increase the vulnerability of Saddam's regime?

A coup d'etat occurs when a new elite seizes control of a state's professional bureaucracy and standing armed forces. Whether one member of a ruling oligarchy replaces the top leader or a new set of leaders replaces the previous ruling group, coups involve the removal of the dominant political leader by those intending to govern the state themselves. In the twentieth century, coups have occurred mainly in Third World states where public commitment to political institutions is weak and the military, which is behind virtually every coup, is a powerful institution, separate from the government but indispensable for rule. Although military defeat or setbacks have sometimes caused coups, coups have never caused a state to abandon successful military operations in this century.

The literature on successful coups suggests that they share three elements. First, conspirators must be able to plan in advance without being detected. Coups involve rapid transitions of power from one ruling elite to another so as to confront potential opponents with a fait accompli. These operations are inevitably complicated and require weeks of planning because they involve not only seizing key instruments of executive power and individual rulers but also blocking resistance from other areas until the new leaders can assert their control over them. Second, the vast majority of the state officials and population must not have a strong interest in opposing the new ruling elite. Any group seizing power which does not have the loyalty of other elites would be quickly replaced by legitimate political authority. Third, poverty is a common denominator among coups. One recent study of 121 countries between 1950 and 1982 found that the poorest were

---

[58] GWAPS, *Summary*, p. 219.

Table 14. Iraqi coup attempts, 1921–1983

Date	Main party	Outcome
10/29/36	left-wing army	success
8/11/37	right-wing army	success
12/24/38	left-wing army	failure
3/31/40	army	success
4/1/41	right-wing army	success
7/15/58	army	success
3/7/59	Ba'athist army	failure
2/8/63	Ba'athist military	success
11/18/63	air force	success
9/17/65	army	failure
6/30/66	Nasserist army faction	failure
7/17/68	Ba'ath army faction	success
1/20/70	foreign-supported faction	failure
6/30/73	police/political faction	failure
7/28/79	Shi'a/Syrian Ba'ath	failure
7/11/82	Shi'a	failure
10/83	unknown	failure

SOURCES: William R. Thompson, *The Grievances of Military Coup-Makers* (Beverly Hills, Calif.: Sage, 1973); Edward Luttwak, *Coup d'Etat: A Practical Handbook* (Cambridge: Harvard University Press, 1978); and Phebe Marr, *The Modern History of Iraq* (Boulder, Colo.: Westview, 1985).

twenty-one times more likely to have coups than the wealthiest states and that a high rate of economic growth dramatically inhibits coups.[59]

Using these criteria, Saddam's regime was a poor target for coup makers. At first glance, it appears highly vulnerable, a typical Third World country with a strong state but weak polity, subject to seventeen coup attempts since 1936, eight of which succeeded (see Table 14). In fact, however, the last successful coup, in 1968, changed the political institutions and transformed Iraq from one of the world's most coup-prone states to one of the least.

In 1968, Iraq adopted one-party totalitarianism. Just as Cuba, North Korea, Outer Mongolia, and Vietnam have not experienced any successful coups since adopting a Marxist-Leninist form of government, so Iraq's vulnerability to coups dramatically lessened when it built a large state apparatus that supports the political domination of the Ba'ath party. An extensive network of secret police numbering more than 250,000 permits the Ba'ath party to monitor Iraq's 18 million people closely, and the Republican Guard and other division-sized units repress opponents. Further, the Ba'ath party has emasculated its main threat, the military, by removing military officers from political office, ending factionalism within the officer corps, and estab-

[59] John B. Londregan and Keith T. Poole, "Poverty, the Coup Trap, and the Seizure of Executive Power," *World Politics* 42 (January 1990): 151–83.

lishing lines of authority parallel to the command hierarchy which are directly responsible to the regime.[60]

Totalitarianism in Iraq reduces the prospects for a coup both by making conspiracies more difficult and by increasing the requirements for success. Conspiracies are more difficult, because the cooperation necessary for opposition within elite circles is severely discouraged by the high incentives individuals have to defect. Moreover, the extent and complexity of the Iraqi regime's instruments of power increases the size of the conspiracy necessary to achieve success. If any one of a multitude of thousand-man units can oppose a coup, many individuals must be co-opted to convince any group of would-be conspirators that the coup could succeed, and the risk that plotters will be discovered before a coup can be attempted increases. Not surprisingly, since 1973, there have been many reports of coup plots foiled by Saddam but relatively few reports of actual attacks on the regime.

Furthermore, the regime established concentric circles of support within Iraq's social structure. The largest circle contains Iraq's 6 million Sunni Arabs, who have dominated the upper economic, political, and military classes for centuries and whose support for Saddam rests on the fear of Shi'a fundamentalist rule and Khurdish separatism. The next is the Ba'ath party, membership in which has become a fact of life for Iraq's nearly 1 million state employees, creating political and economic ties to the current regime. Next are the instruments of state security, numbering several hundred thousand, which are accomplices and executors of Saddam's brutal rule. The next circle contains the thirty thousand "full members" of the Ba'ath party, who control all leadership posts, not just those in Baghdad, through eighteen branches, one in each province, and three in Baghdad. Within this group lies the core leadership group, numbering about two thousand, nearly all of whom come from Saddam's home area, Tikrit, and are bound to

[60] On the generally low vulnerability of totalitarian states to coups, see Steven R. David, *Third World Coups d'Etat and International Security* (Baltimore: Johns Hopkins University Press, 1987), pp. 106–37. Known intelligence services are estimated to total 260,000 and include the Mukhabarat (party intelligence), the Amn (secret police), and Estikhbarat (military intelligence). In addition to the Republican Guard forces, at least three independent division-sized military units are dedicated to protecting the leadership from coups or armed uprisings: the Border Guards, the Mobile Police Strike Force, and Saddam's personal security force, Amn al-Khas. The best available account of the Iraqi security apparatus is Samir Khalil, *Republic of Fear* (Berkeley: University of California Press, 1989), esp., pp. 3–45. See also Islam al-Khafaji, "State Terror and the Degradation of Politics in Iraq," *Middle East Report* 22 (May–June 1992): 15–21; Andrew Rathmell, "Iraqi Intelligence and Security Services," *International Defense Review* (May 1991): 393–95. On the limits of our information on contemporary Iraq, see Marion Farouk-Sluglett and Peter Sluglett, "The Historiography of Modern Iraq," *American Historical Review* 96 (December 1991): 1408–21. On the changing role of the army in Iraqi politics since 1968, see Amatzia Baram, "The Ruling Political Elite in Ba'thi Iraq, 1968–1986: The Changing Features of a Collective Profile," *International Journal of Middle East Studies* 21 (1989): 447–93; Hanna Batatu, *Old Social Classes and Revolutionary Movements of Iraq* (Princeton: Princeton University Press, 1978), pp. 29, 764–807; and Khalil, *Republic of Fear*, pp. 25–28.

him by tribal affiliation. Finally, there are the key individuals who control state organizations, and these are related to Saddam by blood or marriage.[61]

Concentric loyalty reduces the regime's vulnerability to a coup by tightly linking devotion to Saddam with access to Saddam, reducing the odds that those he meets with would support his removal. It also encourages those in each circle to oppose Saddam's overthrow by someone in the next larger circle, since it would also jeopardize their position.

The Ba'ath party stressed modernization and more equal distribution of wealth by egalitarian distribution of income and services, by creating a socialist economy, and by rapid economic development. Between 1968 and 1983, the Ba'ath regime redistributed vast portions of land, developed a welfare state funded by oil in which education and health services are free, and rapidly developed heavy industry and manufacturing—all of which improved social mobility for the lower and middle classes.[62]

The improvement of economic well-being for the Iraqi population reduced the risk of coup because it removed a major source of grievance among would-be plotters: poor economic performance by the regime. In addition, although Iraq's economy was impoverished by the embargo and air war, Saddam diverted resources away from sectors of the population most likely to oppose his regime (Kurds and Shi'as) and toward parts that would more likely remain loyal (central region Sunnis), thus mitigating their hardship and demonstrating the regime's willingness to treat loyal groups better than disloyal groups.[63]

Strategic air attack could increase the chances of a coup against Saddam only modestly. Destruction of leadership bunkers and national communications could impede the ability of Iraq's security services to talk to each other and to monitor phone conversations but would not have prevented the security services from discovering plots, partly because plotters too were denied access to national communications and partly because the ability of the security services to monitor the population rests not on elite-to-elite communication but on spy-to-individual observation. Nor could Instant Thunder solve the most important execution problem of potential coup makers: knowing Saddam's location at a specific time. Although Instant Thunder destroyed a handful of locations Saddam could use, mobile communication systems permitted him to remain in contact by radio or messenger wherever he was. Moreover, Saddam's military advantage over potential coup makers dwarfed any benefit they would obtain from a breakdown of elite commu-

---

[61] Amatzia Baram, *Culture, History, and Ideology in the Formation of Ba'thist Iraq* (New York: St. Martin's, 1991), pp. 4–5, 19; Helen C. Metz, *Iraq, a Country Study* (Washington, D.C.: GPO, 1990), pp. 185–93; Khalil, *Republic of Fear*, pp. 36–38.

[62] Phebe Marr, *The Modern History of Iraq* (Boulder, Colo.: Westview Press, 1985), pp. 240–81.

[63] Simon Edge, "Iraq Goes Hungry after Merchant Purge," *Middle East Economic Digest*, 18 September 1993, p. 10.

nications. Throughout the war, about a third of Iraq's 1.2 million armed men were stationed away from Kuwait and southern Iraq: one infantry corps of three divisions in central Iraq south of Baghdad; two corps of eighteen infantry divisions in the north near Mosul; two infantry divisions and two armored regiments in western Iraq; and two to four Republican Guard brigades and one mechanized infantry division in Baghdad itself.[64] Although destroying communications among these forces would slow their response to rebel forces beyond their positions, they were already located in the most important strategic areas for any coup forces to control. Accordingly, the imbalance of force favoring Saddam was so great that it overwhelmed any effects of slow communication between the forces. Yet, even if Instant Thunder had provoked a coup, other elites were not likely to have accepted a new government willing to withdraw from Kuwait. Any new regime sympathetic to American wishes would be immediately condemned as unpatriotic, and so would become an easy target for a countercoup by an anti-American elite.

In short, Instant Thunder assumed that Saddam's regime rested on its physical ability to provide secure leadership areas and telecommunications to support forces that were vulnerable to air attack. In fact, it rested on a political structure that air attack could not alter.

If it could not precipitate a coup, perhaps Instant Thunder could have toppled Saddam's government by instigating a popular revolt against the Ba'ath party. Unlike a coup, which would transfer control of the state from one set of individuals to another, a revolt would destroy the state and replace it with a regime based on new political principles.[65] Specifically, the destruction of Iraq's key economic infrastructure along with visible air superiority might have persuaded the population that the Ba'ath party could not provide for its welfare, whereupon the people might rise up against the party.

This projection has more credibility than the hopes for a coup because, in the war's aftermath the Kurds and Shi'as did rebel against the Ba'ath party, making it appear that strategic air power in fact came close to producing a revolt which would have ended the war on favorable terms to the Coalition.[66] There are two flaws in this argument however: first, the uprisings were not the result of strategic attack but occurred only among groups already disaffected with the regime; and second, the failure of the uprisings even after the Coalition had decimated Iraq's army in the KTO suggests that the popular revolt would have been even less likely to succeed had military

[64] DoD, *Conduct of the Persian Gulf War*, p. 83.
[65] This definition follows Stephen M. Walt, "Revolution and War," *World Politics* 44 (April 1992): 321–69.
[66] For a history of the rebellions, see "Civil War in Iraq," a Staff Report to the Committee on Foreign Relations, United States Senate, 102d Cong., 1st sess., May 1991, pp. 1–4.

pressure been limited to strategic air attack alone. Furthermore, the area most heavily subjected to strategic air attack, Baghdad, contained the lowest popular resistance against the Ba'ath party. Whereas large mobs roamed cities in the Shi'a south and Kurdish north, in Baghdad popular opposition never escalated beyond individual acts of civil disobedience easily contained by local police. The only groups to revolt were those already so disaffected that they required no additional encouragement by strategic air attack to rebel.

The timing of the uprisings suggests that it was the defeat of the Iraqi army in Kuwait rather than strategic air attack that precipitated rebellion. The Iraq civil war began in the Shi'a south on 2 March, two days after Iraq's army was defeated but a month after Iraq's national telecommunications, electric power, and oil-refining networks had been destroyed. Moreover, the instigators of the uprisings were not impoverished civilians but conscripted Shi'a infantry soldiers who wanted revenge for being abandoned to their fate in the ground war. One officer described their mood:

> We were anxious to withdraw, to end the mad adventure, when Saddam announced withdrawal within 24 hours—but without any formal agreement with the allies to ensure the safety of the retreating forces. We understood that he wanted the allies to wipe us out. . . . In Zubair we decided to put an end to Saddam and his regime. . . . Hundreds of retreating soldiers came to the city and joined the revolt. . . . In a matter of hours, the uprising spread to Basra.[67]

In short, the timing of the revolts combined with the fact that they occurred in areas farthest from strategic air attack and already hostile to the regime suggests that the revolts would likely have occurred even had no bombs fallen on Baghdad.

In addition, there is no evidence that strategic air attack made the rebellions more likely to succeed. As I have pointed out, Saddam had already stationed large army formations separate from those in the KTO near likely trouble areas. This strategy reduced the need for communication between the leadership and the instruments of repression as well as the need to move forces long distances to suppress opposition. That the army was able to respond with force in a matter of days to both revolts suggests that Instant Thunder did little to reduce the capability of Saddam's instruments of repression below the level they required to operate effectively.

Instant Thunder actually created serious coordination problems for the rebel forces. Given Iraq's two-decade-long campaign against opposition to the Ba'ath party, only small, fragmented opposition groups could have existed prior to the war. Therefore, successful overthrow of the Ba'ath regime

[67] Quoted in Faleh Abd al-Jabbar, "Why the Uprisings Failed," *Middle East Report*, 22 (May–June 1992): 9.

by a popular revolt would require opposition leaders to coordinate the activities of local populations without the benefit of past mobilization plans. In particular, they would need access to reliable and timely national communication networks to gather intelligence on and organize a regional defense against Saddam's loyal forces.[68] Thus, when Instant Thunder destroyed Iraq's national communication network, it made it virtually impossible for the rebels to prevent Saddam's forces from regaining control over the rebellious towns one-by-one. In short, Instant Thunder made rapid coordination of force inside Iraq difficult, but in so doing, it harmed the less-prepared rebels more than the well-prepared security forces. Of course, if Saddam had been killed, the outcome might have been different, since his personal authority provided the political cohesion that tied the various security forces to a single cause.

Instant Thunder also failed to isolate Saddam's regime from the battle in Kuwait, despite official statements to the contrary.[69] For military decapitation to have smashed Iraqi military power, attacks against national leadership and command and control should have rendered Iraqi forces incapable of offensive or defensive operations even if their operational and tactical capabilities had remained intact. Accordingly, evaluation of the effect of military decapitation depends on three issues: how much direction Iraqi army operations required from Baghdad; how significantly communication between Baghdad and the KTO was degraded; and whether that degradation accounts for Iraq's poor performance during the land war.

Iraqi military operations did not use high-volume, real-time communication with Baghdad. In comparison to the multibillion-dollar apparatus deployed by the Coalition, Iraq's command-and-control infrastructure prior to the conflict was exceedingly primitive. Senior leaders were used to taking orders from Saddam in face-to-face meetings, and communication above division level relied on Iraq's elementary post, telephone, and telegraph system.[70] As a result, Saddam lacked the capability to orchestrate the movement of many combat units while a battle was in progress. Iraqi army doctrine called for local commanders to construct detailed plans, which were then passed up the chain of command for approval. Similarly, the lo-

---

[68] For instance, the Kurds inherited vast quantities of Iraqi military equipment (tanks, trucks, artillery, mortars, and light arms) and claimed to have more than 400,000 men under arms, but lacked the logistics (POL) and communications capability to get the equipment to the men on short notice. Al-Jabbar, "Why the Uprisings Failed," p. 12; "Civil War in Iraq," pp. 4–5.

[69] The Department of Defense report to Congress says that air strikes on Iraqi leaders and national communication targets paralyzed Iraq's ability to direct battlefield operations by seriously degrading communication between Baghdad and the KTO: "In Iraq's rigid, authoritarian society, where decision-making power is highly centralized in the hands of Saddam Hussein and a few others, destruction of the means of Command and Control had a particularly crippling effect on forces in the field." DoD, *Conduct of the Persian Gulf War*, p. 199.

[70] National Training Center, *The Iraqi Army: Organization and Tactics*, Handbook 100-91, (Fort Erwin, Calif.: Operations Group of the National Training Center, 3 January 1991), p. 37.

gistic and supply procedures of the Iraqi army also did not depend on high-volume communication from the theater to Baghdad. The Iraqis followed a Soviet-style pattern of "pushing" supplies from central Iraq to forward depots (which would match resources to immediate needs) according to preplanned criteria that did not rely on communicating demand from the field.[71] Thus, Baghdad required the ability to communicate approval for theaterwide plans, not to orchestrate the action of many divisions, regiments, and battalions in battle.

The air war degraded communication between Baghdad and the KTO significantly but not enough to cripple Saddam's ability to direct theaterwide operations. Although the civil telecommunications system through which 60 percent of military landline communications passed appears to have been destroyed in the first days of the air war, air power did not destroy a dispersed network of command posts between Baghdad and Kuwait with high-frequency radio transmission capability, and it did not stop couriers.[72] Specifically, by 23 February the Joint Chiefs of Staff battlefield damage assessment for the president indicated that 75 percent of national command telecommunications and 30 percent of military communications were still

---

[71] Ibid., pp. 46, 173–76. On Iraq's unsophisticated command-and-control procedures during the Iran-Iraq War, see Michael G. Cooper, "The Iran-Iraq War and Lessons for the Future" (Newport, R.I.: Naval War College, Department of Operations, 1989), pp. 49–52; and, M. G. Ellison, "Operational Art: The Missing Link in the Iran-Iraq War" (Fort Leavenworth, Kans.: U.S. Army Command and General Staff College, 1988).

[72] This channel provided the Coalition with intelligence on Iraqi plans, preparations, and morale, which means that such information was in fact being transmitted among senior commanders. DoD, *Conduct of the Persian Gulf War*, pp. 151–52; and Desmond Ball, *The Intelligence War in the Gulf*, Canberra Papers on Strategy and Defense no. 78 (Canberra: Strategic and Defense Studies Centre, Australia National University, 1991), pp. 80–82; R. W. Apple, "Raids Said to Badly Delay Baghdad Messages to Front," *New York Times*, 11 February 1991, p. 12; and S. Gregory, *Command, Control, Communications, and Intelligence in the Gulf War*, Strategic and Defense Studies Centre Working Paper no. 238 (Canberra: Australian National University, 1991), pp. 15–18. It is not clear whether the failure to destroy this channel was deliberate, whether it was kept open so as to pinpoint the location of the Iraqi leader. Whereas Secretary of Defense Cheney declared that the United States was "not in the business of targeting specific individuals," he also said, "As commander of those forces, as part of the national command authority, [Hussein] might be well affected." Another Pentagon official stated in mid-February: "We have adopted a strategy of leaving Saddam with some communications so that we can track him." Also, it was reported on 25 January that "a Central Intelligence Agency task force has coordinated an intensive effort to identify and locate Saddam's electronic 'fingerprints,' or the characteristic patterns of movement and communication that accompany his travel around Iraq." Moreover, Tariq Aziz reported in a postwar interview that Saddam believed U.S. intelligence could pinpoint his location electronically, and therefore he never used a telephone after 2 August 1990. Richard Cheney, interviewed on NBC, *Meet the Press*, 27 January 1991, transcript in *Current News* (Washington, D.C.: Office of the Assistant Secretary of Defense for Public Affairs, 28 January 1991), p. A7; James Adams, "The Day Saddam Escaped Death," *Sunday Times* (London), 17 February 1991, p. 3; Barton Gellman, "Air Strike against Saddam Foiled by Storm: Iraqi Leader Is Part of Command-and-Control Structure Allies Seek to 'Decapitate,'" *Washington Post*, 25 January 1991, p. 1; and Milton Viorst, "Report from Baghdad," *New Yorker*, 24 June 1991.

"operational." Moreover, numerous prisoner of war reports affirmed that communications from Baghdad to Kuwait were continuously available.[73]

Clearly, Iraq remained able to direct its ground forces throughout the war. It had sufficient command and control to organize the Al-Khafji attack on 29 and 30 January, an attempt by the Iraqi army to prompt a ground war by seizing a Saudi Arabian town, which combined battalion-sized spearheads with division-sized follow-on forces. More significant, in response to the surprise left hook in the Coalition's ground attack, Iraq was able to order a withdrawal from the theater and to direct five Republican Guard divisions to screen the retreat by blocking a breakthrough by the Seventh Corps into the Iraqi rear.[74]

The air war did succeed in paralyzing Iraqi combat units, but movement stopped more because of lack of intelligence about the nature of the Coalition's advance and because of air power's ability to destroy enemy forces on the move than because of any cutoff of timely communication with Saddam. Unlike the Coalition, Iraq had no intelligence satellites and instead relied on a small number of airborne early warning and reconnaissance aircraft, which could not operate given the Coalition's air supremacy. Iraq also had ground-based systems, but these were jammed.[75] Thus, until Coalition forces made contact with them, Iraqi forces could not move because they had no way of knowing the Coalition's plan of attack.

Moreover, tight Iraqi coordination of division- or corps-sized ground units hardly mattered because air power's ability to destroy Iraqi forces on the move was so overwhelming. As the experiences of the Al-Khafji attack and general retreat indicate, the Iraqi forces were significantly more vulnerable to air attack when on the move than in concealed revetments. Total Iraqi equipment attrition as recorded by Central Command increased fourfold during the Al-Khafji incursion over what it had been for the entire campaign up to that point.[76] Given the open desert terrain and Iraq's inability to contest control of the air, degrading Saddam's ability to conduct sophisticated schemes of ground maneuver could not make Iraq's forces any more vulnerable than they already were.

EXECUTION AND EFFECTS OF DENIAL

Unlike decapitation, the denial campaign generated powerful coercive pressure on Iraq to withdraw from Kuwait. Specifically, Iraq's willingness to

[73] GWAPS, *Effects and Effectiveness*, pp. 224, 289.
[74] GWAPS, *Summary*, p. 70; Freedman and Karsh, *Gulf Conflict*, p. 397; and U.S. News & World Report, *Triumph without Victory: The Unreported History of the Persian Gulf War* (New York: Times Books, 1992), p. 335.
[75] Gregory, *Command, Control*, p. 16.
[76] GWAPS, *Summary*, pp. 109–10.

abandon Kuwait grew as air power crippled its military strategy for holding the seized territory.

Iraqi Goals and Strategy

With its invasion, Iraq attempted to incorporate Kuwait and its oil resources quickly and cheaply. Success would permit Saddam to dominate the Organization of Petroleum Exporting Countries and the Persian Gulf region, if not to set the world price of oil. In his 25 July 1990 interview with the American ambassador to Iraq, April Glaspie, Saddam said, "Iraq came out of the war [with Iran] burdened with a $40 billion debt. . . . We began to face the policy of the drop in the price of oil. . . . Kuwait and the UAE [United Arab Emirates] were at the front of this policy aimed at lowering Iraq's position and depriving its people of higher economic standards. . . . Twenty-five dollars a barrel is not a high price."[77]

By September it became apparent that Saddam had chosen a "fortress Kuwait" military strategy aimed at deterring the Coalition from a ground attack by threatening a lengthy and bloody attrition battle. America's Vietnam experience appears to have been a key factor in Iraqi calculations that the specter of high casualties would either deter a Coalition attack or compel the United States to abandon it once begun. Saddam told Glaspie, "Yours is a society which cannot accept 10,000 dead in one battle."[78] One Iraqi assessment early in the crisis was even more clear: "During the Vietnam War, millions of Americans criticized the war because casualties were disproportionate to the 'gains' which could be achieved. There is no doubt that the families of the soldiers sent to Saudi Arabia to threaten Iraq's security . . . will not remain silent about the death of their sons in the Arabian desert at the hands of Iraqi soldiers, and will raise their voices high against President Bush."[79]

The heart of Saddam's military strategy was the forty-two Iraqi army divisions in the KTO. They were deployed for in-depth defense in three primary layers. The first layer comprised a front line of sixteen infantry divisions along the Saudi-Kuwait border, eight infantry divisions defending the Kuwaiti coast against a possible amphibious invasion, and one infantry

[77] "The Glaspie Transcript," in *The Gulf War Reader: History, Documents, Opinions*, ed. Micah L. Sifry and Christopher Cerf (New York: Random House, 1991), inter alia, pp. 122–33.

[78] Ibid., p. 125.

[79] *Al-Jumhuriyya*, 14 August 1990, p. 4, quoted in Norman Cigar, "Iraq's Strategic Mindset and the Gulf War: Blueprint for Defeat," *Journal of Strategic Studies* 15 (March 1992): 5. Many Western analysts considered the range of 10,000 to 20,000 casualties likely. See Joshua Epstein, *War With Iraq: What Price Victory?* (Washington, D.C.: Brookings, 1991); Center for Defense Information, "U.S. Invasion of Iraq: Appraising the Option," *Defense Monitor* vol. 19, no. 8, p. 7; and Trevor Dupuy, *How to Defeat Saddam Hussein* (New York: Warner, 1991). For a view that cut against the conventional wisdom at the time, postulating quick and decisive Coalition ground victory with "probably less than 1000 fatalities," see John Mearsheimer, "Liberation in Less than a Week," *New York Times*, 8 February 1991, p. A31.

Table 15. Estimated KTO order of battle, 17 January 1991

CENTCOM estimates	Divisions	Troops	Tanks	APCs	Artillery
Strategic reserve	8	103,000	1,123	699	592
Operational reserve	9	116,000	2,071	1,984	666
Front line	25	321,000	1,086	187	1,852
Totals	42	540,000	4,280	2,870	3,110

SOURCES: CENTCOM estimates for totals and divisions in each layer, derived from standardized organizational charts, see GWAPS, *Effects and Effectiveness*, pp. 163, 165, 169. The position of different types of divisions in the KTO is from Central Intelligence Agency, *Operation Desert Storm: A Snapshot of the Battlefield*, IA 93-10022 (Washington, D.C.: GPO, 1993); and GWAPS, *Planning*, pp. 204–205. Tables of organization and equipment for the Iraqi army are from *Iraqi Army*, National Training Center, which was the training manual used by U.S. forces to train for Desert Storm. Analysis based on these sources accounted for all but 354 tanks, 22 armored personnel carriers, and 86 artillery pieces, which I evenly divided across the forty-two divisions and aggregated accordingly.

division in south-central Iraq. The second layer was nine regular army mechanized and tank divisions deployed between the front and Kuwait City as an operational reserve. The third layer was a strategic reserve of eight Republican Guard divisions in southern Iraq.

Coalition planners overestimated the strength of the Iraqi forces in the KTO. Table 15 shows U.S. estimates at the start of the war. After the war, information gathered from Iraqi prisoner of war interrogations and intelligence imagery indicated a far different picture. Most Iraqi units were authorized 15 to 20 percent fewer troops than U.S. intelligence estimated and deployed at less than their authorized strength in manpower and equipment. Moreover, Iraq had a policy of allowing up to 20 percent to take leave, few if any of whom returned after the air war began. Table 16 estimates the distribution of Iraqi ground forces in the KTO based on the best postwar data.

Although it involved smaller forces than Coalition planners feared, the Iraqi defensive scheme emphasized attrition warfare. It was designed to make the attacker pay dearly in both the breakthrough and exploitation phases of the battle.

To prevent breakthroughs, the Iraqis deployed sixteen infantry divisions supported by tanks, artillery, mines, and other obstacles in a continuous line, approximately 225 kilometers long, from the coast to a point about 50 kilometers west of the western edge of Kuwait.[80] This represents a very

[80] Only one division was deployed farther west probably because the Iraqis thought, along with many Western observers, that it was logistically impossible for the Coalition to mount an attack there. They may also have thought that the Arab members would veto large ground operations into Iraq itself. The eight divisions assigned to the coast were also unavailable for the breakthrough phase of the battle. These divisions would not have mattered in the exploitation phase either, since, as Iraqi tactical doctrine recognized, they did not have sufficient mobility. National Training Center, *Iraqi Army*, p. 98.

Table 16. Actual KTO order of battle, 17 January 1991

	Divisions	Troops	Tanks	APCs	Artillery
Strategic reserve	8	70,000	966	812	583
Operational reserve	9	79,000	1,999	1,888	529
Front line	25	187,000	510	380	1,363
KTO totals	42	336,000	3,475	3,080	2,475
Deviation from 17 January estimate		−39%	−19%	+7%	−20%

SOURCES: Personnel figures are based on GWAPS estimates, *Effects and Effectiveness*, p. 168, which in turn were based on Iraqi prisoner of war interrogations, which included many high-ranking officers who knew the troop strength of their units. Equipment totals are CIA estimates cited in GWAPS, *Effects and Effectiveness*, p. 170. The equipment analysis was built from detailed CIA counts of equipment in Iraq's twelve armor and mechanized infantry divisions in the KTO in *Operation Desert Storm: A Snapshot of the Battlefield*, which account for all but 180 tanks, 456 armored personnel carriers, and 1,656 artillery pieces, which I divided evenly across the other thirty divisions and aggregated accordingly.

dense defense by Iraqi standards. On paper, the front included an average of one division per fourteen kilometers; since Iraqi divisions in the KTO were on average about 40 percent under strength, the actual density was closer to one division-equivalent for every twenty-three kilometers of front.[81] This distribution compares to typical frontages of twenty-four to forty-five kilometers per division called for in Iraqi tactical doctrine.[82] Their mission was to inflict as much attrition as possible on attacking forces and, even more important, to hold the line long enough for the mobile units of the operational reserve to counterattack and restore the line. If all went right, the attrition battle at the front would be prolonged indefinitely, and the combined firepower of the operational reserves and frontline infantry would inflict rapidly mounting casualties on the attacker.[83] If significant penetrations did occur, the Iraqis would blunt these by counterattacking the flanks of the advancing spearheads using previously uncommitted units of the operational reserve. Once the enemy became bogged down—or if the operational reserve were defeated—the Republican Guard forces would launch a decisive counterattack against the Coalition's main effort.[84] The timing, location, and size of counterattacks would depend on the number and seriousness of enemy penetrations.

[81] This number is very approximate, because it assumes that all divisions were equally under strength and focuses solely on personnel, ignoring heavy weapons.

[82] National Training Center, *Iraqi Army*, p.96.

[83] Iraqi tactical doctrine emphasizes counterattacking rather than containing any penetrations. Ibid., pp. 97–98.

[84] James W. Pardew Jr., "The Iraqi Army's Defeat in Kuwait," *Parameters* 21 (Winter 1991–92): 19–21; Scales, *Certain Victory*, pp. 65–69; and Swain, *Lucky War*, p. 106.

Air Operations against Iraq's Army

The denial campaign began in earnest in the second week, on 23 January, by which time it had become clear the Iraqi air force had decided not to fight and the core strategic targets had been destroyed. Air operations to cut Iraqi movements into and out of the KTO began as precision aircraft (F-111Fs, A-6s, and F-15Es) were directed against bridges. At the same time, non-laser-designating aircraft (F-16s, B-52s, F-18s, A-10s) shifted to attacks against Iraqi ground forces, major highways into the KTO, and supply areas.[85]

The denial campaign received an unexpected boost when Iraq sent parts of two of its operational reserve divisions to attack Al-Khafji. On 29 January striking with several hundred tanks and other armored vehicles but without air cover, the Iraqis presented lucrative targets to a steady stream of Coalition aircraft, which mauled them. On 30 January additional units from these divisions were detected by the Coalition's Joint Surveillance Target Attack Radar System (JSTARS) massing for a follow-on attack. Coalition air power repeatedly attacked the two divisions until they retreated in disarray.[86] The carnage inflicted on the units involved in this battle warned any Iraqi force that left dug-in defenses to conduct a mobile operation that it would face overwhelming air attack.

On 8 February attacks against dug-in Iraqi forces became significantly more effective when laser-designating aircraft were also directed to attack Iraqi armor, artillery, command and control, and logistics throughout the KTO in an operation that became known as "tank plinking."[87] Iraqi armored vehicles were dug in up to their turrets, sandbagged, and surrounded by berms, which protected them from the near misses that frequently occurred because nonprecision aircraft struck from medium altitude. In early February, F-111 crews returning to base near sunset reported that buried armor could be detected by their infrared sensors, because the metallic surfaces cooled faster than the surrounding sand. Thus, air power could strike dug-in armor at night, when the threat from ground fire was least, and with great accuracy.[88]

The front line received more attention after 15 February when B-52s began to target frontline infantry divisions almost exclusively. Also, the effects of the interdiction campaign tightened considerably in February. With many permanent bridges across the Tigris and Euphrates out of commission, Iraq shifted to widespread use of pontoon bridges. Starting in mid-February, F-16s, F-15Es, and F-111s flew armed reconnaissance missions

---

[85] DoD, *Conduct of the Persian Gulf War*, p. 174; GWAPS, *Summary*, p. 18.

[86] DoD, *Conduct of the Persian Gulf War*, pp. 175–76.

[87] Between 23 January and 8 February, F-111Fs devoted approximately 60 percent of their strikes to aircraft shelters. GWAPS, *Summary*, p. 18.

[88] DoD, *Conduct of the Persian Gulf War*, pp. 183–84.

along key river segments to keep them free of usable bridges, destroying a total of thirty-one pontoon bridges and forcing the Iraqis to hide their temporary spans, thus reducing their usability.[89]

When the ground offensive began, air power shifted from stationary to moving Iraqi forces. Its main role was to pursue and destroy the Iraqi army after it began a general retreat early on the morning of 26 February.[90] Armed reconnaissance concentrated on highway choke points along major roads to Basra, destroying over two thousand vehicles. That fewer than fifty of them were tanks or other armored vehicles suggests that, except for the Republican Guard forces which had the best chance of escaping intact because they were in the northern part of the theater, the Iraqis abandoned their equipment rather than attempt to withdraw it under air attack.[91]

The general lack of enemy resistance and superior quality of Coalition ground power made close air support a peripheral aspect of this war. Even on the first morning many aircraft returned with their ordnance because they could not find useful targets. Over a third of A-10 close air support sorties did not drop bombs, AV-8Bs had more missions canceled than completed, and some B-52 strikes against breaching sites were redirected to other targets because ground forces had already passed over them.[92]

Air Power's Effects on Iraq's Military Strategy

How effective in degrading the Iraqi army's combat power was the denial campaign, especially prior to the Coalition's ground attack? Specifically, what were the main requirements of Iraq's military strategy for holding Kuwait and how did the denial campaign affect these requirements?

The key to Iraq's military strategy for holding Kuwait was the ability of its three-layer defensive plan to inflict large numbers of casualties on Coalition forces. Two elements were critical. First, the frontline infantry had to fight tenaciously against the attacking spearheads, channeling them into killing zones where artillery would inflict most of the damage. Otherwise the Coalition forces would be able to bypass frontline units and quickly break into the Iraqi rear before operational reserves were ready to counterattack. Second, the operational and Republican Guard mechanized forces

---

[89] GWAPS, *Effects and Effectiveness*, p. 186.

[90] Of course, air power was not able to stop all movement by the Iraqi mobile reserves, since parts of five Republican Guard divisions were able to maneuver into blocking positions that delayed the Coalition's right hook while other Iraqi forces escaped. Exactly what limited the effectiveness of air power in this case remains a mystery, although Air Force claims that problems in coordination with the Army account for the limited effectiveness of close air support in general should not be completely discounted as a possible explanation.

[91] GWAPS, *Summary*, pp. 113–15.

[92] Ibid., p. 110.

had to be able to move to counterconcentrate against any penetration of the front, both to block the advance of the armored spearheads, prolonging their attrition in the front area killing zones, and to counterattack and halt more serious penetrations. Otherwise the advancing coalition spearheads would quickly overrun the thinly armored infantry units and then run amok in the Iraqi rear, defeating the dispersed mobile forces piecemeal and destroying the command and logistics backbone of the Iraqi forces in the KTO.

Although Saddam expected an air attack, he appears to have believed that it would not weaken Iraq's ability to inflict casualties. Specifically, he sought to protect the army's ability to fight a protracted war by stockpiling large amounts of war materiel and sustenance in the theater and by digging in and dispersing his manpower and equipment. Moreover, Saddam appears to have believed the air campaign would be short. In a transcript of a secret meeting of senior officers inside Kuwait in October 1990, Saddam predicted that the war would start with allied air raids and told his commanders to "stay motionless under the ground just a little time. If you do this, their shooting will be in vain. . . . On the ground the battle will be another story. On the ground the Americans will not be able to put forces as strong as you are."[93]

The air campaign in Kuwait succeeded in undermining the key tenets of Iraq's military strategy. Although Iraq retained sufficient supplies and equipment in the theater as a whole to wage a significant defense of Kuwait and potentially to inflict large numbers of casualties, air power thwarted the twin pillars of its military strategy: the willingness of the frontline units to fight and the ability of the reserve forces to counterconcentrate.

First, air power froze the Iraqi mobile reserves. The threat of attack by hundreds of theater-based aircraft made it impossible for the mobile reserve forces to concentrate and move in significant numbers inside the theater, thus rendering them incapable of blunting penetrations of the front after they occurred. This state of affairs existed as soon as the Coalition gained air superiority, but the Al-Khafji battle clearly demonstrated that Iraq's ability to maneuver under air attack was practically nonexistent.[94] Not only were the initial battalion-sized attacks defeated, but the decimation of the two divisions massing for the follow-on attack indicated that Iraq's plan to mass heavy forces against enemy ground units as they broke through front lines

---

[93] Cigar, "Iraq's Strategic Mindset," p. 18.

[94] The Iraqis knew that intelligence satellites could monitor ground force movement because the Reagan administration had shared this information with Baghdad during the Iran-Iraq War. The Iraqis thus had clues as to how to exploit gaps in the coverage of the American spy satellites, but they did not understand the full extent of the intelligence resources available to the Coalition, such as JSTARS, a 747 with sophisticated radars for monitoring the movement of ground forces. Michael R. Gordon and Bernard E. Trainor, *The Generals' War: The Inside Story of the Conflict in the Gulf* (Boston: Little, Brown, 1995), p. 270.

was not likely to succeed. The failure at Al-Khafji may have demonstrated the vulnerability of Iraqi ground forces to air attack not only to Saddam but to his local commanders as well, who, calling for air support during the battle, may not have realized the degree of air supremacy achieved by the Coalition.[95]

Second, air attack caused massive desertions in the frontline infantry divisions, destroying their morale to the point that they lost the capacity to offer significant resistance. Prisoner reports indicate massive desertions from nearly every frontline division just prior to the start of the ground war. Postwar studies suggest that about 100,000 desertions occurred across the theater compared to approximately 30,000 to 36,000 casualties inflicted by air attack.[96] Furthermore, deserters from frontline units who surrendered before the ground war told their interrogators that most of those remaining in their units would surrender without resistance, as they in fact did once the ground war began.[97]

Air power destroyed morale primarily by direct attrition attacks on frontline units and by battlefield air interdiction of Iraqi logistics within the KTO. Theater-level interdiction of supplies entering the KTO played only a minor role.

Bombing, especially by B-52s, posed a significant threat to the lives of the soldiers below. As the lowest on the pecking order, the frontline units received the least help from Iraqi engineers in preparing bunkers and other fortifications against air attack. Thus, as the air campaign shifted emphasis toward the frontline units, it moved away from the least vulnerable units toward the most. The enemy prisoner of war reports indicate that the B-52 strikes on the frontline troops, which began on 7 February and consumed almost all their effort after 16 February, were the most devastating. The Gulf War Air Power Survey estimates that of the 30,000 to 36,000 troops killed or injured during the air war, most would have been in the frontline units.[98]

Air power also destroyed Iraq's system for distributing supplies within the KTO. Although there was no lack of food in the theater as a whole, battlefield air interdiction cut the flow of supplies to frontline infantry divisions below subsistence levels. The supply doctrine practiced by the Iraqi army called for frequent replenishing of frontline units, with individual soldiers carrying only one day's supply of ammunition, rations, and water, di-

---

[95] DoD, *Conduct of the Persian Gulf War*, p. 175; Freedman and Karsh, *Gulf Conflict*, pp. 365, 479. For evidence that Iraqi military commanders reported the unexpected success of air power at Khafji back to Saddam, see Gordon and Trainor, *Generals' War*, pp. 282–83.

[96] Estimates of desertions range from 84,000 to 153,000. GWAPS, the most authoritative, estimates 100,000. GWAPS, *Effects and Effectiveness*, p. 220; House Armed Services Committee, *Defense for a New Era: Lessons of the Persian Gulf War* (Washington, D.C.: GPO, 1992), pp. 32–33.

[97] GWAPS, *Effects and Effectiveness*, p. 225.

[98] Ibid., p. 220.

visions five days, and the theater as a whole thirty days.[99] Without rail lines or usable waterways south of the Kuwaiti border, this system totally depended on movement of supplies by trucks, which F-16s, F-15Es, F/A-18s, and A-10s attacked either as secondary targets or during armed reconnaissance missions along roadways. By the time the ground war began, according to Iraqi prisoner reports, air attack had destroyed about half the trucks in the theater. Moreover, because drivers were typically killed when their vehicles were destroyed, Iraqi drivers became unwilling to make supply runs. As a result, while there were adequate provisions in the theater to supply Iraq's army, the units farthest from the rear and least favored in Iraq's military hierarchy suffered severe shortages of food, water, medicine, and clothing. Coalition ground forces discovered large supplies of food and water in Republican Guard areas, but they found frontline infantry units generally in wretched health and malnourished.[100]

Theater air interdiction, by contrast, did not make much difference because the Iraqis had more transport capacity than they needed and because they had stockpiled large reserves in the theater. Before the war, Iraqi forces in the KTO were estimated to require 17,000 tons per day of supplies to sustain themselves when not in combat; total route capacity between Baghdad and the Kuwaiti border stood at more than 200,000 tons per day. After air attacks against highway bridges, rail lines, and temporary spans such as pontoon bridges began, total capacity into the KTO fell to 110,000 tons per day by 1 February, to 75,000 tons per day by 15 February, and to 60,000 tons per day by 22 February, still well above subsistence levels.[101] Moreover, the Iraqis did not need to push the limits of this capacity, moving a steady flow of 10,000 to 15,000 tons per day during the air war (about half of the 20,000 to 40,000 tons per day they averaged during the prewar buildup), because Saddam had stockpiled large quantities of supplies in the theater.[102] Coalition forces estimated after overrunning Iraqi positions that the Iraqi army had sufficient petroleum, oil, and lubricants in Kuwait to have supported thirty-five to forty days of defensive combat or three hundred days of continued static defense without combat, food for thirty days, potable water for several weeks, and about 300,000 tons of ammunition, sufficient to last longer than any of the other categories.[103]

---

[99] National Training Center, *Iraqi Army*, p. 176.

[100] GWAPS, *Effects and Effectiveness*, pp. 199–201; GWAPS, *Summary*, p. 98.

[101] However, attacks on Iraqi lines of communication into the KTO had, just prior to the ground offensive, approached the point where the residual route capacity would not have been able to sustain the Iraqi army in prolonged defensive operations, which before the war were estimated to require 42,000 tons per day. GWAPS, *Effects and Effectiveness*, p. 189.

[102] GWAPS, *Effects and Effectiveness*, pp. 189, 191–92, 195; DoD, *Conduct of the Persian Gulf War*, p. 179.

[103] GWAPS, *Effects and Effectiveness*, pp. 196–97.

Third, air power also destroyed significant amounts of Iraq's heavy military equipment (tanks, armored personnel carriers, and artillery), especially after the F-111s began "tank plinking" on 6 February. Since the end of the war, there has been considerable controversy over how much Iraqi heavy equipment was killed and how much of the total was killed prior to the ground campaign. During the war itself, CENTCOM reported that as of 23 February some 39 percent of tanks, 32 percent of APCs, and 47 percent of artillery had been destroyed. After the war, detailed studies were conducted by the CIA, Marines, and Army, each of which had a comparative advantage on a different part of the KTO (the CIA using overhead imagery could best assess Republican Guard areas in Iraq, and the Marines and Army conducting physical inspections of tanks mainly in their operating areas of operations could best evaluate damage in Kuwait). Despite different methodologies, these studies all come to remarkably similar conclusions: air power destroyed about 20 percent of Iraq's heavy military equipment (see Tables 17 and 18).

By freezing Iraqi mobile reserves, depleting the frontline infantry divisions, and destroying large amounts of equipment in place, theater air power unhinged Iraqi military strategy. It dramatically reduced the likelihood that Iraq's plan to turn a Coalition blitzkrieg into a protracted war of attrition would succeed. Theater air power made it impossible for the Iraqis to stop a breakthrough at the front, for it created huge holes in the front. The average frontline division, which was deployed at no more than 80 percent strength on 17 January, lost 50 percent of its already depleted numbers through desertions and casualties and averaged only four thousand men or fewer.[104] As a result, the Iraqis could not cover the entire front. Some of the Coalition's breaches were two kilometers wide and essentially involved large numbers of fast-moving mobile forces driving along four-lane highways deep into the Iraqi rear areas. Moreover, theater air power made it impossible for the Iraqis to stop these penetrations for long because their reserves could not counterconcentrate. In fact, the Coalition's attack advanced almost twice as fast as expected, largely because the Iraqi mobile reserves hardly opposed the breakthroughs at the front.

Perhaps the most striking evidence that air power thwarted the Iraqi defensive strategy is that far from presenting staunch resistance against the Coalition's attack, Iraqi forces were in a race to the Euphrates only one day after the Coalition's ground war started. By eight o'clock on the evening of 25 February, Marine intelligence began recording large-scale Iraqi pullouts from Kuwait City, and other sources indicated that Baghdad had ordered a general withdrawal, with priority given to commanders and their staffs.[105]

---

[104] Gordon and Trainor, *Generals' War*, p. 354.
[105] Ibid., p. 369.

Table 17. Estimated KTO order of battle, 23 February 1991

CENTCOM estimates	Divisions	Troops	Tanks	APCs	Artillery
Strategic reserve	8	86,000	924	702	432
Operational reserve	9	96,000	1,237	1,233	402
Front line	25	268,000	394	0	810
Totals	42	450,000	2,592	1,951	1,648

SOURCE: Totals calculated by subtracting CENTCOM's 23 February 1991 kill totals from CENTCOM's estimates before air war as found in DOD, *Conduct of the Persian Gulf War*, p. 188.

Although some Iraqi divisions tried to delay the oncoming Coalition spearheads so that other forces could make a hasty retreat, large amounts of heavy equipment were simply abandoned. Of the 163 tanks inspected by the Marines after the war, half had not been hit by munitions at all, and only some thirty tracked vehicles were found among the thousands of others on the "highway of death," the principal route used by Iraqi forces to escape the KTO during the ground war.[106]

This evidence strongly supports the denial model, because changes in the vulnerability of Iraq's military strategy correspond to changes in its willingness to abandon Kuwait (see Table 19). With its military strategy in tatters, Iraq's political calculations began to change. Saddam first blinked on 15 February, when Baghdad suddenly announced that the Revolutionary Command Council was preparing to accept a withdrawal from Kuwait, provided certain conditions were met. From this point on, Iraq began dropping conditions and moving toward a timetable for withdrawal. By 22 February Iraq had agreed to leave Kuwait two days after a cease-fire without a parallel withdrawal by the United States from Saudi Arabia or resolution of Palestinian issues.

Moreover, the denial model also explains why Saddam failed to accept Bush's "last chance" ultimatum, which had more to do with compelling Iraq to abandon its offensive military equipment in Kuwait than to abandon Kuwait itself. Since Saddam had no reason to believe that he would lose more of his forces by retreating after a defeat than by accepting U.S. terms to abandon nearly all his military equipment, the denial model would not expect Saddam to accept the loss of his army in addition to withdrawing from Kuwait.

Both strategic air power and theater air power advocates wrongly estimated the potential for coercing Iraq to leave Kuwait. Strategic air power advocates were overoptimistic about the effect of bombing a very tiny target

[106] GWAPS, *Summary*, p. 113.

Table 18. Actual KTO order of battle, 23 February 1991

KTO	Divisions	Troops	Tanks	APCs	Artillery
Strategic reserve	8	44,000	773	650	466
Operational reserve	9	50,000	1,599	1,510	424
Front line	25	106,000	408	304	1,090
totals	42	200,000	2,780	2,464	1,980
Deviation from 23 Feb. estimate	−56%	+7%	+21%	+17%	
Deviation from 17 Jan. actual	−41%	−20%	−20%	−20%	

SOURCES: The personnel total estimate is from GWAPS, *Effects and Effectiveness*, p. 220, which is based on Iraqi prisoner of war interrogations. Equipment losses for heavy equipment are estimated by CIA imagery for the strategic reserve (Republican Guard) and by U.S. Army and Marine on-site surveys of Iraqi equipment after the war for the operational and frontline forces. The CIA compared positions of equipment prior to 24 February and on 1 March. If it failed to move it was counted as killed by air power. This analysis shows that approximately 20 percent of the equipment was "killed" by air attack. U.S. House of Representatives, Committee on Armed Services, *Intelligence Successes and Failures in Operations Desert Shield/Storm* (Washington D.C.: GPO, August 1993). The Army and Marine teams physically inspected targeted Iraqi tanks and armored personnel carriers to determine whether air-delivered or ground-delivered weapons hit it. Although the teams conducted their evaluations independently, they both concluded that about 20 percent of the equipment had been destroyed by air attack. Battlefield Assessment Team, Armor/Antiarmor Team, *Armor/Antiarmor Operations in South-West Asia*, Marine Corps Research Center, Research Paper no. 92-0002 (Washington, D.C.: Department of the Navy, July 1991). After the war, Iraq retained possession of 842 tanks, 1,412 APCs, and 279 artillery pieces, according to CIA, *Operation Desert Storm: Snapshot of the Battlefield*.

set in overthrowing, isolating, or intimidating Saddam's regime. Theater air power advocates underestimated the coercive potential of large-scale bombing of Iraq's fielded forces, expecting simply to pave the way for the ground war. In fact, Saddam was coerced before the ground war began and would have been coerced even if no bombs had fallen on Baghdad or "leadership" targets.

It is not clear that bombing Iraq's national communication network contributed to coercion at all. If we posit its usefulness, however, it would have been better to attack it not during the first few days of the war but just before the beginning of the ground campaign. The demands on military communications networks in static warfare are minimal. It is only during rapidly changing mobile operations that command-and-control capabilities are stretched. Thus, by attacking Iraqi communications at the beginning of the air war, the Coalition merely gave Saddam Hussein thirty-nine days to repair, work around, or substitute for damaged communications.

The success of denial in Desert Storm cuts against claims that the Gulf War heralds a new paradigm for conventional warfare. In fact, denial has always been the only consistently effective coercive air strategy. Denial has an important limitation, however. The target state can be made to concede only

Table 19. Air power and Saddam's willingness to leave Kuwait

Date	Air power	Military impact	Saddam
17–19 January	Instant Thunder executed	nil	no change
29–30 January	Al-Khafji	maneuver impossible	no change
6 February	tank plinking	attrition begins	no change
12 February			Baghdad talks
15 February	Al-Firdos bunker	ends Baghdad strikes	mentions withdrawal
16–18 February	B-52s focus on front	desertions rise	Aziz to Moscow
22–23 February		100,000 deserters 20% attrition	accepts Soviet plan

territory that the coercer can demonstrate it would lose anyway. Desert Storm is no exception. Saddam Hussein did not concede Kuwait from August to January because the Coalition had not yet demonstrated his inability to hold it. Similarly, the Coalition could not demand Saddam's removal as a condition for ending the war, because although it may have had the military capacity, it had not demonstrated the unity or political will to fight to Baghdad.

Desert Storm does serve as a caution to those who might employ coercion by denial for a goal they do not think is worth the price of winning a complete victory. This case shows that sometimes coercers must come exceedingly close to complete defeat of an adversary for coercion to succeed. How close depends on the nature of the opponent's military strategy. Saddam's strategy was not very demanding. He believed if he could inflict ten thousand casualties with his force of 300,000 men, 3,500 tanks and 2,500 artillery pieces, the United States would go home. Consequently, for coercion to succeed, the United States had to approach the complete defeat of this adversary more nearly than in other cases, such as North Vietnam in 1972, with a more demanding strategy.

The "revolution" in precision weapons has not changed the dominance of denial over decapitation. Although guided weapons boosted the efficiency of air power in destroying either denial or decapitation targets, accuracy alone cannot make decapitation a viable coercive air strategy. First, the size of decapitation target sets is generally so small that they can be destroyed even without precision weapons. Second, killing leaders and degrading communications networks is more a problem of military intelligence than combat effectiveness. Without precise intelligence, precise weapons can precisely destroy targets that are not in use. Third, even if leaders can be hit and communication networks severed, estimating whether military effects can be translated into coercive success is a problem of political forecasting—and an uncommonly difficult one. We have no theories that can predict in either democratic or nondemocratic polities whether and when military pressure will cause a change of regime or in what direction. Finally, the failure of decapitation in the Gulf War is especially telling, because the case of a single authoritarian leader with little enthusiastic popular support, highly reliant on rudimentary national communications should have been an easy test for this strategy. That it failed here indicates that it is likely to be even less successful in future cases where conditions may be much less favorable.

Decapitation's worst feature, however, is not its ineffectiveness but its seductiveness. Decapitation advocates promise to solve conflicts quickly and cheaply with few aircraft, little collateral damage, and minimal or no friendly casualties. History shows that air power can coerce but not without a lot of it and a lot of ground power to back it up. Western political leaders should resist the decapitation temptation.

[8]

Germany, 1942–1945

The end of World War II in Europe is perhaps the most important coercive failure to study, for it is not predicted by the parsimonious version of the denial theory. Although the Allies successfully undermined its military strategy, Germany still did not surrender. Why did this nation, under continuous attack on all fronts by enormously superior enemy forces and suffering intense air bombardment, continue to fight until its forces were incapable of coherent operations and the country was completely occupied? In contrast to 1918, when the German government sought an armistice rather than continue fighting under hopeless conditions, the Nazi government never gave up and had to be completely obliterated. This coercive failure was tremendously costly for all sides. In the last ten months of the war alone, U.S. forces in the Atlantic theater suffered 583,000 dead and wounded, the British over a quarter million, and the Soviets and Germans well over a million each, not counting millions of civilian casualties due to aerial bombing, ground fighting, displacement of refugees, and the continuing operation of the "final solution."[1]

From the standpoint of coercion, what matters is why Germany did not surrender even though the Allies had both inflicted tremendous punishment and undermined its military capacity to resist. During the war, the Allies dropped 1.3 million tons of bombs on Germany, destroying over 40 percent of the urban area of the seventy largest cities and killing 305,000

---

[1] U.S. Adjutant General's Office, *Army Battle Casualties and Nonbattle Deaths in World War II* (Washington, D.C.: Department of the Army, 1953), p. 6; British casualties in 1944 and 1945 were about 356,000, H. M. D. Parker, *Manpower: A Study of War-time Policy and Administration* (London: HMSO, 1957), p. 485; John Keegan, *The Second World War* (New York: Viking, 1990); and Matthew Cooper, *The German Army, 1933–1945* (New York: Bonanza, 1984), p. 485.

civilians.[2] At the same time, the Allies had rendered untenable all of Germany's military strategies, not only the original offensive program for dominating Europe but also the later defensive strategies for preserving the territorial integrity of Germany against the Allied counteroffensives. Thus, both punishment- and denial-based theories would have predicted success.

Compared to Japan, Korea, and Vietnam, the German case has generated relatively little scholarly debate. The conventional wisdom is that Hitler's absolute power and ideological fanaticism prevented any possibility of surrender. The wider implications for coercion are generally ignored. Hitler's rule is considered so exceptional that broader theories of foreign policy decision making neither can nor should be expected to account for Germany's behavior.[3]

This argument is misleading, however. In fact, Hitler's power was not absolute. German decision making was not different in kind from that of all other possible targets of coercion, only in degree. Modern nation-states in serious disputes are normally quite resistant to coercion; Germany in 1945 was extremely so.

To understand Germany's failure to surrender, it is helpful to divide the problem into two parts. The first is why air attacks against German civilians failed to cause Germany to accept unconditional surrender. Although German leaders tried to mitigate the damage, aerial punishment played no important role in decisions about surrender. The reason is that the most significant threat to the German population was the prospect of Russian occupation, which could not be avoided by surrendering unconditionally.

The second is to explain why Germany did not surrender when its military strategy for defense of the homeland became untenable. Germany might have surrendered at three points: July 1944 when Allied offensives shattered German lines in both France and Russia and demonstrated that the Allies had sufficient military power to conquer Germany unless they could be deterred or diverted; January 1945 when the failure of the German Ardennes Offensive and the successful Russian offensive in Poland showed that Germany was likely to be overrun and could not inflict enough casualties to deter the Allies; and March 1945 when Hitler's ability to control his subordinates broke down.

---

[2] United States Strategic Bombing Survey (USSBS), *Summary Report (European War)* (Washington, D.C.: GPO, 1945), p. 36; and Kenneth Hewitt, "Place Annihilation: Area Bombing and the Fate of Urban Places," *Annals of the Association of American Geographers* 73, no. 2 (1983): 257–84.

[3] There is also an argument that Germany would have surrendered had the Allies abandoned unconditional surrender. Anne Armstrong, *Unconditional Surrender: The Impact of the Casablanca Policy upon World War II* (New Brunswick, N.J.: Rutgers University Press, 1961). My explanation based on changes in Germany's military vulnerability is broadly consistent with this view, although the exact terms the Allies could have obtained at a given time would have depended on the military situation at that moment.

In July 1944 Germany did not surrender because senior leaders did not believe that the conquest of Germany itself had become inevitable. The Nazis believed that a severe blow could still shock the West into breaking the coalition with the Soviet Union and making a separate peace. Most Army leaders believed that strategic withdrawals could still establish defensible positions. The dissidents who tried to overthrow Hitler in July 1944 hoped to sign an armistice with the western Allies, because they believed that, while a two-front war was hopeless, continuation of the war against Russia alone was not.

In January 1945 Germany's military position had become untenable, because German forces could not prolong the war long enough to inflict significant attrition. Nevertheless, surrender did not take place, because most Nazis believed that enough new resources could be generated to extend the fighting long enough for cumulative losses or divergent interests to split the Allies. Moreover, the generals had been too demoralized by the aftermath of the July 1944 coup to overthrow Hitler.

By March 1945 both Nazis and the military saw that final defeat was certain and that Hitler's grip on power was significantly looser. Still, immediate surrender did not occur, because continued resistance was expected to mitigate the civilian costs of eventual defeat. At this point, although further resistance could not avoid defeat and would involve additional costs, German leaders believed that it would avoid even greater civilian costs inflicted by a vengeful Russian army. They hoped to buy time for refugees and soldiers to escape from the areas to be occupied by Russia into areas under the control of the Western Allies.

The failure of Germany to surrender emphasizes the importance of the relation between the costs of surrender and the costs of resistance. Leaders abandon territorial objectives only when the costs of continued resistance exceed the expected benefits of further fighting. Because of the refugee problem in the east, Germans believed in spring 1945 that surrender would increase, not decrease, civilian costs. Thus, although Germany's failure to surrender is inconsistent with the most parsimonious version of my theory (which simply predicts that military vulnerability will coerce although civilian vulnerability will not), on closer inspection it is consistent with the underlying causal logic of the theory.[4]

To understand why Germany failed to surrender, we must examine Allied goals and strategies, how faithfully and capably they were executed, and the links among Allied military pressure, the prospects for Germany's diplomatic and military strategies, and changes in German leaders' willingness to surrender.

[4] We could represent the effects of costs of surrender on the decision making of target states by adding two terms to the equation presented in Chapter 2 as follows: $R = Bp(B) - Cp(C) + C(s)\, pC(s)$. Note that such "costs of surrender" must be separate from the loss of the territorial values at stake, which are already accounted for as B.

ALLIED GOALS AND STRATEGIES

The final form of the Allied goals for the war against Germany was set at the Casablanca Conference in January 1943.[5] The Allies, as Franklin Roosevelt stated, "were determined to accept nothing less than the unconditional surrender of Germany, Japan, and Italy."[6] Unconditional surrender, it later became clear, meant not only complete military victory but also the destruction of German sovereignty, the democratization and denazification of political institutions, and the reeducation of the population. In addition, the United States, Great Britain, and the Soviet Union agreed to the division of Germany into zones of occupation, resettlement of ethnic Germans in Eastern Europe, and transfers of forced labor to the Soviet Union.[7]

The unconditional surrender goal was motivated by three concerns. First, the decision reflected the prevalent belief that a major cause of World War II had been the insistence of the Germans after World War I that their army had never been defeated but had been "stabbed in the back" by politicians. Occupation would be necessary, it was thought, to bring home the lesson of defeat. Second, unconditional surrender was necessary to permit extensive social engineering of German society. The Nazi party and the German military, particularly the "Prussian" officer corps, were widely viewed as criminal organizations consisting of militarists, warmongers, and committed enemies of democracy. To eradicate militarism, no negotiated settlement that allowed either the Nazis or the military command to retain any influence could be accepted. Third, unconditional surrender mitigated the Allies' worries about collective action. The Western Allies and the Soviet Union each feared that the other would sign a separate peace with Germany. Thus, a general commitment to fight on until total victory served to buttress al-

[5] Before this point, the main goal had been to prevent German domination of the Eurasian continent. By the start of 1943, however, three factors had made it possible for the Allies to begin formulating policies for Germany's defeat: the reverses suffered by the German army on the eastern front, expectations of containing the German naval threat in the Atlantic, and the rapidly increasingly flow of war materiel provided by full mobilization of the American economy, which would ultimately supply much of the forces of the United Kingdom and Soviet Union as well as equip and maintain the five million men in the U.S. expeditionary force. Alan S. Milward, *War, Economy, and Society, 1939–1945* (Berkeley: University of California Press, 1977), pp. 63–74; Haywood S. Hansell Jr., *The Air Plan that Defeated Hitler* (Atlanta, Ga.: Higgins-McArthur, 1972), pp. 62–63.

[6] Robert E. Sherwood, *Roosevelt and Hopkins*, rev. ed. (New York: Harper and Brothers, 1950), pp. 693–94.

[7] Allied plans for Germany were considerably harsher than those for Japan, which did not envision the division of Japanese territory, resettlement of overseas Japanese, or a purging of the entire governmental structure beyond the military and top civilian leadership. The most detailed history of Allied postwar objectives is Paul Y. Hammond, "Directives for the Occupation of Germany: The Washington Controversy," in *American Civil-Military Decisions*, ed. Harold Stein (Tuscaloosa: University of Alabama Press, 1963), pp. 313–461.

liance solidarity. This was important in 1943 because although battlefield events were changing in favor of the Allies, victory was not yet in sight and the costs of achieving it were certain to be high.[8]

During the war, Allied military and civilian leaders conceived four strategies to finish Germany, all of which depended heavily on strategic air power. The first was the "industrial web" strategy, which would use precision attacks on key economic bottlenecks to cripple the German economy as a whole, fatally weakening the social and political cohesion needed for resistance. The second, strategic air interdiction, would also use precision bombing but would focus on industries critical to war production rather than seek a general economic collapse. The third was a Douhet strategy using area incendiary bombing of population centers. All three approaches aimed to break German resistance through air power alone, so that a cross-Channel invasion would be either unnecessary or simply a coup de grace to an already beaten opponent.[9] The fourth strategy, by contrast, aimed to destroy the German army through the combined weight of Soviet and Western ground offensives. Strategic air power would support this strategy through operational interdiction attacks designed to have a direct and immediate impact on ground operations.

Support for these strategies fluctuated, mainly according to views on the necessity for, and scale and timing of, an Anglo-American landing on the Continent to roll back the Wehrmacht from Western Europe. To assess the effects of the Allies' military strategies on German political calculations, we must investigate the advocates, goals, targets, and plans of each.

Destruction of Economic Bottlenecks

American airmen entered World War II believing that Germany could be forced to surrender by air bombardment of industry, without invading the Continent or resorting to terror bombing of civilians. The initial plans followed the 1930s "industrial web" theory, which predicted that small amounts of destruction, if concentrated on weak nodes critical to the system as a whole, would bring the whole economic house of cards down. Eco-

[8] Armstrong, *Unconditional Surrender*, chap. 1.
[9] Strategic bombing was seen as an alternative to confronting German military might, not a way to make that confrontation cheaper. The hope was that these efforts would be so successful that they alone might induce Germany to sue for peace. The role of the British army would thus be limited to occupation instead of invasion, avoiding the horrors of land combat ala World War I. For evidence on Churchill's views regarding the matter in July 1941, see Richard J. Overy, *The Air War, 1939–1945* (New York: Stein and Day, 1980), pp. 134–35. For evidence that the British based early planning with the United States on hopes for victory through air and naval coercion, see Wesley Frank Craven and James Lea Cate, *The Army Air Forces in World War II* (Washington, D.C.: GPO, 1948), 1: 142–43.

nomic collapse, in turn, would render the enemy incapable of sustaining military operations and would also incite the civilian population to pressure the government to stop the war. The chief motive behind this strategy was to force Germany to capitulate at minimum cost to American and British land forces regardless of the outcome of Germany's war with the Soviet Union.

The industrial web theory was embodied in the first *Air War Planning Document (AWPD-1)*, of 1941, which proposed destroying some common servicing system on which all major German industrial sectors depended instead of hitting isolated industrial plants.[10] War demands required 17 million Germans to move out of civilian pursuits and production and into military-related activities, forcing the remainder of the economy to function with reduced labor and other resources. Therefore, the German industrial economy was stretched so taut that destruction of a few carefully selected nodes by air attack might snap its strained strands. The resulting general economic collapse would not only ruin Germany's ability to produce war materiel but even more immediately produce widespread social disruption that would destroy German morale and possibly topple the state.

To cause a general collapse of the economy by hitting just a few targets, the key was to destroy targets that affected both the war effort and civilian welfare. The target priorities recommended in *AWPD-1* were the German air force (aircraft factories, aluminum and magnesium plants), followed by the electric power grid, the transportation network (rail, inland waterways, and highways), and the petroleum industry.

The German air force was seen not as a final objective but as a preliminary requirement to clear the way for attacks on the decisive targets. Of these, electric power had top priority because it was "vital to the German war effort, and . . . highly important to civil life." Loss of electricity-generating capability would affect weapons manufacturing, cold storage of food, manufacture of warm clothing, and transportation within cities. National transportation, especially of primary resources, came next: "In addition to the effect upon war industry, crippling the German transportation system would bring severe suffering to the German people by denying them the necessary coal for heating. The winters in Germany are cold and clothing is

---

[10] The basic aim of *AWPD-1* was "the application of air power for the breakdown of the industrial and economic structure of Germany. This conception involves the selection of a system of objectives vital to continued German war effort, and to the means of livelihood of the German people, and tenaciously concentrating all bombing toward destruction of those objectives." By these means, *AWPD-1* hoped to achieve the surrender of Germany "even in the event of Russian collapse." Office of the Chief of the Army Air Forces, *AWPD-1: Munitions Requirements of the Army Air Forces*, 12 August 1941, pp. 1–2, USAF Historical Research Agency, Maxwell Air Force Base, Ala., 145.82–1. That *AWPD-1* should draw on the industrial web theory is hardly surprising given that its authors (Laurence S. Kuter, Kenneth N. Walker, Harold L. George, and Haywood S. Hansell Jr.) had all taught at the Air Corps Tactical School.

becoming scarce. Breakdown of the transportation system would interfere with the orderly distribution of foodstuffs and common utilities." In short, the idea was to cause a shortage of key components, which would halt nearly all of Germany's production of manufactured goods, military as well as civilian.[11]

Although this strategy contained elements of both punishment and denial, the punitive elements were dominant. Advocates occasionally alluded to how strategic air attack would support a future land invasion, but air officers doubted that the Normandy invasion would succeed and believed that "if the air offensive is successful, a land offensive may not be necessary."[12] Whereas military collapse was also expected, the major justification for this doctrine was the expectation that economic devastation would also undermine civilian morale.[13]

Bombing Cities

British air strategy consistently stressed direct attacks on German population centers as the key to bringing Germany to terms. Unlike the Americans, who attacked population centers only at the end of the war, the British had detailed plans from the beginning and diverged from them only when Western land forces required immediate support.

The British had plans to attack German civilian morale even before France was attacked, and they bombed railway centers beginning in July 1941, according to the British Bombing Survey, as a means of "destroying the morale of the civilian population as a whole and of the industrial work-

---

[11] *AWPD-1*, pp. 1–3.

[12] *AWPD-1*, p. 2; Hansell, *Air Plan that Defeated Hitler*, pp. 74–76. In November 1943 Carl Spaatz told President Roosevelt's close adviser Harry Hopkins that given three months of clear weather, he could defeat Germany, rendering the invasion unnecessary. Harry C. Butcher, *My Three Years with Eisenhower: The Personal Diary of Harry C. Butcher, USN Naval Aide to General Eisenhower, 1942–1945* (New York: Simon and Schuster, 1946), p. 447.

[13] As Major Muir Fairchild, director of air tactics and strategy, remarked, "Obviously we cannot and do not intend to actually kill or injure *all* the people. Therefore our intention in deciding upon this method of attack must be to so reduce the morale of the enemy civilian population through fear—fear of death or injury for themselves and their loved ones—that they would prefer our terms of peace to continuing the struggle, and would force their government to capitulate." Quoted in Ronald Schaffer, *Wings of Judgment: American Bombing in World War II* (New York: Oxford University Press, 1985), p. 31. Similarly, Major General Donald Wilson, another ACTS lecturer, also stressed that the anticipated economic disintegration would disrupt the daily routine of the civil population and in so doing result in defeatism "to such an extent that public clamor would force the government to sue for peace." Quoted in Larry J. Bidinian, *Combined Allied Bombing Offensive against the German Civilian, 1942–1945* (Lawrence, Kans: Coronado Press, 1976), p. 21. By contrast, denial played a relatively minor role in these industrial web plans. Although destruction of the economy would naturally affect military production, nowhere did these plans state what level of decline in fighting power or production would be sufficient to weaken the Wehrmacht fatally, or indeed, how strong the Wehrmacht actually was. This lack of analysis suggests lack of interest.

ers in particular." They did not adopt incendiary bombing tactics in earnest, however, until early 1942.[14] In March 1942 the target set for Douhet-style incendiary bombing of cities was established. Fifty-eight major cities with population over a hundred thousand would be destroyed in four to six months.[15] RAF planners declared that to break German morale, "we must achieve two things: first, we must make [German towns] physically uninhabitable and, secondly, we must make the people conscious of constant personal danger. The immediate aim is therefore two-fold, namely to produce: (i) destruction; and (ii) the fear of death."[16]

Sir Arthur Harris, chief of the RAF Bomber Command, and other British decision makers had more concrete expectations from this bombing than is indicated in secondary sources. In November 1942 the Chief of the Air Staff, Sir Charles Portal, laid bare the assumed effects of dropping 1.250 million tons of bombs on German towns:

(i) the destruction of 6,000,000 German dwellings, with a proportionate destruction of industrial buildings, sources of power, means of transportation and public utilities;
(ii) 25,000,000 Germans rendered homeless;
(iii) an additional 60,000,000 "incidents" of bomb damage to houses;
(iv) civilian casualties estimated at about 900,000 killed and 1,000,000 seriously injured.[17]

---

[14] In the months prior to the German attack on France, the British Air Staff produced three plans: W.A. 5, which sought to cripple German war industry in the Ruhr, Rhineland, and Saar by destroying electric power, gas and coking plants, and the railway system; W.A. 6, which focused exclusively on oil production; and W.A. 8, which aimed to attack morale by targeting the electricity, gas, and oil plants mentioned in W.A.5 and W.A.6 at night. In the event that the British government would give authority for unrestricted air action without a German attack on the Low Countries, plan W.A. 8 (morale) was to be put into effect immediately. British Bombing Survey Unit, *The Strategic Air War against Germany, 1939–1945* (London: HMSO, 1947), pp. 1–2, 5–6, USAF HRA K512.552-11.

[15] Charles Webster and Noble Frankland, *The Strategic Air Offensive against Germany, 1939–1945* (London: HMSO, 1961), 1: 331–36.

[16] Air Staff, "The Value of Incendiary Weapons in Attack on Area Targets," 29 September 1941, in Towns Panel of the British Bombing Survey Unit, *Effects of Strategic Air Attacks on German Towns* (London: HMSO, 1947), p. 50, USAF HRA K512.552-3. This view was supported by civilian advocates, such as Lord Cherwell, the prime minister's scientific adviser, who said in March 1942: "Investigation seems to show that having one's house demolished is most damaging to morale. People seem to mind it more than having their friends or even relatives killed. At Hull signs of strain were evident, though only one-tenth of the houses were demolished. . . . we should be able to do ten times as much harm to each of the fifty-eight principal German towns. There seems little doubt that this would break the spirit of the people." Quoted in ibid.

[17] Ibid., pp. 10–11. Similarly, a 30 March 1942 paper by Lord Cherwell to the Cabinet expected that "if even half of the total load of 10,000 bombers were dropped on the built-up area of these 58 towns, the great majority of their inhabitants (about one-third of the German population) would be turned out of house and home." Quoted in BBSU, *Strategic Air War*, p. 7.

Portal's key assumption was that citizens' morale (willingness to continue supporting the war) depended on their welfare, which was most dependent on their possession of homes. Destroying homes would depress morale to the point at which the population would abandon economic activity. The German state would then face a terrible dilemma between achieving its territorial goals and continuing to provide for its population: "A substantial proportion of the total industry of Germany is necessary to maintain a minimum standard of subsistence amongst the German people. As the German economic structure is now stretched to the limit this proportion cannot be further reduced. Consequently, the loss of one-third of German industry would involve the sacrifice of almost the entire war potential of Germany in an effort to maintain the internal economy of the country or else the collapse of the latter."[18] According to this logic, destroying homes lowers civilian morale, which diminishes all economic production, which compels a choice between achieving territorial objectives or civil unrest.[19]

American airmen also became attracted to the idea of bombing civilians as the war entered its final phase in 1945. From the beginning American air planning considered that in addition to hitting economic bottlenecks, the air offensive might end with final attacks on urban areas. *AWPD-1* emphasized that "timeliness of attack is most important in the conduct of air operations directly against civil morale. If the morale of the people is already low because of sustained suffering and deprivation and because the people are losing faith in the ability of the armed forces to win a favorable decision, then heavy and sustained bombing of cities may crush that morale entirely." Similarly, "immediately after some very apparent results of air attack on the material objectives listed above or immediately after some set-back of the German ground forces, it may become highly profitable to deliver a large scale, all-out attack on the civil population of Berlin. In this event, any or all the bombardment forces may be diverted for this mission."[20]

Strategic Interdiction

By the time the United States deployed a significant bombing force in early 1943, American air strategy had shifted from the industrial web theory

---

[18] Portal quoted in Towns Panel, *Effects on German Towns*, pp. 10–11.

[19] Evidence that British civilians held up well under air attack was discounted because Germans were considered especially vulnerable to morale bombing. One report declared: "The Germans have been undernourished and subjected to a permanent strain equivalent to that of war conditions during almost the whole period of Hitler's regime, and for this reason also will be liable to crack before a nation of greater stamina [i.e., Britain]. It can be argued that concentrated attacks on the main centres of population in Germany . . . might comparatively quickly produce internal disruption in Germany." Chief of Staff Report, 7 January 1941, in Webster and Frankland, *Strategic Air Offensive* 1: 297.

[20] *AWPD-1*, p. 7, tab 1, p. 9, tab 2, p. 5.

to a new strategy that focused more narrowly on sectors of industry directly linked to the combat power of the Wehrmacht.[21] The main catalyst of the change was the January 1943 report by the Army Air Forces Committee of Operations Analysts, whose recommendations were supported in the field by General Ira C. Eaker, the commander of the Eighth Air Force.

The cornerstone of strategic interdiction is to reduce the enemy's capacity to field forces by destroying the production facilities for manufacture of weapons systems. Like the industrial web theory, strategic interdiction is a kind of precision-bombing strategy that seeks to destroy an entire industrial system by striking only a small number of targets. Unlike the industrial web theory, it aims to coerce by denying the enemy the ability to control territory rather than through pressure against the civilian population, by destroying military manufacturing narrowly defined rather than the national industrial structure as a whole. The key assumption is that destroying certain identifiable components early in the military production cycle will make the large-scale manufacture of finished military equipment such as tanks, aircraft, and artillery impossible. Ideal targets for this strategy were thought to include primary and semifinished products with special military use such as ball bearings, machine tools, rubber, aluminum, magnesium, nickel, steel, and nitrates.

Although early American war plans focused on industrial-web targets such as electric power and transportation, as the war progressed, committees were established to study the German economy in detail. These panels, comprising economists, political scientists, and experts in industrial management, as well as air men, quickly realized that earlier plans failed to recognize the possibility of substitution.[22] It was not enough to establish how much of a commodity was needed and to reduce production below that level, for other means of production or other products could often be substituted, especially if the defender possessed stockpiles and the ability to repair damaged factories. Further, dual-use commodities, such as oil, could be taken from the civilian sectors of the economy so that the combat power of German forces would not be reduced until the civilian cushion had been destroyed.

The net effect of this analysis was the replacement of electric power and transportation with ball bearings as the primary target. What had been the

---

[21] Some histories and some participants have lumped together the strategies I differentiate as strategic interdiction, operational interdiction, and the industrial web theory, including the official histories of Craven and Cate and Webster and Frankland. My framework not only captures fundamental differences among the air strategies but also explains why certain targets, such as electric power, which were considered critical early in the war and which the United States Strategic Bombing Survey says could have been struck later, were completely abandoned. By the time it had become feasible to strike these targets they were no longer considered desirable because a fundamentally different strategy guided target selection.

[22] Craven and Cate, *Army Air Forces in World War II* 2: 351–52.

chief attraction of these targets—that they formed an interlocking system in which the effects of destroying one node rippled throughout the system—now became their main liability. So long as capacity could be shifted to replace what was lost at any one point (current in the case of power and rail cars in the case of transportation), many nodes would have to be struck simultaneously to affect the system. The targets were too numerous and dispersed to be struck at the same time with available aircraft.[23] Ball bearings emerged as the main industrial target because the Schweinfurt plants alone manufactured one-half of the total Axis production, thus offering a peculiarly concentrated target within practicable flying range. Bearings were thought to be in such short supply (the inventory cushion was estimated to be only one month's supply) that any curtailment of production would be felt almost immediately. If the planned attacks were successful, the resulting shortages were expected to reduce German armaments production by 30 percent.[24]

The shift in targeting philosophy can be traced by comparing the target priorities of the original *AWPD-1* to those of *AWPD-2* (August 1942) and to the Combined Bomber Offensive (May 1943). All three list the German air force as a preliminary objective, but electric power is progressively downgraded from second in *AWPD-1* to fourth in *AWPD-2* and disappears altogether in the CBO plan (see Table 20). "Morale" appeared only in *AWPD-1*; *AWPD-2* retained transportation and oil and added submarine yards and rubber; the CBO plan added ball bearings and military vehicles to the list.[25]

Invasion and Operational Interdiction

The first three strategies—the industrial web, Douhet, and strategic interdiction—were intended primarily for coercive purposes. The Western Allies thought of a large-scale invasion of Europe primarily as an alternative to coercion, a means to achieve decisive military victory if coercion failed. A major ground offensive could also coerce, however, if the threat or the actual conquest of part of the German homeland led to the complete surrender of Germany.

[23] Since individual industries depended on networks that pooled electricity rather than on single generating plants, specific industrial regions had to be deprived of electricity in general to impede production. Study of the industrial regions in the Ruhr and central Germany revealed that a large number of targets (sixty) would have to be destroyed and kept inoperative to immobilize production in the local region. Similarly, internal transportation within Germany had such a large cushion that production would not be significantly curtailed until more than 30 percent was taken out of service. Craven and Cate, *Army Air Forces in World War II* 2: 351–55.

[24] USSBS, *The German Anti-Friction Bearings Industry* (Washington, D.C.: GPO, 1947).

[25] Many targets, with the possible exception of electric power generating and switching equipment, could be reconstructed or repaired within a period of two to four weeks. Accordingly, targets capable of being regenerated had to be hit at least twelve times during the six-month period. Hansell, *Air Plan That Defeated Hitler*, pp. 86, 163.

Table 20. Target priorities

	AWPD-1	AWPD-2	CBO
	German air force[a] electric power transportation oil morale	German air force submarine yards transportation electric power oil rubber	German air force submarine yards ball bearings oil rubber military vehicles
Total targets	191	177	76

[a] Includes aircraft factories, engine plants, aluminum plants (in *AWPD-1* and *AWPD-2*), magnesium plants (in *AWPD-1*), and attrition by fighter sweeps over Germany (in the CBO plan).

The British, especially, wanted to avoid the costs of a major land campaign on the Continent, preferring instead a peripheral strategy that would rely on the Western Allies' sea and air power, in combination with Soviet land power, to undermine Germany's capability and will to resist. "The Russian Army," the British Joint Planning Staff stated in autumn 1942, "is today the only force capable of defeating the German Army. . . . We must therefore employ our resources to wear down the German war machine . . . until German morale has definitely cracked."[26] The final western offensive would be simply the occupation of an already defeated enemy.

American opinion was divided. Air leaders such as Hap Arnold, Ira Eaker, and Carl Spaatz thought that strategic air bombardment, not large-scale ground operations, would be the main instrument of Germany's defeat.[27] They favored several strategies at different times. At the start of the war they supported the industrial web strategy; later they advocated strategic interdiction; and still later some advocated a Douhet strategy. Some air commanders doubted that invasion would be necessary.

Despite the preferences of air strategists, invasion became Allied policy both because the USSR demanded it and because the U.S. Army and top American civilian leaders were convinced that a major ground offensive would be absolutely necessary to overthrow German power. Anglo-American differences over the timing of the Allied landing at Normandy gradually narrowed in a series of meetings in 1943 until, at Quebec in August, the plan was adopted that was finally executed as Operation Over-

[26] Michael Howard, *Grand Strategy IV: August 1942–September 1943* (London: HMSO, 1972), p. 197.
[27] For a superb biography of World War II American Air Leaders, see David Mets, *Master of Airpower: General Carl A. Spaatz* (Novato, Calif.: Presidio Press, 1981).

lord in June 1944.[28] The plan was to defeat the German army on the ground in a two-step process. The first was to obtain a lodgment on the Continent. Thus, the cross-Channel invasion aimed to seize and develop an administrative base from which future offensive operations could be launched, not to win a decisive battle against German forces in northwest Europe. The second step made the Ruhr, the industrial heart of Germany, the primary objective. After sweeping through western France, the Allies would advance into Germany along two routes, one to the north of the Ardennes directly into the Ruhr and one to the south of the Ardennes into Saarbruecken. Success on either axis was expected to force enemy withdrawals from both areas.[29]

To support land conquest, air power would increasingly focus on the German army in an attempt to impose operational interdiction on German land operations. Unlike strategic interdiction, operational interdiction would attack the last steps in the logistic chain by targeting finished military goods and the means of bringing them to the battlefield.[30] Operational interdiction target sets included road, rail, and canal transportation in Germany and especially in France, oil, and fielded forces. When necessary, strategic bombers might also be diverted to direct tactical support to specific Allied ground operations. Despite disagreements over priorities, in the event the Allies devoted considerable effort to all these targets.[31]

---

[28] On planning for the cross-Channel invasion, see Kent Roberts Greenfield, *American Strategy in World War II: A Reconsideration* (Baltimore: Johns Hopkins University Press, 1963); G. A. Harrison, *Cross-Channel Attack* (Washington, D.C.: GPO, 1951); and Tuvia Ben-Moshe, "Winston Churchill and the 'Second Front': A Reappraisal," *Journal of Modern History* 62 (September 1990): 503–37.

[29] Roland G. Ruppenthal, *Logistical Support of the Armies* (Washington, D.C.: Department of the Army, 1953), 1: 178–79, 485.

[30] The Enemy Objectives Unit of the Office of Strategic Services believed that neither generalized bombing of industry nor area bombing of cities would bring about the collapse of German resistance; collapse would come "as a result of the military and military supply situation literally defined." Since the goal of the air offensive was to weaken the Wehrmacht in conjunction with land campaigns, target systems fairly late in the production cycle should be selected; the sites of final production of armaments or the manufacture of components closely related to completed products would produce direct military effects in fairly short order. Memorandum, W. W. Rostow, OSS, to Wing Commander Burgess A.I.3 (c)2, 14 November 1943, in W. W. Rostow, *Pre-invasion Bombing Strategy* (Austin: University of Texas Press, 1981), p. 112.

[31] On Allied strategy in World War II, see Greenfield, *American Strategy*; Ray S. Cline, *Washington Command Post: The Operations Division* (Washington, D.C.: Office of the Chief of Military History, U.S. Department of the Army, 1951); Maurice Matloff and Edwin S. Snell, *Strategic Planning for Coalition Warfare, 1941–1942* (Washington, D.C.: GPO, 1953); Maurice Matloff, *Strategic Planning for Coalition Warfare, 1943–1944* (Washington, D.C.: U.S. Department of the Army, 1959); and J. R. M. Butler, ed., *History of the Second World War*, 6 vols. (London: HMSO, 1956–75).

EXECUTION OF MILITARY OPERATIONS

Military pressure against Germany passed through four stages, as more coercive instruments and strategies were brought to bear. In the first stage, starting in May 1940, the RAF launched an operational interdiction campaign, but without sufficient resources to be effective. In the second, which began in March 1942, the RAF undertook Douhet-style bombing of cities. In the third stage, beginning in May 1943, the British continued their Douhet campaign, while the Americans pursued a strategic interdiction strategy based on precision bombing of industrial targets. In the final stage, starting in May 1944, strategic bombing was supplemented with an invasion threat from both the west and the east. In the air, the British persisted in pounding German cities, while the Americans employed a mix composed primarily of operational interdiction, lesser effort on strategic interdiction, and some morale bombing at the very end (see Table 21).

British Operational Interdiction

Although the British favored attacks on German cities, they were initially unable to pursue such a strategy for two reasons. First, they were deterred. During the 1930s, British political and military leaders feared that in future wars the Luftwaffe would deliver an early "knock-out" blow by bombing British cities, and this fear was sharpened by the German bombing of Warsaw in 1939 and Rotterdam in 1940. Since the Luftwaffe enjoyed numerical superiority, Britain decided to conserve resources until the gap in air strength was narrowed.[32] Second, the British were often distracted by immediate operational needs. The German attack on France and subsequent threat to the British Isles made reduction of German fielded military strength the dominant concern.

Accordingly, from May 1940 through July 1941, Bomber Command waged an operational interdiction campaign.[33] During the Battle of France, bombing was directed against oil plants and marshalling yards in the Ruhr and German forces in France. Once France fell and it became clear that a German invasion of England would require the Luftwaffe to establish air superiority over Britain, Bomber Command turned its attention to reducing the German air threat by attacking aluminum plants, airframe assembly factories, and air stores parks in Germany, as well as German ports and shipping useful in the

[32] Wesley K. Wark, *The Ultimate Enemy: British Intelligence and Nazi Germany, 1933–1939* (Ithaca: Cornell University Press, 1985); BBSU, *Strategic Air War*, pp. 1–2.

[33] Bombing was also justified during this period as part of a general strategy of using economic pressure to create widespread revolt in occupied Europe. Blockade of foodstuffs would produce widespread starvation throughout Europe, and air attack, especially against oil, would weaken German military control by immobilizing its forces. J. R. M. Butler, *Grand Strategy II: Sept. 39–June 41* (London: HMSO, 1957), pp. 212–15.

Table 21. Bombing effort against Germany, 1940–1945.

	1940	1941	1942	1943	1944	1945
Percentage dropped on:						
Towns	1%	39%	74%	68%	21%	16%
Industry[a]	25	8	7	9	13	7
Military[b]	44	21	1	5	45	67
Other[c]	30	32	18	18	21	10
Total tons (thousands)	14	36	54	227	1,189	477

SOURCE: British Bombing Survey Unit, *Strategic Air War against Germany*, tables 10, 11, and 12.

[a] Includes airframe and aircraft engine plants, military vehicles, ball bearing, ordnance, powder, steel, and coke producers, and other war industries. RAF data generally include airfields and radars because statistics of subdivisions of target systems are available only for 1944.

[b] Includes army installations, oil plants, fuel dumps, rail yards, bridges, and other transportation targets.

[c] Includes German air force, navy and V-weapons targets. Early in the war, effort in this category was devoted mainly to submarine bases; later it was devoted mainly to airfields and V-weapons.

invasion itself. As the threat of imminent invasion receded in fall of 1940, however, Bomber Command returned to oil, abandoning it in favor of marshalling yards in July 1941 after Germany occupied the Balkans and improved its access to oil. In November 1941 bombing operations were terminated as losses mounted and results appeared negligible.[34]

The campaign failed, hardly slowing the Wehrmacht's defeat of France or preparations to attack Russia. Further, although the British denied the Luftwaffe the air superiority necessary for a successful invasion, the deciding factor was the shortage of skilled German pilots, not aircraft. Thus, it was attrition in the air, not the bombing of German industries, which made the difference.

Bombing failed partly because it did little damage. Because of a shortage of bombers, the RAF could drop only two hundred tons on any given day on targets in Germany. Meanwhile, German air defenses forced the RAF to abandon daylight raids early in the war and bomb only at night, thus increasing navigation and aiming errors to the point that only one-third of the bombs fell within five miles of the target area.[35]

More important, any damage inflicted by bombing the primary resources of oil and transportation could contribute little to reducing Germany's fighting capacity, for oil was relatively abundant and most of the Reich's transportation could not be reached. Germany's conquests in 1940 and 1941 opened the door

[34] Webster and Frankland, *Strategic Air Offensive* 1: 146–47, 156, 256, 302.
[35] This was the conclusion of the famous Butt report of August 1942, which was the first systematic use of photographic reconnaissance to assess bomb damage. Ibid., 1: 178, 4: 205.

to the oil resources of nearly all of Europe, from stockpiles in the west (e.g., France) to production centers in the east (e.g., Romania). Consequently, Germany was considerably less dependent on indigenous oil installations than it had been before the war. Destroying transportation targets that could be reached was also futile, because only those in the Ruhr could be bombed. Even if all nine of the designated railway centers in this area had been hit with the fifteen tons thought necessary to disrupt operations for a week, repairs could have been so easily accomplished during this period that no disruption of traffic large enough to affect the German economy would have occurred.[36]

Douhet, March 1942–1945

Early in 1942, the British strategic bombing effort shifted from an operational interdiction strategy to a Douhet strategy of inflicting maximum damage on population centers.[37] Attacks against population centers remained the main focus of RAF bombing for the rest of the war, although in 1944 and 1945 some effort was diverted to operational interdiction in support of the Western Front and to suppress V-weapons sites.[38]

The change in British air strategy resulted from three factors. First, after German air raids on London and other English cities in 1940, the British government felt increasing pressure to retaliate against German cities.[39] The Cabinet, in fact, had already come to favor area bombing over precision industrial attacks before sustained bombing of Germany had even begun. Second, the failure of precision operations to produce significant results, even though the Cabinet had given Bomber Command first call on British war production in 1941, was politically unacceptable. Third, since a shift to night operations was unavoidable, the British needed targets which were large enough in area to make even a widely spread bomb pattern effective. Only urban areas fit this bill.

On 22 February 1942, the precision-oriented chief of Bomber Command, Sir Richard Pierse was replaced by Air Marshal Arthur Harris, who was to execute the new Douhet strategy that had been ordered by the "Towns Directive" of 14 February. Tactics for the raids were optimized to burn down

[36] BBSU, *Strategic Air War*, pp. 1–6.

[37] A modest move in this direction can be detected after July 1941, when night attacks against marshalling yards in the center of cities began as a compromise between interdiction and morale bombing, "since it was recognized that on only some six moonlight nights a month could specific objectives be bombed, and that on the remaining twenty-four or five conditions were likely to be so bad that attacks, owing to their necessarily 'indiscriminate' character, could be regarded as directed only against morale." BBSU, *Strategic Air War*, p. 6.

[38] As in the case of Japan, the transition in strategies can be dated by tracing changes in targeting, mission profiles, and munitions. For a detailed account of the development of American incendiary tactics, see John W. Mountcastle, "Trial by Fire: U.S. Incendiary Weapons, 1918–1945" (Diss., Duke University, 1979).

[39] Webster and Frankland, *Strategic Air Offensive* 1: 297.

German cities by producing not many small fires but great city-destroying "fire storms." Harris's strategy was to husband resources for periodic massive strikes on one city at a time.[40] He also supported the development of navigation techniques that could dependably locate the centers and residential areas of cities.

Following a series of small, experimental raids against Essen (8 March), Cologne (13 March), Lubeck (28 March), Rostock (23 April), and Stuttgart (4 May), the incendiary campaign began in earnest with the "thousand bomber" raid against Cologne on 30 May. This raid was by far the most devastating of the war up to that point, destroying as much of the city as had 70 previous raids combined. Incendiary raids continued until on 24 July 1943 Harris finally achieved his goal of creating a fire storm, which largely destroyed the city of Hamburg; it was the first time in history such an inferno was produced by air attack. This single raid destroyed one-third of the houses of the city and killed between 60,000 and 100,000 people. The RAF proceeded to destroy one major urban center after another, leaving only cities in the extreme eastern part of the Reich unscathed.[41]

Late in the war, the U.S. Army Air Forces joined the morale bombing campaign. Some effort was made to disguise the purpose of these raids. For example, railroad yards or administrative centers were nominally designated as the "military" targets of the strikes. That these were usually located in city centers, however, and the large fraction of incendiaries in the bombloads shows that the principal aim was to wreak havoc directly on civilians.[42]

[40] "The destruction of a city by fire can only [be] obtained by creating a large-scale conflagration in the vulnerable built-up area of the city, which generally lies about its centre. In this form of attack, the basic requirement is to drop a sufficient number of potential fire-raisers in the form of incendiary bombs to saturate the fire guard and fire brigade service. In addition, high explosive bombs must be used to harass and lower the efficiency of the fire fighters, to break water mains and to deny access to the fires by blocking structures, etc." Department of Bombing Operations, *Incendiary Attacks on German Cities* (London: British Air Ministry, January 1943), pp. 66–67, USAF HRA K512.547.

[41] USSBS, *Summary Report (European War)*, p. 10; Webster and Frankland, *Strategic Air Offensive*, 2: 138–67; and Martin Caidin, *The Night Hamburg Died* (London: New English Library, 1966).

[42] Plans for Operation Shatter, a scheme to "demonstrate to the German people through their own eyes their vulnerability to direct attack" by bombing a hundred German towns on a single day, which was developed in 1944 but never executed, make clear the intent behind these target choices: "To free such an operation as this from the stigma of being merely retaliatory terror bombing exact targets would have to be bombed in each of the cities to be attacked. They would be public utilities, transportation facilities, minor industries, or governmental buildings. The following program implies the disruption of administrative processes as the immediate objectives. It equally well could be fitted, for morale effect, to any other type of targets." But terror bombing was very definitely the purpose: "If the SHATTER criteria are followed, it is found that the cities selected, which have been previously free from heavy attack, do not contain a great proportion of important German transportation installations. Attack on them, therefore, will have very little effect on the transportation system." Memo, Director of Intelligence, Headquarters, U.S. Strategic Air Forces in Europe, to B. G. George C. McDonald, Director of Intelligence, USSTAF, 27 June 1944, pp. 1, 3, app. G of Target section, USSTAF, "Suggested Plans for Attack on German Transportation Systems," September 1944, USAF HRA K519.322-1.

The first major American morale bombing raid was Operation Thunderclap on 3 February 1945. Thunderclap had its genesis in a 22 July 1944 meeting of the British Foreign Office, Ministry of Economic Warfare, and the British and American air staffs, which concluded that the ideal form of attack on German morale would be a massive raid on Berlin which would substantially destroy the city and "influence the minds of the German authorities in such a way that they prefer organized surrender to continued resistance." American operational commanders were not immediately attracted to the plan, but as the end of the war approached they became more receptive to countermorale operations, as originally envisioned in *AWPD-1*. The acting AAF commander, Lieutenant General Barney M. Giles, observed on 31 January 1945: "Indications are that pandemonium reigns in Berlin as a result of Soviet advances in the East. . . . have all available day and night heavy bomber aircraft directed against Berlin for the next few days with a view towards accentuating this condition."[43] Following Thunderclap, a few additional American incendiary raids were launched, against Dresden (14 February), Munich (25 February), Berlin (26 February), Leipzig (27 February), Halle (27 February) and Chemnitz (3 March) before strategic bombing operations were stood down in April 1945.[44]

The overall pace of the city-bombing campaign can be gauged by the rate at which urban area was destroyed in the fifty-eight principal population centers. Up until February 1942 practically no built-up area in these cities had been destroyed. By June 1943 fourteen square miles had been burned out, by March 1944 thirty-six square miles, and by March 1945 sixty-seven square miles, after which no further damage was recorded.[45] In all, Allied bombers attacked sixty-one major cities and thirty-one towns, of which 128 square miles were razed, amounting to 50 percent of their urban area. Seven

[43] Quoted in Richard G. Davis, "Operation 'Thunderclap': The U.S. Army Air Forces and the Bombing of Berlin," *Journal of Strategic Studies* 14 (March 1991): 90–111.

[44] The purpose of these raids, especially that against Dresden, remains controversial, but certain facts speak for themselves. The 311–plane American operation against Dresden was mounted in combination with a British night raid of 770 planes; against rail yards in the center of the city; through cloud cover, using radar bombing methods with an average error of two miles; and using a bomb mix including 40 percent incendiaries, the same percentage as the British. Compare this figure to an average of 11 percent for four other American raids against Dresden's marshaling yards from October 1944 to April 1945. (A second American raid, which dropped only high explosives, hit Dresden as a secondary target because their primary target that day, a synthetic oil plant, had poor weather). Moreover, rail yards were poor targets for incendiaries, because such weapons do little harm to heavy equipment or tracks. Of the 9,042 tons dropped by the Americans on French rail yards in spring 1944, only 33 tons were incendiaries. Similarly, during Operation Clarion in 1945, when the Americans bombed dozens of transportation targets in Germany, only 3 of 7,164 tons were incendiaries. Melden E. Smith Jr., "The Bombing of Dresden Reconsidered" (Diss., Boston University, 1971), pp. 6–36, 279; Gary J. Shandroff, "The Evolution of Area Bombing in American Doctrine and Practice" (Diss., New York University, 1972), p. 102; and Richard G. Davis, *Carl A. Spaatz and the Air War in Europe* (Washington, D.C.: Center for Air Force History, 1993), pp. 569–70, 572.

[45] BBSU, *Effects on German Towns*, p. 13.

and a half million people, 11 percent of Germany's entire population, were rendered homeless, 305,000 civilians were killed and 780,000 wounded.[46] In addition, the catastrophic losses inflicted on such cities such as Cologne, Hamburg, and Dresden shocked the entire German people. The destruction probably approached the limits of what conventional fire bombing could achieve against German towns, and thus the campaign can be considered to have satisfied the requirements of an ideal Douhet strategy.[47]

Nonetheless, the strategy failed. There is no evidence that it produced any political pressure on German leaders or contributed much to the collapse of the German economy. As in the case of Japan, bombing did depress individuals' spirits, though it is unlikely that it was the main cause of low morale.[48] Nevertheless, it failed to stimulate—indeed impeded—collective political action against the government. There were no mass demonstrations against the government or any other form of popular political activity. Civil disobedience was insignificant. Far from discouraging loyalty to the Nazi regime, bombing tightened political ties, because the civilian population became more dependent on the functioning of Nazi relief organizations, without which their suffering would be even worse. People were moved not to collective action against the government but to political apathy; they became obsessed with finding individual solutions to their personal problems.

There are three reasons why public feeling did not directly influence German political calculations to any important degree. First, German nationalist sentiments made the population willing to countenance significant punishment in order to achieve the objectives of the state. Second, the government controlled information media and used them to indoctrinate the population to sacrifice for national goals and to believe in the evil nature of their enemies. Third, the state anticipated dissent and subversion and took active measures against them. As a revolutionary movement, the Nazis had long allocated large resources to instruments of repression.

Aside from producing no political effects, the Douhet strategy also failed to contribute significantly to Germany's economic problems. Although total

[46] Bidinian, *Combined Allied Bombing Offensive*, pp. 29, 35; Webster and Frankland, *Strategic Air Offensive* 4: 50; USSBS, *Summary Report (European War)*, p. 15.

[47] The actual damage inflicted on German towns was between a third to a half the damage originally expected by the British in 1942. The British had assumed that the American air forces would also devote their efforts mainly to morale bombing, but they did not. In addition, the predominance of stone rather than wood construction in German cities inherently limited their combustibility. See Horatio Bond, *Fire and the Air War* (Boston: National Fire Protection Association, 1946).

[48] The minor difference in morale between bombed and unbombed communities seems to suggest that German defeats on the eastern and western fronts did more to lower morale than did fear of harm from bombing. Whereas 60 percent of civilians in heavily bombed towns may have demonstrated low morale, 50 percent of those in unbombed towns also had low morale by the end of the war. USSBS, *The Effects of Strategic Bombing on German Morale* (Washington, D.C.: GPO, 1947), p. 13.

absenteeism approached 20 percent during the last months of the war, the countercivilian raids had only a minor effect on the overall economy and practically no effect on war production.[49]

Three factors account for the poor economic results. First, despite depression, most workers simply continued to work in routine fashion. The German armament industry sustained a steady increase in munitions production until July 1944 and even in January 1945 had declined by only 30 percent from the peak. The U.S. Strategic Bombing Survey was largely correct when it concluded: "Allied bombing widely and seriously depressed German civilians, but depressed and discouraged workers were not necessarily unproductive workers."[50]

Second, various methods of industrial rationalization (standardization, concentration in larger firms, substitution, and redistribution of resources and manpower used in civilian supply industries) enabled German industry to sustain the country's war effort. These measures introduced efficiencies more than adequate to counter the effects of bombing on morale at least until late 1944.[51]

Finally, few industrial plants were located in city centers. Hence, bombing the population did not contribute much to damaging heavy industrial complexes, which were located on the outskirts. In fact, most German authorities believed that expending bombs in countercivilian raids prolonged the life of German war industries and so helped sustain the war effort. As the USSBS observed, "Political, industrial, and military spokesmen frequently expressed both amazement and gratification over the Allied choice of targets; their belief, concurred in by practically every civilian interrogated, was that the cities could be rebuilt but that industry was vital to the pursuit of war."[52]

American Strategic Interdiction, June 1943–1945

American strategic bombing of Germany began in earnest in June 1943 and aimed at strategic interdiction.[53] Although the industrial web theory had justified the procurement of a large strategic bomber fleet, it was never actually implemented. Instead, attacks were made against military equipment plants and especially key basic industries critical to a wide range of

---

[49] USSBS, *Effects on German Morale*, pp. 53–60, 65. The British Bombing Survey estimates that during 1944 and 1945 overall production losses attributable to town-area attacks ranged from 4.4 to 9.7 percent, and war production losses ranged from 0.9 to 1.2 percent. BBSU, *Effects on German Towns*, p. 40.

[50] USSBS, *Summary Report (European War)*, pp. 4, 48, 99.

[51] Bidinian, *Combined Allied Bombing Offensive*, p. 93; USSBS, *Effects on German Morale*, p. 7.

[52] USSBS, *Oil Division Final Report* (Washington, D.C.: GPO, 1947), p. 124.

[53] Although American strategic bombing began in October 1942, the initial operations were carried out with very small forces against operational interdiction targets, mainly submarine bases, primarily in France, but including a few in Germany.

war production. Of these, the most important product was thought to be ball bearings.

Strategic interdiction came under a critical test during the fall of 1943. In a series of raids beginning on 17 August 1943, the ball-bearing plants at Schweinfurt were attacked. As a result, September production of bearings fell 65 percent. To keep production low, the plants were reattacked on 14 October, and again the target was badly damaged. Nevertheless, despite further attacks during 1944, production at Schweinfurt was back to preraid levels by 1944, and there is no evidence from factory records or testimony of production officials that these attacks produced any measurable effect on essential war production.[54]

The ball-bearing offensive caused only a temporary setback in production because machines and machine tools were damaged far less severely than factory structures—a phenomenon common to raids on industrial targets. As a result, the Germans had the equipment to disperse part of their production between the initial attacks in the autumn of 1943 and their resumption in February 1944. Moreover, stocks of bearings turned out to be relatively generous, sufficient to tide the Germans over during the period when output was being restored. The Germans were able to cannibalize damaged equipment and weapons, draw down stocks, and redesign some equipment to use fewer bearings.[55] Meanwhile, these unescorted daylight raids suffered prohibitive losses, including 62 of the 228 bombers in the second raid on Schweinfurt, which was well above the 5 percent rate of losses that airmen would generally consider tolerable in sustained bombing operations. As a result, strategic bombing operations were stood down until long-range fighter escort became available in early 1944.[56]

During January, operations resumed against aircraft and ball-bearing plants, which, although inflicting damage similar to past raids, did little to depress production. The USAAF did largely destroy the Luftwaffe during 1944 but almost entirely by air-to-air combat, not by bombing. From January to March, more than four thousand German aircraft were destroyed, after which the Luftwaffe conceded air superiority to the Allies, contesting missions only on occasion. The problem was not lack of aircraft, which were still being produced at a rate that could contest the Allied air forces, but lack of experienced pilots, which gave the decided advantage to the Allies in en-

[54] USSBS, *Summary Report (European War)*, pp. 14–15.
[55] Ibid., p. 15; Craven and Cate, *Army Air Forces* 2: 703–4.
[56] Both the Americans and the British thus began with daylight raids by unescorted bombers, and both were forced to abandon this mode of operation because of prohibitive losses, but their reactions were different. Instead of resorting to city burning, the Americans shifted temporarily to attacks on operational targets in France and the Low Countries before returning to strategic bombing of Germany in 1944. The difference can be accounted for by the absence of pressure for revenge, the Americans' greater interest in a cross-Channel invasion, and the imminent availability of a long-range escort fighter (P-51).

gagements. Although one might argue that bombing Germany proper was necessary to force the Luftwaffe to fight, bombing military targets in France in preparation for the Allied landing would have had the same effect unless the Germans were prepared to concede the success of the invasion.[57]

The aircraft and ball-bearing campaigns illustrate the difficulties of applying strategic interdiction to a continental power such as Germany which controls vast resources. Germany was not exceptionally vulnerable to economic shortages over the long term so long as it could extract resources from Europe as a whole. Temporary shortages of particular materials might occur, but these could often be resolved by state intervention because the huge size of the resource base provided many opportunities for substitution and conservation. As a result, there was no Achilles heel, no small, vulnerable set of factories whose loss would cripple all war production, not even any important category.

Even if they existed, moreover, it was nearly impossible to identify soft spots in the German war economy. In order to take substitution fully into account, it would have been necessary to monitor the daily performance of all sectors of the economy, involving hundreds of industries and many thousands of individual plants, to predict accurately how the destruction of a handful of factories would ripple through the rest of the war economy. Even in peacetime, when access to information is relatively open, forecasts of enemy defense allocations at this level of detail are often in error. In war when the opposing government is seeking to prevent access to such information, estimates of current and prospective economic performance are even less reliable. The Allies were forced to base economic estimates mainly on agents' reports, press reports, and public statements by German officials rather than on primary documents or firsthand evidence.[58] The Allies thus estimated that Germany had gone to a total war economy early in the war, when in fact it had not, and they underestimated the effects that Albert Speer's reorganization had on production.[59] Information was inadequate to produce reliable macroeconomic analysis, let alone the comprehensive microeconomic analysis required for strategic interdiction by precision bombing.

Most important, strategic interdiction aims at wrecking the manufacture of military equipment on the assumption that shortages of tanks, aircraft, guns, and other such materiel will cripple the fighting power of the enemy army. In the German case, however, such shortages never occurred. Through the final surrender, tens of thousands of tanks, artillery pieces, air-

[57] Craven and Cate, *Army Air Forces* 3: 47–63.

[58] F. H. Hinsley, *British Intelligence in the Second World War* (New York: Cambridge University Press, 1993), vol. 3, pt. 1, p. 54.

[59] Germany's failure to mobilize fully for war until 1942 is discussed in Burton H. Klein, *Germany's Economic Preparations for War* (Cambridge: Harvard University Press, 1959); and Alan S. Milward, *The German Economy at War* (London: Athlone Press, 1965).

craft and other vehicles remained in German hands. In other words, although many parts of the German economy ceased to function by the end of the war, no meaningful military equipment shortages were generated.

Operational Interdiction, May 1944–May 1945

As the date for the invasion grew nearer, the air services were asked to develop plans to support the ground offensive. This objective required a shift away from both Douhet and strategic interdiction plans, because the lag phase between inflicting damage on specific targets and measurable weakening of German resistance was too long and uncertain. The pressure to reduce Allied ground casualties compelled a shift to an operational interdiction strategy designed to produce immediate reductions in German ground force mobility and fighting capacity.

By March 1944 operational interdiction was supported by Dwight Eisenhower, commander of the Supreme Headquarters Allied Expeditionary Force, British Air Chief Marshal Arthur Tedder, Eisenhower's deputy, Charles Portal, chief of the British Air Staff, Carl Spaatz, commander of the U.S. Strategic Air Forces in Europe (USSTAF), the Joint Intelligence Staff, the British Ministry of Economic Warfare, and the Enemy Objectives Unit (EOU) of the Office of Strategic Services. The only major dissenter was Arthur Harris, chief of RAF Bomber Command, who advocated the primacy of area attacks on German cities.[60]

Although nearly all the senior Allied leaders approved of this shift in air strategy, there were significant differences over target selection. All agreed that gaining air superiority over Europe was the highest priority, but once this was achieved early in 1944, a major dispute arose as to whether oil or transportation should be hit next.[61]

The transportation plan developed by Solly Zuckerman, Tedder's scientific adviser, aimed to destroy the rail, road, and river communications on which the German army depended. The core target set was the German railway network because it carried the vast majority of very heavy loads, including military vehicles and other heavy equipment. Rather than cut railway lines themselves, which could be easily repaired, the idea was to create roadblocks by bombing the principal marshalling yards, which acted as transportation hubs, coordinating the distribution of cars between in-

---

[60] Major accounts of the shift in bombing strategies in early 1944 are Craven and Cate, *Army Air Forces* 3: 67–79, 138–66, 172–81; Webster and Frankland, *Strategic Air Offensive* 3: 10–41; Arthur William Tedder, *With Prejudice: The War Memoirs of the Marshal of the Royal Air Force* (Boston: Little, Brown, 1966), pp. 499–600; Solly Zuckerman, *From Apes to Warlords* (New York: Harper and Row, 1978), pp. 216–45; Rostow, *Pre-invasion Bombing Strategy*; and Alfred C. Mierzejewski, *The Collapse of the German War Economy, 1944–1945: Allied Air Power and the German National Railway* (Chapel Hill: University of North Carolina Press, 1988), pp. 61–85.

[61] Craven and Cate, *Army Air Forces* 2: 364.

coming and outgoing trains. The goal was to make it impossible for the Germans to move significant reinforcements into France. The plan also called for the destruction of seventy-six rail centers in France, Belgium, and Western Germany.[62]

Americans, led by Spaatz, preferred oil to rail targets. Their brief was carried by the EOU, which rejected railways on the grounds that there was too great a cushion of capacity for civilian and long-term industrial use above the minimum required by fighting units: "Military traffic forms a small proportion of total traffic; at its maximum it will not be more than about one-fifth of total traffic. A reduction of at least 30% could be made in European rail traffic without affecting enemy military potential for a year."[63] Oil, by contrast, was the foundation of German military operations. Assuming that Germany had stocks of finished petroleum products sufficient for only several months of military operations, the EOU estimated that the loss of more than 50 percent of Axis output would quickly reduce German tactical and strategic mobility as well as frontline delivery of supplies.[64] Specifically, the destruction of fifty-four oil installations was expected to force Germany to cut present military consumption by 25 percent, even if it retained possession of the Romanian oil fields. An immediate effect on the western front could not be guaranteed, because the Allies could not estimate how the consumption reductions would be allocated between air and land forces and between the various fronts. Nevertheless, the EOU planners were confident that there would be a major impact within six months.[65]

On 23 March 1944 Eisenhower decided in favor of transportation because it appeared to offer the greatest military effect on the Western front in the shortest time. Oil was assigned second priority. Even so, between 1 May 1944 and 31 March 1945, the Eighth and Fifteenth Air Forces and RAF Bomber Command conducted 555 separate attacks on 133 oil industry tar-

[62] Tedder, *With Prejudice*, pp. 502–4, 509, 529–40; Zuckerman, *From Apes to Warlords*, pp. 222, 232–33, 289–90; and Mierzejewski, *Collapse of the German War Economy*, pp. 81–82. The French transportation system was clearly an operational target, but transportation in Germany, as well as oil, was more ambiguous, since these targets could also be hit in support of a strategic interdiction or even an industrial web strategy. I have characterized them as operational interdiction targets, first, because that was the rationale on which Allied air planners selected them; second, because the German civilian economy, including electric power generation, heating, and other civilian fuel requirements were met primarily by coal; and third, because substantial attacks on transportation targets in Germany proper did not begin until September 1944, by which time they were needed for the direct logistic support of frontline forces.

[63] EOU, "The Use of Strategic Air Power after 1 March 1944," 28 February 1944, pp. 3–4, app. 8, USAF HRA K519.3171–2.

[64] Memorandum, Carl Spaatz to General Dwight D. Eisenhower, Supreme Allied Commander, "Plan for the Completion of the Combined Bomber Offensive," 5 March 1944, USAF HRA K519.318–1.

[65] Rostow, *Pre-invasion Bombing Strategy*, pp. 31–35; Mierzejewski, *Collapse of the German War Economy*, p. 83.

gets, plus numerous raids on reserve oil depots and POL dumps. In addition, when the Soviet forces overran Romania in August 1944, Germany lost access to Ploesti oil fields, which accounted for 25 percent of production. By November Germany's oil production had dropped to about 30 percent of what it had been in the spring.[66] By February 1945 the oil campaign had succeeded in lowering the output of fuel below the levels necessary for German forces to fight efficiently. After January large-scale operations by either the Luftwaffe or by motorized units of the German army were impossible. The failure of the Germans to gain much ground in the Ardennes offensive and their inability to prevent the Soviet breakout from the Baranov bridgehead in January, which led to the loss of Silesia, were both direct results of fuel shortages affecting the tactical mobility of motorized forces.[67]

The transportation offensive opened in May 1944 with heavy attacks on French rail yards and bridges designed to prevent the Germans from moving reinforcements from Germany or redeploying reserves already in France to meet the Normandy landing. Once the invasion forces were securely ashore, the effort against transportation was reduced in favor of intensified attacks against oil. The transportation campaign resumed in earnest from September 1944 onward, with heavy attacks on targets in Germany proper with the aim of shutting down rail movement in the entire area between the Rhine and the Western border. Tactical air forces interdicted bridges, lines, and train movements, and strategic air forces hit marshalling yards.[68]

The structure of German logistics combined rail and motor transportation. Approximately 300 to 450 tons of supplies of all types were required daily to support a German frontline division, depending on whether it was infantry or armor, during a normal day's fighting. To maintain a division's supply, trains would bring cargo from supply centers to army railheads (the average train was capable of transporting 450 tons), and then trucks and horses would deliver it to the fielded forces, with trucks carrying 30 percent and horses 70 percent.[69]

Under the persistent pressure of the oil and communications offensives, the German army progressively lost the ability to provide combat formations with the supplies essential to their operations. During the Battle of Normandy, air interdiction reduced total deliveries to the German armies from the 5,250 tons per day thought necessary by German commanders to 3,300.[70] Initially, the effects of these shortages were mitigated by the exis-

[66] Thomas A. Fabyanic et al., "Army Air Forces' Intelligence and Its Effects on Plans and Operations during World War II," mimeograph (Washington, D.C.: Office of Air Force History), p. 326; Craven and Cate, *Army Air Forces* 3: 640–45.

[67] Webster and Frankland, *Strategic Air Offensive* 3: 234.

[68] Ibid., 3: 244–48.

[69] USSBS, *The Impact of the Allied Air Effort on German Logistics* (Washington, D.C.: GPO, 1947), pp. 133–34.

[70] Ibid., pp. 135–36.

tence of local stockpiles located near the front in anticipation of the Allied cross-Channel attack. As the invasion progressed, however, the German logistic position deteriorated because the fluidity of the fighting reduced the usefulness of prepositioning supplies, while air interdiction made the movement of logistics more and more difficult.

Starting in September 1944, heavy attacks were launched against marshalling yards, bridges, lines, and train movements, producing a serious disruption in traffic throughout western Germany. Freight car loadings, which were approximately 900,000 in August, fell to 700,000 by the end of October, to 550,000 by the end of December, and to 214,000 by the first week of March 1945. Despite reduced industrial production from lost transportation, there was no immediate shortage of weapons for the German fighting forces.[71] Rather, the main effect of lack of transport was the inability to put weapons and supplies in the hands of divisions actually fighting. On 23 March when the German forces retreated across the Rhine, combat formations were short almost all supplies other than food, especially fuel and ammunition, even though rear depots contained large stocks until the end of the war.[72]

Strategic air power, however, was not the decisive cause of these effects. Whereas strategic forces damaged 20 of 25 marshalling yards, tactical air forces destroyed 12 of the 18 major bridges, 101 minor bridges, 4,000 locomotives, and 28,000 cars and created over 5,000 line cuts.[73] The important point is that operations were interdicted mainly by tactical air attacks and these effects would have occurred even if the strategic offensive had not taken place.[74]

Invasion

The Allies' landing in France signaled a shift from coercion to conquest as the primary strategy for ending the war. The failure of previous bombing operations, the growing superiority of the Soviet army on the eastern front, and the need to knock out Germany rapidly so resources could be concentrated against Japan—all persuaded the Allies that the main military pressure applied to Germany should come from land forces.[75] Rather than attack the economy or morale, the armies would simply overrun Germany.

[71] Tanks were scarce, but because of high demand, not lower supply. Webster and Frankland, *Strategic Air Offensive* 3: 258.

[72] USSBS, *Impact on German Logistics*, p. 128; USSBS, *Summary Report (European War)*, p. 31.

[73] USSBS, *The Effects of Strategic Bombing on German Transportation* (Washington, DC: GPO, January 1947), p. 14.

[74] Webster and Frankland, *Strategic Air Offensive* 3: 258.

[75] By the spring of 1944, Churchill was increasingly worried about Soviet advances as well as the defeat of Germany, although it was too late to affect Allied invasion plans. Ben-Moshe, "Churchill and the 'Second Front.' "

On both the eastern and western fronts, ground strategy was based on attrition warfare. The Allies simply tried to destroy German military capability by annihilating military equipment and manpower faster than they could be replaced.[76] Decline in its ground power would leave Germany less and less able to hold any defensive front, allowing Allied forces to advance faster and faster.Since attrition warfare, if it lasts more than a few months, requires the full national mobilization of human and industrial resources, the determinants of ultimate victory are industrial capacity and population size. Although the second leading industrial power in 1938, Germany was exceptionally vulnerable to the combined attrition efforts of the United States, Great Britain, and the Soviet Union. As Table 22 shows, Germany and its partners were outmatched two to one in both industrial resources and population. In 1938 Germany, Italy, and Japan accounted for 20.7 percent of world manufacturing production, compared to 51.1 percent for the Allies.[77] In 1937 the populations of Germany, Italy, and Japan totaled 183 million, compared to 344 million for the United States, Great Britain, and the Soviet Union.[78]

The most serious of Germany's vulnerabilities was manpower (see Table 23). Although military production remained quite high until the very end, Germany no longer had an army that could use it. Casualties from 1941 to the end of the war were more than double the army's size in 1941. As a result, virtually all units fell more and more under strength as the war continued. Even more important, the quality of replacements progressively declined, and Germany was forced to rely on leaders as well as soldiers who were increasingly unskilled and unfit and often killed before they had time to learn from experience.[79] At the same time, the experience and competence of the Allied armies, which had much deeper population reserves, improved, and the immense productivity of Allied war industries equipped them with aircraft, fighting vehicles, and other heavy weapons that Germany could not match.[80] As a result, from mid-1944 onward, the Wehrmacht was no longer able to contain major Allied offensives. The question became

[76] Russell F. Weigley, *The American Way of War: A History of United States Military Strategy and Policy* (New York: Macmillan, 1973), pp. 312–62.

[77] I do not include France on either side. Adding France to the Axis powers only raises their total to 25.1 percent of world-manufacturing production. See Paul Bairoch, "Industrialization Levels from 1750 to 1980," *Journal of European Economic History* 11 (Spring 1982): 297.

[78] Quincy Wright, *A Study of War*, 2d ed. (Chicago: University of Chicago Press, 1942), 1: 672.

[79] By spring 1943 the Eighteenth Panzer Division had less than half its original strength and consisted largely of soldiers over thirty-six years old. During the spring it received replacements that made it one of the best-staffed divisions on the eastern front, although the officers it received were a mix of untrained cadets and recalled elderly men. The skills of the enlisted soldiers were also deficient. During and after Kursk, the division suffered such heavy losses that it had to be disbanded. Omer Bartov, *Hitler's Army: Soldiers, Nazis, and War in the Third Reich* (New York: Oxford University Press, 1991), pp. 52–53. Bad as the manpower situation was in 1943, losses in 1944 were even higher and the quality of the replacements that Germany could scrape up were even lower.

[80] Weigley, *American Way of War*, pp. 312–59.

Table 22. Comparative economic power of warring states in Europe, 1943

	Population (millions)	Steel (millions of tons)	Hard coal (millions of tons)	Aircraft (units)	Tanks (units)
Britain	42	13.2	202.1	26,263	7,476
United States	137.3	82.1	535.3	85,898	29,497
Soviet Union	170.5	8.4	92	34,900	24,012
Greater Germany	81.1	30.6	268.3	25,200	19,824

SOURCE: Mierzejewski, *Collapse of the German War Economy*, p. 66.

Table 23. Cumulative German manpower losses, 1941–1945

	Eastern front	Western front	Total
March 1942	1,000,000		1,000,000
June 1942	1,300,000		1,300,000
October 1942	1,600,000		1,600,000
October 1943	3,100,000		3,100,000
October 1944	4,600,000	700,000[a]	5,300,000
March 1945	6,200,000	750,000	6,950,000
April 1945	6,700,000	3,000,000	9,700,000

SOURCES: Bartov, *Hitler's Army*, pp. 36, 38, 39, 44, 45; H. P. Willmott *The Great Crusade* (New York: Free Press, 1989), pp. 451, 455; John Erickson, *The Road to Berlin: Stalin's War with Germany* (London: Weidenfeld and Nicolson, 1983) 2: 422; Albert Seaton, *The German Army, 1933–1945* (New York: St. Martin's, 1982), p. 243; and Cooper, *German Army*, pp. 496, 512, 527.
[a] I combine Cooper's number of 550,000 for June to August with Seaton's number of 150,000 for September through October.

less whether the Allies would reach Berlin than which Allied army would get there first.

Contrary to early expectations at the time, strategic bombing was not decisive. The question is whether it helped significantly or hardly mattered. The answer is that it made virtually no difference. Even if there had been no strategic bombing campaign at all, the war would have ended in the same way and at just about the same time. It is not true, as strategic bombing advocates insist, that bombing destroyed the German war economy, reducing replacements to the German army and leaving it less able to resist Allied offensives. Although German industry was in drastic decline from mid-1944 onward, the existence of significant stockpiles of semifinished goods such as steel and refined oil products meant that German armaments production and the mobility of German forces were not seriously affected for several months more. Even as late as March 1945, armaments production was half of the July 1944 peak and almost 50 percent higher than in January 1942 (see Table 24).

Table 24. Index of armaments output, 1944–45

	July	September	December	March
(January–February 1942 = 100)				
Panzer	589	527	598	273
Motor vehicles	117	84	63	37
Weapons	384	377	408	208
Ammunition	319	335	263	154

SOURCE: USSBS, *Effects on German Economy*, p. 275

In contrast to Japan, where war production ended before the war did, in Germany the Allies invaded before the war economy collapsed. Weapons and munitions production, while reduced, was still substantial in early 1945, although the fuel situation was more serious. The Ardennes offensive was the first major operation to suffer from serious fuel shortages, and by February and March 1945 most Panzer units on both fronts were effectively unable to move for offense or defense. Even if the German tanks had had fuel, the last round of Allied offensives would still have succeeded because of the enormous numerical and material superiority of the Allies. Virtually all major Allied offensives after July 1944 succeeded.

Moreover, decline in the war economy was due mainly to territorial losses, not strategic bombing. Steel production was undermined by the loss of iron ore from Western Europe, and the loss of the Romanian (August 1944) and Hungarian (February 1945) oil fields crippled oil production. Finally, the collapse of German domestic transportation in February 1945, which caused the final disintegration of German war production, was due mainly to the operations of tactical air power flying from bases liberated by the Allied armies as they advanced across Europe rather than to strategic bombing.

It could be argued that strategic bombing helped by compelling Germany to invest in antiaircraft defenses and by destroying the Luftwaffe in air-to-air combat with escort fighters, mainly during the first half of 1944. Even if there had been no strategic bombing effort, however, the Luftwaffe would still have been destroyed by Allied tactical air power as the advance of ground forces extended its range. Even in 1943 and early 1944 Allied fighters had already achieved control of the air as far as they could reach into Belgium, France, and Italy, and the same pattern was repeated wherever Allied fighters flew.[81]

In summary, the Douhet, strategic interdiction, and operational interdiction strategies all satisfied their basic requirements, but at different times.

[81] For a rich discussion of the battle for air superiority over Western Europe, see Williamson Murray, *Luftwaffe* (Baltimore: Nautical & Aviation Publishing Company of America, 1985), pp. 143–97.

[282]

The Douhet strategy was implemented quite effectively, destroying large parts of Germany's largest cities by the end of the war. The goal of the strategic interdiction strategy, to destroy the German economy, was achieved by March 1945, although air attack was a less important cause than land power. Operational interdiction was the most effective air strategy because it impeded the flow of supplies that could have significantly improved the fighting power of the German armies.

Explaining German Behavior

Allied coercion failed, not because the Allies' coercive strategies were not well implemented but because Nazi Germany was virtually immune to conventional coercion. The efforts to manipulate civilian vulnerability failed, though the Allies inflicted substantial costs, because Germany, even more than most modern nation-states involved in war, was willing to pay a high price to preserve its territorial control. The effort to manipulate military vulnerability failed not because the Allies could not convince German leaders of their inability to defend the homeland, but because Hitler saw no point to a surrender that would bring the end of National Socialism, and the army generals who could have overthrown him believed that the Soviet army would exact such horrific revenge that the costs of immediate surrender would be higher than the costs of resistance to gain time for refugee movement westward.

In order to explain why Germany did not surrender prior to complete military defeat, we need to understand how the German state made consequential decisions. We also need to know Germany's political objectives in the European war, and its military and diplomatic strategies for achieving them. We must correlate the increasing vulnerability of Germany's population and military strategy to changes in German leaders' willingness to surrender. Since Germany did not surrender before complete defeat, we must determine the point at which the denial theory would have predicted capitulation and ask why it did not come about. Finally, we must assess whether the factors that prevented surrender were unique to the German case or were simply extreme examples of the domestic political dynamics that make coercion of all modern nation-states difficult.

German Decision Making

Unlike some cases in which the military and political calculations of the target state's leadership cannot be measured directly and so must be inferred from the behavior of the state as a whole, in the German case there is sufficient evidence to reconstruct the positions of the major groups within the governing elite.[82] The political elite was divided into four main parts: Hitler, the Nazi civilian leadership, the military leadership, and the anti-Nazi resistance. Germany was governed by a revolutionary one-party system, which subjugated the major elites and political forces in German society (Junkers, industrialists, the military, the Catholic church, Social Democrats, and Communists) in order to maintain its own power and advance the goals of National Socialism. The Nazi system of government was based on the leadership principle. Each minister was personally responsible to Hitler; there was no collective cabinet responsibility, and consultation between ministries to coordinate policy was frowned upon. As a result, far from being monolithic, the Third Reich was in reality a battleground for powerful quasi-feudal interest groups, all struggling for influence, which Hitler was able to play off one against another to maintain and expand his own authority.[83]

Hitler was undoubtedly the central decision maker, but his control over state policy fluctuated. After his ascendancy over the armed forces was firmly established in February 1938, there were no institutional constraints on his exercise of power and no decision of any significance could be taken without his approval. In essence, his power was absolute. After 1943, however, Hitler's rule began to disintegrate. As long as he was alive, there was no question of replacing him, but his single-handed control of German policy gradually eroded. The transition to total war vastly increased the number of decisions requiring the fuhrer's authority while Hitler's physical condition deteriorated. As events accelerated, Hitler involved himself in policies at his own discretion—that is, impulsively and spasmodically. As a result, the autonomy of other decision-making groups increased, especially regarding the implementation of policies. By the last months of the war, Hitler's control had eroded to the point where even his direct orders were sometimes ignored or disobeyed.[84]

The second group, the civilian leadership, was completely dominated by Nazi officials. The leaders of national socialism were a collection of lower-middle-class intellectuals and political adventurers who were motivated by varying combinations of frustration over Germany's weakened interna-

---

[82] Although there is good evidence for the major coalitions, however, we do not have sufficient evidence for all involved individuals to treat each as a separate case.

[83] On the power structure of the Third Reich, see Karl Dietrich Bracher, *The German Dictatorship* (New York: Praeger, 1970); Eberhard Jaekel, *Hitler in History* (Hanover: University Press of New England, 1984); Martin Broszat, *The Hitler State* (London: Longman, 1981); and Edward N. Peterson, *The Limits of Hitler's Power* (Princeton: Princeton University Press, 1969).

[84] For a description of Hitler's waning control during the last years of the war, see Ian Kershaw, *Hitler* (New York: Longman, 1991), pp. 163–87; Albert Speer, *Inside the Third Reich*, trans. Richard Winston and Clara Winston (New York: Macmillan, 1970), pp. 405–62; Hugh Trevor-Roper, *The Last Days of Hitler* (New York: Macmillan, 1949); and Hans Mommsen, *From Weimar to Auschwitz*, trans. Philip O'Connor (Princeton: Princeton University Press, 1991), pp. 163–88.

tional status, fanatical racism, fascist ideas, and simple ambition. Despite varying degrees of personal commitment to different aspects of Hitler's foreign and domestic programs, all were willing to support and implement Hitler's decisions. Although Nazi leaders competed fiercely to extend their power over each other, all remained loyal to Hitler, partly because of their confidence in his ability, and even more because their personal power depended on their standing in the Nazi party, whose stability in turn depended on Hitler's charismatic leadership and unifying control.

The civilian leadership comprised three separate empires, obedient to the fuhrer and in deadly competition with one another. The first was the Nazi party machine, controlled by Martin Bormann, which had tentacles deep in society. The party had its own press, control over education and regional government, and a myriad of paramilitary organizations such as the Hitler Youth. Second was the internal security hierarchy, headed by Heinrich Himmler, which included the Gestapo, the Reich Central Security Office, the assassination squads of the Sichersheitdienst (SD), and Hitler's private army, the Waffen SS. The third empire consisted of the tools for state control over the economy, including all the resources and productive capability that supplied German military forces; this domain was first headed by Hermann Goering and later by Albert Speer.

The third leadership group was the military, of which the most important component was the Army. Following the penetration of the Nazi social revolution throughout German society during the 1930s, the Army was the only remaining institution that could oppose the civilian leadership. Although the Nazis went to great lengths to assimilate the officer corps and Hitler took control of military operations himself in 1942, they did not entirely succeed in extinguishing Army independence because many officers were politically conservative and not attracted to Nazi ideology.[85] Most important, the only way to change German state policy decided by the Nazis was to oust them from power, and only the Army had sufficient force to do so.

The German officer corps was itself divided into two main camps. The so-called Nazi generals, mostly younger and from middle-class backgrounds, either owed their rapid promotion to Hitler or identified with National Socialism.[86] This group is represented by Erwin Rommel, Heinz Guderian,

[85] Even though Hitler had succeeded in transforming the 1930s tactical alliance between conservative officers and the Nazis into party domination over the military, for many conservative officers, class and institutional loyalties remained much stronger than commitment to the Nazi regime. On party-army relations, see Robert J. O'Neill, *The German Army and Nazi Party* (London: Cassell, 1966); Harold Deutsch, *Hitler and His Generals* (Minneapolis: University of Minnesota Press, 1974); and John Wheeler-Bennett, *The Nemesis of Power: The German Army in Politics, 1918–1945* (London: Macmillan, 1964).

[86] There was also a less important group of genuine pro-Russian anti-Communists who hoped that the collapse of bolshevism would be followed by a regime with which Germany could cooperate. Wheeler-Bennett, *Nemesis of Power*, pp. 611–12.

Wilhelm Keitel, Alfred Jodl, Walter Model, Adm. Karl Doenitz, Albert Kesselring, Walter von Reichenau, and Walter Warlimont. In the other camp were conservative, largely aristocratic officers who followed the tradition of the old Prussian officer corps. Domestically, this group opposed the class-leveling tendencies of both the Weimar republic and National Socialism, preferring to maintain their leading class and institutional position in society. In foreign policy they strongly supported the Nazi goal of reviving Germany's international position but were much less enthusiastic about a far-ranging campaign of conquest and not at all desirous of the major war that such a campaign could be expected to provoke. They saw Germany's conflicts, especially in the east, in geopolitical and ideological but not racial terms; they were interested in overthrowing bolshevism and in gaining access to resources to expand Germany's industrial base but not in extermination. Whereas the Nazis saw the Slavs as subhumans to be exploited or killed, conservative officers preferred to enlist the Soviet population to help overthrow bolshevism.[87] Nearly all the major army figures in the July 1944 coup came from this group: Colonels Claus von Stauffenberg and Hans von Dohnanyi, Generals Ludwig Beck, Henning von Tresckow, Guenther von Kluge, Reinhardt Gehlen, Karl-Heinrich von Stülpnagel, Hans Speidel, Admiral Wilhelm Canaris, and Field Marshal Erwin von Witzleben. Most members of this group remained politically inactive; among the high-ranking officers who refused to join against Hitler were Field Marshal Erich von Manstein and General Franz Halder, and Field Marshal Gerd von Rundstedt actually helped to suppress the plot.[88]

The fourth element in German society was the anti-Nazi resistance, including many subgroups, among them Weimar democrats, the Catholic church, trade unionists, aristocrats, and civil servants.[89] The chief aim of these groups was to regain the positions they had held in Weimar society. For them, the outcome of the war was important to the extent it discredited Nazi leadership and created opportunities to replace the Nazi regime with one dedicated to maintaining the traditional social structure. Historians debate how committed and how widespread was resistance to Nazism; certainly, the resistance had no influence on German policy during this period. Since the Army was the only force independent of the Nazis, the civilian op-

[87] Alex Alexiev, *Soviet Nationalities in German Wartime Strategy, 1941–1945*, R-2772 (Santa Monica, Calif.: Rand Corporation, 1982), pp. 7–8.

[88] A key problem for resisting generals was predicting the loyalty of the troops. Many junior officers and most of the troops had been indoctrinated in the Nazi-controlled education system; 30 percent of all officers were party members. Omer Bartov, *The Eastern Front, 1941–1945: German Troops and the Barbarisation of Warfare* (New York: St. Martin's, 1986), p. 49.

[89] On the anti-Nazi resistance, see Peter Hoffmann, *The History of the German Resistance, 1933–1945* (London: Macdonald and Jane's, 1970); Hans Rothfels, *The German Opposition to Hitler: An Appraisal* (Chicago: Henry Regnery, 1962); Allen Dulles, *Germany's Underground* (New York: Macmillan, 1947); and Hermann Graml, ed., *The German Resistance to Hitler* (London: Batsford, 1970).

position could influence whether Germany would continue the war only by gaining Army cooperation to mount a coup.[90]

German Goals and Strategies

What matters for understanding the effects of Allied coercive strategies on German surrender decisions is not initial war aims, but German political and territorial objectives at the time coercion was being applied and strategies for achieving those objectives. The keys, therefore, are German goals and strategies during 1943–1945, when the Allied coercive campaigns reached full force. To understand these fully, it is helpful to trace the earlier evolution of German policy, particularly from the start of the war against the Soviet Union.

The Nazi leaders and the German generals each entered the war against the Soviets for their own reasons, which were not mutually exclusive. The generals believed Germany needed to expand eastward to achieve economic and military autarky. Many believed that the growing Soviet industrial base posed a long-term threat to Germany, as well as an immediate threat to Romania and the Wehrmacht's oil supply. They also believed that agricultural shortages had significantly contributed to Germany's defeat in World War I and that colonizing food-producing areas in Eastern Europe would remove this vulnerability.[91]

Nazi goals in the war against the Soviet Union were driven by National Socialist ideology. Their principal imperative was lebensraum ("living space") for the German nation, to be achieved through territorial control of parts of Eastern Europe and the western Soviet Union (Baltic lands, Belorussia, western Ukraine, and the Crimea).[92] Within the annexed areas, all

---

[90] On the resistance, see Ernst Wolf, "Political and Moral Motives behind the Resistance," in *German Resistance to Hitler*, ed. Graml, pp. 193–271; Ulrich von Hassell, *The von Hassell Diaries, 1938–1944* (Garden City, N.Y.: Doubleday, 1947); Rothfels, *German Opposition to Hitler*; Dulles, *Germany's Underground*; Hoffmann, *History of the German Resistance*.

[91] These concerns essentially followed the grand strategic thinking of the German general staff before and after World War I. Arden Bucholz, *Molke, Schlieffen, and Russian War Planning* (New York: Berg, 1991); Imanuel Geiss, *German Foreign Policy, 1871–1914* (Boston: Routledge and Kegan Paul, 1976).

[92] Operation Barbarosa was intended to achieve both sets of goals. On 30 March 1941 Hitler explained to his generals that achieving all Germany's goals would require more than inflicting a decisive victory over enemy forces in the field. The slogan for his Soviet policy was "Destruction of Fighting Forces—Dissolution of State," which Halder in his diary interpreted as the "struggle between two opposing world outlooks. Destructive decision on Bolshevism; is equal to social criminaldom. Communism extraordinary danger for future. We must disavow the point of view of soldierly comradeship. The Communist is not a comrade before and not a comrade after. It is a question of a war of destruction. If we don't conceive of it that way, then we will indeed beat the enemy, but in thirty years the Communist enemy will again confront us. We do not conduct war to conserve the enemy." Halder's diary entry for Hitler's speech to the generals on 30 March 1941 as found in Lucy S. Dawidowicz, *The War against the Jews, 1933–1945* (New York: Bantam, 1975), p. 110.

persons of suitable racial origins were to be Germanized, and "racially unfit" groups were to be destroyed and their lands resettled. The implications for the "unfit" were clear: "If we take from the land what we need many millions will undoubtedly starve to death."[93] As the war continued and hopes of military victory receded, the importance of achieving these racial goals mounted, so that the liquidation of races was accelerated rather than abandoned as the war continued.[94]

German strategy for the war in the east passed through four phases. In the first, Germany tried a blitzkrieg campaign expected to last only five months.[95] Although this strategy succeeded in destroying the bulk of the Red Army mobilized near the frontiers and in overrunning many of the industrial centers of the western Soviet Union, intensive mobilization of remaining industrial and manpower resources allowed the Soviets to field fresh armies and block the German advance, so that from the winter of 1941 onward the Germans were always outnumbered on the eastern front.

The second phase began in late 1942 after El Alamein, the Allied landing in North Africa, and the disastrous defeat at Stalingrad had shifted the initiative to the Allies. The eastern front remained the main front, where Germany sought to maintain control of all occupied territory in order to keep resources needed to achieve victory in a long war of attrition. Hitler and his generals, however, disagreed over how attrition should be pursued. Instead of manning a broad front they could not hope to hold, the generals preferred a defensive attrition strategy under which German forces would withdraw to a narrower front where they could defeat Soviet offensive blows. Hitler, however, would not permit retreat and insisted on a strategy of offensive attrition based on limited attacks to disrupt the preparation of future enemy offensives. Offensive attrition failed with the bloody repulse of the attack at Kursk in July 1943, after which the Germans were forced into defensive attrition by continuous Soviet offensives.[96]

The third phase ran from summer 1944 to winter 1945. The second front in the west together with continuing Soviet advances eliminated any hope that Germany could ultimately defeat the combined resources of its enemies. Hitler nevertheless continued to rely on an attrition strategy in the hope that

[93] According to the most detailed plan for postwar lebensraum policy, General Plan Ost, between 46 and 51 million people were earmarked for deportation as "undesirables." German official quoted in Alexiev, *Soviet Nationalities*, p. 4.

[94] Dawidowitz, *War against the Jews*, pp. 140–43.

[95] For the history of German strategic planning for Operation Barbarossa, see Bryan I. Fugate, *Operation Barbarossa: Strategy and Tactics on the Eastern Front, 1941* (Novato, Calif.: Presidio Press, 1984); and Alan Clark, *Barbarossa: The Russian-German Conflict, 1941–45* (New York: Quill, 1965); and Earl F. Ziemke, *Stalingrad to Berlin: The German Defeat in the East* (Washington, D.C.: Office of the Chief of Military History, U.S. Army, 1968).

[96] Keegan, *Second World War*, pp. 209–10; B. H. Liddell Hart, *History of the Second World War* (New York: Putnam's, 1970), pp. 169, 485, 493; Ziemke, *Stalingrad to Berlin*, p. 122; Cooper, *German Army*, pp. 461–63; Clark, *Barbarosa*, p. 322.

the prospect of enormous casualties would deter one or all of the Allies from prosecuting the war to the end. To achieve this goal, German forces were directed to maintain a forward defense of occupied territories and to launch limited offensives against enemy forces. In particular, Hitler hoped that the Western Allies would be unwilling to see the Soviets in control of Central Europe and so would seek accommodation with Germany. Although German military leaders became increasingly pessimistic during this period, they had no influence on strategy. The Allied breakthroughs on both eastern and western fronts in July sparked the unsuccessful coup by some officers; other officers continued fighting but with no hope of success.[97]

The final phase was triggered by the defeat of the German Ardennes offensive and the breakthrough in Poland which brought Soviet forces to within 45 miles of Berlin by the end of January 1945. At this point German strategy disintegrated. German forces continued to resist on both fronts and to inflict significant casualties on the advancing Allies, but Germany no longer had the ability to present the Allies with the prospect that attrition would continue for a protracted period. Hitler was reduced to hoping that the Allied coalition would dissolve of its own accord, while many other Nazi officials and generals began acting independently to limit further war costs. For example, Himmler and Kesselring made attempts to negotiate with the Allies; Speer countermanded Hitler's scorched-earth policies; and Doenitz began military operations to protect the westward flow of refugees rather than to extend the survival of the Nazi state.

Civilian and Military Vulnerability

Although Germany was not coerced, this case can provide important evidence about the relative effectiveness of coercive strategies based on civilian vulnerabilities and military vulnerabilities. If one factor had more effect than the other on decision makers' positions on whether and how much Germany should surrender, then this evidence can be compared to the general patterns of other cases, even if this effect was ultimately insufficient to change the behavior of the German state.

To evaluate the relative effects of civilian and military vulnerability on German decision making, we must trace the effects of changes in either type of vulnerability on the positions of the important groups making up the German leadership. To do so, I divide the case into several discrete time slices and measure the degree of Germany's vulnerability to each type of threat in each period. If I can show that the preferences of a particular group changed at the same time a certain type of vulnerability increased and the

---

[97] Alan Bullock, *Hitler and Stalin: Parallel Lines* (London: Harper Collins, 1991), p. 865; idem., *Hitler: A Study in Tyranny*, rev. ed. (New York: Harper and Row, 1962), p. 760; Heinz Guderian, *Panzer Leader* (New York: E.P. Dutton, 1952), pp. 370–73.

other remained constant, it would show that the first and not the second was the cause of that group's decision.

Carrying out this analysis reveals that the only factor to influence any of the principal groups was military vulnerability to invasion (see Table 25). Changes in civilian vulnerability correlate with changes in groups' political behavior in only one instance (July 1943), when there was a simultaneous increase in military vulnerability. The most significant attempt to change German policy occurred when military vulnerability rose to high with the collapse of both the French and Russian fronts in July 1944, although the attempted failed. Even when military vulnerability rose to very high in January 1945, German leaders did not surrender, not because they thought that continued resistance could affect the territorial settlement in any way but because resistance was expected to reduce the civilian costs of Soviet occupation by permitting refugee flows westward. In March, when resistance in Italy and on most of the western front could no longer help reduce civilian costs, leaders in these areas began to surrender piecemeal.

The two independent variables are civilian vulnerability and military vulnerability. Civilian vulnerability is coded as "low," meaning that although there is some risk to individuals, no major part of the population must make adjustments or compromises in their daily lives to avoid the threat; "medium," meaning that the risks to individuals has risen to the point that major parts of the population must make compromises or adjustments in their daily lives, such as evacuation or substitution, to lower the threat; "high," meaning that 1 percent or more of the population may die despite the best countermeasures; and "very high," meaning that 5 percent or more of the population is at risk.

Military vulnerability is coded according to change in the prospects of Germany's attrition strategy for preventing or, later, deterring invasion of the homeland. Vulnerability is coded as "low," meaning there was risk that the current position could not be maintained but only uncertainty about whether any threat to the homeland would emerge; "medium," meaning that the current position definitely could not be held but threats to the homeland could be reduced by added defensive measures; "high," meaning that the homeland could not be defended unless attrition deterred further Allied offensives and the success of attrition was uncertain; and "very high," meaning that the likelihood of complete defeat approached certainty because both defense and heavy attrition of enemy forces was impossible.

Prior to the summer of 1940, German society was not subject to attack.[98] Starting on 24 August 1940, with the first British raid against Berlin, German

[98] In May 1940 the British started to drop bombs on German soil but did not target civilians and civilian losses were negligible. Although Germany was under blockade, it controlled most of the resources of continental Europe and so was not short of food or other civilian needs.

Table 25. Changes in vulnerabilities and leaders' surrender policies

Date	Event	Vulnerability		Leaders		
		Civilian	Military	Nazis	Army	Resistance
August 1940	1st Berlin raid	low	nil[a]	ns	ns	ns?
December 1940	Regular British bombing	medium	nil	ns	ns	ns?
November 1942	Stalingrad, Torch, El Alamein	medium	low	ns	ns	ns?
July 1943	Hamburg, Kursk, Sicily	high	medium	ns	ls	ls
July 1944	Breakthroughs in Russia and France	high	high	ns	ls+	ls+
October 1944	Red Army enters East Prussia	very high	high	ns	(ls)	—[b]
January 1945	Breakthrough in Poland	very high	very high	(is)	(ls/is)	
March 1945	Breakthrough in West/economic collapse	very high	very high	is	is	

[a] Meaning that there was no current or foreseeable threat, although one might arise in the future. From at least December 1941, for instance, Germany faced a coalition with superior overall resources, so ultimate defeat could not be ruled out.

[b] In the aftermath of the July 1944 coup attempt, the civilian resistance was totally supressed.

ns = no concessions
ls = some in the group will make concessions but not surrender the homeland
is = some in the group will surrender homeland
() = some would prefer concessions but are not willing to act
+ = larger number willing to act than previously
? = little information available

civilians were vulnerable to air attack. Vulnerability remained low until December 1940; although the British launched raids against urban centers which caused an estimated 349 deaths, no extraordinary resources were devoted to the protection of urban areas.[99]

With the RAF's first area attack against a German city, Mannheim, in December 1940, civilian vulnerability rose to medium. Although raids on German cities became a regular part of the war, the numbers of casualties were kept relatively low by a combination of effective air defense, fire fighting, and civil defense measures. Municipal fire departments were nationalized and augmented by fire-fighting sections of the German armed forces and by "plant brigades" organized in individual industrial factories. Civilian deaths in 1941 and 1942 are estimated at 2,785 and 4,327 respectively.[100]

[99] Bidinian, *Combined Allied Bomber Offensive*, p. 41.
[100] Bond, *Fire and the Air War*, pp. 98–99; Bidinian, *Combined Allied Bomber Offensive*, p. 41.

In July 1943 civilian vulnerability increased to high as more effective incendiary techniques and larger numbers of bombers increased civilian damage by an order of magnitude. The large numbers of incendiaries caused fires too numerous for fire-fighting forces to contain, and the heat of the fires was often so intense that shelters offered little protection. The increasing weight of attack together with the destruction of the Luftwaffe after winter 1944 meant that German protective measures could not significantly reduce casualties. Civilian deaths in 1943, 1944, and 1945 (to May) are estimated to be 103,271, 201,000 and 101,000.[101]

In October 1944 civilian vulnerability rose to very high, not because of any increase of the bombing but because Russian forces reached the outer borders of the Reich in east Prussia, triggering, in the midst of intense combat along a broad front, the flight to the west of approximately four to five million civilians.[102] Soviet occupation was expected to be very brutal in retaliation for the German treatment of the Soviet population earlier in the war, and indeed, this fear was hardly unjustified. The total number of German soldiers and civilians who died after the war, roughly four million, equals the number killed in combat during the war itself.[103]

Prior to fall 1942, military vulnerability was nil. Germany's strategy for defeating the Red Army had not yet lost its momentum. The German army was still advancing in the late summer and early fall of 1942, reaching its high-water marks in Stalingrad and the Caucasus in September and October.[104]

Military vulnerability rose to low in November 1942, with the Soviet encirclement of the quarter-million-man German Sixth Army at Stalingrad and the almost simultaneous defeat of Rommel in Egypt and the Anglo-American landing in northwest Africa. Although the front was still deep in the Soviet Union, these events placed Germany on the strategic defensive. Some loss of occupied territory was certain, and even attacks on Germany proper had to be considered as an eventual possibility, as evidenced by Hitler's new slogan "defense of the Homeland," used in rallying the armies on the eastern front.[105] Germany's defeats of 1942, however, did not constitute conclusive evidence that its army would eventually suffer decisive defeat. Germany had not yet fully mobilized its economy for total war, and it was unclear whether the Western Allies could successfully invade the Continent. Moreover, there existed an alternative—strategic withdrawal—which might

[101] Bond, *Fire and the Air War*; Bidinian, *Combined Allied Bomber Offensive*, p. 41.

[102] Alfred M. de Zayas, *Nemesis at Potsdam: The Anglo-Americans and the Expulsion of the Germans* (Boston: Routledge and Kegan Paul, 1977), p. xx.

[103] Douglas Botting, *From the Ruins of the Reich: Germany, 1945–1949* (New York: Crown, 1985), pp. 125–26, 129.

[104] Ziemke, *Stalingrad to Berlin*, p. 47.

[105] Ibid., p. 118.

considerably improve the odds of avoiding defeat by achieving more favorable attrition ratios, possibly good enough to resist indefinitely.[106]

In summer 1943 military vulnerability increased to medium. Tunisia fell in June; the Allies invaded Sicily in July and Italy in September; and Mussolini's government collapsed. Also in July, Germany's Kursk offensive failed, and in August the Soviets began a counteroffensive that started to roll the Wehrmacht back, inflicting heavy losses. Given their manpower shortage and the immense width of the front, the Germans could not defend any line in sufficient strength to check the Soviet advance completely. At the same time, Allied invasion of France was becoming an increasingly likely possibility.

Although current positions could not be held, Germany still retained substantial attrition capabilities, which could be increased by further mobilization of Germany's economy and society. German forces could still exact a heavy toll on the enemy for taking each measure of territory. The Wehrmacht reckoned that between 1 September 1943 and 1 January 1944 the Soviet losses in killed, disabled and POWs amounted to 1.2 million men compared to 243,743 for the Germans. Industrial output was rising, providing enough tanks and weapons to equip new divisions for the western front and replace some of the losses in the Soviet Union.[107] The success of this attrition strategy was by no means assured, however, because the USSR was pulling far ahead of Germany in all major categories of military power, and the huge productive capacity of the Allies would be added. Thus, whereas it might still be possible for Germany to achieve a military stalemate, this was not a foregone conclusion. Occupation of Germany itself had to be considered a growing possibility, although the Soviets were still over 550 miles from Berlin.

In mid-1944, military vulnerability increased to high. In July the Allies broke through the German lines encircling the Normandy beachhead, and at the same time the Red Army launched a massive offensive in Belorussia. These two offensives destroyed the bulk of Germany's frontline combat strength in both theaters. Given its rapidly declining industrial output and

[106] The military history of this period is discussed in Paul Kecskemeti, *Strategic Surrender: The Politics of Victory and Defeat* (Stanford: Stanford University Press, 1958), pp. 119–21; Liddell Hart, *Second World War*, pp. 477–97. The only military alternative, flexible operational warfare based on strategic withdrawals, might have had equally disastrous results in view of the balance of force that obtained after the end of 1942; it is also possible that it would only have hastened Germany's final defeat. To withdraw in order to re-form would have been to play into the hands of the Allies, for Germany's weakness lay not merely in the dispersal of its fighting forces but in the inferiority of all its resources to those at the enemy's command. The Allies were in a position to exploit any German withdrawals more effectively than Germany could have used them. By saving effort for the Allies and more rapidly concentrating their strength at Germany's borders, strategic withdrawal would probably have brought defeat more rapidly than Hitler's choice. F. H. Hinsley, *Hitler's Strategy* (New York: Cambridge University Press, 1951), p. 235.

[107] Ziemke, *Stalingrad to Berlin*, pp. 214, 312.

increasing manpower problems, Germany could no longer replace its losses; German strength on the eastern front stood at 1.79 million in October, down nearly 700,000 from January 1944.[108] At the same time, Allied strength continued to increase.

Germany could still impose considerable attrition, but the unmatchable materiel superiority of its enemies meant that Germany could no longer stalemate the Allied advances. From this point onward, Allied advances were constrained more by weather and the need to establish forward logistics bases for each successive advance than by German resistance.[109] Attrition could succeed in averting the occupation of the German homeland only if one or more of the Allies could be deterred from prosecuting the war to the end by the prospect of even greater casualties than they had already suffered.

In January 1945 the failure of the Ardennes offensive and the successful Soviet offensive in Poland increased Germany's military vulnerability to very high. Existing German forces could no longer hold any line for very long. Against a monthly demand of 1.5 million tank and antitank artillery rounds, January output was 367,000. The Luftwaffe had practically no aviation gasoline. Even before the Soviet offensive in Poland, the force balance on the eastern front was hopelessly uneven; afterward, it was even worse (see Table 26). Although Allied losses continued at a steady rate during the last months of the war, German forces could no longer hope to impose attrition for a protracted period of time because the distance between the eastern and western fronts had become so short that the Allied advances could be expected to meet in the very near future.[110] American and Russian forces meet at Torgau on the Elbe on 22 April.

The dependent variables are the policy preferences of German leaders in each of the four main groups—Hitler, the Nazi civilian leadership, the military leadership, and the resistance. Ideally, to determine the effect of increasing civilian and military vulnerability on German decision making, we would measure the views of every important individual for each period when there was an increase in either type of vulnerability. Policy views are measured as "no surrender," which means not willing to surrender prior to occupation of Germany; "limited surrender," which means willing to negotiate with either the western Allies or the Soviets to surrender all occupied territories on that front so as to continue on the other; and "immediate sur-

---

[108] Ibid., p. 412.

[109] The only significant offensive failure, Operation Market Garden in the Netherlands in September 1944, was due mainly to weather, which prevented reinforcement and resupply of the parachute units, and to logistic constraints caused by the rapidity of the advance across France, which limited the ground "linkup" force to three divisions. Larger ground forces, which were available if they could have been supplied, would almost certainly have rescued the parachute bridgeheads sooner. For a superb account, see Cornelius Ryan, *A Bridge too Far* (New York: Simon and Schuster, 1974).

[110] Ruppenthal, *Logistical Support of the Armies*, 2: 317; Cooper, *German Army*, p. 527.

Table 26. Numerical balance of forces, January 1945

	Soviet forces	German forces
Men	6,900,000	2,100,000
Guns	103,700	6,700
Tanks	13,400	3,700
Aircraft	14,800	—

Source: David Glantz, *From Vistula to the Oder: Soviet Offensive Operations, October 1944–March 1945* (London: F. Cass, 1991), p. 48.

Note: German figures are used for German forces and Soviet figures are used for Soviet forces.

render," which means willing to accept the Allied demand of unconditional surrender. Since Hitler was never willing to surrender, a meaningful measurement of other German leaders' willingness to surrender must include whether they were willing to act independently of Hitler, either by supporting efforts to overthrow his rule or by disregarding his orders in the field. Further, since at certain times certain groups, especially the military leadership, were divided, measures of these groups' potential impact on German policy must monitor changes in the number of each group willing to act.

Much of the evidence for German views is problematic because it comes from statements made by the principals to American interrogators or from memoirs published after the war. In fact, unlike the Japanese case, there are very few contemporaneous primary sources in which leaders' views are documented. The problem is that evidence may be biased toward presenting officials as favoring surrender earlier or more strongly than they in fact did. Given the anticipation of war crimes trials, senior officials had powerful incentives to maximize the extent to which they had personally favored surrender and the degree to which they had opposed Hitler's policies. Also, because many of the interviews were conducted by the U.S. Strategic Bombing Survey, which was concerned to demonstrate the effectiveness of strategic bombing, the interviewees had an incentive to agree that air power had played a key role in affecting their views.

Ideally, one would control for slanted self-reporting by comparing several reports of each individual's views and by comparing statements to different audiences, and where possible I have done so.[111] To the extent that unde-

[111] For instance, after the war, Speer told different Allied interviewers that practically every component of the bombing—raids against ball-bearing plants, morale, electric power—had been the crucial factor. Compare the quotes by Speer in Davis, *Spaatz and the Air War*, p. 398; John Terraine, *A Time for Courage: The Royal Air Force in the European War, 1939–1945* (New York: Macmillan, 1985), p. 548; and Hansell, *Air Plan That Defeated Hitler*, p. 261. Speer's claim he wanted to surrender in February 1945 is more credible because we have his contemporary reports to Hitler as well as corroboration from Guderian and others. See Alfred C. Mierzejewski, "When Did Albert Speer Give Up?" *Historical Journal* 88 (June 1988): 391–97.

tected biases may remain, they would tend to exaggerate the effectiveness of coercion in general, strategic bombing in particular, and especially the strategies most favored by Allied commanders, namely morale bombing and strategic interdiction.

Hitler himself probably never shifted from the position of no surrender. Although there is evidence that on a few occasions he conversed with Foreign Minister Joachim von Ribbentrop and with Rommel about seeking a negotiated solution with one side or the other, it is doubtful that he was ever serious about the possibility. There is no evidence that Hitler participated in the formulation of plans to approach the Allies or encouraged others to do so. He appears to have lent support to the idea of a limited surrender only a few times and never to have supported unconditional surrender. In May 1943 when Rommel told Hitler he was convinced that a complete victory was irretrievably beyond Germany's grasp, Hitler said, "Yes, I know it is necessary to make peace with one side or the other, but no one will make peace with me."[112] Similarly, in February 1945, when Ribbentrop suggested offering the Western Allies an armistice so that Germany could continue fighting in the east, Hitler reportedly replied, "Very well, you can try but I don't expect anything to come of it." On 16 March, when neither the Vatican nor Portugal nor Switzerland nor Sweden nor Ireland responded positively, Hitler forbade further conversations with any foreign power.[113]

The only civilians other than Hitler who could have influenced policy on the war were the top leaders of the Nazi party. Few members of this group advocated surrender at any point, and none was willing to act against Hitler until February 1945 at the earliest. They realized that surrender would mean not only their personal prosecution and imprisonment or execution as war criminals but also the complete destruction of their party, political program, and ideology. Unlike army officers (especially conservative officers) or the Japanese elite, the Nazis had no class or institutional base that could allow them to retain any influence in a postwar society.

Nazi socialist ideology emphasized elitism, the idea of a "new aristocracy," a new leadership order. Nazi leaders were primarily political adventurers with no sources of wealth, influence, or status other than their membership in the ruling party. Party leaders were young men whose careers had advanced with lightning speed; the average age of Cabinet members was forty, compared to fifty-six in the United States and fifty-three in England. The Nazi party was a middle-class movement, composed predominantly of the World War I and postwar generations, and its leadership

---

[112] Wheeler-Bennett, *Nemesis of Power*, p. 604.

[113] Fritz Hesse, *Hitler and the English* (London: Wingate, 1954), pp. 197–99, 200, 214. Ribbentrop reports that Hitler refused to support his similar requests to approach Stalin in 1943 and 1944. *The Ribbentrop Memoirs*, introduction by Alan Bullock (London: Weidenfeld and Nicolson, 1954), pp. 170–72.

came primarily from the lowest, rootless, or "alienated" middle class and farmers, and secondarily from military and professionally dissatisfied intellectuals. Most of the top leaders (Goering, Himmler, Joseph Goebbels, Bormann, Ribbentrop) had joined the movement before 1933 and had spent every moment since as party activists. Only in the military and the SS hierarchy (or in conquered areas) could latecomers rise to the top.[114]

Staunch long-committed Nazi leaders saw no point in surrender, since nothing of Nazi ideals would survive if Germany were occupied. Goebbels wrote on 14 November 1943: "As far as we are concerned, we have burned the bridges behind us. We no longer can turn back, but we also no longer want to. We are forced to extremes and therefore also ready for extremes. . . . We will go down in history either as the greatest statesmen or as the greatest criminals."[115]

Younger "Nazi" generals were also largely concerned with the historical mark and influence of Nazi ideas in future German politics. According to Jodl, the

chief argument [of the resistance] in every cautious contact with commanders was that the war was lost and that it could only be ended without Hitler. I had long thought this, but along with the majority of responsible commanders I saw no way out. Our enemies did not seek the overthrow of the Nazi regime; they had proclaimed the destruction of Germany. Could we prevent this fate for Germany by overthrowing Hitler? This was the decisive question. . . . It is my firm conviction that the people and especially the workers would have remained peaceful, but in the chaos of self-destruction the enemy could have invaded without the order of a capitulation. Exactly the same misery would have descended on Germany as has now arrived, perhaps in a still worse form, but the public might have believed that it was not the result of military defeat but of a 'stab-in-the-back.' . . . Even when I consider the losses which followed until May, 1945, I still believe that the way to the bitter end was better for Germany. It cannot give rise to false legends.[116]

To the extent that Nazi party leaders considered surrender at all, changes in their positions corresponded to increases in Germany's military vulnerability, not civilian vulnerability. The principal figures on whom we have evidence are Himmler, Goebbels, Speer, and Ribbentrop, none of whom shifted toward surrender in response to the escalations of city bombing in December 1940 or July 1943. By contrast, all were influenced by the worsening of Germany's military vulnerability, particularly from February 1945 onward.

---

[114] Bracher, *German Dictatorship*, pp. 273–74, 276–77.
[115] Quoted in ibid., p. 283.
[116] "Excerpts from a Note about the July 20, 1944, Plot by Colonel General Alfred Jodl, Nurenberg, 1946," in Armstrong, *Unconditional Surrender*, p. 277.

The attitudes of these leaders changed with loss of confidence in Germany's ability to prevent Allied occupation, but some required more evidence than others. Goebbels was willing to negotiate in spring 1944; Ribbentrop and Speer seem to have come to this conclusion in February 1945; Himmler appears not to have changed his position until April.

Prior to spring 1944, as military vulnerability increased from nil to medium, no important Nazi leaders favored surrender. Although some had doubts about Germany's military position in 1943 and 1944, none had concrete plans for surrender at this point. All spoke and behaved like ardent supporters of continuing the war, and most important, none backed the July 1944 plot to overthrow Hitler.

Starting in April 1944, Goebbels shifted from no surrender to limited surrender to the Soviet Union. He submitted a memorandum to Hitler declaring, "Never has the Reich won a two-front war"; therefore, he proposed, Germany should agree to return to the position of 1939–1940 under the Nazi-Soviet Pact and should surrender to the Soviet Union all of Eastern Europe from northern Norway to Greece, inclusive. Goebbels was willing to surrender to the Soviets, but not to the West right up until the end.[117]

Following the disasters of January 1945 on the battlefield and the collapse of the German war economy in March, several leaders went directly to Hitler to advocate surrender. In February Ribbentrop advocated limited surrender; in March Speer appears to have been willing to surrender immediately to the West. A principal factor in Speer's change of attitude was a study he completed in March 1945 which showed:

> It is impossible to maintain Germany's economic life for any length of time with the amount of hard-coal still available and the raw steel production capacity. . . . It is possible to delay this threatening collapse of the German economy for several months. . . . After the loss of Upper Silesia German armament *will no longer be even remotely in a position to meet the requirements of the front and the demands for new lists of equipment. The material superiority of the enemy can therefore no longer be balanced by the bravery of our soldiers.*[118]

Finally, military vulnerability persuaded Himmler to shift to immediate surrender on 23 April: "In the situation that has arisen I consider my hands free. I admit that Germany is defeated. In order to save as great a part of

---

[117] On Goebbels's surrender position, see Rudolf Semmler, *Goebbels* (London: Westhouse, 1947), pp. 119–21; and Hugh Trevor-Roper, ed., *Final Entries, 1945: The Diaries of Joseph Goebbels* (New York: Putnam's, 1978), p. xxvi; Percy Schramm, *Hitler: The Man and the Military Leader* (Chicago: Quadrangle, 1971), p. 163.

[118] Speer quoted in Milward, *German Economy*, pp. 176–77. I date Speer's shift to a memorandum he submitted to Hitler which portrayed the collapse of German industry unambiguously and pleaded for an end to hostilities. For indications that his views began to shift at the end of January 1945, see Mierzejewski, "When Did Albert Speer Give Up?"

Germany as possible from a Russian invasion I am willing to capitulate on the Western front in order to enable the Western Allies to advance rapidly toward the East. But I am not prepared to capitulate on the Eastern front."[119]

Military leaders were the crucial group in determining the outcome of the German case, because they were the only group with sufficient force to be able to act and sufficient ideological independence to be likely to act. As the war progressed, however, this group became increasingly divided. Most Nazi generals did not change their views on surrender, but a significant number of conservative generals moved toward a policy of limited surrender. This shift corresponds with changes in military, not civilian, vulnerability. These generals seem to have appreciated the degree of military vulnerability sooner than civilians did and were more willing to surrender given the same degree of perceived military vulnerability. Unlike Nazi civilian leaders and Nazi officers whose political, institutional, and social standing would be destroyed by surrender (if they were not simply killed), conservative officers could expect to preserve much of their position in society even if Germany lost the war. The main disagreement among the conservatives was whether overthrowing Hitler would soften Allied demands; it was the dividing issue between those who joined the coup and those who did not.

Following Hitler's early successes against Czechoslovakia, Poland, and France, most German military leaders came to believe that ultimate victory against Germany's remaining enemies was possible so long as they could be fought successively.[120] The first major blow to this optimism occurred after the Battle of Stalingrad, when the loss of more than the entire German Sixth Army in the most disastrous battlefield defeat in German history affected the political calculations of military leaders. Manstein believed that decisive German victory was no longer possible and that the chief goal must now be the prevention of total disaster: "On the German side there could no longer be any question of this being one last bid for the palm of final victory. . . . the principal aim . . . could only be, in the words of Schlieffen, 'to bring defeat underfoot.' " Kesselring concurred but stressed that since the German war machine held great potential and the entire homeland was still intact, Germany would be in a good bargaining position if the Allies wished to negotiate a settlement. Rommel hoped that Germany's remaining military power could persuade the Allies to "conclude a tolerable peace."[121]

At this point, a small group of mostly junior officers led by Stauffenberg, Dohnanyi, and Canaris started plotting against Hitler. During 1943, they

[119] Bullock, *Hitler and Stalin*, p. 889.
[120] Armstrong, *Unconditional Surrender*, p. 113.
[121] Erich von Manstein, *Lost Victories* (New York: Methuen, 1958), p. 367; Interview with Kesselring in Armstrong, *Unconditional Surrender*, p. 118; Erwin Rommel, *The Rommel Papers*, ed. B. H. Liddell Hart (New York: Harcourt, Brace, 1953), p. 427.

made several attempts to kill him, including placing a bomb on Hitler's plane which failed to explode. Several senior generals were approached for support but turned the plotters down at this stage.[122] Thus, some senior generals were searching for an alternative to continuing the war, but they had not yet adopted a surrender policy.

Military confidence about the ability to defend the homeland was radically undermined in summer 1944, leading a number of conservative generals to a shift to limited surrender. The more unavoidable a two-front war became, the more did significant portions of the army leadership, particularly in the west, join the anti-Hitler resistance. By March 1944 Rommel, Speidel, Günther Blumentritt (chief of operations), von Kluge, and von Rundstedt began to plan for an armistice. They meant not to surrender unconditionally but to negotiate a settlement with the west so that the eastern front could be held. Field Marshal von Kluge in his suicide letter in late July 1944 warned Hitler: "Make up your mind to end the war. The German people have borne such untold suffering that it is time to put an end to this frightfulness. There must be ways to attain this end, *and above all, to prevent the Reich from falling under the Bolshevist heel.*"[123] Rommel told his son shortly before his suicide: "Our enemy in the East is so terrible that every other consideration has to give way before it. If he succeeds in overrunning Europe, even only temporarily, it will be the end of everything which has made life appear worth living."[124] Still, the opposition was not interested in immediate surrender. Rather, they planned for evacuation of the western theater and withdrawal to Germany's 1937 western border in return for immediate termination of British and American hostilities toward Germany. On the eastern front fighting would continue.[125]

There is a clear correlation between the decline in confidence that Germany's military strategy would succeed and movements toward surrender by the elite in Germany. The crucial events began in May 1944, when Rommel and Generals von Stülpnagel and Alexander von Falkenhausen joined the conspiracy to overthrow Hitler and make a separate peace with the west. The impending Allied landing in France, the generals recognized, would lead to a two-front war, which Germany would lose decisively. More generals joined the plot in June and July, leading to the 20 July attempt to assassinate Hitler, which failed only because the bomb was placed on the wrong side of the conference table.[126]

---

[122] See Wheeler-Bennett, *Nemesis of Power*, pp. 587–88.
[123] B. H. Liddell Hart, *German Generals Talk* (New York: William Morrow, 1948), p. 260n. my emphasis.
[124] Rommel, *Rommel Papers*, p. 502.
[125] Armstrong, *Unconditional Surrender*, p. 131.
[126] Kecskemeti, *Strategic Surrender*, pp. 129–32.

After the assassination attempt Hitler's hatred of the professional military erupted with destructive fury; approximately five thousand men were executed and many others imprisoned. Thereafter, only a small circle was granted personal audiences, and then never alone.[127] Thus, the coup's failure ended organized anti-Nazi resistance in Germany, and it became virtually impossible for individuals to act against Hitler.

When the defensive lines of the Reich were breached in the east and west in January 1945, the position of even loyal military officers approached the surrender policies of the 20 July plotters. For instance, Chief of General Staff Guderian favored shifting resources to the east to check the further advance of the Soviets, even though the western forces would have quickly succumbed to the overwhelming material superiority of the Western Allies.[128] After March despite Hitler's orders to defend on both the eastern and western fronts to the bitter end, military commanders in the west either surrendered piecemeal, stopped fighting, or disbanded their forces. The Allied advance into southern and central Germany became a walkover. Meanwhile German forces in the east continued their all-out effort to hold off the Soviet Union.

Throughout the war, the anti-Nazi resistance opposed both national socialism and the war, but this group had no political power at all in the Third Reich. It could influence policy only with military support, which was not forthcoming as long as the war appeared to go well. After an aborted assassination attempt against Hitler in fall 1939, German successes in Poland and France made all further action impossible until after Stalingrad. Serious plotting against Hitler and attempts to recruit sympathetic military officers resumed in 1943, leading to six planned coup attempts between September and December 1943, culminating in the events of 20 July 1944.[129]

The resistance did not pursue unconditional surrender. Its members opposed communism as much as the Nazis, and therefore, they wanted a limited surrender to the west which would permit continued military resistance on the eastern front. They saw removing Hitler as both a gesture to the Western Allies and a dagger in the heart of an ideology they despised.[130] The resistance had frequent communications with the Western Allies, although the westerners never opened serious negotiations. The most

---

[127] Armstrong, *Unconditional Surrender*, p. 195.

[128] General Heinz Guderian, "The Interrelationship between the Eastern and Western Fronts," in *World War II German Military Studies*, ed. Donald S. Detwiler (New York: Garland, 1979), 21: 35.

[129] Wheeler-Bennett, *Nemesis of Power*, p. 598.

[130] Ulrich von Hassell wrote in his diary on 27 December 1943: "With Hitler the war will certainly be lost because it will be fought to a catastrophic end by both sides. . . . The one definite point upon which the other side is united is that Hitler must first of all be laid low. . . . Only after this goal has been reached can (and will) their differences come to the surface." Quoted in ibid., p. 592.

detailed offer was in May 1944, when Beck sent Dulles a plan for simultaneous action by the Anglo-American forces and the conspirators, with the object of facilitating the occupation of Germany and at the same time holding the Soviets on the eastern front. After the putsch, three western airborne divisions were to occupy Berlin while large-scale landings were made on the French and German coasts. London and Washington rejected the offer, demanding surrender to all the Allies simultaneously.[131]

Why Germany Did Not Surrender

The main reason that German army leaders continued to fight after they determined that defeat was inevitable was fear of Soviet occupation, which they believed would be exceedingly brutal, partly in retaliation for German crimes in the east. Because of their own direct and indirect participation, they knew they could not escape retribution. Despite heavy costs, they continued to fight in order to buy time to permit soldiers and civilians to flee the advancing Red Army.

Germany might have surrendered in July 1944, when Allied offensives shattered German lines in both France and Russia, making defeat certain if Germany could not deter its enemies by fear of high casualties. Germany might have surrendered in January 1945 when the failure of its Ardennes offensive and the successful Russian offensive in Poland made it impossible to continue attrition warfare for long. Or it might have surrendered in March 1945 when Hitler's ability to control his subordinates broke down and the final Allied offensives began. At each of these points, however, fear of Soviet occupation outweighed concern for the costs of continuing the war. It was that fear that prevented many officers from joining the coup in July 1944. Both Guderian and Manstein, for example, withheld support largely because they doubted the coup would soften Allied treatment of Germany after the war.[132] In January 1945 continued resistance in the west mattered because it provided resources for Germany to hold off the Soviets in the east. In March the main concern was buying time for refugees to escape from the areas to be occupied by the USSR into areas under the control of the Western Allies.

Since my argument hinges on Wehrmacht behavior in the east and German military leaders' expectations of Russian occupation, it is important to con-

---

[131] Ibid., p. 620.

[132] Manstein believed that "it would have led to an immediate collapse of the front and probably chaos inside Germany. . . . it was already clear by that time that not even a coup d'etat would make any difference to the Allied demand for unconditional surrender." Guderian wrote: "Not one leading political figure among the enemy had shown the slightest inclination to make any agreement with the conspirators. It is no exaggeration to say that if the assassination had succeeded Germany's condition would be not one jot better than it is today. Our enemies were not solely interested in destroying Hitler and Nazism." Manstein, *Lost Victories*, pp. 287–88; and Guderian, *Panzer Leader*, p. 345.

sider these in detail. The first wave of western historiography treated Germany's war against the Soviet Union like any other military contest between opposing armies. Early works, supported by the apologetic postwar memoirs of former Wehrmacht generals, sharply separated the atrocities committed by Nazi henchmen from the purely military operations of the army.[133]

In striking contrast to claims of innocence or indifference, German historians have now unearthed mounds of primary evidence showing that the Army participated willingly and fully in the Nazi program. Although the Einsatzgruppen of the SS and SD and the civilian-administered death camps spearheaded Nazi extermination policies in the east, the Wehrmacht not only supported these but itself carried out much of the genocide.

The Wehrmacht was sympathetic to the Nazi program and heavily involved in planning it. Military leaders participated not merely in the passive sense of knowing about the "political activities" and the work of the Einsatzgruppen, but also in the active sense of issuing orders to ensure they were executed efficiently.[134] The military leadership in general accepted the National Socialist propaganda regarding the Soviet people and believed that the Jews were largely responsible for communism. Although few older officers were committed Nazis, the Prussian officer corps had a long tradi-

---

[133] The most significant was Liddell Hart, who declared: "The German Army in the field on the whole observed the rules of war better than it did in 1914–18." Alexander Dallin supported this view, suggesting that the German Army ameliorated harsh policies in the rear areas it governed: "The fortuitous subordination of military government to the Quartermaster General's office contributed to the relatively more 'realistic' policy which prevailed in some areas of military government, since General [Eduard] Wagner and his staff were not genuinely committed to the extreme measures dictated by the Fuhrer and Keitel." Similarly Martin Van Creveld writes, "The German Army was inclined to develop a single-minded concentration on the operational aspects of the war to the detriment, not to say neglect, of everything else." Liddell Hart, *German Generals Talk*, p. 29; Alexander Dallin, *German Rule in Russia*, 2d ed. (Boulder: Westview Press, 1981), p. 98; Gordon A. Craig, *Politics of the Prussian Army, 1640–1945* (New York: Oxford University Press, 1955), pp. 500–503; and Martin Van Creveld, *Fighting Power: German and U.S. Army Performance, 1939–1945* (Westport, Conn.: Greenwood Press, 1982), p. 164. Soviet historians were never under such illusions. For a relatively early example of a Western work that brings out the brutal nature of the eastern front, see Alexander Werth, *Russia at War, 1941–1945* (New York: Dutton, 1964).

[134] Field Marshal Walter von Reichenau, commander in chief of the Sixth Army, ordered on 10 October 1941: "The most essential aim of the campaign against the Jewish-Bolshevist system is the complete crushing of its means of power and the extermination of Asiatic influence in the European region. This poses tasks for the troops that go beyond the one-sided routine of conventional soldiering. In the Eastern region, the soldier is not merely a fighter according to the rules of the art of war, but also the bearer of an inexorable national idea and the avenger of all bestialities inflicted upon the German people and its racial kin. Therefore the soldier must have full understanding for the necessity of a severe but just atonement on Jewish subhumanity. An additional aim in this is to nip in the bud any revolts in the rear of the army, which, as experience proves, have always been instigated by Jews." Reichenau's directive was distributed as a model for all commanding generals. Conservative generals such as Manstein also issued such orders. For more on the Army's role in planning, see Dawidowicz, *War against the Jews*, pp. 123–25; Christian Streit, "The German Army and the Politics of Genocide," in *Policies of Genocide*, ed. Gerhard Hirschfeld (Boston: Allan & Unwin, 1986), p. 7; and Arno Mayer, *Why Did the Heavens Not Darken?* (New York: Pantheon, 1988), p. 251.

[303]

tion of anticommunism, anti-Semitism, and anti-Slavicism. Further, the immense expansion of the Wehrmacht brought in large numbers of Nazis, so that party members composed a higher proportion of the officer corps than of the German population at large.[135]

The Wehrmacht facilitated the work of the Einsatzgruppen, the three-thousand-man task force dedicated to administering "special treatment" to groups designated as enemies of the Reich. With the Wehrmacht's support, the Einsatzgruppen killed a total of 2.2 million Soviet Jews, including 550,000 during the first six months of the war against the USSR. Most important, the Army divided POWs into racial and political categories and handed over the designated groups to the Einsatzgruppen. Of course, the Einsatzgruppen depended on the Army for munitions, fuel, and food.[136]

Moreover, the Wehrmacht directly killed millions of prisoners and civilians. In sharp contrast to French prisoners of war, Red Army POWs met a harsh fate. The infamous Commissar Order called for the summary execution of all agents of "Judeo-Bolshevism" and estimates of the number shot range from 140,000 to 580,000. Of the 3.5 million Soviet prisoners captured during 1941, over 60 percent had died by February 1942, compared to a death-rate for POWs inside the Reich of 18.5 percent.[137] German figures count total deaths in POW camps in the East as 1,981,000, in addition to "Exterminations; Not accounted for; Deaths and disappearance in transit," which totaled 1,308,000. Furthermore, the Army was also directly involved in the war against partisans, which involved punishing towns and villages and killing over a million civilian "traitors."[138]

Finally, the Wehrmacht ruthlessly exploited large parts of the occupied territories (Ukraine, Belorussia, western Russia, the Crimea, and the northern Caucasus). Food supplies were extracted from the land not only to support German soldiers but also to feed civilians in Germany proper with the full understanding that the locals would starve.[139] Further, after 1943, when

[135] Omer Bartov's detailed examination of three divisions finds that about 30 percent of the officers were registered Nazis, compared to 16 percent of the middle class in Germany. Bartov, *Eastern Front*, p. 49.

[136] Theo J. Schulte, *The German Army and Nazi Policies in Occupied Russia* (New York: St. Martin's, 1989), pp. 214–27; and Streit, "The German Army and the Policies of Genocide," p. 4.

[137] Before the attack on France, the Wehrmacht made special arrangements for transporting, feeding, and clothing POWs to prevent undue hardship. By contrast, the German army made no preparations for the enormous numbers of prisoners it expected to capture in its battles of encirclement in the east. A September 1941 Wehrmacht report stated that "in contrast to the feeding of other captives [i.e., British and French], we are not bound by any obligation to feed Bolshevik prisoners." Schulte, *German Army and Nazi Policies*, pp. 203, 209–10, 219; Bartov, *Eastern Front*, p. 110; Clark, *Barbarossa*, pp. 206–7.

[138] Clark, *Barbarossa*, pp. 206–7; Timothy Mulligan, "Reckoning the Cost of the People's War: The German Experience in Central USSR," *Russian History* 9 (1982): 27–48.

[139] Alexiev, *Soviet Nationalities*, p. 4; Tim Mason, "The Primacy of Politics—Politics and Economics in National Socialist Germany," in *The Nature of Fascism*, ed. S. J. Woolf (London: Weidenfeld & Nicolson, 1968).

the eastern front, which had remained virtually static for two years, began to collapse, the German Army pursued scorched-earth policies that increased chaos and destruction. German troops were directed to lay waste to everything that could not be removed, including livestock, crops, buildings and equipment, turning vast tracts of the occupied territories into a desert.[140]

As the Soviets advanced westward in late 1943 and 1944, German military leaders understood that the Red Army would exact a heavy vengence. In the spring of 1944, Soviet public declarations emphasized the stark demand that the entire Wehrmacht should be employed as slave labor by the victorious Allies.[141] As the advance continued reports about the degree of punishment to be extracted from German society increased, and the Soviet armies that entered Germany were brutal. In January 1945 the German government obtained a copy of an Allied map showing the proposed partition of Germany among the USSR, the United States, and Britain. This confirmed the beliefs of many that acceptance of unconditional surrender would be exceedingly costly, putting an end to Germany as a national entity and leading to the loss of many lives under Soviet occupation. As Admiral Doenitz said,

> In the event of our submitting we should have no rights whatever, but would be wholly at the mercy of our enemies, and of what that meant, some idea can be gathered from Stalin's demand at the Teheran Conference, for four million Germans to serve as forced labor in the USSR.
>
> The sort of treatment we might well have expected to receive is well exemplified by the 'Morgenthau Plan,' which was accepted by Churchill and Roosevelt at the Quebec conference in September 1943 and which envisaged the destruction of German industry and all the German mines and transformation of Germany into a purely agricultural country.[142]

Guderian also appears to have based his further resistance on similar premises: "The soldiers, at least, were convinced from now on that our enemies had decided on the utter destruction of Germany, that they were no longer fighting . . . against Hitler and so-called Nazism, but against their efficient, and therefore dangerous rivals for the trade of the world."[143]

The initial advance of the Red Army into Germany was accompanied by mass murder, rape, and pillaging. The Nemmersdorf Massacre is the best documented. Major General Erich Dethleffsen, Chief of Staff of the German Fourth Army in East Prussia, stated: "When in October 1944 Russian units . . . broke through German defenses and advanced as far as Nemmersdorf,

---

[140] Werth, *Russia at War*, pp. 265–68, 629–48.

[141] Wheeler-Bennett, *Nemesis of Power*, p. 619.

[142] Karl Doenitz, *Memoirs: Ten Years and Twenty Days*, trans. R. H. Stevens (Annapolis: Naval Institute Press, 1990), pp. 308–9.

[143] Guderian, *Panzer Leader*, p. 284.

they tortured civilians in many villages south of Gumbinnen, nailed some on barn doors and shot many others. A large number of women were raped. The Russian soldiers also shot some fifty French prisoners of war."[144] Events after hostilities ceased confirmed many of the fears of German leaders. In Berlin alone, over 90,000 women sought medical attention as a consequence of rape.[145] A total of 13,841,000 Germans were expelled from Eastern and Central Europe, of which 2,111,000 died during the expulsion. Another million Germans were deported to the Soviet Union to serve as forced labor, of which some 350,000 died.[146]

If military defeat was inevitable, then the costs of surrender could not be avoided, but German generals did not see the costs of surrender as a constant. Rather, they thought the costs could be reduced if, by holding off the Soviet troops a little longer, they could buy time to evacuate refugees (and soldiers as well) from the areas soon to be occupied. Doenitz, for instance, believed that capitulation during the winter months of 1944–1945 would have sent an appalling number of the 3.5 million German soldiers on the eastern front to their deaths and would have sacrificed the opportunity to transfer millions of civilians out of the expected zone of Soviet occupation and into the western zones. "Painful though it was to be compelled by these pressing considerations to continue the war in the winter of 1944–45, to sacrifice more soldiers and sailors on all fronts and all the world over and to endure yet more casualties among civilians in air-raids, there was no option, for the losses were smaller than had we prematurely given up our eastern territories."[147] Jodl gave a similar explanation for not surrendering after the Ardennes offensive:

> Even if we had any doubt as to what faced us, it was completely removed by the fact that we captured the English "Eclipse." . . . It was exact instructions about what the occupying power was to do in Germany after the capitulation. Now, unconditional surrender meant that the troops would cease to fight where they stood on all the fronts, and be captured by the enemy facing them. . . . Millions of prisoners would suddenly have to camp in the middle of winter in the open. Death would have taken an enormous toll. Above all, the men still on the Eastern front, numbering about three and a half million, would have fallen into the hands of the enemy in the East. It was our task to save as many people as possible [by evacuating them to] the Western area.[148]

[144] Quoted in Zayas, *Nemesis at Potsdam*, p. 62. For many accounts of Russian brutalities in Romania, Hungary, and Czechoslovakia, see Theodor Schieder, ed., *Documents on the Expulsion of the Germans from East-Central Europe*, 4 vols. (Bonn: Federal Ministry for Expellees, Refugees, and War Victims, 1960).
[145] Botting, *Ruins of the Reich*, p. 70.
[146] Zayas, *Nemesis At Potsdam*, p. xxv, 203–4.
[147] Doenitz, *Memoirs*, p. 431.
[148] *The Trial of Major German War Criminals* (London: HMSO, 1948), pt. 15, p. 371.

Fear of the Soviet occupation explains why the army did not want to sur-render in the east but not why it did not surrender to the Western Allies. Al-though Allied plans for occupation of Germany were harsh, including reparations as well as possible political and economic dismemberment of the country, they did not pose the murderous threat that the Red Army did. Moreover, by January 1945 further German resistance could not possibly af-fect Allied occupation policy. At worst, surrender would save the Western Allies the costs of pointless resistance. At best, it might offer opportunities to shift some forces to shore up defenses in the east.

So why were the Germans willing to pay the cost of further resistance in the west? In fact, as I have shown, there were many attempts by members of the German resistance and some members of the Army to seek a one-sided armistice—that is, any agreement that would not require Germany to stop fighting on all fronts simultaneously. Opposition representatives proposed a two-stage surrender—an armistice in the west to be followed by total sur-render after the eastern front was stabilized. The resistance was willing to go so far as to assist Anglo-British forces in France and to facilitate their entry into Germany. The plan fitted the belief of Rommel and others that it was better for Germany to become a British dominion than be ruined by fighting the war to completion. These terms, however, were repeatedly re-jected by the Western Allies.[149]

Even if the Allies would not cooperate, however, and forces could there-fore not be shifted, why did not the Germans surrender unilaterally in the west anyway and save the costs of resistance on that front? Unilateral sur-render does not appear to have been considered. Yet even without Allied agreement, we would expect German commanders in the west to have sur-rendered if they could do so without jeopardizing operations in the east. That such surrender would expose the rear of troops fighting in the east to the advancing Western Allies need not have been a concern, since if the Al-lies therefore advanced farther than planned, the extension of Western Al-lied occupation would have protected the endangered civilians from the Soviets.

The reason the Germans did not surrender unilaterally in the west in Jan-uary 1945 is that they believed the Western Allies would not occupy all of Germany but would leave a significant portion to Soviet control. As John Keegan explains, "By one of the most bizarre lapses of security in the entire war, the demarcation line agreed between Moscow, London and Washing-ton had become known to the Germans during 1944, and the last fight of the Wehrmacht in the west was motivated by the urge to hold open the line of retreat across the Elbe to the last possible moment."[150] Further, the combat

---

[149] Armstrong, *Unconditional Surrender*, pp. 140, 204.
[150] Keegan, *Second World War*, pp. 532–33.

potential of German forces on the eastern front depended on flows of supplies and equipment from industries in western Germany, which would be lost if the western front collapsed.[151]

By March 1945 the Ruhr was producing little and only a small portion of that could be shipped east, and that motive for defending in the west disappeared. Hitler's personal authority also declined as he isolated himself in his Berlin bunker, and both civilian and military leaders had more freedom of action. The motive for defending in the east, however, remained unchanged, although the prospects of holding on for long had become quite dim. Yet, German leaders still did not surrender unilaterally in the west. Nevertheless, except in a few places still needed to protect escape routes for refugees, German officers and troops on the western front and some Nazi civilians began to surrender piecemeal, in a way that supports my interpretation. German forces in areas that could not expect to receive refugees (southwest Germany and Italy) surrendered soonest, and those sites most important to the refugee traffic (Hamburg, Kiel, and the Baltic coast) held on the longest.

Whereas the Germans spent their last ounce of strength to stop the Soviets, their resistance in the west quickly dissolved. In the first half of April British and American forces roared through western Germany, reaching the Elbe in just eighteen days, often meeting no opposition. At this point, German commanders formally liquidated hostilities. Field Marshal Model, in charge of Army Group B defending the Ruhr, dissolved his command on 17 April, and its 300,000 men were dismissed from service, told to go home, or permitted to join other units. Others negotiated capitulation agreements. Field Marshal Kesselring, theater commander in Italy, agreed to surrender on 28 April, and the commanders of forces in Munich and Innsbruck surrendered during the next few days.[152]

The refugee problem was especially acute late in the war. By April 1945 millions of civilians, particularly from northern Germany, were fleeing westward to escape the Soviets.[153] Admiral Doenitz, who succeeded Hitler, said that his "first task is to save German men and women from destruction by the advancing Bolshevist enemy. It is to serve this interest that the military struggle continues." He hoped to enable evacuations to continue for a few more weeks. To do so some continued resistance against the Western Allies was necessary, so that they would not shut the door to the refugees. Doenitz wrote in a letter forbidding the premature surrender of Hamburg:

---

[151] Through January 1945, forty-nine trains a day from west and central Germany supplied German forces on the eastern front, a number which dwindled to only eight or nine a day in February. Mierzejewski, *Collapse of the German War Economy*, p. 173.

[152] Kecskemeti, *Strategic Surrender*, pp. 138–44.

[153] Zayas estimates that from January to May 1945, two to three million Germans were evacuated by sea alone from eastern territories to the west. *Nemesis at Potsdam*, p. 74.

The main preoccupation of the military authorities in the present situation is to save German territory and the German race from Bolshevism . . . or at least to hold it up for as long as possible, to enable the maximum number of Germans to leave the province. This evacuation is practicable only as long as a door through the zonal demarcation line agreed at Yalta remains open. If the Elbe-Trave canal is closed by the British, we shall be handing over seven million Germans to the mercy of the Russians.[154]

Indeed, 2.5–3 million German soldiers and civilians escaped from the Soviet troops during the last weeks of the war. On 2 May Doenitz, in keeping with the idea of saving as many Germans as possible from Soviet captivity, wanted to surrender to General Bernard Law Montgomery some German units then fighting the Soviets east of the Elbe. Montgomery declined this offer and also refused to permit civilian refugees to cross the Allied lines.[155]

The final surrender in May indicates that the Western Allies would not have been cooperative in any event. When the German Chief of Staff, General Jodl arrived at Supreme Headquarters, Allied Expeditionary Forces on 6 May, his goal was to continue to play for time to permit thousands of Germans to withdraw westward and thus evade captivity and death at the hands of the Soviet forces. A total of 1.2 million German soldiers were still fighting their way westward out of Soviet encirclement as were many thousand civilians, whose withdrawal to the west, Jodl maintained, would help the United States and Great Britain deal with the Soviet Union. In response, Eisenhower's chief of staff, General Walter Bedell Smith told Jodl: "You will have to deal with the Russians alone. . . . Our lines will be closed even to individual German soldiers and civilians. I don't understand why you don't want to surrender to our Russian Allies." The best Jodl could get was forty-eight hours until the western lines closed, which is why hostilities formally ceased two days later at midnight on 9 May.[156]

As this account makes clear, Germany's failure to surrender was not irrational in terms of expected costs and benefits. Given expectations of truly brutal Soviet occupation, largely precipitated by Germany's own callous disregard for human life and genocidal policies earlier in the war on the eastern front, avoiding this result provided enormous benefits and was worth the marginal costs of a few months of continued resistance. Since a unilateral surrender to the West would have sealed Germany's borders and so cut off all significant refugee movement, this too was not in Germany's interest.

The most important lesson to draw from this case is that, although Germany's failure to surrender in March 1945 is inconsistent with the parsi-

---

[154] Doenitz message to Kaufmann, 30 April 1945 in Doenitz, *Memoirs*, p. 437.
[155] Kecskemeti, *Strategic Surrender*, pp. 149–51.
[156] Botting, *From the Ruins*, p. 87.

monious version of the denial theory of coercion, it is completely consistent with its logic. The parsimonious version holds that if a state loses confidence in its military strategy to achieve specific territorial goals, then it will stop pursuing those goals to avoid wasting resources in a futile effort. This theory clearly assumes that the political decisions of modern nation-states are rational in the sense that they are motivated by cost-benefit calculations.

The German case could easily fall outside this theory of coercion if Germany's geopolitical decisions were not rational. Indeed, conventional wisdom attributes Germany's refusal to surrender to Hitler's irrational personality, which determined the outcome because of Hitler's unique position in the government of German policy. According to this view, Hitler was the main reason why Germany failed to surrender, and cost-benefit political calculations were irrelevant. If this conception were correct, it would imply that the denial theory could not be applied until a metatheory was developed which could predict the conditions under which states will behave rationally.

The "irrational dictator" explanation is wrong, however. Hitler's irrationality does not explain Germany's failure to surrender, for Hitler could have been overthrown had a majority of the senior military leadership opposed his rule. Germany failed to surrender largely because German military leaders would not accept unconditional surrender so long as it meant Soviet occupation, which they expected to be exceptionally brutal. In theoretical terms, Germany chose to continue the war because it expected the price of surrender to be greater than the price of resistance. That these fears were rational is confirmed by the realities of postwar occupation. In other words, the correct implication is not that irrationality can dominate surrender decisions but in fact the opposite: states will not voluntarily make themselves worse off.

The question is often asked, Is the German case unique? In one sense, Germany is hardly unique. It is always hard to coerce modern nation-states engaged in disputes over consequential issues, largely because domestic factors such as nationalism and institutional and individual political interests mitigate the coercive effects of punishment and denial strategies, although to different degrees. The German case supports this finding. To the extent that German leaders shifted their positions on surrender at all, it was in response to military pressures that threatened to thwart their military strategy for controlling the contested territory. Punishment of the population did nothing to encourage a popular revolt or to compel the government to abandon national objectives.

Still, the German case is rare in one important respect. Modern nation-states have rarely gone to war to achieve largely racial goals, which in the German case unleashed a fountain of feverish nationalist hatreds that ended in a contemporary version of a Carthaginian peace. Coercion may not apply against states that practice genocide, less because they are invulnerable to coercive military pressure than because they want more than control over territory.

The end of World War II in Europe also offers three additional lessons on coercive air power. First, whereas strategic air power is capable of inflicting widespread destruction on targets located in a state's homeland, strategic bombing will significantly affect a state's political calculations only to the extent it alters events on the battlefield. Second, when the opponent is a continental power, strategic air power is most effective in altering events on the battlefield when it is used to disrupt ongoing operations rather than for long-term effects. Third, the ultimately misplaced confidence with which air planners sought to achieve victory through air power at the expense of building ground forces serves as a warning for future defense policy.

Perhaps the most surprising fact to emerge from studying German surrender decisions is that Allied strategic air power played such a minor role in the contemporary thoughts of German leaders. By far, the most crucial concern on the part of civilian and military leaders alike was the land war; the air war was a distant second. Hitler personally managed land operations of the Wehrmacht, but he paid far less attention to air defenses and even canceled the ME-262, a jet fighter that might well have prevented the Allies from gaining air superiority over Germany.

The main reason is that Germany's vulnerability to air attack was tightly determined by its vulnerability on the ground. Although many air advocates claimed after the war that air power was "decisive" in Western Europe, its effects could not have been achieved without the progress of Allied land armies.[157]

Consider the main independent effect air power is said to have had in this case: the destruction of the German economy. Even if one accepts the superb analysis of Alfred Mierzejewski that bombing transportation late in the war crippled the German economy, it would not have done so without Soviet progress in the east and the Allies' progress in the west. Destroying Germany's internal railway system mattered because it stopped the movement of coal from mines in the Ruhr and Upper Silesia (Poland) to industries across Germany. The first determined bombing of internal German rail lines in September and October produced an immediate transportation (and coal) crisis, which the Speer ministry met by reallocating labor from the armaments industry to transportation construction, enabling coal shipments to continue at about half their August 1944 rate.[158]

---

[157] For instance, see USSBS, *Summary Report (European War)*, p. 37.

[158] For details on Germany's reallocation of labor to offset the coal crisis, see Milward, *German Economy*, pp. 173–75. For monthly figures on Reichsbahn hard coal car placings, see Mierzejeski, *Collapse of the German War Economy*, p. 192.

The Germans were not able to offset the effects of the second round of transportation bombing from February to March largely because ground power had blockaded coal shipments from Poland and had enabled the Allies' large tactical air forces to augment the strategic air forces. Following the Soviet advance through Upper Silesia, which was not accompanied by transportation bombing, coal shipments from this area collapsed to 10 percent of the August rate.[159] Coal shipments from the Ruhr declined radically between February and March (also to 10 percent of the August rate), when a combination of strategic and tactical air power was applied to stop all rail movement into (or out of) the Ruhr in preparation for its occupation by land forces.[160] The bottom line is that without the progress of Allied ground forces, strategic air attack on transportation would likely have produced the dismal results expected by the Committee of Operations Analysts in January 1943.

The German case also illustrates the central weakness of applying the industrial web theory of air attack to a continental power. At bottom, the industrial web theory seeks to impose an economic blockade from the air, the main criterion of success being whether the attacker can cause severe shortages of indispensable goods or services. The main problem is that whether critical shortages can be created is a function not of how goods are currently employed but of how well the economy as a whole can substitute for scarcity in individual products. Two factors are important: the size of the resource base and the efficiency of the government in reallocating resources. As a continental power with a highly educated population and sophisticated government administration, Germany was well endowed on both. Accordingly, Germany could not be brought to the point of economic collapse by wartime shortages.

Instead, the shortages that mattered were those relating directly to immediate demands on the battlefield. Oil is the principal case. Destroying Germany's production of fuel oil affected the fighting capability of the Wehrmacht not only because production was limited but also because German forces consumed enormous amounts of oil in trying to defend the hundreds of miles of front in the both the east and west. In other words, Germany's need to consume oil was driven by the need to maintain tactical mobility, which could not be replaced by horse- or manpower without significant cost in effectiveness. Hence, once a shortage of oil actually occurred, it translated directly into lower fighting effectiveness, but it would not have been so important had not ground forces been pressing the battle.

Finally, the German case serves as a warning to those who advocate near complete reliance on air power to win wars. The air planners who prepared

---

[159] Mierzejewski, *Collapse of the German War Economy*, p. 192.

[160] USSBS, *The Effects of Strategic Bombing on German Transportation* (Washington, D.C.: GPO, January 1947), p. 14.

AWPD-1 had spent years in a sincere attempt to devise an air strategy that would win even without large ground forces. Indeed, the original plans of the United States to build 240 divisions were stalled at 90 by the need to assign over 1.3 million men to the Army Air Forces at their peak and countless thousands to building an air force that reached twenty-eight thousand planes at its peak.[161] Nonetheless, air power played a secondary role to land power, and we must question the wisdom of any long-term defense policy relying exclusively on air power.

[161] USSBS, *Summary Report (European War)*, p. 5.

[9]

Beyond Strategic Bombing

The most important reason to study the determinants of coercive success and failure is to draw lessons for future policy debates. Coercion, and strategic bombing, will not go away. Air power is becoming increasingly important to American grand strategy. It projects force more rapidly and with less risk of life than land power and more formidably than naval power. These are valuable attributes for unpredictable crises that occur in places where the American public is unwilling to shed much blood. Thus, from Iraq to Bosnia to North Korea, increasingly the first question in debates over American intervention is becoming, Can air power alone do the job?[1]

The answer is no. First, coercion is very hard. It hardly ever succeeds by raising costs and risks to civilians. When coercion does work, it is by denying the opponent the ability to achieve its goals on the battlefield. However, even denial does not always work. Sometimes states can succeed only by decisively defeating their opponents. Second, strategic bombing does not work. Strategic bombing for punishment and decapitation do not coerce, and strategic bombing is rarely the best way to achieve denial. The "precision-guided missile revolution" is not likely to enhance the coercive effects of strategic bombing. Nevertheless, despite its ineffectiveness, strategic bombing is likely to persist because of bureaucratic interests and political pressures for cheap solutions to difficult foreign policy problems. The solution, if there is one, is knowledge, for ignorance allows advocates of bad

---

[1] The clearest call for the air force to conduct power projection by relying on strategic bombing is found in Donald B. Rice, *The Air Force and U.S. National Security: Global Reach—Global Power* (Washington, D.C.: Department of the Air Force, June 1991). For a diverse debate on the role of air power in American grand strategy, see Richard H. Schultz Jr. and Robert L. Pfaltzgraff Jr., eds., *The Future of Air Power in the Aftermath of the Gulf War* (Maxwell Air Force Base, Ala.: Air University Press, 1992).

strategies to escape serious questioning. Historically, we have not studied military coercion in peacetime; we should.

Coercion Is Hard

The cases studied in this book show that the requirements for successful coercion are very high. Even when coercion succeeds, moreover, it rarely gains very much.

Conventional attack on civilians was pursued as a major coercive strategy in four of the five cases (Germany, Japan, Korea, and Vietnam) and played a minor role in the fifth (Iraq). In two of the five (Germany and Japan), it was operationally unrestrained and very destructive. In three cases it was restrained (Korea, Vietnam, and Iraq). In no case can it be shown to have produced concessions to any part of the coercer's demands.

Conventional denial strategies were seriously pursued in all five cases. In four cases they succeeded, although in all but one instance the gains were minor. The greatest success was the Gulf War: Iraq agreed to the most important Coalition demand (withdrawal from Kuwait) but not to others (abandonment of equipment and a humiliating admission of defeat). By contrast, in November 1951 the Chinese conceded a small area of territory but rejected other UN demands, prolonging the war for another twenty months. In 1972 the North Vietnamese agreed to a cease-fire, but it forced them only to defer, not to abandon, their offensive plans. Japan surrendered, but only on the doorstep of total defeat. Coercion of Germany failed altogether; the war went on until Germany was completely overrun.

Nuclear coercion was tried twice. In one case actual bombs were used (Japan); in the other only a veiled threat (Korea). Neither, however, yielded much additional coercive leverage. Nuclear devastation was only one of several pressures on Japanese elites, and not the decisive one. Nuclear threats did have coercive impact in the Korean War but succeeded only in resolving peripheral issues such as prisoner repatriation, and only after the target had lost its own nuclear ally.

Although planners often excuse the failure of coercive programs by citing political constraints and operational problems (e.g., weather), in fact, these seldom crippled the effectiveness of coercive air campaigns. Weather is a problem in all air campaigns and is always taken into account in planning. Similarly, political constraints are common. Although American airmen typically cite Johnson's micromanagement as the reason for coercive air power failed in Vietnam from 1965 to 1968, they usually fail to mention Nixon's interference in rules of engagement during the coercive success of 1972. Overall, operational and political constraints only infrequently stopped air campaigns from reaching the military objectives the airmen believed they needed to achieve. In fact, these military objectives are normally reached, and airmen do a terrific job of overcoming the constraints of weather and politics. These coercive campaigns failed *despite* effective implementation because they were badly conceived.

The bottom line, then, is that coercion is extremely hard. Success in conventional coercion can be attained only if the coercer is fully prepared to impose its demands by force and usually only after fighting a long way toward a military decision. Oddly, even nuclear coercion has made only small differences, usually because the side with nuclear superiority has a large conventional advantage as well. Political leaders who rely on coercion by air power to gain their objectives without having to fight for them are likely to be disappointed, often disastrously.

STRATEGIC BOMBING DOESN'T MATTER

Coercive air power is usually identified with strategic bombing. This is a mistake. History shows that strategic bombing strategies are the least effective ways to use air power for coercion.

First, punishment does not work. Modern nation states have extremely high pain thresholds when important interests are at stake, which conventional munitions cannot overcome. Low to moderate levels of punishment inspire more anger than fear; heavy bombardment produces apathy, not rebellion.

Second, risk does not work. Risk strategies are merely a weaker form of punishment. Although they depend on credibility, their credibility is often low because they have usually been employed by governments that were domestically constrained from unleashing full-scale punishment. Nuclear coercion is the exception; the prospect of nuclear devastation is so horrible that even threats with low credibility can coerce.

Third, decapitation does not work. Political decapitation is not feasible because individual leaders are hard to kill, governments are harder to overthrow, and even if the target government can be overthrown, the coercer can rarely guarantee that its replacement will be more forthcoming. Military decapitation is ineffective because air power cannot isolate national leaders from control over battlefield forces for long, and short disruptions do not matter unless other instruments are poised to exploit them immediately.

Fourth, denial can work, but strategic bombing is not the best way to achieve it. No strategic bombing campaign has ever yielded decisive results, nor were any significant opportunities missed.

Strategic bombing is much more expensive than theater air power, but advocates justify the added cost on the grounds that strategic bombing destroys much higher-leverage targets.[2] They are wrong. Modern war economies are not brittle. Although individual plants can be destroyed, the opponent can reduce the effects by dispersing production of important items and stockpiling key raw materials and machinery. Attackers never anticipate all the adjustments and work-arounds defenders can devise, partly because they often rely on analysis of peacetime economies and partly because intelligence of the detailed structure of the target economy is always incomplete.

Further, even substantial reductions in the production of essential items may have no military impact because the opponent can economize by eliminating lower-priority uses first. That is why, even if strategic bombing aims at denial, it usually punishes civilians before it reduces military capability. To contribute meaningfully to denial, strategic bombing must practically eliminate production of crucial items,[3] and even coercers much stronger than their opponents have found it impossible to do so.[4] Even if it could be done, considerable time would elapse before lost production would seriously affect the opponent's combat strength at the front, and only if theater stocks were drawn down by simultaneous intense pressure by friendly land and theater air forces.

Thus, strategic bombing can matter only in long wars of attrition which are decided by overall material superiority, not in short conflicts fought mainly with existing stocks. Even then, it matters only against mechanized conventional forces with heavy logistic requirements, not against guerrillas. And in this case, it matters only if simultaneous intense pressure by friendly land and theater air forces generates large needs for replacement of equipment and weapons. After all that, it still takes considerable time to wear down theater stocks enough to meaningfully reduce the opponent's combat power. Still, strategic air power cannot be decisive. The most it can do is to reduce the costs that friendly land and theater air forces have to pay to defeat enemy forces on the battlefield.[5]

---

[2] Strategic bombing is inherently harder than interdiction, requiring more expensive, longer-range bombers and more extensive air defense suppression, refueling, and other support. This is why strategic bombers have generally cost more than ten times tactical aircraft of the same era, a ratio that may be increasing for today's generation. For cost comparisons of the B-17 to tactical aircraft in World War II and the B-2 to the A-10 today, see Wesley Frank Craven and James Lea Cate, *The Army Air Forces in World War II* (Washington, D.C.: GPO, 1948), 6:360; and Northrop Corporation, *B-2 Stealth Bomber 1992 Fact Book* (September 1992).

[3] Although strategic bombing of Germany reduced ball-bearing production by 70 percent, Germans adjusted by curtailing non-essential (especially civilian) uses and by re-designing equipment to use fewer bearings. Craven and Cate, *Army Air Forces in World War II*, 2:686, 699, 703–4.

[4] The only war economy seriously disrupted by air attack was that of a nearly defeated Germany in February 1945, but the economic damage was done largely by massive numbers of tactical aircraft, which could blanket the German rail and road networks because the Allies had advanced so far that Germany itself had become the combat theater.

[5] Of course, the likelihood that strategic air power can actually reduce the costs of defeating the enemy on the battlefield is declining as the cost of strategic bombers rises. B-2 stealth

Theater air power is a much stronger coercive tool, useful in short wars as well as long and against irregular as well as regular forces.[6] Although, like strategic bombing, theater air attack is effective only when combined with simultaneous pressure from ground forces, it gives the opponent much less scope to minimize consequences because effects are more immediate. Dispersing forces leads to piecemeal defeat, and reallocating scarce reserves or supplies to priority sectors can be obstructed by interdicting transportation routes. The isolated units can then be overwhelmed by friendly ground forces and close air support before logistic links can be reestablished. This hammer-and-anvil approach, if carried out repeatedly or on a large enough scale, undermines the opponent's ability to take or hold the disputed territory.

The lesson of air power history is that strategic bombing is a very marginal coercive tool. In principle it could help shorten a coercive campaign, but it never has. Strategic bombing cannot substitute for ground and theater air pressure, but the combination of theater air power and land power can deny the opponent the capacity to control disputed territory, whether or not strategic bombing is also used.

STRATEGIC BOMBING WON'T MATTER IN THE FUTURE

In the aftermath of America's near bloodless victory in the Gulf War, strategic bombing has gained more popularity than at any time since Vietnam. Proponents claim not only that strategic bombing was the decisive factor but also that the Gulf War heralds a new age in which strategic bombing will be the strongest form of military power, dramatically enhancing America's coercive capability and options.[7]

Although these arguments are as yet vague and incomplete, they all center around the ability of PGMs to destroy strategic targets more easily and

---

bombers cost approximately 600 million dollars each (if the United States buys more than twenty)—or the equivalent of some ten thousand very good laser-guided bombs or Maverick precision-guided missiles, roughly two-thirds of the number of PGMs fired in in the Gulf War.

[6] Ground support is sometimes effective against guerillas, whereas interdiction generally is not.

[7] Foremost is Colonel John A. Warden III, one of the principal architects of the strategic air campaign against Iraq and the commander from 1992 to 1995 of the Air Command and Staff College, the air force school for promising midlevel officers. Warden, "Employing Air Power in the Twenty-first Century," in *Future of Air Power*, ed. Schultz and Pfaltzgraff, pp. 57–82. Others include Jason B. Barlow, "Strategic Paralysis: An Air Power Strategy for the Present," *Airpower Journal* 7 (Winter 1993): 4–15; Edward Mann, "One Target, One Bomb: Is the Principle of Mass Dead?" *Airpower Journal* 7 (Spring 1993): 35–43; Buster C. Glosson, "Impact of Precision Weapons on Air Combat Operations," *Airpower Journal* 7 (Summer 1993): 4–10; and Phillip S. Meilinger, "Towards a New Airpower Lexicon; or, Interdiction: An Idea Whose Time Has Finally Gone?" *Airpower Journal* 7 (Summer 1993): 39–48.

more rapidly than nonprecision weapons. The claim is that PGMs overturn previous limitations on strategic air power, greatly enhancing the effectiveness of all the coercive strategies that depend on strategic air power—punishment, risk, and decapitation.[8]

The premise of these arguments is true, but the logic is faulty. PGMs make it possible for fewer aircraft to destroy more targets than in the past, but this enhanced efficiency makes little difference to the coercive effectiveness of any of these strategies.

Consider punishment. Strategic bombing advocates claim that PGM-equipped aircraft can suddenly and simultaneously knock out the all the critical nodes of a national economy. Once these are destroyed, civilian living conditions will rapidly become intolerable, forcing the government to make peace. According to John Warden, "The number of key production targets in even a large state is reasonably small and all of the targets in key industries such as power production and petroleum refining are fragile." He believes that "the growth in cities around the world, and the necessity for electricity and petroleum products to keep a city functioning have made these two commodities essential for most states." Therefore, he says, "Unless the stakes in the war are very high, most states will make desired concessions when their power generation system is put under sufficient pressure or actually destroyed."[9] Moreover, advocates believe that economic research can further multiply the impact of strategic attack. Since World War II, they say, nuclear weapons have made serious study of economic vulnerabilities seem irrelevant. We simply have not studied how modern economies and specific industries are constructed, but if we did, we would find that every industry has just a few critical nodes whose loss would effectively destroy the whole industry.

---

[8] Two additional arguments are not PGM dependent. Some contend that future crises will occur unpredictably, with little warning and no time to deploy ground and tactical air forces to the conflict region. This argument supports the use of extremely long-range aircraft such as the B-2. Christopher J. Bowie, *The New Calculus: Analyzing Airpower's Changing Role in Joint Theater Campaigns* (Santa Monica: Rand, 1993). However, no one has shown that the large, slow-flying B-2 can survive the difficult-to-predict air defenses accompanying enemy ground forces. Other strategic air power advocates maintain that the American public has not only a low tolerance for casualties in its own ranks but also a low tolerance for protracted operations of any kind or even for enemy casualities. Glosson, "Impact of Precision Weapons," p. 8. As a result, in future conflicts the United States may not have the political staying power to wait for theater air attack to clear the way for ground forces. Recent evidence does not support this argument. Despite concerns before the start of Desert Storm that there would pressure to terminate the air war after just a few days, it was in fact continued for thirty-nine days until Iraq's ground forces were decimated. There was no public outcry when it was reported immediately after the war that over 100,000 Iraqi troops had been killed, nor did estimates that 100,000 more Iraqis would die if sanctions were not lifted quickly generate noticeable public pressure against sanctions.

[9] Warden, "Employing Air Power," pp. 66, 65–66, 64. Warden makes clear (p. 64) that the purpose of taking down the economy is *not* denial: "Note that destruction of the power system may have little short-term effect at the front—if there is a front."

This argument is fatally flawed. Even if these economic effects could be caused as easily as advocates claim, they do not represent very severe punishment by historical strategic bombing standards. Bombing knocked out nearly all power generation in North Korea (90 percent), North Vietnam (85–90 percent), and Iraq (over 90 percent), but in no case caused the population to rise up against the regime.[10] The populations of Germany and Japan suffered vastly worse punishment—they were fire bombed! Nearly 1 percent of each country's population was killed and 20 percent made homeless; yet there was no public pressure on either government to surrender. If modern nation-states can withstand so much, they will not give in under the relatively bloodless harassment envisioned by today's strategic bombing advocates.[11]

Strategic bombing advocates say that PGMs bolster coercive strategies based on risk by enabling the coercer to turn punishment on and off at will, as well as to modulate it in fine increments. PGMs permit the coercer to destroy a designated fraction of a critical economic system, such as power, fuel, or telecommunications, as an indicator of capability to destroy the entire system if concessions are not made.[12] They claim that knocking out power generation with PGMs has the additional advantage that only a few critical components need be attacked, enabling the coercer to hold out the promise of speedy restoration as a carrot. Said Warden, "Assistance with repair of electric power can take place quickly—and is very desirable as soon as the Iraqi government adheres to Coalition terms."[13]

Even if damage can be controlled as finely as advocates claim, however, PGMs do nothing to remedy the inherent weaknesses of risk-based coercive strategies. Given the limited destructiveness of conventional weapons, even with PGMs, risk strategies amount to nothing more than slower and weaker punishment campaigns. Such strategies are generally used by coercers that are politically constrained from inflicting maximum punishment, and are thus incredible. After the Gulf War, Iraqi officials said that they had taken U.S. strategic air strikes as evidence that there would be no extensive bom-

---

[10] Thomas E. Griffith Jr., *Strategic Attack of National Electrical Systems* (Maxwell Air Force Base, Ala.: School of Advanced Airpower Studies, 1993). In Iraq, the groups that revolted—the Kurds in the North and the Shi'ites in the South—did so because of long-standing grievances against oppression by Hussein's Sunni-dominated regime, not because of sudden economic deprivation.

[11] PGMs are thought of as increasing the destructiveness of conventional war because they are much more effective against military and certain economic targets. The most devastating way to attack civilians, however, is with incendiary bombs, which need not be guided because they work by starting massive fire storms, not by destroying individual houses one by one.

[12] In effect, strategic bombing enthusiasts are claiming that we are fully able now to implement the strategies of coercive diplomacy proposed by Thomas Schelling and Alexander George.

[13] Warden, "Employing Air Power," p. 72.

bardment of Baghdad and Basra and that therefore they should "hold tight and the Americans will go away." The Interior Minister said, "We would have understood carpet bombing, but we didn't understand this other"; he thought the United States was just being spiteful.[14]

Further, punishment cannot be as finely modulated as risk proponents assert, both because coercers rarely have good enough intelligence about opponents' stockpiles of key components and because they cannot accurately predict how opponents will adjust to damage. During the Gulf War, Coalition aircraft did more damage to Iraqi power plants than intended. Although targeting was supposed to be limited to transformers and switching yards, the generator halls and turbines of nearly every major plant were also destroyed.[15] Repair assistance is also not a powerful incentive, because targets are often capable of restoring the damaged systems themselves. For instance, in the negotiations during and after the Gulf War, Iraq never asked for assistance with its power systems but was able to restore 68 percent of 1990 peak capacity and 75 percent of transmission lines by August 1991.[16]

Third and most important, enthusiasts say that PGMs have made possible a new coercive air strategy—decapitation—which attacks leadership and national communications in order to achieve victory by changing or paralyzing an enemy government. Modern nation-states, it is argued, whether First World or Third World, increasingly rely on sophisticated communication systems connecting elite to elite and capital to field. As these systems become more sophisticated, they also become more brittle. Central telephone exchanges, television stations, and radio transmitters are prominent, stationary, and easily destroyed by one or a few weapons. The result is strategic paralysis, which renders battlefield forces useless even if undamaged, as well as domestic political vulnerability as leaders are cut off from internal security organs. According to Warden,

Capturing or killing the state's leader has frequently been decisive. In modern times, however, it has become more difficult—but not impossible—to capture or kill the command element. At the same time, command communications have been more important than ever, and these are vulnerable to attack. When command communications suffer extreme damage . . . the leadership has great difficulty in directing war efforts. In the case of an unpopular regime, the

---

[14] Interviews by William Arkin, quoted in "Defeat of Iraq Sparks Debate on Which Air Role Was Crucial," *Aviation Week and Space Technology*, 27 January 1992, pp. 62–63.

[15] In addition, most plants were restruck from two to five times each because imagery could not confirm levels of damage. Gulf War Air Power Survey, *Operations and Effects and Effectiveness* (Washington, D.C.: GPO, 1993), vol. 2, pt. 2, pp. 298, 306.

[16] Walid Doleh et al., "Electrical Facilities Survey," in International Study Team, *Health and Welfare in Iraq after the Gulf Crisis: An In-depth Assessment* (October 1991), p. 1.

lack of communications not only inhibits the bolstering of national morale but also facilitates rebellion on the part of dissident elements.[17]

Vulnerability of the enemy regime can also be enhanced by direct attacks on security forces, their headquarters, and even their files. The ability of PGMs to modulate punishment also facilitates decapitation because civilian hardship can be timed to coincide with attacks on government anticoup resources.

Decapitation has the advantage of minimizing collateral damage, and more important, the critical target sets are so small that it seems a war can be won by a few squadrons of F-117s in a matter of days. Like the Texas Ranger slogan, "One riot, one Ranger," decapitation promises "One war, one raid."

Accuracy alone, however, cannot make decapitation a viable coercive air strategy because the ability to destroy the target sets is not the problem. Precisely because decapitation target sets are so small, they can easily be destroyed even without precision weapons.[18] Decapitation is primarily a problem of intelligence, not combat effectiveness.

Consider political decapitation. The core problem is obtaining the intelligence needed to kill enemy leaders who are making every effort to evade detection. Further, endangering regimes by cutting communications between leaders and their domestic security services requires detailed understanding not only of their formal communication links but also of backup and informal control systems, as well as the loyalties and motivations of individual leaders and units. Without precise intelligence, precise weapons can precisely destroy targets that are not in use. Unknown to the Coalition, Iraq removed the key equipment from its central telephone exchange in Baghdad before the Gulf War began, so we destroyed a building, not a system.[19] The Iraqis had evidently made plans to do without it. Finally, even if leaders can be hit and communication networks severed, estimating whether military effects can be translated into regime change is a problem of political forecasting, and an uncommonly difficult one. We have no theories that can predict in either democratic or non-democratic polities whether

---

[17] Warden, "Employing Air Power," p. 65. See also Barlow, "Strategic Paralysis"; and Dennis Drew, "Hyperwar," *Air Force Times*, 6 May 1991, p. 31. These ideas are spreading beyond the U.S. Air Force. For example, see Gary Waters, *Gulf Lesson One — the Value of Air Power: Doctrinal Lessons for Australia* (Canberra: Air Power Studies Centre, 1992), p. 170.

[18] PGMs are sometimes said to be essential for destroying hardened targets such as command bunkers. During Desert Storm the United States developed a five-thousand-pound laser-guided bomb to destroy a bunker that two-thousand-pound laser-guided bombs could not penetrate. The advantage of PGMs is accuracy, not penetration, however. An equally heavy dumb bomb can destroy the same targets provided a direct hit is achieved. It may be necessary to drop considerably more bombs to hit the target, but it is still feasible if the number of such targets is small. That is not to say that PGMs are not desirable for strikes on command and control targets. They require fewer sorties, which can be important if air resources are very limited, and they cause far less collateral damage.

[19] Arkin, "Defeat of Iraq Sparks Debate," p. 62.

and when military pressure will cause a change of regime or, if it does, in what direction.

Military decapitation, or "strategic paralysis," is infeasible for three reasons: strategic direction does not demand high-volume, real-time communication; links cannot be cut for long; and authority can be predelegated to theater commanders. PGMs do not change this state of affairs. As with political decapitation, the problem is one of intelligence, not target destruction. Large and stationary electronic communication systems can be knocked out with relative ease, but nation-states today have so many backup and work-around alternatives (such as dedicated land lines; small, mobile radios including cellular telephones; couriers traveling by car, rail, helicopter, or plane; and face-to-face meetings between leaders) that an attacker cannot hope to locate and disrupt them all.[20] After the Gulf War an Iraqi army corps commander said that he had direct contact with Baghdad only once during the war, not because his links were destroyed but out of fear of being intercepted.[21]

Strategic-bombing proponents also say that PGMs advantage strategic air power over theater air power simply because PGMs are expensive, and strategic targets are always limited in number whereas theater targets are always virtually infinite. In fact, however, some of the most effective types of PGMs are not expensive; a typical laser-guided bomb (the GBU-12) costs about ten thousand dollars. Compared to the cost of building and maintaining the aircraft, training the crew, and providing basing, communications, aerial refueling, air superiority, and other support, the difference between this and a cheaper dumb bomb is very small. Theater targets such as a $1.5 million T-72 Soviet-made tank can easily justify their use.[22] Of fifteen thousand PGMs used by U.S. aircraft in Desert Storm, at least ninety-five hundred were used against theater targets.[23]

Since strategic bombing advocates claim that PGMs enhance punishment, risk, and decapitation, it may seem surprising that they have not raised the question of whether PGMs enhance strategic bombing for de-

---

[20] Cheap, mobile, and flexible communications technology is proliferating throughout the Third World. Fiber-optic land lines, which can handle thousands of channels, can be dispensed from a reel mounted on the back of a truck. The average per-capita gross domestic product of countries launching cellular telephone networks has fallen from $14,500 in 1979–1982 to about $1,500 today and a projected $600 in 1998. In 1994 the command system of the Rwandan Patriotic Front was based on mobile cellular phones. "Survey of Telecommunications," *Economist*, 23 October 1993).

[21] Arkin, "Defeat of Iraq Sparks Debate," p. 62.

[22] Glosson, "Impact of Precision Weapons," p. 4. An F/A-18 E/F costs $60 million, plus $111 million in twenty-year operating costs. Assuming that it flies a hundred combat missions over its lifetime and that it drops four LGBs per mission, the aircraft alone costs $43,000 per bomb dropped. Northrop Corporation, *B-2 1992 Fact Book*.

[23] These figures exclude some two thousand antiradiation missiles. Department of the Air Force, *Air Force Performance in Desert Storm* (Washington, D.C.: GPO, April 1991).

nial.[24] There is a reason for this omission. Since strategic bombing can affect denial only in long wars of attrition, anyone proposing this approach would be in the position of advocating a long-war strategy, probably involving heavy casualties even for the winner—hardly an attractive prospect.[25]

Beyond this, there is an even more powerful reason why strategic bombing for denial is unlikely to matter in the foreseeable future: there is no possible opponent against which strategic bombing would be both useful and possible. The twin military-technological revolutions of nuclear weapons and PGMs ensure this. Any opponent that is not one of the world's major economic powers cannot possibly replace equipment as fast as a PGM-armed attacker can destroy it, and will be defeated when prewar stocks are used up. If the opponent is one of the world's economic powers, it will almost certainly be nuclear-armed and able to deter strategic attack.

Modern PGMs, including air-to-ground, surface-to-air, and antitank weapons, have increased loss rates on the conventional battlefield far beyond the capacity of all but the largest economies to replace. In the 1973 war Israel lost 200 tanks, Egypt 1,150, and Syria 1,150 in eighteen days, and in 1991 Iraq lost 2,633 in forty-three days—or annual rates of 4,056, 23,000, 23,000, and 22,000, respectively.[26] None of these countries produced any tanks during these wars; Israel now produces fewer than a hundred per year.[27] Although any country involved in a long war can dramatically increase military production, months or years are required. Against a PGM-equipped opponent, any country at all, with the possible exception of a few of the world's largest economies, would lose its entire

---

[24] "One does not conduct an attack against industry or infrastructure because of the effect it might or might not have on field forces. Rather, one undertakes such an attack for its direct effect on national leaders and commanders who must assess the cost of rebuilding, the effect on the state's economic position in the postwar period, the internal political effect on their own survival, and the cost versus the potential gain from continuing the war." Warden, "Employing Air Power," pp. 67–68.

[25] States rarely initiate conflicts that they expect to become wars of attrition. John J. Mearsheimer, *Conventional Deterrence* (Ithaca: Cornell University Press, 1983).

[26] In fact, Egypt and Syria suffered these losses against a non-PGM-equipped opponent; had Israel fielded PGMs on a large scale, their losses would have been even higher. Chaim Herzog, *The Arab-Israeli Wars* (New York: Random House, 1982), p. 341; and Frank Gervasi, *Thunder over the Mediterranean* (New York: David McKay, 1975), pp. 406–7. Although these were both desert wars, terrain makes less difference to the destructiveness of PGMs than to which types of PGMs inflict the damage. In close terrain, in which small ground units are harder to detect, air-launched PGMs would do less damage, but ground-launched ones would do more. An analysis of aircraft losses would show the same patterns as do tanks, although terrain makes no difference.

[27] Approximately one thousand Merkava tanks were produced between 1977 and 1993. Christopher Foss, ed., *Jane's Armour and Artillery, 1993–94* (Alexandria, Va.: Jane's Information Group, 1993), pp. 58–59.

prewar force before replacement production could make even a tiny contribution to the need.[28]

It would be difficult for even a superpower patron to make good such losses. American tank production from 1984 to 1993 averaged 840 per year.[29] If such a case nonetheless arose, strategic bombing of the client would remain irrelevant, but PGMs would enhance the effectiveness of air interdiction, either to prevent delivery to the client or from rear areas to the front.

The only opponents against which strategic bombing can matter are the world's largest military and industrial powers. These countries, however, generally possess strategic nuclear weapons.[30] Thus, any argument for conventional strategic bombing in such a conflict requires assuming that one side will permit the other routinely to fly missions throughout its airspace with nuclear-capable aircraft that could deliver a nuclear first strike without warning at any time—without resorting to nuclear threats or preventive actions.[31]

The coercive strategy that benefits most from the PGM revolution is theater air attack. This is because many of the most important theater interdiction targets, as well as ground support targets, are point targets requiring direct hits: tanks, armored personnel carriers, self-propelled artillery, bunkers used for communications, logistic storage, or other purposes, and bridges.[32] Without PGMs, well-constructed bunkers and bridges can usually be destroyed only with tremendous effort, while dug-in combat vehicles are next to impossible to hit from the air. With PGMs, these missions become feasible, although still far from easy.[33] PGMs also allow aircraft to attack from a safer distance and altitude, avoiding the densest ground fire.

---

[28] At the indicated loss rates, Israel, Egypt, Syria, and Iraq would have lost their entire tank inventories, including reserves and obsolete models, in 180, 35, 28, and 78 days respectively. Anthony H. Cordesman, *After the Storm: The Changing Military Balance in the Middle East* (Boulder, Colo.: Westview Press, 1993), pp. 182–83.

[29] U.S. M1 main battle tank production has averaged seventy per month since January 1984. The United Kingdom Challenger 2 production will be thirty per year through 1998. France's Leopard 2 production has averaged three hundred per year since 1982. Russian T-80 production is estimated at two thousand per year from 1983 to 1993. Foss, *Jane's, 1993–94*, pp. 11, 41, 93, and 110.

[30] Although some actual or potential global powers, such Germany, Japan, and India, do not possess them today, it is impossible to imagine a scenario involving a major war between the United States and one of these countries in which the opponent did not possess strategic nuclear weapons.

[31] On routes by which conventional conflicts can inadvertently lead to nuclear conflict, see Barry R. Posen, *Inadvertent Nuclear Escalation: Conventional War and Nuclear Risks* (Ithaca: Cornell University Press, 1991).

[32] Many other types of theater targets, such as towed artillery, trucks, and unhardened communications sites and depots are vulnerable to near misses. Thus, although easier to hit with PGMs, attacking them with unguided munitions is feasible.

[33] During the Gulf War, the Coalition launched approximately 9,500 PGMs of types commonly used against armored vehicles, and destroyed 2,500 tanks and APCs, yielding a kill rate of 26 percent, although since we cannot be sure that none of these weapons was used against any other target types or that all the tank and APC kills were due to PGMs, the true rate may be either higher or lower.

Whereas tactical air power has long supported friendly ground operations, PGMs have made it possible to conduct a sustained independent air
attrition offensive against a stationary, dug-in ground force and substantially destroy it.[34] That is not to say that air power can coerce by itself; it cannot drive the enemy off disputed territory or occupy the territory itself, but
it can do most of the work, leaving friendly ground forces to mop up. Tactical air power has always been the weaker member of the theater combined
arms team; now it is the stronger.[35]

In short, strategic bombing advocates have it exactly backward. PGMs
have done nothing to enhance the coercive strength of strategic air power.
Punishment, risk, and decapitation strategies had little merit before PGMs,
and they have little merit now. Denial remains the most effective coercive
air strategy, and PGMs have further increased the superiority of theater air
power over strategic bombing.[36]

WHY STRATEGIC BOMBING PERSISTS

If strategic bombing doesn't work, why does it persist? Coercers have
demonstrated a remarkably consistent tendency toward overreliance on
strategic bombing in general and punishment strategies in particular. Further, confidence in the efficacy of punishment frequently persists despite
disconfirming evidence. The most egregious example was the continued
British fire-bombing of German cities throughout World War II. British leaders found ways to believe that German citizens were more squeamish than
their own even after years of terror bombing produced no significant results. In the Pacific the United States fire-bombed smaller and smaller
Japanese cities after burning the largest ones had no discernible effect. In
Korea the United States waged three separate punishment campaigns, in
1950, 1952, and again in 1953, despite the fact that the earlier efforts produced no coercive results at all. Finally, in 1991 American strategic bombing
advocates assumed that levels of punishment far lower than those visited
on Germany, Japan, Korea, or Vietnam would bring Iraq to its knees.

Strategic bombing persists for four main reasons. First, it serves the bureaucratic interests of air forces. Second, both civilian and military leaders

---

[34] Of course, PGMs may some day be cheaply countered. For a history of competition between offensive and defensive weapons which shows that each new advance tends to trigger
countermeasures, see Bernard Brodie and Fawn M. Brodie, *From Crossbow to H-Bomb: The Evolution of the Weapons and Tactics of Warfare* (Bloomington: Indiana University Press, 1973).

[35] At least in open terrain and clear weather. With PGMs, anything that can be seen can be
hit, so the more closed-in the weather or terrain, the less they matter.

[36] Thus, most air forces would be better off investing in detection (e.g., air-to-ground radar)
to enhance their ability to destroy theater targets rather than in penetration (e.g., stealth)
which is most useful for strategic attack.

want cheap and easy solutions to difficult international confrontations. Third, ignorance allows strategic bombing enthusiasts to sway policy decisions with unsupported assertions. Fourth, deliberate obfuscation of the brutality of strategic-bombing campaigns to shield them from criticism also impedes evaluation.

The most important institutional interest of air forces, like other bureaucracies, is maintenance of institutional independence and autonomy. Of the three main air combat missions—air superiority, tactical bombing, and strategic bombing—strategic bombing serves this interest best because it is an inherently independent mission, requiring little coordination with other services.[37] Theater air attack, because it must be closely coordinated with the plans and movements of ground forces, risks loss of control over air operations in wartime to ground commanders and could threaten control over missions and budgets even in peacetime.[38] Air superiority enhances air force autonomy but only to the extent that it is associated with strategic bombing, which requires control of air space over enemy territory. Absent strategic bombing, air superiority could in principle be limited to control of air space over fielded forces and homeland territory. Thus truncated, air superiority would not unambiguously justify an independent air service. Armies already participate in air defense of the battlefield and friendly rear areas with anti-aircraft artillery and missiles; arguably, taking over control of interceptor aircraft could improve air defense coordination. After all, navies traditionally provide all aspects of their own air defense—guns and missiles as well as aircraft.[39]

Civilians and the other military services have their own reasons for going along with strategic bombing. Sometimes civilian leaders are hardly involved in military strategy, as in the cases of Roosevelt in World War II and Bush in the Gulf War. Sometimes, like Johnson and Nixon in the Vietnam War, they actively support strategic bombing as a cheap alternative to long, costly, and politically unattractive ground campaigns. Civilians also sometimes turn to strategic bombing for revenge or to maintain morale when the public is suffering heavy costs, as did Churchill against Germany and the United States against Japan in World War II.[40] Finally, it is hard for the other

---

[37] Strategic bombing was the justification for the creation of the RAF in 1917, the quasi independence of the U.S. Army Air Forces during World War II, and the establishment of the independent U.S. Air Force in 1947.

[38] Carl H. Builder, *The Icarus Syndrome: The Role of Air Power Theory in the Evolution and Fate of the U.S. Air Force* (New Brunswick, N.J.: Transactions, 1994), pp. 141, 204.

[39] Russia has an independent air defense service, separate from both the army and the air force, which controls both interceptor aircraft and surface-to-air missiles for homeland defense against strategic attack. Tactical air defense is divided between the army and air force in the same way as in Western militaries.

[40] Philip E. Converse and Howard Schuman, " 'Silent Majorities' and the Vietnam War," *Scientific American* 222 (June 1970): 21; Harvey B. Tress, "Churchill, the First Berlin Raids, and the Blitz: A New Interpretation," *Militargeschichtliche Mitteilungen* 32, no. 2 (1980): 65–78; John W. Dower, *War without Mercy: Race and Power in the Pacific War* (New York: Pantheon, 1986).

services to object to anything that might reduce casualties. In Desert Storm, General Schwarzkopf took the initiative to request a strategic bombing plan; it did not have to be imposed on him.

Bad strategy thrives on ignorance, which is a special problem for coercive air power. One property common to every single coercive air campaign is that none of the coercers took the problem of coercion seriously enough in the years prior to the actual dispute to dedicate analytic resources to understanding it. In particular, the mechanisms by which military effects are supposed to translate into political results are hardly ever studied.[41] Reviewing literally thousands of planning documents for the preparation of this book, I found innumerable studies of how forces would be applied to destroy a given target set but no document, at any level of government, of more than a page to explain how destroying the target was supposed to activate mechanisms (popular revolt, coup, social disintegration, strategic paralysis, or even thwarting enemy military strategy) which would lead to the desired political change. Given the vast availability of previously classified documents, I can only conclude that they do not exist.

As a result, coercive disputes generally provoke hurried scrambles to assemble ad hoc policies by individuals few of whom had thought much about such problems before and who are under tremendous time pressure to produce recommendations that not only stand a chance of success but also can win out in bureaucratic competitions of power and authority. Such a situation practically guarantees poor evaluation. In this environment, a "man with a plan" that promises quick, cheap success is likely to prevail. Possible weaknesses in the plan's assumptions about coercive mechanisms are likely to pass uninvestigated or even unnoticed.

Finally, obfuscation has impeded effective evaluation. Although most strategic bombing campaigns have employed punishment strategies, coercers have generally tried to hide the true purpose of such attacks from possibly squeamish publics or allies. During World War II, the British government denied that it was carrying out "indiscriminate" area bombing and privately defined fire raids as countermilitary attacks because they targeted "industrial workers." At the same time, the chief of the U.S. Army Air Forces admonished commanders in both Europe and the Pacific to stress in public the military rather than counter-civilian reasons for bombing German and Japanese cities. In Korea American air planners added transportation targets to strike packages that attacked enemy dams so as to declare publicly that the missions had a military purpose. In Vietnam American commanders claimed that destroying the North's

---

[41] The efforts of the Air Corps Tactical School in the 1930s and of the Air Command and Staff College under John Warden are lonely exceptions. Even in these cases analyses have focused on identifying target sets, and political mechanisms are simply assumed, not subjected to critical research.

main industrial targets would produce military effects, even though they knew that the North produced almost no significant war materiel. Probably the most absurd misrepresentation of punishment was the statement of the Manhattan Project's Target Committee that Hiroshima and Nagasaki had been selected as atomic bomb targets because of their military importance.[42]

Today, leaders obfuscate the purpose of decapitation as well as punishment campaigns. During the Gulf War, General Powell and Secretary Cheney maintained that the Coalition was not seeking to kill Saddam Hussein even as air planners were targeting all known locations he might visit.

Although not the main purpose, one result of all these misrepresentations has been to reduce both elite and public awareness of the extent to which punishment and related strategies have been used and to prevent evaluation. Strategies cannot be criticized as failures if it is not admitted that they were tried.

WHAT IS TO BE DONE?

The end of the Cold War has reduced major national security threats to the United States and other Western powers, correspondingly increasing their freedom of action in foreign policy. At the same time, failed states, ethnic conflicts, nuclear proliferation, and bids for regional hegemony have increased the number of incidents in which Western intervention must be considered. The problem of the Cold War was deterrence; the problem of the post-Cold-War era is coercion.

Social scientists should respond to this challenge just as vigorously as they did deterrence. This book is only a small beginning. The key problem in coercion is the validity of the mechanisms that are supposed to translate particular military effects into political outcomes. We must learn more about how agricultural, industrial, and post-industrial societies adjust to compensate for economic shortages and how their adjustment capabilities and choices are affected by international conflict.[43] We must learn more about the relationship between civilian suffering and popular unrest and how it is affected by war. We must learn more about how governments defend themselves against domestic overthrow and how senstive their defenses are to external disruption. We must learn

---

[42] Letter from General Henry H. Arnold to General Ira C. Baker, 29 June 1943, Library of Congress, Eaker papers, box 16; Robert F. Futrell, *The United States Air Force in Korea, 1950–1953* (New York: Duell, Sloan, and Pearce, 1961), p. 481; and Michael S. Sherry, *The Rise of American Air Power* (New Haven: Yale University Press, 1987), pp. 318–20.

[43] In addition to the effects of bombing, we should also study blockades, embargoes, domestic unrest, natural disasters, and possibly commodity price inflation.

more about the circumstances in which state policy is dependent on the personality of a single leader. Finally, since denial appears to be the most effective coercive strategy, we must learn more about how governments and publics evaluate the success or failure of national policy, and how evaluation changes in crises and wartime. These are all problems of social science, not military art. For their part, governments should create permanent organizations composed of individuals with expertise in a variety of military and civilian fields and disciplines to study the various political effects that alternative uses of force might produce. Such groups would not actually design a set of contingency plans to coerce countries across the globe. Even if they were given such a fantastic charter, such plans could not hope to bear on the exact context of any specific future dispute. Rather, such groups should serve as repositories of knowledge about the general political, economic, and social effects of various applications of force, which would be available to policy makers considering intervention in international disputes.

The objection could be raised, Will not increased study of military coercion lead to increased use of it? It is not impossible that someone could discover a previously unimagined coercive approach, but such a theory should not be accepted unless the causal mechanisms on which it relies can be empirically proved. History suggests, however, that ignoring coercion is likely to do more to engender false optimism than to deter the use of force. Policy makers are often more optimistic about the chances for coercive success than situations warrant. Only thorough investigation in peacetime of the capabilities and limitations of coercive air power can defeat unwarranted confidence in crisis or wartime policy making.

Further, an understanding of coercion based on denial is much less likely than other coercive theories to produce unwanted military quagmires, because fielding the forces necessary to thwart the opponent's military strategy for control of the disputed objective will often be so obviously expensive ex ante that the potential coercer will be self-deterred. Thus coercion would be likely to be attempted only over issues so important to the coercer that it would be willing to pay the full costs of military victory. In this situation coercive failure would be much less catastrophic, since military commitments will not have been based on false hopes of obtaining a cheap solution, and since the nation's forces will already be constituted to obtain the objective by force if the opponent is not forthcoming.

For their part, the military services should re-orient their doctrines and organization to focus more on the problem of destroying armies from the air. Although theater air attack is, and will likely remain, the most effective coercive air strategy, neither the U.S. Air Force nor the Army has seriously studied the vulnerabilities of field armies to air attack, either separately or jointly.[44] To realize fully the potential of theater air power requires understanding the set of possible strategies for controlling territory; the dependence of each strategy on logistics, communications, firepower, mobility, and personnel; and how damage to each of these components affects the viability of these strategies. The Air Force and Army should cooperate to solve this problem. Admittedly, to do so both services would have to put aside concerns about loss of institutional autonomy, and that is inherently difficult for bureaucracies to do, but it is the way to maximize military and, hence, coercive effectiveness in an era of declining forces. America's stunning success in the Gulf War without addressing these issues is no cause for confidence, for in that war the United States could deploy forces so superior to the enemy's that either the Army or the Air Force could have won the war virtually unassisted and, in effect, each did.

Finally, both publics and policy makers should stop thinking of coercion as a a silver bullet to solve intractable foreign policy dilemmas. Coercion is no easier, only sometimes cheaper, and never much cheaper, than imposing demands by military victory.

If all coercion were a function of civilian vulnerability, then coercion would indeed often be cheap and easy. Quite small military forces can usually raise civilian costs enough to cause observable declines in the general welfare of population centers. Coercion would then be simply a matter of designing the correct formula of threats and actions, of sticks and carrots, to persuade that opposing population that they had something to lose by not altering their behavior.

Fortunately this is not the world we live in. If it were, military coercion would be far more common than it is. This means that advocates of counter-civilian coercion not only recommend harming innocent civilians, but they do so for no good purpose. Civilian threats are thus both wasteful and immoral. This lesson applies not only to the United States, but also to all states, including those in the Third World, which are increasingly acquiring modern aircraft and missiles that can strike at the homeland of other states. If a state faces the grim necessity of using air power for coercion, its leaders should think carefully about how to maximize the effects on the opponent's military strategy. This approach will not only be more effective but also harm fewer civilians.

---

[44] The Army's AirLand Battle Doctrine assigns air power a supporting role during intense ground engagements but does not explore how air power can exploit the vulnerabilities of enemy ground forces not currently in contact with friendly units.

Appendix: Coding Cases
of Coercive Air Power

BRITAIN–GERMANY, 1917

Germany tried to coerce Great Britain to withdraw from World War I by crippling British civilian morale through submarine blockade and the bombing of British cities.[1] The coercive campaign failed, as the denial theory would have predicted.

British civilian vulnerability in 1917 was medium, meaning that the risks to individuals had risen to the point that major parts of the population made adjustments in their daily lives to lower the threat. David Lloyd George, former prime minister, later recalled, "At the slightest rumor of approaching aeroplanes, tubes and tunnels were packed with panic-stricken men, women and children."[2] In London, it was common for 100,000 to 300,000 people to take shelter in the underground railways on the night of an attack.[3]

In 1917 Allied military vulnerability in the west was medium. The current situation was unstable because the French army was near to collapse, but the British were able to solidify the front by taking added military measures. By 1917 the British were reaching the peak of their ability to mobilize resources and so had large new armies to bring pressure to bear on Germany which would relieve pressure on the French. In May 1917, 3.2 million Allied troops faced 2.8 million Germans on the

---

[1] For overviews of this case, see George H. Quester, *Deterrence before Hiroshima* (New York: John Wiley, 1966), pp. 17–49; H. A. Jones, *The War in the Air* (Oxford: Clarendon Press, 1935), vol. 5; Douglas H. Robinson, *The Zeppelin in Combat* (London: Foulis, 1962).

[2] David Lloyd George, *War Memoirs* (Boston: Little, Brown, 1934), 6: 117–18. Also see *Air Raid Damage in London*, Report no. 20 (London: British Fire Prevention Committee, 1923); L. E. O. Charlton, *War over England* (London: Hutchinson, 1936).

[3] Jones, *War in the Air* 5:89–90.

western front.[4] In the summer the British were thus able to take the offensive at Passchendaele; this offensive, though it did not portend an Allied victory in the west, did divert German effort from the French and bought time to bring the United States into the war. Germany's air raids had little effect on this strategy. None of Britain's war industries was significantly affected, although production at some individual factories occasionally dropped because of temporary absentism following a nearby strike.[5]

BRITAIN–SOMALI REBELS, 1920

Since 1900 a group of rebels led by Sayyid Muhammed, the so-called Mad Mullah, had occasionally attacked isolated British military posts in Somaliland. After the Mullah and his fighters had captured a fort and a naval blockade failed to dislodge them, in January 1920 the British decided to use air power against the rebels. A dozen bombers were allocated to the task and bombed for three weeks. Coercion succeeded as the denial theory would have predicted and the Mullah and his followers fled across the border into the Ogaden region of Ethiopia, abandoning their military operations throughout Somaliland. Before the end of the year, Sayyid Muhammed died and the rebellion was over.

Rebel civilian vulnerability was nil, because RAF bombing was directed only against a fort occupied by enemy fighters and made no efforts to threaten civilian targets.

Military vulnerability was high, because the air assault on the rebel stronghold destroyed the fort, leaving the Mullah's fighters completely exposed to attack by British ground forces.[6]

BRITAIN–TURKEY, 1920S

Although the RAF throughout the 1920s was engaged in suppressing tribal rebellions in Iraq, between 1922 and 1924 it was also called on to repel

[4] Correlli Barnett, *The Swordbearers: Supreme Command in the First World War* (Bloomington: Indiana University Press, 1963), p. 203.

[5] On British strategy, see Paul Guinn, *British Strategy and Policy, 1914–1918* (Oxford: Oxford University Press, 1965); and Paul M. Kennedy, "The First World War and the International Power System," *International Security* 9 (Summer 1984): 20–23. For the effects of Germany's air attack against London in World War I, see Basil Collier, *A History of Air Power* (London: Weidenfeld and Nicolson, 1974), pp. 61–82.

[6] Bruce Hoffman, *British Air Power in Peripheral Conflict, 1919–1976*, R-3749-AF (Santa Monica: Rand, 1989), pp. 4–8; David J. Dean, "Air Power in Small Wars: The British Air Control Experience," *Air University Review* 34 (July–Aug. 1983), pp. 24–26; Chaz Bowyer, *History of the RAF* (Greenwich, Conn.: Bison Books, 1977), p. 51.

an external threat to Iraq's territorial integrity from Turkey. British rule in the oil-rich Mosul region in the northwest corner of Iraq was simultaneously challenged by the restive indigenous Kurdish population and by Turkish efforts to incorporate the area into its republic. Many skirmishes occurred between Turkish and local ground forces until 1924 when RAF bombers routed a large Turkish cavalry formation that had crossed into Iraq.[7] The denial theory would have predicted success, and indeed, British bombers succeeded in compelling Turkey to abandon efforts to control Mosul, despite the large numbers of Turkish soldiers still massed on the border capable of continuing military operations.

Turkish civilian vulnerability was nil, because RAF bombing struck military targets away from population centers, mainly enemy troop concentrations and lines of communication, and because British leaders made no efforts to signal an intention to hit civilian targets in the future.

Military vulnerability was high, meaning that Turkey could not control the Mosul region with its current forces and the success of future efforts was very much in doubt, although the balance of theater forces favored the Turks eighteen thousand to fifteen thousand.[8] As the local RAF commander noted, "There can be no doubt that any advance against us would have been very seriously hindered." The RAF's ability to blunt Turkey's 1924 incursion, in the words of the main historian of the period, "convinced the local tribesmen that any attempt to recover Mosul would be firmly resisted." With its strategy blunted, Turkey withdrew all troops in October 1924.[9]

ITALY-ETHIOPIA, 1936

In 1936 Italy tried to coerce Ethiopia to accept annexation to the Italian colonial empire.[10] Coercion failed, as the denial theory would have predicted. Ethiopia was annexed to the Italian empire but only after battlefield victory.

---

[7] David E. Omissi, *Air Power and Colonial Control: The Royal Air Force, 1919–1939* (New York: St. Martin's, 1990), pp. 29–33; Sir John Salmond, "The Air Force in Iraq," *Journal of the Royal United Service Institution* 70 (August 1925): 483–84. For a general description of this case, see Bruce Hoffman, *British Air Power in Peripheral Conflict, 1919–1976* (Santa Monica, Calif.: Rand Corporation, 1989), pp. 18–19; and E. J. Kingston-McCloughry, "The Gordon-Shephard Memorial Prize Essay," *Royal Air Force Quarterly* 5 (July 1934): 208.

[8] Omissi, *Air Power and Colonial Control*, p. 30; Salmond, "Air Force in Iraq," pp. 486, 487.

[9] Salmond, "Air Force in Iraq," p. 490; Omissi, *Air Power and Colonial Control*, p. 35.

[10] For overviews of the war, see Thomas M. Coffey, *Lion by the Tail: The Story of the Italian-Ethiopian War* (New York: Viking, 1974); Angelo Del Boca, *The Ethiopian War, 1935–1941* (Chicago: University of Chicago Press, 1969); John H. Spencer, *Ethiopia at Bay: A Personal Account of the Haile Selassie Years* (Algonac, Mich.: Reference, 1984); and Anthony Mockler, *Haile Selassie's War: The Italian-Ethiopian Campaign, 1935–1941* (New York: Random House, 1984).

Ethiopian civilian vulnerability was high, meaning that the numbers affected and the consequences were so severe that major parts of the population were uncertain about whether they would survive. Although total damage statistics are unavailable, Italian planes regularly bombed towns throughout Ethiopia and used poison gas on at least eighteen occasions, which significantly increased civilian costs. Ethiopian Emperor Haile Selassie said, "In order to kill off systematically all living creatures, in order more thoroughly to poison waters and pastures, the Italian Command made its aircraft pass over again and again. The very refinement of barbarism consisted of carrying ravage and terror into the most densely populated parts of the territory. The object was to scatter fear and death over a great part of the Ethiopian territory."[11] Best estimates are that Ethiopian deaths totalled 225,000, or approximately 2 percent of the population.[12]

Ethiopia's military vulnerability during most of the strategic bombing campaign was medium, meaning that although its prospects of success were uncertain, its leaders believed that additional defensive measures would prevent the loss of their homeland. The Ethiopians tried to exploit superior numbers against a better-equipped enemy by mass attacks with lightly armed forces designed to inflicting large numbers of casualties on the Italians. Since the Ethiopians were able to deploy their forces in large independent groupings, dispersed across the country, they were able to pursue this strategy until each major area of the country was conquered.[13] Although there is no evidence of the Ethiopian emperor's military assessments before and during the war, a close adviser on foreign affairs believed as late as 15 April, just weeks before the final Italian offensives, that "we were but a few weeks away from the heavy rains, during which period the military advantage would clearly be on the side of the Ethiopian regular and guerrilla troops."[14]

SPANISH CIVIL WAR, 1936–1939

Nationalists and Loyalists contended for control of Spain.[15] Coercion failed. The Nationalists won the war but were unable to coerce the Loyalists

---

[11] Selassie quoted in J. F. C. Fuller, *The First of the League Wars* (London: Eyre and Spottiswoode, 1936), pp. 79–80.

[12] Del Boca, *Ethiopian War*, p. 206; Melvin Small and J. David Singer, *Resort to Arms: International and Civil Wars, 1816–1980* (Beverly Hills, Calif.: Sage, 1982), p. 90.

[13] This account follows the excellent operational history of Pedro A. del Valle, *Roman Eagles over Ethiopia* (Harrisburgh, Pa.: Military Service, 1940).

[14] Spencer, *Ethiopia at Bay*, p. 55.

[15] General histories include Hugh Thomas, *The Spanish Civil War*, rev. and enlarged ed. (New York: Harper and Row, 1986); Pierre Broue and Emile Temime, *The Revolution and the Civil War in Spain* (Cambridge: MIT Press, 1970); Gabriel Jackson, *The Spanish Republic and the Civil War, 1931–1939* (Princeton: Princeton University Press, 1965); Herbert R. Southworth, *Guernica! Guernica!* (Berkeley: University of California Press, 1977); and Raymond L. Proctor, *Hitler's Luftwaffe in the Spanish Civil War* (Westport, Conn.: Greenwood, 1983).

into surrendering before they were completely defeated. The denial theory would have rightly predicted failure in 1936–October 1938 and wrongly predicted success in October 1938–April 1939.

Loyalist civilian vulnerability is coded as low to medium in the earlier period, meaning that, despite some risk to individuals, no major part of the population made adjustments or compromises in their daily lives to avoid the threat. The Nationalist air force, consisting of German and Italian formations, mounted many operations against urban targets (e.g., Madrid, Granollers, Nules, Durango, Costellon de la Plana), the largest of which, against Guernica, killed about a thousand people.[16] An observer of the March 1938 raids on Barcelona noted: "The ever-present menace of death from the air . . . , the uncertainty and suspense of that peril appeared to have shaken the nerve of even the bravest. In spite of this . . . the people realized the importance of calm and made gallant efforts to carry on unperturbed as if everything were normal."[17]

At that time Loyalist military vulnerability is coded as medium, meaning that although the Loyalist front was not strong at any time, Loyalist leaders believed that added defensive measures, mainly in the form of greater foreign assistance, could reduce the threat. In general, the Spanish Civil War was fought in a series of set-piece battles, because logistics constrained both sides from fighting more than one battle at a time. The Loyalists waged a war of attrition to protract the conflict until international support could shift decisively in their favor. By forcing the Nationalists into long battles for every gain, the Loyalists were able to remain in control of large sections of the country.

After October 1938 the military vulnerability of the Loyalists increased to high, meaning that although they still had considerable forces and could impose high costs on the Nationalists, they could not stave off defeat if the fighting persisted. The key changes were the Munich Accord, signed at the end of September 1938, which removed any hope of British or French aid, and the beginning of the Nationalist offensive in Catalonia on 23 December which eliminated one of the two major Loyalist enclaves. General fear of reprisals at the hands of the victors and, on the part of the Communists, ideological hatred of the Fascists prevented surrender.[18]

Although the war did not end until 31 March 1939, when the last cities were occupied by the Nationalists, the Loyalist forces had already lost their capacity for armed resistance. After the rebels captured Barcelona on 26 January, large numbers of Loyalist soldiers either surrendered piecemeal or left

---

[16] The most detailed analysis of the air war against civilians in the Spanish Civil War is Hilton P. Goss, *Civilian Morale under Aerial Bombardment, 1914–1939* (Maxwell Air Force Base, Ala.: Air University Press, 1948), pp. 143–278. The most recent numbers on Guernica's casualties are found in Thomas, *Spanish Civil War*, p. 625.

[17] Quoted in Goss, *Civilian Morale*, p. 219.

[18] Thomas, *Spanish Civil War*, pp. 579–95.

Spain altogether. When Franco launched his final offensive on 26 March, the war quickly came to an end with little resistance.[19]

JAPAN–CHINA, 1937–1945

Japan tried to control northern China and parts of central China (areas around Hopei, Shantung, Chahar, Suiyuan, Shansi, and Shensi, and Nanking-Shanghai). The main period of strategic bombing occurred from 1939 to 1941 when the Japanese launched many raids against Chinese cities.[20] As the denial theory would have predicted, China refused to accept Japanese control over this territory.

Chinese civilian vulnerability was high, meaning that the numbers affected and the consequences were so severe, that major parts of the population were uncertain about whether they would survive. From April 1938 to December 1941, the period for which detailed numbers are available, 266,000 civilian casualties were inflicted by air strikes on urban areas. As part of their countercivilian strategy, the Japanese made many incendiary raids against residential or commercial centers of cities. About half of the downtown business district of Chungking, for instance, was burned out.[21] In all, it is estimated that some 6 million Chinese civilians were killed.[22]

Chinese military vulnerability to Japan was medium, meaning that although the Chinese government's ability to retain control over the north was tenuous, its leaders believed added defensive measures could improve their prospects. After losing two major battles in 1937 and significant territory, Chinese leaders adopted a new strategy of mobile and guerrilla warfare to restore the antebellum status quo by attriting Japanese strength over time. Chinese leaders believed that Japanese military strength would decline because Japan had exhausted its reserves and could never reduce its defense against the Soviet Union. Chinese confidence may actually have increased in later years. Even though the Chinese military continued to lose ground in the north, it delivered one blow after another against Japanese

---

[19] Jackson, *Spanish Republic*, pp. 265–477; Raymond L. Proctor, "A Military History of the Spanish Civil War, *1936–1939*," in *Historical Dictionary of the Spanish Civil War, 1936–1939*, ed. James W. Cortada (Westport, Conn.: Greenwood, 1982), pp. 530–31.

[20] Chinese Ministry of Information, *China Handbook, 1937–1943: A Comprehensive Survey of Major Developments in China in Six Years of War* (New York: Macmillan, 1943); Hsu Long-jsen and Chang Ming-kai, *History of the Sino-Japanese War (1937–1945)*, trans. Wen Ha-hsiung (Taiwan: Republic of China, 1971); Hsi-Sheng Ch'i, *Nationalist China at War: Military Defeats and Political Collapse* (Ann Arbor: University of Michigan Press, 1982); and John H. Boyle, *China and Japan at War, 1937–1945* (Stanford: Stanford University Press, 1972); and, F. F. Liu, *A Military History of Modern China, 1924–1949* (Princeton: Princeton University Press, 1956), p. 198.

[21] Chinese Ministry of Information, *China Handbook*, pp. 715, 724, 818.

[22] Vincent J. Esposito, *A Concise History of World War II* (New York: Praeger, 1989), p. 401.

forces in Burma until it scored a victory and cleared the ground for an accelerated flow of American lend-lease material into China in the spring of 1945. At the same time, Japanese forces were fast becoming a hollow army as a result of the American blockade.[23]

GERMANY–BRITAIN/FRANCE 1938

Germany attempted to acquire the Sudetenland in Czechoslovakia, which was important to France and Britain, albeit to varying degrees, in the context of a general European war. The Sudetenland was vital to the effective defense of Czechoslovakia during war because it housed a series of fortifications, and so its loss would jeopardize Czechoslovakia as an independent military power in Eastern Europe. The existence of an independent Czechoslovakia was the linchpin of the European security system devised after World War I. Its location and military strength ensured that an aggressive Germany would have to fight a two-front war rather than deal with its opponents piecemeal.[24] The denial theory would have predicted success, and indeed, Germany compelled Britain and France to put pressure on Czechoslovakia to abandon the Sudetenland.

During the Czech crisis, British and French civilian vulnerability was high, meaning that the expected losses and consequences were so severe that major parts of the population would not survive. Throughout the 1930s, British leaders feared the Luftwaffe could launch an aerial knockout blow against civilian morale. The basis of British leaders' expectations of the likely costs of a countercivilian air campaign by the Luftwaffe was a 1937 study by the Committee on Imperial Defence, which estimated 600,000 deaths and 1.2 million injuries over the first sixty days, estimates that were still believed in September 1938.[25]

The French also feared massive air attacks against their cities. The chief of the French Air Staff predicted on 26 September 1938 that Germany would immediately launch an all-out air offensive against France at the outset of

[23] For an excellent discussion of Chinese decision making during the Sino-Japanese war, see Ch'i, *Nationalist China at War*, pp. 40–82. For the importance of Chinese logistics, see R. Ernest Dupuy and Trevor N. Dupuy, eds., *The Encyclopedia of Military History from 3500 B.C. to the Present*, rev. ed. (New York: Harper and Row, 1977), p. 1125.

[24] If Germany were to command Czech territory, it would be able to deal with a war on its eastern border in short order. Germany could then surround Poland on three sides and isolate it and have a corridor that reached deep into the Balkans to provide a frontier with Hungary and Romania. Williamson Murray, *The Change in the European Balance of Power, 1938–1939: The Path to Ruin* (Princeton: Princeton University Press, 1984), pp. 290–93.

[25] Wesley K. Wark, *The Ultimate Enemy: British Intelligence and Nazi Germany, 1933–1939* (Ithaca: Cornell University Press, 1985), pp. 67–68; Uri Bialer, *In the Shadow of the Bomber: The Fear of Air Attack and British Politics, 1932–1939* (London: Royal Historical Society, 1980), p. 127; Richard M. Titmuss, *Problems of Social Policy* (London: HMSO, 1950), p. 13.

any war. The French foreign minister is reported to have said in early September 1938 that "French and British towns would be wiped out and little or no retaliation would be possible."[26]

The vulnerability of British and French military strategy was very high, meaning that the likelihood of a German victory over Czech forces approached certainty, regardless of the measures that could be taken. As Neville Chamberlain confided in private correspondence as early as 20 March 1938:

> You have only to look at the map to see that nothing that France or we could possibly do could save Czechoslovakia from being overrun by the Germans if they wanted to do it. . . . Therefore we could not help Czechoslovakia—she would simply be a pretext for going to war with Germany. That we could not think of unless we had a reasonable prospect of being able to bend her to her knees in a reasonable time, and of that I see no sign. I have therefore abandoned any idea of giving guarantees to Czechoslovakia or to France in connection with her obligations to that country.[27]

Similarly, the French ambassador in Berlin wired the French prime minister in July 1938 that "according to the plan which the Fuehrer had decided on, the first useful pretext offered by the Prague government will be seized. An unexpected and lightning attack will be launched against Czechoslovakia, whose fate will be militarily settled before any of the allies of this state have had time to move."[28]

GERMANY–BRITAIN/FRANCE, 1939

Germany wanted to acquire Danzig and rights to the German corridor in Poland. Britain, France, and Germany all saw their interests in the Polish crisis as strategic in nature, affecting whether German expansion would be deterred by the prospect of a two-front war.[29] The denial theory would have predicted that the Germans would prevail, but in fact, they did not. Britain and France were not compelled to put pressure on Poland to concede.

---

[26] Quoted in Herbert S. Dinerstein, "The Impact of Air Power on the International Scene, 1933–1940," *Military Affairs* 19 (Summer 1955): 69.

[27] Chamberlain quoted in Norman H. Gibbs, *Grand Strategy* (London: HMSO, 1976), 1: 314.

[28] François-Poncet to Daladier, July 6, 1938, quoted in Anthony Adamthwaite, *France and the Coming of the Second World War, 1936–1939* (London: Frank Cass, 1977), p. 195. Although many military historians now believe Germany would have lost a war in 1938, what matters for coercion is the expectations of the leaders of the target states. Murray, *Change in the European Balance of Power*.

[29] Martin Wright, "Germany," in *Survey of International Affairs, 1939–1946: The World in March 1939*, ed. Arnold Toynbee and Frank T. Ashton-Gwatkin (New York: Oxford University Press, 1952); Anita J. Prazmowski, "The Eastern Front and the British Guarantee to Poland of March 1939," *European History Quarterly* 14 (April 1984): 183–209.

British and French civilian vulnerability was high, meaning that large parts of their population were uncertain about whether they would survive. Although British air defenses improved in 1939 and the British became more optimistic that they could ride out a countercivilian air campaign by the Luftwaffe, the survival of large parts of the population remained in jeopardy. In April 1939 the Air Staff estimated that German bombers could deliver seven hundred tons a day in the opening two weeks of an air campaign, which, according to the then-current estimate of fifty casualties per ton, translated into thirty-five thousand casualties per day. A June 1939 Air Raid Defence League pamphlet estimated that 200,000 casualties would be suffered in the first ten days, and the government planned to evacuate 4 million urban dwellers (half of the total) in the first days of the air war; 1.5 million to 3.75 million actually evacuated.[30] French estimates are unavailable.

The vulnerability of British and French strategy was very high, meaning that the likelihood of a German victory over Polish forces approached certainty regardless of the measures that could be taken. During the winter of 1938–1939, British military assessments improved, not because of improvement in the numerical ratio of forces (which in some areas was worsening), but because of greater emphasis on latent economic strength. Nevertheless, the British still did not consider 1939 the optimum moment for a military challenge, nor were they confident that they could prevent Poland's defeat.[31] Thus, the denial theory would have forecast that the British would not maintain a commitment to Poland during the summer of 1939, but they did.

GERMANY–POLAND, 1939

The German invasion of Poland began on 1 September 1939, quickly breaking through Polish defensive lines. On 17 September, Russian divisions invaded Poland from the east. The next day, the Polish government fled to Romania, practically ending organized resistance, except for a few pockets in the southeastern portion of the country and the capitol city, Warsaw. To force Warsaw to capitulate, the Germans launched heavy air attacks at the residential portions of the city on 26 September. The same day German ground forces encircled the city and began overrunning its outer defenses. Coercion succeeded, as the denial theory would have predicted, and Warsaw and its 120,000 troops surrendered on 27 September.[32]

[30] Basil Collier, *The Defence of the United Kingdom* (London: HMSO, 1957), p. 77; Titmuss, *Problems of Social Policy*, pp. 10, 97, 102.

[31] Prazmowski, "Eastern Front," p. 208.

[32] Robert M. Kennedy, *The German Campaign in Poland, 1939* (Washington, D.C.: 1956); Williamson Murray, *The Change in the European Balance of Power, 1938–1939* (Princeton: Princeton University Press, 1984), pp. 310–53; Erich von Manstein, *Lost Victories* (Novato, Calif.: Presidio Press, 1982), pp. 21–63.

Civilian vulnerability was high. Although numerical casualty estimates were not reliably tallied, the Nazis made a propaganda film, "Baptism of Fire," assembled from newsreel pictures of the campaign, which showed that substantial sections of Warsaw had been flattened.[33]

Military vulnerability was very high. Encircled by approximately 880,000 men of Germany Army Group South and with the Red Army advancing from the east, Warsaw had little hope, because both defense against and heavy attrition of enemy forces were impossible.

SOVIET UNION–FINLAND, 1939–1940

After occupying Latvia, Estonia, and Lithuania in October 1939, the Soviet Union demanded that Finland concede significant parts of its territory. Soviet aircraft bombed Helsinki and Viipuri on 30 November. The denial theory would have predicted success, and in fact, the Finns conceded on 12 March 1940 after a Soviet offensive captured part of southeastern Finland. They surrendered the parts of Finnish soil that the Soviets demanded and that they believed they could not defend, even though they retained the capacity for continuing military operations.[34]

Finish civilian vulnerability was medium, meaning that the risk to individuals had risen to the point that major parts of the population made adjustments in their daily lives to lower the threat. The Russians launched 2,075 bombing attacks against civilian targets in 516 localities. Although these raids inflicted only modest direct costs, killing about 650 civilians and wounding 2,000 or so, historians credit the aerial offensive with wreaking havoc on the private lives of civilians, who were forced to abandon bombed-out buildings and to adhere to strict civil defense measures during the war. Over 10 percent of civilians lost their homes from all causes during the war.[35]

Finnish military vulnerability was high, meaning that the Finns lacked the ability to control the disputed territory by defeating Soviet forces but retained the ability to inflict attrition to reduce the Soviet commitment to remain on Finnish soil. Soviet armies entering Finland totaled nearly one million men, which were opposed by 300,000 Finnish fighters.[36] Finnish strategy was to engage Soviet conventional troops in guerrilla and light-infantry warfare in massive forest regions, where heavy Russian troops

[33] Fritz M. Sallagar, *The Road to Total War: Escalation in World War II* R-465-PR (Santa Monica: Rand, 1969), p. 36.

[34] Dupuy and Dupuy, *Encyclopedia of Military History*, pp. 1054–55.

[35] William R. Trotter, *A Frozen Hell: The Russo-Finnish Winter War of 1939–1940* (Chapel Hill, N.C.: Algonquin, 1991), pp. 188, 263; and Allen F. Chew, *The White Death: The Epic of the Soviet-Finnish Winter War* (East Lansing: Michigan State University Press, 1971), p. 127.

[36] Ibid., p. 1054.

would bog down in the snow. This strategy achieved some initial successes, but broke down as the Finns could not replace casualties suffered in repeated Soviet offensives. Soviet countercivilian air raids had no effect on Finnish morale. Once the war began, the Finns were fighting not only for the initial territory at issue but for sovereignty. Although the ultimate concessions cost Finland its standing military forces, the Soviet military losses made Stalin eager for a negotiated settlement, because they endangered the Soviet position against the Japanese and Germans.[37]

GERMANY–NETHERLANDS, 1940

On 10 May 1940 German forces moved into the Netherlands, and on 13 May they bombed the business section of Rotterdam. The Netherlands surrendered on 14 May with its main formations still intact, as the denial theory would have predicted.[38]

Dutch civilian vulnerability was high, meaning that the numbers affected and the consequences were expected to be so severe that major parts of the population were uncertain about whether they would survive. On the morning of 14 May the Dutch received the German threat that, unless resistance were discontinued, Rotterdam and Utrecht would be destroyed from the air, and other towns would meet the same fate.[39] A member of the Dutch General Staff recalls: "Everyone who knows Dutch towns . . . will realize what the execution of this threat on centers of population numbering from 400,000 to 800,00 people would have meant. The fate of Rotterdam, where the threat was carried into effect by an attack of at least fifty bombing aircraft, is an eloquent example of what would have ensued."[40]

Dutch military vulnerability was very high, meaning that the likelihood of complete defeat had approached certainty because neither defense nor heavy attrition of enemy forces was expected to be possible. The Dutch strategy, to blow up all bridges across the Rhine in the event of attack to prevent the Germans from entering the Netherlands, was thwarted when Germany dropped paratroopers behind the lines to prevent the destruction of several key bridges until the arrival of heavy ground forces on 14 May.[41]

---

[37] Dupuy and Dupuy, *Encyclopedia of Military History*, p. 1054; and Tomas Ries, *Cold Will: The Defense of Finland* (London: Brassey's 1988), pp. 83–84.

[38] B. H. Liddell Hart, *History of the Second World War* (New York: Putnam's, 1970), p. 67.

[39] Estimates of civilians killed in Rotterdam vary from one thousand to thirty thousand. J. R. M. Butler, *Grand Strategy* (London: HMSO, 1957), vol. 2, app. 1, pp. 569–70; Eelco Nicolaas van Kleffens, *Juggernaut over Holland: The Dutch Foreign Minister's Personal Story of the Invasion of the Netherlands* (New York: Columbia University Press, 1941), p. 131.

[40] Quoted in P. L. G. Doorman, *Military Operations in the Netherlands from 10th–17th May, 1940*, trans. S. L. Salzedo (London: George Allen and Unwin, 1944), p. 81.

[41] Van Kleffens, *Juggernaut over Holland*, pp. 117–18.

The Dutch Foreign Minister summarized the position on 14 May: "Either the Allies were to send adequate assistance without delay, and in that case we would fight on, or, if such adequate assistance could not be sent, the Dutch military commanders were to be empowered to act as they judged best. ... [Mr. Churchill] was completely frank, and various measures of assistance were at once taken, but they could not be extensive enough to save the situation."[42]

GERMANY–BRITAIN, 1940–1941

Germany tried to coerce Britain to withdraw from the war by threatening to invade the British home islands and by bombing raids against British cities. Had Germany succeeded, the British would have accepted German hegemony on the Continent. As the denial theory would have predicted, coercion failed, and Britain refused to withdraw from the war.

British civilian vulnerability was high, meaning that the numbers affected and the consequences were expected to be so severe that major parts of the population were uncertain about whether they would survive. In 1940 and 1941 over 44,000 were killed, 143,000 were hospitalized, and 98,000 were treated in local first-aid stations. Between September 1939 and September 1941, after 1.5 to 3.75 million had already evacuated large cities, the government evacuated an additional 1.6 million people.[43]

British military vulnerability was medium, meaning that although the current military situation was uncertain, risks could be reduced by attrition of the Luftwaffe and bombing Germany. In the event of invasion the balance of available ground forces favored Germany, which had thirty-nine army divisions in the west to Britain's twenty-nine home forces divisions and eight brigades.[44] Thus, Britain lacked sufficient land strength to defeat the Germans once ashore. Accordingly, its strategy relied on the Royal Navy to block any invasion, and the navy depended on air power to defend the fleet against German air attack. The Luftwaffe attempted to gain air superiority by knocking out the main airfields of the Royal Air Force in southern England. Initially the campaign achieved considerable success in wearing down British airfields, fighter direction systems, and pilot reserves. When, in retaliation for British terror bombing, the Germans shifted their attacks from these weak points in the British air defense

---

[42] Quoted in Ibid., pp. 139–40.

[43] Titmuss, *Problems of Social Policy*, pp. 559, 560, 563. For a detailed account of the effects of strategic bombing on British morale, see Tom Harrison, *Living through the Blitz* (New York: Schocken, 1976).

[44] Liddell Hart, *Second World War*, p. 89; Peter Fleming, *Operation Sea Lion* (New York: Simon and Schuster, 1957), p. 179.

system to bombing the city of London, however, the air defenses were able to recover.[45]

UNITED STATES–ITALY, 1943

The United States tried to compel Italy to surrender by invading and bombing the homeland. The denial theory would have forecast success, and Italy did indeed surrender on 8 September 1943, before its forces were decisively defeated or the country was occupied.[46]

Italian civilian vulnerability was medium, meaning that the risk to individuals had risen to the point that major parts of the population made compromises or adjustments in their daily lives, but large parts of the population were not uncertain of their survival. From October 1942 to August 1943, Allied air raids against Italian cities caused about 3,700 deaths and 8,400 injuries, compelling large parts of the population to adopt civil defense measures.[47]

Italian military vulnerability was very high, meaning that the likelihood of complete defeat approached certainty because neither defense against nor heavy attrition of enemy forces was possible. The confidence of Italian leaders in their ability to defeat an Allied invasion was completely undermined when the conquest of Sicily took only a few days. Requests for additional German help were refused.[48] In a memorandum to Mussolini on 14 July, the Italian chief of staff stated that the Allies would be able to invade the Italian peninsula at will unless the main weight of the Axis effort was shifted to the Mediterranean. If not, "it pertained to the highest political au-

---

[45] Len Deighton, *Fighter: The True Story of the Battle of Britain* (London: Johnathan Cape, 1977); Derek Wood and Derek Dempster, *The Narrow Margin: The Battle of Britain and the Rise of Air Power, 1930–1940* (London: Hutchinson, 1961); and John Terraine, *A Time for Courage: The Royal Air Force in the European War, 1939–1945* (New York: Macmillan, 1985). For evidence that Churchill was deliberately trying to provoke the Germans into countercivilian attacks by sending bombers against German civilians in Berlin, see Harvey B. Tress, "Churchill, the First Berlin Raids, and the Blitz: A New Interpretation," *Militargeschichtliche Mitteilungen* 32, no. 2 (1982): 65–78.

[46] The main accounts of Italy's surrender are Albert N. Garland and Howard McGraw Smyth, *Sicily and the Surrender of Italy* (Washington, D.C.: Department of the Army, 1965); F. W. Deakin, *The Brutal Friendship: Mussolini, Hitler, and the Fall of Italian Fascism* (New York: Harper and Row, 1962); Melton S. Davis, *Who Defends Rome? The Forty-Five Days, July 25–September 8, 1943* (New York: Dial Press, 1972); Peter Tompkins, *Italy Betrayed* (New York: Simon and Schuster, 1966); and Paul Kecskemeti, *Strategic Surrender: The Politics of Victory and Defeat* (Stanford: Stanford University Press, 1958).

[47] Histories generally do not estimate Italian civilian casualties due to air attack. My estimates were calculated from Martin Middlebrook and Chris Everitt, *The Bomber Command War Diaries: An Operational Reference Book, 1939–1945* (New York: Viking, 1985), pp. 318, 319, 325, 327, 331, 351, 406, 419, 421, 422; and Henry Adams, *Italy at War* (Alexandria, Va.: Time-Life Books, 1982), p. 156.

[48] Tompkins, *Italy Betrayed*, p. 34.

thorities to consider if it be not appropriate to spare the country further fighting and defeats, and to anticipate the end of the struggle, given that the final result will undoubtedly be worse within one or two years."[49]

GERMANY–BRITAIN, 1944–1945

Germany launched flying bomb (V-1) and rocket (V-2) attacks against British cities from 12 June 1944 to 27 March 1945 to coerce the Allies to reduce their demands for unconditional surrender.[50] The British made no change in their demands, as the denial theory would have predicted.

British civilian vulnerability was medium, meaning that the risks to individuals had risen to the point that major parts of the population made adjustments or compromises in their daily lives to lower the threat. Before the attacks, the Air Ministry estimated that the maximum scale of the attack would be less than half the size of the heaviest previous raids. After the attack, there was a much shorter period of evacuation than in 1940–1941, lasting only two months and involving about a million people, who quickly returned. Shelters were used by only one-seventh as many people. All told, flying bomb and rocket attacks killed about nine thousand and seriously injured about twenty-five thousand.[51]

British military vulnerability was low, meaning that there was some risk its military strategy against Germany would fail but not enough to warrant additional efforts. In the last year of the war, Allied military strategy called for a series of large-scale offensives against the western and eastern borders of Germany to defeat German ground forces. This strategy depended not only on Allied superiority in aggregate resources but also on Allied willingness to suffer the costs of attriting German forces defending many lines in succession. Germany's air attack did not substantially reduce British prospects because it had no practical effect on the British economy, added little to the much greater costs the British were paying on

[49] Quoted in Garland and Smyth, *Sicily and the Surrender of Italy*, pp. 240–41. Mussolini appears to have shared these views, writing to Hitler on 18 July: "The sacrifice of my country cannot have as its principal purpose that of delaying a direct attack on Germany. . . . My country . . . has exhausted itself, burning up resources in Africa, Russia, and the Balkans. . . . the time has come for us to examine the situation . . . in order to draw from it the consequences conforming to our common interests and to those of each of our countries." Quoted ibid., p. 242.

[50] Overviews include Jozef Garlinski, *Hitler's Last Weapons: The Underground War against the V-1 and V-2* (New York: Times Books, 1978); Richard Brown Baker, *The Year of the Buzz Bomb: A Journal of London, 1944* (New York: Exposition Press, 1952); and Collier, *Defence of the United Kingdom*, pp. 331–422.

[51] Titmuss, *Problems of Social Policy*, pp. 427–29; Terence H. O'Brien, *Civil Defence* (London: HMSO, 1955), pp. 650–51, 657, 667; Collier, *Defence of the United Kingdom*, p. 528.

the Continent, and induced the Allies to shift only 6 percent of their bombing effort to V sites.[52]

UNITED STATES–GERMANY, 1945

The United States tried to force Germany to surrender by invading and bombing the homeland. Though the denial theory would have predicted successful coercion, the Germans refused to surrender and the Allies achieved a battlefield victory.

German civilian vulnerability was very high, meaning that large parts of the population were certain not to survive if military operations continued.

German military vulnerability was also very high after January 1945, meaning that German forces in being could no longer hold any line for very long and could not impose attrition on the advancing forces for long.

UNITED STATES–JAPAN, 1945

The United States tried to force Japan to surrender by bombing and threatening to invade the homeland. This coercion succeeded, as the denial theory would have predicted. Japan agreed to American occupation of the home islands.

Japanese civilian vulnerability was very high, meaning that major parts of the population were certain not to survive American air attacks on cities.

Japanese military vulnerability was also very high, meaning that continued military operations to defend against an American invasion or inflict large casualties on invading forces were certain to fail.

U.S.–CHINA AND NORTH KOREA, 1950–1953

During the Korean War, the United Nations set out to compel the Chinese and North Koreans to accept a territorial division of Korea as well as a permanent U.N. military presence to guarantee the security of the South. As the denial theory would predict, on 26 November 1951 Communist negotiators agreed to U.N. territorial demands. The war did not end at this point because the U.S. further insisted that prisoners could only be repatriated voluntarily, which the Communists accepted, after nuclear risk threats, on 4 June 1953.

[52] O'Brien, *Civil Defence*, p. 654; Collier, *Defence of the United Kingdom*, pp. 367–422; British Bombing Survey Unit, *The Strategic Air War against Germany, 1939–1945* (London: HMSO, 1947), table 13.

In 1950 and 1951, civilian vulnerability was medium. North Korean cities were bombed in 1950, but it caused no fire-storms similar to those in World War II. The bombing of Pyongyang reportedly gutted the industrial areas of the city but hardly damaged civilian neighborhoods.

Military vulnerability was high. In spring 1951 U.N. forces were advancing against overextended Communist troops and defeated major Communist counter-offensives in early Summer. By mid-June it was clear that the UN could defend the military status quo and that any attempt by the Communists to retake ground would be prohibitively costly. As the denial theory would have predicted, the Communists conceded the existence of an independent South Korea supported by large numbers of American troops.

In May 1953, the Eisenhower administration used credible nuclear threats to compel the Communists to accept UN demands on prisoner repatriation. The denial theory would have predicted success, and in fact, the Communists agreed to end the war.

In 1953, Chinese and Korean civilian vulnerability was very high, meaning that if the U.S. had employed significant numbers of nuclear weapons, major parts of these populations would have been certain not to survive.

The military vulnerability of the Chinese and North Koreans was medium. The loss of their offensive military prospects did nothing to undermine the Communists bargaining power on the POW issue. Neither side could get its prisoners back without the consent of the other and the Communists faced no danger of total defeat.

FRANCE–ALGERIAN REBELS, 1954–1962

On 31 October 1954 the nationalist Front de la Liberation Nationale opposed French control of Algeria. The French responded with air and ground forces to compel the rebels to abandon their aims.[53] Coercion failed, as would have been expected from the denial theory. Algeria became independent in 1962.

The French routinely used harsh methods against civilian groups suspected of being loyal to the rebels, but accounts of the numbers of incidents and casualties vary widely and there is no systematic history of the reaction of the population to these attacks. Since most accounts include numbers of

---

[53] For general accounts, see Joseph Kraft, *The Struggle for Algeria* (Garden City, N.Y.: Doubleday, 1961); Concepts Division, Aerospace Studies Institute, *Guerrilla Warfare and Airpower in Algeria, 1954–1960* (Maxwell Air Force Base, Ala.: Air University Press, 1965); Edgar O'Ballance, *The Algerian Insurrection, 1954–1962* (Hamden, Conn.: Archon, 1967); Alistair Horne, *A Savage War of Peace: Algeria, 1954–1962* (New York: Viking, 1978); and William B. Quandt, *Revolution and Political Leadership: Algeria, 1954–1968* (Cambridge: MIT Press, 1969).

civilian casualties in the tens of thousands, civilian vulnerability is coded as medium to high.[54]

Military vulnerability was low, because the rebels adopted a guerrilla strategy to persuade increasingly large parts of the population to use in subversion against the French. The rebel strategy was to seize control of remote villages where French presence was especially light or nonexistent; draft the young men into committing subversive acts, which branded them and their families as outlaws; and then after having won the minds of a local populace through a spreading circle of complicity, start the process over in nearby villages.[55] Air power could do little against this strategy. It could destroy some military capability and punish sympathizers, but the rebel strategy required little logistical support and the rebels could easily redirect their ideological campaign toward new parts of the population.

BRITAIN/FRANCE–EGYPT, 1956

Gamal Abdel Nasser, president of Egypt, nationalized the Suez Canal on 26 July 1956, precipitating a major international crisis which ended with the Suez operation of October–November. On 31 October 1956, following Israel's assault in the Sinai, France and Britain issued an ultimatum calling on Egypt to withdraw from the Suez Canal, which Egypt rejected. Franco-British forces then began bombing Egyptian air bases and on 5 November invaded the canal zone. Nevertheless, as the denial theory would have predicted, Egypt did not accept a cease-fire, relenting only when Soviet and American intervention compelled an end to the war on 7 November.[56]

Egyptian civilian vulnerability was low, meaning that although there was some risk to individuals, no major part of the population made adjustments or compromises in their daily lives to avoid the threat. Prior to the crisis, Britain and France tried to precipitate a popular revolt against Nasser by raising Egyptian civilian vulnerability to the point that the population would overthrow him. The plan was to gain air superiority in the first days, then launch an eight-to-ten-day "aero-psychological" campaign, bombing economic targets such as oil installations, bridges, and railway stations and dropping leaflets and haranguing the population with loudspeakers, but not actually inflicting civilian casualties.[57] Although parts of this plan were

[54] Horne, *Savage War*, pp. 26–27, 112–22; Kraft, *Struggle for Algeria*, p. 103.

[55] Alf Andrew Heggoy, *Insurgency and Counterinsurgency in Algeria* (Bloomington: Indiana University Press, 1972), pp. 95–98.

[56] Dupuy and Dupuy, *Encyclopedia of Military History*, pp. 1228, 1278. General accounts include Keith Kyle, *Suez* (New York: St. Martin's, 1991); Hugh Thomas, *Suez* (New York: Harper and Row, 1966); A. J. Barker, *Suez: The Seven Day War* (New York: Praeger, 1964); Donald Neff, *Warriors at Suez* (New York: Simon and Schuster, 1981); and W. Roger Louis and Roger Owen, *Suez, 1956: The Crisis and Its Consequences* (Oxford: Clarendon Press, 1989).

[57] André Beaufré, *The Suez Expedition, 1956*, trans. Richard Barry (New York: Praeger, 1969), pp. 54–55.

implemented—leaflets were dropped and the transmitter of Cairo Radio was destroyed—international pressure to end hostilities persuaded Britain and France to invade and shift the air campaign to military targets sooner than they had planned.[58]

Egyptian military vulnerability was medium, meaning that although the current position was in jeopardy, the threat could be reduced by additional defensive measures. Egypt's strategy was to concentrate its forces in the Canal Zone and attack the invasion force as it advanced after landing. A top Egyptian source recalls: "Nasser thought that in general the British and French invasion forces were not strong enough. His estimation was that if they continued to advance they would be vulnerable once they came out of the protected strip from Port Said to El Qantara."[59]

SOVIET UNION–BRITAIN/FRANCE, 1956

On 5 November 1956, the Soviet Union responded to the Anglo-French invasion of Egypt by issuing a nuclear ultimatum through official messages to Britain, France, and Israel, which were also broadcast over Moscow radio. "In what position would Britain have found herself," read the letter to Prime Minister Anthony Eden, "if she herself had been attacked by more powerful states possessing every kind of modern destructive weapons? And there are countries now which need not have sent a navy or air force to the coast of Britain but could have used other means, such as rocket technique."[60] On 6 November, as the denial theory would have predicted, Britain and France agreed to withdraw.

British and French civilian vulnerability was very high, meaning that large parts of their populations would have been certain not to survive a Soviet nuclear attack. Britain and France had no nuclear weapons capable of destroying targets in the Soviet Union, but the Soviet Union had over three hundred warheads capable of reaching targets in Britain and France.[61]

---

[58] M. J. Armitage and R. A. Mason, *Air Power in the Nuclear Age* (Urbana, IL: University of Illinois Press, 1985), pp. 214–23; Roy Fullick and Geoffrey Powell, *Suez: The Double War* (London: Hamish Hamilton, 1979), pp. 109–22.

[59] Mohamed H. Heikal, *The Cairo Documents: The Inside Story of Nasser and His Relationship with World Leaders, Rebels, and Statesmen* (Garden City, N.Y.: Doubleday, 1973), p. 119.

[60] Quoted in Richard K. Betts, *Nuclear Blackmail and Nuclear Balance* (Washington, D.C.: Brookings, 1987), p. 62.

[61] France had no nuclear warheads in 1956. Although Britain had outfitted some Canberra bombers to deliver nuclear weapons, these could not have reached the Soviet heartland unless they were deployed to Germany. Lawrence Freedman, "British Nuclear Targeting," and David S. Yost, "French Nuclear Targeting," in *Strategic Nuclear Targeting*, ed. Desmond Ball and Jeffrey Richelson (Ithaca: Cornell University Press, 1986), esp. pp. 113, 330; Robert P. Berman and John C. Baker, *Soviet Strategic Forces: Requirements and Responses* (Washington, D.C.: Brookings, 1982), p. 42.

British and French military vulnerability was medium, because Anglo-French operations against the Egyptians were well behind schedule and commanders realized that adjustments would be necessary to achieve success. There was also some risk that the Soviets would intervene with conventional forces, but this was a lesser concern. Although the Soviets had not ruled out unilateral conventional military intervention and had asked the United States to participate in a joint operation, they did not make actual preparations to intervene or indicate what level of intervention, if any, they might consider.

UNITED STATES–SOVIET UNION, 1962

The United States demanded that the Soviet Union remove the nuclear-capable missiles it had stationed on Cuba and went on nuclear alert. The Soviet Union removed the missiles, as the denial theory would have foretold.[62]

Soviet civilian vulnerability was very high, meaning that large parts of the population would have been certain not to survive an American nuclear attack. In October 1962 the number of U.S. nuclear weapons able to reach the Soviet Union was estimated at 3,000, compared to about 24 Soviet warheads definitely able to reach the United States.[63] A U.S. government report in September 1961 estimated 2 million to 15 million American fatalities if the United States struck first. The United States, of course, could have inflicted far greater damage on the Soviet Union.[64]

Soviet military vulnerability was very high, meaning that the Soviets would certainly have failed in any conventional defense of their missiles in Cuba against the large-scale air attack and invasion being prepared by the United States.

UNITED STATES–NORTH VIETNAM, 1965–1968

The United States tried to compel North Vietnam to cease support of the insurgency in the South and negotiate a settlement. It failed, as denial theory would have predicted.

[62] Welcome additions to the voluminous literature on the Cuban missile crisis include Betts, *Nuclear Blackmail*, pp. 109–22; Marc Trachtenberg, "The Influence of Nuclear Weapons in the Cuban Missile Crisis," *International Security* 10 (Summer 1985): 137–203; Raymond L. Garthoff, *Reflections on the Cuban Missile Crisis* (Washington, D.C.: Brookings, 1989); James G. Blight and David Welch, *On the Brink: Americans and Soviets Reexamine the Cuban Missile Crisis* (New York: Hill and Wang, 1989); and Strobe Talbott, *Khrushchev Remembers: The Glasnost Tapes* (New York: Little, Brown, 1990).

[63] Michael C. Desch, " 'That Deep Mud in Cuba': The Strategic Threat and U.S. Planning for a Conventional Response during the Missile Crisis," *Security Studies* 1 (Winter 1991): 323.

[64] Betts, *Nuclear Blackmail*, p. 175.

North Vietnamese civilian vulnerability was medium, meaning that, although significant numbers were affected, major parts of the population were not uncertain about whether they would survive. From 1965 to 1968, bombing killed an estimated 52,000 civilians out of a population of 18 million. Only relatively small parts of Hanoi and Haiphong were evacuated, and damage to smaller population centers was occasionally high. Thanh Hoa, for instance, suffered extensively and was largely deserted.[65]

The military vulnerability of the North Vietnamese was low, meaning that although their military strategy was not certain to succeed, there was little risk in continuing military operations. During the Johnson years, North Vietnam pursued a guerrilla strategy that air power could not seriously hinder, because air strikes could not cut off the minimal supplies and reinforcements required by the strategy.

UNITED STATES–NORTH VIETNAM, 1972

The United States tried to compel North Vietnam to cease conventional aggression in the South and accept a cease-fire, and it succeeded, as the denial theory would have predicted. In October 1972 Hanoi agreed to American cease-fire terms, which were finalized in January 1973.

North Vietnamese civilian vulnerability was medium, meaning that the risks to individuals rose to the point that major parts of the population made adjustments in their daily lives to reduce the threat. Air raids against the North in 1972 caused an estimated 13,000 deaths; the intense Linebacker II raids killed 1,318 in Hanoi and 305 in Haiphong. Although individuals may have been frightened and some evacuated, there is no evidence that major parts of the population doubted their survival. Telford Taylor, a prosecutor at the Nuremberg war crimes trials and a critic of the Vietnam War, who was in Hanoi, remarked: "Despite the enormous weight of bombs that were dropped, I rapidly became convinced that we were making no effort to destroy Hanoi. The city remained largely intact and it seemed quite apparent that if there were an effort to destroy Hanoi it could have been done very readily in two or three nights."[66]

Military vulnerability was high, meaning that the ability of the North Vietnamese to control the South through further military operations had become doubtful even with additional commitment of force. During the Nixon years, Hanoi had shifted to a conventional offensive strategy, which

[65] Mark Clodfelter, *The Limits of Air Power: The American Bombing of North Vietnam* (New York: Free Press, 1989), pp. 136–37; Guenter Lewy, *America in Vietnam* (New York: Oxford University Press, 1978), p. 398.

[66] Taylor quoted in John Morocco, *Rain of Fire: Air War, 1969–1973, the Vietnam Experience* (Boston: Boston Publishing, 1985), p. 157.

required high volumes of logistics and reinforcements vulnerable to U.S. air attack.

ISRAEL–EGYPT, 1969–1970

Israel threatened civilian targets in an attempt to compel Egypt to cease military action against Israeli forces in the Sinai. Coercion failed, as the denial theory would have predicted, and superpower intervention ultimately brought hostilities to an end.

Egyptian civilian vulnerability was low. Nearly all Israeli raids were aimed at purely military targets, while total Egyptian civilian casualties were not more than four thousand, probably fewer, and there is no evidence that major parts of the population doubted their survival.[67]

Egyptian military vulnerability was medium, meaning that although the air raids did not prevent Egypt from continuing current operations or reduce Israeli casualties, they did cause sufficient concern that the Egyptians sought and obtained Soviet air defense assistance.[68]

ISRAEL–PLO, 1970s

From 1970 to 1978, Palestine Liberation Organization forces operating from Lebanon carried out many terrorist attacks against Israel. Israeli policy was to strike back with air raids as well as border raids and artillery fire.[69] These raids failed to compel the PLO to abandon its policy of terrorism, as would have been expected from the denial theory.

Palestinian civilian vulnerability was medium to high, meaning that the numbers killed in retaliation by Israel for terrorist activity was high enough to cause major parts of the Palestinian population in south Lebanon to doubt their survival. In the early 1970s, some 160,000 Palestinians lived in southern Lebanon; over 2,000 of them were killed.[70]

Palestinian military vulnerability was low, meaning that air strikes against PLO camps in Lebanon posed practically no risk of thwarting their

[67] Ahmed S. Khalidi, "The War of Attrition," *Journal of Palestine Studies* 3 (Autumn, 1973): 76.

[68] Yaacov Bar-Simon-Tov, *The Israeli-Egyptian War of Attrition, 1969–1970* (New York: Columbia University Press, 1980), pp. 170–71.

[69] For overviews, see Richard A. Gabriel, *Operation Peace for Galilee* (New York: Hill and Wang, 1984), p. 54; Ze'ev Schiff, *A History of the Israeli Army: 1874 to the Present* (New York: Macmillan, 1985), pp. 164–77; and Lon Nordeen, *Fighters over Israel* (New York: Orion, 1990), pp. 149–88.

[70] Aryeh Y. Yodfat and Yuval Arnon-Ohanna, *PLO Strategy and Politics* (New York: St. Martin's, 1981), p. 31.

operations. In the 1970s Lebanon became the main base of PLO activity. The PLO strategy was to conduct terror strikes either by infiltrating small teams into northern Israel or by indiscriminately shelling targets across the border. Israeli air strikes could not affect this strategy, because it required few resources and because any destroyed resources could be easily replaced.[71]

SOVIET UNION–AFGHAN REBELS, 1979–1988

During the Afghan War, the Soviet Union bombed rebel camps and villages throughout Afghanistan to coerce the rebels to abandon their resistance, but the rebels refused to surrender, as the denial theory would have predicted.

Civilian vulnerability was high to very high. Numerous bombing raids, together with Soviet ground operations, killed approximately one million out of a prewar population of less than 20 million. Significant numbers of the 3 to 5 million Afghan refugees living in Pakistan were also killed.[72]

Afghan military vulnerability was low, meaning that although Soviet forces could interfere with rebel operations, Soviet air power could not interdict the trickle of supplies necessary to support the guerrillas.[73] As a result, the threat was not so great as to compel the rebels to make adjustments in their military posture. In fact, their position improved over time due to military aid from the United States, China, and other countries.

SOVIET UNION–PAKISTAN, 1979–1986

During the Afghan War, the Soviet Union bombed Afghan rebel camps and villages in Pakistan not only to affect rebel behavior but also to dissuade Pakistan from serving as the main conduit for arms supplies to the rebels and from permitting guerrillas to cross the frontier. In March 1986 the Soviet news agency warned Pakistan: "The Zia ul-Haq regime should recognize into what dangerous ventures Pakistan's overseas patrons are trying to draw the country, with results which could be disastrous for it."[74] Pakistan refused to reduce its support for the rebels, however, as denial theory would have forecast.

---

[71] On the PLO's strategy in Lebanon, see ibid.; Yair Evron, *War and Intervention in Lebanon* (Baltimore: Johns Hopkins University Press, 1987); and Itamar Rabinovich, *The War for Lebanon, 1970–1985* (Ithaca: Cornell University Press, 1985).

[72] Rasul Bakhsh Rais, *War Without Winners: Afghanistan's Uncertain Trainsition after the Cold War* (Karachi: Oxford University Press, 1994), p. 8, n. 28; Towle, *Pilots and Rebels*, p. 202.

[73] On the effectiveness of Soviet air power, see Denney R. Nelson, "Soviet Air Power: Tactics and Weapons Used in Afghanistan," *Air University Review* 36 (January–February 1985): 31–43.

[74] Quoted in Philip A. Towle, *Pilots and Rebels: The Use of Aircraft in Unconventional Warfare, 1918–1988* (Oxford: Brassey's, 1989), p. 202.

Pakistani civilian vulnerability was low, meaning that although there was some risk to individuals, no major part of the population made adjustments in their daily lives to reduce the threat. Although Soviet bombing and shelling appear to have caused many casualties among Afghan refugees living in Pakistan, there is no evidence that most of the Pakistani population believed they were at risk.

Pakistani military vulnerability was low, meaning that although Soviet forces could interfere with rebel operations in Pakistan, the threat was not so great as to compel the Pakistanis to make adjustments in their military posture. Throughout the war, Pakistan maintained far more forces on the India-Pakistan border than in the west and in early 1985 had one more division on the Indian border and one less facing the Afghan frontier than in 1980. A September 1985 article in the *Pakistan Times* by a retired general claims that the Soviets would require another fifteen to twenty divisions to attack Pakistan.[75]

ISRAEL–PLO, 1982

In 1982 Palestine Liberation Organization forces operating from Lebanon carried out many terrorist attacks against Israel. Israel responded with a large-scale air and ground offensive designed to drive the PLO out of Lebanon. Israel rapidly occupied southern Lebanon and on 1 July 1982, with air and artillery bombardment and the threat of a ground attack, tried to coerce the PLO to leave Beirut. They succeeded; on 6 August 1982 the PLO agreed to leave Beirut.[76] The outcome fit the denial theory.

Palestinian civilian vulnerability was high, meaning that despite their best countermeasures, large parts of the population could not avoid risk of death. Israeli air strikes on Palestinian residential areas began on 22 July and continued daily through 12 August. Total casualties in the siege of Beirut were 5,000–6,000 dead of 400,000 trapped in the city.[77]

PLO military vulnerability was high because the Israelis completely cut off the city, Israel, which had an overwhelming advantage in firepower, began ground operations to clear the city on 4 August. The PLO was unable to prevent Israeli advances, although it was inflicting enough casualties to

---

[75] For instance, in 1985 Pakistan deployed twelve of sixteen infantry divisions and its two armored divisions along the India-Pakistan border. Theodore L. Eliot and Robert L. Pfaltzgraff Jr., *The Red Army on Pakistan's Border* (New York: Pergamon-Brassey's, 1986), pp. 30–31. The Soviets maintained about 120,000 troops in Afghanistan and 30,000 across the Amu River in the Soviet Union for immediate reinforcement during most of the war, compared to Pakistani standing forces of about 482,000. Salman Beg, "The Problems of Pakistan's National Security Since 1979" (Thesis, Fort Leavenworth, Kans.: U.S. Army Command and General Staff College, 1987), p. 73; Eliot and Pfaltzgraff, *Red Army on Pakistan's Border*, p. 29.

[76] Gabriel, *Operation Peace for Galilee*, p. 155.

[77] Ibid., pp. 164, 165, 137.

give Israeli leaders cause for concern. Israeli forces committed to the campaign numbered 78,000, compared to PLO forces in southern Lebanon of 15,000, with perhaps a few thousand more elsewhere in Lebanon, for a total of approximately 20,000. Syrian forces numbered 30,000.[78]

UNITED STATES–LIBYA, 1986

In 1986 the United States tried to persuade Libya to end its sponsorship of terrorism by using a coercive strategy that culminated in an air raid on 14 April.[79] The denial theory would have forecast failure, and although the raid was widely hailed as a success at the time, subsequent evidence indicates that Moamar Qaddafi did not abandon terrorism. Although its sponsorship became less visible after the raid, Libya remained deeply involved in terrorism worldwide. The State Department noted in 1987: "We have little doubt that the US air raids on Libya in 1986 contributed heavily to Qaddafi's subsequent caution. At the same time, however, we are equally sure that he continued planning for anti-US attacks involving the use of surrogate groups to disguise Libyan responsibility." Libya was suspected just weeks after the raid of shooting two State Department officers, murdering three hostages in Beirut, and nearly bombing an El Al flight in London. In December 1988, Libyan agents bombed Pan Am flight 103, killing 270 people. In 1987 and 1988 Libya was the third most active state sponsor of terrorism, training, arming, and financing about thirty insurgent and terrorist groups worldwide. The number of incidents remained above 800 a year from 1986 to 1988.[80]

Libyan civilian vulnerability was low, meaning that although there was some risk to individuals, no major part of the population was threatened. The raid, though it inflicted relatively minor damage, threatened to increase the costs of Libyan terrorism by demonstrating the vulnerability of the Libyan leadership and economy to air attack.[81]

---

[78] Ibid., pp. 151–54, 47, 53, 81.

[79] Tim Zimmermann, "The American Bombing of Libya: A Success for Coercive Diplomacy?" *Survival* 29 (May/June 1987): 195–214; Robert E. Venkus, *Raid on Qaddafi* (New York: St. Martin's, 1992); Brian L. Davis, *Qaddafi, Terrorism, and the Origins of the U.S. Attack on Libya* (New York: Praeger, 1990).

[80] David Johnston, "Flight 103: A Solution Assembled from Fragments and Debris," *New York Times*, 15 November 1991, p. A8. Lillian Craig Harris, "America's Libya Policy Has Failed," *Middle East International*, 10 October 1986, p. 14; Victor E. Dodds, "Naval Air Strike as a Response to State-Sponsored Terrorism" (Thesis, Newport, R.I.: Naval War College, 2 June 1986), pp. 12–14; *Patterns of Global Terrorism* (Washington, D.C.: Department of State, 1986–89). The quotation is from 1987 volume, p. 37.

[81] For evidence that the raid demonstrated the vulnerability of political and economic targets, see Seymour Hersh, "Target Qaddafi," *New York Times Magazine*, 22 February 1987; Zimmermann, "American Bombing of Libya."

The vulnerability to air attack of Libya's ability to sponsor terrorism was low because terrorist training facilities, leaders, and organizations were difficult to attack comprehensively from the air and easy to regenerate. Three of the five targets attacked were directly linked to the terrorists, but there were over thirty terrorist training facilities operating in Libya at the time.[82]

IRAQ–IRAN, 1980–1988

Once the Iran-Iraq War evolved into protracted attrition, Iraq tried to compel Iran to abandon the conflict by sending air attacks against Iranian population centers and by improving the fighting effectiveness of its army. Iraq's main countercity offensives occurred from January to February 1987 and from February to April 1988.[83] Iraq's success fits the denial theory prediction. In July 1988 Iran did agree to end the war, although more as a result of events on the battlefield than Iraqi air strikes on cities.

Iranian civilian vulnerability was medium, meaning that the risk to individuals had risen to the point that major parts of the population were uncertain about whether they would survive. In the main Iraqi countercivilian campaigns, six thousand Iranian civilian deaths were reported. Although the numbers of deaths were not high, rumors of possible Iraqi chemical attack caused several million to flee Tehran and other major cities by late April.[84]

Iranian military vulnerability was high, meaning that the likelihood of failure of Iran's strategy for overrunning southeastern Iraq approached certainty. Throughout the war, Iraq maintained more men in arms than Iran. Iraq's advantage in 1980 was 535,000 to 240,000, and in 1985, 675,000 to 555,000. Iran's strategy had been to bleed Iraqi forces in protracted attrition battles, which killed large numbers on both sides. This strategy began to collapse by the summer of 1988. Although Iran retained some capability to inflict losses on Iraqi forces, Iranian casualties were much heavier and Iraqi offensives using gas and improved tactics rolled back territorial gains Iran had made earlier in the war. The Ayatollah Khomeini is said to have agreed to a cease-fire in July only when his chief military commander said it would take five more years of war to win. Iran's economy was near collapse, how-

---

[82] U.S. Senate, Committee on the Judiciary, Subcommittee on Security and Terrorism, *Libyan Sponsored Terrorism*, 99th Cong., 2d Sess, 1986, pp. 88–91.

[83] Anthony H. Cordesman and Abraham R. Wagner, *The Lessons of Modern War*, vol. 2: *The Iran-Iraq War* (Boulder, Colo.: Westview Press, 1990); Stephen C. Pelletiere, *The Iran-Iraq War* (New York: Praeger, 1992); Ronald Bergquist, *The Role of Airpower in the Iran-Iraq War* (Maxwell Air Force Base, Ala.: Air University Press, 1988); and Efraim Karsh, ed., *The Iran-Iraq War: Impact and Implications* (New York: St. Martin's, 1990). For a detailed record of the air raids, see Cordesman and Wagner, *Iran-Iraq War*, pp. 501–2.

[84] Cordesman and Wagner, *Iran-Iraq War*, pp. 206, 255, 500; Thomas L. McNaugher, "Ballistic Missiles and Chemical Weapons: The Legacy of the Iran-Iraq War," *International Security* 15 (Fall 1990): 10–11; "A Battered City under Siege," *McLean's*, 18 April 1988, p. 34.

ever, and Iraq was on the verge of further military offensives, so this strategy was clearly infeasible.[85]

UNITED STATES–IRAQ, 1991

The United States wanted to compel Iraq to withdraw from Kuwait.[86] The success to be predicted from the denial theory was forthcoming. By the end of February, before the ground attack, Iraq had indicated its willingness to abandon Kuwait. The main obstacle to an agreement was the U.S. demand that Iraq also abandon its military equipment.

Iraqi civilian vulnerability was low, meaning that although there was some risk to individuals, no major part of the population made adjustments in their daily lives to avoid the threat. The U.S. Bureau of the Census estimates Iraqi losses above peacetime expected deaths as 145,000, but only 5,000 of these were civilians who died during the war. There were also 40,000 military deaths during the war and 100,000 postwar civilian deaths due to violence and health conditions.[87]

Iraqi military vulnerability was high, meaning that Kuwait could not be defended against a determined American ground invasion and the success of an attrition strategy was uncertain. Iraq hoped to draw the Coalition into a premature ground offensive in the hope that heavy casualties would lead Western publics to demand an early cease-fire, leaving Iraq in control of the most economically valuable portions of Kuwait. Although the American air offensive began on 16 January, it was not until mid-February that Iraq's heavy ground forces began to be destroyed in large numbers, rapidly reducing Iraq's ability to inflict casualties on American ground forces.

IRAQ–SAUDI ARABIA, 1991

In the hopes of persuading the Saudi government to reduce its support for the U.S.-led coalition against it, beginning on 18 January 1991 Iraq launched 37 Scud missiles at Saudi population centers over six weeks. This coercive attempt failed as the denial theory would have predicted and Saudi Arabia continued to energetically support the war effort against Iraq.

Civilian vulnerability was medium. Although there was only 1 civilian killed and 77 injured, there was widespread fear and extensive civil defense

[85] Cordesman and Wagner, *Iran-Iraq War*, pp. 192, 395–99.
[86] Lawrence Freedman and Efraim Karsh, "How Kuwait Was Won: Strategy in the Gulf War," *International Security* 16 (Fall 1991): 37.
[87] Frank Hobbs, "Population Estimates for Iraq," Population Studies Branch, Center for International Research, U.S. Bureau of the Census, January 1992.

measures were taken. 28 U.S. soldiers and a number of other Coalition soldiers were also killed.[88]

Military vulnerability was low. While the Scuds themselves did almost no damage to rear bases supporting the Coalition war effort, the Iraqi army in Kuwait remained an obstacle, albeit one that the Coalition could and did defeat at relatively low cost.

IRAQ–ISRAEL, 1991

In order to disrupt the integrity of the U.S.-led coalition against it, beginning on 18 January 1991 Iraq launched 39 Scud missiles against Israeli population centers over six weeks hoping to provoke an Israeli military response, putting Arab states in the coalition in the uncomfortable position of being co-belligerents with Israel. This coercive attempt failed as the denial theory would have predicted because the Scud attacks posed no threat to Israeli military security.[89]

Civilian vulnerability was medium. Although only 13 people died in the attacks, virtually the entire population of Israel wore gas masks and accepted other disruptions to their daily routes in order to minimize risk.

Military vulnerability was nil, because the Scuds were insufficiently accurate to hit military targets.

[88] Middle East Watch, *Needless Deaths in the Gulf War* (Washington, D.C.: Human Rights Watch, 1991), pp. 318, 385.
[89] Ibid., p. 317.

Index